Mystery Movie Series of 1930s Hollywood

ALSO BY RON BACKER

*Mystery Movie Series of 1940s Hollywood* (McFarland, 2010)

# Mystery Movie Series of 1930s Hollywood

Ron Backer

McFarland & Company, Inc., Publishers
*Jefferson, North Carolina, and London*

LIBRARY OF CONGRESS CATALOGUING-IN-PUBLICATION DATA

Backer, Ron, 1951–
Mystery movie series of 1930s Hollywood / Ron Backer.
p.   cm.
Includes bibliographical references and index.

ISBN 978-0-7864-6975-8
softcover : acid free paper ∞

1. Detective and mystery films — History and criticism.
2. Motion pictures — United States — History — 20th century.
I. Title.
PN1995.9.D4B325    2012        791.43'6556—dc23        2012023083

BRITISH LIBRARY CATALOGUING DATA ARE AVAILABLE

© 2012 Ron Backer. All rights reserved

*No part of this book may be reproduced or transmitted in any form or by any means, electronic or mechanical, including photocopying or recording, or by any information storage and retrieval system, without permission in writing from the publisher.*

On the cover: Poster art for the 1933 film *The Kennel Murder Case*
Front cover design by Cindy LaBreacht

Manufactured in the United States of America

*McFarland & Company, Inc., Publishers
Box 611, Jefferson, North Carolina 28640
www.mcfarlandpub.com*

For my daughter, Emma,
whose accomplishments so far
have overwhelmed me and
whose best is yet to come.

# Table of Contents

*Introduction*   1

1. Philo Vance: The Upper Class Detective   5
2. Bulldog Drummond: The English Adventurer   40
3. Charlie Chan: The Chinese Detective   85
4. Arséne Lupin: The Gentleman Thief   160
5. Hildegarde Withers: The Teacher Detective   168
6. Thatcher Colt: The Police Commissioner   185
7. Inspector Trent: The Police Detective   195
8. Nick and Nora Charles: The Thin Man Series   200
9. Perry Mason: The Defense Attorney   215
10. Sophie Lang: The Lady Thief   235
11. Sarah Keate: The Nurse Detective   241
12. Torchy Blane: The Investigative Reporter   258
13. Alan O'Connor and Bobbie Reynolds: The Federal Agents   274
14. Mr. Moto: The Japanese Detective   282
15. Bill Crane: The Private Detective   300
16. Joel and Garda Sloane: The Husband and Wife Team   308
17. Nancy Drew: The Teenage Detective   317
18. Mr. Wong: The Other Chinese Detective   327
19. Barney Callahan: The Roving Reporter   339
20. Brass Bancroft: The Secret Service Agent   344
21. Tailspin Tommy: The Young Aviator   352
22. Persons in Hiding: The FBI Story   361

*Appendix: 1930s Mystery Series Listed*   371
*Bibliography*   373
*Index*   375

# Introduction

*Mystery Movie Series of 1930s Hollywood* is a companion book to *Mystery Movie Series of 1940s Hollywood*, which was published by McFarland in 2010. When I first decided to write about mystery movie series, it was clear to me that there were too many relevant movies to include in a single volume. Therefore, I had to draw the line somewhere. Dividing the topic by decades seemed to make sense and even though there are 23 more films covered in the 1930s volume than in the 1940s volume, there is at least a rough split between the number of films covered in each book.

Dividing the books into separate decades was, of course, convenient but it was also arbitrary. Perhaps there was a better place to draw the line. After all, many of the film series discussed in these books contain movies which were released in both decades. In fact, even though the Charlie Chan movies are all covered in the 1930s volume, there were actually more Chan films released in the 1940s than in the 1930s. However, after working my way through all of these mystery movie series, I finally decided that while the split along decades may have originally been arbitrary, there are actually important distinctions between the mystery series created in the 1930s and those created in the 1940s.

The mystery series of the 1930s relied significantly on mystery literature as inspiration. Just about every major mystery film series of the decade was inspired by a series of crime stories from literature, such as Charlie Chan, Nick and Nora Charles, Thatcher Colt, Bill Crane, Nancy Drew, Bulldog Drummond, Sarah Keate, Sophie Lang, Arséne Lupin, Perry Mason, Mr. Moto, Persons in Hiding, Joel and Garda Sloane, Philo Vance, Hildegarde Withers and Mr. Wong. Many of the movies in the series were based substantially on, or at least inspired by, a novel or short story. For example, all of the Perry Mason, Hildegarde Withers, Sarah Keate and the 1930s Philo Vance and Bulldog Drummond movies were purportedly based on written works about the characters.

By contrast, in the 1940s, the film detectives came from multiple sources, including radio and comic strips, and many more of the films had totally original scripts. While it was obviously a positive for the 1940s films to be inspired by multiple sources, the fact that many more of the 1940s films had original scripts gave those features more of a "cookie cutter" or assembly line feel. Arguably the best films of both the 1930s and 1940s mystery series were based on written works.

In the 1930s, several series featured female detectives, young and old, from Nancy Drew and Torchy Blane to Sarah Keate and Hildegarde Withers. By contrast, in the 1940s, there were none. Indeed, with the exception of the Miss Marple films from the 1960s, it is rare, to this day, to find a mystery movie with a female detective that had even one sequel. Paradoxically, the 1930s movies, at least in this regard, seem more modern than their counterparts in the 1940s.

In the 1930s, most of the major studios were involved in the production of mystery movie series. MGM had Nick and Nora Charles and Joel and Garda Sloane, Warner Brothers had Perry Mason, Torchy Blane, Brass Bancroft and Nancy Drew, Paramount had many of the Philo Vance and Bulldog Drummond films, RKO had Hildegarde Withers, Universal had Bill Crane and Fox (later 20th Century–Fox) had Charlie Chan and Mr. Moto. Additionally, Columbia and some Poverty Row studios were also involved in 1930s series productions. The variety of studios putting out the product added to the variety of mystery films released.

By the 1940s, MGM, Warner Brothers and Paramount had essentially exited the field and by 1942, 20th Century–Fox also gave up on mystery movie series. The sub-genre was essentially left to RKO, Columbia, Universal and several minor studios. Once again, this reduced the variety of the mystery product in the 1940s as contrasted with the 1930s.

As a result, the 1940s films were almost always B–productions, with stars who were past their prime, such as Chester Morris, Warner Baxter and Warren William. The 1930s films were sometimes A–productions (*The Canary Murder Case* [1929], *The Black Camel* [1931], *Arsène Lupin* [1932] and *The Thin Man* [1934]) which often featured major personalities who were still in their prime, such as William Powell, John Barrymore, Melvyn Douglas, Ronald Colman, Basil Rathbone, Myrna Loy and Rosalind Russell. How exciting it is to watch major stars perform in a series of crime films!

That is not to say that the films of the 1930s were better than the films of the 1940s, only that they were different. For example, several of the earliest 1930s films were diminished by their difficulty in adapting sound to the cinema. On the other hand, many of the 1940s films were enhanced by the development of film noir techniques, allowing the studio to create an excellent product on a small budget. For mystery movie fans, there is much to enjoy in each decade and there is no doubt that when the mystery movie series as a sub-genre disappeared in the 1950s, there was a significant hole left for those viewers who loved to watch mystery movies, a hole that television could not completely fill. Perhaps that is the reason why the movies of the Hollywood mystery series, even though some are now over 70 years old, are still enjoyed today by the true mystery fan.

*Note on the Films*: There are 167 films addressed in this book. Each is from a Hollywood mystery series whose movies were primarily released during the 1930s. While there were some Lone Wolf and Sherlock Holmes movies released during the 1930s, those movies are not covered in this book because most of the releases for those film series occurred in the 1940s. Those and similar series were completely covered in *Mystery Movie Series of 1940s Hollywood*.

Similarly, although the Charlie Chan series, the Bulldog Drummond series, the Thin Man series and others had a number of films released during the 1940s, they are better known for their 1930s entries. Indeed, the first Charlie Chan and Bulldog Drummond sound films were released in 1929. All of the films in those series and similar series are considered herein, even the ones released during the 1920s and 1940s.

By definition, a mystery series contains at least three movies. Therefore, I have not addressed those situations where there was only one sequel made to the original film. Consistent with the title of the book, I have not addressed crime series that were primarily produced in England or other foreign countries, except to complete the discussion of the movies in the Bulldog Drummond series.

*Note on the Source Material*: For each film discussed herein which was based on a written work, I have tried to find and read the work and then compare and contrast it with the film that it spawned. In some cases, it was not easy to find the written works, as many have been out of print for some time. However, after scouring libraries, used book stores and the Internet, I was able to find almost all of the written works for which I was searching. In all, I read or re-read 52 novels, nine short stories and one play, and in addition, based upon secondary sources, references are made to other source materials in the instances in which I was unable to locate the original work.

*Spoiler Alerts*: Although there are no detailed synopses of the plots of each of the movies discussed herein, as that would be excruciatingly boring, this book does contain short synopses and a detailed analysis of the plots, usually addressing the issues of whether the mystery makes sense, is fair to the viewer and the like. In order to do the subject justice, many of the plot twists, surprise endings and identities of the murderers must also be discussed. However, to preface each spoiler with a warning, such as "Spoiler Alert," would disrupt the flow of the chapters and make them hard to read. Therefore, if you do not want to read a spoiler, carefully skim over the discussions of those movies that you have not already seen and then come back to those discussions once you have viewed the film.

# 1

# Philo Vance
## *The Upper Class Detective*

The comic poet Ogden Nash famously wrote, "Philo Vance/Needs a kick in the Pance." In his well-known essay "The Simple Art of Murder," Raymond Chandler referred to Vance as "the most asinine character in detective fiction."

Anyone who has read any of the Philo Vance novels knows that there is more than a little truth in those critical quotations. There is the way Vance talks, using old-fashioned expressions and often dropping the "g" at the end of his words. There are his references to obscure literature and classical art which no one can understand. There are his constant deprecations of standard police procedure in favor of his own questionable psychological methods. There are his upper class affectations, such as his valet, Currie, and his membership in the exclusive Stuyvesant Club. The list could go on and on.

Despite all of these shortcomings, the Philo Vance novels were the most popular American detective stories of the 1920s and early 1930s. The novels were then made into some of the earliest sound detective movies. Fortunately, because of the time constraints of the cinema, when the novels were translated into films, most of Vance's affectations disappeared, making the Vance character much more likable and accessible on the screen than in the books. Perhaps it is for that reason that the Philo Vance movie series was one of the most successful classical detective series ever filmed.

## BACKGROUND

### *The Novels*

Willard Huntington Wright was born on October 15, 1887, in Charlottesville, Virginia. While he was still a teenager, the Wright family moved to California where Archie Wright, Willard's father, became a successful hotel entrepreneur. Despite several attempts, young Willard never earned a college degree. He did, however, spend much time abroad, soaking in the European culture, often with his brother Stanton who became a well-known artist. Despite the lack of a college diploma, Willard eventually became a famous, if controversial art and literature critic, editor of a literary magazine, and author of several books before he entered the mystery field.

Wright's health was seldom great, with his illnesses often caused by a drug addiction. Around 1922, during one of those illnesses, his friend, Dr. Jacob Lobsenz, suggested that Willard take a break, put aside his art and philosophy texts and read some detective fiction. Another friend, Norbert Lederer, had a vast collection of detective fiction and permitted

Wright access. Wright then read all of the authors of crime fiction, old and new, from Arthur Conan Doyle to Dorothy Sayers, and decided that he could do better.

Recognizing that a detective series would be more profitable than a single book, Wright decided to approach a publisher with a package of three novels starring the same detective, whom he named Philo Vance. Vance was clearly patterned after Wright himself, with his interest in the arts, literature and other minutia and his snobbish disdain for those he believed were inferior to him. Because Wright was too conceited to allow his colleagues to find out that he was writing popular fiction, he created the pseudonym "S.S. Van Dine," supposedly based on the abbreviation for steamship and an old family name.

The first three novels, *The Benson Murder Case*, *The "Canary" Murder Case* and *The Greene Murder Case*, published in 1926, 1927 and 1928, respectively, were huge successes, making Wright very wealthy, at least for a time. Hollywood beckoned and each of those works was turned into a film at Paramount Pictures.

Despite announcing that he would only write a total of six Philo Vance novels, Wright continued writing Vance books until his death in 1939. In all, there were 12 Philo Vance novels published although the last one, *The Winter Murder Case*, was published in an early draft which is all that Wright had completed at the time of his death. By the mid–1930s, American crime fiction had passed Philo Vance by, and at the time of Wright's death the sales of Philo Vance novels were substantially lower than they were in the 1920s.

## The Film Series

The first Philo Vance film was *The Canary Murder Case*, released in 1929 by Paramount Pictures. It was originally intended to be a silent film but part way through production, it was changed into a sound movie by re-shooting and re-dubbing some scenes. Purportedly the first sound detective movie ever released, *The Canary Murder Case* starred William Powell as Philo Vance. A success, it was followed later that year by *The Greene Murder Case*, also starring Powell.

Powell was born in 1892 in Pittsburgh, Pennsylvania. He entered the silent cinema in 1922, appearing that year in *Sherlock Holmes*, one of the many mystery films in which he would perform. He then appeared in numerous other silent films, playing a variety of roles, before obtaining better parts late in the silent era. *The Canary Murder Case* was his second talking film. Powell's career is discussed further in this book's chapter on the Thin Man series.

The third Vance film, *The Bishop Murder Case* (1930), was released by MGM, the studio where Powell would later have his greatest successes in films. However, Powell was under contract to Paramount in 1930 and therefore Basil Rathbone was brought in to portray the great detective. Rathbone was born in South Africa in 1892. He began working in silent films, first in England and then sporadically in America, before achieving great success during the 1930s, playing villains in adaptations of famous works from literature, such as *David Copperfield* (1935) and *Anna Karenina* (1935), and dueling with Errol Flynn in *Captain Blood* (1935) and *The Adventures of Robin Hood* (1938). *The Bishop Murder Case* was the only movie in which Rathbone played Philo Vance.

The series then returned to Paramount for one last film, *The Benson Murder Case*, released in 1930. Powell once again undertook the role of the great detective and, ignoring the intervening film starring Rathbone, the characters refer to Vance's prior case as the Greene murder case.

Powell then moved over to Warner Brothers and that studio acquired a Vance novel so that Powell could reprise his role as the famous detective. Indeed, the credits to *The Kennel Murder Case* (1933) trumpet Powell's chance to play Philo Vance again, stating, "William Powell Returns as Philo Vance." *The Kennel Murder Case* is usually considered one of the best detective movies of the 1930s. It was the last appearance of Powell in the part that he originated four years before.

The series continued at Warner Brothers with *The Dragon Murder Case* (1934), starring Warren William. William, who was born in 1894 in Minnesota, began appearing in films on a regular basis in 1931. Around the time he was playing Philo Vance for Warner Brothers, he was also playing Perry Mason for the same studio. William's career is discussed in greater detail in this book's chapter on the Perry Mason mystery series.

The Philo Vance series then moved back to MGM for two films. The first was *The Casino Murder Case* (1935), starring Paul Lukas. The Hungarian–born stage actor first appeared in Hollywood films at the end of the silent era. He is well-known today for his Oscar–winning performance as Kurt Muller in *Watch on the Rhine* (1943). The second MGM film was *The Garden Murder Case* (1936), starring Edmund Lowe. Born in 1890 in San Jose, California, Lowe appeared in numerous silent films (the most famous being *What Price Glory?* [1926]) before making the transition to sound films.

Interestingly, when the Vance films returned to MGM in 1935, William Powell was a major star at that studio based, in part, on his success as Nick Charles in *The Thin Man* (1934). However, by the middle–1930s, the Philo Vance films had become B–movies, now beneath the dignity of a major star such as Powell.

It was then back to Paramount for two more films. The first was *Night of Mystery* (1937), which was a remake of *The Greene Murder Case*. It starred Grant Richards, an actor who appeared in very few films in his undistinguished career. Next came *The Gracie Allen Murder Case* (1939), based on a book conceived by the studio but written by S.S. Van Dine. The film starred Gracie Allen, and, oh yes, Warren William played the part of Philo Vance.

The last film of the era was *Calling Philo Vance* (1940), a remake of *The Kennel Murder Case*. It was made at Warner Brothers and starred James Stephenson, a British actor who had a few good roles in Hollywood before his untimely death in 1941 at the age of 52. Stephenson received an Oscar nomination for Best Supporting Actor for *The Letter* (1940).

In addition to the great detective, a number of characters from the novels, such as the district attorney, John Markham, the coroner, Dr. Doremus, and the policeman, Sergeant Heath, were carried over to the films. Markham and Doremus were played by several different actors over the course of the film series. So was Sergeant Heath, although one actor, Eugene Pallette, played Sergeant Heath in six of the films, making him the actor who appeared most often in the Philo Vance movies. Pallette, who was born 1899 in Winfield, Kansas, began acting in silent films in the early 1910s, appearing in over 100 such films. One of his earliest talking pictures was *The Canary Murder Case* (1929). With his froggy voice and rotund figure, Pallette was so memorable in that role that when the Philo Vance series moved from Paramount to Warner Brothers, Pallette was brought along to play the hardworking policeman.

By the time of *Calling Philo Vance* (1940), Willard Huntington Wright was dead and the Philo Vance novels were out of vogue. It was assumed that the film series was over for good, but in 1947, Producers Releasing Corporation (PRC), an independent studio which specialized in very low-budget films, revived the name of Philo Vance, if not the character, in a series of three movies. Interestingly, and perhaps appropriately, S.S. Van Dine was not referred to anywhere in the credits to the films. In these three films, all of the affectations of the Philo Vance of the books and the subsidiary characters created by Van Dine had disappeared. Vance, as critic William L. DeAndrea noted, was now as tough as the next guy; he just happened to have a funny name. Indeed, in two of the features, much like Boston Blackie and the Falcon, Philo Vance had an assistant, Ernie Clark, who fulfilled the same duties that the Runt and Goldie Locke performed in those other mystery movie series of the 1940s.

The three films were released in a different order than they were produced. In two of the films, both from 1947, *Philo Vance's Gamble* and *Philo Vance's Secret Mission*, the part of Vance was played by Alan Curtis. Curtis was born in 1909 in Chicago, Illinois. Although Curtis had been appearing in films since 1936, he had an undistinguished career with no significant credits in the mystery movie genre prior to the Philo Vance films. The other film, also from 1947, was *Philo Vance Returns*, starring William Wright as the title character. Wright was born in Utah in 1911 and began appearing in films in 1936. Wright also had an undistinguished film career although he had small roles in two Boston Blackie movies in the 1940s.

## THE WILLIAM POWELL ERA

### *The Canary Murder Case* (1929)

*The Canary Murder Case* is interesting as a curio, being the earliest distributed film discussed in this book. Production was started as a silent film in 1928, but the film was released as a talkie (a number of the scenes had been re-shot and some of the dialogue dubbed in). Oddly, despite the original intent to release the movie as a silent, with presumably little dialogue and many action sequences, the sound film which was finally released is stagebound and lacks pace, making it a disappointing first entry in the long line of Philo Vance films.

*The Canary Murder Case* is an account of the murder of Margaret O'Dell, a beautiful Broadway musical star whose stage name is "The Canary." O'Dell's beauty has bewitched a number of successful gentlemen and, being just as merciless as she is beautiful, the Canary seems to have blackmailed each of those men at one time or another. Therefore, when the Canary is murdered (strangled in her apartment with a piece of her own jewelry), there are a number of male suspects. One is young Jimmy Spotswoode, who is now engaged to Alys La Fosse, who lives down the hall from O'Dell. The Canary intends to marry young Jimmy, whether he wants to marry her or not, thus bringing Jimmy's father Charles into the mix.

On the night of the murder, Charles visits the Canary to try to convince her to give up his son. She refuses and so Charles leaves her apartment. His last look into the apartment shows the Canary with her back to the door, reclining on the davenport with a cigarette in her hand. While Spotswoode is talking with the desk clerk about calling for a taxi, they hear a scream from the apartment. The two rush to the Canary's apartment but when Charles yells in to her, the Canary says, through the door, that everything is fine and that she will see him in the morning. Thus, Spotswoode and the desk clerk assume she is safe.

The next morning, Spotswoode returns to the Canary's apartment building, intending to have further discussions with her. The Canary's strangled body is then discovered

In the opening scene of *The Canary Murder Case* (1929), soon-to-be murder victim Margaret O'Dell (Louise Brooks) is on her swing and flying above the stage, dressed as "The Canary."

by Spotswoode and the desk clerk in her locked apartment, which the desk clerk opens with a skeleton key. Philo Vance is called in by District Attorney Markham to help with the investigation. After playing a round of poker with all of the suspects, Vance determines who the murderer is, simply by psychological analysis. However, Markham needs proof, not theories, and Vance is finally able to provide the same, after the murderer is killed in a car-train collision while he is on the way to confess his crimes to the police.

*The Canary Murder Case* does not work well either as a mystery or a film. There is so much time spent ensuring the viewer that Charles Spotswoode is not the murderer, as the Canary was clearly alive when he left her apartment, that the experienced mystery fan will know that Charles must be the killer. Vance discovers the murderer by playing poker with all of the suspects and then, by analyzing the way they play, determines that only Spotswoode has the personality to be the murderer. This approach to crime detection strains credulity and is a technique which is probably not taught in many criminal justice programs these days.

The solution to the crime also lacks credibility. Spotswoode is supposed to have brought a phonograph record with him to the Canary's apartment, using it to create the impression that the Canary was still alive when he left the apartment. The record has perfect pauses in it, so that Spotswoode can pretend he is talking to O'Dell through the door with the desk clerk listening in. But, what if the desk clerk had asked her questions through the door? How did Spotswoode time his responses to the recording so accurately?

The sloppy plotting of the crime cannot sustain even casual scrutiny. If Vance's analysis of the murder is accurate, then when the authorities arrived the next morning to investigate the crime, the phonograph should still have been on, with the arm at the end of the record. No one mentions seeing that because if someone had observed that situation, the record would have been played and Spotswoode's guilt would have been conclusively determined almost immediately. In addition, Spotswoode had placed a burning cigarette in the Canary's dead hand in the event the desk clerk had looked through the keyhole when the Canary supposedly screamed. The next day, the dead body of the Canary should have had burns on her fingers, or perhaps a fire would have started in the apartment when the cigarette fell to the floor. Nevertheless, nothing is discovered the next morning — not even any ashes on the floor. Thus, Vance's theory of the crime is contradicted by the lack of physical evidence in O'Dell's apartment.

As to cinematic techniques, *The Canary Murder Case* is also disappointing. The direction is uninspired, at best, and if the viewer is not told so, he would never suspect that this film was originally intended as a silent. Other than the early scenes with the Canary performing on her swing in her show, with a number of the suspects looking on, there is almost no movement in the film. The story is stagebound and static. It is all dialogue and no action. Surprisingly, there is a significant lack of close-ups of the performers, resulting in an overuse of medium and long shots. This is a relic from the early sound era and not from the dynamic visual phase of the late silent era.

Yet, for all its faults, there is some interest in *The Canary Murder Case*. Jean Arthur appears in a small role as Alys La Fosse and although she has few close-ups, any knowledgeable moviegoer would recognize her from her distinctive voice. It is interesting to see Louise Brooks in one of her few sound film roles, although her voice was dubbed by a different actress. It is easy to discern why so many characters fell in love with the tantalizing beauty. William Powell was always good at playing a sophisticated detective and the part of Philo Vance was particularly well-suited to him. Nevertheless, Powell is not quite yet the film personality that he would become in later mystery movies and, for example, delivers his explanation for the crimes in a pretentious manner. Gruff–voiced Eugene Pallette as Sergeant Heath, while always respecting Vance's detective abilities, is also always willing to take partial credit for Vance's successes. Heath is not portrayed here as a bumbler but rather as a quite competent policeman, making the role much more interesting than the standard mystery movie cliché of the dumb cop.

Pure whodunits can be difficult to film. In a traditional mystery novel, after a murder, the detective usually solves the crime by investigating the crime scene and then interviewing the various witnesses, often more than once. That approach works in print because it is often quite interesting. Moving pictures, however, are supposed to move and therefore long scenes set in the murder room and then interview after interview of witnesses can quickly become tedious. That is much of the problem with *The Canary Murder Case* and several of the other early Philo Vance movies. Until the filmmakers were able to solve the conundrum of portraying a classic murder mystery on the screen without the film becoming boring, it would be difficult to produce a successful Philo Vance film.

*Note on the Source Material*: The film was based on the 1927 book of the same name by S.S. Van Dine. Much like the movie, the novel concerns the murder of a blackmailing courtesan named Margaret O'Dell, also known as the Canary. There are four suspects although one of them, Spotswoode, seems to be ruled out because after he left the Canary's apartment on the night of the murder, the Canary screamed and Spotswoode, in the presence of the apartment building's night receptionist, talked to her through her apartment door.

The murderer and the method of murder are the same in each version, although in the novel, Spotswoode is directly infatuated with the Canary and not just interceding with her on behalf of his son. Also, Spotswoode does not put a cigarette in O'Dell's dead hand, a device which, as noted above, makes little sense in the context of the physical clues discovered in the apartment after the Canary's death. In both the book and the film, a thief is trapped in the clothes closet of the apartment when the murder occurs and he is later killed when he attempts to blackmail Spotswoode. The device of Vance playing poker with all of the suspects to divine the killer also comes from the book. The concept is no more convincing in the written work than it is in the movie.

The most significant difference between the two works is the locked room nature of the Canary's murder in the book, a fact which is de-emphasized in the movie. At first in the book, it seems that it was impossible for anyone to have murdered the Canary, since no one walked past the night receptionist, and the outside door to the side hallway was bolted from the inside. After learning that the bolted door was open at some time during the evening, it then seems that all of the suspects had the opportunity to kill the Canary except, of course, for Spotswoode, who apparently left the building while the Canary was still alive. Once Vance determines how the side door could have been bolted from the outside, matters start to come into focus.

The locked room puzzle of the book is one of its most entertaining qualities. Eliminating the locked room aspect of the murder in the film is a significant negative.

In both versions of *The Canary Murder Case*, Spotswoode creates his own alibi, by reproducing the Canary's voice on a record and playing that record on the Canary's phonograph. In both versions, the record contains the false label of the Andante (Second) Movement to Beethoven's Fifth Symphony although in the book, the often irritating Vance refers to the orchestral piece as Beethoven's C-Minor Symphony, instead of by its more common name.

*Note on the Production*: *The Canary Murder Case* was originally shot in 1928 as a silent film. The director was Malcolm St. Clair. Immediately after shooting ended, Louise Brooks left for Germany to appear in *Pandora's Box* (1929), to be directed by G.W. Pabst. In that film, she played a character named Lulu, who was not dissimilar to the Canary.

Back in America, the Hollywood studios finally determined that sound was here to stay, and Paramount decided to retool *The Canary Murder Case* as a sound production. A new director, Frank Tuttle, was brought in, parts of the film were re-shot, and in other parts the silent footage was retained, with the voices dubbed in. Since Louise Brooks refused to return from Germany to complete the dubbing of the dialogue of the Canary, her lines were dubbed in by Margaret Livingston, the actress-wife of bandleader Paul Whiteman. Livingston, who had been appearing in silent films for many years, also took Brooks's place in some newly shot footage.

The book was based on the then famous murder of Dorothy "Dot" King which occurred in 1923. Dot was a young beauty who appeared in one Broadway show before she took up her real career of being a companion to a number of wealthy and well-known male citizens of New York City. She lived on the fourth floor of an apartment building on West 57th Street, paid for by one of her admirers, J. Kearsley Mitchell.

On the night of the murder, Mitchell and Dot spent the evening together, with Mitchell leaving the apartment about 2:30 A.M., according to the elevator operator. No one else was seen going into the apartment that night, but there was a private staircase that could have provided access to Dot's apartment from a side entrance. The next morning, the maid found Dot's apparently strangled body in her ransacked apartment but she was actually killed with chloroform (the bottle was found at the scene). The two leading suspects provided air-tight alibis and the crime was never solved.

The Dot King murder was also the basis for *The King Murder*, released by Chesterfield in 1932. Much like *The Canary Murder Case*, *The King Murder* is highly fictionalized, with the victim's name changed to Miriam King. While the two films are decidedly different, what they have in common is an attempt to provide an alibi by having the supposed murder victim talking in her apartment after one of the suspects leaves (with Miriam King already dead) and the involvement of a record player in the crime. It is referred to as a Victrola in *The King Murder*.

## *The Greene Murder Case* (1929)

S.S. Van Dine was a proponent of the classic style of whodunit wherein a murder is committed within a large group of suspects, often in a large mansion with a butler and other servants afoot, among characters who exist not just in the upper class of society but on the wealthiest rung of the upper class. The murder is then solved, not by professional police detectives but by a talented amateur. Van Dine did not invent this formula but he was one of the most successful practitioners thereof.

Van Dine did concoct one interesting variation to the aforesaid whodunit theme. In several of his mysteries, after the initial murder, the remainder of the suspects start to be killed one by one, until there are only a few left. *The Greene Murder Case* was the first of the Philo Vance novels brought to the screen that employed this unusual plot device. Perhaps for that reason, even though the movie is told in a static and talkative manner, it never becomes boring, as murder follows murder until there are only two suspects left.

The Greene family is quite unusual. Its members are matriarch Mrs. Tobias Greene, who has been bedridden for many years because of her weakened legs, her two sons, Chester and Rex Greene, and her two daughters, Sibella and Ada Greene. All seem to dislike each other but all are destined to live together for 15 years, based upon the provisions of the will of Tobias Greene. Tobias bequeathed his vast estate to whomever of his wife and children who are still alive after 15 years and have lived in the Greene mansion during that entire time period. The one exception is for Ada who, because she is adopted, is permitted to move from the mansion if she ever marries.

The end of 1929 brings trouble to the Greene family. On New Year's Eve, Chester Greene is shot to death while sitting in his favorite chair and Ada is wounded by a gunshot just a few minutes later. Vance offers to assist Sergeant Heath but does not accept his theory that the murder and attempted murder resulted from a failed burglary attempt. However, before Vance can solve the crimes, Rex is shot and killed, Ada is poisoned but survives, and Mrs. Greene is poisoned and expires. When there are only two potential suspects left, Vance finally solves the crimes and then saves Sibella Greene from a last effort by Ada to murder her sister by pushing her off the roof of the mansion into the river below.

The film is quite stagebound, with most of the scenes taking place in the Greene mansion, with little action but with lots of dialogue. There are a disproportionate number of long shots of the parties talking, adding to the languorous pace of the story. Most of the murders take place off screen, resulting in the viewer being told about the events rather than learning about them through the visuals. All of these film techniques should have brought the flow of the film to a screeching halt but for reasons hard to discern, they do not. The movie always remains interesting.

One reason, paradoxical though it may be, is that the murderer is obvious from the beginning. While it is tantalizing to suspect the bedridden Mrs. Greene, one rule of thumb in solving classic whodunits is that if there is an attempted murder of one of the characters and that character survives, that character is the murderer, almost for sure. In *The Greene Murder Case*, the "killer" misses on two attempts on Ada's life but is totally successful in every other murder attempt the killer makes. That ensures that Ada is the killer. Knowing that, it is interesting to see Ada set up an alibi for the murder of Rex by making a phone call to Rex from the district attorney's office on a thin excuse, resulting in the sound of a gunshot over the phone connection. The viewer is well ahead of Vance in recognizing that Rex was killed by a gun trap set up in advance by Ada. Later, Ada is caught in a lie about Mrs. Greene's ability to walk, sealing the deal on Ada's guilt. Thus, the viewer has fun by finally solving a mystery on his own and, knowing the killer in advance, watching Vance as he slowly comes to the right conclusion.

The film is aided by good performances in large roles and small. William Powell gives a much more natural performance here as Vance, as contrasted with *The Canary Murder Case*, apparently becoming more comfortable with both the role and with performing in a sound movie. Perhaps it is his raspy voice or his rotund figure but Eugene Pallette is once again enjoyable as Sergeant Heath. He is clearly one of the most watchable policemen in a mystery movie featuring a private detective. Jean Arthur is quite attractive and convincing as Ada Greene. Brandon Hurst is good as the butler, Sproot, acting just suspiciously enough that the viewer may start to have doubts concerning Ada's guilt.

Instead of the film ending in a set scene where Vance announces the identity of the murderer to all of the characters gathered, *The Greene Murder Case* ends with an exciting rescue of Sibella Greene from a murder attempt by Ada Greene and the surprise death of Ada by a fall into an icy river. It is the most cinematic scene in the entire film and is a great climax to a very appealing mystery movie. Despite all of the murders that has gone before, it is a slightly happy ending as Sibella has just been married and she will eventually inherit the entire Greene family fortune.

*Note on the Source Material*: *The Greene Murder Case* was based on S.S. Van Dine's 1928 novel of the same name. Almost every scene in the film comes from the novel, with a serial killer loose in the Greene mansion, killing off the Greenes one by one, until only Ada and Sibella are left.

While the novel is interesting at times, it drags through its inordinate length. The filmmakers were clever enough to make just enough changes to *The Greene Murder Case* when they adapted it for the cinema to substantially improve the work. One modification was that the killing of Julia Greene, the first murder to occur in the book, was eliminated from the film, streamlining the story somewhat but also eliminating some of the repetitiveness of the tale. Another alteration was the elimination of the unexciting conclusion of the book wherein Vance races his car through the streets of New York City in an attempt to rescue

Sibella. That scene is replaced in the film with the much more exciting incident of Ada attempting to kill Sibella on the Greene mansion rooftop, ending with Ada's eventual fall into the East River.

The most important change, however, is that Philo Vance's interminable ramblings about art, literature, psychoanalysis, crime and other matters in which the reader has no interest are eliminated in the film. The Philo Vance of the movie is a much more engaging character than the Philo Vance of the book.

*Note on the Remake*: *The Greene Murder Case* was remade as *Night of Mystery* (1937).

## *The Bishop Murder Case* (1930)

When it comes to mysteries based on nursery or children's rhymes, Agatha Christie's name immediately comes to mind, with her many novels employing that concept, such as *Crooked House*, based on a children's rhyme that commences with the phrase, "There was a crooked man," or *A Pocket Full of Rye*, based on the nursery rhyme which starts with the phrase, "Sing a song of sixpence." Christie was not, however, the first writer to tie the killings in a murder mystery to a nursery rhyme theme. Surprisingly, that milestone belongs to the snobbish and erudite S.S. Van Dine, in a novel about his snobbish and erudite detective, Philo Vance, the last two people, real or fictional, one would ever expect to know anything about children's rhymes.

In the film *The Bishop Murder Case*, the first killing is of a young man known as Cock Robin, apparently shot through the chest with an arrow, perhaps by his rival, Raymond Sperling, whose last name is German for "sparrow." The reference to the rhyme which starts, "Who killed Cock Robin?" is obvious. There are then three more killings in the movie, each based on a nursery rhyme: Johnny Sprig, Humpty-Dumpty and the House That Jack Built. Much like the film version of *The Greene Murder Case*, so many people are murdered in *The Bishop Murder Case* that as the film comes to its end, there are only two suspects left who could have possibly committed the crimes. At that point, it is not too surprising that the less-likely one is actually the killer.

Even though this film was made at MGM while the first two films in the series were made at Paramount, *The Bishop Murder Case* suffers from the same problems. Large portions are all talk, with little movement within the frame. The effectiveness of those scenes are further undercut by a stationary camera, with long set shots of entire large rooms with the actors talking, interrupted with few cuts and even fewer close-ups. In 1930, Hollywood still seemed to be feeling its way in developing the most effective approaches to employing dialogue in sound films and those difficulties are manifested in this film. Also, several of the actors overact outrageously, as if they were still appearing in silent films. In particular, George F. Marion as Adolph Drukker, Zelda Sears as his sister and Charles Quartermaine as Pardee are less than convincing, despite their strange faces which make them obvious suspects for the crimes.

Yet, for all of these flaws in the presentation, director Nick Grindé does, from time to time, employ an interesting variety of shots to ameliorate some of the static nature of the film. These include shots of people's reflections in a mirror, shots from above down a set of steps, very long outdoor shots to indicate the location of a balcony and a bay window, and shadows of hands on a wall, building a house of cards. Grindé also attempts to give the film a sense of movement by, for example, having one talking scene occurring in a mov-

Philo Vance (Basil Rathbone), far left, and District Attorney Markham (Clarence Geldert), far right, begin their investigation of the murder of Cock Robin by interviewing suspect Amesson (Roland Young), standing, and Professor Dillard (Alec B. Francis), sitting, in *The Bishop Murder Case* (1930).

ing car and one murder taking place outdoors in a park as the victim steps behind a large rock. In this film without background music, Grindé makes the most of the sounds of the Dillard home, particularly near the end as the viewer can hear the sound of typing on an old-fashioned typewriter, a baby doll crying as its carriage is rocked and the sound of birds flying. The prior two films in the series made little use of the sound element to convey the story.

Basil Rathbone is quite good as Philo Vance, much more staid and serious than William Powell in the role and much less flamboyant than Rathbone's later film impersonations of Sherlock Holmes. Roland Young is also quite good as one of the suspects.

While the film does keep the viewers' attention, and a film with multiple killings has much going for it, the announced solution of the crimes makes little sense. The motive of the killer is hard to believe, even after repeat viewings of Vance's explanation. Vance has no clues and he never even tries to explain how he determined the identity of the killer. With just two suspects at the end, he probably just flipped a coin.

From the perspective of many years later and with the knowledge that Basil Rathbone would one day become the most recognizable film Sherlock Holmes of many generations, it is interesting to see Philo Vance sarcastically referred to as Sherlock Holmes by one of the characters. Later, in the tradition of Holmes, Vance deduces Sergeant Heath's recent activities solely from an ink mark on his finger, a smudge on a handkerchief, his recently shaved face and his constant looking at his watch.

However, *The Bishop Murder Case* is not a Holmes story nor is it an Agatha Christie mystery. Even though the film is based on a nursery rhyme murder, a key clue comes from the name of an obscure character in an obscure Henrik Ibsen play. Only in a Philo Vance story could such a thing happen.

Despite the imperfections in both the plot and the production, *The Bishop Murder Case* has its inherent interests. It is worth a view both for historical reasons, as one of the first sound whodunits, and also for its satisfactory rendering of an older style of mystery story which would disappear from the screen within a few years.

*Note on the Source Material*: The movie was faithfully based on S.S. Van Dine's 1926 novel *The Bishop Murder Case*. All of the murders are the same and all of the suspects are the same. As a result, the solution of the murders in the book is as questionable as the solution in the film. If Professor Dillard committed all of the crimes to frame Arnesson with the idea of getting Arnesson out of his life, why not simply kill Arnesson? The film does not address that issue at all. The book does but the reasoning of Vance on that issue is less than credible. Also, if Dillard was trying to frame Arnesson, why set up the initial killing of Cock Robin to implicate Sperling? In fact, for someone as smart as Professor Dillard, if he was really trying to frame Arnesson for the crimes, why did he not leave any clues to Arnesson's guilt at any of the crime scenes for the police to discover?

The two significant changes between book and film occur at the conclusions. The film version uses the movie cliché of the beautiful young heroine being carried off by the killer and Vance rescuing her just in time. In the book, there is a similar event but to keep the story in line with the Mother Goose theme, the killer kidnaps a young girl named Madeleine Moffat. Vance eventually rescues the young girl but not before the connection is made to the nursery rhyme, "Little Miss Muffet." Thus, the ending of the book is more satisfying than that of the film, since the book completes the circle of having all of the crimes relate to a Mother Goose rhyme.

In addition, at the end of the book, Dillard sneaks poison into a cup of wine intended for Arnesson. Vance notices Dillard's actions and surreptitiously switches the glasses, causing Dillard to drink the poisoned wine. Dillard dies almost instantly. When Markham accuses Vance of murder, Vance replies, "Oh, doubtless.... I say, am I by any chance under arrest?" In the film version of this scene, Dillard dies from shock and not from poisoning by Vance. While the film goes the less controversial route for the demise of the villain, it is still the better approach to this scene. Much like the elimination of Vance's speeches about uninteresting topics from the novels, every effort in the films to reduce Vance's arrogance improves the effectiveness of the story.

Despite the problems with the solution to the murders, *The Bishop Murder Case* is one of the best of the Philo Vance novels, possibly because of the inherent appeal of the nursery rhyme theme, the multiple murders, and the fact that Vance's lectures on obscure topics are kept to a minimum. Nevertheless, the lectures did not disappear completely. In particular, in Chapter XXI, when Vance is ostensibly analyzing the crimes, he actually gives a full chapter speech on mathematics, physics and some other boring subjects. At one point in the chapter, Vance stops in the middle of the lecture and says to Markham, "Do I bore you?" Markham, to the cheers of all of the novel's readers, replies, "Unquestionably." For

From left to right, Mrs. Menzel (Bodil Rosing), District Attorney Markham (Clarence Geldert) and Philo Vance (Basil Rathbone) find the dead body of Mrs. Drukker in *The Bishop Murder Case* (1930).

a book that is over 80 years old, it is likely that no reader has ever read Chapter XXI without skimming over at least a few of the lines.

## *The Benson Murder Case* (1930)

This is the third Philo Vance mystery starring William Powell and it is the last one filmed at Paramount Pictures. Even though *The Benson Murder Case* was released in 1930, a few years after sound came to the cinema, the film still epitomizes the problems with early sound films: little camera movement and lack of close-ups of the performers. At least there are a few high-angle camera shots to spice up the presentation. Yet despite these production flaws, *The Benson Murder Case* is, at the very least, somewhat entertaining.

Sometimes it is a surprise to the reader or viewer as to who the victim will be in a murder mystery. Not in this case. The story is set at the beginning of the stock market crash, at a time when a number of clients of Anthony Benson, a wealthy stockbroker, are ruined when Benson sells out all of their stock positions. Everyone hates Benson and it is hardly a surprise when he is killed one night at his country estate. There are a number of suspects, including bootlegger Harry Gray and dowager Paula Banning, both of whom lost a substantial sum of money as a result of Benson's actions. Also high on the list of likely killers are Adolph Mohler, a gigolo whose forged check Benson is holding, and Fanny Del

Roy, a woman of some ill repute, who claims that Benson is holding valuable pearls that are rightfully hers.

Benson invites Gray to spend the night at his country estate where, by coincidence or design, all of the suspects also appear along with Philo Vance and District Attorney Markham. While Vance is debating crime issues with Gray downstairs, a shot is heard upstairs and Benson's murdered body falls down the steps. Vance, who has been bored since solving the Greene murder case, decides to take on this new mystery and it is not too long before he brings all of the suspects back to Benson's estate and unmasks the true killer.

One problem with the three Paramount Philo Vance movies is that the killer is easy to spot, because the same plot trick is used in each. In all three films, there is one suspect who could not have committed the murder. Therefore, that person must be the killer. In this case, Harry Gray must be innocent since he was talking to Vance downstairs at the exact time Benson was shot upstairs. Vance, however, is not fooled by Gray's alibi and deduces that Gray shot Benson a few minutes earlier with a gun with a silencer and then created a contraption which would mimic the sound of a gun and allow Benson's already dead body to drop down the steps at just the right time to confuse Vance.

Unfortunately, Vance's explanation of the crimes is far from convincing, particularly since it requires Gray to have conceived his clever contraption and then built it on almost a moment's notice when he spotted the opportunity to kill Benson. Vance mentions clues of a puddle of blood on the house stairs and Gray reaching into his pocket after the murder, but these important pieces of evidence are never brought to the viewer's attention while the crime is being investigated. There is, however, one good clue that the viewer definitely learns: Benson was not wearing his toupee when he was shot. Since the vain Benson was unlikely to leave his room without his hair piece, it was unlikely he was shot at the top of the stairs.

It is much easier to identify the problems with the film rather than its positive attributes, but there are a few. Some of those positives are the excellent performances, once again by William Powell as Philo Vance and Eugene Pallette as Sergeant Heath. Also, Paul Lukas is sufficiently shifty as lothario Adolph Mohler and William Boyd is convincingly arrogant as shady Harry Gray that their performances add significantly to the effectiveness of the feature.

In addition, the first half of *The Benson Murder Case* works particularly well, as all of the suspects visit the Benson mansion on a stormy night. For a time, the film seems more like an old dark house mystery than a whodunit, and who does not like an old dark house mystery?

The film gives an interesting portrayal of the wealthy at the end of the roaring '20s. Vance is willing to pay $3000 for a Japanese print and even interrupts his murder investigation to visit an exhibition of other Japanese prints. Harry Gray has a barber come into his lavish apartment each day to shave him and hires Benson's valet simply because he ties his neckties so well. Everyone seems to have bought stocks on margin and then does not have sufficient funds to make the necessary payments when the margin calls are made. The Philo Vance films and novels were always set among the rich but these people seem to be the richest of the rich (at least for a time). There may be some historical value to this portrayal of the wealthy in America just before the start of the Great Depression.

*The Benson Murder Case* is a flawed film and a flawed mystery and yet it does have its unfathomable interest. Much like *The Greene Murder Case* and *The Bishop Murder Case*, it is well worth a view.

*Note on the Source Material*: The first Philo Vance novel was *The Benson Murder Case*, published in 1926. It involves the shooting death of stockbroker Anthony Benson in his New York apartment. At the time of his death, Benson has a forged check and a confession to that forgery by one of the suspects locked in his safe. Vance eventually solves the crime.

Other than that, there are no similarities between the film and the written work. Even though its first two Vance films were based substantially on their source material, Paramount chose to go with an original script for the movie version of *The Benson Murder Case*.

## *The Kennel Murder Case* (1933)

For mystery aficionados *The Kennel Murder Case* is one of the best-known and best-loved movies of the 1930s. With its complex plot, innovative direction and likable performances, it is a true mystery classic.

The film opens at the Long Island Kennel Club where the annual dog show is taking place. Captain MacTavish, Philo Vance's favorite pet, is in the competition but for the first time in the movie series, the erudite detective suffers a significant defeat. MacTavish is a loser, falling in this round to a hound owned by wealthy Archer Coe and one owned by Sir Thomas McDonald. Coe's ward, Hilda Lake, is in love with McDonald and there is more than a friendly competition between Coe and McDonald when it comes to show dogs.

While light-hearted in tone, this opening sequence is used to begin to acquaint the audience with some of the important characters and the eventual suspects in the murder of Archer Coe. It may also have been inserted to justify the title of the movie, as there are no persons named "Kennel" murdered in the film and no further action in the film takes place at a dog kennel.

Matters quickly turn serious as that evening, McDonald's show dog is mysteriously murdered and McDonald suspects Coe of the misdeed. The next morning, Archer Coe's body is discovered in his locked bedroom, with a bullet hole in his head and a gun in his hand, apparently a suicide. Vance, however, disputes the suicide conclusion and his suspicions are then confirmed by the coroner, Dr. Doremus, who determines that the bullet wound occurred after death. Indeed, Doremus discovers that Coe was also hit across the head with a blunt instrument and knifed in the back, so suicide is out of the question. But, then, how did Coe's body end up in a locked room?

There are a number of suspects. In addition to McDonald, who is upset over the death of his dog, there is Archer Coe's brother Sebastian, who did not like his arrogant sibling. There is Hilda Lake, who also disliked Coe, particularly because Coe controlled her finances too closely. Raymond Wrede, Coe's secretary, is in love with Hilda and was upset with Coe for disapproving of the relationship. Coe had a mistress, Doris Delafield, who lives in the apartment building next to the Coe mansion. Delafield was also romantically involved with Eduardo Grassi, a visitor from Italy who was attempting to purchase a substantial number of Coe's Chinese antiques for a company back in his native land. When Coe found out about the relationship between Delafield and Grassi, Coe cancelled the transaction to the chagrin of Grassi. Also lurking in the background at the Coe home are Gamble, the butler, and Liang, the cook. Given Coe's arrogant and superior disposition, any one of those characters could have been involved in the killing.

In addition to the multiple wounds on Coe's body, there are a number of puzzling clues. An injured Doberman pinscher is found in the house, a broken Chinese vase with blood

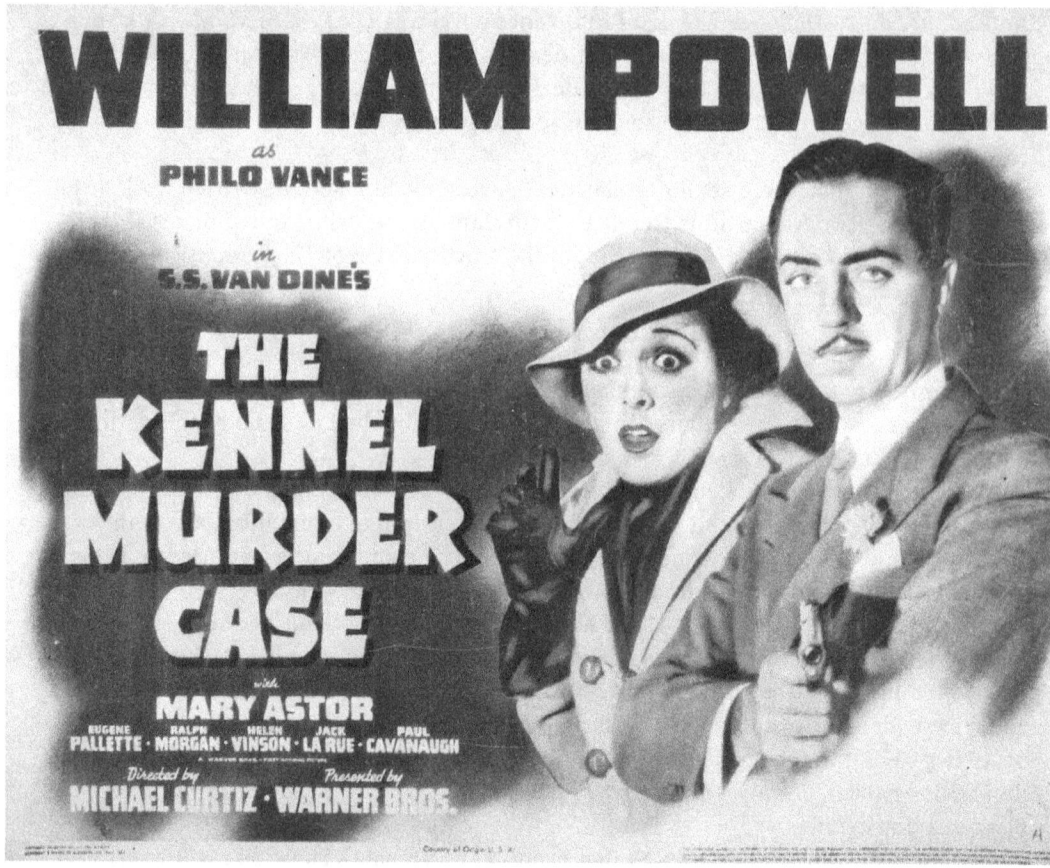

This lobby card for *The Kennel Murder Case* (1933) highlights two of the stars of the feature, Mary Astor, who plays suspect Hilda Lake, and William Powell, who plays Philo Vance for the fourth and last time in his career.

on some of the pieces is discovered by Vance, and a strange device with strings, pins and a darning needle is found in the pocket of another victim. Then there is the locked room aspect to the murder of Archer Coe. Despite all of these complexities, Vance still manages to piece the intricate tale together and deduces that there were two killers operating independently on the night of Coe's murder. Vance then plays a trick on the one killer who is still alive, forcing him to confess to the crimes.

Michael Curtiz's direction of *The Kennel Murder Case* is superb, as he uses a number of cinematic techniques to move the story forward. In order to maintain a variety of shot compositions so as never to allow the film to become static, there are camera shots from low- and high-angle perspectives, shots of characters' reflections in mirrors, and shots of characters speaking with an extra, inanimate object in the frame. There are the passing camera shots of a train station's clocks which establish Sebastian Coe's alibi for Archer's murder, which require the viewer to pay close attention. There are quick camera pivots within and between scenes as the camera moves from one party to the other, dissolves and wipes between scenes and even a split screen employed during a telephone conversation. There is a striking shot of Coe's body through the bedroom door keyhole, with the camera somehow moving through the keyhole to focus in on the corpse. All of these cinematic tools transform a story which is essentially a talkfest into a story that is always moving and never boring. The contrast with the earlier films in the Vance series is stark.

But cinematic technique alone cannot make a great detective movie. In the end, a mystery needs a great plot and *The Kennel Murder Case* has it. As noted above, there are numerous viable suspects and many puzzling clues, all of which keep the viewers on their toes. The story is one of the most complex ever filmed and yet the viewer can easily understand the denouement, as Vance explains the crimes through the use of building models and a brilliant flashback sequence describing the murders. The flashback sequence is silent, except for the narration of Vance and some important sounds such as falling bodies and a gunshot. The camera seems to prowl through the Coe house as the murders and other strange goings-on occur. Many other mystery films simply have the detective explain the solution to the murder to a group of suspects gathered at the end of the film, in a very boring sequence. Curtiz demonstrates the better way to handle the denouement of a movie whodunit, using cinematic techniques rather than long speeches to explain the situation. The flashback sequence from *The Kennel Murder Case* is one of the highlights of the mystery movies of the 1930s.

William Powell had really grown into the role by the time of *The Kennel Murder Case*, never becoming the arrogant Vance of the books, always being a likable seeker of the truth. His character is aided by his obvious affection for his dog, an attribute of the story which does not come from the book. The performance of the film, though, is that of Etienne Girardot as the irascible coroner, Dr. Doremus, interrupted in his meal times by the multiple calls to the Coe home. Girardot is delightful in the role, resulting in him being brought back for two subsequent features in the Vance series. Doremus is one of the first in a long line of humorous coroners in film, television and print mysteries.

*The Kennel Murder Case* has its flaws. The police are made into bumblers for the first time in the series, as Heath seems ready to put the handcuffs on everyone without any proof, and the police somehow fail to discover the other body and the injured dog in the Coe mansion. While Vance's explanations of the crimes hold together, there is never any explanation as to how he discovered the perpetrator and on that one issue, Vance seems to be guessing. These are, however, minor matters. *The Kennel Murder Case* cleverly illustrates that an intricate murder mystery can be created for the screen, and be both interesting for the viewer but not so difficult that the storyline cannot be followed. It is a shame that more Hollywood mystery movies did not follow the example of *The Kennel Murder Case*, the best of the Philo Vance movies.

*Note on the Source Material*: *The Kennel Murder Case* was based on the 1933 novel of the same name by S.S. Van Dine. The essence of the film's murder mystery comes from the novel as in both the film and the book, Archer Coe is found shot, stabbed and bludgeoned in his locked bedroom, another body is later discovered in the downstairs closet of the mansion, and an injured canine provides an important clue. Oddly, the film has more suspects than the novel, as Sir Thomas McDonald does not appear in the book and Doris Delafield is only mentioned therein.

The mystery in the book makes more sense than the film, as Vance explains how he knew who the killer was by a convincing analysis of the clues. There is no guesswork on the part of the great detective, as there seems to be in the film. However, the movie is far more entertaining, as the audience does not have to be bored by Vance's tedious monologues on Scottish terriers, Doberman pinchers and Chinese antiques. Also, the flashback

Heavyset Sergeant Health (Eugene Pallette) and the erudite Philo Vance (William Powell, both on the left, interview two of the suspects in the murder of Archer Coe, Eduardo Grassi (Jack LaRue), with whom Coe recently canceled a business deal, and Doris Delafield (Helen Vinson), Coe's mistress, in *The Kennel Murder Case* (1933).

sequence gives a visual explanation to the crimes that is hard to replicate in print. That in no way takes away from the plot of the book, which is exceptionally clever.

The dog who followed the killer into the Coe mansion and then was severely injured is a Scottish terrier in the novel, rather than the Doberman pinscher used in the film version. Vance's tracing of the owner of the terrier provides him with the solution to the crimes. At the end of the novel, Vance adopts the injured animal who, the reader is told, then went on to live with Vance for the rest of its life. The terrier's name in the book is Miss Mac-Tavish, and that name is obviously the inspiration for the name of Vance's dog in the film.

*Note on the Remake*: *The Kennel Murder Case* was remade as *Calling Philo Vance* (1940).

## THE POST-WILLIAM POWELL ERA

### *The Dragon Murder Case* (1934)

For the true detective story aficionado, *The Dragon Murder Case* commences in a comfortable manner, with a number of wealthy, sophisticated people gathered at a large mansion for a dinner party, with drinks being served by a tuxedoed butler and with many of the characters having an unconcealed antipathy toward one or more of the others. Surely, murder is afoot and of course, the viewer will not be disappointed. This type of film is clearly one of those classic puzzle mysteries (or cosies) which epitomizes the Golden Age of the Detective Story. And, while this type of story is usually associated with English writers such as Agatha Christie, it was in fact S.S. Van Dine who popularized the form in America in the 1920s and the 1930s.

The wealthy Stamm family seems to have a number of problems. Pretty Bernice Stamm is engaged to marry Monty Montague even though she is in love with her childhood friend, Dale Leland. Bernice's brother, Rudolph, is so upset about something that he has decided to drink himself into an unconscious stupor. Bernice's mother, old Mrs. Stamm, is a raving lunatic. The Stamms seem to have so few friends that they have decided to invite several people who generally dislike each other to the same party.

To relieve the tension, Montague suggests that everyone go for a swim in the mansion's swimming pool, which is actually a backed-up stream with a shady history, prophetically dubbed the Dragon Pool. Montague decides to jump into the pool off of the high dive and, after a fabulous swan dive, disappears for good. It may be a case of murder and so Philo Vance takes over the investigation.

*The Dragon Murder Case* is helped immensely by the number of excellent performances by the actors playing the suspects, from a very young Lyle Talbot as Leland, a gruff William Davidson as Greeff and a sarcastic George E. Stone as Tatum. Margaret Lindsay is fetching as Bernice Stamm. Etienne Girardot returns as the coroner, Dr. Doremus, and he is the funniest thing in the film, twice criticizing the police for calling him out on an assignment when they do not even have a dead body available for him to carve up. Eugene Pallette is back as Sergeant Heath but this is his least interesting performance in the series. Much like *The Kennel Murder Case*, the character of Heath is written, once again, as somewhat of a bumbler, willing to arrest almost any suspect with scant evidence. Also, it is amazing to see how much weight Pallette has gained since the original Philo Vance films produced at Paramount in the late 1920s.

This is Warren William's first film as Philo Vance and unfortunately, he comes in a distant second in a comparison with William Powell, the man who originated the role. Warren William simply does not convey much enthusiasm for the role and seems to be just going through the paces. It can be difficult, however, to truly evaluate William's performance as Philo Vance. William is so familiar playing a detective in the Perry Mason and Lone Wolf series, as well as in an Arsène Lupin film, that it is simply boring watching him play the same type of role again and again. William is not a clever enough actor to distinguish between these several film detective roles, so, perhaps with the exception of Perry Mason in *The Case of the Howling Dog* (1934), William plays all of the roles in the same manner. By contrast, William Powell's Philo Vance is completely distinguishable from William Powell's Nick Charles.

However, the true stars of *The Dragon Murder Case* are not the actors but rather the sets. In addition to the impressive sets within the Stamm mansion, the set of the Dragon Pool is truly amazing. The pool is not a traditional swimming pool but is more of a pond, with irregular shores and rock formations setting its boundaries. Director H. Bruce Humberstone often shoots the scenes at the pool from a distance and on high, to show the size of the set and the detail therein. Indeed, the key scene in the film is the dive by Montague into the Dragon Pool, his disappearance underwater and the rescue attempts by Greef and Leland. The effectiveness of the scene is aided immensely by the incredible studio-created backdrop.

With the cackling ranting of Mrs. Stamm, a slight horror element to the story, and the re-staging of the death scene at the pool, *The Dragon Murder Case* never becomes boring. Nevertheless, the end of the film seems particularly rushed, with Vance disclosing that Rudolph Stamm is the killer only because he accidentally discovered liquor in the dirt of the plant near Stamm's chair. Thus, Stamm was not actually drunk on the night of the murder and could have committed the killing of Montague. Of course, that does not mean that he actually committed the murder and there is no real proof that he did. Thus, to help Vance out, Stamm confesses to the murder for no reason.

Once the culprit is disclosed in a murder mystery, the whole scenario should make sense when looking back over everything the murderer previously did in the story and if it does not, the solution lacks credibility. Here, Stamm has planned in advance to kill Montague by placing diving equipment near the Dragon Pool. On the night of the murder, Stamm pretended to be drunk so that he had an alibi for the killing of Montague. However, Stamm had no idea, in advance, that Montague would dive into the pool that night, or, if he did so, when he would dive into the pool. The suggestion to go swimming came from Montague and it appears to have been a spur-of-the-moment decision. Thus, in retrospect, the killing of Montague by Stamm makes little sense.

On the other hand, for those who say that they knew Stamm was the killer from the beginning, because he was the only suspect who could not have committed the crime, note the clever trick by the filmmakers. Tatum left the swimming pool just before Montague's murder to get some drinks so that just like Stamm, it appears that Tatum also could not have committed the crime. Either of the two is therefore just as unlikely a suspect as the other. Thus, the solution to the original murder in *The Dragon Murder Case* is cleverly disguised. Unfortunately, the explanation of the crimes and Vance's reasoning cannot survive much scrutiny. The rushed ending of the film undercuts most of the virtues of the rest of *The Dragon Murder Case*.

*Note on the Source Material*: The movie was substantially based on the novel of the same name, first published in book form in 1933. There are, however, some significant differences between the two works. For example, there is one more suspect in the Stamm house on the night of the murder in the novel than in the movie and the killing of Greef is handled in a substantially different manner in the book than in the film. However, the murderer, the method of murder and the technique by which the murderer attempts to give himself an alibi are the same in both works.

One of the drawbacks of the novel is that though there are a number of suspects for the killer of Montague, so little time is spent with each of them they are hard to distinguish from one another. Oddly, this is a shortcoming usually exhibited by mystery movies, such as many of the movies in the Charlie Chan series. It is seldom a problem in a mystery novel which usually has enough time to flesh out each of the suspects for the reader. With *The Dragon Murder Case*, however, while the novel has this problem, the film version does not. The viewer actually becomes more familiar with the suspects in the film than the reader does in the book. Also, in the book Tatum is down at the swimming pool when Montague dives into the Dragon Pool, so unlike the movie, there is not that extra clever attempt to divert suspicion from the real killer. Thus, in several ways the movie is better than the novel.

One of the most common improvements in the Philo Vance movies over the books is the deletion of Vance's esoteric lectures. In *The Dragon Murder Case*, it is Chapter XIV and

Vance's ceaseless lecture on dragons in mythology and culture. For perhaps the only time in the entire Vance movie series, the lecture is carried over into the film although, luckily, only for a few seconds, and Markham and Heath participate in the discussion. Because of its brevity, it is actually bearable to listen to the lecture in the movie while it is nearly impossible to read the lengthy speech in the book.

## *The Casino Murder Case* (1935)

After only a few minutes of viewing, it is clear that *The Casino Murder Case* is a cut below all of the previous films in the series. All of the earlier Philo Vance features, whether excellent, good or fair, were serious matters, with little intentional humor other than the interactions with the coroner, Dr. Doremus. In *The Casino Murder Case*, the filmmakers chose to go the easy route, very common in movies of the 1940s mystery series, by adding comedy, to the detriment of the film.

For example, for the first time in the film series, Vance's valet, Currie, is featured and since he appears in the person of Eric Blore, the role is obviously played for humor. The character adds nothing to the plot. At the Llewellyn house, there is a servant who eavesdrops at doors and a butler, carrying a heavy trunk up some long steps, having to reverse directions over and over again depending upon who gives him instructions about where to move the crate. Abbott and Costello, where are you? Eugene Pallette is gone and in his place as Sergeant Heath is Ted Healy, most famous today for working with The Three Stooges in vaudeville. Since the role of Sergeant Heath is now written as comedy relief only, Healy is properly cast but he is egregiously unfunny. Pallette was much more entertaining as Heath, even when the part was written more seriously, with the opportunity for only light humor. Also, for the first time in these films, Vance has a sidekick. It is not, however, his loyal Van from the novels but rather is Doris, the secretary to Mrs. Llewellyn. There even seems to be a bit of a love interest between Philo and Doris. While Rosalind Russell is fine in the role, the insertion of this type of part into a Philo Vance film is totally inappropriate. For those who disagree with that opinion, please wait around just four more years until the release of *The Gracie Allen Murder Case*, where Vance has a different female "assistant" in his criminal investigations.

The plot of *The Casino Murder Case* is typical for the Philo Vance films, with a myriad of suspects in a murder committed in a large mansion among New York's wealthy class. Vance's involvement in the affairs of the Llewellyn family commences when Vance receives a note, signed by "A Friend," asking Vance's assistance in preventing a dreadful tragedy to Lynn Llewellyn at the local casino that night. That leads Vance to the Llewellyn home where he meets the neurotic and overbearing matriarch of the family, Priscilla Llewellyn, her son Lynn, his wife Virginia, Lynn's sister Amelia, her boyfriend Dr. Kane and Priscilla's brother, Richard Kinkaid, the owner of the casino. On the occasion of Vance's visit, there is substantial tension at the Llewellyn manor caused by the acerbic Virginia and her desire to quit the household and return to the stage.

At the casino, Lynn is poisoned while gambling, is rushed to the hospital and survives. Back at the mansion, Virginia is poisoned and dies. Later, Mrs. Llewellyn commits suicide — or so it appears. Even Doris is poisoned and almost dies. Then, after an inexplicable detour in pursuit of heavy water, Vance, to the surprise of no one, unmasks Lynn as the killer of Virginia.

S.S. Van Dine was both a popular and clever mystery writer but his popularity waned

**Philo Vance (Paul Lukas) may have his first screen love interest in Doris (Rosalind Russell), Mrs. Llewellyn's secretary, in this scene from the last seconds of *The Casino Murder Case* (1935).**

quickly in the middle 1930s. One of the reasons, perhaps, is that Van Dine had few whodunit tricks in his writing arsenal. Looking back at the previous movies in the series, it seems that the person who was physically unable to have committed the murder, whether by way of an alibi or physical distance from the crime, was usually the murderer. As a corollary of that trick, if there was an attempted murder of a suspect and that suspect survived, the murderer was then obvious. Both tricks are used in *The Casino Murder Case* as Lynn Llewellyn survives a poisoning and he was far away from the Llewellyn mansion when his wife was killed. Any ardent mystery fan will know the identity of the murderer, just minutes after Virginia's murder is committed.

There are other problems with the mystery aspects of the movie. If Lynn was setting up an alibi for himself at the casino, why write a letter to the greatest detective in New York City, asking him to become involved in the investigation even before the crime is committed? Vance's presence at the casino provided no additional cover for Lynn's crimes and the letter itself was the best piece of evidence pointing Vance toward Lynn. During one of the long story arcs of the film, Vance, due to Lynn's clever misdirection, goes off in pursuit of heavy water, leading him away from Lynn as the murderer. The problem there is that Vance is the only person in the entire world who is clever enough to fall for the trick. The whole idea is way above Sergeant Heath's acumen, or, for that matter, of anyone else, so why employ the ruse at all?

The police do not investigate the crime, never analyzing a box of candy that could contain poison, never finding the gun in Llewellyn's room, never using gloves when handling the evidence, and, for that matter, never interviewing the suspects. At the end of the film,

Vance has set a trap for Lynn at the casino, which requires the police to overhear Llewellyn's confession. However, just before Vance heads to the casino, Markham tells Vance that he is not going with him because he believes the case is closed. Yet, without the viewer knowing it in advance, Heath ends up at the casino anyway and overhears the confession as planned. Thus, Markham makes his statement to Vance about the casino, not for any plot purposes, but solely to trick the viewer into believing that Vance will be at the casino on his own. That is a shamefully crude trick to play on the viewer.

Paul Lukas was usually a fine actor in his many screen appearances, but he is woefully miscast as Philo Vance. He plays the part in such a light manner that his act in causing the police to execute Lynn near the end of the film is not very credible. It is very hard for the viewer to get past Lukas' thick accent, also undermining his credibility as the erudite detective. Of course, Vance's explanation for the crimes and how he solved them is unconvincing in any event, so it may not have mattered who played the role in this particular film. Even William Powell would have been hard-pressed to make *The Casino Murder Case* into an intelligible work.

*Note on the Source Material*: *The Casino Murder Case* was based on S.S. Van Dine's 1934 novel of the same name. The film is generally true to the novel although in the novel, a fake suicide note is discovered after the murder of Virginia Llewellyn, and the second person who almost dies from poisoning is Amelia Llewellyn, as the character of Doris is new to the film. The side plot concerning heavy water comes from the novel, and may actually be more unconvincing in the book. The conclusion of the film, with the apparent killing of Vance, comes from the novel, but the scene is actually more suspenseful in the book, with District Attorney Markham and the hapless narrator Van also in peril.

An interesting characteristic of the Vance novels is highlighted when one watches a movie in the series and then reads the book. If there is an unconvincing and unexplained plot point in the movie, Van Dine usually recognized it in his book and attempted to explain it away. For example, the action of Lynn Llewellyn in writing to Vance in advance of the killings is noted by Vance at the end of the book, during the explanation of the crimes. Vance says to Lynn, "Your letter to me, begging for my presence at the Casino Saturday night, was your first miscalculation.... And really, y'know, it wasn't necess'ry to have me witness your collapse at the Casino; any one could have given me the details." This is the exact point made above in the discussion of the film. The explanation given in the book is that it was all part of Lynn's plan to frame Kincaid, based on the linkage between the water at the crime scenes and the heavy water being manufactured. Lynn needed Vance at the scene because he was the only one astute enough to fall for the trick. As unconvincing as that explanation is, at least Van Dine made an attempt.

Although the Philo Vance novels are little read today, the early ones are actually quite good. However, all of them are deleteriously affected by Vance's long monologues on uninteresting subjects. That is why the most amusing, yet telling, dialogue from the film comes when Doris tells Vance that she has read all of the books about Vance's cases. When asked what she thinks of them, Doris tells Vance that while she liked the books, they "are a trifle long-winded in spots."

## *The Garden Murder Case* (1936)

With *The Garden Murder Case*, the eighth Philo Vance film produced in America, Edmund Lowe becomes the fifth actor to play the role of the erudite detective and the fourth actor in as many films to play the part. In addition, the role of Sergeant Heath is turned over to Nat Pendleton, the third different actor in as many films to play that role. After *The Garden Murder Case*, there would be additional cast turnover, undercutting the cohesiveness of the Philo Vance movies as a mystery series.

Lowe turns out to be an excellent choice to undertake the part in *The Garden Murder Case* (and is a major improvement over Paul Lukas from the prior film). Lowe is handsome and sophisticated and is also able to portray the softer side of Vance, which is important for this film because for the first time the detective seems to fall in love during the course of the proceedings. It is a shame that Lowe was not brought back for the few remaining Philo Vance films of the era.

*The Garden Murder Case* commences at a steeplechase race track where wealthy Lowe Hammle has a horse in the last race. His jockey is young Floyd Garden, who seems quite depressed. Madge Fenwick-Ralston, the wife of Major Fenwick-Ralston, is having an affair with Floyd and begs him not to ride in the race. Floyd insists that he ride, telling everyone that he will break his neck during the race. Floyd goes on to ride in the steeplechase race, taking a nasty spill and breaking his neck, just as he had predicted. The police initially believe Floyd's death to be a suicide but Vance disagrees.

The action then moves to more familiar surroundings for Vance: the large Hammle mansion with a butler, a cook, Hammle's bedridden aging mother in an upstairs room, a bitter nurse attending to her and a few other excellent suspects, such as the Fenwick-Ralstons. Two of those suspects are then killed, leaving only a few good ones left, a familiar scenario for Vance fans. The erudite detective is then able to solve the crimes, two of which were committed by use of a hypnotic trance, surely not familiar territory for Vance, making the ending more like the supernatural than the serious.

*The Garden Murder Case* is graced by a number of excellent performances in addition to that of Lowe's. Virginia Bruce plays Hammle's niece Zalia, who is both a suspect and a love interest for Vance. Bruce is particularly attractive in this film, easily matching wits with Vance as they fall in love, even though she may still be the killer of three people. Jessie Ralph as the impatient and inconsiderate Mrs. Hammle is outstanding in the few moments she has in the film. Etienne Girardot returns as Dr. Doremus, the coroner, and he is irascible as ever. The actors and actresses playing the other suspects at the Hammle abode, down to the butler and cook, are all quite good.

The disconcerting performances in the film involve Nat Pendleton as Sergeant Heath and Grant Mitchell as District Attorney Markham. Pendleton cannot compare to Eugene Pallette's fabulous performances in the role, particularly since Heath appears to becoming dumber and dumber with each new film. The part of Markham is written differently in this film than in the prior movies and books, with Markham seeming to have a tension-filled relationship with Vance. Then why let Vance come along on the investigations in the first place?

The mystery in *The Garden Murder Case* is quite intriguing, with two characters apparently committing suicide after telling people that they were about to die. There is also a surprise killing of Hammle in his library, which does not fit the pattern of the other two deaths. In a clever solution, Hammle has been killed by a different character and for a different reason than the other two murdered people.

In the end, though, *The Garden Murder Case* does not really work at all. It turns out that the two characters who predicted their own deaths were hypnotized into killing themselves. Suddenly, the very rational Philo Vance murder cases have turned into supernatural affairs, with no basis in the reality of hypnosis. A hypnosis-induced death is an exceptionally unconvincing solution to the crimes, making the entire film, as good as it may have been up to that point, fall like a house of cards. Murder mysteries are often not much better than their solutions and for *The Garden Murder Case*, that means that the entire film is mediocre, at best.

At the end of the film, the killer apparently hypnotizes Philo Vance into jumping off a high ledge. At the last instant, Vance steps back from the edge, revealing that he was only pretending to be hypnotized so that he could wring a confession out of the killer. Interestingly, the same ending is used in *The Woman in Green* (1945) from the Sherlock Holmes series. The ending is no more convincing in *The Woman in Green* than it is in *The Garden Murder Case*.

*Note on the Source Material*: Every film in the Philo Vance series to date with the exception of *The Benson Murder Case* was substantially based on S.S. Van Dine's book of the same name. That pattern ended with this movie and S.S. Van Dine's 1935 book of the same name.

The novel concerns the apparent suicide of Woode Swift after he loses a substantial sum of money betting on a horse race. The bets are placed over the phone from the large Garden mansion, with the races broadcast over a radio system to all who are participating in the afternoon of betting at the Garden estate. Vance, who is in the house at the time of Swift's death, quickly deduces that Swift's demise was a murder and not a suicide. After another death and a failed murder attempt, Vance unmasks the surprise killer.

The novel and the film have little in common except for the joint use of the names of some of the characters, a tangential connection to horse racing, Vance almost falling to his death at the end of each work, and Vance acquiring a mild interest in one of the suspects, pretty Zalia Graem. The entire hypnosis angle is a Hollywood creation.

## *Night of Mystery* (1937)

[*This is one of only a few films discussed in this book which the author did not view.*]

*Night of Mystery* was the second adaptation of *The Greene Murder Case*, the 1928 novel by S.S. Van Dine. Based on secondary sources, *Night of Mystery* appears to be an even more faithful adaptation of the novel than the 1929 film. However, just as in the 1929 film, the ending of the novel (although not the identity of the murderer) was changed with, in this version, Ada Greene attempting to commit suicide but surviving and then confessing to all of the murders. William K. Everson wrote that even though Grant Richards looked the part of Philo Vance, he was still miscast because he projected a kind of insincerity. Everson thought, however, that the direction of the film was lively and atmospheric.

## *The Gracie Allen Murder Case* (1939)

*The Gracie Allen Murder Case* is the nadir of the Philo Vance series and, perhaps, the worst mystery movie in any of the Hollywood mystery series. The film features Gracie Allen to such an extent that Philo Vance seems to be only a supporting player, on the level of Sergeant Heath or District Attorney Markham. *The Gracie Allen Murder Case* is primarily a comedy, with the mystery elements seemingly thrown in as filler material.

The plot, such as there is one, involves the poisoning of escaped convict Benny "The Buzzard" Nelson and the later poisoning of his wife Dixie Del Marr, a dancer at the Diamond Slipper, a New York nightclub. The owner of the Diamond Slipper is Daniel Mirche,

Philo Vance is nowhere to be seen in this still from *The Gracie Allen Murder Case* (1939), which is fitting since the real star of the movie is Gracie Allen, right. Bill Brown (Kent Taylor) is flirting with Gracie to make his girlfriend jealous.

who had previously framed Nelson for some crimes they jointly committed. At the end of the film, Mirche is fingered for the slaying of Nelson, and Mirche's attorney, Richard Lawrence, is announced as the killer of Del Marr, although it is not clear exactly how the murders were solved or who solved them.

Gracie Allen is Gracie Allen in this film, rattling off inconsistent lines and non sequiturs at the rate of what seems like dozens a minute. There are some funny lines in all of that dialogue but there is simply too much of Gracie. As ingratiating and funny a character as she was on radio and television, Gracie simply cannot carry a full-length movie on her own. Things might have been better if George Burns had appeared in the film. Gracie needed George's straight lines and comedy timing for her material to work better.

The true shame is the way the filmmakers demeaned the Philo Vance character and the legacy created by S.S. Van Dine. Whatever fair criticism there may be of the Vance novels, they were always complex mysteries with multiple suspects and many clues. Here, it is obvious from the beginning that Mirche killed Nelson; there are simply no other suspects. As for attorney Lawrence being the killer of Del Marr, he does not even appear in the film until the end (except for a brief comedy moment at the Diamond Slipper) and he inexplicably gives himself away by refusing to represent the arrested Mirche. Mirche then turns on Lawrence, accusing him of being involved in the murders and after some dithering around, the police finally arrest Lawrence. There are no clues to these killers; the murders are simply resolved at the end of the film by means hard to explain. Even in a comedy, Vance deserves a real mystery to solve.

In many ways, the Philo Vance of the novels has been ignored in *The Gracie Allen Murder Case*. Vance's valet is Asian instead of the reliable Currie from the novels. Vance is an adversary of Markham, not his ally. Vance makes a promise to the press about solving the murder in 48 hours, something Vance would never have done in the novels. At one point, Vance acts like a lawyer, saying he will obtain a writ of habeas corpus for one character who has been arrested. Vance must also believe he is a doctor, as he determines the cause of death of one of the victims before the coroner does. To create a tension-filled climax, Vance, not realizing that one of the cigarettes in his case contains poison, smokes four of them in the space of five minutes, hardly something Vance would have done. Since this is not the Philo Vance of the books or the previous films, perhaps Gracie Allen was correct in giving him a new name: Fido Vance.

A complete misfire, *The Gracie Allen Murder Case* is an embarrassment to all involved, including S.S. Van Dine, who contributed to it. (See the Note on the Production below.) Philo Vance, the most conceited of all the literary detectives, had no pomposity left by the time this disaster was released.

*Note on the Source Material*: The film was based on the novel *The Gracie Allen Murder Case*, published in 1938. The book involves the death of criminal Benny the Buzzard by a poisoned cigarette, although throughout most of the story it appears that the body is that of Philip Allen, the brother of Gracie. Much of the book is set at the Domdaniel café, a name of some literary significance, at least according to Philo Vance. In the movie, the name of the nightclub was changed to the Diamond Slipper, a somewhat sexier name. In the book, Dixie Dell Marr is not murdered and the character of the attorney-killer, Richard Lawrence, is not present.

The book is aided by its short length (about 100 pages less than the prior novels) and its original setting for a Vance novel, i.e., outside the seemingly ubiquitous large mansion with its many suspects and a butler walking around. Happily, Vance is still the focus of the book, with Gracie Allen a subsidiary character. Even George Burns makes a short appearance. However, the book is surely one of the weakest of all the Philo Vance novels. The mystery itself is as feeble as the one in the movie, with almost no suspects and no clues.

*Note on the Production*: According to *Alias S.S. Van Dine*, by the late 1930s, the popularity of the Philo Vance novels had waned to such a degree that Charles Scribner's Sons, which had earlier made a fortune off the Van Dine works, refused to publish another Vance mystery after *The Kidnap Murder Case* unless any new book was serialized in a magazine first, much like the other books in the series. Since that appeared to be unlikely, the Philo Vance series seemed to be at an end.

Paramount Pictures, however, came to the rescue, advising Wright that if he would incorporate the famous comedienne Gracie Allen into his next work, the studio would be happy to film it. Wright agreed and at that point Scribner's was happy to publish the novel, believing that the star power of Gracie Allen would contribute to large sales. Wright therefore wrote the book with the forced title of *The Gracie Allen Murder Case*, in consultation with the representatives of Paramount. Wright also agreed that Paramount could make any changes it wanted from the book in its transformation to the screen.

Wright met Burns and Allen once for lunch in 1938. They were agreeable to the project, believing the publicity would be good for them even though they received no payment for the use of their names. Of course, Gracie then starred in the movie version, receiving compensation for that work.

*Note on the Titles*: S.S. Van Dine was the first detective story writer to recognize that if the titles of his mystery novels followed a pattern, each of his books would be more recognizable to the reading public. Thus, out of the 12 Philo Vance novels, 11 are in the format of *The ___ Murder Case*, with the blank being filled in by a six-letter word such as "Bishop" or "Dragon." That is another reason why *The Gracie Allen Murder Case* is such a disappointing novel. It breaks the name pattern of the rest of the titles to the Philo Vance stories.

The early Ellery Queen novels, which were greatly influenced by the Philo Vance works, had their own title pattern, such as *The Spanish Cape Mystery*, *The Chinese Orange Mystery* and *The Roman Hat Mystery*. It would have been difficult for Queen to have sustained that pattern of titles over 30 years of Ellery Queen novels, and the author dropped the pattern after nine novels. Other examples of this titling technique are the Perry Mason novels, always beginning with *The Case of the ___* and usually ending with an adjective and a noun, such as *The Case of the Caretaker's Cat* and *The Case of the Curious Bride*. The Travis McGee novels by John MacDonald always had a color in the title, such as *A Purple Place for Dying* and *A Deadly Shade of Gold*. Perhaps the most successful practitioner of this titling art is Sue Grafton, with her alphabet titles *"A" Is for Alibi*, *"B" Is for Burglar* and so on.

## Calling Philo Vance (1940)

Warner Brothers was infamous for remaking films only a few years after the original was released. There was *20,000 Years in Sing Sing* (1932), with Spencer Tracy taking a rap on a murder charge to protect his girlfriend, remade as *Castle on the Hudson* (1940), with John Garfield taking the same fall. There was *Dr. Socrates*, a 1935 film starring Paul Muni playing a doctor slowly drawn into a life of crime, remade as *King of the Underworld* (1939), with Kay Francis playing a similar role. There was *The Life of Jimmy Dolan* (1933) in which Douglas Fairbanks, Jr., playing a boxer charged with murder, finds refuge in a children's home, remade as *They Made Me a Criminal* (1939) with John Garfield playing the accused boxer. Then, of course, every movie mystery fan knows that there were three versions of *The Maltese Falcon* made by Warner Brothers between 1931 and 1941.

Similarly, *Calling Philo Vance* is a Warner Brothers remake of its 1933 film *The Kennel Murder Case*. Given the strong reputation of the earlier film, it was unlikely that *Calling Philo Vance* would ever be able to reach the same level of appeal as the 1933 film and it does not. Nevertheless, it is a somewhat interesting mystery because, at its core, it is based on Van Dine's complex and cunning plot from the original novel, *The Kennel Murder Case*.

The film opens in Vienna on dark, foggy streets with two well-dressed gentlemen making their way to a secret rendezvous. One is Philo Vance, now a spy for the U.S. State Department, who is given the assignment from the other gentleman to find evidence that one Archer Coe from America is selling plans for his airplanes to a foreign government in violation of an exclusive arrangement with the American government. In order to accomplish this task, Vance is required to steal plans from Austria's Department of Aeronautics. Vance is initially successful in his mission, using the cover of being a husband to a peasant wife and their young son. But when Vance tries to flee the country, the young boy, in an amusing moment, tells the inspecting officer that Vance is not his father and continues to cry for his real papa. Vance is arrested but eventually flees the country and returns to America.

These early scenes with Vance in Vienna are actually the highlight of the film. The scenes are well-directed and well-performed. The sets of Vienna are large and convincing. In fact, the opening of the film evokes the style of the early Basil Rathbone films in the modern Sherlock Holmes series wherein Holmes undertakes wartime activities on behalf of his government. These scenes also evoke memories of the television program *Mission: Impossible*, with the viewer almost expecting Vance to be told that if he is caught or killed on his secret mission, the secretary will disavow any knowledge of his actions. The moments with the young boy who inadvertently foils Vance's plans are fabulous.

Once back in America, the spy story disappears (except for an ongoing interest in secret airplane plans) and Vance becomes involved in investigating the death of Archer Coe, whose dead body is found in his locked bedroom, an apparent suicide except for the blow across his head and the knife wound in the back. Later, another body is found in the house; after that, a large dog, still alive, who was also beaten across the head, is discovered. Vance finally solves the complex tale, unmasking the killer with a trap involving the injured dog.

It is almost as if there are two separate films being shown here. One is a spy drama, the other a murder mystery. The two do not fit together very well. It is as if the filmmakers were unable to decide what type of movie they were trying to create.

James Stephenson is actually quite satisfactory in the role of Philo Vance and he is quite a handsome fellow. Nevertheless, his performance pales in comparison to William Powell's performance in *The Kennel Murder Case*—suave, sophisticated and witty. Powell had an incredible screen presence; Stephenson has very little. Edward Brophy as policeman Ryan tries way too hard to be funny. It is the same role as Sergeant Heath in the 1933 film, and, once again, it is nearly impossible to top Eugene Pallette in that particular role.

The direction is adequate but nothing more. The shot composition is mundane and even the final flashback scene is disappointing. The one cleverness in the direction occurs at the end when the dog assaults the killer as part of Vance's scheme to disclose the killer's identity. As the dog attacks, it is difficult to see which of the final two suspects the canine is assaulting. It is only when the dog is pulled off his victim that the killer's identity is finally disclosed. This is a clever method of delaying the denouement of the film to the last possible moment.

For a mystery lover who has not read the book nor seen the earlier film version, *Calling Philo Vance* is interesting enough. However, rather than taking the time to watch this version, it is well worth the effort to locate the original movie version of the novel, which is one of the best mystery movies of the 1930s.

*Note on the Source Material*: *Calling Philo Vance* was based on S.S. Van Dine's 1933 novel *The Kennel Murder Case*. It is the second film version of the novel, the first being *The Kennel Murder Case* (1933). In fact, *Calling Philo Vance* was based more on the 1933 film than on the 1933 novel.

Of course, the metamorphosis of Philo Vance from upper class, dilettante detective into an international spy comes neither from the book nor the first film. That is a Hollywood wartime concoction for the character. However, once the film focuses in on the murders at the Coe mansion, the script's reliance on the prior film becomes apparent.

The character of Sir Thomas (or Taylor) MacDonald was first created for the 1933 film and carried over into this version. Doris Delafield, Coe's mistress (although that fact is made more readily apparent in the earlier film than the later film), never actually appears in the novel, although she is mentioned therein. Doris appears in both film versions. The outing of the murderer by the use of the dog who was previously struck by the murderer across the head with a poker, used in the second film, was first created for the 1933 film. The killer is discovered in a different manner in the book. Vance's Dog, Captain McTavish, is carried over from the prior film; he does not appear in the book.

Even the final explanation of the crimes in *Calling Philo Vance* comes from the earlier film. Stephenson's use of diagrams of the relevant buildings and an extended, almost silent flashback sequence were first devised for the 1933 film. Since so much of *Calling Philo Vance* comes from the film, *The Kennel Murder Case*, that is another reason to view the original film version rather than the inferior remake.

## The Later Films

### *Philo Vance's Gamble* (1947)

After being off-screen for seven years, famous amateur detective Philo Vance returned to the silver screen in 1947 in three very low-budget productions from Producers Releasing Corporation. One of the three films is *Philo Vance's Gamble* (1947). But, is the lead detective really Philo Vance? He does have that strange first name and he hails from New York City. However, he is now a professional private detective with an assistant named Ernie Clark. Sergeant Heath and District Attorney Markham are nowhere to be found (although Markham's name is mentioned by the district attorney of Los Angeles, where the story takes place). There are new lead actors in the cast, as Alan Curtis takes over the role of Philo Vance and Frank Jenks plays Ernie Clark. But, while the story has an interesting set-up, the low budget, poor acting, limp direction and weak plot result in a very forgettable film.

Jeffrey Connor is a swindler par excellence. He has talked a group of investors into paying him $150,000 to acquire a stolen emerald after having it smuggled into the country. He promises the group that he will sell the jewel for twice that amount, resulting in a quick profit for all involved. He also advises his fiancée, Gigi Desmond, that they will be eloping on board a ship the next day with the emerald as their joint bounty. Instead, Connor intends to flee with the emerald alone, by plane to South America, jilting both his investors and his girlfriend. It is not surprising, therefore, that Connor is shot and killed. The emerald cannot be found since Connor hid it in a jar of skin cream.

While not necessarily well-acted or -directed, these early moments of *Philo Vance's Gamble* are the highlights of the film, with at least the part of Jeffrey Connor well-played by familiar character actor Dan Seymour. Vance becomes involved in the case because Conner had allayed the suspicions of his investors by telling them that he had hired Vance to protect the jewel. Since Vance hails from New York City and the story takes place in Los Angeles, that seems like an unconvincing representation but the group apparently believed it. Vance also receives a call from the local district attorney's female secretary to meet with the D.A., Ellis Mason, but when Vance arrives, Mason knows nothing about the call. Indeed, the district attorney's only secretary is male. As he is leaving Mason's office, Vance runs into a former acquaintance from New York, lovely Laurian Marsh, who asks Vance for help concerning her suspicions about Jeffrey Conner. Marsh is interested in the situation because Oliver Tennant, who is bankrolling the new play in which Marsh is to perform, may have to close the play if he does not get his investment back from Conner.

In addition to the opening sequence, *Philo Vance's Gamble* has a few other plusses, including multiple murders, always of interest to the crime fan. The murders, though, are all clichés, with several people killed just as they are about to reveal information about the killer, meaning that the murderer always seems to be just in the right location at just the right time. How does a killer do that? The killer also seems to have the habit of hiding behind some curtains but still allowing the gun barrel to show through, a true movie cliché.

However, the real mystery cliché is the identity of the murderer. Since Vance knew Laurian Marsh in New York City and there is a budding romance between the two, who does not know that Marsh will turn out to be the killer? At least there is a clue to her deception, as she was the only person who benefited from the fake call from the district attorney, allowing her to "accidentally" meet Vance and get him involved in the investigation. But, why get Vance involved at all if she intended to go to Connor's house that night with a gun?

After the publication of Dashiell Hammett's novel *The Maltese Falcon* in 1929 and the release of the film versions, no book or film should have ever tried to use the apparent female love interest of the hardboiled detective as the surprise villain, without employing at least a little variation in the telling and a lot of style in the presentation. *Philo Vance's Gamble* does neither. In the denouement moment, the dialogue is poor, the direction is tepid and the scene is quite boring. Whatever justifiable criticism there may be of Mickey Spillane's novel *I, the Jury* (1947), which has the same resolution, no one can say that Spillane's denouement is not done in a different style than the Hammett novel. Unfortunately, *Philo Vance's Gamble* does the identical scene with no style at all.

The low budget of *Philo Vance's Gamble* also undercuts any effectiveness the film might have had. The entire story seems to have been filmed on indoor sets and to cut costs, most dialogue scenes have no close-ups and are filmed in a single take, thus avoiding multiple set-ups. Although Alan Curtis, Frank Jenks and Dan Seymour are good in their roles, most of the rest of the cast gives the impression that this is amateur night at the local theater. *Philo Vance's Gamble* is neither a Philo Vance story nor a good mystery movie. Given the lack of effort put into this film, it is hard to understand why PRC wanted to dust off the Philo Vance franchise at this late date.

## *Philo Vance's Secret Mission* (1947)

It is hard to determine the exact order in which the last three Philo Vance films were produced and then released, but it makes sense to next consider *Philo Vance's Secret Mission*. Just as in *Philo Vance's Gamble*, Alan Curtis stars and Frank Jenks plays Vance's assistant, Ernie Clark. This second feature is an improvement over the first, mainly because of its superior plot.

Vance is called in by Martin Jamison, the owner of Argo Publications, a company which publishes pulp mystery stories, ostensibly to assist with a new mystery novel. In reality, Jamison wants Vance to investigate the unsolved homicide of his partner Haddon

Phillips, who was murdered almost seven years before. In front of all of the potential suspects for the murder, Jamison asks Vance to come to his home that night so that he can give him some new insights into the killing. For someone who has experience in publishing mystery thrillers, Jamison should have realized that it was not a good idea to talk to Vance in the company of all of the suspects, as it gives Phillips' murderer the incentive to also dispose of Jamison. To the surprise of no one, Jamison is found murdered later that night and then, to the surprise of no one (as ridiculous as it may seem), Vance is deputized by the local police into assisting with the investigation.

Although Vance displays very little detective acumen in this film, preferring to try to trick the killer into exposing himself rather than investigating the facts, he does reach the obvious conclusion that if he can discover the murderer of Jamison, he would also discover the killer of Phillips. That should have triggered a very interesting "cold case" investigation, but Vance does little in that regard, other than consulting with the insurance investigator who originally looked into Phillips' murder. Instead of showing flashbacks to Phillips' murder, the insurance investigator reads his file aloud to Vance, a much more boring method of conveying important information to the viewer than actually showing the crime as it occurred. The filmmakers thus missed a number of opportunities with regard to Phillips' murder.

Nevertheless, there are many interesting aspects to the story. Seven years before, Phillips' body was seen on the floor of his home through a window but when the police arrived, the body was missing and was never found. Both Mrs. Phillips and Paul Morgan, the other partner in Argo Publications, are just about done waiting the seven years for Phillips to be declared dead so that each can collect on separate insurance policies on Phillips' life. Mrs. Phillips is about to marry the county attorney and go on her honeymoon in South America. All of the suspects seem to have an alibi for Jamison's murder.

This is another one of those film mysteries where there are numerous suspects but little attempt is made to distinguish between them. That means that either the killer will be the least likely suspect, i.e., one of this anonymous group, or the killer will be someone very obvious. In *Philo Vance's Secret Mission*, it is the latter situation. Most mystery fans will be able to figure out at least part of the solution to the crimes, since whenever the body of a murder victim is not found, whether in a novel or a movie, suspicions are immediately raised as to whether a murder actually occurred.

Curtis is fine as Vance as he was in the prior film, handsome and suave, always bantering with the beautiful Mona Bannister, his constant companion in this film. Sheila Ryan is quite attractive as Mona although her performance seems less than genuine, as she does not always deliver her banter with Vance in a convincing manner. Most of the other performances are satisfactory. The direction of Reginald LeBorg is adequate.

It is easy to pick out the flaws in *Philo Vance's Secret Mission*, whether the cheap production (note how the rear projection shots of a car or motorcycle following Vance's car never quite match the shots of the two vehicles together) or the filler material (Clark's romantic endeavours with the elevator operator), but there is a better plot than one might expect from this type of film. There is even a suspenseful car ride and chase through the woods, as Philo and Mona are being pursued by a gun-toting killer, a rare outdoor scene for such a low-budget film. This is not *The Kennel Murder Case* (1933) but so long as expectations are lowered, *Philo Vance's Secret Mission* is not too bad for a late 1940s mystery movie from PRC.

Philo Vance (Alan Curtis), center, leaves the offices of Argo Publications with Mona Bannister (Sheila Ryan), left, after he has accused her of murder in order to trap the real killer, in *Philo Vance's Secret Mission* (1947). Also on the elevator, from left to right, are Sheriff Harry Madison (James Bell), Vance's sidekick Ernie Clark (Frank Jenks) and the elevator operator (unidentified).

## *Philo Vance Returns* (1947)

Philo Vance returns again, this time in the person of William Wright, the ninth actor to portray the great detective in this series of films that were released over a period of almost 20 years. (Only three actors played Charlie Chan during the same approximate time frame.) Once again, the film and the portrayal of Vance owe nothing to the Van Dine novels. The only attribute of those stories which has been used for *Philo Vance Returns* is the name of the character.

Wealthy playboy Larry Blandon meets pretty singer Virginia Bernaux and, after one night of dancing, decides to marry her. Larry brings the singer to his mansion so that he can introduce her to his grandmother, Stella Blandon. There, Stella advises Virginia of Larry's past romantic history which includes four ex-wives and one ex-fiancée, all of whose pictures, for some inexplicable reason, remain hanging on a wall of the mansion like a sort of rogues gallery. Despite Larry's history and Stella's quiet suggestion that she reconsider the marriage, Virginia decides to go forward with the nuptials. However, when Larry drops Virginia back at her apartment later that night, Virginia is shot by a mysterious assailant, who flees in a car. Returning to his mansion, Larry calls his friend Philo Vance, and while on the phone Vance hears Larry being shot and killed.

Vance immediately undertakes the investigation of the two murders. Thereafter, two more of Larry's ex-wives are killed, the second husband of one is killed, and two of the ex-wives are almost killed. Finally, Vance concludes that Stella Blandon is the killer and rushes to the Blandon estate, just in time to prevent the killing of another of Larry's ex-wives.

While that broad outline of the mystery plot would seem to suggest that the film has some interest, *Philo Vance Returns* is, in fact, awful. The acting is below par, even for a second feature, and for once, the actor playing Vance, William Wright, gives a weak performance. The budget is so low that there may not be any outdoor scenes in the entire feature. What is a certainty is that there are not any exciting or suspenseful scenes.

Just as in the other 1947 Vance films, Vance does almost no investigation; he simply talks to the suspects. Indeed, Vance is so uninterested in the murders in *Philo Vance Returns* that he uses Virginia's singing coach and manager to do some of his leg work. In actuality, this is done solely for purpose of adding comic relief. While Leon Belasco is sometimes funny as Alexis Carnova, the whole idea of Vance using an incompetent amateur for investigative assistance undercuts the supposed reputation of Vance for being a great detective, the important underpinning of the entire Philo Vance series.

As for the plot, is there any viewer who does not know, almost from the beginning, that Stella is the murderer? Yet at the end of the film, when Stella confesses, she states that one of the ex-wives, Catherine, killed Larry, that she then killed Catherine, and that she then started after the other ex-wives because they had made Larry weak or because they had divorced Larry or maybe just because Stella was crazy. If Stella's story is true, however, who killed Virginia at the beginning of the story? It had to be Stella, but then, why did Catherine kill Larry and on the same night that Stella killed Virginia? The story makes absolutely no sense.

Some of the actresses are attractive. Purely by accident, the writers have used one theme of the Philo Vance novels, which is the killing-off of all of the suspects one by one, severely reducing the number of potential killers by the end of the film. However, despite a few slight positives, *Philo Vance Returns*, with its abysmal plot, weak acting and infinitesimal production values, is a true disaster of mystery cinema. It was as though PRC, through its final debasement of an authentic icon of detective literature and movie fame, was seeking to ensure that the character of Philo Vance would never again return to the silver screen.

## Afterwards

The first three actors to play Philo Vance on the screen went on to become better associated with other film detective roles. William Powell is best known today for playing sophisticated detective Nick Charles in *The Thin Man* (1934) and in the other five films in the Thin Man series. Basil Rathbone is best remembered for playing Sherlock Holmes in the long-running series which began with *The Hound of the Baskervilles* (1939). Warren William is most closely associated with the part of Michael Lanyard, a.k.a. the Lone Wolf, in a long series of movies commencing with *The Lone Wolf Spy Hunt* (1939).

Paul Lukas did not portray any more series detectives after *The Casino Murder Case*, but he did appear in crime movies from time to time. He died in 1971. After *The Garden Murder Case* (1936), Edmund Lowe continued working in films for another 25 years, with no significant appearances in crime films. On television, Lowe played newspaper columnist and amateur detective David Chase in *Front Page Detective*, broadcast live on the Dumont Network from 1951 to 1953. Lowe died in 1971.

Alan Curtis' movie career ended soon after his two appearances as Philo Vance in 1947. He passed away in 1953. Similarly, William Wright made only a few more film appearances after portraying Philo Vance in 1947. He died in 1949.

Given the lack of popularity of the Philo Vance novels by the late 1930s and the end of the main movie series shortly thereafter, it is surprising that there were three radio series starring the upper class detective. A short-lived one starred John Emery as Vance in the mid–1940s, perhaps as a summer replacement series. In 1945, Jose Ferrer starred as Vance in a short run series. He was assisted by Frances Robinson playing Lane Randall, his personal secretary. The best remembered radio series starred Jackson Beck as Philo Vance, George Petrie as District Attorney Markham and Joan Alexander playing Ellen Deering, also a secretary and assistant to Vance. The show was on the air from 1948 to 1950.

Vance did not have a female secretary or personal assistant in the books, but the narrator S.S. Van Dine, usually called "Van" by Philo Vance in the books, is, essentially, the same part that was incorporated into the two radio series. However, unlike the radio secretary, Van did not have one line of dialogue in all of the 12 books written by S.S. Van Dine, even though Van was with Vance throughout all of his written adventures.

In addition to the Vance novels, Willard Huntington Wright, writing under the name S.S. Van Dine, contributed ideas and scripts for a 12–film series of mystery shorts for Vitaphone featuring an amateur detective called Dr. Crabtree. Starring Donald Meek, the shorts were released between 1930 and 1932. Under his own name, Wright edited a famous anthology of detective stories, titled *The Great Detective Stories*, published in 1927, which included a lengthy introduction about the history of detective fiction.

As noted above, Van Dine's novel *The Gracie Allen Murder Case* was conceived first as a script for a movie starring Gracie Allen and only secondly as a novel. Similarly, just before his death, Van Dine was working on a story which was intended as a motion picture vehicle for popular skating star Sonja Henie. After Van Dine's death, the novel *The Winter Murder Case* was released in the format of the second draft of the book, without, as the introduction to the book states, its "final elaboration of character, dialogue, and atmosphere." There was never a film version of the novel.

Except for *The Winter Murder Case* (1939) and *The Kidnap Murder Case* (1936), all of the Philo Vance novels were filmed. Except for *The Scarab Murder Case* (1930), which was filmed by British Paramount in 1936 with Wilfrid Hyde-White portraying the erudite detective, all of the films were produced by Hollywood studios.

Willard Huntington Wright passed away on April 11, 1939, in New York City. His body was cremated two days later. Although the Philo Vance novels are seldom read today, they were the most popular American crime novels of their era.

# 2

# Bulldog Drummond
## *The English Adventurer*

In England, the term "Sapper" refers to a private in the Royal Engineers or to a soldier who digs trenches (saps) to approach or sneak inside the enemy's territory. The term is also used in the lexicon of the military of other countries such as the United State Army, where the term refers to combat engineers who advance with the front-line infantry. Recently, the Army has begun to award a Sapper tab for combat engineers who have completed a rigorous leadership course. The Sapper tab is worn on the left shoulder of a soldier's uniform.

In the mystery field, "Sapper" means something completely different. It is the well-known pseudonym of Herman Cyril McNeile, the creator of Bulldog Drummond. McNeile served in the Royal Engineers from 1907 to 1919. He started writing while in military service and due to military regulations, he was not permitted to use his own name on his works. His publisher therefore dubbed him "Sapper," a name McNeile continued to use once he returned to civilian life.

The Drummond novels by Sapper were very popular during the 1920s and 1930s, leading to the production of a number of movies about the character, both in the United States and England. Those films stretched from the silent era to the 1960s.

## BACKGROUND

### The Novels

Herman Cyril McNeile was born at Bodmin, Cornwall, England, on September 28, 1888. His father, who was a captain in the Royal Navy, was then serving there as the governor at the Naval Prison. At the age of 19, McNeile, following his studies at the Royal Military Academy, was commissioned into the army. He served in the Royal Engineers for the next 12 years, until his retirement as a lieutenant colonel in 1919. During World War I, McNeile fought in France, receiving the Military Cross for bravery in the field, among several other medals.

While in France, McNeile began writing stories about the lives and experiences of soldiers in war. The stories were published in an English newspaper under the pseudonym "Sapper." McNeile continued to use that pen name when, in 1920, he published his first novel, *Bulldog Drummond*, about the demobilized officer who sought adventure and excitement after the end of World War I. (The actual title of the novel was *Bull-Dog Drummond*, but the dash disappeared in later books and in reprints of the first novel.) In that book, Drummond first met his arch-enemy Carl Peterson, and their battle would go on through three more novels, ending with *The Final Count* (1926). Carl's associate, Irma Peterson, who appeared in all four of these novels, then showed up in several of the later books to challenge Drummond. The Petersons were part spies and part international thieves, usually embarking on insidious plots to somehow make a profit from war or insurrection.

Indeed, the Bulldog Drummond books are not necessarily mysteries; they are actually action stories which combine mystery, spy and adventure elements around what would now be called a James Bond–like character. The tall and strong Captain Hugh "Bulldog" Drummond leads a crew of ex-officers from World War I into battle against Communists, terrorists, spies and other villains, sometimes with the support of the government and sometimes as an independent gang of vigilantes. No adversary is too tough for Drummond and his gang.

There were a number of continuing characters in the stories. One was Drummond's wife Phyllis, whom he met at the beginning of the first novel and married at the end of the book. They stayed together throughout all of the stories. Some of the other recurring characters were Algy Longworth, who wore an eyeglass for effect and often seemed quite silly (although not as silly as he appeared in some of the films), Peter Darrell, who often appeared to be the second-in-command just under Drummond, and Denny, Drummond's servant.

In all, Sapper wrote ten novels and several short stories about the British adventurer, with the last book being *Challenge* (1937). McNeile also wrote novels and short stories about other detectives and adventurers. In August of 1937, at the age of 48, McNeile died of throat cancer. On his death bed, he asked his friend Gerard Fairlie to take over the series and to protect the good name of Bulldog Drummond. Interestingly, Sapper may have based the character of Bulldog Drummond, in part, on Fairlie.

Fairlie was born in London on November 1, 1899. In 1914, at the start of World War I, he entered officer training school and received his commission about four years later. He joined the British Army late in 1918, as the Great War was just about over. Fairlie continued his army career for the next six years, resigning in 1924. During his early time in the military, he met Sapper, who eventually became a good friend. Indeed, since Fairlie was interested in writing, Sapper became somewhat of a mentor to him. After working in newspapers for a time, Fairlie began writing fiction. His first novel was published in 1927. He also wrote a play about Bulldog Drummond, along with Sapper, titled *Bulldog Drummond Hits Out*. It opened in London in late December of 1937 but only had a short run. Thereafter, with the death of Sapper, Fairlie fulfilled his promise to Sapper and continued the Bulldog Drummond series, writing seven additional novels about the character from 1938 through 1954.

The majority of the Bulldog Drummond movies were released prior to 1939. Accordingly, to the extent a Bulldog Drummond movie was based on a written work, it was always one by Sapper. The one partial exception was the last film of this era, *Calling Bulldog Drummond* (1951). Fairlie contributed to the screenplay and then wrote a book based on the screenplay using the same title. Fairlie also contributed to the screenplay for *Charlie Chan in Shanghai* (1935).

## The Film Series

Captain Drummond commenced his screen career with the 1922 English silent film *Bulldog Drummond*. The film starred Carlyle Blackwell as the title character and is purported to be an adaptation of the first Drummond novel by Sapper, also titled *Bulldog Drummond*. In 1925, Jack Buchanan played the title character in *Bulldog Drummond's Third Round*, once again based on a novel by Sapper. In both of these films, Drummond matched wits with arch-enemies Carl and Irma Peterson.

At the beginning of the sound era, the Bulldog Drummond films moved to America for United Artists' *Bulldog Drummond* (1929). Much like the first silent film, the first talking Drummond feature was based upon the first Drummond novel and the stage play that was adapted from it. Drummond meets and matches wits with Carl and Irma Peterson. He also meets his wife-to-be, Phyllis Benton. In this film, Bulldog Drummond was played by Ronald Colman.

Colman was the first of a number of famous actors who essayed the role of Drummond on the screen during the sound era. Born in England in 1891, he began his acting career on the stage in England, before coming to America in 1920 for more stage work. He began appearing regularly in silent films in 1923, performing in both romantic and adventure films. With his cultured voice, he made an easy transition into sound films, being nominated for an Oscar for his performances in two 1929 films, one being *Bulldog Drummond*. Thereafter, he starred in many well-known films, including *A Tale of Two Cities* (1935) and *Lost Horizon* (1937). He seldom appeared in mysteries, except for his roles as Bulldog Drummond, but he did play the title character in *Raffles* (1930) and gave an Oscar-winning performance in *A Double Life* (1948). Colman died in 1958.

In 1934, Colman played Drummond one last time in another United Artists film, *Bulldog Drummond Strikes Back*. The feature is about the fight for a coded radiogram and the surprise information contained therein. In between Colman's two appearances as Captain Drummond, Fox released *Temple Tower* (1930), an adaptation of another Sapper novel. That film is now considered lost.

The series then moved to England for two films. The first was *The Return of Bulldog Drummond* (1934), starring Ralph Richardson as Captain Drummond. The film is about a band of vigilantes led by Drummond who fight Carl Peterson and his gang, who are attempting to make an illegal profit on England's rearmament between the two World Wars. Drummond's wife Phyllis is also an important character. Richardson, who was born in Cheltenham, England, in 1902, had his greatest successes in his long career on the British stage. However, he was also quite successful in film, receiving Oscar nominations for *The Heiress* (1948) and *Greystoke* (1984). His only significant mystery roles were as the hero in *The Return of Bulldog Drummond* (1934) and as the villain in *Bulldog Jack* (1935). Richardson died in 1983.

The other British film of this era was *Bulldog Drummond at Bay* (1937), about the fight to recover the plans for a top secret airplane. In that film, John Lodge played Captain Drummond. Lodge, who was the brother of Henry Cabot Lodge, Jr. (who ran as the vice-presidential candidate in 1960 with Richard Nixon), was born in 1903 in Washington, D.C. Lodge had a short film career in the 1930s, before becoming a naval officer during World War II. Thereafter, he entered politics, eventually becoming the governor of Connecticut. Lodge died in 1985.

Between those two English films, a feature titled *Bulldog Jack* (1935) was also produced in England. That film, which also goes by the title *Alias Bulldog Drummond*, is a spoof of the Bulldog Drummond movies, with Drummond himself making only a brief appearance. The majority of the film was carried by British actor Jack Hulbert, playing an upper class Englishman who impersonates Drummond.

Ronald Colman appears in his most famous mystery role as the English adventurer Captain Hugh "Bulldog" Drummond.

The Bulldog Drummond features then moved back to America, where a true series about the character commenced. Produced at Paramount Pictures, the series consisted of eight films released between 1937 and 1939. The first film was *Bulldog Drummond Escapes* (1937), an essentially original story, but it tells a new version of the initial meeting between Hugh and Phyllis, which would lead to their eventual marriage in the film series but only after a long and winding road, indeed.

In this film, Ray Milland made his only appearance as Bulldog Drummond. Milland, who was born in Wales in 1907, began his screen career in 1929, first appearing in small roles, such as playing one of the suspects in *Charlie Chan in London* (1934). *Bulldog Drummond Escapes* was one of his earliest significant starring roles in films, but by the 1940s, Milland was a major star in Hollywood, appearing in such important films as *The Major and the Minor* (1942) and the film for which he won an Oscar, *The Lost Weekend* (1945). His career waned in the 1950s but he continued to appear in films and television well into the 1980s, with a best-remembered role from this later period as Ryan O'Neal's condescending father in *Love Story* (1970). Milland died in 1986.

John Howard then took over the role for the next seven films, with Drummond's upcoming marriage to Phyllis always in the background as Drummond fought spies or other evil villains in stories usually based on works by Sapper or, at least, purportedly based on works by Sapper. Howard was a rare actor of American birth to play the English adventurer, having been born in Cleveland, Ohio, in 1913. He attended college at Western Reserve

University in Cleveland, where he first became interested in the theater. Howard made his film debut in 1934 and soon became a contract player for Paramount, appearing in many minor films. His first memorable role was as Ronald Colman's younger brother in *Lost Horizon* (1937), which would become an interesting coincidence later that year, when Howard began playing Bulldog Drummond, a role Colman had originated for the sound cinema in 1929.

After the conclusion of the Bulldog Drummond series, Howard had few significant roles in films, one exception being his part as the wealthy fiancé of Katharine Hepburn in *The Philadelphia Story* (1940). Howard served in the U.S. Navy during World War II, receiving several military honors. However, after the war, his film career suffered and he turned to television work. He then became a high school teacher in California, teaching for 17 years. Howard died in 1995.

In the Paramount series, the Phyllis Benton of the original novel became Phyllis Clavering, Drummond's intended. The role was originated by Heather Angel in *Bulldog Drummond's Escape* (1937) and she reprised the part in four of the remaining films in the Paramount series. Angel was born in Oxford, England, in 1909. She began working regularly in films in the early 1930s, appearing in several mystery movies such as *Hound of the Baskervilles* (1932) and *Charlie Chan's Greatest Case* (1933). In the 1940s, she had small parts in significant features, such as two Alfred Hitchcock movies, *Suspicion* (1941) and *Lifeboat* (1944), plus a lead role in *Time to Kill* (1942) from the Michael Shayne series. She ended her career with guest appearances in television. Angel died in 1986.

In three of the films, Louise Campbell played Phyllis Clavering. Campbell was born in 1911 in Chicago, Illinois, so that when she appeared with John Howard, the characters of Hugh and Phyllis were both surprisingly played by American actors. Campbell was a contract player at Paramount, where her film career essentially began with *Bulldog Drummond Comes Back* (1937) and basically ended just a few years after she completed her third Bulldog Drummond movie. Campbell retired from films after marrying character actor Horace MacMahon. In all, Campbell appeared in only about a dozen films. She passed away in 1997.

What would a Bulldog Drummond film be like without the character of Algy Longworth? For the Paramount series, British character actor Reginald Denny was given the part and, unfortunately, he was sorely miscast in the role. Born in Surrey, England, in 1891, he began acting on the stage at a very young age and even made a world tour while a teenager. In the silent era he began appearing in films such as *Sherlock Holmes* (1922) with John Barrymore and William Powell. Denny was never out of work in the 1920s and with the advent of sound, he settled in as a dependable character actor, usually playing upper class Englishmen. He made numerous appearances in mystery movies such as *Rebecca* (1940), *Sherlock Holmes and the Voice of Terror* (1942) and *The Crime Doctor's Strangest Case* (1943).

Starting in the 1950s, Denny's acting work was primarily in television. However, Denny was also involved in the aviation industry, manufacturing radio-controlled aircraft such as drones, which his company produced for the Army during World War II. Denny passed away in 1967.

In the novels, Bulldog Drummond's butler, cook and confidante, James Denny, lived with his wife at Drummond's various homes. The Dennys also sometimes became involved in Drummond's adventures, such as running errands, relaying messages and acting as decoys. Through it all, though, they were generally minor characters.

For the Paramount series, Denny (but not his wife) became a major character, although he was renamed Tenny so as not to confuse anyone with Reginald Denny who was then playing Algy Longworth. Tenny was in the films primarily for comic relief but he often made significant contributions to the plot, such as rescuing Drummond on several occasions. In all eight films, Tenny was played by E.E. Clive, one of the most likable of all the British character actors in America. Clive was often one of the best things about the Paramount Drummonds.

Edward E. Clive was born in Wales in 1879. He initially planned a career in medicine, but at the age of 22 turned to the stage. After touring the British provinces, he moved to the United States in 1912 and continued to work on the stage. He started in films in the early 1930s and although his movie career only lasted about eight years, his performances were usually memorable. He generally played minor characters such as magistrates, burgomasters, policemen or butlers, in horror films such as *The Invisible Man* (1933) and *Bride of Frankenstein* (1935) and mysteries such as *Charlie Chan in London* (1934) and *The Adventures of Sherlock Holmes* (1939). Clive died at age 60 in 1940.

In the Paramount series, Drummond alternately feuded with and assisted Colonel ("Don't call me Inspector") Nielson of Scotland Yard. Nielson was the equivalent of Inspector McIver (or MacIver) from the written works by Sapper and Gerard Fairlie. McIver appeared in just about all of the published stories about Drummond's adventures. C. Aubrey Smith played Colonel Nielson in *Bulldog Drummond Strikes Back* (1934) and Sir Guy Standing inaugurated the role for Paramount in *Bulldog Drummond Escapes* (1937). Standing, who was born in London in 1873, was prominent in stage work in both England and America before moving into Hollywood films in the early 1930s. Standing died at the age of 63 of a rattlesnake bite shortly after making *Bulldog Drummond Escapes*.

The Paramount series then scored a casting coup by securing John Barrymore, the famous MGM star of the early 1930s, for the part of Colonel Nielson. By 1937, alcoholism had taken its toll on Barrymore, which can be easily discerned by comparing the way he looks in *Arsène Lupin* (1932) with his appearance in *Bulldog Drummond Comes Back* (1937). Barrymore's career is discussed further in this book's chapter on Arsène Lupin.

Once Barrymore left the series, familiar character actor H.B. Warner took over the role of Colonel Nielson for the last four films. Born in London in 1875, Warner, much like Sir Guy Standing, had his early successes on the stage, both in England and America. However, unlike Standing, Warner began appearing in silent films as early as 1914, with a particular success being his role as Jesus in *The King of Kings* (1927). When sound came to the cinema, Warner was seldom out of work, often having good supporting roles, particularly in films directed by Frank Capra. He made a few appearances in mystery films, such as *The Garden Murder Case* (1936) and *Ellery Queen and the Perfect Crime* (1941). Warner died in 1958.

The last of the Paramount Drummonds was *Bulldog Drummond's Bride* (1939), in which, on the eve of World War II, Captain Drummond and Phyllis Clavering are finally married. Drummond was off the screen during the war years but he was brought back in the late 1940s for four new adventures. In them, Drummond was now unmarried and his investigations were related to crimes rather than international intrigue.

The first two films came from Columbia Pictures and starred Ron Randell as Bulldog Drummond. *Bulldog Drummond at Bay* (1947) was the first starring role in a Hollywood for the Australian actor who was born in 1918. He reprised the role of Captain Drummond in *Bulldog Drummond Strikes Back*, released in the same year. In 1949, Randell played that other famous cinema sleuth, Michael Lanyard, in *The Lone Wolf and His Lady*. Randell's film career thereafter was sporadic. He also performed on television and Broadway over the next several decades. He died in 2005.

The series then moved to a small studio, Reliance Pictures, for two 1948 films starring Tom Conway as Drummond, namely *The Challenge* and *13 Lead Soldiers*. Conway is well-known to mystery fans, having played the Falcon in nine films starting with *The Falcon's Brother* (1942). Conway, whose real name was Thomas Charles Sanders, was born in Russia in 1904 but was educated in English schools. He was the older brother of actor George Sanders. Around 1940 Tom followed George to Hollywood, where he changed his name to Tom Conway to avoid confusion with his brother. Conway began appearing in films in the early 1940s and in addition to the Falcon series, he is best known for appearing in three Val Lewton horror films of the 1940s. On the radio, Conway played Sherlock Holmes once Basil Rathbone left the radio series. Conway passed away in 1967.

As was always the case in the films about Bulldog Drummond, Algy Longworth was a character in the Randell and Conway films, played by Pat O'Moore in the Randells and by John Newland in the Conways. Neither are well-known today, although O'Moore may seem familiar because of his numerous guest performances on television and Newland may be remembered by some as the host and director of *One Step Beyond*, a television show that was supposedly based on true stories of the occult or paranormal activities.

These four Drummond movies had another character in common, namely Seymour, a young newspaper reporter. Seymour was a character in the novel *Bulldog Drummond at Bay*. This character was then carried over first into the 1947 film version and then remained for the next three films, even after the series switched studios. Seymour was always played by the same actor, Terry Kilburn. Kilburn, who was born in London in 1926, was originally a child actor in Hollywood before graduating to the slightly older part of young Seymour for these four films.

*13 Lead Soldiers* was the 18th sound film about Bulldog Drummond (if *Bulldog Jack* is included in the tally), with eight different actors playing the lead role. However, there was still one last film for this era of Drummonds, namely *Calling Bulldog Drummond* (1951), in which well-known film star Walter Pidgeon played Bulldog Drummond. Born in New Brunswick, Canada, in 1897, Pidgeon started appearing in films during the silent era, with some of his first starring roles as master detective Nick Carter in a three-film series released by MGM starting in 1939. Thereafter, Pidgeon had a very successful career, becoming a leading man in Hollywood and starring in famous and successful movies such as *How Green Was My Valley* (1941) and *Mrs. Miniver* (1942). He continued appearing in important films throughout the 1950s and 1960s, although usually in significant character parts, such as playing the Senate majority leader in *Advise and Consent* (1962). Pidgeon passed away in 1984.

## The Early American and British Films

### *Bulldog Drummond* (1929)

By today's standards, this is pretty tame stuff. There are no long car chases or violent gun battles. There are no special effects employed and almost no stunts attempted. While there is some violence, it occurs off screen. And yet for a film produced by Hollywood so early in the sound era, *Bulldog Drummond* still retains its charm and sense of adventure, making the film a worthwhile beginning to the more than two decades worth of movies about the exploits of Captain Hugh "Bulldog" Drummond.

After a brief prologue to the main story, *Bulldog Drummond* opens with a whimsical moment that sets the tone for all of the Bulldog Drummond movies to come. It seems that Captain Drummond, a young British army officer recently demobilized after World War I, finds civilian life quite tedious. Seeking any kind of adventure at all, he places an advertisement in the personal column of *The London Times*, announcing his situation. The ad reads, in part, "Demobilized officer, finding peace unbearably tedious would welcome any excitement. Legitimate, if possible, but crime of humorous description, no objection." Surprisingly, and even though the advertisement was only semi-serious, Drummond receives so many letters in response to his plea that he can hardly keep up with them.

One in particular attracts his attention. It is signed by Phyllis Benton and states that if Drummond's intentions are truly serious, the young lady would like to meet him at the Green Bay Inn at midnight that night. She has reserved two rooms for him under the name John Smith. Drummond goes to the rendezvous and meets the young girl, who asks Drummond for help in freeing her wealthy uncle, Hiram T. Travers, from a hospital where he is being held against his will by master criminal Carl Peterson (although his first name is not used in the film), his "sister" Irma and Dr. Lakington, a physician who runs the hospital and who has been drugging Travers. Drummond is somewhat skeptical of Phyllis' story but when she appears to have been kidnapped from the inn, Drummond is on the case.

Thereafter, Drummond does have the adventure of his life, jousting with the Petersons, rescuing Travers and Phyllis on more than one occasion, being captured himself and then almost being murdered, killing Lakington by strangulation and finally being tricked by Carl Peterson, thereby allowing the Petersons to escape. Through it all, Drummond is a modern movie hero—courageous, cool, clever and composed, even in the most serious of situations.

Given its release at the beginning of the cinema's sound era, the production of *Bulldog Drummond* is surprisingly sophisticated. Even though the film is somewhat stagebound, the direction is not. Director F. Richard Jones employs a mixture of shots, from extremely wide shots to extreme close-ups. There are no long segments of conversation where the camera remains fixed, as if a hidden microphone is holding the characters in place. (By contrast, see the early Philo Vance films.) While some of the acting is disappointing, there is none of the overacting or uneasiness with sound that sometimes occurred when silent movie performers made their first transition to sound films. (By contrast, see *Behind That Curtain* [1929] from the Charlie Chan series.)

Other important attributes of *Bulldog Drummond* are the sets, designed by William Cameron Menzies, still famous today for his production designs on films as diverse as *Gone with the Wind* (1939) and *Invaders from Mars* (1953). Some of the sets are particularly massive, such as the high look of the gentlemen's club in which the film opens to the strangely Gothic feel of the Green Bay Inn. Most of the edifices and rooms in the film have an expressionistic architecture, with impossible windows, walls with strange angles, crooked staircases, and low cross-beams in ceilings and doors which are wildly out of proportion to the rest of the building. Menzies provides *Bulldog Drummond* with a look that is different from most other mystery movies. It is not surprising that he was nominated for an Academy Award for Best Art Direction for the film.

Director Jones adds to the atmosphere created by the sets by conveying parts of his story by use of shadows of the characters projected on the walls. While this is hardly an unusual cinematic technique in crime films, here the shadows are often huge, filling the high walls, adding to the eeriness and even the horror of the *mise-en-scène*. All of these devices give the film a look of a German silent film, but, more importantly, also give *Bulldog Drummond* a unique appearance, thereby holding the viewer's attention even when the presentation may be stagy.

In terms of performances, Ronald Colman carries the film. With his suave good looks and cultured voice, he epitomizes the fictional concoction of a sophisticated, upper class adventurer, imbuing a role that has no basis in reality with a verisimilitude that is always convincing. Colman received a well-deserved Academy Award nomination for Best Actor of 1929 for his collective work in this film and *Condemned* (1929). Claud (or Claude) Allister is always entertaining as Algy, Drummond's best friend and another fictional concoction, the British upper-class silly ass. Comic relief roles often become quite boring, quite fast in a mystery movie, but Algy wears very well throughout the entire film, still engendering some mild smiles late in the picture.

The female performances, however, are very disappointing. Joan Bennett makes her film debut in the role of Phyllis Benton and at the age of 19, she was simply too young for the part. The Benton character was written as a strong woman, often battling the Petersons on her own, but in the hands of Bennett, Phyllis becomes a weak and almost petulant character, young beyond her years. Mystery fans would rather remember a more mature Bennett as the seductive title character in Fritz Lang's *The Woman in the Window* (1944). Lilyan Tashman plays Irma Peterson, a role written for a beautiful and tantalizing woman. Unfortunately, Tashman is neither of those. She exudes no allure and if not for Algy, from time to time, commenting on how attractive Irma is, no one else would ever come up with the idea. Tashman's line reading is also inadequate.

Fans of comedy films will spot Charles Sellon, who plays the captured Travers, from his role as the blind man, Mr. Muckle, in the W.C. Fields vehicle *It's a Gift* (1934). Fans of movie musicals will recognize the opening of *Bulldog Drummond* in a stuffy men's club where talking is not permitted as similar to the scene at the opening of *Top Hat* (1935) with Fred Astaire.

Whether it is Dr. Lakington's disgusting implications of what he intends to do to the body of Phyllis Benton while she is unconscious, to Drummond brutally strangling Lakington to his death, to the surprise ways in which Drummond foils the Petersons' plans, the script for *Bulldog Drummond* never becomes banal. Even at the end, when the picture seems to be over, there is one final surprise in the story, with the usually clever Drummond suffering a defeat at the hands of his enemy. While *Bulldog Drummond* is hardly an innovative work, even by 1929 film standards, it is not just a relic of the early sound era. *Bulldog Drummond* is a film that can be truly enjoyed today and not just admired for its historical value.

*Note on the Source Material*: The credits to the film make it very clear as to its source material. They state, "Based on the international stage success by Sapper." The reference is to the play *Bulldog Drummond*, which opened in London in 1921. It starred Sir Gerald du Maurier (Sapper's co-playwright) and ran for 428 performances. The play also ran on Broadway for 162 performances starting in late 1921.

The film is surprisingly faithful to the play although, as would become customary when plays were adapted for the cinema, the story was opened up for the film, with more sets used and some outdoor scenes inserted. Also, as would be the custom in most of the

Bulldog Drummond films, Algy Longworth, who was only a minor character in the play, became an important player in the film, with an emphasis on his value as a figure of comic relief. Perhaps the only change of significance between the two versions is that in the movie, the millionaire being held hostage by the Petersons is Phyllis Benton's uncle while in the play (and the novel) he has no familial relationship to Phyllis. The film adopts the ending of the play, with the Petersons escaping capture by employing "the old circus gag." Claude Allister was in the original cast of the play in London. However, he did not play Algy Longworth; he played the captured American, Hiram Travers.

The play was loosely based on Sapper's first novel about the English adventurer, titled *Bulldog Drummond*, and published in 1920. Accordingly, the film is also loosely based upon the novel. In the novel, bored ex-military man Bulldog Drummond puts an ad in the paper seeking adventure. It is answered by Phyllis Benton, who tells Drummond that two men, Peterson and Lakington, have been troubling her father. Recently, the two have kidnapped a wealthy American, Hiram C. Potts, and have been holding him against his will. Drummond takes up the challenge, rescuing and losing Potts several times, before finally defeating the enemy and killing Lakington.

After the early part of the book, there is little similarity between the novel and the movie. Most of the specific incidents in the book were not carried over to the film. In the written work, Drummond is aided in his endeavors by a coterie of friends, not just Algy. In the end of the novel, Drummond marries Phyllis. Peterson and Irma are arrested by the police but Drummond later learns, in what is really the epilogue to the book, that they have escaped. It will take three more rounds with Peterson before Drummond permanently dispatches him.

Also, the novel has an important backstory to it. Peterson and Lakington are after Potts' money to help fund the overthrow of the British government by Communists, somehow bringing a fortune to Peterson and his partners. That latter point may have seemed a bit too melodramatic an idea for the filmmakers to write into the storyline of a 1929 American movie.

## *Temple Tower* (1930)

[*This is a lost film and one of only a few films discussed in this book which the author did not view.*]

This is the first film based on *Temple Tower*, the 1929 novel by Sapper. The other film which lists *Temple Tower* in its credits is *Bulldog Drummond's Secret Police* (1939). According to Lawrence P. Treadwell, Jr., the film is about murder and robbery at a locked, guarded estate which contains a secret passageway, and if that is an accurate summary of the film's plot, the film was based, at least in part, on Sapper's book of the same name. William K. Everson has characterized *Temple Tower* as a dull film, now justifiably forgotten, with Kenneth MacKenna probably the weakest actor ever to play the role of Bulldog Drummond.

## *Bulldog Drummond Strikes Back* (1934)

Given that *Bulldog Drummond Strikes Back* is the long-awaited sequel to the excellent *Bulldog Drummond* (1929), and since both features star Ronald Colman in his only two appearances as Bulldog Drummond, the film is a much anticipated view by the ardent mystery fan. This anticipation has been fuelled by the film's excellent write-ups by many reviewers, including one by William K. Everson in his widely read book *The Detective in Film*.

In this scene from *Bulldog Drummond Strikes Back* (1934), Drummond (Ronald Colman) agrees to be arrested by two English policemen in order to avoid capture by Prince Achmed (Warner Oland), center. The bobby on the left is played by Yorke Sherwood and the character on the far right, Singh, one of Achmed's henchmen, is played by George Regas. The second bobby is played by E.E. Clive, who would go on to play Drummond's man, Tenny, in eight Drummond movies at Paramount. The other character on the right, Hassan, is played by Mischa Auer.

Despite those expectations, however, *Bulldog Drummond Strikes Back* is, in fact, very disappointing, never living up to the reputation it has acquired over time.

Paradoxically, the sequel starts off in exactly the opposite manner in which *Bulldog Drummond* does. In *Bulldog Drummond Strikes Back*, Captain Drummond has finally had enough excitement in his life. He wants to simply walk into the fog, disappear from his hectic London life and raise Hollyhocks in Sussex. In furtherance of that goal, Drummond does disappear into that thick London fog, but instead of peace and quiet, he encounters a puzzling mystery. Drummond enters an unlocked, empty mansion, for reasons hard to explain, and discovers a dead body. When Drummond returns with the police, the edifice is occupied and the body is gone.

This inexplicable event sets Drummond off on a struggle with the owner of the house, Prince Achmed, on behalf of a pretty young lady, Lola Fields, whose uncle has disappeared. Achmed is most interested in a coded radiogram which was originally in the possession of that uncle but is now in the hands of one of the members of the Fields family. On the other hand, Drummond is most interested in protecting the Fields family from Prince Achmed and his gang of henchmen and one henchwoman. After multiple kidnappings and druggings, the film concludes on board Achmed's boat, which Drummond sets on fire to prevent the cholera-infected goods contained therein from being unloaded onto English soil.

While that brief synopsis may convey the impression that *Bulldog Drummond Strikes Back* has a strong storyline, the film, in fact, does not. The MacGuffin is that radiogram that Prince Achmed desires and Captain Drummond refuses to relinquish. It is not until the end of the film that the audience learns of the significance of that document. Until then, the film seems to be much ado about nothing, with everyone chasing after a piece of paper that seems to have little importance. Drummond invades Achmed's house at will, even with a police guard on the outside, and rescues the Fields women on several occasions. Similarly, Prince Achmed kidnaps the women at will from Drummond's flat, even though Drummond leaves them alone for just a few minutes. There never seems to be any progress made in the story by either of the adversaries, as everyone seems to be walking around in circles.

With so little plot to carry the film, two running gags are inserted to fill up the long running time of the feature. One repetitive joke involves Algy leaving his bride on their wedding night, over and over again, to assist Bulldog Drummond on his case. The gag is not only not funny, it also makes Algy seem cruel and heartless to his sweet bride. The second running gag involves Drummond repeatedly waking up Colonel Nielsen in an attempt to get him involved in the case. To convince Nielsen of the seriousness of the situation, Drummond brings the policeman down to Drummond's flat to meet either Lola Fields or her aunt. On each occasion when this happens, Achmed has kidnapped the woman in the short interval when Drummond has left the woman alone, and Drummond is unable to persuade the policeman that a serious crime is afoot.

Of course, each time Lola or her aunt is kidnapped just seconds before Colonel Nielsen arrives, Drummond's butler had to have been tied up by Achmed's men. Drummond never thinks to show the tied-up butler to Nielsen or have Nielsen interview the butler, so that Nielson can understand the gravity of the situation. That would have ruined the running joke.

Ronald Colman, a little bit older but still quite handsome, is good once again in the role of Bulldog Drummond, although Colman treats this case in a lighter manner than the one in the first Bulldog Drummond sound picture. Loretta Young, already a screen veteran by 1934, was still in her early 20s when this film was made. Surprisingly attractive, Young is convincing in the part of Lola Fields, never yielding to the temptation to overact as a damsel in distress. Warner Oland, as Prince Achmed, is menacing yet sophisticated as the villain, a type of role for which Oland was still well-known in 1934. There is also an excellent supporting cast, including C. Aubrey Smith as Colonel Nielsen and Una Merkel as Algy's bride. The sultry Kathleen Burke, best known for playing the Panther Woman in *Island of Lost Souls* (1932), has a minor role as an associate of Achmed's. It helps that she somewhat resembles Myrna Loy.

The one disconcerting performance is that of Charles Butterworth as Algy. It is easily the worst performance of that character in the entire series. Sometimes Butterworth appears to be doing a poor imitation of Stan Laurel, as he responds to the unusual remarks of some of the other characters. At other times he seems to be sleeping his way through the part, with little energy for the role or for his new wife. In either way he performs the role, Butterworth is an irritant to the viewer, even though he does have a few funny lines.

Some of the positives for *Bulldog Drummond Strikes Back* are the direction of Roy Del Ruth and the impressive sets, particularly Prince Achmed's house. However, there is little background music in the film and its intermittent use, from time to time, is jarring and obtrusive.

Another problem with *Bulldog Drummond Strikes Back* is that it is more of a spoof than a mystery, but it is spoofing a genre of films that was practically non-existent at the time. By 1934, there had been only two sound Bulldog Drummond films released, and there were few (if any) other characters like him in the other films of that era. So, what exactly is being spoofed here? For a modern audience, steeped in spy spoofs like the James Bond films and mystery spoofs like the Inspector Clouseau movies, whatever is being spoofed here has little traction with the audience.

The film starts out in a ridiculous manner, with a disappearing body in what may be a haunted house, surely a cliché now if not back then. The coincidences and illogical action that get Drummond into the house in the first place make no sense and there is never an explanation given as to why the body was lying there for Drummond to find. In the middle of the film, there are more coincidences and more nonsensical events. *Bulldog Drummond Strikes Back* then ends in a ridiculous manner, with Drummond about to marry Lola even though he has known her for less than one day.

Perhaps if the film is considered as a spoof or a satire, it could be enjoyable. As a mystery, however, *Bulldog Drummond Strikes Back* clearly comes up short.

*Note on the Source Material*: The credits to the film indicate that the movie was based on *Bulldog Drummond Strikes Back*, the 1933 novel by Sapper. The book was originally published in England under the title *Knock-Out*. Yet, despite the credit and the similarity in title to the book, the film *Bulldog Drummond Strikes Back* has no similarity to the novel. The book starts out with the killing of a man named Sanderson and ends with Drummond and his gang preventing a terrorist attack on an English train carrying a shipment of gold, all part of a scheme to devalue the currency of England so that the villains can make a quick profit. None of the scenes in the movie comes from the book.

## *The Return of Bulldog Drummond* (1934)

The Bulldog Drummond series moved to its native England for *The Return of Bulldog Drummond*, the first sound movie about the character to be produced by a British studio. Ronald Colman, happily ensconced in Hollywood in 1934, was obviously not available for the title role. In his place is a young Ralph Richardson, in an early film in his long screen career. (Richardson is probably better known today for his work on the stage.) He is fine as a very earnest Captain Drummond, although he displays little emotion in the role, even when his wife is kidnapped by the evil Carl Peterson. Unlike the prior American films, the character of Drummond in *The Return of Bulldog Drummond* is humorless, probably appropriate for a vigilante who is fixated on ridding England of war profiteers. With the part written in such a serious manner, Richardson is undoubtedly more convincing in the role than Ronald Colman ever would have been. Nevertheless, Colman is by far the more engaging actor, handsome and suave and not always taking everything as seriously as perhaps he should. Despite the strong performance by Richardson, Colman is still missed in this film.

Claud Allister, however, is back playing Algy Longworth, a role he had in the original 1929 film. Just seeing that face again and hearing him speak is a real joy. Unfortunately, the part of Algy is particularly small in this film.

The focal point of the film is the Black Clan, a gang of ex-soldiers led by Captain Drummond. The Clan is a new vigilante group in England, waging a war against people speaking out in favor of the re-armament of Britain. While some could see the Clan's actions as part of a political statement, addressing a controversial issue in England between the

Bulldog Drummond (Ronald Colman), right, and Algy Longworth (Charles Butterworth), center, are captured by Prince Achmed and locked in his basement in *Bulldog Drummond Strikes Back* (1934). They are about to make their escape by cracking one of the villains, Dr. Owen Sothern (Arthur Hohl), on the head.

World Wars, that is not really the case. Drummond and his gang are only after those who are drumming up support for re-armament solely to make an illegal profit from the activity. More importantly, Drummond is once again after the Peterson gang, which is advocating re-armament for profit purposes only. Indeed, Peterson is not been above killing those who are honestly advocating peace and disarmament. In an early scene, an advocate for peace is machine-gunned from a car driven by the Peterson gang and apparently that was the third suspicious death of a peace advocate in recent months.

The heart of the film, though, is not the underlying crimes nor is it the vigilantism of the Black Clan. Rather, it is the tussle between Drummond and Peterson, here in the second round of their epic battle. Drummond and the Clan humiliate several members of the Peterson gang and then steal secret documents from one of them. Peterson responds by capturing Drummond's wife Phyllis and using her as the lure to capture Drummond. After paralyzing Drummond with a strange drug he concocts, Peterson attempts to drown Drummond by driving a car off a bridge into a river, with Drummond trapped inside. Drummond manages an escape and then he is off to the Peterson abode in an attempt to rescue Phyllis. After some ups and downs and narrow escapes, the deed is accomplished, the Clan comes to the rescue and Peterson meets a grisly death.

There is not much plot to *The Return of Bulldog Drummond* and much of the film seems stagy. Even many of the outdoor scenes appear to be studio-bound. The character of Phyllis Drummond is sketchy at best, with Ann Todd having little to do in the role. Similarly, the female villain, Irma Peterson, does not seem very menacing and Joyce Kennedy has little to work with in that part.

Nevertheless, *The Return of Bulldog Drummond* is always enjoyable to watch. Part of its appeal comes from the feud between Drummond and Peterson. The intensity of their dispute rivals that of the Holmes-Moriarty struggles, although without the clever dialogue. Drummond does not just want to defeat Peterson; he wants to humiliate him. Peterson drags Phyllis into the dispute, an act that Drummond believes is particularly low and outside the bounds of their rules of engagement. The titanic struggle between Peterson and Drummond is at the core of the film and when the adversaries are in the same scenes together, the movie truly comes alive. It is easy to see why their dispute stretched over several of the Sapper novels.

Another important attribute of the film is Francis L. Sullivan, who plays Carl Peterson. The overweight Sullivan deftly portrays the evil that is Carl Peterson by paradoxically underplaying the role just a bit. Much like the Bulldog Drummond of this film, there is almost no humor in the Peterson character, which helps to emphasize the malevolence of the international criminal.

While somewhat slow-moving, *The Return of Bulldog Drummond* is energized by several interesting scenes, such as Drummond's escape from his watery grave, Drummond throwing Phyllis over an electrified fence to facilitate her escape, and Phyllis being recaptured by Peterson just a few minutes later. The ending is particularly exciting, with the rescue of Hugh and Phyllis by the Clan and the surprise death of Peterson.

Even though *The Return of Bulldog Drummond* has a slimmed-down plot with little mystery, the film never fails to engage the viewer with its stark contrast between good and evil. While different in attitude and style from the previous two Ronald Colman films, it is, in its unique way, every bit as appealing as *Bulldog Drummond* (1929).

*Note on the Source Material*: According to the credits, *The Return of Bulldog Drummond* was based on Sapper's 1922 Bulldog Drummond novel *The Black Gang*. It was the second of the four rounds of the struggle between Drummond and Carl Peterson, which ended in the death, or so it seemed, of Peterson in *The Final Count* (1926).

The film bears a substantial similarity to the novel. Both involve the vigilante group run by Drummond known as the Black Gang, although, for some reason, the name was changed to the Black Clan for the film. As in the film, the Gang of the novel is after Carl Peterson and his assistant, Irma, but in the novel, the two villains are fomenting the rise of Bolshevism in England, often through terrorist activities. Once again, it is hard to discern the profit to Peterson in these activities, but it is a continuation of his pattern of crimes from the original novel, *Bulldog Drummond* (1920). It is interesting that in the film of the novel, Peterson's activities involved British re-armament, not Communism, so perhaps, in fact, the movie may have been making more of a political statement than now seems apparent from the distance of 75 years.

Although the first halves of the film and the novel diverge, once Peterson makes his appearance disguised as the Reverent Theodosius, with a daughter who turns out to be the dangerous Irma, the stories converge. In the novel, Peterson is after some diamonds that Drummond has obtained (secret documents in the film), and in order to lure Drummond into danger, kidnaps Phyllis Drummond. Thereafter, there is the incident of the linen on a chair containing a poison which paralyzes Drummond, an actor imitating Drummond's voice on the phone to allay the fears of the rest of the Black Gang, the car with Drummond trapped inside going over a swinging bridge into the river below, the rescue of Phyllis from the villains' house, Drummond throwing her over the electrified fence, Phyllis being quickly recaptured by Peterson and a last-minute rescue of the Drummonds by the Black Gang.

The one significant difference in the endings of the two works is that Carl Peterson survives in the novel. He still had two more rounds to go with Bulldog Drummond in Sapper's novels.

## *Bulldog Jack (Alias Bulldog Drummond)* (1935)

*Bulldog Drummond Strikes Back* (1934) was a mild spoof of the English adventurer film; *Bulldog Jack* is an out-and-out madcap satire of the genre. However, what may have seemed funny to a British audience in 1935 has little humor for an American audience viewing the film more than 75 years later. *Bulldog Jack* is the true disaster of the early Bulldog Drummond movies.

Bulldog Drummond's only significant appearance in the film occurs at the beginning when criminals sabotage the brakes on his car, causing it to go out of control and crash on a winding mountain road. Drummond's arm is broken and that puts him out of action on his latest case — a call from a damsel in distress. For no discernible reason, Drummond deputizes amateur Jack Pennington to take his place on the adventure. Pennington then impersonates Drummond and, after some shenanigans, learns that jewel thieves have captured a jeweler and are forcing him to prepare fake jewels to substitute for real ones at the British Museum. With the help of Algy Longworth, Pennington captures the gang of jewel thieves, more by luck than anything else.

If one has a taste for over-the-top acting, some clever dialogue interspersed among unfunny witticisms and a bit of obvious physical comedy, then *Bulldog Jack* is the film to see. For most people, however, *Bulldog Jack* will be a major disappointment. Jack Hulbert, the fake Bulldog Drummond with a very prominent chin, overacts outrageously. His brother, Claude Hulbert, as Algy Longworth, mugs shamelessly. English audiences may have found those types of performances amusing back in the 1930s but it is unlikely that American audiences ever did. Simply put, the humor in *Bulldog Jack* is just too British to be funny. It is if the actors are saying to the audience, "Aren't we funny?" The answer to that question, unfortunately, is "No." The humor is obvious, which in and of itself may not be all that bad, but it is also not funny. There are very few genuine laughs in this relatively long film.

*Bulldog Jack* is not without its interest. An unrecognizable Ralph Richardson plays the chief villain, Morelle, and he is a standout in the part, perhaps because he plays the role completely straight. In the main, the humor is left to the Hulbert brothers. Richardson had just played Bulldog Drummond in *The Return of Bulldog Drummond* (1934) so this film was a true change of pace for him. Fay Wray plays Ann Manders, the damsel in distress who seeks Bulldog Drummond's help. It is hard to dislike any film in which Fay Wray appears, and, indeed, this may be the prettiest she has ever appeared in films, with the exception, of course, of *King Kong* (1933).

The opening of the film, with the attack on the real Bulldog Drummond, is told in the style of a serious mystery, without any attempted humor. Much of it is cleverly shot with little dialogue, making it a highlight of the film. The climax is also quite suspenseful, with

Morelle fleeing on a speeding underground train carrying Pennington, Algy and Ann, with the end of the line upcoming. As good as its opening and closing are, however, *Bulldog Jack* is primarily a comedy, and it is faint praise for a comedy film when its best scenes are the non-comedy ones.

*Bulldog Jack* is often tedious, usually neither a good comedy film nor a good suspense film. It is a struggle just to get through it. If the viewer is somehow able to do so, the ending on the Underground has some appeal.

## *Bulldog Drummond at Bay* (1937)

*Bulldog Drummond at Bay* would be the last of the British Bulldog Drummonds for quite some time, with most of the rest of the Drummond films being produced at Paramount or other Hollywood studios. The film sports a primarily British cast, which gives the movie a sense of authenticity, as Bulldog Drummond and Algy are stereotypical British characters. Paradoxically, however, two of the most important actors in the film are American and Canadian. John Lodge makes his only screen appearance as Captain Drummond. Somewhat forgotten as a result of the more famous portrayals by Ronald Colman and John Howard, Lodge is handsome enough as the title character and is surely satisfactory in the role. Nevertheless, he is easily forgettable, possibly because the part is underwritten somewhat, in the sense that Drummond is not always the focal point of the movie as he was in the prior Bulldog Drummond features.

Canadian–born Victor Jory plays Gregoroff, the secondary villain, who is really no more than a henchman until the finale. Gregoroff, however, is a particularly vicious villain for the 1930s, happily torturing one of his victims and then punching out a female adversary. Jory is all animosity in the role; there is nothing underwritten about the part or his performance. When Gregoroff becomes a more important character in the second half of the film, Jory's vehement performance provides a spark to the movie.

*Bulldog Drummond at Bay* does not have a cohesive plot. Rather, it proceeds in several story arcs or predicaments from which Drummond must extricate himself. In the first, while Drummond is resting at a country home, a rock with a message on it is thrown through the window. (Unbeknownst to Drummond, it was thrown by Caldwell, the inventor of a top secret airplane.) Thereafter, two men come to the home questioning Drummond as to whether he has seen a stranger in the area. Drummond is unaware that the men are agents of a munitions dealer named Kalinsky, but nevertheless puts the two men off by pretending to be a country bumpkin. The dialogue is droll and Lodge is quite good in one of the most amusing scenes in the film.

Because there is a concern by the villains that there might have been a note attached to the rock, the next morning two people are sent to search Drummond's cottage. One is Doris Thompson, who gains entry by claiming that her car has broken down. Drummond is quickly onto her ruse and drives back with her to London. The wordplay between the two is entertaining and suggestive of a possible romance on the way. When Drummond returns to the country home, he finds his housekeeper drugged and a tea salesman searching the home. Before Drummond can elicit important information from the miscreant, the interloper is killed. Later, the body disappears.

These first two vignettes are quiet, civilized exchanges between heroes and villains, with little action or suspense. Nevertheless, they are very entertaining moments and excellent setups for the next two exciting story arcs. The first involves a fight in a laboratory, amid chemicals and smoke, with the odds seemingly stacked against Drummond. It ends with Drummond and Algy trapped in the laboratory, with deadly gas being pumped in the room. This episode is the highlight of the film, with the escape of Drummond and Algy being particularly clever.

Next comes a scene on a train to Scotland, with the villains intent on killing Drummond when the train proceeds through a small tunnel. The sounds of the train and the claustrophobic feeling inside the train add to the suspense of the vignette. The film ends with the villains caught and Gregoroff dying in a crash of Caldwell's special plane.

*Bulldog Drummond at Bay* is another Drummond entry that holds the interest despite its many flaws, and the flaws in the film are easier to identify than its attributes. The opening segment features a display of big, bold newspaper headlines on large white sheets (with the filmmakers not even taking the trouble to produce fake front pages of newspapers) relating the backstory of Kalinsky's European travels. At these times, the movie becomes an exercise in reading rather than a viewing experience, hardly an impressive filmmaking technique. On two occasions, the film uses the movie cliché of the killing of a speaker just as he is about to reveal crucial information, such as the name of the leader of the villains. For a film that has a number of clever moments, reverting to a mystery movie chestnut on two different occasions is quite disappointing. Also, while it is hard not to love Claud Allister playing the role for which he was born, Algy Longworth, Algy's part in this film has fallen to comic relief only, making him a "very silly ass," not just his usual "silly ass."

The major structural problem is that Captain Drummond does little to solve the crimes, rescue Caldwell or capture or kill the victims. Those acts are really accomplished by Doris Thompson, who turns out to be a British secret service agent, and by Caldwell himself. However, rather than pick at flaws in the feature, it is better to relish the several clever suspense scenes amid the sophisticated British dialogue that is spoken by all. Even in its quieter moments, *Bulldog Drummond at Bay* never becomes boring, and at other times it is quite exciting and suspenseful. What better recommendation can be given to a mystery movie?

*Note on the Source Material*: The beginning of *Bulldog Drummond at Bay* was based on Sapper's 1935 novel with the same title. Thus, as the novel opens, a rock with a note on it is thrown through the window of Drummond's country home, two thugs accost Drummond to see if he has seen a stranger in the area, Drummond pretends to be a country bumpkin to deceive his two visitors, and the next day, two people come to the house in an attempt to determine if there was a note tied to the rock. The second person, a man who is about to reveal the truth about the incident, is killed when Drummond leaves the room.

Thereafter, although there are some similarities between the two works, such as the involvement of the pacifist organization known as the Key Club and the search for the secret airplane designs of Caldwell, the film goes off in a different direction than the book. That was a good choice by the filmmakers since the novel is an unusually talkative work by Sapper, with very few action sequences. Instead, the film makes good use of some novel action and suspense sequences created especially for the film.

The book employs an interesting idea for modern readers. The villains use a new drug to attempt to elicit information from one of their captives. It is a Mexican drug called marijuana. According to Sapper, in Chapter XII of *Bulldog Drummond at Bay*, marijuana instills "such fear into the mind of the taker that he ceases to be a man. He is mad with terror ... his brain refuses to function ... [a]nd finally he finishes up in a suicide's grave or a lunatic asylum." It is a shame that this information was not available to young people in the 1960s and 1970s. (In fairness to Sapper, he is describing the effects of marijuana if injected directly into the bloodstream, rather than being inhaled in cigarette form.)

*Note on the Remake*: The novel, *Bulldog Drummond at Bay*, was also the basis for the 1947 film of the same name.

*Note on Drummond's Gang*: Another significant difference between the book and film versions of *Bulldog Drummond at Bay* are the associates of Drummond who appear in each of the works. In the book Drummond is assisted by Peter Darrell, an ex–Army officer who is almost the equal of Drummond. According to *The Bulldog Drummond Encyclopedia*, Darrell appeared in every book in the series but never made it to the movies. (However, since Darrell does not appear in Gerard Fairlie's *Calling Bulldog Drummond*, that statement must be corrected to provide that Darrell appears in every Drummond book written by Sapper.) Another associate of Drummond's in the book is Ronald Standish, who was associated with the War Office (and was the subject of two non–Bulldog Drummond books written by Sapper). Standish also did not make it into the movie.

The character who did make it into the movie version of *Bulldog Drummond at Bay* is, of course, Algy Longworth. Longworth was a natural for the movies, partly as comic relief, partly as the caricature of a certain type of upper-class Englishman and partly as a helpful associate of Drummond. Longworth appeared in every sound film about Bulldog Drummond (not counting the "James Bond era" films of the 1960s). Surprisingly, Longworth did not appear in the novel, *Bulldog Drummond at Bay*.

## THE PARAMOUNT SERIES

### *Bulldog Drummond Escapes* (1937)

*Bulldog Drummond Escapes* is not based on any of Sapper's books, but its inspiration in *Bulldog Drummond* (1920), the first of the Drummond novels, is patent. Drummond is established early in the film as the quintessential English adventurer, looking for any type of excitement to keep from boredom. And if the escapade involves a damsel in distress whom he can rescue from the clutches of an evil villain, that is all for the better.

Luckily for Drummond, and to the exasperation of Colonel Nielson, Drummond has just such an experience in *Bulldog Drummond Escapes*. In this case, the damsel's first name is Phyllis, the same as in the original novel, and by the end of the film nuptials seem to be imminent, the same as in the original novel. In a sense, *Bulldog Drummond Escapes* updates some of the background of the original book, jettisoning its post–World War I aspects and political overtones but retaining the sense of adventure created when the demobilized officer first put his ad in the newspaper after the end of World War I.

To set the stage for the film's characterization of Captain Drummond, *Bulldog Drummond Escapes* commences at a London airport in a very thick fog, with Drummond about to land his plane. Officials on the ground try to convince him to avoid the attempt as he is sure to crack up. Drummond demurs and in a thrilling display of flying ability, lands the plane without a scratch on either the vehicle or the person. It is an exciting way to commence the film.

Bulldog Drummond (Ray Milland) is on the phone, tricking Algy into coming to his assistance by pretending he has been shot, in *Bulldog Drummond Escapes* (1937). At the time, Algy is at the hospital as his wife is about to give birth to their first child.

The main storyline begins with Drummond driving on a back country lane when he believes he has hit a young woman with his car. Drummond gets out of the vehicle and finds the woman lying by the road. He also discovers the body of a man who has been shot. While Drummond is with the man's body, the woman, later identified as Phyllis Clavering, takes Drummond's car and drives off. When Drummond returns to the body, it is sinking into the marsh and then disappears.

Drummond's butler Tenny recovers the car and through a set of coincidences hard to believe, Drummond locates Phyllis at Greystone Manor, where she says she is being held prisoner by Norman Merridew. After a number of tussles with the villains, Drummond rescues Phyllis from the clutches of the evil Merridew, who was holding Phyllis captive so that he and his associates could prepare counterfeit copies of Phyllis' war bonds in order to steal her inheritance.

Ray Milland, who was particularly handsome at this point in his career, is good as Drummond, bringing a light-hearted and ingratiating manner to his performance. Heather Angel is pretty as Phyllis but in her early scenes in the film, her performance is too understated for the role, making her seem legitimately disturbed, just as Merridew contends. Angel is much better in later scenes when she plays the part with more gusto, allowing her strong personality to finally break through. Porter Hall, who usually played mild characters in a screen career of generally minor roles, is surprisingly wicked and convincing as the evil Merridew. The performance of the film, however, is given by E.E. Clive as Drummond's very English butler Tenny. The gentleman's gentleman is a much better assistant to Drummond than Algy Longworth. Clive is given some clever lines which he delivers in his understated English manner, adding to the humor of the situation. *Bulldog Drummond Escapes* lights up when Clive is on the screen. It was an astute move by the filmmakers to make Tenny (Denny in the books) a much more important character in this new film series than he was in the original Sapper works.

Despite some good performances, *Bulldog Drummond Escapes* is only mildly entertaining. It is dragged down by its flimsy plot. Drummond meets Phyllis and immediately decides to rescue her, even though she has just stolen his car. Then it is simply back and forth with the villains, with Drummond entering their mansion on several different occasions to try to either make contact with Phyllis or to rescue her. There is no true mystery to the story; it is all just back and forth.

To fill in the time, there is a running joke about Algy's wife having a baby and Drummond convincing Algy to come with him rather than stay at the hospital. It is not at all funny and, in fact, Drummond's actions with Algy seem particularly mean-spirited. It is similar to Drummond repeatedly interrupting Algy on his wedding night in *Bulldog Drummond Strikes Back* (1934). Reginald Denny, as Algy, is far from funny in the role. He cannot seem to decide if he is playing a buffoon or a competent assistant to Drummond. Where is Claud Allister when you need him?

Much of the story makes little sense. If Phyllis wanted to escape from Merridew and she had Drummond's car, why not drive away at that time and deliver the mystery note directly to the police? Instead, she goes right back into the clutches of Merridew. If Inspector Nielson knew about Merridew's villainy all the time, what was the purpose in sparring with Drummond over the matter and even locking him up for a time?

Even the characterization of Phyllis is so inconsistent as to be unbelievable. Through most of the film, she is a meek, subservient character who needs to be rescued by Drummond. At the end, she is bopping her adversaries across the head with heavy objects and, in a sense, she rescues Drummond more than he rescues her. As inconsistent as those last scenes are, though, they are among the most enjoyable in the film, at least bringing *Bulldog Drummond Escapes* to a satisfying conclusion. Thus, the film does have its interest but its lack of a substantive plot or an intriguing mystery makes it difficult to recommend.

*Note on the Source Material*: The credits state that the film was based on a play by H. C. "Sapper" McNeile and Gerard Fairlie titled *Bulldog Drummond Again*. Little is known about the play and it may never have been produced. What is most interesting about the credit is that it cites both authors of the Drummond novels as a source for the same film.

## *Bulldog Drummond Comes Back* (1937)

*Bulldog Drummond Comes Back* is a pleasant but forgettable film. Even though it involves the serious subjects of the kidnapping of Phyllis and the attempted murder of both Hugh and Phyllis, the style of the film is always light, undercutting whatever suspense there may be, at least until the film's exciting conclusion.

The story takes place around the time of the expected marriage of Hugh and Phyllis and the christening of Algy's baby. Because Drummond helped send Erena Soldanis' husband to the gallows, Erena has decided to seek her revenge on Drummond by kidnapping his fiancée Phyllis and then leading Drummond on a wild chase as he tries to save Phyllis.

The body of the film involves clues given by Erena to Drummond, some on gramophone records, some on notes and some forcibly provided orally by Phyllis to her fiancé. Captain Drummond, along with Algy and Tenny, follow those clues back and forth between Drummond's home and a fishing village, with little progress being made in the storyline. Finally, Drummond and Algy are led to an old house, where they discover Phyllis. However, the three are then locked in the mansion where there is a time bomb set to explode, effectuating the final revenge of Erena. Fortunately, at the last instant, the trio is rescued by an unlikely party, so perhaps Hugh and Phyllis may eventually get married and perhaps Algy can finally attend a family event.

Once again, the joy of these Bulldog Drummond films is often in the performances. Here, E.E. Clive is wonderful once again as Drummond's butler, Tenny. He often has the best lines in these films and in *Bulldog Drummond Comes Back*, he also is the hero. Helen Freeman as Erena Soldanis, with her strange voice and evil accent, is particularly menacing. Probably the most interesting performance is that of top-billed John Barrymore as Colonel Nielson. *Bulldog Drummond Comes Back* must surely have been a career letdown for Barrymore, yet he essays the role of Nielson with relish, particularly in the two disguises he employs to hide his identity from Drummond and the villains. Barrymore, who is virtually unrecognizable in those disguises, is a joy to watch as he dominates most of the scenes in which he appears.

*Bulldog Drummond Comes Back* marks the debut of John Howard in his most famous screen role. Howard is surely handsome enough for the role of Captain Drummond but he really has little to do in this film. Reginald Denny is a zero once again as Algy. It is not quite clear why that character is still inserted into these films, since in the Paramount series, Tenny is surely the more entertaining and often the more effective of the two assistants to Bulldog Drummond.

*Bulldog Drummond Comes Back* has its intrinsic interest, as any game of puzzles does. In this case, though, the clues themselves are not very challenging and they seem to be without purpose. Since they all lead Drummond back and forth over the same ground amid some scenes in foggy settings, the true purpose of the clues is apparently to hide the low budget of the feature. Also, despite the fact that Erena tells Drummond several times that she is leading him on this chase, rather than simply plugging him in the back, so that Drummond can suffer like her husband did, that really makes no sense. The brutal killing of Phyllis would have caused more suffering for Drummond than this wild chase game on which he is forced to embark. Only in the cinema would a villainess concoct such a silly scheme of revenge. The underpinnings of *Bulldog Drummond Comes Back* are weak.

The ending, though, is quite exciting, with Hugh, Phyllis and Algy trapped in a mansion with a time bomb about to explode. Tenny makes a last-minute rescue of the group just before a terrific explosion demolishes the building. This last scene is quite suspenseful. As a result, as lightweight as the film may be, *Bulldog Drummond Comes Back* is a pleasant enough diversion and at a running time of less than an hour, it is an easy way to spend a little of the leisure time of a mystery movie devotee.

*Note on the Source Material*: *Bulldog Drummond Comes Back* was loosely based on *The Female of the Species*, the 1928 novel by Sapper. The time period of the book is after the completion of the four rounds that Drummond fought with Carl Peterson, ending with *The Final Count* (1926), in which Drummond killed Peterson. Irma Peterson, Carl's mistress, vowed revenge and she almost attains it in *The Female of the Species*.

In the book, Irma captures Drummond's wife Phyllis and then leads Drummond and his gang on a treasure hunt to locate Phyllis. In the process, she gives them several clues, two of which were used in the movie. One of those clues involves the Angler's Rest hotel in Drayminster and the other involves the question of whether Drayminster was the fifth or sixth most beautiful village in England. Other than that, the movie goes off in a different direction than the novel.

*The Female of the Species* is one of the best of the Sapper novels, being far superior to the movie. The fact that the book, unlike the movie, involves Irma Peterson, not some unknown foe of Captain Drummond, adds to the spice of the novel. There are fewer clues in the novel than in the movie, giving each clue in the novel more significance. Also, the story in the novel does not simply meander back and forth, but instead, Drummond often seems to be making real progress in his search for Phyllis. Another important attribute of the novel is that it is written in the first person by Joe Dixon, who accidentally becomes involved in the intrigue on the side of the Drummond gang. Dixon has a unique perspective on the goings-on, and the style of the book and Dixon's interesting viewpoint on matters make the novel very engaging. So, if one can get past the book's derogatory language about minorities, it is well worth a read.

## *Bulldog Drummond's Revenge* (1937)

At the beginning of *Bulldog Drummond's Revenge*, Drummond just happens to be in Colonel Nielson's office discussing his upcoming wedding in Switzerland when a foreign agent, Sumio Kanda, informs Nielson that Sir John Haxton has invented a super-explosive known as Hextonite and that he is flying it to France to confer with another scientist. Kanda informs Nielson that an attempt will be made to steal the explosive that night.

Later, while on the plane, Haxton's secretary, Draven Nogais, kills Haxton and tosses the Hextonite, attached to a parachute, out of the airplane. The plane crashes but not before Nogais also parachutes to safety. The parachuted valise happens to land right where Drummond, Algy and Tenny are driving, on their way to Phyllis' house. The three take the suitcase with them, but it is stolen in the dark by Nogais and an accomplice, the latter being severely scratched in the fight.

Later, Drummond, Phyllis, Hugh and Tenny board the train to Dover with the intent to go on to France by ferry. The first person Algy spots on the train is the man with the scratched face. He and Nogais are boarding the train, along with the Hextonite, with the intent to sell it to a foreign agent at the end of their journey. Drummond is therefore off on the search for the missing explosive, to the chagrin of Phyllis.

Later, Colonel Nielson tells Captain Drummond, "You certainly have a way of stumbling into things that don't concern you." With that line, Nielson identifies one (but not the only) problem with the plot of this film: too many coincidences fuel the story. No wonder Drummond keeps getting involved in a criminal enterprise which does not concern him. No matter what he does to get away, the plot keeps turning back to Drummond, but only by several unconvincing coincidences.

Even without the coincidences, the plot of *Bulldog Drummond's Revenge* is weak. Much of the story is taken up with the upcoming marriage of Hugh and Phyllis, and Phyllis' doubts about marrying a man who is always involved in trouble. Phyllis' professed worries are far from believable and one suspects they are inserted in the film just to give the character more screen time, justifying the character's appearance in the film at all. There

There's another setback for the upcoming marriage of Hugh Drummond (John Howard) and Phyllis Clavering (Louise Campbell), both center, as Phyllis tells Hugh that she no longer wants to marry him because she does not want so much excitement in her life. Algy Longworth (Reginald Denny) and his wife Gwen (Nydia Westman) look on in this scene from *Bulldog Drummond's Revenge* (1937).

are the usual antics of Algy as he keeps becoming accidentally separated from his wife, a source of "comic relief" which is becoming particularly tiresome after its repetitive use in so many of these Drummond movies. While there are some funny moments in the film, including some involving a severed hand recovered from the plane crash, these are few and far between. Only E.E. Clive, as the redoubtable English gentleman's gentleman Tenny, is consistently amusing in this film series, with his witty humor delivered in the driest of dry manners.

John Barrymore, as Colonel Nielson, once again receives top billing but he has little to do. Nevertheless, it is refreshing to see a serious performer in the role of the lead policeman rather than the official investigator being a bumbler who is primarily used for comic relief. Since both Algy and Tenny are already comic relief characters (and the consistently unfunny Algy is already one person too many for that function), also using Captain Nielson for comic relief would have been way too much for any one mystery series to absorb.

There are some clever mystery points in *Bulldog Drummond's Revenge*, such as Drummond immediately deducing that the severed hand is not that of Nogais since it is too cold to have been separated from the body in the airplane crash, or Drummond noticing the smell of jasmine perfume in the train compartments, indicating that the villain on the train is a female (or, as it turns out, a male dressed as a female). There are also some unexpected bursts of violence, in the killings on the train of both Nogais' accomplice and Sumio Kanda and the earlier killing of Sir John.

However, it is all bland and unoriginal. The MacGuffin of the powerful explosive has been used many times in mystery or spy movies. The fight over the suitcase at Phyllis' house unfolds in the dark, diffusing any excitement that scene may have engendered. (Is there any doubt in any viewer's mind that when Algy shouts, "I've got him," that when the lights come on, he will be choking Tenny?) There is little action in the feature and the ordinary direction of *Bulldog Drummond's Revenge* by James Hogan adds nothing. Indeed, the performances of John Howard as Hugh Drummond and Louise Campbell as Phyllis Clavering are as bland as everything else in the movie, as they treat the serious subject matter of a stolen explosive as only a slight interruption to their wedding plans.

In *Bulldog Drummond's Revenge* the filmmakers seemed to be trying to fill an hour's worth of film with as little entertainment as possible. This is undoubtedly the weakest Drummond movie in the Paramount series to date.

*Note on the Source Material*: The credits to *Bulldog Drummond's Revenge* state that the film is based on *The Return of Bulldog Drummond*, the 1932 novel by Sapper, which was published in the United States under the title, *Bulldog Drummond Returns*. Perhaps the most interesting mystery about the film is why the credits make any reference to *The Return of Bulldog Drummond*. The book is about an escaped convict, a murder of a young lawyer, some missing securities, the kidnapping of a millionaire and stock market manipulations. There is not one scene, incident, portion of the storyline or non-recurring Drummond character in common between the book and the film. Thus, the reference in the film's credits to *The Return of Bulldog Drummond* is a true mystery, surely worthy of the attention of the great Captain Drummond.

This is similar to *Bulldog Drummond Strikes Back* (1934) where there is a reference in the film's credits to the book written by Sapper of the same name, even though there is no similarity between the book and the film. Perhaps the filmmakers believed that the reference to a written work by Sapper would give the film more credibility than it otherwise deserved.

## *Bulldog Drummond's Peril* (1938)

This is the fourth film in the Paramount series about the demobilized officer from World War I and the third film in a row which commences around the time of Drummond's expected marriage to his true love Phyllis. While the film is moderately interesting, it just seems like it has all been done before.

Hugh and Phyllis, in Switzerland for their wedding, have received a number of wedding gifts which Bulldog refers to as "the loot." (Didn't their friends know by now that a wedding was unlikely to take place and that it made more sense to wait until after a wedding occurred before sending a gift?) Among the presents is a perfect synthetic diamond manufactured by Algy Longworth's father-in-law, Professor Goodman, pursuant to his own secret formula. Hugh and Phyllis were supposed to keep the diamond a secret but they open the letter in front of Sir Raymond Blantyre, the head of an international diamond syndicate, who just happens to be among the wedding guests. Blantyre immediately realizes that if Goodman is allowed to publish his formula, it could ruin the diamond industry.

This leads to the killing of the detective who is watching the wedding gifts and the theft of the manufactured diamond. Back in London, Blantyre unsuccessfully tries to convince Goodman to sell his formula. That leads to Blantyre deciding to kill Goodman by way of an explosion at his house. Dr. Mac Botulian, a scientist and competitor of Goodwin's, becomes involved in the plot, kills Blantyre's thug and kidnaps Goodman in order to obtain the secret formula for himself. Unfortunately for both criminals, Bulldog Drummond is on the matter and, after escaping from his own kidnapping by Botulian, finally solves the case and captures the villains.

On the plus side, the plot of *Bulldog Drummond's Peril* is a little more complicated than the usual Drummond film. The straightforward storyline of Blantyre going after Goodman is turned on its head when Botulian appears in the film with a much more complicated crime caper involving Goodman's formula. Of course, it is a little hard to believe that a research scientist such as Botulian could concoct such a complex criminal scheme on the spur of the moment, but then a lot of the plots of these films do not make much sense.

Another plus is the limited screen time for Algy Longworth who, as played by Reginald Denny, is a particularly unfunny character in these Paramount features. The screen time for Tenny is also reduced, which is unfortunate as Tenny, as played by E.E. Clive, is a particularly funny character in these Paramount features.

Then there is that strange laboratory sequence (Goodman shows how he manufactures his synthetic diamonds) that has to be seen to be believed. It actually looks like Paramount borrowed the necessary electrical props from Universal Studios and that the Frankenstein monster might suddenly appear in place of the synthetic diamond.

Once again, John Barrymore, reflecting his lingering star status, receives top billing. Unhappily, his Inspector Nielson has become a character merely of comic relief and Barrymore, the great thespian, overacts outrageously. By the time of this film, it seems merely sad that Barrymore was stuck performing in such a humiliating role for one who was such a star just a few years before. Barrymore left the series after this film and John Howard then received top billing in the subsequent films, billing which he obviously deserved.

Porter Hall gives the best performance in the film, playing the part of the evil Dr. Botulian in a quiet and understated manner. Nevertheless, Hall's appearance in the film is one reason why the movie seems so familiar. Hall played a similar role, that of the evil Merridew, in *Bulldog Drummond Escapes* (1937), in the same manner that he plays Botulian in *Bulldog Drummond's Peril*. Then there is the recurring background setting of the marriage of Drummond and Phyllis, which has not come to fruition in any of the prior films and will not actually occur in the next few films either. Phyllis is captured again by the bad guys, making this the third in the last four films in which that has occurred. Tenny provides the surprise method of escape for Drummond from the clutches of the evil ones, something that also seems quite familiar.

It should not have been a problem for the filmmakers to bring some variety to the Paramount Drummonds, since most of the films are purportedly based on a novel or short story by Sapper, each with its own unique plot. The problem, however, is that even though a script may start with a work by Sapper, the plot of each film has to be squeezed into the Paramount Drummond formula, which includes the background story of the wedding of Hugh and Phyllis and the necessary screen time for Tenny, Algy and Colonel Nielson. Even the most innovative mystery plot would seem familiar and tiresome if it were forced into the same film blueprint as the prior movies in the series.

For a viewer who has never seen one of these Paramount Drummonds, *Bulldog Drum-*

*mond's Peril* will be an enjoyable viewing experience. For others, it would be nice to see a little more variety in the storylines and the settings after four somewhat similar films.

*Note on the Source Material*: *Bulldog Drummond's Peril* was based on Sapper's 1924 novel *The Third Round*, which is sometimes known as *Bulldog Drummond's Third Round*. True to the title, this is the third Drummond novel by Sapper and the third of the four encounters which Drummond had with master criminal Carl Peterson.

The film starts out with the same premise as the novel, as the Professor Goodman of the novel, who is the father of the fiancée of Algy Longworth, has discovered a method of making synthetic diamonds on the cheap. Raymond Blantyre, the head of a diamond syndicate, offers Goodman 250,000 pounds to keep his formula secret. Goodman refuses and so the syndicate hires Edward Blackton to accomplish its goal of keeping Goodman's formula from being made public, without necessarily caring how that goal is accomplished. Unfortunately for the syndicate, it has unknowingly employed arch-villain Carl Peterson, in disguise, and Peterson immediately concocts a scheme to obtain the money from the syndicate by disposing of Goodman—but not before Goodman produces a number of valuable diamonds for Peterson to sell. In fact, Peterson intends to double-cross the diamond syndicate by ending up with the money from the syndicate, the diamonds from Goodman and the formula itself, so that he can later blackmail the syndicate over and over again.

Peterson's scheme includes blowing up Goodman's laboratory with another body inside, leading everyone to believe that Goodman is dead. However, Goodman had previously left the notes for his formula with Bulldog Drummond, requiring Drummond to go toe to toe with Peterson again, although Drummond does not initially know he is dealing with Peterson.

Although there is obviously a similarity between the book and the film, after the first third of *Bulldog Drummond's Peril*, the film has little in common with *The Third Round*. In addition, the book is much more complicated and clever than the film, one reason being that the viewer is alternately told the story from the point of view of both Peterson and Drummond. One of the strengths of Sapper's writings was his often clever variation on point of view and the differing observations of the protagonists, and he uses that skill to great effect in *The Third Round*.

*The Third Round* is one of the best of the Drummond books, and that highlights one of the problems with the Paramount Drummonds. Even though *Bulldog Drummond's Peril* is based on a book by Sapper about the titanic and ongoing struggle by Drummond with Carl Peterson, the movie forgoes Peterson, one of the best villains ever created by any writer of thrillers, in favor of a Dr. Batoulian, a character of little charisma. Similarly, *Bulldog Drummond Comes Back* (1937) is based on another quality Sapper novel, *The Female of the Species*, which has as its lead villain Irma Peterson, who is almost as villainous as Carl and an ongoing enemy of Drummond throughout the novels. For the movie, Irma was replaced with an interesting character, Erena Soldanis, but one who does not have the criminal credentials or the history with Drummond that Irma has. While *Bulldog Drummond Comes Back* and *Bulldog Drummond's Peril* are interesting enough films, they are not as memorable as the books on which they were based, one significant reason being the difference in the quality of the villains.

As noted above, the filmmakers on the Paramount Drummonds often seemed to take a cookie cutter approach to the films, making them enjoyable enough but easily forgettable. If, instead, those filmmakers had chosen to use Carl and Irma Peterson as the villains of some of the pieces, with the special aura of villainy that they would have brought to any film in the series, the Paramount Drummonds would have been much better and probably much more distinctive and memorable. As support for that thesis, the two films from other studios which did feature Carl and Irma, namely, *Bulldog Drummond* (1929) and *The Return of Bulldog Drummond* (1934), are two of the best features in the entire series. It is hard to imagine a Nayland Smith movie without Fu Manchu, just as it is hard to imagine eight Bulldog Drummond movies without either Carl or Irma Peterson. For viewers familiar with the Sapper novels, the Paramount Drummonds seem to be a series of missed opportunities.

## *Bulldog Drummond in Africa* (1938)

This is a publicity photo for *Bulldog Drummond in Africa* (1938), where Phyllis (Heather Angel) and Hugh (John Howard), on the eve of their wedding night, have concerns about the safety of the kidnapped Colonel Nielson.

The Bulldog Drummond films were seldom mysteries (except for some of the films of the late 1940s) and although they often involved foreign intrigue in some manner, they were seldom spy tales (*Bulldog Drummond's Revenge* [1937] being a possible exception). In the original book and original sound movie, both titled *Bulldog Drummond*, Drummond advertised in the newspaper for an "adventure," so perhaps these Drummond films are justly labeled as adventure films. In modern times, however, a new classification is often used for this type of film, namely "thriller." In particular, *Bulldog Drummond in Africa*, with its slimmed-down plot and exciting second half, surely falls within that category of movies.

The film commences, as many of these Paramount Drummonds have, on the eve of the wedding of Hugh and Phyllis. In an amusing opening scene, Phyllis has relieved Drummond and Tenny of their pants so that it would be impossible for them to become involved in a new caper. Drummond even cuts the phone lines of his own house, so that he cannot possibly be tempted to delay his upcoming nuptials for a new adventure. Thus, it is surprising that it is Phyllis who causes the diversion in this film, when she happens to see Colonel Nielson being kidnapped by Richard Lane, an international villain. Phyllis rushes to Drummond's house and the chase is on as Hugh, Phyllis, Tenny and Algy fly to Morocco to rescue Nielson.

The first half of the film is amusing at times, particularly in those early scenes at Drummond's house and later when Drummond eludes a Scotland Yard policeman so that he can fly to Morocco despite official disapproval. Once again, however, these scenes fall in the category of "seen that before" and, in fact, fall in the category of "seen that many times before." The second half of the film, though, has a completely different tone and structure, justifying the thriller category.

Once Drummond and his gang reach Morocco, the film takes off. There is a time bomb on the plane which explodes just after they land back at Lane's residence, a night raid on the Lane mansion, a shootout, Colonel Nielson almost mauled by a lion, Tenny suddenly shooting a villain who is about to shoot Drummond, and a fight between Drummond and Lane on a rooftop balcony, which finally results in Lane going over the side and being chewed up by his own lion. These scenes are quite suspenseful, helped by the fact that most of the comedy elements disappear at this time in the story, allowing the viewer to concentrate on the thriller elements of the plot. It is in scenes such as these that Bulldog Drummond can be viewed as a forerunner to James Bond.

Many viewers, when they first see the lion on the short chain at Lane's estate, may suspect that Lane will experience his demise at the hand (well, paws) of his own creature. That has become somewhat of a movie cliché, with, for example, J. Carrol Naish again, playing Dr. Daka, being killed by his own alligators at the end of the serial *Batman* (1943). However, cliché or not, it is an exciting moment in the film, with the fight on the balcony between Drummond and Lane going back and forth, with shots of the lion on his hind legs interspersed with scenes of the fight above, amidst roars from the lion. Even though no graphic violence is shown, what viewer does not wince along with the cast when the lion is on top of and devouring Lane?

H.B. Warner replaces John Barrymore as Colonel Nielson. While Barrymore was good in the Paramount Drummonds, by his third appearance in the series his overacting started to detract from the effectiveness of the films. Warner, on the other hand, is calm and subdued as Nielson, never losing his temper or sophistication, no matter what evil Lane and his cohorts throw at him. Warner gives the performance of the film. J. Carrol Naish is always good in a villain's roles, as he is here, and it is fun to see a pre-stardom Anthony Quinn in a small part as Lane's duplicitous assistant.

Not enough mention has been made in these essays about John Howard's performance as Captain Drummond. Since well-known performers Ronald Colman, Ray Milland, and Ralph Richardson had previously portrayed the English adventurer in the cinema, Howard had big shoes to fill, but he is clearly up to the challenge. By this fourth film as Drummond, Howard is very comfortable in the part, witty when necessary, loving when dealing with Phyllis and heroic when confronting the villain. While he is not really British enough for the role, being American- born, Howard's obvious charm and good looks paper over that one hitch in his casting as the most famous British adventurer of them all.

*Bulldog Drummond in Africa* never aspires to greatness; it is only second-feature entertainment. In that category, however, it excels, making it a good diversion for the fan of either mysteries or thrillers.

*Note on the Source Material*: The credits state that *Bulldog Drummond in Africa* was based upon *Challenge*, the 1937 novel by Sapper. In fact, the movie and the novel have absolutely nothing in common. The book involves the mysterious death (and perhaps murder) of Jimmy Latimer, a British officer, on a ferry traveling from France to England across the English Channel. Captain Drummond and Ronald Standish are called in by the War Office to investigate the matter. At the end, Drummond and his gang thwart a terrorist plot against

England. There is nothing about a secret formula that the villains are trying to coerce out of a Scotland Yard inspector.

*Challenge* was the last full-length novel written by Sapper about Bulldog Drummond. In 1948, 20th Century–Fox released a Drummond adventure film titled *The Challenge*. Its plot also had nothing in common with Sapper's 1937 novel.

## *Arrest Bulldog Drummond!* (1938)

The Paramount series about the English adventurer reached its nadir with *Arrest Bulldog Drummond!* The film runs less than one hour and even at that, there is not enough of a story to fill that short running time. In fact, for most of the movie, there is no story at all.

Richard Gannett, an old friend of Drummond's and an odd individual to say the least, has invented a ray gun that can destroy firearms and explosives from half a mile away. On the night of his bachelor party, Bulldog visits Gannett's flat because of some strange letters that Gannett has written. There he finds Gannett near death from a strange wound. With his dying breath, Gannett utters, "Look out for the stinger." Later, after the police have left the murder scene, Gannett's killer, Rolf Alferson, steals Gannett's contraption, which he then takes by ship to St. Anthony's Island. Alferson attempts to sell the device at a profit, but Drummond thwarts his intentions, capturing Alferson and his co-villains.

The title of the film comes from the fact that during the movie Drummond is arrested on three separate occasions for crimes he did not commit. Presumably that is supposed to be funny. Additional schtick includes Colonel Nielson being called "Inspector" by Drummond on several occasions, antics with Drummond's bow tie, some mild slapstick moments, and a blackbird which becomes important to the storyline. These vignettes are seldom amusing and become quite tiresome, quite fast.

Coincidences abound. Every time Alferson tries out the ray machine over a long distance, Drummond, Algy or Tenny happen to be there and almost suffer the consequences of an explosion. The villains just happen to depart on the same boat carrying Phyllis and her aunt on a long ocean cruise. One of the villains on St. Anthony sends his assistant to locate two men who are interested in purchasing Gannett's device. He brings back Algy and Tenny, because Tenny blurts out something about the ray gun to this man whom he does not even know. At the time, Algy is posing as a tourist so there is no logical reason for him to say what he did. Of course, the actual reason for doing so was as a blatant plot device for the assistant to misidentify Algy and Tenny as the two people for whom the assistant was looking and accidentally place Algy and Tenny into Alferson's clutches. This is an example of lazy plotting.

Another example: Since Gannett's machine uses a substantial amount of electricity, the lights in his neighborhood usually blink or become less intense when the machine is in operation. Drummond canvasses the neighborhood and every neighbor confirms the light situation except one, Beryl Ledyard. Thus, Drummond knows that she must be one of the villains. Given that Beryl is at least a semi-bright person, the only reason she refuses to admit the obvious to Drummond is so that Drummond can have a clue to the location of Gannett's device. To be frank, did the writers make any effort to develop clever plot ideas for this film?

Then there are the clichés, the most important one being the ray gun that could effectively neutralize opposing armies, the scientist who invents the device for the good of mankind, and the villain who purloins it for a profit motive only, consequences be damned. Also, the effectiveness of Gannett's invention is surprising since it appears to be made from spare parts and chewing gum.

Although George Zucco, one of the great movie villains, is totally wasted in the role of Alferson, it is still the performers that provide the only spark for the film. Heather Angel is back as Phyllis, spurned once again at the altar, but looking quite beautiful in her wedding dress and later quite fetching in the short outfit she wears when she goes biking. Claud Allister, the best of the Algys, has a small role as an associate of Colonel Nielson and he is wonderful in the part, with his affected British mannerisms and attitude. How much better would the Paramount Drummonds have been if Claud Allister had played Algy instead of Reginald Denny, who, once again, is unimpressive in the role?

The ending has its mild excitement with Algy and Denny trapped in a life-threatening situation and Phyllis in danger of being harmed by a ray gun explosion. However, a fistfight then ensues, and the film, which up until then has had no background music, suddenly has a completely inappropriate musical track, severely undercutting the excitement.

*Arrest Bulldog Drummond!* has very little going for it. Isn't it about time that Hugh and Phyllis finally marry and live happily ever after in peace?

*Note on the Source Material*: According to the credits, *Arrest Bulldog Drummond!* was based on Sapper's 1926 novel *The Final Count*. The book details the final encounter between Hugh Drummond and Carl Peterson, with Peterson dying at the end of the novel. *The Final Count* involves a deadly poison discovered by a scientist, Robin Gaunt, which he hopes can be employed to end all wars for all time. It is purloined by Peterson, with the intent to spray it onto ships on the high seas from a dirigible hovering above and then robbing the dead passengers and stealing anything of value in the ship's hold.

The book is one of the weakest of Sapper's works, particularly disappointing since it relates the story of the final encounter between Drummond and Peterson, after their three previous titanic struggles. Unfortunately, and unlike the previous novel about their battles, *The Third Round* (1924), Peterson is hardly in *The Final Count* until the end, undercutting the intensity of the struggle. The novel also has one of Sapper's weakest plots, which is perhaps one reason why the storyline was not employed in the film version.

Indeed, other than the fact that *Arrest Bulldog Drummond!* has, as its MacGuffin, a ray gun (slightly similar to the deadly poison of the novel) that a scientist hopes will end all wars, which is then stolen by a gang of criminals, the two works have nothing in common. None of the scenes or incidents from the novel is employed in the film. Once again, it is unclear why *The Final Count* is mentioned in the credits to the movie. Without that mention, it is unlikely that any person who read the book and then viewed the film would make any connection between the two works.

## *Bulldog Drummond's Secret Police* (1939)

*Bulldog Drummond's Secret Police* takes the Paramount Drummond series in a new direction, away from larger-than-life villains and into an old dark house mystery. However, the novelty of the setting is wasted as the short feature has the flimsiest of storylines, even flimsier than most of the prior films in the series.

It is the evening before the marriage of Hugh Drummond to Phyllis Clavering, although Aunt Blanche has serious doubts that the marriage will actually occur. The seasoned Bulldog Drummond fan will probably have some serious doubts also. Hugh has decided to open up his family homestead, Rockingham Tower, for the big event. The trouble begins when Professor Downie arrives at the estate to advise Hugh that there is a large fortune hidden deep in the catacombs of the manor. Downie is close to finding the location of the treasure, by trying to solve a cipher that has come into his possession. However, the villainous Frank Seaton is also after the treasure. Posing as the new butler, Albert Boulton, Seaton kills Downie and absconds with the cipher and Downie's partial solution. After solving the cryptogram by using Downie's work product, Seaton, towing a reluctant Phyllis with him, is off to the subterranean tunnels of the tower in order to locate the hidden fortune. Despite long odds, Hugh and the gang finally come to Phyllis' rescue. Seaton loses the fortune and he then drowns in the effort. Needless to say, by the time the film ends, there is still no marriage for Hugh and Phyllis.

Since the viewer knows almost from the beginning that the new butler, Albert Boulton, is actually Henry Seaton, the villain of the piece, there is not much mystery to the story. Therefore, in order to stretch the feature out through its short 56 minutes of running time, there is a dream sequence in which Drummond imagines his wedding day and also thinks about the other times he almost married Phyllis, allowing the insertion of clips from the prior Paramount films, a very inexpensive way to pad the feature. There is also comedy padding, mainly involving the unfunny Algy. Actually, there is so much comedy in *Bulldog Drummond's Secret Police* that it seems that the film may actually have been intended as a comedy and it is the mystery elements which are the padding.

With all the supposed comedy, if the viewer sometimes becomes confused and believes he is watching an Abbott and Costello feature, that is understandable, with slapstick humor such as a swivel door in the library leading into a tunnel of a cave and a suit of armor falling down the steps, although Algy, as usual, seems to be doing an imitation of Stan Laurel and not Lou Costello (who, in any event, had not yet made it to the cinema by the time the film was released). A more apt analogy may be to Sherlock Holmes and "The Musgrave Ritual," turned into an entertaining feature with Basil Rathbone titled *Sherlock Holmes Faces Death* (1943), which has a similar search for a hidden treasure on a large estate. Whatever comparison anyone can think of, *Bulldog Drummond's Secret Police* will always come in second.

As usual, with the exception of Reginald Denny as Algy, the acting in this Paramount Drummond is excellent, with E.E. Clive, once again, outstanding as Tenny. Forrester Harvey, as the absent-minded Professor Downie, is particularly engaging, actually providing some real humor to the film such as wearing winter clothes in August, apparently because he forgot to turn over the pages of his calendar.

For all of the justifiable criticism of *Bulldog Drummond's Secret Police*, the ending is first-rate. Once Phyllis enters the tunnels, dragged along by Seaton, the tale becomes quite suspenseful. Drummond and his gang are caught in a death trap, with a ceiling of spikes slowly descending onto them. Their attempts to block it by piling stones as a barrier or trying to escape out a small opening which Phyllis manages to create several times when Seaton is not looking are constantly thwarted. At the end, Phyllis and Seaton fall into another death trap of rushing waters, with Hugh rescuing Phyllis at the last instance. The set on which all of this occurs is magnificent, giving the film the feel, for a few minutes, of a high-budget feature, surely one higher than the movie serials on which these scenes are clearly based. This sequence is one of the highlights of all of the Paramount Drummonds.

However, the excellent ending to *Bulldog Drummond's Secret Police* does not adequately compensate for what little has gone before. It seems that Paramount was quickly losing interest in the series by the time of this film. Audiences had to be losing interest also. Luckily, there was only one movie left in the series and based upon its title, it seems that Hugh and Phyllis may finally tie the knot.

*Note on the Source Material: Bulldog Drummond's Secret Police* is the seventh film in the eight-film Bulldog Drummond series from Paramount. Except for the first film, *Bulldog Drummond Escapes* (1937), which is purportedly based on a play by Sapper and Fairlie, the next six films, including *Bulldog Drummond's Secret Police*, are purportedly based upon novels by Sapper. However, only *Bulldog Drummond Comes Back* (1937) (based on *The Female of the Species*) and *Bulldog Drummond's Peril* (1938) (based on *The Third Round*) have any similarity to the work of Sapper which is identified in the credits. Even in those cases, the films are hardly faithful adaptations of the novels that inspired them

*Bulldog Drummond's Secret Police* is, according to its credits, based on Sapper's 1929 novel *Temple Tower*. The book is about a man who hides in a fortress known as the Temple Tower with jewels that were stolen many years before, living in fear that a silent strangler will kill and rob him. There is no similarity between the written work and the film, other than the fact that the setting of each involves a tower, a secret tunnel leading into the tower contains a death trap, and Bulldog Drummond is a character in each. Of the other recurring characters from the books, only Peter Darrell is along for the ride with Drummond in the written work, although Denny has his usual small part.

The novel *Temple Tower* has a strong enough plot that it could have been adapted into a solid film. (That may already have occurred in *Temple Tower*, the 1930 film from Fox, which is now lost and cannot be evaluated.) However, as noted in the discussion of *Bulldog Drummond's Peril*, because each of the Paramount Drummonds was required to have Phyllis, Algy, Tenny and Colonel Nielson in the story, not to mention the oft-postponed wedding of Phyllis and Hugh as a sub-plot, the storyline of *Temple Tower* would have been difficult to adapt to the screen, since none of those characters (or their print counterparts) are in the novel (or, in the case of Tenny, have significant roles) and Hugh and Phyllis had been happily married in Sapper's works since the conclusion of the very first novel. Once again, this illustrates the problem with the Paramount Drummonds. It was nearly impossible to shoehorn a good Sapper plot into the rigid Drummond formula of Paramount.

## *Bulldog Drummond's Bride* (1939)

In looking back at the discussions of the previous seven films in the Bulldog Drummond series, two of the films were referred to as the worst movie to date in the series and almost all of them were criticized for their flimsy plots. It is therefore fitting that the last film in the series, *Bulldog Drummond's Bride*, is actually the worst film in the series and features the flimsiest plot.

Once again, it is just a few days before the planned wedding of Hugh and Phyllis and the two are optimistic enough about their planned nuptials that they are having their London flat painted for their upcoming occupancy. Unfortunately, it is just at that time that a London bank is robbed by well-known criminal Henri Armides, who coincidentally hides the loot in a radio in the Drummonds' apartment. Armides then poses as a mad house painter so that he can escape the police cordon around London. Later, Armides escapes the asylum to which he had been sent, and when he returns to Drummond's apartment to collect the loot, he has a run-in with Drummond and his gang. Armides is unable to steal the radio on that occasion, but he luckily learns that the radio has been sent by Hugh to Phyllis in Targemont, France, a small town where the wedding is to take place. Armides is therefore off to Targemont to recover the radio, with Hugh close on his trail. After some absurd antics and comedy schtick, Hugh recovers the bank funds, kills Armides and marries Phyllis.

In some respects it can be difficult to evaluate *Bulldog Drummond's Bride* because this book is about mysteries, not comedy. However, when a particular mystery movie is more about comedy than mystery, there is no choice but to address the comedy elements. In a way, that is fitting, since good mysteries and good comedies have at least one element in common — surprise. Without surprise, comedy cannot be funny. When Drummond and Armides become involved in a fight in the dark in the London flat and Drummond tells Algy to tie Armides' legs, and Algy does so, how many viewers do not guess in advance that Algy actually ties Drummond's legs? (A similar joke was previously used in *Bulldog Drummond's Revenge* [1937].) The trio then hears a sound on the steps and, believing the villain has returned, jumps the man and beats him to the ground. How many viewers do not figure out in advance that the man being attacked is Colonel Nielson? It is hard for a comedy moment to be funny when the finish is telegraphed many seconds in advance. This problem re-occurs many more times in the film.

In addition to there being no surprises or humor in the humor of the film, there are also no surprises or mystery in the mystery of the film. After its excellent opening with the explosion in a bank stunning an otherwise busy but mundane London street, the rest of the film continues with an uninteresting storyline concerning the chase after the radio, with Armides usually being accidentally frustrated at every attempt he makes at stealing the radio. Immediately thereafter, the radio is put in a place where it is once again within Armides' grasp. That is the entire storyline of the film. "Flimsy" may not adequately describe the plot of *Bulldog Drummond's Bride*; "feeble" or "pathetic" may be more accurate.

That fine character actor and great movie villain, Eduardo Ciannelli, plays Armides, but he is wasted in the role, having almost no lines other than in his ridiculous "mad" scene. The incomparable E.E. Clive, playing Tenny, is also wasted since his part was diminished to give Reginald Denny, playing Algy, the chance to do more slapstick humor such as having buckets of paint poured over his head and then slipping in the paint. The film is partially stolen by Gerald Hamer, who is so good in the Sherlock Holmes film *The Scarlet Claw* (1944). Here he plays Garvey, Armides' assistant, who is really his intern in crime. The part of Garvey is written and performed with some subtlety and there is therefore more real humor with the Garvey character than there is in all of the other outrageous incidents in the film combined. John Howard and Heather Angel are attractive and very likable as the finally married Drummonds. Those two have been rare strong points of the series; it is a shame they never had very good material with which to work.

All of these Paramount films were supposed to be based on written works by Sapper, although they usually were not. Instead of addressing serious matters of international importance or crimes of a significant nature, the films were often no more than fluff pieces. Whatever happened to that demobilized officer who was seeking adventure at the end of World War I?

*Note on the Source Material*: The credits of *Bulldog Drummond's Bride* state that the film was based upon "Bulldog Drummond and the Oriental Mind," a short story by Sapper published posthumously in the *Strand* in October 1937. Keeping with the tradition of the

Paramount Drummonds, the film has nothing in common with the short story, which involves a request by a female acquaintance of Algy's for assistance in helping her uncle, whose house has been invaded by a distant cousin of questionable motives and a frightening Oriental manservant.

## The Later Films

### Bulldog Drummond at Bay (1947)

After an absence of eight years from the silver screen, Bulldog Drummond returned to the cinema with a new Captain Drummond, Ron Randell, a new Algy, Pat O'Moore, and a new studio of origin, Columbia Pictures. Unfortunately, over the course of those intervening years, Drummond appears to have lost his style and daring. While *Bulldog Drummond at Bay* has its slight interest, it never comes close to the quality of the early Drummond films.

Drummond is vacationing at his country cottage when one evening his peace is suddenly disturbed by a rock thrown through his front window. Drummond goes outside to investigate and he is accosted and threatened by two men, who want to know if Drummond has seen a stranger in the area. After the thugs leave, Drummond examines the rock and discovers a torn claim check attached to it. The pasteboard contains some cryptic writing, which Drummond cannot decipher.

The next day a young woman, Doris Hamilton, appears at the cottage, claiming she is experiencing trouble with her car. The always gallant Drummond invites her in for breakfast but then sees in a mirror that she is drugging his tea. That sets Drummond off on a long quest to determine the secret of the claim check and Doris' true motives. With the assistance of Algy Longworth and a newspaper reporter named Seymour, Drummond discovers that villains are after a fortune in stolen jewels. Drummond then rescues the Scotland Yard policeman who threw the rock through the window and also gets the girl.

As can been seen from the 1937 film version of the same story, there is an intrinsic interest in the incident of the note and the various methods by which the villains try to obtain possession of the document. However, the 1947 film version spends too much time on that issue. It actually comprises more than half of the film. That, unfortunately, turns *Bulldog Drummond at Bay* into a talkfest rather than an action feature, and an audience is expecting much more action than talk in a film about the English adventurer. A little tightening of the script in this area would have gone a long way toward improving the film.

The storyline of *Bulldog Drummond at Bay* cannot sustain much scrutiny. What an incredible coincidence that Doris works for Meredith, the jeweler who has the jewels, and Scotland Yard has her brother substituted as the courier for the jewels! The villains then blackmail Doris, an assistant in a jewelry store, into going down to Drummond's cottage to drug him and then to search his house for the elusive note. No wonder that scheme did not work. Perhaps the next time, these professional thieves will not employ a rank amateur to do their dirty work. Crime should always be left to the professionals.

Despite all of these problems, *Bulldog Drummond at Bay* might have worked if there were a more accomplished actress in the role of Doris Hamilton. Anita Louise, a seasoned veteran of the screen by 1947, has the part. While she is slightly attractive, she conveys no allure or sexuality. Her performance is bland and unconvincing. She is no femme fatale

Bulldog Drummond (Ron Randell, on the right) has just rescued Scotland Yard agent Richard Hamilton (Oliver Thorndike) from a gang of jewel thieves, with the help of Hamilton's sister Doris (Anita Louise), in *Bulldog Drummond at Bay* (1947).

and it is frankly hard to see why Drummond has any interest in her, or for that matter, any interest in continuing to investigate whatever crimes may have occurred.

The very handsome Ron Randell is fine in his first American screen performance, although the role of Captain Drummond is written without wit or flair, making it hard for him to stand out in the part. Pat O'Moore is also fine playing Algy Longworth, although once again, the role is written in an undistinguished manner, unlike the prior film characterizations of Drummond's best friend. Algy provides little humor, except at one point, when he tries to warn Drummond of trouble by whistling like a whippoorwill, as a prearranged signal. Unfortunately, Algy's imitation sounds just like a whistle, bringing all of the villains quickly to the scene.

The direction by Sidney Salkow is pedestrian and in some of the few action sequences, the direction is so poor that it is difficult to determine who is shooting whom or who is fighting with whom. The one interest in viewing *Bulldog Drummond at Bay* is to see a different take on the character of Bulldog Drummond, once his grounding in World War I is so far in the past that it can have no more impact on his nature, and the villainy he is investigating no longer involves international issues.

*Note on the Source Material*: Most commentaries assert that the 1947 film has no connection with the 1935 novel of the same name by Sapper. That is patently incorrect. More than half of the 1947 movie is based on the opening of the novel. Thus, the scenes where the rock is thrown through the window, Drummond is accosted by two men, a woman comes the next day to locate any note that accompanied the rock, the attempt to drug Drummond, Drummond having his housekeeper telegram a fake note to him, the shooting of his dog and the later killing of one of the henchmen in Drummond's cottage all come from the book. Indeed, in these early scenes, the 1947 film is based more on the book than the 1937 film.

One major difference between the two works comes from the time period of the post–World War II film as contrasted with the time period of the between-the-wars novel. A MacGuffin based on an organization of pacifists known as the Key Club and issues of rearmament would have hardly worked in 1947. Thus, the MacGuffin of the movie was changed to the more mundane but slightly more realistic bag of valuable jewels. The other major difference is that after the scenes at Drummond's cottage are concluded in the movie, all of the events in the film are original to the film.

*Note on the Remake*: The novel *Bulldog Drummond at Bay* was also the basis for the 1937 film of the same name.

## *Bulldog Drummond Strikes Back* (1947)

Given that it comes so late in the Hollywood mystery movie cycle, *Bulldog Drummond Strikes Back* is a surprisingly good mystery. By the late 1940s, the Hollywood studios were paying little attention to their crime series, and, indeed, despite being produced at Columbia Pictures, *Bulldog Drummond Strikes Back* is a B–movie, with a very small budget. The direction by Frank McDonald is standard; the dialogue is uninspired. There are no stars in the cast, not even any future stars. The acting is adequate, at best. There are really no action scenes except for some fistfights, and they occur primarily in the dark so they are very hard to view. In fact, *Bulldog Drummond Strikes Back* has little style at all.

Nevertheless, *Bulldog Drummond Strikes Back* is a mystery, not a work of art, and as a mystery, it is quite entertaining. Captain Drummond spots a friend, Inspector Sanderson, sitting at a bar with a pretty girl. When Sanderson leaves, it appears that he is being followed. Drummond is so worried that he, along with Algy Longworth and young Seymour, their companion from the prior film, proceed to Sanderson's house, where they discover his body in his study, shot from outside through a window. Drummond also finds Ellen Curtis hiding in the room and it is from her that Drummond learns the backstory of the murder.

Sanderson had been investigating a "fake heir" racket, where imposters have been making claims to large estates, using the fact that many birth records were lost during the bombings of World War II. In this case, there are two claimants to the estate of Jane Cosgrove, each claiming to be Ellen Curtis. Each has a birth certificate whose authenticity cannot be conclusively determined. Drummond is immediately attracted to the pretty Ellen he finds at Sanderson's house (Ellen #1) and sets out to help her prove her claim.

*Bulldog Drummond Strikes Back* is always interesting because the viewer is constantly guessing as to which Ellen is the true heir. Both actresses playing the Ellens are attractive so on that criteria, it is a draw. Ellen #2, however, has her uncle testifying to her bona fides and she also has more knowledge than Ellen #1 about country neighbors of her aunt. Paradoxically, that helps Ellen #1's standing in the viewer's eyes, as everyone likes an underdog and Ellen #2's proof seems just a little too pat. Also, the uncle appears somewhat disagreeable and Ellen #1 seems just a little bit nicer than Ellen #2, again pushing the audience to root for Ellen #1. (This is actually a trick often employed by Agatha Christie, making the villain seem nice and the good person a little disagreeable, subtly forcing the reader to be disinclined to suspect the character who eventually turns out to be the villain.)

Then there is that interesting moment when two of the villains sneak into Drummond's home. Even though they get the upper hand on Drummond and Algy, they simply leave without trying to obtain the documents they supposedly intended to steal. However, they do "accidentally" drop a hotel room key. When it turns out that Ellen #1 has been kidnapped from Drummond's home and is being held in that hotel room, Drummond starts to become suspicious. He then decides to resolve the matter by bringing both Ellens to the home of their childhood nanny, who should be able to identify the real Ellen.

There is true suspense at that point in the film, as no viewer can be quite sure whom the nanny will select. When she identifies Ellen #1 as the legitimate claimant, everyone gives a huge sigh of relief, until Drummond suddenly trips up the nanny on her testimony, finally revealing Ellen #2 as the true claimant to the Cosgrove estate. There is then one last surprise, as the identity of the murderer of Sanderson is revealed.

*Bulldog Drummond Strikes Back* always keeps the viewer guessing as to the identity of the real Ellen Curtis. Looking back over the feature, there are some fair clues to the real Ellen's identity and also to that of Sanderson's killer, so *Bulldog Drummond Strikes Back* is a mystery film whose solid substance trumps its poor style. It is a shame that this plot was not employed in a bigger picture.

Sapper's Bulldog Drummond was an adventurer and not really a detective and he seldom dealt with issues as small as competing heirs to an estate, large though the estate may be. Nevertheless, while there is little of the true Bulldog Drummond in *Bulldog Drummond Strikes Back*, it is an excellent mystery and very enjoyable, being quite a pleasant surprise for a viewer who has preconceived notions about the film because of the year in which it was released.

*Note on the Source Material*: According to the credits, this film is based upon the novel by Sapper. That presumably means *Bulldog Drummond Strikes Back*, the 1933 novel by Sapper. The book does start with the killing of a man named Sanderson, but he is not an inspector from Scotland Yard. The novel ends with Drummond and his gang preventing a terrorist attack on an English train. There is nothing in the book about competing heirs to an estate. Other than the purloining of the name "Sanderson" for the initial murder victim, the film and the book have nothing in common.

That gives Sapper's novel, *Bulldog Drummond Strikes Back*, a unique distinction. Two films about Drummond were made with that title, one in 1934 and one in 1947, and neither one was based upon the book.

## *The Challenge* (1948)

*The Challenge* is deadly dull. While there may be other appropriate adjectives to use, such as tedious and boring, deadly dull is surely accurate. The reasons for this are many. Bulldog Drummond movies could often be exciting but this is a Bulldog Drummond film in name only. Sure, there are characters named Captain Drummond, Algy Longworth and Inspector McIver, but Sapper's Drummond was usually involved with matters of international importance or he did battle with archvillains the likes of which the world seldom knew. Captain Drummond rarely lowered himself, as he does in this film, to investigating more trivial matters such as the death of an elderly ship captain and buried treasure.

While very British terms such as "Scotland Yard," "pub" and "quid" are used from time to time in *The Challenge*, there is no real sense that *The Challenge* takes place in England. Its setting could have just as easily been America or in any other country with a coast and some shipping. The direction by Jean Yarbrough is so poor that there are almost no close-ups of any of the actors. Rather, Yarbrough generally employs long shots or shots with two or three actors in the frame. As to quick cutting or montage to create excitement, forget about it. A number of scenes are shot in the semi-dark, probably to hide the threadbare sets being used rather than to create any tension.

Tom Conway plays Bulldog Drummond and the 44-year-old actor seems to have aged considerably since playing the Falcon earlier that same year. That observation may not be 100 percent accurate because, as noted above, there are no good close-ups of Conway in *The Challenge* to accurately judge his appearance. However, his performance as Hugh Drummond is the same as his performances as Tom Lawrence in the Falcon series, once again supporting the conclusion that *The Challenge* is a Bulldog Drummond film in name only.

Poverty Row studios often attempted to beef up their mysteries, boring though they might be, by at least having an exciting conclusion. Even in that regard, *The Challenge* falters. The crooks follow clues to the location of a treasure chest on a beach and walk right into the arms of the waiting police. They do not even put up a fight. Of course, what does one expect when the lead villain is the aged housekeeper of Captain Sonnenberg? Where is Irma Peterson when you need her?

As to the plot, it has something to do with a buried treasure, with a clue to the location thereof hidden in the sails of a model sailing ship built by Captain Sonnenberg. The model accidentally comes into the hands of Algy Longworth, thereby involving Drummond in the matter. Early in the film, Sonnenberg is pushed off a high cliff to his death near the sea, a murder which is never fully explained in the film. The three potential heirs to the Sonnenberg estate are the most likely suspects for the villain of *The Challenge*, but there are no good clues given for the viewer to discern the actual culprit.

Note the two not-so-clever plot devices used in *The Challenge*. Seymour and Drummond work on Morse code at the beginning of the film, leading most viewers to suspect that the code will come in handy late in the film. It does, as Drummond's coded message to Seymour leads to the capture of the heavies and a rescue of Drummond. (If these films were shot in a different order, Seymour would not have known Morse code and the killers would have gotten away.) That sequence also addresses the only true mystery in the film — why Seymour is a character at all.

Late in the film, Drummond proceeds to the Sonnenberg estate and, for the first time in the film, does not ask Algy to accompany him. That heavy-handed moment is inserted into the story so that Drummond can be captured by the villains. If Algy had come along, which would have made complete sense, Drummond could not have been captured and the ending sequences of the film could not have occurred.

By 1948, it is highly unlikely that the Bulldog Drummond stories were still very popular in America, with Gerard Fairlie's novels being published on an irregular schedule in the 1940s. *The Challenge* did not incorporate a storyline of either Sapper's or Fairlie's. Thus, it is hard to fathom why *The Challenge* was made as a Drummond movie. For that matter, given how poor *The Challenge* is, it is hard to fathom why the film was made at all.

*Note on the Source Material:* This is the second film supposedly based on Sapper's 1937 novel *Challenge*, with the first being *Bulldog Drummond in Africa* (1938). Neither film has any relationship to the novel, which involves a complex terrorist plot against England which is thwarted by Drummond and his associates. The setting and time period of the novel is during the increased tensions in Europe just a few years prior to World War II and therefore the plot may not have been easily adaptable to a post–World War II film.

## *13 Lead Soldiers* (1948)

This is the second consecutive film to star Tom Conway as Bulldog Drummond and the second one in a row that does not have the feel of a real Bulldog Drummond story. The film could have come from the Falcon series or the late 1940s Philo Vance films or from any other mystery series of the era. Almost none of the cast is English and, although the story supposedly takes place in England, none of the film was shot on location and there are no establishing shots of London or other English landmarks. This decidedly non–English atmosphere of the movie is surprising for a film about one of the greatest English adventurers of them all. Drummond is called on to investigate an affair about toy soldiers, which seems a tad insignificant compared to his epic struggles with Carl and Irma Peterson. Once again, it is hard to understand why this film was made at all but it is particularly difficult to understand why it was made as a Bulldog Drummond movie.

*13 Lead Soldiers* opens with the murder of Ashley Stedman and the theft of his two miniature lead soldiers and the parchment which he was studying. Stedman had recently acquired the items at an auction. He had then refused to sell them to an aggressive man named Edward Vane who had offered a high price. Drummond comes into the picture when an acquaintance of his, Philip Coleman, brings to Drummond two toy soldiers that he owns, similar to the ones stolen from Stedman. Coleman has received anonymous death threats from someone demanding Coleman's toy soldiers, and Coleman has some obvious concerns for his own well-being. Drummond, as always, is willing to help, in this case by setting himself up as a target of the murderer. He places an announcement in the press to the effect that Drummond has now acquired two soldiers that are similar to Stedman's. The ruse first brings fake newspaper reporter Estelle Gorday to his flat. Later, Edward Vane himself shows up to try to steal Drummond's lead soldiers. It seems clear that Vane had killed Stedman but when Vane himself ends up murdered, Drummond must look elsewhere for the killer. In that process, Drummond figures out the secret of the 13 lead soldiers and discovers a treasure that has been hidden for over 900 years.

*13 Lead Soldiers* is an uninspired effort even for the late 1940s, which was an uninspired era for series mystery movies in general and Bulldog Drummond features in particular. This is the second film in a row with a hidden treasure MacGuffin. The direction is unimaginative, the performances are routine and the production is threadbare. Much of the film is shot in the semi-dark and since it is difficult to obtain a good print of the feature, much of the detail of the movie, if there is any, can be lost on the modern viewer. Once Philip Coleman reappears about halfway through the film, it is clear that he is the killer, and so, unlikely a suspect as he may be, there is no surprise at the end of the feature.

The film attempts to create some interest by having Algy and Bulldog masquerade as each other, with the real Bulldog Drummond nevertheless always receiving the most attention from the women the two meet in the movie, proving that looks and personality are more important than a name. These scenes do have their appeal and humor but they are not enough to rescue the film. Also, the same idea was done before in *Secrets of the Lone Wolf* (1941), with Michael Lanyard and his valet Jamison exchanging places.

Despite all of its shortcomings, the finish of *13 Lead Soldiers* has its interest. When the 13 lead soldiers are placed in the correct positions on a pedestal, there is a lot of shaking as some counterweights move and then a door slides up, revealing the ancient treasure. Then, Drummond and his allies are almost entombed in the hidden room when Coleman tries to make his escape, leading to Coleman's grisly death in the sliding door. These are excellent moments for *13 Lead Soldiers*, bringing to mind modern treasure hunt movies such as *National Treasure* (2004) and *Indiana Jones and the Kingdom of the Crystal Skull* (2008). However, it is highly unlikely that *13 Lead Soldiers* was an inspiration for those features. It is doubtful that many people now alive have seen *13 Lead Soldiers* all the way through.

*Note on the Source Material*: According to the credits, *13 Lead Soldiers* was adapted from an original story by Sapper. The reference must be to "Thirteen Lead Soldiers," which was published posthumously in the *Strand* in December 1937. The last Drummond work written by Sapper, it involves an attempted assassination of a high French official at an overnight conference in England, with his aide using the order in which 13 lead soldiers are aligned on a tray on a window sill to signal the assassin as to which of 13 rooms the French official would be sleeping in that night. There is obviously no relationship between the short story and the film starring Tom Conway, except that a character in the short story is named Stedman.

## *Calling Bulldog Drummond* (1951)

With *Calling Bulldog Drummond*, it is refreshing to view the first A–production of a Bulldog Drummond movie in over a decade. The films from the late 1940s were bargain basement endeavors and even the Paramount Drummonds from the late 1930s were hardly top-of-the-line affairs. With this 1951 feature, it is also refreshing to see a Bulldog Drummond film shot in its natural locale of England, with a cast that is almost all British. The main exception to the all–British cast is Walter Pidgeon as Captain Drummond, but since Pidgeon was Canadian–born, perhaps that is the same thing. Although the Hugh Drummond of *Calling Bulldog Drummond* is not a veteran of World War I, there is an early reference in this film to his work for England during World War II, so there is some faithfulness to the original character developed by H.C. McNeile in the early 1920s. The film stars one of the most recognizable of the Hollywood stars of the 1940s, Walter Pidgeon, and if he seems just a bit too old to play the part, it is still interesting to see the first major star to play the role since Ronald Colman, over 15 years before. All in all, there is a lot to like in *Calling Bulldog Drummond*. However, there are difficulties with the film, arising mainly with the storyline. It is not that the plot is bad; it is just that it has been done so many times before.

Responding to a string of major thefts, Scotland Yard's Inspector McIver has decided to tap that talented amateur, Captain Hugh Drummond, to go undercover to attempt to infiltrate the gang. Drummond poses as Joe Crandell, a career criminal who has just returned from Italy, and Sergeant Helen Smith poses as his significant other, Lily. The one clue the police have involves a waterfront nightclub, The Last Word, and so Drummond works a scheme wherein Lily meets the owner, Arthur Guns, worms her way into his affections and

In *Calling Bulldog Drummond* (1951), Captain Drummond's (Walter Pidgeon) undercover operation has gone awry and he and Sgt. Helen Smith (Margaret Leighton) are awaiting word as to how the villains intend to get rid of them.

then attempts to get Drummond incorporated into the gang. Drummond's scheme almost works but it unfortunately unravels quite suddenly when the secret head of the villains, Colonel Webson, a member of Drummond's club, accidentally learns at the club that Drummond is working undercover for the police. Webson directs his subordinate, Guns, to capture Drummond and Sergeant Smith. However, it is hard to keep an ex-military man tied up for long. Drummond escapes with the help of Algy and captures the villains.

Of course, a hero pretending to be a villain to infiltrate a gang of criminals has been done many times before, from Warner Brothers' gangster movies to the Torchy Blane and Brass Bancroft mystery series to spy films such as *The Counterfeit Traitor* (1962). In *Calling Bulldog Drummond*, the scenario is actually handled quite well, with substantial time taken to establish Drummond's bona fides with the gang, whose very skeptical leader Guns is not easily fooled. Unfortunately for Guns, his attraction to Lily undermines his better judgment. Margaret Leighton, masquerading as Lily Ross, and Robert Beatty, as Arthur Guns, are particularly good in the scenes detailing their cat and mouse seduction. Drummond's additional tricks to establish his authenticity involve a fake shooting of some Scotland Yard policemen while Guns is looking on. Indeed, *Calling Bulldog Drummond* is probably one of the best of these undercover film capers. Nevertheless, it has just been done so many times, both before and after, that it is hard for the scenario to entice a viewer once again.

Of course, the undercover angle is not all there is to the film. *Calling Bulldog Drum-

*mond* opens with a beautifully structured scene of the robbery of a bank, timed to the second, and with radar used to help the villains escape over fog-enshrouded London streets. The finale involves the precision robbery of an airplane that has just landed, also very well-directed, both from a cinematic and criminal viewpoint. There is also the ingenious way the gang tricks Algy into providing McIver with the wrong information about the location of the gang's next heist. However, when Drummond, Algy and Smith have been captured and are being held in the Last Word basement at gunpoint by one of the thieves, it is, needless to say, cliché time once again as the viewer knows that Drummond will somehow engineer his escape and probably not in a very clever manner. And, of course, that is what occurs, with Drummond bowling over the gunman when he moves from his seat to obtain a cigarette for Smith. In the 21st century, now that there is much less smoking going on in the world, one expects that heroes will have a much harder time escaping from their villainous captors.

Pidgeon's performance as Bulldog Drummond will not be to everyone's taste. Pidgeon is too old to be dashing and adventurous and he has little clever dialogue with which to work. From the perspective of 60 years later, Drummond's reluctance to work with a female police officer makes Drummond seem even older than he looks. Given Pidgeon's size and age, the stunt work at the end of the film in the fisticuffs between Drummond and Guns is hardly convincing. Even though Pidgeon has star power, a younger actor would probably have been more effective in the part. David Tomlinson is excellent as Algy Longworth, bringing just the right measure of the caricature of a silly ass Englishman to a role that also requires him to display genuine concern for Drummond during the film and some true bravery at the end of the picture. Next to Claud Allister, Tomlinson is the best of the Algy Longworths.

There is a special moment at the conclusion of *Calling Bulldog Drummond*, when Drummond confronts Colonel Webson, a representative of a stiff upper class Englishman, and asks him why he has turned to a life of crime. Webson replies, "Excitement, I suppose. Life in peacetime seemed unbearably flat. I was bored, Hugh, bored stiff." Drummond replies, knowingly, "Yes, I know the feeling." In those few lines, the writers tie *Calling Bulldog Drummond* back to the genesis of the character of Captain Drummond in Sapper's first novel and in Ronald Colman's first film, bringing the film series to a fitting conclusion. It is a poignant moment, particularly for those who have seen the early Drummond films or read the Sapper novels. So, while *Calling Bulldog Drummond* is disappointing in several ways, it has its merits. It is clearly better than many of the Bulldog Drummond films that had been released in the prior 20 years.

*Note on the Source Material:* The credits to *Calling Bulldog Drummond* state that the film was based on a story by Gerard Fairlie. Fairlie is also credited as one of the three scriptwriters, as is Howard Emmett Rogers. According to the Turner Classic Movies website, though the film was released in 1951, it was shot in England in 1950. The novel, *Calling Bulldog Drummond*, was first published in August, 1951. Since Fairlie dedicated the book to Howard Emmett Rogers, calling him "a splendid script craftsman with whom to work," it seems clear that the book was based on the movie and not the other way around. Fairlie probably wrote the story which was used for the film's screenplay and then after the script of the film was completed, expanded that story into a full-length novel.

As a result of Fairlie's involvement with the film version, it is not surprising that there is much similarity between the two versions of the story with, in the novel, Drummond going undercover as Joe Crandell, a small time crook. Along with Sergeant Smith, posing as Lily, he infiltrates a gang of brazen thieves. The main difference is that in the novel, Algy Longworth is along for the ride from the beginning, posing as Wally Nelson, the third member of Drummond's gang. Also, in the novel, the police create a fake death scene for Drummond, which permits him to leave his upper class society and go undercover, while in the film, Drummond has supposedly gone out of the country after being caught cheating at cards at his club. Perhaps more surprisingly, the film is much more appealing then the novel, which forgoes the scenes in the film in which Guns' confederate Molly tricks Algy into telling McIver the wrong location for the upcoming robbery or Molly on her own discovering that Crandell may be Bulldog Drummond. In fact, the Molly character in the book is killed by Guns early in the story.

While the endings of the two works are nearly identical, the novel does not have that exchange between the Mr. Big character and Drummond about being bored after the excitement of war, a truly significant moment for the film series, as described above. It is surprising that Fairlie did not include that exchange in his novel given its significance to the entire Bulldog Drummond saga. Also, in the novel, when Drummond and Algy are attempting to escape from their captor before Guns returns to kill them, Drummond signals to Algy that he wants Algy to tackle the man with the gun, by making a cryptic remark about football, which, of course, is called "soccer" in the United States. The film version has the same moment, except that Bulldog and Algy refer to the sport as "soccer," an incredible mistake for the screenwriters to make about two of the most English gentlemen in all of mystery literature. In this one instance, it made sense for Fairlie to not incorporate this dialogue of the film into his novel.

## AFTERWARDS

Bulldog Drummond truly was a forerunner of James Bond and with the popularity of Bond spy adventures in the 1960s, it was natural for other filmmakers to attempt to revive the Bulldog Drummond franchise. The first film was *Deadlier Than the Male* (1967), with Richard Johnson as Hugh Drummond and Nigel Green as Carl Peterson. Here Drummond is an insurance investigator interested in several mysterious deaths. The sequel is *Some Girls Do* (1969), with Drummond investigating acts of sabotage surrounding England's first supersonic airliner. Johnson reprised his role as Drummond and James Villiers appeared as Carl Peterson.

Neither of these films is true to the spirit of the Bulldog Drummond of literature. By the end of the 1960s, the James Bond craze quieted down and no more Bulldog Drummond movies have since been made.

*Bulldog Drummond* was a long-running radio program on the Mutual Network, starting in 1941 and continuing through 1949. George Couloris originally starred as the title character, being replaced in later years by Santos Ortega and Nick Wever, with Wever playing the role the longest. Denny was a regular character in the stories, played originally by Everett Sloane. In these programs, Drummond was a private detective. After setting the story in England for the first two months of the show, the series then moved to America, leading to its famous opening, "Out of the fog ... out of the night ... and into his American adventures ... comes ... Bulldog Drummond." There was a short-lived (1953–54) revival of the program with Cedric Hardwicke in the lead role. There were no American television programs about the character.

After the last film in 1951, Gerard Fairlie wrote one more book about Captain Drummond, titled *The Return of the Black Gang*. In the 1954 novel, Carl Peterson, long thought dead, made a surprise reappearance. Thereafter, Fairlie wrote several books unrelated to Captain Drummond. He died in 1983.

# 3

# Charlie Chan
## *The Chinese Detective*

According to one dictionary definition, the word "aphorism" means a terse statement which expresses an astute observation. For most people, that definition will suffice. For mystery fans, however, the dictionary definition is wholly inadequate. For them, a better definition of "aphorism" would be a short statement of truth spoken by the famous Honolulu policeman, Charlie Chan. Indeed, and to adapt an old joke, when one looks up the word "aphorism" in the dictionary, there is always a picture of Charlie Chan with it.

Of course, the Chan novels and movies are more than aphorisms; they are often very good mysteries. However, even when a Chan movie might not be all that good, the character of Chan, his attitude toward crime and his Oriental demeanor are always at the forefront, making it a worthwhile viewing experience. And, when a Chan movie is really bad, there are always the aphorisms.

## Background

### The Novels

Earl Derr Biggers was born in Warren, Ohio, in 1884. He graduated from Harvard University in 1907 and then obtained a job on a newspaper, *The Boston Traveler*, for which he wrote a humor column and some drama criticism. In 1913, Biggers published his first novel, *Seven Keys to Baldpate*, about a writer who goes to a deserted resort to write a book but is interrupted by several mysterious characters. In addition to the book becoming a bestseller, the work was adapted into a long-running play of the same name, which became a huge success for the original lead actor, George M. Cohan (who also adapted the novel for the stage). The play, first produced in 1913, has been revived many times since and, in addition, it has been adapted into several films including two during the silent era. Even without the later Chan novels, Biggers' name would still be remembered today as a result of *Seven Keys to Baldpate*. Biggers also wrote other novels and plays containing mystery elements.

While vacationing in Hawaii in 1920, Biggers became interested in setting a mystery in the tropical islands. As the story goes, in 1924 he visited the New York Public Library and read newspaper stories about Chang Apana, a Chinese detective on the Honolulu police force. Apana, a well-known figure in Hawaii, lived on Punchbowl Hill as would Charlie Chan. He had many children as would Chan. However, Apana was thin, not heavy, and he was a tough, physical detective, generally involved with opium smuggling, not homicides, and famous for his use of a bullwhip to subdue the villains.

Although Biggers did not meet Apana at that time (that would not come until much later), the idea of an Oriental detective intrigued him so much that he decided to write a mystery story about one. The first Chan book, *The House Without a Key*, was originally published in 1925. There, detective Charlie Chan investigates the murder of Dan Winterslip, who was stabbed in the heart. Surprisingly, but as was often the case in the Chan novels, the Honolulu policeman, while he does solve the crime, sometimes seems like a subordinate character, less important than the young hero, John Quincy, who also solves the crime amid his own romantic difficulties.

The next book was *The Chinese Parrot* (1926) in which Charlie goes undercover as a Chinese cook to protect some valuable jewels and also to expose a murderer and his gang. Much of the action takes place in the California desert, presaging Charlie's world tour in the movies and the fact that most of his film mysteries do not take place in Hawaii. In all, Biggers wrote only six novels about the great Chinese detective. If not for Biggers' untimely death in 1933, it is assumed that Biggers would have written many more stories about the Chinese detective since the Warner Oland films made Chan quite a popular character in the early 1930s.

## The Early Films

The transition of Charlie Chan from novels to the cinema was quick but not with much early success. Just a year after *The House Without a Key* was published, the novel was turned into a ten-chapter serial of the same name, released by Pathé in 1926. The chapterplay starred Walter Miller and Allene Ray, who acted together in many silent serials, and was directed by Spencer Gordon Bennet, well-known today for the many silent and sound serials he directed. Charlie Chan was played by George Kuwa, an actor of Japanese descent, making this a rare film in which Charlie was played by an Asian actor. However, the part of Charlie seems small, with Kuwa being billed very low in the cast listings. The film is lost.

The second Chan film, also from the silent era, was *The Chinese Parrot* (1928), based upon Biggers' 1926 novel. It was released by Universal and directed by Paul Leni, best known today for the silent horror films he directed such as *The Cat and the Canary* (1927) and *The Man Who Laughs* (1928). Once again, Charlie was played by a Japanese actor, Sojin, and once again the actor was billed low in the cast. Interestingly, George Kuwa also appeared in this film, playing the Chinese servant Louis Wong, who is killed during the course of the proceedings. This film is also lost.

The first sound film about Charlie Chan (and the earliest film about the Honolulu policeman still in existence) is *Behind That Curtain* (1929). Released by Fox, which would eventually start the long-running mystery series about Chan starring Warner Oland, *Behind That Curtain* was more of a love story than a mystery, although at the end Chan (played by Korean actor E.L. Park) made an appearance just in time to shoot the villain. The role of Charlie was not much more than a cameo. The 1929 movie was loosely based on Biggers' novel *Behind That Curtain*, published in 1928.

## The Film Series

In 1931, Fox decided to produce another film about Charlie Chan, but the studio made two important improvements over its release of *Behind That Curtain* in 1929. First, it brought in Warner Oland to play the charismatic Honolulu policeman and no longer relegated the role of Charlie Chan to a minor supporting character. Also, the studio decided to faithfully adapt one of the Biggers novels, which in this case was *Charlie Chan Carries On*, first published in 1930. As a result of being faithful to the novel, Chan first appears rather late in the film but he is still such an important character, and Oland fit the role so perfectly, that a new film series was started — one which would last until 1949, with 44 films being produced.

In 1931, Warner Oland was already well-known to movie fans. He was born in Sweden on October 3, 1879 or 1880, and his family immigrated to the United States in 1892. After working in the theater for several years, Oland first appeared in films as John Bunyan in *The Pilgrim's Progress*, produced around 1910, before appearing regularly in silent films starting in 1915, often playing character heavies. Oland's facial features were such that with a little bit of makeup it was easy for him to play Oriental roles. His first such part was in *The Lightning Raider* (1919). In the early sound era, he portrayed the greatest Oriental villain of them all, Dr. Fu Manchu, first in *The Mysterious Dr. Fu Manchu* (1929) and then in two sequels. Oland was then tapped to play the most famous Oriental detective of them all, Charlie Chan, in *Charlie Chan Carries On* (1931). Previously, Oland had played Cantor Rabinowitz, Al Jolson's father, in *The Jazz Singer* (1927), the first part-talkie.

The first several Chan movies starring Oland were adapted from novels written by Biggers. The only Chan novel which was not turned into a film was *Keeper of the Keys*, published in 1932. Unfortunately, most of these early Chan films are now lost, with the only one fully in existence being *The Black Camel* (1931), also starring Bela Lugosi and Robert Young.

*Charlie Chan in London* (1934) marks two important changes in the film series. It is the first film not based on a Biggers novel and it also starts the first leg of Chan's world tour, on which he would eventually make stops in Paris, Egypt, Shanghai and San Francisco. Thereafter, Chan started investigating murders at events or attractions, such as the circus, the race track, the opera, and the Olympics, amid stops on Broadway and at Monte Carlo.

*Charlie Chan in Paris* (1935) is a seminal film in the series, as it introduces No. 1 son Lee Chan. The characterization of Lee in this film is slightly different here than in later films, as Lee is in Paris on business and stops in to see his father while he is close by. Lee is not as much a figure of comic relief as he would later become in the series, and Lee's affection and respect for his father is one of the highlights of the film. Lee Chan is missing when Charlie visits Egypt but on the next stop on Charlie's world tour, *Charlie Chan in Shanghai* (1935), Lee is back. He assisted his father in the remainder of the Oland films except for one, *Charlie Chan's Secret* (1936).

While none of the actors who played Charlie Chan in the series were of Chinese descent, the actors who played his sons always were. Keye Luke was born in Canton, China, on June 18, 1904, and came to America when he was only four months old. Luke was raised in Seattle, Washington, where his father owned an art store. Luke became a talented illustrator and commercial artist, eventually coming to work in Hollywood at Grauman's Chinese Theater. RKO then hired him to do artwork and publicity, and he eventually did work for other studios, including some work on the Charlie Chan films. Luke's first screen performance was a small supporting part in *The Painted Veil* (1934), for which Luke received good reviews. When the producers of the Charlie Chan series were looking for a younger performer to keep the series fresh, Luke was a natural hire for the role of Lee Chan.

Early on in the Chan series, Oland still appeared in other roles, such as another Oriental villain in *Shanghai Express* (1932) with Marlene Dietrich, and as the first werewolf in screen history in *Werewolf of London* (1935). Oland's pictures over the last three years of his life, however, were all Charlie Chan films. In 1938, during the filming of the next picture for the series, *Charlie Chan at the Ringside*, Oland suffered a nervous breakdown and disappeared from the set. Oland went home to Sweden where he died on August 6, 1938.

Since the Charlie Chan films were still moneymakers for 20th Century–Fox, the studio decided to continue the series with a new actor, and after many screen tests of potential replacements for Oland, chose Sidney Toler, an American actor born in Warrensburg, Missouri, on April 28, 1874. Toler's early acting successes were on the stage, in both local and touring companies. In 1903 he came to Broadway where he spent many years acting, directing and writing stage plays. In 1929, he moved to Hollywood and performed in his first film, *Madame X*. Thereafter, Toler worked regularly in films in character roles, appearing in almost 50 films before receiving the sought-after role of Charlie Chan. Once settling into his most famous role, Toler seldom appeared in any other movies.

Whether for contract reasons or because he did not want to continue playing Lee Chan without Oland, Luke left the series after Oland's death. A new character was created, No. 2 son Jimmy Chan, and Victor Sen Yung (often billed just as Sen Yung) was chosen to play the role. Sen Yung was born in 1915 in San Francisco, California. His parents had emigrated there from China. After graduating from college, he started in films as an extra, appearing in *The Good Earth* (1936) as well as *Mr. Moto Takes a Chance* (1938) and *Torchy Blane in Chinatown* (1939), the latter two films from mystery movies series. He was asked to audition for the role of Charlie Chan's second son and, after receiving the part, appeared steadily in the role through the end of the series at 20th Century–Fox. At that time, Sen Yung joined the United States Air Force.

Sidney Toler and Sen Yung played the Chinese detectives in 11 films at 20th Century–Fox, ending with the well-regarded *Castle in the Desert* (1942). However, by 1942, Fox appeared to have lost interest in its B–series films, ending its Michael Shayne and Cisco Kid series around that same time. Toler was undeterred and believed that if he could obtain financing for the films, Fox would have a renewed interest in the series. Therefore, Toler purchased the screen rights to Charlie Chan from Earl Derr Biggers' wife and, when Fox still had no interest in the character, he moved the series to Monogram Studios. His first film there was *Charlie Chan in the Secret Service* (1944).

At Monogram, several changes were made in the cast. Victor Sen Yung left the series and Benson Fong was brought in to play Tommy Chan, a college student and No. 3 son. (Layne Tom, Jr., had previously played Tommy Chan at a younger age in *Charlie Chan in Honolulu* [1939].) Fong, an actor of Chinese descent, was born in Sacramento, California, on October 10, 1916. In 1943 he began appearing in small parts in films, eventually playing Tommy Chan in six films with Toler at Monogram. Fong continued to appear in movies and television for 40 years. Later, he became well-known in the Los Angeles area as the owner of the Ah Fong Restaurant. He passed away in 1987.

Interestingly, for the last three Toler movies at Monogram, Fong was out and Victor Sen Yung returned to play Jimmy Chan. Other Chan offspring who assisted Charlie Chan at Monogram were daughters Iris Chan (played by Marianne Quon in *Charlie Chan in the Secret Service* [1944]) and Frances Chan (played by an actress also named Frances Chan in *Black Magic* [1944]). No. 4 son, Eddie Chan, who appeared in *The Jade Mask* (1945), was played by Keye Luke's brother, Edwin.

However, the most important addition to the cast for the Monogram Chans was Birmingham Brown, played by black actor Mantan Moreland. Brown was introduced in *Charlie Chan in the Secret Service* (1944) as the chauffeur of one of the suspects, drove a taxi for Charlie in *The Chinese Cat* (1944), and eventually became Charlie's regular chauffeur, justifying his appearance in most of the remaining films. Moreland, who was born in Monroe, Louisiana, on September 3, 1902, began running away from home in his teens to perform with circuses and medicine shows. By the late 1920s, he had acquired considerable experience on vaudeville and the stage. He then started appearing in low-budget movies aimed at African-American audiences. He eventually graduated to small parts in mainstream films, although most were low-budget, before receiving his continuing role in the Charlie Chan series.

In his films, including the Chan series, Moreland almost always played a stereotypical black comic relief figure, a wide-eyed character who worked in menial jobs and who was always frightened of dead bodies. However, Moreland could also be quite charismatic and very funny. Although his performances are not attuned with contemporary sensibilities, even a modern-day audience can still sometimes be amused by Moreland's antics. Indeed, Moreland was so important to the Monogram Chan films that he often had second billing.

After making 11 Chan films at Monogram, Toler died of cancer on February 12, 1947. Monogram still believed there was profit to be made from the series so they brought in a new actor, Roland Winters, to play the part of the detective. Winters was born in Boston in 1904, making him the second American–born actor in a row to play the role and also the youngest actor to play the role in the Fox-Monogram series. Prior to undertaking the role of Charlie Chan, Winters' experiences in the performing arts were on the stage (including some appearances on Broadway), radio-announcing baseball games, appearing in a few bit parts in the movies and working on radio programs in the 1940s.

In all, Winters appeared in six films at Monogram as Charlie Chan. Victor Sen Yung returned for these films, but for some reason he played Tommy Chan rather than Jimmy Chan. In the last two films, *The Feathered Serpent* (1948) and *The Sky Dragon* (1949), Keye Luke reprised his role as No. 1 son Lee Chan. Like Winters, Luke was born in 1904, although earlier in the year than Winters. Thus, in the last two Charlie Chan films of the era, the actor playing No. 1 son was actually older than the actor playing Charlie Chan!

## THE FIRST SOUND FILM

### *Behind That Curtain* (1929)

This is the third film based on a Charlie Chan novel and the first one from the sound era. It was produced at Fox Film Corporation which thereafter started the long series of successful movies about the great detective from Honolulu. Those Chan films emphasized the personality of the Oriental detective, his great deductive skills and some of the other members of his family. In *Behind That Curtain*, early in the film, Chan is mentioned once by Sir Frederic Bruce, a famous Scotland Yard detective, as "the ablest detective in the world," and then at the end of the film, Chan makes a short appearance when the story moves to San Francisco, where Chan is apparently a detective on that city's police force. The main detective in the film, though, is Sir Frederic Bruce, who travels the world trying to solve a murder that occurred many years before in London. So, for those who are looking for another film about their favorite Chinese detective, this is not the movie. Chan makes what amounts to a cameo appearance only.

In London, solicitor Hilary Galt is employed by Sir George Mannering to dig up some dirt on Eric Durand, who is interested in marrying Mannering's niece Eve. In the process, Galt may have also dug up some dirt on John Beetham, another friend of Eve's and one who also has a romantic interest in her. As the film opens, Beetham threatens Galt, demanding the return of all of the materials about himself, or else. That night, Galt is killed in his office and all clues point to Beetham, particularly since the killer had placed a unique and valuable pair of Chinese slippers on the body after the killing. Sir Frederic mentions that Charlie Chan, a detective in San Francisco, provided the evidence that the slippers belonged to Beetham.

Over her uncle's objections, Eve marries Eric and they immediately leave for India. Mannering's suspicions about Eric turn out to be correct, as he is unfaithful to Eve in India, even taking up with their native housemaid. When a letter unexpectedly arrives from England from a blackmailing witness to Galt's murder, Eve learns that Eric killed Galt, which Eric then candidly admits. Eve runs off on an expedition with Beetham but their burgeoning love cannot come to fruition with the disgrace of Eric's misdeeds hanging over them. Also, the two have serious concerns about Sir Frederic, who seems to be chasing them all over the world in the pursuit of Galt's killer.

*Behind That Curtain* is a love story, more in the nature of a Jane Austen novel than an Earl Derr Biggers mystery. Thus, there are two people, Eve Durand and John Beetham, who are truly in love but due to circumstances and Eve's misplaced sense of honor, apparently will never allow their love to blossom. The story, while old-fashioned, is nevertheless quite interesting, if one is not anticipating a clever murder mystery just because the film is based on a Charlie Chan novel.

The execution, though, is another matter. Shot near the beginning of the sound era, the film is representative of its generation with, during the first half of the film at least, people seldom moving when they are talking, apparently being tied to the microphone nearby. Much of the acting is abysmal, also reflecting the era in which it was made. Lois Moran plays Eve, sometimes talking too loudly when she emotes, and other times employing long pauses between her words. Gilbert Emery, as Sir Frederic, also unnaturally paces his sentences in a long and inconsistent manner. Warner Baxter as Beetham gives the best performance but even his delivery is inconsistent at times.

E.L. Park plays Chan and it is interesting to see a real Asian performer in the role. Unfortunately, he also seems to have a limited acting range (although the role is so small, that is not entirely certain). Clearly, if Fox were going to start a long-running series about Chan and make Chan the principal detective, another actor was needed.

The second half of the movie opens up somewhat, with scenes in the Arabian Desert, including one stunning horizon shot of a line of camels walking up and over a sand hill. There are also some scenes shot in San Francisco on real city streets, giving a verisimilitude to the presentation. Despite its flaws, *Behind That Curtain* is not a low-budget film.

As to the mystery, there really is none. Eric Durand is identified as the murderer of Hilary Galt quite early in the film, and thereafter, it is just a matter of time before Scotland Yard unravels the crime. Thus, *Behind That Curtain* is a Charlie Chan mystery without a murder mystery and for that matter, for all intents and purposes, without Charlie Chan. Nevertheless, the film has some interest, as an example of a crime story from the early sound era, as an interesting romantic melodrama, and for a brief appearance by Boris Karloff before he became a star, as Beetham's manservant. Fans of the Charlie Chan movies will want to see this film for its historical value and also because its remake, *Charlie Chan's Chance* (1932), appears to be permanently lost.

*Note on the Source Material*: *Behind That Curtain* was based on a 1928 Biggers book by that same name. Sir Frederic Bruce, a retired Scotland Yard detective, is visiting San Francisco, coincidentally at the same time that Charlie Chan is visiting from Honolulu. There is a party at the house of Barry Kirk where famous explorer John Beetham is showing film of his previous expeditions. During the film, Sir Frederic is shot and killed. There are a number of suspects and it is believed that the murder relates to two crimes that Sir Frederic was still investigating, even though he was retired from the London police force.

One crime Sir Frederic was investigating was the killing, 16 years before in London, of Hilary Galt, a solicitor. When the body was discovered, Galt's polished boots had been removed from his feet and two velvet slippers with Chinese writing on them were found in their place. The other investigation involved the mysterious disappearance 15 years before of an English woman, Eve Durand, from Peshawar, India, where she was living with her husband Eric. Attention soon focuses on the woman operating one of the elevators in the building as possibly being the missing Eve.

The novel *Behind That Curtain* is a classic whodunit of the era, with multiple suspects, physical clues, conflicting stories and suspicious events and motives unrelated to the main crime being investigated. It is quite good, aided substantially by the charm of detective Charlie Chan. Surprisingly, the 1929 movie eliminated all of the mystery and only told the backstory of the novel — the killing of Galt, the disappearance of Eve Durand, the romance between Beetham and Eve, and Eve turning up in San Francisco many years later as an elevator operator. While the film is still entertaining, after reading the book it is clear that the filmmakers missed a number of opportunities for creating a better film, if only they had used more of the mystery elements from the novel.

*Note on the Remake*: This film was remade as *Charlie Chan's Chance* (1932).

## THE WARNER OLAND FILMS

### *Charlie Chan Carries On* and *Eran Trece* (1931)

[Charlie Chan Carries On *is a lost film. However, the author was able to view* Eran Trece, *the contemporaneous Spanish-language version.*]

In *Eran Trece*, Charlie Chan is played by Manuel Arbo, a Spanish actor who receives last billing in the film, much like the low billings that were given to the actors who played Chan in the previous film versions of the Biggers novels. Chan does not appear until the second half of *Eran Trece* but once he does appear, the film makes Charlie its focal point. It can be difficult to evaluate the performance of an actor who is speaking in a foreign language but Arbo seems quite effective in the part, even though he is a Spanish actor playing a Chinese character living in Hawaii. Warner Oland appears to be the more charismatic actor of the two, although that evaluation may be partially the result of Oland being the more familiar of the two.

*Eran Trece* commences in London with the murder of wealthy Louis Potter who, along with twelve other Americans, was on a world tour conducted by a Dr. Lofton. Potter was strangled at Broome Hotel in London with a strap of a suitcase owned by Dr. Lofton. Inspector Duff of Scotland Yard and a friend of Chan's from the time of their experiences together in the novel *Behind That Curtain* (1928), believes that Potter was murdered in a different room of the hotel and that the body was then carried back to Potter's own hotel room. Duff suspects that the killing was committed by a member of the tour, but since he has no evidence against any one of them, the tour is allowed to continue.

There are two more killings associated with the tour and when the boat reaches Honolulu, Duff has traveled there directly from London to assist in the investigation. After a short meeting with Chan, Duff is wounded by an unknown assailant. Chan carries on by taking up the case, boarding the cruise ship, avoiding an assassination attempt and discovering the murderer just before the boat docks in San Francisco.

*Eran Trece* (and therefore, presumably, *Charlie Chan Carries On*) often seems like a talkfest, with witnesses and suspects being interviewed over and over again. The film, however, never seems boring, probably because of the multiple murders, several additional attempted killings, the change in locales as the tour group travels around the world, and even because of an appealing romantic subplot. There are also some memorable moments in the film, such as the shooting of Sybil Conway through the roof of a descending elevator, and Charlie, through a window, grabbing the hand of a gun-toting assailant, but only managing to hold onto the shooter's glove as the shooter makes his escape. Then there is also that almost surreal moment at the last dinner on board ship when the Minchins entertain the other tour members with songs and impersonations.

*Eran Trece* suffers from many of the same problems that would afflict several of the later Chan films. There are unexplained matters, such as the inexplicable shooting of Inspector Duff (actually just a device to get Charlie into the investigation), and the key which was taped to the suitcase of Dick Kennaway, which disappears near the time the boat is to dock. There are numerous suspects for the murders but little differentiation between them. Charlie is forced to create a trap for the killer since the great detective, much like the viewer, does not have any clue as to who the killer is.

Despite its flaws, *Eran Trece* is always an interesting film and when Chan first appears, even though in the person of Manuel Arbo, what mystery fan does not experience some excitement at seeing the first true sound version of the Charlie Chan character? This film is recommended as an entertaining mystery film but its historical interest cannot be overlooked.

*Note on the Source Material*: *Eran Trece* was based on *Charlie Chan Carries On*, the 1930 novel by Earl Derr Biggers. It was the next-to-the last Charlie Chan novel written by Biggers, with the last being *Keeper of the Keys* (1932), the only Chan novel which was never filmed. *Eran Trece* is very true to the plot of the Biggers novel, although, as is often the case, the novel is more detailed and nuanced than the film. For example, the book spends some time relating Scotland Yard's painstaking investigation into the crimes before the tour group finally reaches Honolulu and Charlie appears. The details of the British investigation are generally missing from the film.

In other instances, *Eran Trece* takes elements from the novel but never follows through on them in the remainder of the film. The elderly lawyer Mr. Tait (Nielson in *Eran Trece*) has a seeming heart attack when he walks into a room of suspects in London. Inspector

Duff is curious about the incident in the film, but the matter is dropped almost immediately, never to be mentioned again. In the novel, it is explained that because Mr. Tait heard a struggle in Honywood's room on the night of the murder, he thought that it was Honywood who was killed. When he walked into the room of suspects the next day, he was so shocked to see Honywood alive that Tait had his attack. This is not an insignificant matter as it is more proof that Drake was not killed in his own hotel room.

When Duff arrives in Hawaii in the novel, several chapters are devoted to his visit there and his meeting with the tour group as the ship arrives. Thus, Duff's shooting in Honolulu by a killer now worried as to why Duff has suddenly re-emerged halfway around the world makes some sense in the novel. In the film, it looks like a mere plot device to get Charlie Chan into the storyline. Furthermore, the strange incident of the key taped to Dick Kennaway's suitcase at the end of the film is fully explained in the novel and makes complete sense. These are all examples of the film using incidents from the book but never tying them into a cohesive storyline as the book does.

On the other hand, the movie does create a few cinematic moments unique to it. Among them is the scene where Pamela Potter yells the name of "Jim Maynard" to all of the major male suspects while they are walking down a street in China. This puts her life in danger, resulting in an attempted killing of Pamela. Neither incident occurs in the book. The endings of the book and the film are different with, in the movie, Charlie using a clever trap to snare the killer while in the book, Charlie catching the killer in a one-word mistake, allowing Charlie to then find the evidence to prove the suspect's guilt. While the ending works well for the book, the filmmakers chose a much more cinematic finish.

Except for the endings, the differences between *Eran Trece* and the novel are generally more of emphasis rather than radical change. The plot of the novel *Charlie Chan Carries On* was strong enough to carry both the English- and Spanish-language versions of the novel. It was also strong enough to start the longest running movie mystery series of all time.

*Note on the Production*: Even those who have forgotten all of their high school Spanish will know that "Eran Trece" is not Spanish for "Charlie Chan Carries On." Loosely translated, "Eran Trece" means "They were thirteen," referencing the number of people who were originally on Dr. Lofton's world tour in the movie. (In the novel, 17 people were initially on the world tour.)

While not a common practice, some studios did produce contemporaneous Spanish or other foreign-language versions of their early sound films so that their films could reach an international audience. The most famous example of this is the Spanish-language version of *Dracula* (1931), filmed at night on the same sets on which the Bela Lugosi version was filmed during the day. (Manuel Arbo also had a small role in the Spanish-language version of *Dracula*.) Once dubbing and subtitling movies into foreign languages became practical, this idea of simultaneously producing different language versions of the same film ended quickly. *Eran Trece* is the only Spanish-language version of a Charlie Chan feature.

Based on a comparison of the script for *Charlie Chan Carries On* with the screen version of *Eran Trece*, the two works are substantially similar. The only significant difference seems to be the inclusion, in the Spanish version, of that strange scene near the end of the movie where the Minchins perform some musical numbers at the last dinner on board ship. A less important but interesting difference is that Charlie's oldest son is named John in *Eran Trece* but in the script for *Charlie Chan Carries On*, he is named Henry. In the book, he is

Charlie Chan (Warner Oland) and the psychic, Tarneverro (Bela Lugosi), discuss the best method for investigating the murder of actress Shela Fane in *The Black Camel* (1931).

also named Henry. For all true Charlie Chan movie fans, however, Charlie's No. 1 son will always be Lee Chan, as played by Keye Luke, with his first appearance in *Charlie Chan in Paris* (1935).

*Note on the Remake*: This film was partially remade as *Charlie Chan's Murder Cruise* (1940).

## *The Black Camel* (1931)

This is the earliest extant Charlie Chan film starring Warner Oland and it is significant for that fact alone. For quite some time, most everyone believed that *The Black Camel* was a lost film, since it was not included among the Chan films which played on local television stations for many years. The recent release of *The Black Camel* on DVD has sparked a renewed interest in the feature.

By just this second film in the series, the studio had yet to decide on the proper approach in presenting the Chan character. The great detective has little screen time in the first third of the film, although he becomes the prime character once the murder is committed. There are no sons to both assist and bother Charlie and provide some comic relief, but in their place is an irritating and not amusing assistant policeman named Kashimo. Unfortunately, there is no chemistry between Charlie and Kashimo, and it would take the arrival, several years later, of Charlie's No. 1 son Lee Chan for that comedy supporting role to become an effective contributor to the success of the series. Although the viewer does meet Charlie's large family at breakfast one day, the scene is short, albeit quite interesting. Charlie's family, usually in the person of his sons, would become much more important in later films.

Although Charlie Chan is the most famous detective in the Honolulu police department, it is surprising how few of his films actually take place in Hawaii. *The Black Camel* is a rare exception. Here, the filmmakers have recreated the atmosphere of the islands in a refreshing manner, with good on-location footage of the islands imparting a degree of authenticity to the film, helped immensely by the native Hawaiian music employed in the background and either Asian or Hawaiian actors in many of the smaller parts.

The story itself is quite complex, with the modern-day mystery related to the unsolved murder of Denny Mayo three years before in Hollywood. Actress Shela Fane admits to a psychic, Tarneverro, that she had been in love with Mayo and was in his house on the night he was murdered. Shortly thereafter, Shela is found stabbed to death in her island pavilion. The body is discovered by Julie O'Neill, Shela's protégé, and Julie's boyfriend, Jimmy Bradshaw, who works for the island tourism bureau. Before Jimmy goes to call the police, Julie insists on removing the emerald ring from Shela's finger and hiding the jewel from the police.

Charlie Chan is called in to investigate the crime. He is assisted, for a time, by Tarneverro and also by his incompetent official assistant, Kashimo. Later, a beach bum and struggling painter known only as Smith blackmails Robert Fyfe, Shela's divorced husband, over something Smith overheard Shela say to Fyfe on the night of the murder. Not surprisingly, Smith is then shot and killed, apparently by Fyfe. However, everything is not as it may seem to be and several of the characters are not who they purport to be. Charlie is finally able to solve both crimes merely by the clue of scratches on a dining room floor made by a part of a pin which was taken from Shela's body on the night of the murder.

This film is aided considerably by the direction of Hamilton MacFadden, who keeps his camera in constant motion whenever possible. Additionally, when Charlie is questioning a suspect and camera movement would be inappropriate, the other suspects are usually lined up in the background as a grim tableau, adding to the interest of the examination. The crucial early scene in the film with Tarneverro, Shela Fane, and the bright crystal ball in the center of the screen, as Shela confesses her involvement with Denny Mayo, is beautifully shot in the semi-dark, with the actors' faces barely visible from the light from the ball as they lean close to the sphere. This adds to the tension of a very tension-filled scene.

Bela Lugosi gives a surprisingly good performance as the turban-clad Tarneverro, nuanced when he is just a suspect but using his horror film reputation in that crystal ball scene where he towers over Shela, intimidating her into a confession. The moment almost appears to come from a horror film and the use of Lugosi in the part adds to the horror element. Lugosi's partner from *Dracula*, Dwight Frye, plays the butler, Jessop, and it is a very tantalizing performance. Frye had a strange voice and face, and his performances remind the viewer of those of Peter Lorre. Could this be the film in which the butler actually did it? Victor Varconi plays Fyfe and he was apparently in a competition with Lugosi to see which one could speak with the thickest accent. Murray Kinnell is engaging and sympathetic as the beach bum Smith, even though he blackmails Fyfe into buying one of his paintings.

For all of that, the film starts to drag in the latter parts as constant talk and little action tend to slow its pace. The ending, however, is quite dramatic, with the killer being the person who will sit at a particular seat at a dinner table when the crime is re-enacted. First, one suspect sits in the seat until he realizes he is in the wrong seat. Then another suspect sits in the seat, but Charlie knows that he is not the killer. It takes Charlie a few moments to realize that the killer sat in the seat after the dinner was completed and with that information, he determines the identity of the killer.

Some of the mystery does not hold together all that well. Four of the guests at Shela's dinner party on the night of her murder are suspects, but the viewer never learns enough about three of them to truly include them in the murder equation. Julie's theft of Shela's ring after the murder is not well-explained, nor is the false confession of Robert Fyfe, Shela's former husband, to the murder of Shela. The motive for the murder of the beachcombing blackmailer is not very believable, and it is still hard to believe that Fyfe was not that killer. There are no clues to enable the viewer to solve the murders and little information to alert the viewer that some of the characters are not who they appear to be. The solutions seem to come out of the blue.

The Charlie Chan films were still in their formative years at the time of the release of *The Black Camel* and the series would not hit its stride for a while. But, with a good murder mystery to tell, excellent direction, good performances and its historical interest (including the film debut of Robert Young as Jimmy Bradshaw), mystery movie fans will want to see this feature, the earliest existing Charlie Chan film starring Warner Oland.

*Note on the Source Material*: *The Black Camel* was based on a 1929 Biggers book of the same name. The unusual title refers to an old Eastern saying, "Death is the black camel that kneels unbid at every gate."

The film was substantially based on the events related in the book although the killing of the beachcomber, Smith, is a Hollywood concoction. The whodunit holds together much better in the novel than the film, with, for example, the questions of why Fyfe confessed to killing Shela Fane or why no one recognized Tarneverro as the brother of Archie Mayo fairly well-explained in the written work, if still not done in a totally convincing manner. Tarneverro is also a much more disruptive influence in the novel than in the film. Kashimo is a character in the novel, but he is not as irritating as the Kashimo of the movie. The film, however, better handles the identity of the murderer, giving the killer some screen time before the denouement whereas, in the novel, the killer barely appears in the story before being fingered by Chan as the wrongdoer.

The written works by Biggers contain numerous Chinese sayings by Charlie but for some reason when the material was transferred to the cinema, the screenwriters usually preferred to write their own. In the novel *The Black Camel*, when a suspect states that he has a perfect alibi, Charlie says, "Perfect alibis have way of turning imperfect without warning." In the film, when the character makes the same statement, Charlie comments, "Alibi have habit of disappearing like hole in water." At least in this instance, the Chan of the screen was much more eloquent than the Chan of the novels.

*Note on the Remake*: *Charlie Chan in Rio* (1941) is a partial remake of this film.

## *Charlie Chan's Chance* (1932)

[*This is a lost film and one of the few films discussed in this book which the author did not view. However, the author was able to listen to an audio recreation.*]

Honolulu policeman Charlie Chan is in New York City to learn big-town police techniques when he learns of the death of retired Scotland Yard Inspector Sir Lionel Grey in the offices of Barry Kirk. The coroner believes that Sir Lionel died of natural causes but Charlie correctly deduces that the inspector was killed by poison gas. Since Sir Lionel had announced that he intended to solve an old murder case that night and had assembled guests at a party to identify the killer, suspicion immediately focuses on those guests. It seems clear early on that the death was caused by Alan Raleigh, who committed a murder back in England which Sir Lionel was investigating. At the time, Shirley Marlowe, Raleigh's former lover and a witness to the crime, disappeared so that she would not have to testify against Raleigh. The question then becomes: Is Raleigh masquerading as one of the guests at the party?

The only version of the film available is the written script read by a modern cast as publicity photos and studio stills are shown. Obviously, under those circumstances, the performances and direction of the film cannot be evaluated. As to the plot, it is a simplified version of the book but it has the same problem that the 1929 film version of the novel had — the killer (Alan Raleigh) is obvious almost from the beginning. At least in this version of the novel, there is a true mystery afoot, with multiple clues and a variety of suspects whom Charlie must investigate before he can identify which character is secretly Alan Raleigh.

*Note on the Source Material*: This was the second film based on the 1928 Charlie Chan novel *Behind That Curtain*. The book is discussed in greater detail with regard to the 1929 film of the same name. Suffice it to say, *Charlie Chan's Chance* is a closer adaptation of the Biggers novel than the prior film, incorporating the murder of a retired Scotland Yard inspector in an office owned by Barry Kirk, the inspector investigating an old murder in England and trying to find a missing female witness to the crime, one suspect breaking her pearl necklace and leaving one pearl in the dead man's room, and even a incident where a young Chinese Boy Scout inadvertently foils a plan of Charlie's to obtain evidence about the mysterious Li Gung. The final clue with regard to the checked valise of the Scotland Yard inspector also comes from the book.

There were significant changes, however, with the method of murder completely different, a sharp reduction in the number of suspects and variety of clues, and the elimination of the incident with the Chinese slippers showing up at each killing. Also, the backstory of the murder in England and the missing lady is far less complicated in the movie than in the book.

*Note on the Remake*: This film was a partial remake of *Behind That Curtain* (1929).

## *Charlie Chan's Greatest Case* (1933)

[*This is a lost film and one of the few films discussed in this book which the author did not view.*]

*Charlie Chan's Greatest Case* is one of those rare Charlie Chan films which is set in his native land of Hawaii. Chan is called in to investigate the murder of Dan Winterslip, who was stabbed in the heart. The main clue to the killer is provided by Minerva Winterslip, Dan's sister. She saw a prowler in the house on the night of the murder, wearing a glow-in-the-dark wristwatch with a blurred numeral two. At the end of the film, Chan gathers all the suspects at Dan's house so that Chan can expose the killer.

*Note on the Source Material*: *Charlie Chan's Greatest Case* was based on the first novel written by Earl Derr Biggers about the Chinese detective, *The House Without a Key* (1925). The title refers to the home of murder victim Dan Winterslip, who always left his house unlocked.

Based on the synopsis of the film, it appears that *Charlie Chan's Greatest Case* was substantially based upon the novel, with the killer being the same person and having the same motive, and the book having similar suspects and similar clues. However, the movie cliché of gathering all of the suspects at the end of the story to reveal the killer does not come from the novel. The explanation of the killings in the written version occurs in the local prosecutor's office.

*The House Without a Key* is only fair as a mystery, with too many of the clues hidden to the reader. The novel focuses on John Quincy, the young hero, more than Charlie Chan and in fact, Quincy, on his own, solves the murder of Dan Winterslip around the time that Chan does. However, the novel has a timeless interest in its evocation of 1920s Hawaii, with most Americans not then knowing the island territory was part of the United States and only a few chosen Americans allowed to attend the native ritual of the luau. The book contrasts the easygoing nature of Hawaii with the more staid nature of Boston, providing many of the highlights of the novel. It is assumed that the screenplay of *Charlie Chan's Greatest Case* de-emphasized those aspects of the novel.

As a matter of hindsight, there is a very interesting moment in the novel. Charlie asks John Quincy to tell him more about Boston as he has never been there. Charlie says, "I have unlimited yearning for travel. But it are (sic) unavailable. I am policeman on small remuneration." Of course, the Charlie Chan of the novel did not know that the Charlie Chan of the movies was soon to become a world traveler extraordinaire.

*Note on the Remake*: This is the second film version of *The House Without a Key*. The first was the silent serial *The House Without a Key*, released in 1926. The silent film was the first screen appearance of Charlie Chan.

## *Charlie Chan's Courage* (1934)

[*This is a lost film and one of the few films discussed in this book which the author did not view. However, the author was able to listen to an audio recreation.*]

For some reason not well-explained in the film (other than that Charlie was once the houseboy to Sally Jordan), Honolulu policeman Charlie Chan agrees to become the personal courier of a string of valuable pearls owned by Sally Jordan which must be brought safely from Hawaii to San Francisco. Jordan intends to sell the pearls to wealthy J.P. Madden, who, for safety concerns, then decides that he wants the pearls brought all the way to New York City before he will agree to take possession of them. Shortly thereafter, Madden calls Jordan, tells her that he has changed his mind, and states that he wants the valuables brought directly to Madden's ranch in El Dorado. The change in plans raises suspicions and Charlie goes undercover at the Madden Ranch as a cook, using the alias Ah Kim. Charlie is aided in his investigations by young Bob Crawford, the son of the jeweler who was helping Jordan arrange the sale.

The first murder in the film is that of a parrot but it is a very interesting parrot indeed. This bird speaks Chinese along with some salty English. Based on what he keeps repeating, the parrot may have been witness to a murder, providing a motive for the bird's killing.

Later, Louis Wong, Madden's Chinese cook, is killed. Charlie eventually discovers a vast scheme to steal Jordan's necklace with at least four characters involved in the plot.

As best as can be determined by the audio recreation, *Charlie Chan's Courage* seems to be a very interesting film. There are some good clues to help unravel the criminal plot, including the killing of the Chinese parrot and the cook, the only two innocent characters who might have discovered the scheme being plotted at the Madden Ranch. Madden's sudden changes of mind on several key issues also provide additional clues for the viewer as to the key trick behind the sinister scheme. It appears to be one of the best of the early Chan films.

*Note on the Source Material*: *Charlie Chan's Courage* was based on Biggers' 1926 novel *The Chinese Parrot*. The title of the book is apt because in both the film and the written work, the parrot, Tony, is one of the most striking characters. Although the bird only survives for a few moments, the fact that his surprising language implies that he has witnessed a murder is the catalyst for Charlie's investigations in both versions of the story.

The film is a true adaptation of the novel, with just about every incident in the film coming from the book. Even the romance between Bob Crawford and Paula Graham, the site locater for a movie studio, comes from *The Chinese Parrot*. Biggers was not above adding a romantic subplot to his mystery novels, a device he also used in *The House Without a Key*. A few incidents from the novel, however, did not make it to the movie, such as the villains diverting Madden's daughter away from the ranch and the villains embezzling some of Madden's other money while they are awaiting the arrival of the pearls.

In both works, Charlie goes undercover as a cook at the Madden ranch, probably the only time the Honolulu policeman ever went undercover in a book by Earl Derr Biggers and a rare occurrence in the films, one other exception being *Charlie Chan in Panama* (1940). Charlie's disguise in *Charlie Chan's Courage* leads to several of the most interesting stills of the movie in existence: the always well-dressed Warner Oland appearing in tattered clothes as the Chinese cook Ah Kim.

*Note on the Remake*: This is the second film version of *The Chinese Parrot*. The first was the silent film *The Chinese Parrot* (1927).

## *Charlie Chan in London* (1934)

This film marks the beginning of Charlie Chan's world tour, which would eventually include trips to Paris, Egypt, Shanghai, Panama, Rio and several parts of mainland America. No matter where Charlie ends up, crime seems to follow him. This is also the first Charlie Chan movie which was based on an original story and not on a work by Earl Derr Biggers. However, the screenwriter of *Charlie Chan in London* was no slouch. Philip MacDonald, a successful mystery and screen writer, was most famous for his books about detective Anthony Gethryn, the most recognizable of which is probably *The List of Adrian Messenger* (1959), which was adapted into a movie in 1963. Much like *Charlie Chan in London*, a fox hunt is the setting of important scenes in that film so fox hunts must have been a significant interest of MacDonald's.

Hugh Gray, the fox hunt secretary to wealthy Geoffrey Richmond, has been convicted of the murder of Captain Hamilton of the Royal Air Force. Hamilton was a guest at the Richmond home at the time of the murder. Hugh's sister, Pamela Gray, is convinced of

Charlie Chan (Warner Oland) is leaving London in just one hour to return to Honolulu, but Pamela Gray (Drue Leyton) implores the great Chinese detective to stay and find the evidence to exonerate her brother, who is to be hanged in three days, in *Charlie Chan in London* (1934). Her fiancé, Neil Howard (Ray Milland), looks on.

Hugh's innocence and when she cannot convince the Home Secretary to prevent the execution, she desperately turns to the world-famous detective Charlie Chan, who is in England to deliver a prisoner he had captured in Hawaii. Chan finally agrees to take the case even though there are only three days left before the hanging of Hugh Gray.

Charlie proceeds to Richmond's summer home in Retfordshire where, since it is the final week of the fox hunting season, everyone who was present at the time of Hamilton's death also happens to be present. Assuming that Hugh is innocent, or why make this movie at all, there are more than enough suspects for the crime, including a suspicious butler who resembles Bela Lugosi, replacement hunt secretary Major Jardine, apparent dimwit Bunny Fothergill and wealthy Geoffrey Richmond himself. There is one more murder and two attempted murders, including one of Charlie himself, before the great detective can solve the case, with barely enough time left to save Hugh Gray's life.

This is a murder in retrospect, even though the crime took place just three months before Charlie arrived in England. Charlie must reconstruct the crime in order to determine who the guilty party is. In doing so, he discovers a number of interesting clues that were overlooked by the police, including the curious incident of the horse who did not raise a fuss when the nighttime murder was committed just outside his stable, the fact that Captain Hamilton was an inventor who was in the process of developing a device to dampen the sound of war planes, and the nervousness of the stud groom, Lake, when questioned about the murder. However, there are no true clues to identify the culprit, and Charlie accomplishes that feat mainly by guesswork and a trick he plays on the killer.

While the mystery story is interesting, the film has a languorous approach, as the characters describe or act out the events of the murder instead of them being shown to the viewer in a series of flashbacks. The present-day murder takes place off screen, also contributing to the unexciting pace of the film. There is much talk but very little action and the unveiling of the killer is anticlimactic, at best.

The acting is uneven. Of course, Oland as Chan is always a joy to watch. The same can also be said for Alan Mowbray, who plays Geoffrey Richmond, and for E.E. Clive, who plays British Detective Sergeant Thacker. Mowbray was in a number of mystery films over the years, including *Terror by Night* (1946) in the Sherlock Holmes series, and *The Lone Wolf and His Lady* (1949), playing Jamison. Clive is remembered for small parts, usually as policemen, in films such as *The Adventures of Sherlock Holmes* (1939), and as a regular in the Bulldog Drummond series, playing Tenny. Did either of them ever give a bad performance?

Some of the other performances are overwrought, though, such as Douglas Walton as Hugh Gray and, upon occasion, Drue Leyton as Pamela Gray. Elsa Buchanan, as the maid Perkins, overacts outrageously.

*Charlie Chan in London* is the second earliest extant Chan film from the Warner Oland era and has significant interest for that reason alone. It is also interesting to see an early screen appearance by Ray Milland, before he was a star, but even though Milland has high billing, he has little to do in the film. The mystery itself is compelling at times, but, unfortunately, it is told in a dull manner. On balance, the film is worth a view, but the Chan films (at least with regard to the films that are available today) still had yet to hit their stride as of the time of the release of this feature.

## *Charlie Chan in Paris* (1935)

While *Charlie Chan in London* may be the better mystery, *Charlie Chan in Paris* is by far the better film. The earlier movie was a talkathon with little action and much dialogue. *Charlie Chan in Paris* has the talk, of course, including numerous aphorisms spoken by the wise Chinese detective, but there is also suspense, some excitement and the introduction of No. 1 son Lee Chan, played by Keye Luke. While relatively unknown today, *Charlie Chan in Paris* is one of the best of the early Chan movies.

Charlie arrives in Paris by plane, ostensibly on vacation but actually to investigate a serious crime. He immediately telephones Nardi, a nightclub dancer who is also doing some investigating for him, and agrees to meet her after her show to discuss the results of her inquiries. Before Nardi can meet with Chan, however, she is killed by a knife thrown by a blind beggar, later identified as Marcel Xavier, who constantly reappears throughout the film. In her last gasp before dying, Nardi tells Chan to look through her apartment. There Chan discovers a diary containing entries about Albert Dufresne, an employee of the Lamartine Bank. It turns out that Charlie is investigating bond forgeries at the bank and Dufresne is one of the chief suspects.

After Chan goes to the bank to tell the officers about the bond forgeries, Dufresne panics and decides to leave the country. The blind beggar, however, believes that Dufresne is double crossing him so he dispatches Dufresne at his apartment with a single gunshot. The beggar then throws the murder weapon into the room. Yvette Lamartine, the bank director's daughter, is in Dufresne's apartment to recover some of her old love letters; she picks up the gun and tries to flee, resulting in her arrest for the murder. Chan must now clear Yvette's name and solve the crime of the bond forgeries, a task made easier for Charlie by the presence of No. 1 son and No. 1 detective assistant, Lee Chan.

The first half of *Charlie Chan in Paris* is quite suspenseful, with two murders, a warning letter to Chan and an attempt on his life. Since both killings and the attempted murder were clearly committed by Marcel Xavier, the film appears to be more of a police procedural than a pure whodunit. However, once it is clear that the blind beggar is a disguise for the true murderer and there really is no Marcel Xavier, the whodunit aspects of the plot come into focus, with numerous suspects. The problem is that each of the suspects was seen in the presence of the beggar, so how could any of them have also been the disguised beggar? The solution is quite clever, probably reflecting the hand of mystery novelist Philip MacDonald, writing his second consecutive screenplay for the series.

The motif that keeps this film gripping throughout its entire length is the constant reappearances of the blind beggar. He is at the airport when Charlie arrives in Paris, he is at the nightclub when Charlie goes there to see a show, and he is at the bank when Charlie goes there for a meeting. He appears to be a figure of menace right from the get-go, making the movie quite suspenseful even before the plot begins to develop.

Unlike the murders in earlier Chan films, such as *Charlie Chan in London*, the murders of Nardi and Dufresne are shown onscreen, at least in part, making those moments quite interesting. The killing of Nardi is well done, coming right at the conclusion of the violent Apache dance, just after she is thrown through a stage window as part of the dance. Before the excitement of the wild Apache dance can dissipate, the surprise killing occurs. The murder of Dufresne, while much less exciting, is more suspenseful as the killer cleverly ensnares Yvette into a situation in which she can be accused of the murder, with Yvette falling into the trap by grabbing the gun and trying to escape. The fact that Yvette is played by the lovely Mary Brian adds to the effectiveness of the moment.

Keye Luke makes his first appearance in the series as Lee Chan, a surprise visitor to Charlie in Paris. Lee is in Europe on business and he did not want to pass up the opportunity to see his father. He is not the figure of mere comic relief as he would later become in the series. Indeed, he is quite the competent detective in this film and his showing of respect for his Chinese father and their mutual affection are some of the highlights of the feature.

The climax in darkened, underground rooms and in the sewer system of Paris is quite striking. The sudden reappearance of the blind beggar, gun in hand, creates just the right amount of suspense. The unmasking of the killer, disguised as Marcel Xavier, is done in a clever manner, adding to the excitement of the moment. And, if the identity of the culprit is not all that surprising, that fact does not detract from the effectiveness.

These later scenes are beautifully composed and photographed, as is much of the remainder of the film. There is a style to the cinematography of *Charlie Chan in Paris* that was missing in the prior Chan movies. This film is well worth a view.

## *Charlie Chan in Egypt* (1935)

The famous Honolulu policeman Charlie Chan comes to Egypt on a mission for the French Archaeological Society. It seems that in exchange for the Society funding Professor Arnold's Egyptian expedition, the Society had the right to receive all of the valuable arti-

Carol Arnold (Pat Paterson), center in white, upset about her missing father, asks Charlie Chan (Warner Oland), far right, for help, in *Charlie Chan in Egypt* (1935). On the far left is Tom Evans (Thomas Beck) and next to him is Professor Thurston (Frank Conroy). The other actress is Rita Cansino, soon to be known as Rita Hayworth, playing the Egyptian servant Nayda.

facts that Arnold's crew discovered. Arnold's undertaking was a success but shortly after Arnold discovered and opened an ancient tomb, artifacts from the site started showing up in the holdings of other museums and collectors around the world. So a Society in France hires a policeman from Hawaii to investigate wrongdoing in Egypt. Oh well, there had to be some excuse to get the famous Oriental sleuth to the interesting locale of Egypt and that is the best the screen writers could come up with.

And what an interesting location Egypt is, even before Charlie arrives. When the tomb of Ahmeti, one of the most powerful priests of the 21st dynasty, was first opened, an Egyptian assistant suddenly collapsed and died for no reason. Could that be the result of an ancient Egyptian curse? Professor Arnold then disappeared with no trace, and his daughter, Carol, has been suffering from hallucinations at night. Edfu Ahmed, the Egyptian servant of the Arnolds and a scary man if there ever was one, seems particularly upset about the violation of the Egyptian tombs. Ahmed claims to be a direct descendent of Ahmeti.

When Charlie begins his investigation, he notices that the varnish on Ahmeti's mummy case is fresh, something that one would not expect on an ancient artifact. Professor Thurston, Arnold's assistant, arranges for an X-ray of the case. It appears initially that a real mummy is inside but when Charlie notices a bullet hole in the body, the mummy case is opened and Professor Arnold's corpse is discovered. That sends Charlie in pursuit of the killer of Professor Arnold and a fortune in Egyptian artifacts.

*Charlie Chan in Egypt* is one of the most atmospheric of the Charlie Chan movies. The beginning sequence involving the opening of Ahmeti's tomb brings back memories of the opening scenes in *The Mummy* (1932). Although there is no walking mummy in this Chan film, there is an overriding air of foreboding from the Egyptian curse, such as when Professor Arnold's son suddenly dies or when Chan and others are exploring, by flashlight, the dark passageways of Ahmeti's tomb. There is a particularly suspenseful moment when young Tom Evans must swim down a dark passage in the tomb, to see what may be revealed at the other end.

Historically speaking, there are some interesting performances in the film. Rita Hayworth, billed under her given name of Rita Cansino, has a very small role as an Egyptian servant. She is barely recognizable as the beautiful actress whom movie audiences would come to know and love in the 1940s. Stepin Fetchit plays the black servant Snowshoes, a gratuitous role that is inserted for the supposed comic relief engendered by a dumb and scared black man. It is hard to believe that the writing and Fetchit's performance were funny back in 1935. They are clearly not amusing today. However, Fetchit was not in that many movies that are still viewed today, so as embarrassing as it may be to watch his performance, *Charlie Chan in Egypt* provides a rare opportunity of seeing one of the earliest and most famous black comedy performers in the cinema.

The direction by Louis King is excellent. He artfully conveys the horror elements that are always in the background of the story, by his emphasis on dark settings and shadowy figures. The sets are immense and the property department went all-out in providing Egyptian replicas for the scenes in the tomb. Jameson Thomas, as Dr. Racine, and Nigel de Brulier, as Edfu Ahmed, are sufficiently menacing and mysterious on their own to create a sense of foreboding throughout the film.

While there are not really any clues to the actual murderer of Dr. Arnold, *Charlie Chan in Egypt* does not rely on the old chestnut of the least likely character being the murderer. When the killer is finally unmasked by Charlie, his identity is believable even to the most jaded of mystery fans. Because of its atmosphere, unusual setting and good mystery, *Charlie Chan in Egypt* is a highly recommended film.

## *Charlie Chan in Shanghai* (1935)

With a "Hi, Pop," No. 1 son Lee Chan, in the person of Keye Luke, reappears in the Charlie Chan series after a one-film absence. Lee was soon to become a permanent member of the cast, which was very good news for Charlie Chan fans because, at the end of the prior film, *Charlie Chan in Egypt*, the black comic relief, Snowshoes, indicated that he was going to follow Mr. Chan on his next journey. Fox may have been considering making Snowshoes the permanent comic addition to the Charlie Chan cast but, luckily, more astute heads prevailed and Lee Chan was chosen for that role.

*Charlie Chan in Shanghai* opens much like *Charlie Chan in Paris*, with Charlie first receiving a warning note on ship telling him not to enter Shanghai, and then Charlie's contact in Shanghai, Sir Stanley, being shot and killed before he can meet with Charlie and advise him about the local evildoings. At that point, Charlie is somewhat adrift as he came to Shanghai to assist Sir Stanley on an investigation, but Charlie does not know what the investigation was supposed to be about. Thereafter, someone tries to kill Charlie and then he is kidnapped by a gang of thugs and almost killed. Still, Charlie does not know what he is supposed to be investigating.

American government agent James Andrews, also an ally of Sir Stanley, arrives in Shanghai and advises Charlie that the issue is opium smuggling. Andrews behaves in a suspicious way and Charlie is not entirely sure about his bona fides. There is also something fishy about Sir Stanley's assistant Philip Nash. He is arrested for making the third attempt on Charlie's life, when his thumb print is found on the gun that was involved in the shooting. In the end, Charlie breaks up the smuggling ring and unmasks the true head of the operation.

The re-introduction of Lee Chan to the film series is an important positive. Given his heft and age, Charlie Chan was seldom involved in physical activity in the movies. His sons usually provided the physical element for the film series as, in this feature, when Lee helps his father escape from imprisonment by slugging one of the guards and then leaping off a high staircase onto another henchman. Additionally, the comic relief of Charlie's sons was often the high point of some of the films, as there could be real humor in their unusual antics.

That is not, unfortunately, the case in *Charlie Chan in Shanghai*, where Lee's interacting with his girlfriend or disguising himself as a beggar fall flat. Indeed, the entire film seems slow-moving and padded. In addition to the scenes with Lee, there is a gratuitous (although charming) moment of padding in the opening scenes on board a ship, when Charlie sings a Chinese song to some young children.

One of the prime problems with the movie is that there is no murder mystery. While the crime story commences with the murder of Sir Stanley, Charlie never does much to investigate the killing and there are no suspects. Indeed, in the first half of the film, Charlie is basically reacting to a threatening note, an attempted murder on his life while he is sleeping, and a kidnapping of Charlie and Lee. Instead of being proactive, Charlie is merely reacting to events, slowing the pace of the film even more.

It is only after United States secret agent James Andrews tells Charlie about opium smuggling out of Shanghai that Charlie finally learns what he is investigating. However, since Andrews turns out to be a fake, there is no reason why he should have told Charlie anything about the smuggling, particularly since the information he provided to Charlie was accurate. Although Charlie's original suspicions of Andrews are allayed when Andrews appears to be acting in good faith, Charlie knows for sure that Andrews is a fake when Andrews smokes and drinks in Charlie's presence. Charlie has a report that the real Andrews did not smoke or drink.

As was often the case in this type of film, the evidence of the report was kept from the viewers, as the screenwriters were afraid to play fair with the mystery audience. It would have been nice if the screenwriters had provided the information from the report to the viewers during the film, so that they would have the same opportunity to solve the crimes that Charlie did. Nevertheless, even without any clues to his guilt, the unmasking of Andrews at the end of the film will surprise no one as it is telegraphed many minutes in advance.

Similarly, few people will be surprised that Philip Nash is not guilty of any crimes and that he was really working with Chan. A good rule of thumb for movie mystery-watching is that when the case is particularly strong against a suspect early in the film, and the leading lady stands by him and truly loves him, that person will not be guilty. That is why there is no surprise at the end when Nash is exonerated. Unfortunately, though, this whole matter makes no sense in retrospect. If Andrews' butler actually took the shot at Charlie, how did the butler get Nash's fingerprints on the gun? Since Andrews knew that Nash did not do the shooting, why was he not immediately suspicious of Charlie's intentions? This is another example of sloppy plotting in a Hollywood mystery film.

There are some interesting moments in *Charlie Chan in Shanghai*, such as the surprise shooting of Sir Stanley at the beginning and a semi-suspenseful capture or killing of the crooks at the end. Irene Hervey is particularly lovely as Sir Stanley's niece, Diana. However, there is little else to recommend it, as *Charlie Chan in Shanghai* has a weak plot filmed at a lackadaisical pace. This is the weakest extant film in the series to date.

## *Charlie Chan's Secret* (1936)

*Charlie Chan's Secret* is an unusual film for the Honolulu policeman. The movie involves an old dark house mystery, a horror-style atmosphere, two séances, and no No. 1 son, Lee Chan. These differences in subject and setting from the prior films in the series are a decided plus for the feature. And, even though the pace of *Charlie Chan's Secret* bogs down somewhat in the middle, it is still quite enjoyable.

The film opens quickly, as a newspaper headline announces in large letters that the S.S. *Nestor*, a passenger ship with many prominent people on board, has been lost in a storm off the coast of Hawaii, providing an excuse for Inspector Chan to become involved. Chan is first shown on a boat, apparently helping with the rescue effort. In fact, though, he is only searching for one person in particular: Alan Colby, heir to the Colby family fortune. It seems that when Colby's father died, Alan could not be located and was therefore presumed dead, so the other relatives, namely his aunt, Mrs. Lowell, and her two daughters, inherited all of the money.

To the chagrin of someone in the family, Alan is not dead and was coming back to San Francisco to claim his inheritance when the shipwreck occurred. A deep sea diver finds a body which is not that of Colby, and also finds a briefcase of Colby's, with his water-soaked diary therein. Charlie is able to read a passage which indicates there were attempts on Alan's life while he was on the boat.

Charlie proceeds to San Francisco to tell Mrs. Lowell that Alan may still be alive. At the same time, Alan arrives at the eerie Colby mansion where he is suddenly knifed in the back. Later that night, during a séance, Alan's luminous body appears, frightening everyone. That leads to the obvious conclusion that Professor Bowan, who ran the séance, and his medium, Carlotta, are involved in the killing.

These opening scenes are excellent as the story moves along quite rapidly, punctuated by Alan's surprise death and his even more surprising re-appearance at the séance. Good use is made of the spooky Colby mansion, essentially uninhabited, with sliding panels, oddly shaped doors, strange animal carvings, high ceilings and at least one strange window. The spookiness is later enhanced by the séance which is lit solely by the light in the center of the table. Even the Lowell house, very inhabited, seems quite spooky with its gothic-type rooms and shadowy interiors. No other Chan film has quite this same atmosphere.

Unfortunately, once the séance is interrupted by the appearance of Colby's body, the film becomes static. Rather than trying to solve Alan's murder, Charlie seems more interested in debunking the bona fides of the séance, thereby spending a large amount of time in the séance room. Even a trip through the secret passages of the Colby house is more dark than scary. Alan's murder seems to be forgotten at this point in the film, which is a serious problem for *Charlie Chan's Secret* because, after all, this is still a murder mystery rather than a horror film. Additionally, since so much time is spent on the side matter of the séance, little time is spent acquainting the viewer with the various suspects for the crime, making it difficult to differentiate between them. The death of another family member reignites the story as the focus returns to the hunt for the murderer. Although the plot twists here may not impress the experienced mystery viewer, they are, nevertheless, still fun to watch. The identity of the killer is a surprise, but it would have been a surprise no matter who was identified as the murderer, because everyone had the same motive and available means to do the killing and there are no significant clues to the murderer.

The comic relief is provided by Herbert Mundin as the often-scared butler, Baxter. Mundin was always quite good in this type of role and he actually provides some real laughs in *Charlie Chan's Secret*, especially when he is almost killed when Charlie tries to recreate one of the murders. After the Chan sons, Baxter is one of the most humorous characters to appear in a Chan film.

The solution to the crimes cannot withstand much scrutiny. How did the killer have the time to set up the stunt at the séance, to throw suspicion on the professor and his medium? How did he manage to have Alan Colby's body appear at the séance? How did he know Colby was coming to the house when he did, so that he could be there to murder him? How was the killer able to attempt to take Colby's life on board the ship, as Colby's diary indicated, when the killer was back in San Francisco?

If a mystery is entertaining enough, it is probably not worth putting too much thought into the logic of the crimes or the cohesiveness of the solutions. That can only lead to severe disappointment. In the case of *Charlie Chan's Secret*, it is better to simply enjoy Charlie's witty aphorisms, the film's dark atmosphere, some excellent acting, a few striking moments and a clever trick on the part of Charlie to snare the murderer. *Charlie Chan's Secret* is an enjoyable, if perhaps a little disappointing, mystery movie.

## *Charlie Chan at the Circus* (1936)

*Charlie Chan at the Circus* has one of the strongest openings of any of the Chan films. There is a fabulous pan from left to right down the curtains of a circus midway containing paintings of different scenes of "big top" activities. Shadows of other circus activities, such as balloons being carried by a child, a fire eater, a revolving Ferris wheel, an acrobat and a juggler, fall on each of the painted frames as the camera continues to move. In the background, there are the sounds of circus music and two midway barkers imploring the audience to attend one of the inside shows. The camera finally rests on the face of one carnival barker who is begging the audience, for just a quarter, to come inside to see the greatest show on Earth. It is a truly stunning opening.

Charlie Chan, his wife and twelve children come into the tent to see the show. The main attractions are two little people, Colonel Tim and Lady Tiny, who perform a very impressive Spanish dance, to the delight of the entire Chan family. The Chan kids then meet the little duo in person while Charlie goes to meet one of the owners of the circus.

In other films, this might all seem like padding but here the time has been appropriately spent to establish the setting and background for the murder mystery to come. For, after all, this is still a Charlie Chan film and there is no doubt that murder will soon be afoot. There is also no doubt as to who the murder victim will be. Joe Kinney, one of the partners in the circus, has been receiving threatening letters and he wants Charlie to investigate them. Kinney is rightfully worried as a number of circus people are quite unhappy with Kinney. His partner, John Gaines, is upset at Kinney for threatening to take the remainder of the circus from him if he cannot make payments on a note that is about due. Kinney has jilted Nellie Farrell, the wardrobe mistress, by deciding to marry Marie Norman, the circus acrobat, also upsetting Nellie's brother Dan. Kinney has just fired Hal Blake, the handler of the circus ape, Caesar. In the ensuing fistfight, the key to Caesar's cage is picked up by a person unknown.

Not unexpectedly, Kinney's dead body is discovered later that night in his locked business trailer. Caesar had been let out of his cage that night and, because of ape hair found on the window of the business trailer, it seems clear that the ape strangled Kinney. But, then, who let the ape out of his cage? Suspicion travels from party to party. After Marie is shot out of the air with a rifle bullet to her trapeze apparatus, Charlie sets a trap, finally revealing the surprise murderer.

*Charlie Chan at the Circus* is shot with more style than most of the other Chan films. In addition to the splendid opening, there are other unusual shot selections, such as the tantalizing shot from high inside the ape cage, over the shoulder of the ape and through the bars, as Charlie is talking to circus people outside the cage. There are shots framed by bunks on the circus train and a very interesting fight between Lee Chan and the killer, wearing a hat, shot in the semi-dark with the scene only lit by a single light hanging from the ceiling near the ape's cage. As the ape escapes once again, his progress is tracked by shadows on a few of the circus tents. The time and attention given to shot selection along with the time and attention brought to convey the real feeling of circus life solves the problem with many other movie whodunits—they become boring talkfests. *Charlie Chan at the Circus* never becomes that.

Unfortunately, the weakest part of the story comes with the explanation to the crimes. The killer is close to, if not actually, the least likely suspect, which is a shame since there are so many other good suspects. The motive for the killings comes out of the blue, unrelated to any of the story previously related. One of the significant clues, that the ape hair on Kinney's business office window was that of a dead ape, indicating that someone dressed in an ape outfit to kill Kinney after letting the real ape loose, is hidden from the viewer. If, in fact, that explanation is correct, how did the fake ape kill Kinney in that locked circus trailer? The viewer should probably not think about that question for very long. The viewer might also want to forget that Dan Farrell, the one who apparently broke into the business office safe and left the fake marriage certificate therein, had no way to get into the safe. He did not know the combination. Also, the viewer should not think long about the fact that there was no reason for the true killer to write those threatening notes to Kinney other than as a plot device to bring Charlie to the circus in the first place.

For all of the unanswered questions, *Charlie Chan at the Circus* is still an interesting film of circus life, midgets and murder, told with a style and wit often missing in this type of film. The film also has an interesting lineage because, even though the murderer is not quite the same as in the first mystery story of them all, "Murders in the Rue Morgue" by Edgar Allan Poe, it is an interesting variation on the same. And the last shot of the escaped ape sitting beneath a circus trailer contentedly eating bananas amid a cornucopia of fruit is a hoot.

## *Charlie Chan at the Race Track* (1936)

This may be the most underrated of the Charlie Chan films. Set in a world of race horses and gamblers, with a story that moves from Australia to Hawaii to California, *Char-*

*lie Chan at the Race Track* is a police procedural of the highest interest. And, unlike many of the other Chan films, it contains an excellent clue so that the viewer has a chance to discover the murderer at the same time Charlie does.

After a short moment at police headquarters in Honolulu, with Charlie giving a lecture to the other officers about the marks that bloodstains make, the film switches to Australia and a very important horse race known as the Melbourne Sweepstakes. The favorite is Avalanche, a horse owned by American George Chester. The horse was given to him by Major Gordon Kent when Chester married his daughter. Also present is Warren Fenton, an apparent friendly competitor of both Kent and Chester.

Avalanche is leading in the race but loses when he is disqualified because of a blatant foul by his jockey, Tip Collins. Kent claims that Collins' action was deliberate, as part of a scheme of an international gambling ring to fix the race. Kent wires his friend Chan to meet his boat back to America when it docks in Hawaii so that he (Chan) can help with the investigation.

These opening scenes are excellent, deftly introducing all of the characters and eventual suspects, and by starting with the thrown horse race, it sets the stage for the racing-related crimes that are about to occur. By the time the boat reaches Honolulu, Kent is dead, having been kicked to death by Avalanche in the horse's stall on the ship. The ship's officers believe it was an accident but Chan is not so easily fooled. He quickly explains why the death of Kent was not an innocent mishap but a deliberate act to prevent Kent from interfering in the gambling ring's activities. Charlie's superior in Hawaii permits Charlie to board the ship with the others as they continue their travels to California for an important race. There, on the day of the Santa Juanita Handicap, when the gamblers believe they have successfully fixed another race, Charlie rounds up the gamblers and discovers the mastermind behind the criminal activity.

*Charlie Chan at the Race Track* is one of the best Chan films as a result of two attributes sometimes lacking in the other films: a mystery that holds together and enough action to prevent the film from becoming a talkfest. At first, the film seems to be a pure police procedural, with Charlie following the evidence like cairns on a mountain trail, gradually reaching his destination amid some sharp and unexpected turns. He analyzes the bloodstains on Avalanche's stall, notices that a pet monkey seems to be bothering a different horse than he did the day before, has Lee Chan search the ship for the typewriter on which a threatening note was written, and deduces that a fire on board ship was not intended to kill any of the horses but was a subterfuge for something else. Charlie's detective activities would have made for an excellent mystery on their own, in the nature of a police procedural, but when Charlie fingers the actual criminal mastermind, he identifies a clue of which the viewer was also previously made aware, which gave the viewer the chance to solve the crime along with Charlie. Thus, a police procedural has turned into a traditional whodunit. This is a vast improvement over most of the other Chan films, where the most important clue is usually withheld from moviegoers so that they never have a real chance of solving the murder.

*Charlie Chan at the Race Track* does reflect another problem with the Chan series, which is that while there are many potential suspects, there is very little differentiation among most of them, undercutting their validity as suspects. In this film, though, that is not a problem as the viewer can easily identify Chester and Fenton as the likely crooks and for once, one of them actually is the crook. The film does not employ the movie cliché of "surprising" the audience by identifying one of the least likely suspects as the criminal.

*Charlie Chan at the Race Track* never becomes a talkfest because there are so many action sequences. There are the races themselves, Charlie and Lee being captured by the crooks and making their escape, a few of the horses going out of control, Charlie being shot in the leg, and the suspense of knowing that if Avalanche is in the lead near the end of the handicap race, the gamblers intend to shoot him with a dart to slow down his progress. Even when that event occurs, can Avalanche still somehow win the race?

The acting is excellent and the direction is more than competent, with good stock footage for the racing scenes blending well with the rest of the film. Lee Chan is both amusing and affectionate to his father; Charlie's aphorisms are of the highest quality. What else could one desire in a mystery film?

*Note on the Source Material*: Although *Charlie Chan at the Race Track* has an original script, the plot idea of Charlie boarding a ship on its trip from Honolulu to California to discover the murderer on board was first used in the novel *Charlie Chan Carries On*, published in 1930.

## *Charlie Chan at the Opera* (1936)

In many ways it is amazing that *Charlie Chan at the Opera* was ever produced. While there is obvious box office appeal to the circus or a race track, the opera might seem to be a little too highbrow for the average Charlie Chan fan, unless the Marx Brothers were involved in destroying the venerable institution. On the other hand, with the addition of Boris Karloff to the cast, perhaps the filmmakers were relying on the memory of the great silent horror film, *The Phantom of the Opera* (1925), to entice the viewing audience. Whatever the thinking, the decision to produce *Charlie Chan at the Opera* was shrewd as the film is usually considered to be one of the best, if not the best, Charlie Chan movie ever produced.

The film starts out emphasizing its horror elements with a shot of a sign for Rockland State Sanitarium, a steady downpour with thunder and lightning, and two guards talking about one of the patients, an amnesiac who is playing the piano and singing operatic songs. The character, who is later identified as Gravelle, is played by Boris Karloff. As another guard talks to him and as a window in the room suddenly blows open from the wind, Gravelle's memory is jarred by a newspaper story about an opera that is opening the next night and a picture of Lilli Rochelle. Gravelle makes his escape and proceeds to the opera.

Coincidentally, Lilli comes to police headquarters in Los Angeles the next day and coincidentally Charlie Chan is there, about to return to Honolulu after solving the race track murders. Lilli, who knew Chan many years before in Honolulu, implores Chan to remain and assist her and the police with the threatening note she has received. Charlie agrees and that night proceeds to the opera where he is called on to solve a double murder and the mystery of a young girl who may be the daughter of Gravelle.

It seems clear that *Charlie Chan at the Opera* was specifically written with Karloff in mind for the role of Gravelle. Horror elements are highlighted throughout the film, as Gravelle sneaks his way around the opera house, frightening many. As expected, Karloff is excellent in the role, not just for his acting abilities (and that crooked smile and strange voice), but also because he is able to use his horror persona to add to the eeriness of the situation. Gravelle, in the hands of Karloff, does in fact become another terrifying phantom of the opera.

Charlie Chan (Warner Oland), far left, and Inspector Regan (Gary Usher) send the masked Gravelle (Boris Karloff) back out on the opera stage to try to trap the killer, in *Charlie Chan at the Opera* (1936). The lighting engineer is not identified.

Nevertheless, *Charlie Chan at the Opera* is still a crime story, not a horror film. The key scene in the movie occurs when Gravelle substitutes for opera singer Enrico Barelli, dons a mask and sings the role of Mephisto on stage. Lilli, who is performing with him, realizes something is wrong, tries to escape, but is constantly pulled back by Gravelle. The scene ends with Gravelle knifing Lilli as part of the opera. Lilli collapses to the floor of the stage, perhaps seriously injured.

The opera is wonderfully staged, with large and convincing sets. As Mephisto walks on stage, the music becomes more intense. The expression on Lilli's face makes it quite clear that she knows she has a serious problem even as she valiantly continues to sing her part. Margaret Irving is marvelous here as Lilli, using only her facial expressions to convey her terror. There is a montage of varying shots, from close-ups of the participants, reaction shots of others, views of the orchestra from the stage and views of the stage from the wings, all of which add to the suspense. The scene ends with the expected knife thrust cleverly foreshadowed by the stage manager's explanation of the storyline of the opera to Charlie and the others who are standing off-stage.

If the rest of *Charlie Chan at the Opera* does not equal this moment, that is not unexpected as this is one of the best scenes in all of the Chan films. It is beautifully directed by H. Bruce Humberstone and, at least for the moment, makes *Charlie Chan at the Opera* seem like a big-budget production. Two murders ensue and the film does return to the usual Chan formula with Charlie, as he often does in the film series, once again tricking the killer into confessing. Similar to *Charlie Chan at the Race Track*, though, the killer is not the least-likely suspect and therefore the mystery does hold together quite well, making the solution satisfactory to the viewer.

The film would have been better if William Demarest had been given less screen time as a not-very-funny and slightly prejudiced policeman. It would have been nice to have had a few more clues to the killer. Nevertheless, while *Charlie Chan at the Opera* may not be the best of the Chan films, it is surely in the upper echelon of films about the great Chinese detective.

## *Charlie Chan at the Olympics* (1937)

While the Chan movies of the 1940s sometimes became formulaic and trite, the Chan movies from the 1930s seldom did. The very early Chan films were based on the novels by Earl Derr Biggers, so they employed plots that were originally conceived for a different medium. When that source material ran out, Charlie went on his world tour, with each new location adding some spice to the proceedings. Around this time, No. 1 son Lee Chan was added to the proceedings. When the setting of the mysteries in foreign locales started to become familiar, Charlie began visiting interesting events such as the circus and the race track. That idea continues in *Charlie Chan at the Olympics*, which makes clever use of the 1936 Berlin Olympic Games as a backdrop. But what makes *Charlie Chan at the Olympics* unique is that this is the first Chan film which is not a mystery. *Charlie Chan at the Olympics* is primarily a spy story and a clever one at that.

It starts out in Honolulu with a test of a device which can remotely control airplanes in flight. The test is initially successful, but then an agent named Miller, who has been hiding on the test aircraft, throttles the pilot and absconds with the plane and the valuable device. Chan, on a fishing expedition with his son Charlie, Jr., discovers the downed plane with the pilot dead and the device missing. With some clever detective work, Charlie identifies the extra person on the plane, but when he proceeds to Miller's apartment finds that Miller has been murdered. One suspect is Yvonne Roland, a brunette who was known to have visited Miller's apartment. The other is Arthur Hughes, an arms dealer, who was in Hawaii at the time of the theft. Both of them have left Hawaii and are on an ocean liner headed to Berlin for the Olympics. Also on board is Lee Chan, an Olympic swimmer, and Dick Masters, an Olympic pole vaulter. Masters is also considered a suspect since he was the one who was originally supposed to fly the plane in Honolulu but begged off because of a shoulder injury. However, Masters is a clean-cut American boy with a sweet and innocent American girlfriend, so there is no way that he could ever be involved.

In Berlin, Charlie recovers the remote control device and captures all of the spies who have been involved, including a foreign diplomat, Charles Zakara, with whom Roland was working. Then, in a surprise ending, Charlie unmasks an American who was collaborating with the German agents.

The spy vs. spy vs. spy element of the story is one aspect of *Charlie Chan at the Olympics* which makes the story very interesting. This is not just a tale of Chan trying to expose a spy; rather, it is a story of two different spies, Roland and Hughes, tangling with each other and Charlie, with other potential suspects involved. *Charlie Chan at the Olympics* always keeps the viewer guessing as to what will happen next. It ends with a kidnapping of Lee Chan and Lee's suspenseful rescue by Charlie. To top it off, when everything seems to be over, there is still one more surprising revelation left.

Another important aspect of the film, particularly from the perspective of a modern audience, is its historical interest. There is much footage from the Olympic Games, including a magic moment when Jesse Owens' name is mentioned and he is shown running on the track. Charlie travels to Berlin in 1936 in the Zeppelin known as the Hindenburg which, in real life, was to have a spectacular fire and crash the following year with all on board killed. (The Hindenburg disaster took place on May 6, 1937, so *Charlie Chan at the Olympics* was in release when the tragedy occurred.) The only historical inaccuracy relates to Lee Chan. Extensive research has failed to locate any proof that Lee won a gold medal for swimming at the Berlin games.

Layne Tom, Jr., plays Charlie Chan, Jr., in the early scenes in Honolulu, substituting for Keye Luke as Lee Chan since Lee is on his way to Berlin. It is fun to see a junior version of Lee Chan make his first appearance in the series and Tom is quite good in the role. Once again, the use of young Tom adds a new element for the series. C. Henry Gordon, in one of his several roles in the Charlie Chan movies, plays Arthur Hughes, one of the suspects. Gordon is one of the fishiest-looking actors ever in a mystery film. Based on looks alone, he is clearly the villain.

*Charlie Chan at the Olympics* has its other small pleasures which greatly add to the fun. There is Miller's landlord, a cranky woman with very strict rules for her building, the maid at the Olympic village who turns out to be a spy and a man at the Olympic Games who can read lips from afar. Thus, in addition to a crackling spy story, *Charlie Chan at the Olympics* features excellent acting, interesting characters, historical insight and even Chinese aphorisms spoken by Lee Chan. This is a highly recommended film.

## *Charlie Chan on Broadway* (1937)

By the time of this 15th entry in the Charlie Chan series, it must have been difficult for the filmmakers to once again come up with new ideas to keep the series fresh. They had already done classic whodunits, murders with horror overtones, crimes around the world and even some spy stories. Nevertheless, for *Charlie Chan on Broadway*, the creators still managed to be quite innovative in the choice of subject matter and location. This time, the emphasis is on gangsters and the locale is now New York City, but needless to say, whatever the subject matter and wherever the location, Charlie Chan is able to solve the crimes.

Chan and his son Lee are on board an ocean liner headed to New York City when the expected shipboard intrigue manifests itself. A suspicious-looking mustachioed man sneaks into a woman's stateroom, puts a chair against an inner door locking the woman in the bathroom, and then proceeds to search her belongings. When the woman screams, Charlie and Lee come to her rescue along with the burglar who pretends he just heard the screams. A search of the cabin discloses that nothing is missing but after everyone leaves, the woman, Billie Bronson, checks a secret hiding place where she has placed a small wrapped package. Later, Billie slips that package into Charlie's luggage so that it will not be found in the usual customs search when the boat docks in New York.

The wrapped package contains Billie's diary, the contents of which, if disclosed, could put a serious crimp in mob activities in New York City. Billie intends to use the diary for monetary gain, either by blackmail or by a sale to the newspapers. Not surprisingly, Billie is found murdered, the diary has gone missing and there are plenty of suspects. Luckily for the New York police, Chan agrees to assist in the investigation and by the end of the film, he is able to identify the surprise killer.

There is a lot to like in *Charlie Chan on Broadway*. Director Eugene Forde, who directed several movies in Hollywood mystery series, including two other Chan films, keeps the pace of the film constantly moving. At the beginning, the story progresses from the attempted burglary of Billie's stateroom to the hiding of the wrapped package in Charlie's luggage to the intrigue as the ship docks to the attempted burglary of Charlie's apartment to the intrigue at the Hoffenstot Club, all with little time wasted. During this portion of the film, there are a few bits of humor between Charlie and Lee but they are kept to a minimum. Even Marie's dance at the Club, which is surely a matter of taste for today's audiences, creates movement within the frame, adding to the pace of the film even though it is just filler material. Also, Forde was clever enough to cut away from the dance on several occasions, so that plot developments could be highlighted.

The acting is generally top notch. Warner Oland and Keye Luke were still at the top of their game in 1937, with great chemistry between the two. The supporting players are Hollywood performers who always gave competent performances. The one dissonance in the bunch is Harold Huber, playing Inspector Nelson. Huber overacts outrageously and his gimmick of asking just about everyone he sees for a cigarette tires quickly. If his performance had been toned down somewhat, the film would have been substantially better. That seems to be a problem with many of the Chan films. Since Charlie operates in such a quiet manner, the filmmakers must have felt that the police character had to be brought up another notch to compensate for Charlie's calm demeanor. In fact, and as shown by *Charlie Chan on Broadway*, that usually turned out to be a bad idea.

The most significant difficulty with the film, as it was with many Charlie Chan films, is that while there are many suspects, there are no clues to the killer. When Charlie identifies the surprise killer at the end, he includes in his explanation the clues he used to solve the murder. Once again, unfortunately, those clues were not previously disclosed to the viewer. Thus, the viewer had no ability to identify the killer other than to guess that the murderer was the least likely suspect. Since there are at least two least-likely suspects in the film, that time-honored approach for solving movie mysteries has only a fair probability of success for this mystery movie.

Despite the criticism, *Charlie Chan on Broadway* is a fun film to watch, for its slick production values, Charlie's aphorisms, Luke's humor, Oland's performance and an interesting backstory for the murders. If only the whodunit aspects of the murders were better handled, this could have been a top film in the series. As it is, *Charlie Chan on Broadway* is an enjoyable but easily forgettable feature.

## *Charlie Chan at Monte Carlo* (1938)

*Charlie Chan at Monte Carlo* is the last film in which Warner Oland played Charlie Chan. After completing 16 films in the series, Oland passed away before the next feature could be completed. Oland, as usual, is good in *Charlie Chan at Monte Carlo* but the film as a whole is disappointing, to say the least. It was not a fitting way to say farewell to the actor who made the character of Charlie Chan so popular in the 1930s.

Charlie and Lee Chan are on their way to Paris to attend an art exhibition in which one of Lee's paintings will be displayed when they encounter crime and intrigue at the famous gambling casino at Monte Carlo. A bank messenger carrying $1,000,000 in metallurgical bonds is killed, and later the chauffeur of the car in which the bank messenger was traveling is found dead. The missing bonds are owned by a man named Victor Karnoff and the obvious suspects are his archrival Paul Savarin and Savarin's accomplice, pretty Evelyn Grey. Karnoff's wife Joan is being blackmailed by the hotel bartender, Al Rogers. Joan had previously given Rogers some of the bonds to keep him quiet, so Joan is also a serious suspect. Near the end of the film, the killing of Rogers and the discovery of a briefcase filled with the missing bonds gives Chan all the clues he needs to identify the triple murderer.

The problems with *Charlie Chan at Monte Carlo* are several. First, and perhaps most importantly, the story is not very interesting. Although there is some surface appeal to the rivalry between Savarin and Karnoff, the stolen bonds and multiple killings, that interest is dissipated by the fact that the first two killings are of characters (the bank messenger and the chauffeur) who barely appear in the film before they are dispatched. Without learning a little more about those characters, the viewer is not all that interested in who did the killings. On the other hand, there is considerable time spent, both before and after the killings, on the prime suspects. However, none of them is the least bit pleasant and all have something negative in their background. Thus, the viewer has no sympathy for any of the suspects, and that is another reason why the viewer is not all that interested in who committed the crimes.

In addition to the flawed structure of the mystery, *Charlie Chan at Monte Carlo* has one of the most irritating characters in all of the film series. Inspector Joubert, the policeman from Monaco, is loud, silly, overbearing, officious and whatever other negative adjectives one can muster. Harold Huber, who plays Joubert, was rapidly becoming a regular in the Charlie Chan series playing some type of policeman and often overacting in those roles. However, Huber never overacted more outrageously than he does here. While Joubert may not have more screen time than Charlie Chan, he is such a dominating character that Charlie often recedes into the background, not a good characteristic for a Charlie Chan movie.

Unlike Chan's trips to Paris, Egypt, Shanghai and Germany, it is nice to see people actually speaking the native language (here, French), instead of always speaking in English, even when two natives are talking to each other. However, that device is used in *Charlie Chan at Monte Carlo*, not for suspense purposes as it was in, say, *The Counterfeit Traitor* (1962) and *Torn Curtain* (1966), but rather as the basis for some attempts at humor by Lee Chan. Since nothing of significance is made of the language usage in *Charlie Chan at Monte Carlo*, all of the characters might just as well have spoken English throughout the film.

As to the solution to the crimes, Charlie hides most of the significant clues from the viewer. The motive for the killings, i.e., that another person has stolen bonds from Karnoff, comes out of the blue with no basis previously laid for it. The killer is easy to spot but only because he is the least likely suspect. Unlike the other major characters, suspicion is never thrown on him at any time.

A number of people believe that the Charlie Chan movies hit their stride in 1936 and 1937, starting with *Charlie Chan at the Circus* (1936) and continuing through the next three or four films. There is a lot of truth to that opinion. However, *Charlie Chan at Monte Carlo*, a misfire from all perspectives (plot, acting, characterization and comedy), put a quick end to that string of Chan mystery successes.

## The Sidney Toler Films at 20th Century-Fox

### *Charlie Chan in Honolulu* (1938)

This film has one of the most amusing titles of just about any detective movie. Since Charlie Chan is a police inspector in Honolulu, most of his cases should have taken place in Hawaii. Producing a film named *Charlie Chan in Honolulu* is no different than filming a movie titled *Spenser in Boston* or *Scudder in New York City*. Where else would Charlie Chan be other than in Honolulu? Of course, the reason for the unusual title is that while the Charlie Chan of the Biggers novel did spend a considerable amount of time on the islands, the movie Chan seems to be everywhere except Honolulu. Thus, it is a true movie event for Charlie to be working on a case for the police department which employs him and pays his salary.

Since *Charlie Chan in Honolulu* introduces Sidney Toler to the series, after the abrupt death of Warner Oland, the filmmakers may have wanted to ease Toler into the role by bringing the series back to its roots in Hawaii. Additionally, and perhaps as part of that plan, for one of the few times in the series, the viewer sees most of Chan's family and Charlie's interaction with them. Also, a family dinner is a good way to introduce Victor Sen Yung as No. 2 son Jimmy Chan, with No. 1 son Lee Chan now off to art school.

Unfortunately, while those ideas may have seemed promising to the filmmakers, none of them works. The domestic scenes go on for way too long and the running theme of Charlie becoming a grandfather for the first time is less interesting than the scriptwriter must have thought it would be. The story gets very silly at the beginning as Tommy Chan takes a message from police headquarters for his father about a murder on a freighter anchored just outside Honolulu. Jimmy Chan decides to investigate the crime on his own, without telling his father about the message. Brother Tommy sneaks onto the boat also. On the ship there is a menagerie of zoo animals and a keeper who is frightened of the animals (and of just about everything else). All of these plot diversions are played for comedy, not mystery, and the purported comedy is hardly funny. The net result of all of these shenanigans is that Charlie does not board the boat to investigate the crime until around 20 minutes into the film. By that time, with little mystery to the tale, the audience's attention is wavering, to say the least.

The murder victim is an unknown man who had just boarded the boat in Hawaii. The murder was witnessed by Judy Hayes, whose attorney-employer back in Shanghai had directed Judy to take $300,000 to Honolulu and give it to a man who presented a wedding ring to her, as a pre-arranged signal. As Judy was about to do so, the man was shot. There are only six passengers on the boat and all of them are suspects. In addition, the $300,000 has disappeared and later there is another murder on the freighter. In the surprising conclusion, the murderer is revealed as a person who does not come from within the group of passengers whom Charlie is investigating.

The unmasking of the killer is surprising because, just as in many of the Warner Oland films, Charlie hides the important clues from the viewer, such as the fact that the scarf which was used to strangle one of the victims was tied in a sailor's knot. As a result, the viewer is unable to solve the mystery on his own. Another problem with *Charlie Chan in Honolulu* is that the shipboard "comedy" does not end when Charlie boards the freighter. The viewer is treated to more humor with the animals, such as a lion that walks around unleashed and frightens everyone, to a monkey who escapes and must be re-captured. Charlie himself gets to do some schtick on the telephone, when the lines are crossed with his chief of police and Charlie's son-in-law when the son-in-law calls Charlie about the baby. It is all pretty lackluster stuff.

In a film of mostly low points, the one joy is watching George Zucco perform the role of Dr. Cardigan, a psychiatrist, mad doctor and prime murder suspect. With his strange hat and round, thick glasses, and his habit of measuring the skulls of all he meets, Dr.

Cardigan is the movie's one truly interesting character. George Zucco underplays the role magnificently, exuding a quiet malevolence, effectively parrying Chan's questioning in the best scene in the movie. When Zucco is on screen, the film comes alive, which it seldom does at any other time. On the other hand, given that Cardigan is innocent and assists Charlie in capturing the real murderer, can anyone explain why Cardigan picks up a gun late in the movie and threatens Charlie?

It is difficult to evaluate the performances of Toler and Victor Sen Yung as, regrettably, their film debuts in the series take place in one of its worst films. There is simply too much comedy and too many poorly scripted moments for this film to rise above the mundane. As to the latter point, did Toler really ask a policeman to have ballistics check a gun to determine how recently that gun had been fired? Warner Oland would never have made such a mistake.

## *Charlie Chan in Reno* (1939)

*Charlie Chan in Reno* is a vast improvement over *Charlie Chan in Honolulu*, Sidney Toler's first effort in the series. Indeed, the beginning of *Charlie Chan in Reno* resembles the openings of many *Perry Mason* television shows, with the cast of suspects and the crime introduced in the long opening segment in which Charlie is nowhere to be found. At the end of the section, the victim's body is discovered with one Mary Whitman standing over the corpse. Needless to say, she is arrested for murder. However, instead of finding a good criminal defense attorney, her estranged husband Curtis Whitman goes back to Honolulu and convinces Charlie to investigate the crime. Luckily, there are apparently no difficulties for Charlie in leaving the full-time job for which he receives a salary and traveling many miles away to Reno, Nevada, to investigate a murder.

That opening section is one of the highlights of the film. There are many people who would have wished for Jeanne Bently's death. Mary Whitman has come to Reno to obtain a divorce from her husband who intends to marry Bently. In the meantime, Bently has been stringing along young Wally Burke, convincing him that she is interested in him. There is a mysterious Dr. Ainsley who has had some involvement with Bently in the past. On the night of the murder, the owner of the hotel, Mrs. Russell, has Bently evicted.

Once Charlie arrives, the mystery thickens. He immediately obtains Mary's release from jail since the scissors with which she supposedly stabbed Bently were not found in the murder room. Thereafter, when Bently's husband George appears, he becomes another good suspect, especially after he attacks Charlie. Missing pages in Bently's scrapbook lead to a blackmail motive. And there is the disappearance of money that Bently won in the casino on the night of her death, creating another motive for someone who may have stolen the currency. Somehow Charlie figures the whole thing out and identifies the real killer, after gathering all of the suspects together in the murder room in the identical clothes they wore on the night of the murder.

One of the main attributes of *Charlie Chan in Reno* is the deft way in which the film mixes the comedy with the mystery elements. There are some true laughs in Jimmy Chan's antics, such as when he gives a lift in his car to two men along the road to Reno. In the next scene, as the car speeds around a corner, Jimmy's body, clothed only in underwear, is thrown out of the car. Later, Charlie spots Jimmy in a police lineup, with his stripped-down body covered mainly by a large coat. These are among the several truly genuine laughs generated by Jimmy Chan in *Charlie Chan in Reno*.

Later, the comedy arises from the local sheriff, Tombstone, who is not happy with Charlie's investigatory techniques. A number of people get off some good lines, as when Tombstone talks to a suspect about the murder. The suspect replies, "I know as little about this as you do." There is also a humorous cab driver who talks incessantly, also bringing a smile to the viewer as the passengers attempt to keep him quiet. In addition, the setting in Reno and the observations on divorce, Nevada-style, are quite entertaining.

However, *Charlie Chan in Reno* is a detective film and the success of the feature depends on the mystery being presented. In addition to the excellent opening, there are a number of good moments, such as Charlie's relentless investigation into mud and scratches on the riding boots of the victim, the stolen money, and the missing pages in the victim's scrapbook. There is also an excellent scene where Charlie visits a ghost mining town at night.

Unfortunately, though, the mystery itself does not hold together that well. The killer is the least likely suspect and this person's motive is unconvincing, especially when surrounded by a number of other excellent motives. The explanation for why the acid was introduced into the murder room on the night of the killing is implausible, and yet that is the key clue in the film. Also, it is hard to understand how the police missed that clue in their investigation, which was completed long before Charlie arrived on the scene. Arguably, the murderer can be discovered by the viewer by identifying the person who did not dress exactly as that person did on the night of the murder when Charlie calls the suspects together. However, who is going to notice that anomaly? (In fact, since Charlie was not there on the night of the murder, he would not know whether the murderer wore a jacket or not. And, when the murder was discovered, the killer was wearing the jacket, to hide some burns.)

Even after Charlie's explanations of the crimes and the arrests of two persons, the ending remains particularly confusing. However, up until that time *Charlie Chan in Reno* is a satisfactory mystery with many fine comedy moments. But if just a little more attention had been paid to the clues and the explanations of the crimes, it could have been an excellent Charlie Chan movie.

## *Charlie Chan at Treasure Island* (1939)

*Charlie Chan at Treasure Island* is usually considered to be the best of the Charlie Chan films starring Sidney Toler. However, while there is much to support that point of view, the film is subtly disappointing.

*Charlie Chan at Treasure Island* commences on an airliner bound from Hawaii to San Francisco. On board are Charlie, Jimmy Chan, who is suffering from acute airsickness, Paul Essex, a mystery writer who has just finished his newest book while on the plane, and Thomas Gregory, an officious insurance actuary. Essex receives a mysterious radiogram which could be a blackmail threat from the famous mystic Dr. Zodiac. Thereafter, just as the plane lands, Essex's dead body is discovered.

That is the first problem with *Charlie Chan at Treasure Island*. If Essex was murdered, the only person who could have been the murderer was Gregory. There are no other persons of interest on the plane. Perhaps for that reason, Charlie suspects that Essex's death was suicide, caused by blackmail, and so once Charlie arrives in San Francisco, he decides to investigate Dr. Zodiac and his possible blackmail racket. Charlie is accompanied in his investigation by Rhadini, a local magician who is famous for exposing fake mystics, and Pete Lewis, a local reporter who has a special interest in exposing Dr. Zodiac. Jimmy Chan also gets into the mix from time to time.

Charlie Chan (Sidney Toler), attending a party at the Hawaiian Village on Treasure Island, talks to Bessie Sibley (Billie Seward), a disciple of Dr. Zodiac, in *Charlie Chan at Treasure Island* (1939).

This middle section of the film is particularly interesting, first in the visit to the Zodiac abode where Zodiac puts on a particularly impressive display of mind-reading, and second, in a late-night burglary of the Zodiac residence, where Charlie and his companions discover some of the tricks of Zodiac's profession and also the file cabinets of information with which Zodiac has been blackmailing his victims. Note, however, that at this point in the film, there is not really much that Charlie is investigating. Indeed, Charlie destroys the files of blackmail evidence, ensuring that Zodiac could never be convicted of extortion.

Charlie then comes up with the idea of Rhadini challenging Zodiac in a public exhibition, offering $5000 to Zodiac if Rhadini cannot expose the mystic as a fraud. Once again, Charlie's purpose in arranging this stunt is unclear given that by this late date, Zodiac could never be convicted of either extortion or murder. Fortunately for the story, Zodiac accepts the challenge. But as the show starts in front of a packed house, Zodiac is nowhere to be found. Rhadini has no choice but to commence his magic act, to keep the audience entertained. During a standard levitation of Eve, Rhadini's assistant, Zodiac makes a surprise appearance. He comes on stage to witness the magic trick, but when the lights come on, Zodiac's body is lying on the stage, with a knife in his chest. The Zodiac mask is removed and it turns out that the dead man is Abdul, Zodiac's assistant.

The police decide to re-enact the crime, and this time Rhadini ends up with a knife wound in the shoulder. Charlie then calls on Eve, a legitimate mind reader, to assist Charlie in exposing the killer of Rhadini. During the course of that exhibition, Charlie, through Eve, identifies a number of the potential suspects. This again exposes a flaw in the feature as none of those suspects are very believable as the killer of Dr. Zodiac and none really had the opportunity to commit the murder. Then, as Eve is about to announce the name of the real murderer, a gun appears from behind a curtain and Eve is almost shot by the person whose name she was about to announce. Of course, what else would one expect, with a vicious murderer loose in the theater and Eve the only person with a spotlight on her about to identify the killer? What was Charlie thinking, putting Eve's life in such danger?

The murderer is revealed to be Rhadini, who was using the stage setting to kill Abdul, the only person who knew that Rhadini was Dr. Zodiac. This will not be much of a surprise to the avid film mystery fan, who will know almost immediately who the killer of Zodiac is. Only Rhadini could have set the timing of the stage show to make the murder work, his baton found in the theater aisleway was the obvious means of delivering the killer knife into Zodiac's person on stage, and to top it off, since Rhadini survived his own attempted murder, he is the automatic killer, by detective story convention.

While the aforesaid analysis may seem overly critical of what is clearly an entertaining film, the critique did not even mention the lack of any true use of the World's Fair background promised by the film's title, the paucity of Charlie Chan's clever aphorisms and the unconvincing use of a legitimate mind reader to solve the crimes. These faults in *Charlie Chan at Treasure Island* are usually overlooked because of the film's quickly moving plot, some good performances and its superb conclusion. Indeed, the last half hour or so of *Charlie Chan at Treasure Island* is one of the best segments in all of the Chan films.

Once the story moves to Rhadini's theater and the challenge is on, the suspense is palpable. The theatre setting is superbly used, with a darkened auditorium, surprise trap doors in the stage and the eerie levitation of Eve. The killing of Zodiac comes as a clear surprise, even for the true film mystery fan. The decision to re-enact the crime, along with the dubious idea of darkening the theater once again, adds to the excitement. The stabbing of Rhadini is another shock for the audience. The idea to darken the stage once again and use Eve's mind-reading act to trap the murderer ratchets the tension up another several degrees. The entire scene cleverly directed by Norman Foster, who attained his experience directing B–mystery movies in the Mr. Moto series. Foster's sure hand is obvious in these final scenes in *Treasure Island*.

Perhaps the best way to watch a Charlie Chan film is to ignore the defects in the plot and/or the flaws in the solution of the crimes, and simply enjoy the presentation, the performances and the comic elements. If that is the way in which the viewer watches *Charlie Chan at Treasure Island*, he may well conclude that it is the best of the Sidney Toler Chans.

*Note on the Exclusionary Rule*: It is quite extraordinary to watch the police detectives of the Hollywood mysteries of the 1930s and 1940s blatantly search a suspect's room or house without first obtaining a search warrant. In *Charlie Chan at Treasure Island*, Charlie shamelessly searches the house of the mystic Zodiac without any prior court approval. Charlie happily admits to breaking and entering which is the exact truth, given that Charlie has no official duties with the San Francisco police. That is a distinction without a difference, however, since if the San Francisco police did exactly what Charlie did in Zodiac's house, they would also be guilty of the crime of burglary.

The Fourth Amendment to the United States Constitution states that the people shall be "secure in their persons, houses, papers, and effects, against unreasonable searches and seizures," and that warrants for a search and seizure can only be issued "upon probable cause," based on a sworn affidavit. However, that Constitutional provision was originally of limited help to the guilty or the innocent, if the police simply decided to do a search without a warrant. For the guilty, the evidence illegally seized was still admissible at trial. For the innocent, they could bring either criminal or civil charges against the police — but with little likelihood of success in court.

In 1914, the United States Supreme Court, in *Weeks v. United States*, 232 US 383, adopted an exclusionary rule applicable only in federal court prosecutions. Designed to deter improper police conduct, the exclusionary rule, in its most basic form, authorizes the courts to exclude, at trial, incriminating evidence found by the police during an illegal search and seizure. In 1961, the Supreme Court, in *Mapp v. Ohio*, 367 US 643, extended the rule to state court prosecutions. A related doctrine is the "fruit of the poisonous tree" rule, which allows the court to exclude, not just the evidence obtained in the illegal search but all other evidence derived from an illegal search, such as a later confession obtained from a defendant who is intimidated by the police by showing the evidence illegally seized from his house.

Today, as a result of the exclusionary rule, it is a rare event, both in fact or fiction, for a policeman like Charlie Chan to burglarize a suspect's house to obtain evidence of a crime. Nowadays, Thatcher Colt (*The Panther's Claw* [1942]) and Mr. Wong and a policeman (*The Fatal Hour* [1940]) would think twice about violating a citizen's rights, even in a good cause.

## *City in Darkness* (1939)

Jimmy Chan, No. 2 son of Charlie Chan, is surprisingly missing from this film but at least there is one prominent son in the feature. Unfortunately, that son is not Lee Chan either, but rather is Marcel, the self-styled son of the prefect of the Paris police. Unfortunately, Marcel is played by Harold Huber, the serial over-actor of the Chan series. Huber is loud, uses exaggerated hand and arm motions, displays an exaggerated French accent and even does a few pratfalls. He often overwhelms the quiet and dignified Sidney Toler as Charlie Chan. Indeed, throughout the film, Toler often seems to fade into the background, giving one of his weakest Chan performances. Huber was missing from the previous three Chan films and watching the movies in chronological order, one can only say, in retrospect, what a relief it was that he was not in those movies. Huber is the focal point of *City in Darkness*, overpowering the other actors and the plot, delivering a fatal blow to what value the film might otherwise have had.

It is late 1938 and the winds of war are blowing in Europe. Despite the unsettled situation, Charlie Chan is in Paris at a reunion of members of the intelligence services from the last World War. Unable to book passage and leave the city, Charlie is drawn into the investigation of the murder of an unscrupulous man named Petroff, who disparages the French military and tries to blackmail a woman into leaving her husband for him. Petroff's murder is the least of Charlie's worries, however, as a ring of foreign agents have infiltrated France and are trying to leave the country with a cache of munitions, posing a serious threat to the French war effort. Charlie is able to break up the munitions ring and almost as an afterthought solves Petroff's murder.

Lurking in this tale of the overwrought son of the prefect of police is a pretty good spy story. The backdrop of the beginning of World War II and the anxiety over whether or not there will be war gives the tale some extra drive, as does the setting in the dark streets of Paris during the wartime blackout (hence the title). Some of that impetus is dissipated by the failed comedy of Parisians coming to the police station to object to the blackout, but nevertheless the setting and time period are a decided plus for the film. Other positive features are some of the typical trappings of a spy tale, such as a forged passport, the search for clearance papers for a ship's special cargo and a desperate attempt at escape by plane.

The one outstanding performance in the film comes from Pedro de Cordoba as Petroff's butler, Antoine. Quiet and dignified, he competently serves his employer, proudly takes his son to the train station to fight for France, and defends the French military from the scoffing by Petroff. He has the funniest lines in the film, such as telling Charlie Chan, referring to Marcel who has just asked one of his idiotic questions, "Monsieur, this man is insane." Or, when Marcel is trying to locate Charlie and asking Antoine where Chan is, Antoine respond that he is "in the cellar, sir.... That's under the house." For all of Huber's screen time and wild performance, de Cordoba is funnier.

Focusing in on the murder mystery itself, there is only one clue to the killer. When Charlie helps Antoine, who was injured in the last war, with tying his shoes, Charlie finds a French franc in one of Antoine's pants cuffs. That, on its face, would seem to have no significance but the veteran Chan film watcher will know instantly that the franc is some kind of clue and that Antoine must be the murderer. Later, Charlie will tie the French coin into proving that Antoine was at the murder scene at just the right time.

The problem with a whodunit which has only one clue is that the killer is obvious; a good murder mystery needs multiple clues and multiple diversions. Thus, *City in Darkness* has a weak murder mystery at its core. On the other hand, at least there is a clue to the killer. Most Chan films have none.

There are obviously a lot of positives to *City in Darkness*. Unfortunately, they are all drowned out by Huber's performance and his disproportionate screen time. As one of his aphorisms, Charlie might have said, "Less is sometimes more." In the case of *City in Darkness*, less of Harold Huber would have made a much better film.

*Note on the Source Material*: The *City in Darkness* credits state that the film was "based on a play by Gina Kaus and Ladislaus Fodor." Born in 1893 in Vienna, Austria, Kaus wrote a number of bestselling novels in the 1920s but had to flee Nazi–occupied Austria in 1938, first moving to Paris and then in 1939 to America. In the 1940s and 1950s, she contributed to a number of Hollywood screenplays. Kaus died in 1985 in California.

Fodor (1898–1978) was born in Hungary. In the 1920s, he wrote several successful stage comedies. Much like Kaus, Fodor fled the Nazis in the late 1930s, eventually moving to America where he did some Hollywood screenwriting in the 1940s.

The Kaus-Fodor play on which *City of Darkness* was based was written in 1939. It was apparently never produced on the stage, being immediately purchased by a Hollywood studio.

## *Charlie Chan in Panama* (1940)

This film is set in Central America at the beginning of World War II as the United States fleet is about to pass through the Panama Canal. There is concern that there may be an attack on the fleet; there does appear to be an exceptionally large number of spies or potential spies in the country. Into this tense setting comes a seemingly innocent group of people who have arrived in Balboa, Panama, by cruise ship and are now flying to Panama

City. The group consists of Dr. Rudolph Grosser, a suspicious-looking scientist, Clivedon Compton, a British novelist, Jennie Finch, a Chicago schoolteacher on her first international trip, Señor Manolo, who owns a local nightclub in Panama City, Kathi Lenesch, a stewardess from the cruise ship who is intending to work as a singer in Manolo's café, Achmed Halide, a cigarette salesman who owns a shop in Panama City, Richard Cabot, a government engineer, and Godley, a government agent. There is enough unusual activity among this group that it is a good guess that one or more of them are either Allied or foreign spies.

The best part of the film is its opening, as two American soldiers attempt to catch a spy who is illegally taking pictures of the American fleet. The scene then cuts to the group of airline passengers as they are about to board the plane. The script gracefully introduces the viewer to all of the passengers, one of whom will turn out to be a dangerous foreign spy. The plane itself is a cramped seaplane with only one seat on either side of the aisle. Given the wartime setting, it is a tension-filled trip, even though nothing really happens on board the plane.

The story then moves to Panama City where Charlie Chan is working undercover as Fu Yuen, the owner of a store which sells Panama hats. This is the first incongruity in the story as no explanation is given as to why the famous Honolulu policeman is working undercover for the United States government, a long way away from his native island. In the other films to date, some explanation, however unbelievable, was given for Charlie's appearances in many different spots around the world. Here, the screenwriters apparently did not have the energy to devise some reason for Chan's inexplicable appearance in Panama.

After the surprise death of Godley from poisoned cigarettes which were probably put in his coat pocket on the seaplane, thus making all of the passengers suspects, Charlie is on the search for Reiner, the international spy who has been the mastermind behind significant sabotage efforts against American interests. From this point forward *Charlie Chan in Panama* is not bad, but there is really nothing new in it. Jimmy Chan shows up for reasons hard to explain; he does his usual pratfalls and schtick. Then there are the Chan clichés of a mysterious figure turning out to be Jimmy (which actually happens twice in this film and how many times in other films), a gun sticking out of a door aimed at a potential victim, and Charlie tricking the killer-spy into making a confession. At least the lights do not go out once the villain is identified.

There are two excellent performances. One comes from Lionel Atwill as novelist Clivedon Compton, who turns out to be an English spy. Atwill is barely in the film before his character is killed, but he is always the center of attention in whatever scene he does appear. Did Atwill ever give a bad performance in a film? Did he always look like the most suspicious character in any mystery movie in which he appeared?

The other terrific performance is from virtual unknown Mary Nash as schoolteacher Jennie Finch, finally sprouting her wings as she escapes from her drab single life in Chicago. There is some true humor in the part and empathy from the viewer as Finch smokes a cigarette for what may be her first time and then appears at Manolo's nightclub, a type of setting she probably never visited before. Unfortunately, as Finch keeps reappearing throughout the film, including at the graveyard scene near the end of the movie, it is painfully obvious that she is the notorious spy Reiner, as innocent and as likable as she appears to be. While her unmasking therefore comes as no surprise, Nash's performance as Finch is excellent, changing from a convincing spinsterish schoolteacher to a convincing diabolical spy in an instant. It is truly the performance of the picture.

Lobby card for *Charlie Chan in Panama* (1940).

*Charlie Chan in Panama* has a very good reputation among Chan aficionados and there is much to like about the feature, such as its setting in Panama at the beginning of the world war and its spy vs. spy tale. However, it all seems just a little too familiar and a little too pat. Given all the security at the Canal, could a spy really have placed a bomb in a water cooler at the military installation in such an easy manner?

Once again, the screenwriters hardly seemed to be trying. There is simply nothing new to see in *Charlie Chan in Panama* because the filmmakers never displayed the imagination to stretch the movie beyond the conventions of the series.

### *Charlie Chan's Murder Cruise* (1940)

Although there were subsequent films in the series based, in part, on a novel by Earl Derr Biggers, *Charlie Chan's Murder Cruise* is the last Chan film to identify its source in the credits. *Charlie Chan's Murder Cruise* is based on *Charlie Chan Carries On*, published in 1930. Since *Charlie Chan's Murder Cruise* is a rare Sidney Toler film which is based on one of the Biggers novels, one would expect that the film would be one of the best of the Toler films. While *Charlie Chan's Murder Cruise* has its pleasures, it is ultimately a disappointing experience.

Inspector Duff of Scotland Yard, who has been traveling incognito on a world tour run by a Dr. Suderman, arrives at Chan's office in Honolulu to enlist his aid in discovering a murderer hidden among the tour group. As Charlie goes out of the room to ask his superior for permission to become involved in Scotland Yard's investigation, Inspector Duff is strangled by a strange man wearing a dark hat, dark coat and glasses and sporting a long gray beard. In the meantime, a call is received about the murder of a tour member at the hotel where they are staying. When Charlie returns to tell Duff about this new development, he finds the investigator dead on the floor. When Charlie shows up at the hotel to begin his investigation, the bearded killer begs him for a handout. Archaeologist Professor Gordon, a member of the group, tries to shoo the beggar away.

Since Charlie cannot solve the murder in Honolulu and he has no legal right to keep the suspects there, he boards the boat as it makes its way on the last leg of its journey to San Francisco. Charlie hopes that he will be able to solve the murders while he is on the ship with all of the suspects. Jimmy Chan also makes his way onto the vessel. After another murder on the boat, Charlie springs a trap and captures the killer in San Francisco.

One serious problem with *Charlie Chan's Murder Cruise* is that much of the story is a retread from prior features. Charlie boarded a boat on its way from Honolulu to San Francisco in order to discover a killer in both *Charlie Chan Carries On* (1931) and *Charlie Chan at the Race Track* (1936). The ruse of the beggar who is also a killer but is seen in the presence of the real murderer was first used in *Charlie Chan in Paris* (1935). The mysterious figure behind a curtain or hiding in the shadows turning out to be one of Charlie's sons was used in many films, as was Charlie creating a trap for the killer when he either did not know who the killer was or, at least, had no proof of the killer's identity. Also, how many times in these films has someone turned out the lights in a room full of suspects at just the right (or, perhaps, just the wrong) moment?

In addition, the mystery does not hold together very well. In order to investigate the murder of a New York judge on board the cruise ship just after it left New York City, Inspector Duff joined the tour in London. That incident (which is only an excuse to have Inspector Duff appear in Honolulu and then to be killed so that Charlie will take up the case) is never tied into the solution of the crimes. Charlie employs one of his most convoluted traps ever to snare the killer when he could have simply staked out Mrs. Pendleton's hotel room in San Francisco and captured the killer in the act of trying to murder her, something the killer was bound to do.

The film is not without its pleasures. The cast is familiar and uniformly excellent, particularly Lionel Atwill playing Dr. Suderman and Cora Witherspoon playing one of the daffy cruise members. There is some humor in the antics of Charlie's sons and particularly Jimmy Chan, who is forced to work on board ship in a menial position. There is a real clue to the killer's identity as he makes an incorrect statement about Chinese history in the presence of Charlie; Charlie points it out for the benefit of the audience, raising a question in the audience's mind as to that character's genuineness. In many Chan films, the audience receives no clues to the identity of the murderer so as obscure as the clue may be in this case, its inclusion in *Charlie Chan's Murder Cruise* is a refreshing improvement over many of the other films in the series.

However, there is little new here, and regular Chan fans have seen this type of story many times before. If the films of the Sidney Toler era were to be effective, they would have to depart from the cookie cutter approach that they now seemed to be taking.

*Note on the Source Material*: *Charlie Chan's Murder Cruise* was loosely based on *Charlie Chan*

*Carries On*, the 1930 novel by Earl Derr Biggers. In the novel, the initial killing takes place in London and is investigated by Inspector Duff of Scotland Yard. As the world tour continues, there are two more murders before the ship reaches Honolulu. There, Inspector Duff is wounded and Charlie boards the ship on its last leg to San Francisco in an attempt to discover the killer.

In the first film versions of the novel, *Charlie Chan Carries On* (1931) and its Spanish language version, *Eran Trece*, and consistent with the novel, Charlie Chan does not appear until past the halfway point. By 1940, with Charlie the clear star of the film series, that would have been an unacceptable way to adapt the novel to the screen. Accordingly, *Charlie Chan's Murder Cruise* commences with the attack on Inspector Duff in Honolulu. The first murder then occurs at a Honolulu hotel and the second murder occurs on the ship while Charlie is on board. Thus, unlike the novel, *Charlie Chan's Murder Cruise* always focuses on Inspector Chan.

The first killing, that of Kenyon (Drake in the novel), is substantially similar to the way in which it occurred in the book with the body dragged into a different room than the one in which the killing occurred, the victim (who was not the intended victim) being deaf, and a bag of 30 silver pieces (pebbles in the novel) found with the body. The motive for the murders is identical. However, the suspects are essentially all different and so is the killer, as is the killer's unusual method of dressing as a blind beggar when attempting his dastardly deeds.

With the necessity of including Jimmy Chan in the proceedings, the tone of *Charlie Chan's Murder Cruise* is substantially lighter than that of the book *Charlie Chan Carries On*. Interestingly, in the book, Charlie's Japanese assistant Kashimo stows on board the ship bound for San Francisco without Charlie's permission, with the idea of assisting Charlie in his investigation. When Kashimo is caught, he must work in a menial position on board the ship while at the same time running undercover errands for Charlie. This exact approach is used in the film for working the character of Jimmy Chan into the storyline on board the boat. Of course, while Kashimo is the source of some humor in the novel, Jimmy Chan is still a substantially funnier character than Kashimo ever was.

While employing some of the plot of the novel, *Charlie Chan's Murder Cruise* is essentially an original story. For a more faithful adaptation of the novel, see *Eran Trece*, the 1931 Spanish–language film version of the novel. Unfortunately, the English–language version, *Charlie Chan Carries On* (1931), is lost.

*Note on the Remake*: *Charlie Chan's Murder Cruise* is a partial remake of *Charlie Chan Carries On* (1931) and *Eran Trece* (1931).

## *Charlie Chan at the Wax Museum* (1940)

In the atmospheric setting of a wax museum crammed with statues of criminals, *Charlie Chan at the Wax Museum* combines a tale of suspense with a classic murder mystery. No other Chan film has quite the same location or structure. As a result, *Charlie Chan at the Wax Museum* finally breaks out of the cookie cutter mode of the last few efforts in the series, making this the best Chan film in quite some time.

The suspense aspect of the film starts early, with a courtroom scene in which Steve McBirney is sentenced to death as a result of a murder investigation by Charlie Chan, which the Honolulu policeman conducted, for some unexplained reason, in New York City. As he is being led back to prison, McBirney threatens Chan. A few minutes later, McBirney escapes from custody and, after a shootout with the police, ends up at Dr. Cream's Museum of Crime. Since Cream is a plastic surgeon to the underworld, in addition to being a wax figure sculptor, McBirney forces Cream to give him the disguise of a new face. A few weeks after the surgery, McBirney sets in motion a scheme to electrocute Chan during the weekly radio broadcast at the wax museum.

The whodunit aspect of the case commences about a third of the way into the film, when McBirney makes that attempt to electrocute Chan. At the last instant, Dr. Otto von Brom switches seats with Chan and it appears that von Brom has been electrocuted. Chan determines, however, that von Brom was killed by a poison dart blown by one of the people at the wax museum during the radio broadcast. Thus, while McBirney is still after Chan and the suspense continues, the thrust of the film turns toward the whodunit. At the end, Chan unmasks the real killer, Dagan, a criminal who was masquerading as one of the participants in the radio broadcast, having also previously changed his facial appearance by surgery so that no one at the museum knew who he really was.

The whodunit aspects of *Charlie Chan at the Wax Museum* are the weakest elements of the feature, displaying the typical problems with a Charlie Chan film: not enough differentiation between the suspects and no true clues for the audience to identify the killer on its own. Those are significant problems with any mystery movie but in this film, those problems are at least partially masked by the suspense features of the picture. Nevertheless, the ultimate identification of the murderer is far from convincing.

As to the suspense aspects of the film, the attempted killing of Chan is quite gripping, with Chan innocently sitting in the murder chair just as the electric switch is about to be pulled. At the last moment, von Brom insists on switching chairs with Chan, apparently saving Chan's life. However, unknown to the viewer, the wires had been cut before the switch was pulled so that Charlie was never in danger. But, then how was von Brom killed? The deliberate murder of von Brom at the same time as the attempted murder of Chan is a clever piece of screenwriting.

The wax museum setting contributes to the effectiveness of the piece, with much of the film shot in the semi-dark in the style of a 1940s horror film. In fact, the bandaged figure of McBirney walking through the museum makes him seem just like a horror film monster. The various wax figures, some of which are people in disguise, add to the tension. The strange actions of the watchman, Willie, who is legitimately crazy, and those of Mrs. Rocke, who only pretends to be crazy, add to the atmosphere of horror and dread. Since the audience knows that the police never received the call that Charlie thought was made after the murder, the isolated setting of the museum with the killer still afoot enhances the chills.

*Charlie Chan at the Wax Museum* is not a traditional Chan film of the 1940s, a time when it often seemed like the writers and directors were only going through the motions, trading on prior successes in the series. Here the filmmakers developed more of a suspense film than a whodunit, and in the best setting for a murder mystery since *Charlie Chan at the Opera* (1936). This film demonstrates that after all these years of Chan movies, there was still some life left in the Chan franchise.

## *Murder Over New York* (1940)

It is hard to take a movie seriously in which a New York City police inspector, learning that a Hindu man is a potential suspect, directs his policemen to round up all the Hindus in the city for purposes of a police line-up. After about 30 Hindu men are brought in, the inspector expresses surprise at how many there are. One of the Hindus has a very familiar voice and when the police, suspicious of his bona fides, wipe his face clean, he turns out to be a con man played by Shemp Howard. One of the Three Stooges actually appeared in a Charlie Chan movie! Who would have thought? Add to that a stereotypical treatment of a black servant and Jimmy Chan stating, "I'll never go on a case again like this without a gat," and sometimes this is pretty silly stuff. Yet, for all of that, *Murder Over New York* is an enjoyable film.

Once again, Charlie has abandoned his policeman's job in Honolulu, this time to attend a police convention in New York City. On the plane to the Big Apple, Charlie runs into his friend Hugh Drake, a former Scotland Yard detective, who is now on the trail of saboteurs. Charlie offers to help in the investigation but that night, Drake is killed by the poison gas in the library of his host, George Kirby, an airplane manufacturer. The killing was clearly related to the case Drake was investigating and it soon becomes clear that the culprit is one Paul Narvo, who was involved in a killing and sabotage in England. But, which of the characters is Paul Narvo? Because of plastic surgery, even his former wife cannot recognize him. At the end of the film, Charlie sets a double trap related to the test flight of a bomber, snaring the killer and his assistant.

It is much easier to identify what is wrong with the movie than what is right. Most of the important clues are hidden from the viewer. Charlie solves the crimes by comparing the handwriting on two documents but does not reveal that information to the audience. Charlie knows that Narvo had plastic surgery due to an auto accident but keeps that information to himself. How can the audience guess the killer ahead of Charlie Chan when it does not have all of the relevant information?

While there are a number of suspects, there is so little difference between them that when Narvo is identified, it is hard to remember who the character actually is. Thus, there is little surprise in the revelation. Surely, no member of the audience slaps his head and thinks, "I should have figured that one out."

The solution to the crimes makes little sense. Knowing that one of the male suspects sabotaged the test plane, Charlie decides to trap all of the suspects in the plane, forcing the killer to disclose his identity. Thus, the evening before the test, Charlie advises all of the suspects to be at the air facility the next day. Charlie, however, did not learn that the plane has been sabotaged until later that night so how did he know to bring all the suspects together? Narvo attempts to kill his assistant in full view of Charlie, the police and the other suspects. How did he ever hope to get away with it? Other elements of the plot also make little sense.

Nevertheless, *Murder Over New York* is fun to watch. Toler is excellent as Charlie Chan, as usual, and Victor Sen Yung is funny without becoming irritating as Jimmy Chan. There is an excellent supporting cast with lots of familiar faces, including Kane Richmond (later to play the Shadow in three features) and Robert Lowery (later to play Batman in the serial *Batman and Robin* [1949]) as two of the suspects, Ricardo Cortez (who had previously played Sam Spade and Perry Mason) as one of the victims, Donald MacBride playing a policeman (as he would in *Michael Shayne, Private Detective* [1941] and *The Thin Man Goes Home* [1945]) and two lovely supporting female performers, Marjorie Weaver (who would appear in several Michael Shayne mysteries) and Joan Valerie (who appeared in a number of mysteries in the 1940s). It is always comfortable watching familiar faces in these mystery movie series.

The direction is also above average, with a moving camera, unusual camera angles and use of shadows to enhance the mystery. The climax on the doomed plane is suspenseful, although the trick is obvious, and there is a double denouement, giving a charge to the end of the movie. Thus, *Murder Over New York*, despite its flaws (and despite the lack of a murder in the skies over New York), is a pleasant enough diversion to warrant a view from the true movie mystery fan.

*Notes on the Source Material*: *Murder Over New York* is a re-working of some of the plot of *Behind That Curtain*, the 1928 Charlie Chan novel by Earl Derr Biggers. Thus, the backstory of the Englishman who, after a killing, fled England with his new wife to the Far East where she eventually escaped from her husband comes from the novel, as do the clues of the pearl found in the room where the body is discovered and the victim's valise being held in the check room of a private men's club.

*Behind That Curtain* was filmed as *Charlie Chan's Chance* (1932). The use of poison gas as the murder weapon was first concocted for that film. Nevertheless, even with all of these similarities to an older Chan novel and movie, *Murder Over New York* is essentially an original story, in terms of its setting amid wartime sabotage of airplanes, the motives for the killings and the identity of the killer.

## *Dead Men Tell* (1941)

*Dead Men Tell* has lots going for it. Although a number of Chan films were set on ships, they were always large cruise ships. *Dead Men Tell* is set on a sailing ship (which never, in fact, sails) and, in accordance with the film's pirate theme, there are shadows everywhere, lots of dark passages and darkened rooms and an apparent ghost on board. In fact, the pirate ghost of *Dead Men Tell* gives the movie the feel of a horror film, somewhat in the nature of the Val Lewton films of the era, with prints of the pirate's peg leg observed on the ground, glimpses of the pirate's hook seen from time to time, and the sound of the peg leg heard more often than the ghost is seen.

The direction of *Dead Men Tell* is the best in quite some time. Harry Lachman, who directed four Chan films in a row, makes great use of the ship's setting and the ghost theme to create an aura of suspense. Lachman's clever camerawork often includes extreme close-ups of the characters, utilizing the expressive faces of the actors to contribute to the mystery, which contrasts with the few direct shots of the pirate ghost itself.

In terms of faces and actors, the highlight of the film is Milton Parsons as a slightly disturbed character, Gene La Farge. Even though Parsons is not playing a mortician, as he often did in films, his understated delivery and strange face add to the spookiness of the setting. If La Farge is not the murderer, there is surely something else wrong about him. At one point, he convinces Jimmy Chan to put on a blindfold and walk a plank, with Jimmy splashing into the river far below. Surely, that means that La Farge is the villain. But no, La Farge has the perfect explanation for what he did: "I've always wanted to do that to someone; not to mention how good it made me feel."

Jimmy ends up in the water four times in this film. The audience may feel that is excessive for the same joke in one film but it does seem funny each time it occurs. Sen Yung, as Jimmy, is one of a number of actors who gives the fine performance expected of the typical cast of a Charlie Chan film. The one disappointing performance is that of Robert Weldon as Steve Daniels. His delivery of lines is so amateurish that his appearances in the film are jarring. It is not surprising that *Dead Men Tell* was his only significant film role.

Yet, for all of these positives, *Dead Men Tell* is ultimately disappointing. A murder mystery needs a good whodunit to be successful and in this most important matter, *Dead Men Tell* falls short. The story involves the search for four pieces of a pirate treasure map (hardly a believable MacGuffin) and the death-by-fright killing of Patience Nodbury, the possessor of one of the pieces. Leaving aside the unlikeliness of that method of murder, even though Miss Nodbury has a heart condition, there is no basis for Charlie to conclude that her death was a homicide other than to create a plot for the film. Another unconvincing matter is that there are a number of suspects on board the ship and when any significant event happens, whether on board or just off the ship, they all seem to be present except, of course, for the actual murderer.

The killer can be easily ascertained by the viewer because, of all the suspects, this character is given the least attention. Chan sets a trap and, just before the disguised murderer is unmasked, Chan announces who it will be. In this case, however, and unlike most of the prior films, Chan gives no explanation as to how he determined who the real killer was. In other words, Chan hides all of the clues from the viewer, even after the film is over. It is easy for a skeptic to conclude that Charlie was only guessing. Thus, *Dead Men Tell* is all style and no substance. Therefore, while it has some appeal for a while, the film is ultimately lacking.

## *Charlie Chan in Rio* (1941)

This is another of those merely competent Charlie Chan movies from the 1940s, slickly produced, ably directed, well-acted and yet having little intrinsic interest. The screenwriters appear to have simply gone through the motions, providing no clues to enable the viewer to solve the crimes and revealing a surprise killer who could have been anyone in the cast.

Charlie, accompanied by Jimmy Chan, is in Rio to arrest singer Lola Dean for the murder of Manuel Cardozo, which she committed a year ago in Honolulu. Lola accepts a marriage proposal from Clarke Denton and schedules a party after her show to celebrate the event. On the way home, Lola stops at the apartment of psychic Alfredo Marana for a reading as suggested by Lola's assistant, Helen Ashby. Marana has other plans and with a hypnotic created by coffee and a special cigarette, obtains and records Lola's confession to the murder of Cardozo. Once Marana confronts Lola with her confession, Lola convinces Clarke to elope with her that night.

Charlie, Jimmy and local policeman Souto arrive at Lola's house to make the arrest, at which time Lola's murdered body is discovered. All of her valuable jewelry is missing from her wall safe. A potential clue is Lola's broken brooch, lying next to the dead body. A pin is missing from the piece and Charlie believes it may be imbedded in the killer's shoe. Since all of the suspects have just had a light meal at the dining room table, Charlie is able to identify the murderer from the scratches on the floor by the chair in which the murderer sat.

This film has some appeal. No. 2 son Jimmy Chan, as played by Victor Sen Yung, is quite funny once again, whether admitting, when under hypnotics, to wrecking Charlie's car back in Hawaii or to romancing Lola's maid in a slightly incompetent fashion. However, his outbursts in front of the suspects when Charlie is investigating the crime and his ridiculous theories about the murder become quite irritating at times. Harold Huber, as policeman Souto, actually gives a toned-down performance for the first time in the series. In terms of feminine pulchritude, this may be the best-ever Chan film cast. Jacqueline Dalya as Lola Dean, Kay Linaker as Helen Ashby and 1940s mystery regular Mary Beth Hughes as one of the suspects are all quite attractive. They make one forget the holes in the plot, at least for a while. The atmosphere of Rio is well-conveyed early on by some songs performed in a local nightclub.

This is, however, a mystery, so where did the mystery go? While there are a number of characters and most are in and around the Dean mansion when Lola's murder occurs, none have any true motive and none had much of an opportunity to commit the deed. Somehow Charlie knows that the murderer was related to Manuel Cardozo, the murder victim in Honolulu, and that he or she killed Lola for revenge, but Charlie never divulges that fact to the viewing audience until the end, and there is no explanation as to how he obtained that information. There is so little differentiation among the characters that if Charlie had fingered another person for the crime, that would have been okay. In fact, Charlie could have identified another character as a relative of Cardozo and the audience would have easily accepted that character as the killer.

The sloppiness of the writing is exemplified by the one apparently significant clue in the story. Lola's watch stopped at the time of her killing and Charlie figures out that the killer set the hands of the watch back about 15 minutes. Police Chief Souto suggests that the killer took that action to provide an alibi for him- or herself. It is a clever bit of police work by Charlie and Souto, but then the watch is never mentioned again, and no one tries to provide himself with an alibi. This incident, taken from the source Chan novel *The Black Camel*, is thrown into the story for no reason other than for the fact that it came from the novel.

At least the finale is quite clever. Charlie identifies the killer from the scratches on the floor but under the powerful hypnotic of Marana, she denies the killing. This denial is accomplished by a clever ruse but one that is not clever enough to fool Charlie. Thus, the film does have its slight interest but the sloppy writing, in particular, prevents *Charlie Chan in Rio* from distinguishing itself from the many other films in the long series.

*Note on the Source Material*: This film is loosely based on *The Black Camel*, the 1929 novel by Earl Derr Biggers, and is therefore something of a remake of the 1931 film titled *The Black Camel*. While most of the plot is original to this film, there are similarities in the scenes of a psychic investigating the death of his brother some time ago and obtaining a confession from a female character, and soon thereafter the surprise death of that character.

The main similarity among all three versions of the story is the use of a broken jewelry pin stuck in the murderer's shoe to identify the killer from scratches the killer made on the floor. However, although the motive is the same, the killer is different in the South American version of the tale than in the novel and prior film version.

## *Castle in the Desert* (1942)

Charlie Chan ended his film career at 20th Century–Fox with *Castle in the Desert*, one of the best Chan films of the Sidney Toler era. With its isolated setting, innovative direction and complex plot, the film was an excellent capper for Fox's Chan series.

There are strange goings-on at the Manderley castle in the Mojave Desert in California, located about 35 miles from the nearest town, Mojave Wells. Professor Paul Manderley, an historian of 16th century culture, and his wife Lucy, a descendant of the Borgias, the famous poisoners of the past, live in the deserted home which has no electricity or telephones. During a round of cocktails at the castle, a guest, Professor Gleason, is poisoned by something contained in his cocktail glass. The last cocktail was given to him by Lucy Manderley just after she found out that Gleason was a genealogist interested in her past. To avoid publicity, the parties decide to move Gleason's body to the local hotel and have it discovered there. After another death by poisoning and one by stabbing, Charlie Chan solves the case, determining that the poisonings were faked, but that the one very real death by stabbing was committed by Lucy Manderley's half-brother, long thought dead, who was disguised as a guest.

As good as *Castle in the Desert* is, the plot deserves substantial criticism. The core story has the premise that Walter Hartford and Dr. Retling, Manderley's attorney and physician, respectively, have faked two poisonings to convince everyone that Lucy Manderley is crazy and should be institutionalized. Then Hartford, who has her power of attorney, will be able to control her vast fortune. Stepping back from the story, that scenario seems to have a low likelihood of success, particularly since it would require Paul Manderley's consent to commit Lucy to an institution. Also, in that event, wouldn't Lucy then give her power of attorney to her husband rather than her attorney?

To make this scheme work, Hartford tricks Charlie into coming to the castle so that the conspirators can convince him that Lucy is crazy. The thinking was that Charlie's imprimatur on Lucy's mental condition would give the scheme some credibility. However, how many criminals would want one of the world's greatest detectives around when they are committing a crime? (Unfortunately, at least based on other films in other Hollywood mystery movie series, the answer to that question is "a lot.") Not only that, in order for the crime to work, Charlie would have to agree not to report the second killing to the police because if he did so, it would become quite clear that there was no body and no poisoning. A renowned detective like Charlie would hardly participate in criminal activity, particularly on behalf of people he hardly knows, so there was no credible reason to bring Charlie to the crime scene. Also, what were they going to do with the second "body"?

As usual, there are no clues to the killer. If Charlie had announced someone else as the villain, no viewer could object. However, there is a blatant cheat in the story. As part of the scheme, after the fake poisoning of Gleason, the parties trick Manderley into agreeing to have the body moved to the hotel in town, rather than disgrace the Manderley family. That was an excuse for the schemers to remove Gleason from the castle without Manderley knowing that Gleason was not dead. Obviously, no body was ever sneaked into the hotel. Then, why, several days later, does the hotel proprietor tell Charlie to tell Dr. Retling not to bring Charlie into his hotel to die, like he did with the fellow last week? No wonder the viewer is unable to determine that the poisonings were faked.

Yet for all of that, *Castle in the Desert* is always entertaining. The setting at an isolated castle with no ability to communicate with the outside world and a killer afoot is fabulous. The film brings back memories of Agatha Christie's *And Then There Were None*. There is an obvious reference to the book and film *Rebecca*, with the Manderlay mansion of the book becoming the Manderley castle of the Chan movie. Note the somewhat similar openings between the two films, as the return to Manderlay by dream in *Rebecca* (1940) is similar to the long drive to Manderley castle in the Chan film, through the desert, through the gate and then on to the giant structure.

Paul Manderley (Douglass Dumbrille), far right, shows his ring to Charlie Chan (Sidney Toler) while Jimmy Chan (Sen Yung) looks on in *Castle in the Desert* (1942). Charlie immediately finds the secret compartment in the ring which can be used to surreptitiously drop poison into an unsuspecting person's glass.

The inside of Manderley castle is eerie, with its flickering candles, dark corridors, angled shadows, high basement steps and rooms filled with unusual objects, such as the armored soldiers. The eeriness of the castle is enhanced by the direction of Harry Lachman, directing his fourth Chan film in a row. It seems as if every camera position he employs is unusual, such as the opening shot out the car window when the vehicle approaches the Manderley gate; unusual long shots mixed with extreme close-ups or two-shots, such as the one of the taxi driver and hotel manager when they are talking to Charlie in Mojave Wells; shots from above and below a character; and unusual framing of shots, such as shots through windows, from behind objects such as candles or shelves, or with an extra inanimate object in the scene, turning mundane two-shots into interesting three-shots. With unusual shot selection and framing, the viewer is always on edge, not knowing what to expect next, adding to the tension of the plot. The style is similar to the one that Roy William Neill employed in *The Scarlet Claw* (1944) from the Sherlock Holmes series. The Holmes films often seemed like A–productions, although on B–budgets, and Lachman gives the same feel to *Castle in the Desert*.

In addition to the setting and direction, the performances are top-notch. Sidney Toler gives his best performance in some time, helped by Charlie's clever aphorisms, often employed in this film more for putting down another character than for their intrinsic wit. Sen Yung is quite amusing without dominating the film. Ethel Griffies, as Madame Saturnia, the strange seer who is always right, provides just the right mixture of horror and comedy to the proceedings. Milton Parsons is only in the film for a few moments, but he is always a highly entertaining performer. Douglass Dumbrille, a regular red herring in Hollywood mystery movies, is fine as Paul Manderley, alternately crabby, professorial and pedantic.

While the plot is often lacking, as noted above, at other times it is excellent. It is hard to take one's eyes off of Paul Manderley's mask (itself a great cinematic effect) and its removal creates a *Phantom of the Opera* moment. Madame Saturnia makes a clearly incorrect (to the viewer) statement that no one has died at Manderley castle yet, which surprisingly turns out to be true. The sudden imposition of a real killer operating at the same time as the fake killers, but for the same motive, adds a complexity to the story that is often missing from a Chan film. It also adds to the excitement of the conclusion.

*Castle in the Desert* is a wonderful film which breaks from the mold of many of the Chan films from the 1940s, making it a unique film for the series. It is highly recommended.

## THE SIDNEY TOLER FILMS AT MONOGRAM

### *Charlie Chan in the Secret Service* (1944)

With the release of *Charlie Chan in the Secret Service*, the Chan films moved from 20th Century–Fox to Monogram Pictures, a significant step down the studio ladder. The differences in the production values between the two studios are readily apparent. *Charlie Chan in the Secret Service* seems to take place almost entirely indoors and in only a few rooms of the set of the Melton mansion. The musical score sometimes goes M.I.A. and at other times it is so loud and inappropriate to the scene being shown that it is a serious distraction. Just listen to the loud stock music soundtrack near the beginning of the film as Charlie exits a government building, enters a taxi and then arrives at the Melton house. The music is all about tension and excitement, even though Charlie is engaged in the most mundane of activities.

The filmmakers had so little confidence in this crime caper that they decided to insert three comedy relief characters in place of Charlie's one son from the prior films. Benson Fong, as No. 3 son Tommy, is a zero, with no personality, especially as compared to Victor Sen Yung as Jimmy Chan. Marianne Quon as No. 2 daughter, Iris, is a complete waste who adds nothing to the film. Mantan Moreland, as a chauffeur to one of the suspects, is not the slightest bit funny in the type of demeaning role in which he often performed. Moreland does have some comedic talent; he just has no opportunity to display it in this film.

Sidney Toler seems older and thinner than he previously appeared in his 20th Century–Fox films. Partially because of that, for the first time in the series, he seems weak and unenthusiastic in the role of the former Honolulu policeman and now mysterious government agent. It is of little help to Toler's performance that the few aphorisms he speaks are far from witty.

The direction of Phil Rosen is also disappointing. On a few occasions when someone makes a significant statement, Rosen cuts to a series of reaction close-ups of each of the suspects, making serious incidents into laughable moments. As was often the case in a low-budget film, time is filled with characters walking from scene to scene, slowing the pace of the film, instead of the director just cutting quickly between the two scenes to accelerate the tempo. There had been some excellent directors for prior Charlie Chan films; Rosen does not live up to that tradition.

The plot of *Charlie Chan in the Secret Service* is basic. It involves the surprise death of George Melton, the inventor of a device to blow up German U–boats. He is murdered at his home, even though he is being protected by Secret Service agents. Also, the secret plans of his military device are stolen. A number of persons are gathered at the home for a cocktail party, and one of them is the famous spy Manlich, who has done the dastardly deed. Chan, who now works for the Secret Service in Washington, is called in on the case.

*Charlie Chan in the Secret Service*, much like many of the prior Chan films, has the problems of failing to distinguish between the suspects and failing to provide any true clues to the killer, resulting in the ultimate revelation of the killer being both disappointing and unconvincing. Here, near the end of the film, Charlie first identifies Peter Lasker as the criminal, gives his reasoning and then has him taken away by the police. The explanation seems convincing to the viewer. A few minutes later, Chan identifies Mrs. Winters as the actual criminal, gives his reasoning, and then has her taken away by the police. Charlie's explanation also seems convincing to the viewer. In fact, Charlie could have kept doing this with all of the suspects until they were all arrested. With no real clues and so little learned about the suspects during the film, any one of the suspects could have been the killer. Thus, *Charlie Chan in the Secret Service* fails miserably as a murder mystery.

Despite Chan's explanations, in actuality no one could have been the killer. Melton was supposedly electrocuted when he pulled the cord on the light in his downstairs closet, which had been tied into a power switch. How could the killer, an invitee to a cocktail party, ever rig-up that device? Another person is killed by a gun which is shot by an electromagnetic device, set off by a switch under the piano. How could the killer, an invitee to a cocktail party, ever rig up that device? How could any of these things been accomplished with the Secret Service guarding the house? In the case of the gun operated by remote control, what was the purpose in setting up the device? The main killer would never know, in advance, that she would have to kill her assistant and in which chair that assistant would be sitting when that second murder became necessary. Thus, the whole film makes little sense.

*Charlie Chan in the Secret Service* has nothing going for it. What the film is missing in production values is not made up by the script. This is a dreadful start to what is really a new mystery series.

## *The Chinese Cat* (1944)

When viewers comment on *The Chinese Cat*, they are apt to say that it is better than *Charlie Chan in the Secret Service*, the first entry in the Charlie Chan Monogram series. While that statement is accurate, it conveys little since just about any mystery film ever made is better than *Secret Service*. It is perhaps more insightful to note that with *The Chinese Cat*, the Monogram series began to create its own little niche in the mystery movie world, a place for sometimes interesting mystery stories with sometimes funny comic relief on always very limited budgets.

One of the reasons that *The Chinese Cat* is better than *Secret Service* and many of the other early films in the Monogram series is that it eschews spy story elements and returns to the staple of the Charlie Chan series—a good murder mystery. The film opens with

Thomas Manning working through a chess problem in his study when a mysterious hand appears and shoots Manning with a gun. As Manning dies, he grabs some of the pieces on the chess board. While Manning's second wife and his stepdaughter Leah bang on the locked door of the study, the killer escapes by way of a secret passage hidden by a swinging wall. When Mrs. Manning and Leah finally enter the room by the secret passage, they discover Manning's body.

While Manning's murder is not quite a locked room mystery, it is close, adding a layer of interest to the story. A series of newspaper headlines describe the police investigation but there is no progress after six months. Then a famous criminologist, Dr. Paul Recknik, releases a book naming Mrs. Manning as the killer and accusing police detective Harvey Dennis of covering up the crime because he fell in love with Leah. That prompts Leah to request that Charlie Chan investigate the crime, which he reluctantly agrees to do. Charlie is only in town for 48 hours so he must move quickly. Thus, the semi-locked room mystery becomes a semi-cold case investigation, which is an excellent set-up for what should have been an excellent detective film.

The strength of *The Chinese Cat* lies in its mystery, as Charlie follows some clever clues to reach his ultimate conclusion. Photographs of the crime scene show that only a bishop was left on the chess board when Manning collapsed from his fatal wound. Was Manning trying to leave a clue to the killer's identity? Charlie traces little figurines in Manning's study back to their Chinese designer, locating stolen jewels inside each of them. Marks on a table indicate that the statue of a Chinese cat was in the study at the time of the murder but is now gone. When Charlie finally locates the Chinese cat, much of the mystery can be solved. However, luck is also important to Charlie, and his investigation is sparked by one of the gang of diamond thieves, Kurt Kazdas, contacting Charlie to provide him with new information. Although Kazdas is killed before he can talk to Charlie, his death starts Charlie on the path to the discovery of the real murderer.

As good as these aspects of the mystery are, the story becomes very convoluted at the end, with Charlie's explanations for the multiple murders less than convincing and his explanation for how he reached his conclusions even less so. However, the finale is somewhat unique for the Chan series, as it involves Charlie's capture and escape from the villains in the unusual setting of a carnival fun house, rather than just the usual dry explanation of how the crimes occurred. There are also some clever moments when suspicion is thrown on the criminologist Recknik, although those moments are handled in such a heavy-handed manner that Recknik cannot be considered a legitimate suspect.

Much of the film is taken up with the comic antics of Birmingham Brown, played by Mantan Moreland. Brown has not yet officially become Charlie's chauffeur in these Monogram movies but he nevertheless functions in that capacity in *The Chinese Cat*. Moreland is an acquired taste and his comedy has not worn well for today's sensibilities. Nevertheless, he can be funny. The real problem with Moreland in this film is that there is just too much of him. The emphasis on Moreland in the movie highlights the fact that while the set-up for the mystery of Manning's murder is good, there are not enough high-quality mystery elements in that story to fill even the short running time of this film.

With Moreland carrying the comedy elements, Benson Fong as No. 3 son Tommy has little to do. However, who does not cringe at the particularly cruel comments that Charlie often makes about his son? When Tommy mentions that Charlie has often said that two men can find a clue quicker than one, Charlie replies, "Where is other man? Do not see other man." When Tommy asks Charlie if he is a mind reader, Charlie touches Tommy's head and replies, "If head not too small." When Charlie spots a figure in the fun house with no head, he tells Tommy, "He remind me of you." It is a wonder that Tommy does not rush back to college rather than be abused by his sarcastic father. Charlie was never quite so mean when he was working at Fox and 20th Century–Fox.

*The Chinese Cat* is no masterpiece but it is a pleasant enough diversion for the true mystery fan. It gives some hope that Monogram was justified in continuing the Chan franchise after 20th Century–Fox dropped the series.

## *Black Magic* aka *Meeting at Midnight* (1944)

Mystery movies that are set amid séances, magician's tricks, old dark houses and the use of hypnosis have an intrigue all their own. Thus, even though *Black Magic* (which was also released under the title *Murder at Midnight*) never reaches its full potential, it is an entertaining film for fans of the Charlie Chan series.

The opening is strong, as psychic William Bonner is conducting a séance at his home with the aid of his wife Jacqueline and two hidden assistants operating from the basement below. As Bonner solicits questions from the participants to ask the spirit that is floating high in the room, an unknown voice asks, "What happened in London the night of October 5th, 1935?" Suddenly, the light of the crystal ball goes out and Bonner's head drops down. He is dead, killed by a bullet that no one can find.

In addition to this tantalizing opening, there are other strong scenes in *Black Magic*, usually involving hypnosis, as Chan discovers Norma Duncan in a trance in his hotel room as a killer enters, Jacqueline Duncan walking off the side of a high office building while in a trance (a particularly brutal scene for this type of film), Charlie almost suffering the same fate, and then Charlie unmasking the killer at a séance, with Charlie almost killed in the same manner as Bonner. When *Black Magic* focuses on its mystery-horror elements, the movie works quite well.

Unfortunately, there is a time in every mystery movie when events have to be explained in a rational manner, and that is when *Black Magic* comes up short. The motive for the murder involves a car accident that occurred on that October 1935 night in London, but the viewer never learns about that fact until the murderer is about to be identified. In order to believe Charlie's explanations for the murders, the audience must swallow the fact that the murderer was so injured in that car accident that after plastic surgery no one can recognize him, even though the two victims, at least, knew him in London. (A similar willing-suspension-of-disbelief is required in *Murder Over New York* [1940] and other Chan films.) No bullet was found in Bonner's body because he was shot with a bullet of frozen blood fired from a spring gun hidden in a cigarette case. Perhaps that is real science but it seems more like James Bond than Charlie Chan. Then there is the drug that allows a person to be easily hypnotized and the idea that the murderer is such a great ventriloquist and thrower of his voice that he could ask the question about London at the séance and no one would be able to determine who was speaking. It is all pretty silly stuff.

There is no son of Charlie Chan to help his pop in this investigation but a daughter, Frances Chan (coincidentally played by an actress named Frances Chan), is around to provide assistance. While it is an interesting variation from the prior films to have a female offspring furnish some aid to Charlie, Frances Chan is truly awful in the part. She displays no emotion or enthusiasm in the role; her line reading appears to be just that — line reading. Also, and unlike her brothers, Frances brings no energy or humor to the film although the part was not necessarily written for humor. That is left to Mantan Moreland, once again playing Birmingham Brown.

Even a viewer who is willing to tolerate much in the demeaning portrayal of African-Americans in these later Chan features, just so the whole film is not thrown out because of some of its parts, *Black Magic* is still pretty hard to take from the perspective of a more enlightened age. Brown tries to make himself invisible (over and over again) by snapping his fingers and saying, "Abracadabra"; he is afraid of "spooks" and other imagined terrors; at one point he believes that Charlie has become a skeleton that talks; and he takes Mexican jumping beans in place of his own pills. It is true that there are some Caucasian characters who act stupidly and are afraid of their own shadows in other Hollywood mystery movies, but nothing was ever done to those white characters in their films that is quite as humiliating as what is done to Birmingham Brown in *Black Magic*. Also, even though there may be a particularly stupid Caucasian character in another movie, there are sophisticated, educated and brave white characters to offset that role. Here, with the exception of another black character who makes a brief appearance (and is also employed in a menial position), Birmingham Brown is the only African-American character in the film. To make matters worse, Moreland has substantial screen time.

Even Sidney Toler is not very good in *Black Magic*, playing Charlie more as a bemused observer rather than a shrewd detective. There are almost none of Charlie's signature aphorisms in the film and surely none that are the least bit memorable.

There is a good mystery lurking somewhere in *Black Magic* but that mystery and some good scenes are squandered, to a significant degree, by the poor writing and poor performances. For viewers who want to see Charlie Chan investigating murders related to séances and visitors from the spirit world, *Charlie Chan's Secret* (1936) is a better choice.

## *The Jade Mask* (1945)

Do all of these Monogram Chans take place on the same few sets? Are the plots of these features getting stranger with each new movie? Are fairly good story ideas being squandered as a result of poor writing and poor productions? While fans may differ as to the first two queries, few would disagree as to the last question, with the creators of *The Jade Mask* once again devising an interesting set-up but then developing it into a mediocre mystery movie.

The film opens with a spooky scene in which a figure in a large coat and a hat worn low on his head, hiding his features, tries to open the gate of the driveway to the Harper mansion. The butler inside asks over the intercom at the gate, "Who's there?" When there is no answer, the butler goes outside the house, where he appears to be shot at by the mysterious man. (Note that in the context of the remainder of the film, the attempted shooting of the butler makes no sense.)

Inside, Harper is conducting a gas chamber experiment with his assistant Walter Meeker. Harper has hidden the secret formula for his work in a booby-trapped room where anyone who enters without Harper's authorization will be killed. A policeman arrives on a motorcycle to see Jean, Harper's niece, and when he is let through the gate, the mysterious figure sneaks in, attacks the policeman and then puts on his uniform. The mystery man then manages to gain entrance to the house. Shortly thereafter, Harper is killed by a poison dart to his head.

*The Jade Mask* has the strongest opening so far of any of the Monogram Chans and it can hold its own against the Fox and 20th Century–Fox features also. The dark exteriors, the gas-filled rooms and the strange man who sneaks into the Harper abode all create a tantalizing beginning to the story. The two quick murders at the start of the film may be a record for a Chan film. A mystery movie fan might reasonably question whether he has actually inserted a Philo Vance movie into the DVD player rather than a Charlie Chan film.

A new Chan offspring, in the person of No. 4 son Edward (or Eddie) Chan is introduced in *The Jade Mask*, although he does not return in any of the subsequent films. Again, the filmmakers were trying to vary the formula, with Eddie, who is more of an intellectual than his other brothers, much less likely to become involved in wacky situations than his siblings. Since Eddie is always teamed with Birmingham Brown throughout the feature, Mantan Moreland has less screen time than usual and his performance is toned down somewhat. That is a decided positive for *The Jade Mask*.

There are, however, several problems with the film. Once Charlie Chan is called in to investigate Harper's killing on behalf of the government, which is interested in Harper's formula, things take a turn for the mundane. The direction of Phil Rosen adds nothing. Unlike the Chan films from Fox and 20th Century–Fox and much like the other Chan movies from Monogram, the supporting actors are mediocre at best. The one exception in this film is Alan (Al) Bridge as the local sheriff, who has a wry outlook on events at the Harper mansion, adding some needed wit to the proceedings.

Although there are a number of good suspects for Harper's murder within the mansion, the audience knows that the killer came from the outside, as evidenced by the mysterious figure disguised as the motorcycle policeman. Thus, when Lloyd Archer, Harper's stepson, suddenly arrives at the mansion and claims his right to the secret formula, the viewer knows that Archer is the killer. For once, the audience has more information about the crime than Charlie does!

However, to accept Charlie's explanations for the crimes, one must believe that Harper brought a life mask of laboratory assistant Meeker with him and that Harper could then perfectly imitate Meeker with no one being suspicious. Also, one must believe that after the butler was killed, he appeared to walk with the aid of a puppeteer's strings and that there was an air gun hidden inside a ventriloquist's dummy which could deliver the poison darts to the bodies of the victims. The whole scenario is hard to swallow.

While *The Jade Mask* is hardly a memorable murder mystery, it cannot simply be dismissed as just "one of those Charlie Chan films from Monogram." It surely has its interest. With the exception of *Charlie Chan in the Secret Service*, which is a true disaster, the other Monogram films to date have had their moments, providing some appeal for the avid Charlie Chan fan.

## *The Scarlet Clue* (1945)

Some of the joys of watching the Abbott and Costello films and the first season of their syndicated television series are those moments when some great vaudeville routines are performed by the great comedy duo. Famous comedy routines such as "Floogle Street," "Niagara Falls," and "Who's on First?" are presented and preserved for posterity on film, so that they can be enjoyed for all time. Similarly, *The Scarlet Clue* provides an opportunity for Mantan Moreland and his vaudeville partner, Ben Carter, to perform their comedy routine where each finishes the thoughts and sentences of the other. Moreland and Carter perform the routine twice in *The Scarlet Clue* and these are the highlights of the film. The two perform the bits as if they were really talking and listening to each other, in a slick yet comfortable manner that makes them entertaining. (The additional analogy to Abbott and Costello is obvious.) Thus, *The Scarlet Clue* provides a real service for comedy fans, preserving for posterity another great comedy routine performed by two consummate actors.

Unfortunately, that is about all that is enjoyable about *The Scarlet Clue*. In fact, much of the film is taken up with the comedy antics of those other famous comedy partners, Benson Fong and Mantan Moreland. Those two, unfortunately, have no comedy timing with each other; they are simply not funny. Even though he is bucking racial stereotyping, Moreland could be very funny on his own. However, with Benson Fong as his partner, Moreland's work seems artificial, probably because it is. What were those two doing in these films, investigating serious crimes on behalf of the federal government? The two together are often cringe-worthy, as they seem to be reading lines to each other rather than talking to each other. Moreland and Carter demonstrate the proper way that a comedy team is supposed to work. Unfortunately, Fong never learned from them.

So much of this discussion of *The Scarlet Clue* has been spent on a consideration of the comedy elements because, just as in many of the other Monogram Chans, so much of the film is spent on the comedy elements rather than the crime story. In what mystery there is in the film, Charlie is working on behalf of the federal government to locate a spy ring that is trying to steal government radar plans. Rausch, the chief suspect and Charlie's one lead to the spy ring, is killed at the beginning of the film, but there are two clues to his killer. One is a shoeprint in blood and the other is a lead to the Cosmo Radio Center, where Charlie finds a footprint which is identical to the one found at the murder scene. What an easy case for Charlie! He simply has to find the radio company employee with the shoe with the scarlet clue. For some reason, however, Charlie fails to take that basic step and thereafter there are three more murders before Charlie finally identifies the villain behind the spy ring.

While the radio setting and its related experimental television studio have some interest, as does a crazy weather tunnel in a scientific laboratory, the film itself has no pace. There is very little action, just a lot of talk and walking around the few sets that are employed. The direction by Phil Rosen is mundane as usual, except for a fairly interesting silent opening to the film as the police tail the spy, Rausch. The story makes little sense, as the villains do nothing much to steal the radar plans, which happen to be located in the same building as the radio studio. Two people are killed by remote control by means that are hardly convincing (and require each victim to voluntarily smoke a cigarette after inhaling a potentially deadly gas). There is an interesting death trap with an elevator whose floor opens by a remote switch, sending the victim on a deadly fall, but one has to wonder how the villain managed to install such a device on an office elevator and, for that matter, why.

The high point is the moment when Charlie realizes that the head of the spy ring is on the elevator of death. Charlie pulls the remote switch, causing the floor to open, sending the villain on a deadly plunge. For this rare occasion only, there seems to be a little of the malicious Mr. Moto in Charlie Chan. Everyone rushes to the basement to learn who the criminal leader is, with Charlie announcing that it is a she before the body of Mrs. Marsh, the nasty radio sponsor, is announced as the leader of the spies. Of course, Charlie had no way of knowing who the killer was in advance, unless he used the same technique as the audience does, which is identifying the least likely suspect. If Charlie had any clues to the chief villain, he kept them hidden from the audience, as usual.

*The Scarlet Clue* has its moments but they are few and far between. While the viewer

Charlie Chan (Sidney Toler), knowing that the head of the spy ring is on a rigged elevator, pulls the switch, causing the elevator floor to open and the culprit to fall to her death, in *The Scarlet Clue* (1945). Helping in the investigation, from left to right, are Tommy Chan (Benson Fong), Birmingham Brown (Mantan Moreland) and Captain Flynn (Robert E. Homans).

cannot expect these Monogram films to match the slick production values of the 20th Century–Fox films, there is no reason why the writing of these stories should also have been so inferior.

## *The Shanghai Cobra* (1945)

Journeyman Phil Rosen directed the first five Charlie Chans from Monogram, but for the sixth film, *The Shanghai Cobra*, Phil Karlson was brought in to helm the feature. The difference in visual styles between the two Phils is striking, particularly in the opening scenes of *The Shanghai Cobra*. Karlson clearly had an interest in film noir (contrast Karlson's direction of *Behind the Mask* [1946] with that of Rosen's in *The Shadow Returns* [1946], both from the Monogram Shadow series), and it shows in this film. The opening shot starts high and then moves down as a beautiful blond in a trenchcoat is walking down the street in the rain. She is being watched by a man in a car, demonstrated by the striking shot of the woman over the man's left shoulder and through the windshield and its fast wipers. The girl then begins to trail a man, later identified as a bank employee, who leaves the Sixth National Bank and goes into a coffee shop. There is an unusual shot of the back of the man as he walks, taken so low that the curb with the rain beating on it is prominent in the frame.

This classic noir style of film direction continues until the surprise death of the bank employee by, perhaps, a cobra bite. Since other bank employees have died in a similar fashion, Charlie Chan, who works for the government, is called into the case. He brings along No. 3 son Tommy and chauffeur Birmingham Brown, who have suddenly become Charlie's official assistants, not just interlopers in the investigation, bringing into question the extent to which the war years devastated the federal government's employee base. Was no one else available to assist the great detective?

*The Shanghai Cobra* does not have the plot of a film noir (with the blond at the beginning not a femme fatale and the private dick who is following her not an important character) and so, after the opening, the direction of the film turns largely to the mundane, with a scene of Charlie in Washington walking to a waiting taxi lifted directly from *Charlie Chan in the Secret Service* (1944). It is a shame that Karlson moved away from his innovative style employed at the beginning of *The Shanghai Cobra*, because thereafter the film becomes visually boring. Shooting scenes in the dark is not enough to make a feature into a noir film.

As the plot of *The Shanghai Cobra* starts to develop, it becomes so muddled that it makes little sense. The bank employee murders are somehow related to the vast radium supply that the Sixth National Bank is holding for the government. A gang of thieves is after the supply and intends to steal it from the bank's vault. Luckily for the thieves, there is a vast underground tunnel into the bank, making their task much easier. But with Tommy Chan and Birmingham Brown on the job, what chance do the thieves have?

This is another of the Chan Monograms which has an unusual killing device, this time a poisonous needle in a juke box. While that is superficially interesting, it has the same problem as the electromagnetic device set off by a switch under the piano in *Charlie Chan in the Secret Service* (1944) and the elevator with the floor that opens in *The Scarlet Clue* (1945): How did the villain install it and how did he know his victims would ever be there so that he could use it? It also has a little of the James Bond quality of the bullets made of frozen blood in *Black Magic* (1944). These Monogram films are a long way from the Charlie Chan books about realistic crimes and solutions based upon ratiocination.

Charlie is trapped in the bombed tunnel but escapes in a ludicrous way: sending a Morse code message over a live telephone wire in the tunnel. After the radium thieves are captured, there are two more mysteries to solve. One involves the identity of a bandaged murderer who escaped from a boat in Shanghai after Charlie arrested him many years before. However, any B-mystery movie fan will recognize the voice of the man under the bandages, so there is no surprise there. Charlie then identifies a bank officer as the surprise leader of the gang, but the real surprise would be if any viewer even remembers who that character is, since he has been missing from the feature for most of its length.

After a strong opening, *The Shanghai Cobra* quickly becomes another letdown in the Charlie Chan series.

## *The Red Dragon* (1945)

*The Red Dragon* displays both the strengths of the Monogram Chans, few though they may be, and exhibits the weaknesses of the films, of which there are many. Thus, *The Red Dragon* is another disappointing Chan entry.

The MacGuffin in this case is information concerning the discovery of a new element that could be used to create a bomb many times more powerful than the atomic bomb. The information is contained in the secret papers of Alfred Wyans, who is living in Mexico

City. Wyans' secretary Dorn is an undercover federal agent and as the film opens, he beseeches Inspector Luis Caverro of the Mexican police to send for Chan. Caverro agrees to do so but the next day, at a luncheon party held by Wyans, Dorn is shot and killed. Just before dying, he types a cryptic clue on his typewriter. Although the shot was heard by Wyans and his five guests, along with Inspector Caverro, no gun is found at the scene. Also, even though only one shot was heard, two bullets are discovered — one in Dorn's body and one in the wall. To add to the mystery of Dorn's death, it is discovered that the bullet that killed Dorn has no firing marks on it, indicating it was not fired by a gun. So how was Dorn's murder accomplished?

Luckily for the Mexican police, Chan arrives to assist in the investigation. Unluckily, he brings along, for no apparent reason, Tommy Chan and Birmingham Brown's cousin, Chattanooga Brown. Chattanooga is introduced as Charlie's chauffeur, and Caverro never thinks to ask Charlie why he would bring a chauffeur along on a plane ride from Washington, D.C., when Charlie will have no car in Mexico. Apparently, waste in government is not just a recent phenomenon.

As poor a film as *The Red Dragon* is, it does have some strengths, just as many of these Monogram Chans do. As was common in these films, the setup is intriguing, as the movie is as much a howdunit as a whodunit. In the end, though, there is another James Bond–like solution for the method of murder, which is not very convincing, undercutting much of what has gone before. Also, the second bullet hole in the wall is never explained, unless this viewer was dozing near the end of the feature.

The death clue on the typewriter is also engrossing, as at first it seems to be all gibberish. Eventually Charlie cleverly realizes that one of the letters is a typo, mistakenly typed by Dorn as he was dying. He is then able to understand what Dorn was trying to communicate about his own murder in the last seconds of his life. In addition, a part of the last section of the film works as a solid police procedural, with Charlie diligently following the clues to the whereabouts of Wyans' secret papers. However, once again, that positive is undercut by Charlie seeming to guess as to the identity of the killer. Of the original five suspects for Dorn's murder (one is later killed), there is nothing to distinguish one from the other. While that was often also the case in the Fox and 20th Century–Fox Chans, here it is worse, because the suspects almost always appear together in the film, as if they are tied together. Thus, when the killer is revealed, it is another one of those "who cares" moments.

Part of the reason why the viewer has trouble distinguishing between the suspects is the direction of Phil Rosen, unfortunately back at the helm for *The Red Dragon*. Most scenes start with a wide establishing shot of all of the people in the room, and that shot, plus perhaps one slightly closer, is all that Rosen employs. The viewer never gets close enough to the suspects to even attempt to start to distinguish them. This type of direction, with so few changes in view, also adds to the languorous pace of the feature.

The one notable performance in the film is that of Fortunio Bonanova as the Mexican Inspector Caverro. The Spanish actor gives a convincing performance, competent and persistent. If this film had been done in the Warner Oland era, it would have been titled *Charlie Chan in Mexico* and Harold Huber would have played Caverro, overacting as usual to the detriment of the movie.

Mantan Moreland as Birmingham Brown is missing, but Willie Best as his cousin Chattanooga, is in the film for comic relief. For those who criticize Moreland for his role in the Chan series (and there is much to criticize in the manner in which the part of Birmingham Brown is written), it is unfair to criticize Moreland personally. Moreland was the consummate performer, clearly bringing some energy to the films and even, once in a while, some humor. He was important enough to the series to usually receive a high billing, second only to Sidney Toler and then Roland Winters. All one has to do is contrast Best's performance in this film with the previous ones of Moreland's to gain a real appreciation of Moreland's comic abilities. Tommy Chan would never have treated Birmingham Brown in the deprecating way he treats Chattanooga in this feature, partly because, paradoxically, Birmingham is a strong character.

As set forth in the introduction to this chapter, when a Charlie Chan movie is really bad, there are always the aphorisms to provide some entertainment. Unfortunately, over the last several films, there have been few, if any, aphorisms. *The Red Dragon* is no exception. Most of Charlie's "clever" expressions in these films have simply been insults thrown at Tommy. Without the aphorisms, are these really Charlie Chan films?

Despite the interesting setup and the suspenseful conclusion, as the murderer is tracked in the dark with his identity being revealed at the last instant, the negatives far outweigh the positives in this feature. *The Red Dragon* is a very poor film, with no pace and little suspense. It may still be worth a view, however, just to watch Sidney Toler dancing the rumba.

## *Dark Alibi* (1946)

Once again, Phil Karlson replaces Phil Rosen as the director of a Charlie Chan film and the contrast in style and quality of the direction is patent. The opening scene is a stunner. There is no dialogue as one crook uses a blowtorch on the large handle of a basement vault while two others, dressed in dark business suits and hats, are on watch. There is very little light in the basement, much of it coming from the blowtorch. A guard comes down the steps; he is seen by the viewer only in shadows. A shot is heard and one of the burglars looks down on the floor, indicating that the guard has fallen there. Suddenly, there is a loud explosion, the screen turns bright and the vault has been blown open. The last shot is of the feet of the villains as they walk to the vault.

Unfortunately, *Dark Alibi* is still a Monogram film and Karlson does not have the budget to sustain this style of direction throughout the feature. The visual style of the rest of the film is more typical of standard mystery fare. At least Karlson's direction does not detract from the efficacy of the storytelling. And, once again, there is a good mystery being told here, although it is undercut somewhat by the over-emphasis on comedy and some sloppy plotting.

Ex–convict Thomas Harley, who lives with his daughter June at a boarding house called the Foss Family Hotel, is arrested for the bank robbery because his fingerprints were found at the scene. Harley denies he was ever at the site, stating that he received a note from his former cell mate, Dave Wyatt, and went to the Carey Theatrical Warehouse to meet him. There, Harley was locked in by mistake. Harley's tale is not convincing, and he is tried and convicted. With only nine days left before Harley's execution, Charlie gets into the case in response to June's plea to prove her father innocent. Charlie begins to suspect the fingerprint evidence since there were two similar bank robberies around the same time with similar fingerprint evidence. He eventually ties the scheme back to the penitentiary where Harley had been incarcerated many years before. Charlie then identifies the multiple culprits involved in the burglary scheme and clears Harley.

The Charlie Chan films from Monogram tended to be better when Charlie was inves-

In *Dark Alibi* (1946), Mrs. Foss (Edna Holland), center, the owner of the Foss Family Hotel, looks on as Charlie Chan (Sidney Toler) shows Emily Evans (Joyce Compton) one of her stage outfits that was recently found at the Carey Theatrical Warehouse, an important location in the film.

tigating a murder, rather than working for the government. Charlie never truly seemed to be in his element when he was working in spy stories; his forte was murder mysteries, as shown by most of the films he made at Fox and 20th Century–Fox. Also, a race-against-time backdrop, with Charlie required to finish his investigation in mere days in order to prevent the execution of Thomas Harley, adds to the spice of the film. However, for all the rush and the deadly consequence if Charlie fails, *Dark Alibi* has a surprising lack of tension. The reason may be that the viewer never really gets to meet and become emotionally involved with Harley and his daughter. The viewer is therefore always a mere observer of what is going on, rather than becoming immersed in the anxiety of the situation. A similar storyline was handled much better in *Charlie Chan in London* (1934).

Part of Charlie's investigation is engrossing, particularly when he ties the most recent burglary to the prior two, including the similarity in fingerprint evidence and the involvement of ex-convicts from the same prison. However, the police expert cannot quite confirm Charlie's suspicions, because he cannot replicate a forging of fingerprints without the right mixture of skin oils. These scenes, along with the opening, are the strongest moments in the film.

However, the whole story does not make a lot of sense, when viewed in retrospect, particularly the fact that just about everyone at the Foss Family Hotel seems to be involved in the crimes. Also, there is a cheat. The prison guard, Hugh Kensey, is fingered as the leader of the gang. Kensey supposedly framed Harley in part because Kensey was interested in June, and Harley objected. However, the viewer only learns about this in retrospect. It is implied, although admittedly not stated, that Kensey first met June when she was visiting her father in prison. How hard would it have been to slip Kensey's relationship with June into some of the film's dialogue, to also give the viewer a chance to solve the crime? However, the writers do deserve some credit for throwing suspicion on the warden, when they have Charlie ask if the same warden was at the prison when Harley served his time there many years before.

The real problem with *Dark Alibi* is the comedy stylings of Mantan Moreland and Benson Fong, a mismatched comedy team if there ever was one. There seems to be more of them in this film than in many of the previous Monogram Chans and they are simply not funny. In scenes which make no sense, they walk through the penitentiary in civilian clothes, getting into trouble. Then there is the walk through the Carey Theatrical Warehouse inserted, not for plot purposes, but so that Moreland can perform his scared routine once again. On this occasion, it is particularly demeaning, with Moreland talking to his shaking legs and then mistaking a skeleton for Tommy Chan. At least Ben Carter is back, with Moreland and Carter performing their vaudeville routine in which they finish each other's sentences, a routine they previously performed in *The Scarlet Clue* (1945).

With a little more emphasis on the mystery and on the team of Moreland and Carter, *Dark Alibi* would have been a substantially better film. Nevertheless, because of the strength of its mystery elements and some of the direction, *Dark Alibi* is still one of the best of the Monogram Chans.

## *Shadows Over Chinatown* (1946)

Because *Shadows Over Chinatown* is a very late film for a Monogram Chan starring Sidney Toler, most viewers, including your author, would expect little out of the feature. In fact, the film is a pleasant surprise. *Shadows Over Chinatown* is more in the nature of a private eye story than a classic whodunit and since that is an unexpected change of pace for the Charlie Chan series, the film is well worth a view.

With the end of World War II, Charlie seems to have lost his job working for the government. He now appears to be a private investigator, in this case working on behalf of an insurance company which has recently paid out two claims on the lives of wealthy individuals who were murdered just after they married. Why Charlie never went back to the Honolulu police force after World War II is never explained.

As *Shadows Over Chinatown* commences, Charlie, son Jimmy and chauffeur Birmingham are on a bus, heading to California to investigate a murder case involving an armless, legless and headless body, which Charlie believes may be the torso of the wife of one of the murder victims. While on the bus, Chan learns that elderly Mrs. Conover is traveling to San Francisco to search for her missing granddaughter, Mary Conover. Charlie agrees to assist in that search also. Not surprisingly, those seemingly unrelated matters come together at the end of the film, as Mary used to work at an escort agency, whose owner has masterminded the insurance scam. Charlie eventually captures the lead villain and returns Mary to her grandmother.

*Shadows Over Chinatown* seems like a private eye story even though Charlie never walks down mean streets, never becomes involved with a dame and never engages in fisticuffs. Rather, the subject is traditional private eye stuff, namely, an insurance scam involving murder, the particularly gruesome torso murder (although it is just talked about and never shown), two additional murders and several other attempted killings. There are scenes at the Missing Persons Bureau, which are set up by a voice-over narration at the beginning of the film, the only time this narrative device was used in any Chan movie. The plot involves an escort service which implies something more adult in nature than the usual Chan subject matter. At the end of the film, two seemingly unrelated matters become intertwined. All of this is conventional private eye material.

Of course, this unusual story is set within the usual trappings of the Charlie Chan movies. Birmingham Brown is back to provide the comic relief, this time supported by Victor Sen Yung, reprising his role as Jimmy Chan. Mantan Moreland and Sen Yung have more chemistry together than Moreland and Benson Fong ever did, helping to make the comic relief more bearable in this feature than in many of the prior films. Also, since Jimmy and Birmingham are involved in the plot, including trailing suspects and assisting in the final trap of the killer, their material is better integrated into the storyline, once again making it more effective.

Another interesting aspect of *Shadows Over Chinatown* is that, probably for the first time, Charlie is unable to solve the crime. Charlie is so bamboozled by private detective Jeff Hay that Charlie never figures out that Hay is the master criminal. This results in Charlie never preventing the police from giving Mary back to Hay at the end of the film, putting Mary's life in danger. Nevertheless, Charlie's error allows the film to have a suspenseful conclusion, always a plus for a mystery movie.

*Shadows Over Chinatown* has an inexplicable beginning. While the bus passengers are warming themselves inside by a fire while the bus is being repaired, a hand appears at the door with a gun, a shot rings out and Charlie is shot. He is luckily saved by the watch in his pocket, which stops the bullet. But who shot at Charlie? It could not have been Jeff Hay, who was in the room at the time. The only logical candidate is the bus driver who was the sole person out of the room at the time. When it turns out that the bus driver was a phony, the conclusion seems accurate. However, the bus driver disappears right after the bus reaches its destination, never to be mentioned again. No explanation is ever given as to who attempted to kill Charlie and why. Also, how often do you see a chauffeur in full uniform riding on a bus?

*Shadows Over Chinatown* is no masterpiece but by this time in the Hollywood mystery cycle, there were few masterpieces being turned out in any of the mystery movie series. Thus, a little bit of innovation in the storyline combined with an adequate production pushes *Shadows Over Chinatown* just a little bit higher on the quality ladder than the other series mysteries of the same time period.

## *Dangerous Money* (1946)

In *Dangerous Money*, Charlie Chan is back on a murder cruise, something he has done several times before in his film adventures. On this occasion the ship is the S.S. *Newcastle*, which is bound from Hawaii to Samoa and then to Australia. Scott Pearson, an undercover agent for the Treasury Department, tells Charlie that he is on his way to Samoa to investigate the sudden appearance of money and artwork stolen from Philippine banks during the Japanese invasion. Pearson is concerned about two previous attempts on his life made during the trip. Pearson's concern is justified because during a cruise show in the salon later that night, Pearson is killed by a knife thrown into his back.

The salon is filled with suspects, including Freddie Kirk, who performs a knife-throwing act for the passengers; blustery P. T. Burke, a trader in cotton; Tao Erickson and his Polynesian wife Laura who own a restaurant on Samoa; stuck-up missionaries Reverend and Mrs. Whipple; absent-minded Professor Henry Martin and his wife; and Rona Simmons, an English tourist who is in love with the ship's purser, George Brace. The problem is that with the exception of Laura, all of the suspects appear to have been in the salon when the knife was thrown at Pearson from the outside. For some reason, Charlie does not address that anomaly in his investigation.

Paradoxically, the later Sidney Toler films at Monogram often seem better than the earlier ones. One possible reason for this, of course, is that they may actually be better. The later films are definitely helped by the fact that they are more like traditional whodunits than spy movies, a particular failing of the prior films in the series. An alternative reason, however, may be that a viewer, watching them in chronological order, becomes so used to their mediocre quality that critical standards drop.

Whichever it is, *Dangerous Money* has its interest, as Charlie conducts a real investigation into a real murder mystery. It is complicated by the question of why Rona Simmons came on board the ship without proper papers, and also by a blackmail attempt of Simmons by P.T. Burke. Once Charlie deals with those side issues, the true inquiry comes into focus. In the end, the solution is a double surprise, as almost all of the passengers appear to be involved in the scheme involving the stolen paintings and money, and the actual killer turns out to be Mrs. Whipple, who is actually a man, Joseph Murdock, dressed as a woman.

Unfortunately, the solution does not hold together all that well. In looking back at the early part of the film, it appears that Whipple-Murdock was in the salon when Pearson was killed, undercutting the entire resolution of the murder mystery. Charlie states that he suspected Mrs. Whipple was a man by the way she/he walked at the restaurant earlier that evening, but the replay discloses there was nothing unusual in her/his manner of walking. Perhaps that is why there are no replays, official or not, in mystery movies.

Nevertheless, the whodunit itself is absorbing, aided by a number of killings late in the film, caused by the unusual murder weapon of a knife shot from a gun. Charlie is particularly aggressive in this film, actually becoming involved in a shootout with some of the suspects. Charlie shows that he is pretty good with a gun, wounding two of the villains. Also, every Chan fan must enjoy the moment when Charlie, held at gunpoint by a villain, turns off the lights so that he can escape and then capture the crooks. In every other Chan film, it is the villain who turns off the lights. A Chan cliché has been turned on its head!

Victor Sen Yung is back as No. 2 son Jimmy and Willie Best once again replaces Mantan Moreland as Charlie's chauffeur. Which famous detective would not bring a chauffeur along on an ocean cruise? Luckily, the two comedians are not too obtrusive in the film, although they are not very funny either. However, since Sen Yung and Best almost always appear together in the film, just as a Chan offspring and Moreland do in most of the other Monogram Chans, the direct humor between Charlie and his sons, often the highpoint of a Fox or 20th Century–Fox film, is lost. Once again, *Dangerous Money* is no masterpiece but it is not too bad, either. It simply goes to show that Monogram had the ability, from time to time, to produce a pretty good murder mystery on a very low budget.

## *The Trap* (1946)

Sidney Toler starred as Charlie Chan in a total of 22 films, 11 at 20th Century–Fox and 11 at Monogram. That is the record number of appearances as the lead in any Hollywood mystery movie series and, one suspects, international mystery film series as well. Toler died of cancer in early 1947. *The Trap*, produced during the summer of 1946 and released late that same year, contains his last screen appearance. Surprisingly, although Toler was in ill health at the time of shooting, he appears quite robust playing Chan, at least until the end of the film when he is slow to get to the vehicle that is supposed to chase after the killer.

Another surprise in *The Trap* is the unusual number of outdoor scenes, some involving cars and motorcycles along the highway and others involving a California beach. This is the first Chan film in almost 15 years that had significant location shooting, and the natural settings give it a nice flavor. Also, much of the cast is comprised of young and pretty female performers, and they bring another breath of fresh air to what had become a stodgy mystery series. Thus, the filmmakers seemed to be making a significant effort to break out of the mold of the prior Chan films, and on the surface, at least, *The Trap* appears to have much going for it. Unfortunately, despite these best efforts, *The Trap* simply does not work.

Showgirl Lois is forced by Marcia, the star of Cole King's performing troupe, to steal some letters from another performer's trunk. Before Lois can complete her task, she is strangled by an unknown assailant with a rope or bathrobe belt. Lois' body is discovered by San Toy, a Chinese member of the troupe, and because suspicion quickly falls on her, she calls her friend Jimmy Chan for help. That brings Charlie, Jimmy and Birmingham Brown to the beach house to solve the murder. Charlie, who has no official status whatsoever, is given free rein to investigate the crime by the local policeman.

Marcia is strangled next, and her body is discovered on the beach. At the end of the film, a trap devised by Charlie smokes out the killer. Then, at the culmination of the slowest 70 MPH car chase in film history, the killer's car goes over a cliff. The killer dies but not before admitting her villainy and explaining her motive.

As it turns out, the murderer is, well, one of the members of the cast but because there are so many female characters it is hard to remember exactly which one she is and, frankly, what her position with the troupe is. However, her motive is, well, something she reveals just before she dies which is something that has never come up previously in the film, so why does anyone care? It may be that the killer's motive was her animosity to Cole King, but if that is the case (and the movie is so mixed up that it may not actually be), then the identity of the killer and her motive make no sense. Why not just murder Cole King instead? Yet, that is not the worst part of the film. Chan's investigation, such as it is, is deadly dull and the characters do and say things that make no sense, such as press agent Rick Daniels vehemently accusing Cole King of the murders, with no evidence, and one of the showgirls continually screaming for no reason.

As for trying to bring something fresh to the series, there is a moment when an intruder is discovered in the house and when everyone goes to investigate, the intruder is, what a surprise, Jimmy Chan. Monogram apparently decided to bring back a chestnut from the Charlie Chan movies from 20th Century–Fox. Then there are the moments when Birmingham investigates something in the dark basement of the beach house, acting scared to death and even being frightened by his reflection in the mirror. Monogram apparently also decided to bring back a chestnut from the prior Charlie Chan movies from Monogram. While Moreland was sometimes funny in these Chan films, by now his attempts at comedy have become so repetitive that there is little chance that he could ever become humorous again in the series.

At the end, Charlie sets a trap for the killer, apparently justifying the title of the feature. However, since that has been done so many times before by Charlie, most of the prior films in the series could also have been titled *The Trap*. Thus, a film that starts out with a breath of fresh air ends up as a typical Monogram Chan with the exception of one more matter, and an unfortunate one at that: Charlie's signature attribute, the aphorisms that he speaks, have totally disappeared.

## THE ROLAND WINTERS FILMS AT MONOGRAM

### *The Chinese Ring* (1947)

For anyone watching these Hollywood mystery movies in chronological order, *The Chinese Ring* can be disconcerting. After 22 straight Charlie Chan films starring Sidney Toler, it is difficult to accept Roland Winters in the lead role. Winters' first impression is not good, as he makes little effort to appear Chinese, although his regular use of the traditional Chan aphorisms, which seemed to be missing from the last few Toler films, is a plus. Then there is the fact that Victor Sen Yung, who has been playing No. 2 son Jimmy Chan since 1938, is now playing No. 2 son Tommy Chan, with no explanation. (It does not help that, in the credits, Yung's name is misspelled "Young.") Also, the plot seems remarkably familiar.

As the film opens, Chinese Princess Mei Ling appears at Charlie's house, asking for help. Birmingham Brown leaves the woman in the front room while he goes to Chan's laboratory to tell Chan about his visitor. As the princess waits for Chan to appear, a window opens, a hand and a blow gun appear, the sound of the firing of a dart is heard, and the princess stumbles to the ground, but not before writing "Captain K" on a note pad. Chan calls the police and gum-chewing Sergeant Bill Davidson arrives to investigate the murder. He is followed by his girlfriend, newspaper reporter Peggy Cartwright.

It turns out that the princess was in America to purchase airplanes for her brother's military back in China. She brought a substantial sum of money, some of which is missing. Suspicion immediately focuses on the two Captain Ks in the film. One is Captain Kong, top man on the ship which brought Princess Ling to America, and the other is Captain Kelso, who was supposedly going to sell her the airplanes. While the two captains are nefarious characters, surely capable of committing murder, Charlie eventually identifies an unexpected character as the killer.

*The Chinese Ring* has little going for it. The film moves at a languid pace, with very little happening during the entire feature. There is almost no background music, adding to the viewer's feeling of ennui. The direction is unremarkable. The performances are consistently uninspired, with Warren Douglas as Sergeant Davidson being particularly irritating as he chews his way through several packs of gum but accomplishes little else.

Indeed, the film is so boring that, for once, the viewer actually wants to see more of Mantan Moreland. At least Moreland brings some energy to the moribund production and, at least once in a while, a slight smile to the viewer's face. However, as a result of the addition of the banter and interaction between the policeman and the female reporter, both Moreland and Sen Yung are relegated to minor supporting parts in the film. Sen Yung, in particular, disappears throughout the entire middle section.

The reason this film seems so familiar is that it is a remake of *Mr. Wong in Chinatown* (1939), itself a disappointing feature. As long as Monogram wanted to save money by recycling an old mystery script, why couldn't it have found a good script to use? Most of the plot problems with the prior feature have not been corrected in *The Chinese Ring*. As noted in the essay on the Wong film, near the end of the film, why do the villains demand that Chan come to banker Armstrong's house and then why do they abduct him? A reason is proffered but the real reason is that it is an attempt to bring some excitement to the end of the film, with Chan captured and his life in danger. (The strategy does not work and the ending of the film is as boring as the rest of the movie.) Because it is necessary for Davidson to rescue Chan on Captain Kong's ship, it just so happens that Captain Kong loses his hotel key at Armstrong's home, giving Davidson that one lucky clue that points to Kong's ship. Since there is no evidence against Armstrong, Chan happens to be at his house when Armstrong takes a call about a headstone at a pet cemetery, allowing Chan to guess that Armstrong killed a young Chinese boy and buried him at the cemetery.

The list of questions and inconsistencies in the plot of *The Chinese Ring* could go on and on. Many more are raised in the essay on *Mr. Wong in Chinatown* in Chapter 18 of this book. Plot inconsistencies can sometimes be overlooked if a mystery movie has an interesting setting, innovative camerawork, striking performances or a tension-filled climax. *The Chinese Ring* has none of these. If at all possible, it is a worse film than *Mr. Wong in Chinatown*.

## *Docks of New Orleans* (1948)

Monogram was still skimping on the budget in this second Charlie Chan movie with Roland Winters, once again recycling a plot from an old Mr. Wong movie. This time, at least, it is one of the better storylines from the Wong series, having been used previously for *Mr. Wong, Detective* (1938). Unfortunately, once again, the plot was handled better in the original version. *Docks of New Orleans* is not much of a film.

Chan, who now makes his home in San Francisco and appears to be a private detective, has, for no apparent reason, moved temporarily to New Orleans with his son Tommy (previously known as Jimmy) and his butler Birmingham Brown (previously his chauffeur). Come to think of it, there has never been any explanation proffered as to why Charlie did not return to the Honolulu police force after the end of World War II and why he abandoned his wife in Hawaii with too many children for one woman to handle. Also, there is nothing so special about New Orleans that required Charlie to move there for this film. The city's name may not even be mentioned in the movie, and *Docks of San Francisco* would have been an adequate title for this programmer — not that much of the action takes place around any docks in any event.

Businessman Simon Lafontanne comes to Charlie with a problem. He believes that he has been followed by an unseen enemy ever since he agreed to transport some containers of chemicals in one of his boats. Charlie agrees to help, particularly since Lafontanne is almost kidnapped in front of Charlie's house by a fake chauffeur. Lafontanne's dead body is later discovered in his office. Oscar Swendstrom is an obvious suspect, since he has been accusing Lafontanne and his two partners of stealing a secret formula for poison gas from him. Swendstrom came to Lafontanne's office on the day of the murder brandishing a gun but since Lafontanne died from poison gas emitted from a shattered radio tube, Swendstrom seems innocent (although the police arrest him in any event). Other obvious suspects are Lafontanne's two business partners, who succeed to his interest in their company, and the group of foreigners who are trying to locate the secret formula for the poison gas. At the end of the film, Chan narrowly escapes death, captures the foreigners and announces the surprise murderer.

Everything about *Docks of New Orleans* is half-hearted. Roland Winters displays little charisma in the role of the great Chinese detective and even less energy. The director seems unable to employ multiple camera set-ups for any scene, and close-ups are at a premium. The only highlight of the film is Carol Forman's appearance in a sexy nightgown. Any viewer hoping to get another good look at Forman later in the film will be disappointed since there are few close-ups of anyone in the feature.

The movie is a half-hearted remake of the earlier Mr. Wong film. In order to create some differences between the two movies, screenwriter W. Scott Darling changed the method of murder from police sirens breaking a vial of poison gas to the high-pitched voice of an opera singer on the radio breaking a radio tube full of poison gas, changing the method of murder from one that is clever to one that is ridiculous. At the end of the film, Charlie is captured by the gang of foreigners, who threaten to kill him unless he gives them the poison gas formula. Why would anyone believe that Charlie, a private detective, has that formula? Then, by Charlie breaking a radio tube and pretending it contains poison gas, the villains start experiencing poison gas symptoms, allowing them to be captured. How unbelievable is that scenario?

In one scene, Birmingham Brown meets old friend Mobile Jones and they start to talk. As part of their byplay, they do the routine where each finishes the other's thoughts, done twice before in these Monogram Chans by Mantan Moreland and his vaudeville partner, Ben Carter. However, Carter had passed away by the time of this film and Haywood Jones is a poor substitute for Moreland's partner. Thus, the routine is short and not funny, just padding to fill the running time of *Docks of New Orleans*, one of the worst of all the Chan films.

## *The Shanghai Chest* (1948)

*The Shanghai Chest* is the first of the Roland Winters Chans which is not a remake of a Mr. Wong film, but it too has an unoriginal script. There are the usual Chan scenes— the suspects brought together in one room at the end of the film, an obvious ploy to trick the killer into confessing, no explanation as to how Charlie solved the murders, No. 2 son getting himself arrested and Birmingham Brown being scared of anything related to death. The central plot device, the use of forged fingerprints, was previously employed in *Dark Alibi* (1946).

A dark figure sneaks into Judge Wesley Armstrong's study and stabs the judge, who was working at his desk. The judge's nephew, Victor Armstrong, enters the study, discovers the body and is slugged in the head by the same assailant. By the time he awakens and starts fingering the murder weapon, the police arrive and arrest him for the murder. District Attorney Frank Bronson is then murdered. At the scene of each crime, the fingerprints of Tony Pindello are discovered, which is surprising since Pindello was executed by the state about six months before. Bronson had prosecuted the Pindello case and Armstrong was the presiding judge. When a member of the Pindello jury is then murdered, it appears that all of the recent murders are related to the conviction of Pindello, who may have been innocent. At the end of the film, however, Charlie fingers an unexpected party as the killer, with a motive unrelated to the Pindello matter.

To say that the identity of the killer is a surprise to the viewer is, quite frankly, a meaningless statement. Whoever Chan identified as the killer would be a surprise. None of the cast (it is unfair to call them suspects) is given any particular attention during the film and

In the opening scene of *The Shanghai Chest* (1948), a mysterious killer is about to knife Judge Wesley Armstrong (Pierre Watkin), the first in a series of alphabetical murders.

they are all ciphers to the viewing audience. While mention is made of an insurance scam that is being investigated (it turns out to be the true motive for the killings), that scam is never tied into any of the cast. Charlie does conduct a feet-on-the-pavement investigation, visiting numerous insurance agencies and funeral parlors to ferret out clues (something the police were better equipped to do than Charlie), but Charlie discovers very little on those expeditions that leads him to the solution of the crimes. On the other hand, perhaps he does discover something important as a result of those efforts. Since no explanation is given as to how Charlie solved the murders, perhaps he found something in his tireless investigations. It would be nice to know.

Of course, since Charlie gives no explanation as to how he solved the crimes, he also has no evidence against the killer. Thus, Charlie employs the obvious device of placing a gun with blanks near the suspect, hoping the suspect will give himself away once Charlie accuses him of the crimes. Apparently the suspect does, even though it is hard to tell whether he really admits to anything or not. Nevertheless, Charlie has solved another case which was too hard for the police or the audience to understand.

There is not much point in addressing the technical aspects of the production since the film's story is such an unconvincing mystery, exemplified by the fact that when the cast is assembled at the end of the film, none of them are potential suspects for the murders, including the person who committed the murders. That leaves time for the viewer to question the economics of Charlie's situation in the Roland Winters films. Chan is apparently a private investigator who undertakes cases on behalf of the police for which he receives no pay. But Charlie must pay a fulltime chauffeur and also provide for a son who is well past the age at which he should have had his own job. Also, Charlie must have huge support and alimony payments each month for his large family which he abandoned in Honolulu many years before.

How does Charlie make it? By the late 1940s, that is the only good mystery contained in these Charlie Chan movies.

## *The Golden Eye* (1948)

It is amazing to view scenes shot in the real outdoors in a Chan film from Monogram. Most of the Monogram Chans are claustrophobic in the extreme, seeming to be shot almost entirely on small sets, with any outdoor scenes shot either indoors or on studio-made city streets without any wide angles to give any feeling of openness. That is why the scenes at the dude ranch in *The Golden Eye* and some other outdoor moments are as refreshing as the outdoor scenes for *The Trap* (1946). In addition, *The Golden Eye* is the first Chan adventure set in the American West in almost 15 years, the last being *Charlie Chan's Courage* (1934) based on the Biggers novel *The Chinese Parrot*.

*The Golden Eye* has an unusual plot for a late Charlie Chan film. Charlie is employed by Manning, an Arizona mine owner who is being followed wherever he goes. In addition, there have been attempts on his life, including one in Chinatown in San Francisco. Charlie goes undercover at a dude ranch adjacent to Manning's Golden Eye Mine. However, by the time Charlie reaches the great outdoors, Manning has had a serious accident in the mine; he lies on his bed with his face completely bandaged, near death. Charlie begins to investigate and learns that significant gold shipments are suddenly coming out of Manning's mine, even though it was believed that the mine had been tapped out. Charlie solves that incongruity, rounds up the gang of villains and unmasks the surprise leader of the gang.

With the production and location changes and a plot that is not a typical Chan whodunit, *The Golden Eye* has some fresh elements to it, making it the best Chan film starring Roland Winters to date. That is not saying much, as the Winters films were all disappointing and that includes, unfortunately, *The Golden Eye*. The production is slow-moving, the performances merely adequate and the direction non-existent. Although Victor Sen Yung stands out in his role as Tommy Chan, it is only because Sen Yung is too old to be playing the part of a No. 2 son. The humor that used to come from Tommy's/Jimmy's youthful exuberance falls flat here.

Oddly, one of the best things about the film is Mantan Moreland, once again playing Birmingham Brown. Even after all of the Chan films in which he has appeared, Moreland's enthusiasm, comic timing and verbal and facial tricks are still worth a look. Though his material is still not very good, Moreland is once again able to turn bad writing into good laughs, by way of performance alone. When Birmingham discovers the leg of a dead body in a mine tunnel, the laughs all come from Moreland's performance, not from the writer or the director.

The plot idea of smuggling cheap Mexican gold into America and selling it through an American mine at higher prices was used previously in *Gold Racket* (1937), from the Allan O'Connor-Bobbie Reynolds mystery series. Few people will notice the purloining of that plot idea because few people have ever watched *Gold Racket* or perhaps, even if watched, can remember the film. However, how many viewers are surprised that the fake nun caring for Manning wears high heels, indicating that she is not a nun? That idea is lifted directly from Alfred Hitchcock's *The Lady Vanishes* (1938) and few mystery fans will fail to recognize Monogram's reuse of that iconic mystery moment.

Other plot twists will fail to surprise knowledgeable mystery fans who will know, even before it actually happens, that another person will be substituted for the completely bandaged Manning who is lying on the bed "unconscious." Those fans will also know, almost from the time that the character first appears in the film, that the least likely suspect, the one who appears to be assisting Charlie, will turn out to be the leader of the villains.

Despite some attributes that permit it to stand out from Winters' previous Chans, *The Golden Eye* is still not much of a movie. Its qualities are drowned out by an inconsistent mystery plot, obvious plot twists and the excruciatingly slow pace.

## *The Feathered Serpent* (1948)

It is nice to see that even very late in the Monogram Chan series, the filmmakers were still attempting to introduce some variety. The first and most obvious novelty here is the return of Keye Luke as No. 1 son Lee Chan. Luke has second billing in the film, with large type announcing, "Featuring Keye Luke." Luke's return justifies the significant credit since he had last played Lee Chan ten years before in *Charlie Chan at Monte Carlo* (1938). This is also the only chance to see Luke and Victor Sen Yung in the same Chan film, although it would have been nice if Sen Yung were playing his signature role of Jimmy Chan instead of the erroneously named Tommy Chan. The location of the film is Mexico, only the second time that country was used for the locale in a Chan film, and the movie opens with some outdoor scenes. From the opening credits of the film, at least through its first few minutes, *The Feathered Serpent* displays a lot of potential.

Vacationers Charlie, his two sons and Birmingham Brown are on their way to Mexico City when they discover an injured and exhausted man lying on the road near the town of San Pablo. When the Chan family drives into San Pablo to locate a doctor, they are advised that the man is Professor Scott, who, along with fellow archaeologist Professor Farnsworth (coincidentally a friend of Charlie's), is in Mexico to attempt to discover the lost Aztec Temple of the Sun and its hidden treasure. The two archaeologists have been missing for months and an expedition was just about ready to start out to try to locate the missing men, as well as the treasure. Among the members of the search party are Farnsworth's sister Joan and his fiancée Sonia. Professor Scott is knifed in the back before he can disclose the location of the Temple. Joan asks Charlie to join the expedition to assist in finding Farnsworth. Charlie agrees and his entourage accompanies him into the mountains where they discover death, betrayal, Professor Farnsworth and a hidden treasure.

As promising as *The Feathered Serpent*'s opening is, that is how disappointing the remainder of the film turns out to be. The opportunity to have two Chan sons in one film is wasted, as they have very little interaction. Indeed, there is no differentiation between the characters of Lee and Tommy; the two are almost interchangeable. It would have been nice if Lee had acted as an older and wiser brother to Tommy, but instead the main difference is that Tommy still performs in a comic duo with Birmingham Brown, with few individual moments of his own. Lee has only mild interaction with Birmingham. Once again, Mantan Moreland is one of the few elements of the film that is somewhat enjoyable. While most of his schtick has been seen many times before, he does get off a few good one-liners.

Another problem is that there is very little mystery. The audience learns about halfway through that the ringleader of the gang is archaeologist John Stanley, the fiancé of Joan and a mole in the expedition. Thus, the film becomes an inverted mystery, with the only question being how Charlie will discover Stanley's villainy on his own. Unexpectedly it is Lee Chan who first deduces that Stanley is the villain, although Charlie deprecates the deduction when it is first broached by Lee. Similarly, Birmingham is the first one to discover the hidden tomb, even though by accident, so that without Birmingham, Charlie would never have solved the case. At the end, Charlie announces the surprise killer of Professor Scott, although Charlie gives no indication as to how he made the discovery and he has no evidence to support his conclusions. Frankly, it appears that he is making it all up, just so that he can be given credit, however undeserved, for solving another murder.

In the end, though, the most significant problem with *The Feathered Serpent* is that it is deadly dull. Sluggish direction, uninterested performances, poor writing, scant mood music and the failure to make better use of the potentially suspenseful setting of the inside of the hidden tomb doomed the movie to failure almost from the beginning. While a little creativity at the beginning of the film is nice, those new ideas are not enough to carry the weak production values and a tepid script. *The Feathered Serpent* is just as disappointing as the rest of the Chan films starring Roland Winters, if not more.

*Note*: *The Feathered Serpent* is a partial remake of *The Riders of the Whistling Skull* (1937), a Three Mesquiteers Western. Oliver Drake is credited as the screenwriter on both films.

## *The Sky Dragon* (1949)

Oddly, this last film of the Charlie Chan series is the best of the six movies starring Roland Winters and it is the equal of the best of the Monogram Chans starring Sidney Toler. That is not to say that the film compares well to the Chan pictures from Fox and 20th Century–Fox; it does not. However, given what it is, the last gasp of the Hollywood mystery movie series of the 1930s and 1940s, it does work within that framework.

Chan and his son Lee are on board a commercial airliner when a daring robbery takes place. Someone drugs the coffee of all of the passengers and the crew and, after everyone passes out, steals a valise containing $250,000 which was brought on board by a courier. Something must have gone awry with the crook's plans because when Lee, the first passenger who wakes up, discovers the robbery, one of the representatives of the insurance company which was protecting the money is dead, having been stabbed in the back. Always willing to help in a murder investigation, Charlie agrees to assist the insurance company and the police in solving the crime, which he does, but then almost loses his life when the killer tries to make a daring escape from a plane flying on automatic pilot, with the gasoline shut off.

Most reviewers do not appreciate *The Sky Dragon*, which has received almost nothing but negative reviews. What those critics are missing, it seems, are some clever variations on the Chan formula. The first 15 minutes or so are set in the confines of a relatively small airplane, which surely helps with the budget of the movie, but also adds to the effectiveness of the scenes, as the claustrophobic effect of the confined setting adds to the tension of the fight. The sound of the airplane engine substitutes for background music as the many suspicious passengers on the flight are introduced. Admittedly, once everyone disembarks, the film hews more closely to the Monogram Chan formula, with Chan routinely assisting the police with bits of Birmingham Brown thrown in from time to time. Even then, Char-

This scene is representative of the increased stature of Lee Chan (Keye Luke), far left, in *The Sky Dragon* (1949). Lee is protecting his father, Charlie Chan (Roland Winters), with mustache, from gun-wielding Andy Barrett (Lyle Talbot). Andy's wife Connie (Elena Verdugo) looks on.

lie and Lee do some real detective work, trying to determine the identity of a passenger's wife through boots-on-the-ground investigative work, making this portion of the film similar to a police procedural.

The crime itself is clever, with all of the passengers and crew on the airplane drugged, so that the valuable shipment of money can be stolen from the courier and presumably thrown out the plane door with a parachute, to be collected by an unknown confederate on the ground. The problem is that if the pilots are drugged, who is going to land the plane? That makes the pilots the chief suspects. Only they would know when the loot should be thrown out of the window so that it could be found by the confederate below, and they are the only ones on board who could be sure that the plane could land safely, with everyone supposedly drugged.

That proposed solution to the criminal enterprise highlights the several good clues to the killer in *The Sky Dragon*. It is actually highly unlikely that any bag thrown out of the plane could ever be found below in a timely manner, so that method of disposing of the money makes little sense. Since it was first suggested by Anderson, the insurance investigator, he becomes a suspect. However, since the plane and the passengers would undoubtedly be searched after landing, how could Anderson get the fortune off the plane? When his employer W. E. French is allowed to talk to Anderson after the landing, the method is obvious. French is the one who will be able to take the scratch away from the aircraft without being searched. Another good clue is that Anderson does not recognize the stewardess, Marie Burke, whose real name is Connie Barrett, even though he had her arrested five years before. Since Marie does not show any signs of recognizing Anderson, perhaps they are in cahoots.

Unfortunately, the formerly astute Chinese detective Charlie Chan does not immediately understand these clues and he allows Anderson to stay involved in the investigation, permitting him to dispose of witnesses who are about to reveal important information about the case. For the mystery fan, such as your author, who cannot pick up subtle clues but always recognizes the obvious ones, it is clear that Anderson is the killer. Any mystery devotee who has watched a number of these B–mystery movies understands one rule of these types of films: Whoever shoots and kills a suspect who is about to reveal important information, even though the killing seems justified at the time, is always the murderer.

Another plus is the characterization of Lee Chan. In *The Sky Dragon*, Lee is not just comic relief. He overpowers a man with a gun, protects his father when Charlie has a risky encounter with one of the suspects, makes good suggestions about what to investigate next, flies a plane, rescues a man from a fire and makes effective use of a disguise at the denouement. This depiction of No. 1 son is closest to the one in *Charlie Chan in Paris* (1935), Lee's first appearance in the series, before all of the Chan offspring became primarily comic relief. At one point in *The Sky Dragon*, Charlie says to Lee, "Increasing wisdom of No. 1 son give much pleasure to humble father." That is a far cry from the somewhat nasty things Charlie said about his children in prior Chan films from Monogram. It is a very satisfying moment for devout Chan fans and a long time coming.

With all of that, *The Sky Dragon* is slow-moving, with indifferent direction, unexceptional acting and almost no background music (and when it does come, the background music is particularly jarring). The plot is marred by the cliché of the killer always happening to arrive in time to eliminate a witness by a shooting or beating over the head or to destroy physical evidence before Charlie can find it. Nevertheless, *The Sky Dragon* cannot be dismissed out of hand, simply because it is the last Chan film, made late in the 1940s at a time when the budgets for this type of film was minuscule. *The Sky Dragon* has a lot going for it.

After 44 films (not counting *Behind That Curtain* [1929]), the Charlie Chan series finally came to an end with *The Sky Dragon*. The films had been produced at three different studios (Fox, 20th Century–Fox and Monogram) and had starred three different actors in the lead role (Warner Oland, Sidney Toler and Roland Winters). Several actors played Chan offspring in the series, but Keye Luke, Victor Sen Yung and perhaps Benson Fong were the most famous. It was truly an incredible run of almost 20 years.

When Oland passed away after completing *Charlie Chan at Monte Carlo* (1938), the quality of the film series still remained high, with Toler undertaking the role with no discernible damage to the product. In fact, *Castle in the Desert* (1942), the last film from 20th Century–Fox, is one of the best in the series. The precipitous drop in quality came when the series moved to Monogram. The quality dropped even more for the Roland Winters films. Three of the six Winters films were remakes, not original scripts. More importantly, Winters never seemed comfortable in the role of the Oriental detective.

Most people find *The Sky Dragon* to be unsatisfactory, just like most of the rest of the Monogram Chans. By 1949, few lamented the end of the Charlie Chan series.

## AFTERWARDS

After the conclusion of the Chan series, Roland Winters continued working sporadically in films and television, with no significant roles. He passed away on October 22, 1989.

After Keye Luke left the Chan series upon the death of Warner Oland, he was never out of work in Hollywood. During the war years, he appeared in several Universal serials and played villainous Asian roles such as a Japanese agent in *Across the Pacific* (1942) but more often performed in positive Asian roles such as a hero in *A Yank on the Burma Road* (1942) and in several films in the Dr. Gillespie series. Later, Luke had recurring roles and made numerous guest appearances on television. Probably his best-known TV role was as the blind monk Master Po on *Kung Fu* with David Carradine, which aired on ABC from 1972 to 1975. Luke also supplied the voice of Charlie Chan in the animated Saturday morning series *Amazing Chan and the Chan Clan*, which began airing on CBS in 1972. Luke passed away in 1991.

Victor Sen Yung was also busy after he left the Chan series, with small roles in feature films and guest appearances on television. His best-known television character was Hop Sing, the cook to the Cartwright family on the long-running series *Bonanza*, which started in 1959. Sen Yung passed away on November 9, 1980.

Mantan Moreland was very busy in films throughout the 1940s but work dried up for him in the 1950s, when his type of comedy began to seem particularly out-of-date. His film and television career had a small resurgence in the 1960s. Moreland passed away in 1973.

Almost from the beginning of the film series, Charlie Chan was a fixture on the radio. In 1932 and 1933, Walter Connolly played Chan on the NBC Blue Network in serial dramatizations of three Biggers novels, *The Black Camel*, *The Chinese Parrot* and *Behind That Curtain*. From 1936 to 1938, Connolly played the role in a series on the Mutual Network. In 1944 and 1945, Ed Begley starred as Chan on various networks and in 1947 and 1948, Begley and Santos Ortega played Chan in a series broadcast, once again, on the Mutual Network. All of the shows were titled *Charlie Chan* or *The Adventures of Charlie Chan*.

Chan first made it to television in 1957 via a syndicated show called *The New Adventures of Charlie Chan*. J. Carrol Naish, a regular guest star in mystery movie film series of the 1940s, portrayed Chan and James Hong played his son, Barry. The television show, which was primarily filmed in England, lasted for only one season. Interestingly, the Chan of the Biggers novels did have a son named Barry. He was born near the end of *Behind That Curtain* (1928) and was named after another character in the story.

There was also the animated show about the Chan children mentioned above. Thereafter, Ross Martin played Chan in the made-for-television movie *The Return of Charlie Chan*, which was filmed in 1971 but was apparently so bad that it did not air until 1979. In terms of films made for the big screen, the only other Chan film produced was *Charlie Chan and the Curse of the Dragon Queen* (1981), a misguided spoof with Peter Ustinov woefully miscast as the Oriental detective.

# 4

# Arsène Lupin
## *The Gentleman Thief*

Of the many oxymorons that have become commonplace in regular speech, such as metal woods in golf or guest hosts in television, mystery stories and mystery films seem to have only one: the gentleman thief. In addition to other gentlemen thieves of literature who also made it to the cinema in the 1930s, such as Raffles and the Lone Wolf, there was France's Arsène Lupin. Actually, the first collection of short stories about Arsène Lupin, published in 1907, was titled *Arsène Lupin, Gentleman-Burglar*. However, "burglar" seems such a nasty term for this type of individual, who only steals from the rich while maintaining the most impeccable of manners. "Thief" is a much more delicate and appropriate term.

Whatever the word employed, the Arsène Lupin stories and films are not for those who enjoy gritty mystery tales of the hardboiled city. However, for those who like fantasy stories of sophisticated thieves mingling with the wealthy as equals, the Arsène Lupin films should not be missed.

## Background

### The Maurice LeBlanc Stories

Maurice LeBlanc was born on November 11, 1864, in Rouen, France. He was educated in France, Germany and England, even attending law school for a time. Thereafter, he worked in the family shipping business, wrote a few novels, became a police reporter and wrote magazine stories. In 1905, the editor of a new French periodical, *Je Sais Tout*, asked LeBlanc to contribute something along the lines of the very popular Sherlock Holmes stories which were appearing regularly in *Strand* magazine. It was then that LeBlanc invented the character of Lupin for the story "The Arrest of Arsène Lupin."

As the title indicates, the short story ends with the arrest of Lupin by Ganimard, the famous French detective, as Lupin is trying to leave a ship with some purloined items hidden in a small camera. However, the character proved so popular that in a subsequent story, Lupin escapes from jail to thereafter pursue a life of crime while taunting the police about crimes he is about to commit. Lupin is aided by the fact that he is a master of disguise. Lupin does battle with the best of the French detectives but also, from time to time, with a thinly disguised Sherlock Holmes, sometimes renamed (for copyright reasons) Holmlock Shears or Herlock Sholmes. Late in his career, Lupin changed attitudes and worked on the side of the law, eventually becoming a full-fledged detective.

## Early Films

Lupin was the subject of many silent European and American films, starting in America with *Arsène Lupin* (1917) with Earle Williams. In 1919 there was *The Teeth of the Tiger*, apparently based upon LeBlanc's 1914 novel of the same name. David Powell played Lupin in that film. In 1920, Wedgewood Nowell played Lupin in *813*, which was presumably based on the 1910 novel with the same title.

None of these films appears to have been a major production and none of them sparked a series. However, early in the sound era, MGM turned to the character for a major motion picture and followed it with a sequel several years later.

## The Film Series

In actuality, there is no American film series about Arsène Lupin. However, in the 1930s and 1940s, there were three Hollywood films released about the French thief. Each starred a different actor in the lead role and the supporting casts were also different.

The first American sound film about Arsène Lupin was titled, fittingly enough, *Arsène Lupin*. Released by MGM in 1932, the film is about several thefts of valuables by the master criminal, including the stealing of the Mona Lisa from the Louvre, even after he notified the police that he intended to commit the crime.

Lupin was played by John Barrymore, one of the top Hollywood stars of the early 1930s. Born in 1882 in Philadelphia, Pennsylvania, Barrymore began acting in silent films in 1914. He appeared in several memorable films from that era, such as playing the title characters in *Dr. Jekyll and Mr. Hyde* (1920) and *Don Juan* (1927). His career hit its peak in the early 1930s in films such as *Grand Hotel* (1932), *Dinner at Eight* (1933) and *Twentieth Century* (1934). While seldom thought of as a performer in mystery films, Barrymore, in fact, has a long résumé in the genre. In the silent era, he played the title characters in *Raffles, the Amateur Cracksman* (1917) and *Sherlock Holmes* (1922). In the sound era, after appearing in *Arsène Lupin*, he appeared in three Bulldog Drummond films in the late 1930s, playing Colonel Nielson. Barrymore passed away in 1942.

The sequel was *Arsène Lupin Returns*, released in 1938. Here, and as usually happened when the character of the sophisticated cracksman was brought to the silver screen, Lupin may now be reformed, trying to assist the police in investigating a series of thefts that someone is trying to pin on Lupin. Or, perhaps, Lupin has actually returned to his life of crime. Although the actors and the director from the first film have changed, this is a true sequel, as mention is made of the ending of 1932's *Arsène Lupin*, (the French police contend that Lupin is dead, having been shot when he attempted to escape the police by jumping off a bridge into the river).

By the time of this second film, Barrymore's alcoholism was affecting his career and most of his films were now being made for studios other than MGM. Melvyn Douglas, a significant star in his own right, was given the role of the famous upper-class thief. Douglas, whose career is discussed in greater detail in this book's chapter on Joel and Garda Sloane, had recently played a gentleman thief in *The Lone Wolf Returns* (1935), based on the works of Louis Joseph Vance.

*Arsène Lupin Returns* was the last Lupin film released by MGM and it seemed that the character's American screen career was at an end. However, in 1944, Universal produced its only Lupin film, *Enter Arsène Lupin*, starring Charles Korvin. In this film, Lupin works as a professional thief while at the same time protecting a young heiress from the murderous schemes of her relatives.

Unlike Barrymore and Douglas, who were well-known Hollywood performers by the time each performed in his Lupin film, *Enter Arsène Lupin* was the first significant screen appearance for Korvin. The actor, who was born in 1907 in Hungary, had a short screen career. He played another jewel thief, although hardly one who could be deemed to be a gentleman, in *The Killer That Stalked New York* (1950). For mystery fans he starred in *Interpol Calling*, a 39-episode series about the international law enforcement agency, shot in England in 1959. Korvin died in 1998.

## THE FILMS

### *Arsène Lupin* (1932)

In addition to being the most famous American movie about the gentleman thief from France, *Arsène Lupin* is significant for being the first of several feature films to co-star the Barrymore brothers, from one of the most famous acting families in all of screen history. John plays Lupin, and it is as if Maurice LeBlanc and the screenwriters wrote the role especially for him. He is handsome and suave, conceited and confident, well-dressed and devious. He carries the film past some of its unconvincing plot issues solely on the strength of his personality and acting abilities. It is easy to see why he was a major star at MGM in the early 1930s.

Lionel Barrymore plays Guerchard, the French policeman hot on the trail of Lupin. Lionel was an excellent actor, particularly well-remembered today for character parts in two of his later films, *It's a Wonderful Life* (1946) and *Key Largo* (1948), but he was also an important player in the 1930s in films such as *Dinner at Eight* (1933) and *You Can't Take It with You* (1938). In *Arsène Lupin*, however, Lionel is disappointing. He displays nervous mannerisms, never seeming to be sure what to do with his hands. He is sometimes semi-slumped over, sometimes not, often cranky, sometimes not. In the war between Lupin (John) and Guerchard (Lionel), it is easy to surmise who the winner will probably be.

*Arsène Lupin* starts out with a robbery at the home of Parisian millionaire Gourney-Martin. Lead policeman Guerchard arrives on the scene with his men. When they stop a fleeing car, they discover the passenger tied up and claiming to have been robbed. Guerchard is suspicious, believing the man to be Arsène Lupin even though the man says he is the Duke of Charmerace. Guerchard handcuffs the passenger and is about to take him to jail when Gourney-Martin identifies the suspect as the real duke, just as he claims. Guerchard, forced to free the man, is humiliated. Luckily, the robbery was not a success because, as Gourney-Martin explains, none of his valuables was in his Paris home; they were actually at his country estate. Perhaps Gourney-Martin should not have been so quick to disclose that information in front of the Duke of Charmerace. The duke still seems to be acting just a little bit suspiciously.

The rest of the film is a cat-and-mouse game between Lupin and Guerchard, with Lupin usually having the upper hand. Lupin notifies Guerchard that he will be at the duke's ball that night, and, in fact, while there, steals jewels from under Guerchard's nose. Later, Lupin steals valuables from Gourney-Martin's estate and the Mona Lisa from the Louvre. Guerchard's main tactical response is to force a beautiful young criminal, Sonia, to go undercover and keep an eye on the duke. When Sonia falls in love with Lupin, that scheme of Guerchard's goes haywire, as do most of his other plans. In the end, though, Guerchard finally has some success and arrests the duke (Lupin). But will Guerchard ever get him to jail?

*Arsène Lupin* is an A–movie, with a good cast and solid production values. In addition to the strong performance by John Barrymore, Karen Morley is a revelation as the enigmatic Sonia, alternately police informant, criminal and love interest for Lupin. It is unusual to see Morley playing the romantic interest in a sophisticated film and she is lovely in the part. There is some fairly mature dialogue between Lupin and Sonia (particularly when they first meet) reflecting the pre–Code nature of the film.

Despite its many virtues, *Arsène Lupin* has not stood the test of time well. The plot is flimsy at best. The tricks that Lupin pulls on the police are unconvincing. He has secret information about many matters, such as where the real Mona Lisa is hidden, which assists him in his crimes, but there is no explanation as to how Lupin obtains his information. Lupin seems to have many people working for him, but there is no explanation as to why they do so. The ending of the film, which is superficially clever, is simply an attempt to try to satisfy both the supporters of Lupin and the supporters of the police, resulting in neither being completely happy. The film is mostly talk, with little action and even less excitement. Clever dialogue seldom fully compensates for a lack of a strong plot, and it does not do so in this film.

For those who are interested in seeing one of the consummate film actors of his generation perform one of his best roles, *Arsène Lupin* is worth seeing. For most others, it will seem dated and slow-moving.

*Note on the Source Material*: According to the credits, this film was based on the play *Arsène Lupin*, written by Maurice LeBlanc and Francis de Croisset, which premiered in Paris in 1908. LeBlanc then adapted the play into the novel *Arsène Lupin, An Adventure Story*, first published in 1909.

There is little similarity between the plots of the novel and the film, although a few of the ideas in the film do come from the novel. In both versions, Lupin masquerades as the Duke of Charmerace but Guerchard quickly suspects it's a ruse. Just as in the movie, there is also a character in the book named Sonia who is not totally honest.

The one scene in the movie that is lifted directly from the novel occurs when Lupin threatens, by a note, to steal some paintings of Gourney-Martin. The police send a number of officers to guard the house and yet the paintings are stolen anyway. It turns out that the guards were not real policemen; they were actually Lupin's men. Lupin had drugged the real policemen and stolen their uniforms. This clever scheme of Lupin is taken from the book and dramatized in the film, although in a different context than in the novel.

## *Arsène Lupin Returns* (1938)

While Arsène Lupin eventually does return in this film, it surely takes him a long time to do so and since his name is now Rene Farrand, the viewer is not really sure that Lupin, in fact, has returned. Indeed, much of the beginning of the film focuses on American detective Steve Emerson, as he first investigates the theft of a valuable jewel in America and then travels to France to protect the jewel on behalf of an insurance company. Emerson is played by Warren William, so the cast of *Arsène Lupin Returns* has two actors who played another

Two of Arsène Lupin's (Melvyn Douglas, center) associates from America, Alf (E.E. Clive), on the left, and Joe Doyle (Nat Pendleton), on the right, have traveled to France to see if Lupin is still interested in a life of crime rather than being a gentleman-farmer, in *Arsène Lupin Returns* (1938).

cinema thief, the Lone Wolf, i.e., Melvyn Douglas in *The Lone Wolf Returns* (1935) and William in a long series of films beginning with *The Lone Wolf Spy Hunt* (1939). Both are prime suspects of the French police for the series of crimes that occur in *Arsène Lupin Returns* and both are also suspicious of each other.

FBI agent Emerson loses his job when his supervisor decides that all the publicity over his exploits has limited his effectiveness on behalf of the government. Emerson goes into private practice but before he can undertake his first job, which is to protect a valuable emerald owned by the Count de Grissac, he finds his client, the client's niece Lorraine and their cousin George Bouchet tied up and robbed. Emerson also discovers a card with the name "Arsène Lupin" written on it and a bullet in the wall shot from an older style of French gun. Has master thief Arsène Lupin started a life of crime in New York?

The thief absconded with only a paste imitation of the necklace and so Emerson is off to France with the Grissacs to help protect the real emerald. There, Emerson meets Lorraine's fiancé, the handsome and sophisticated Rene Farrand, and a rivalry ensues, both over the affections of Lorraine and their mutual suspicions that the other is a jewel thief. While in France, there are other attempts to steal the emerald, and then a murder occurs before the real criminal is finally identified.

While he only has third billing, *Arsène Lupin Returns* is, in many ways, Warren William's film. The first part of the film in New York is all about him and even when the tale moves to France, William has considerable screen time. This is a much better role for William than Perry Mason, whom he had recently portrayed in four films at Warner Brothers, as William's light-hearted yet sophisticated personality better fits the part of the suave investigator, Steve Emerson. When Columbia was later looking for an actor to play the reformed jewel thief, the Lone Wolf, in a series of films, it is likely that *Arsène Lupin Returns* was the film that brought William to the mind of the studio decision makers.

Melvyn Douglas is also quite good as Arsène Lupin, although he is not as striking in the role as John Barrymore was in *Arsène Lupin* (1932). Virginia Bruce is lovely as Lorraine Grissac but the part is really filler material, ancillary to the main plot of locating the jewel thief. There are other well-known character actors throughout the film, such as George Zucco in the atypical role of French police detective and Nat Pendleton and E.E. Clive as two former partners in crime of Arsène Lupin. Since everyone speaks English, whether in New York or France, there is no problem having English–speaking actors in all of the roles, large or small.

*Arsène Lupin Returns* is a pleasant enough diversion, with likable performers and witty dialogue performed in the Hollywood fantasy world of wealthy sophisticates. Unfortunately, the film is little more than a diversion. The plot is flimsy, which is why so much time is spent with the banter between Virginia Bruce and her two co-stars. Instead of using comic relief as filler material, *Arsène Lupin Returns* uses romantic relief to stretch the film's running time. While there is a true mystery as to who the real jewel thief is, when the perpetrator is finally identified, his identity makes no sense whatsoever.

Amid all the fluff involving the goings-on of the sophisticated class, the filmmakers never took the time to create a sophisticated mystery. Thus, while *Arsène Lupin Returns* has much appeal early on, in the end, it turns out that it is all surface appeal, without an effective mystery structure at its foundation. *Arsène Lupin Returns* will be disappointing for the true mystery fan.

## *Enter Arsène Lupin* (1944)

By the 1940s, the Lone Wolf, a famous jewel thief, and Boston Blackie, a former prison inmate, had given up their respective lives of crime and were now attempting to assist the police in their criminal investigations. Around that same time, it seemed that Arsène Lupin had gone the identical route because in *Arsène Lupin Returns* (1938), the prior film in the Lupin series, Lupin appeared to have permanently given up his life of crime. But in *Enter Arsène Lupin*, Lupin returns to his roots as a thief extraordinaire, giving the film a hero and a storyline which are refreshingly different from those of most of the mystery movie series of its era.

Lupin opens the film with the theft of a valuable emerald from Stacie Kanares while en route to Paris on the Orient Express. However, upon meeting Stacie and seeing how beautiful she is, Lupin returns the emerald to her, pretending he found it under the seat in her train compartment. Lupin then follows Stacie to England, where he immediately purloins the valuable Rembrandt painting "Laughing Girl" and a valuable psalm book. Lupin's crime wave would have continued unabated except that he encounters Stacie once again, when she is driving out of control down a winding mountain road in a car with brakes that have failed. Lupin rescues her but is suspicious because there is an excessive amount of grease

Arsène Lupin (Charles Korvin), in top hat, ushers Ganimard (J. Carrol Naish), the French policeman, into his abode to show him that there are no stolen valuables inside, in *Enter Arsène Lupin* (1944). Constable Ryder (Leyland Hodgson) and his assistant Pollett (Tom Pilkington) look on.

on the brakes. Lupin's suspicions are confirmed the next day at a picnic with Stacie, when a poisonous snake is discovered in the picnic basket. The remainder of the film concerns Lupin trying to save Stacie from her murderous cousins (who are desirous of Stacie's emerald) and eluding the tenacious Etienne Ganimard, a policeman who has come all the way from France to capture the notorious thief.

The acting is particularly strong in *Enter Arsène Lupin*, led by Charles Korvin as the title character. The Hungarian–born actor is particularly handsome, with his arresting chin cleft and European features. He imbues the role with a cosmopolitan suavity, even when treating matters with a bemused attitude. Ella Raines is exceedingly good-looking as Stacie Kanares, with a hairstyle reminiscent of Veronica Lake. Gale Sondergaard and Miles Mander, two performers who played villains in the 1940s Sherlock Holmes films from Universal, are also in the cast and they give excellent performances as always, this time playing Stacie's murderous cousins.

The versatile J. Carrol Naish plays Ganimard, the persistent French policeman. This is an unusual role for Naish and he overplays it a little, sometimes appearing more like Inspector Clouseau than a competent investigator. Yet it is Ganimard who cleverly traces the whereabouts of Lupin through his purchase of a case of rare wine and who finally puts the handcuffs on him (although not before Lupin has placed the handcuffs on Ganimard), so perhaps Ganimard is appearing to be a foreign eccentric in order to trap Lupin.

*Enter Arsène Lupin* works because the filmmakers deftly intertwined two stories that were absorbing on their own, creating one particularly effective storyline. While Lupin is surely a thief, he falls within the fictional subcategory of a gentlemen thief. The ambiguity in his character is shown by his giving the stolen psalm book to an orphanage, providing it with a chance to obtain needed funds by returning the ancient tome for a large reward. Thus, it is not surprising that even though Ganimard is hot on his trail, Lupin tries to protect Stacie from her avaricious relatives, even at some risk to himself. As a result, it is Stacie's emerald that eventually provides Ganimard with the evidence to arrest Lupin after many long years of the chase. It may be true that beauty killed the beast, but it was also Lupin's good heart.

The end of the film is particularly stunning. Lupin appears to have made a clean escape, until through an unforeseen circumstance he is arrested for stealing Stacie's jewel. However, it soon appears that Lupin has tricked Ganimard one last time and escape is inevitable. But no, Scotland Yard is on the job and Lupin is captured for good. *Enter Arsène Lupin* has more plot twists in the last few minutes than practically any other mystery movie of its kind, making the picture stand out from the other movies of the Hollywood mystery series.

The title *Enter Arsène Lupin* implies that this was to be the first film in a new mystery series. That turned out not to be the case, and no other Lupin films were produced by Universal. Given the quality of *Enter Arsène Lupin*, that is a huge disappointment for the mystery fan, even after all the years that have gone by.

## Afterwards

Maurice LeBlanc continued writing Arsène Lupin stories well into the 1930s. He died on November 6, 1941.

Lupin was always more popular in Europe, particularly France, than in America, from the time of the earliest works through the present day. This lack of popularity in America is reflected in other media interpretations of the character of the gentleman thief. While there have been several other films about the character from around the world, the last being a 2004 European production, *Enter Arsène Lupin* (1944) is the last U.S. feature film to date. Similarly, while there have been several television versions of the character, from as far away as the Philippines, there have been no American television (or even radio) productions.

LeBlanc wrote a number of stories about the duels between Lupin and a character who was obviously patterned after Sherlock Holmes. Because LeBlanc wrote the stories, Lupin always outwitted the famous English detective. However, over time and particularly in America, Holmes has become the undisputed winner of that rivalry. Today, Holmes is still one of the most recognized fictional figures of all time while Lupin is virtually unknown in this country.

# 5

# Hildegarde Withers
## *The Teacher Detective*

In the modern era of crime fiction, female detectives are tough, action-oriented and, on occasion, even hard-boiled. This type of character is epitomized by Sharon McCone (created by Marcia Muller), V.I. Warshawski (created by Sara Paretsky) and Kinsey Milhone (created by Sue Grafton).

In the first hundred years or so of crime fiction, however, that was not usually the case. The female detective, to the extent there even was one, was usually older, more sedate and often referred to as a spinster. There was Miss Cornelia Van Gorder, a middle-aged spinster created by Mary Roberts Rinehart for *The Circular Staircase* (1908). There was Miss Maud Silver (created by Patricia Wentworth) an elderly governess who in retirement became a private investigator. And of course there was Miss Jane Marple, Agatha Christie's very famous elderly detective, from the village of St. Mary Mead.

In terms of mystery movie series, the first female detective to receive a movie series during the sound era was Hildegarde Withers, the schoolteacher with the acerbic wit. Each of her films was based on a novel or short story by Stuart Palmer, the creator of the spinster detective. Actually, and although it is customary to refer to this group of female detectives as spinsters, the term does not really apply to Withers since, at the end of her first recorded case, *The Penguin Pool Murder* (1931), she received a marriage proposal which she accepted (at least until the next book about the character).

## Background

### The Novels

Stuart Palmer was born in Baraboo, Wisconsin, in 1905. He attended the Chicago Art Institute and the University of Wisconsin before undertaking a variety of jobs, such as iceman, sailor, taxi driver, editor and ghost writer. He contributed some stories to *College Humor* magazine and then, in 1931, wrote his first mystery, *Ace of Jades*. Later that year, his first Hildegarde Withers novel, *The Penguin Pool Murder*, was published, leading to a very successful series about the character. In all, Palmer completed 13 Withers novels during his lifetime (another one was completed after his death) and also wrote numerous short stories about his amateur detective.

Withers is an elementary school teacher at the Jefferson School in Manhattan. She is about 40 years old and a strict disciplinarian when it comes to her students. Her first case,

*The Penguin Pool Murder*, begins during a field trip with her students to the New York Aquarium. A later case, *Murder on the Blackboard*, involves a murder at Withers' school. In almost all of the stories, Withers assists Inspector Oscar Piper of the New York police, whom she first met during the penguin pool murder case. Piper, a man of indeterminate age, usually has a badly lighted cigar hanging from one corner of his mouth.

At the end of *The Penguin Pool Murder*, Piper proposes marriage to Withers and she accepts, even though they barely know each other. As the novel ends, they are off to City Hall to procure a license. In later books, however, although they remain friends and respect each other, the romance and marriage is gone. As Miss Withers remembers, in *Murder on the Blackboard*, their engagement, which occurred in the flush of excitement over solving the aquarium murder, lasted for about half an hour, as Piper was forced to speed off on another case, giving Withers the opportunity to change her mind.

## The Film Series

Starting in the early 1930s, RKO produced a six-film series about Hildegarde Withers and Oscar Piper. The first was *Penguin Pool Murder* (1932), based on Palmer's 1931 novel *The Penguin Pool Murder*. Just as in the book, the film tells the story of the initial meeting between Withers and Piper, when a murder is discovered at an aquarium during a field trip by one of Withers' classes. Luckily for Piper, Withers sticks around and solves the crime for him.

In subsequent films, murder was always the puzzle to be solved, whether occurring in a school, on an airplane, a bridle path, a park or backstage in a Broadway theater. In each film, Inspector Piper was always fortunate to have Withers around to unravel the mystery and identify the killer.

In one of those rare, inspired moments of movie casting, Edna May Oliver was chosen to play Hildegarde Withers. Oliver was born in Malden, Massachusetts, in November 1883, making her about the right age to play Miss Withers during the early 1930s. Oliver was a descendant of John Quincy Adams, the sixth president of the United States. At an early age, Oliver became interested in performing and in her teenage years, she quit school to pursue a career in entertainment. She was on Broadway by 1916 and in the 1920s was receiving significant roles on the stage. At the same time, she also began appearing in silent films. She eventually became a contract player for RKO, with an important early sound success in *Cimarron* (1931), which won the Oscar for Best Picture. The Hildegarde Withers series followed shortly thereafter.

James Gleason played Inspector Oscar Piper in all six films. Gleason was born in 1882 in New York City, making him a natural to play the New York policeman, who usually pronounces the word "murder" as "moider." After fighting in the Spanish-American War, Gleason married Lucile Webster, an actress, and the two began appearing in theaters on the West Coast. His earliest success in films was as writer, drafting the screenplay for the musical *Broadway Melody* (1929), which won the Best Picture Oscar. He also had a small part in that movie. Although Gleason appeared in silent films, his acting career did not take off until the 1930s, when he began appearing regularly in films. Even though *Penguin Pool Murder* was made in 1932, Gleason had already appeared in over 20 sound features and shorts by the time of that film's release,

After the third film in the series, *Murder on a Honeymoon* (1935), Oliver left RKO to sign with MGM. While that was a positive career move for her, it left a big hole in the Hildegarde Withers series, since Oliver was so perfectly cast as the schoolteacher-detective. For the fourth film in the series, *Murder on a Bridle Path* (1936), Helen Broderick played Withers. Broderick was born in 1891 in Philadelphia, Pennsylvania. As a teenager, she became a chorus girl with the Ziegfeld Follies. She later worked in vaudeville with her husband, Lester Crawford, and had success on Broadway in the 1920s. In films, she usually had comedy roles playing the friend or chaperone of the heroine, most notably in the Astaire-Rogers films *Top Hat* (1935) and *Swing Time* (1936). The mother of actor Broderick Crawford, she passed away in 1959.

For the last two films in the series, *The Plot Thickens* (1936) and *Forty Naughty Girls* (1937), ZaSu Pitts was brought in to play Withers. Pitts was born in 1894 in Parsons, Kansas. Her strange first name is a combination of two of her aunt's names, Eliza and Susan. In the early 1900s, she and her family moved to California, where she began appearing in silent films in 1917, the most notable of which was *Greed*, Erich von Stroheim's 1924 movie which is now considered a classic. Pitts had a dramatic part in that film and a few others, but her primary screen work was in comedies, sometimes starring in shorts and features but usually performing as a character actress in bigger-budgeted films. Starting in the 1940s, in addition to her screen work, she also appeared regularly on the stage, on radio and then on television. Her last screen appearance was in a major comedy, *It's a Mad Mad Mad Mad World* (1963). Pitts passed away that year.

## The Films

### *Penguin Pool Murder* (1932)

*Penguin Pool Murder* is a strong start to a new mystery series. Even though the whodunit is quite good on its own, its strong reputation comes from its clever writing and the acting of Oliver and Gleason.

The setting is a New York City aquarium, where there is a surprising amount of intrigue. The director of the facility, Bertrand B. Hemmingway, is upset at Gerald Parker, his stockbroker, believing that Parker has caused him significant losses in the recent stock market crash. Parker's wife Gwen has asked her former lover, Philip Seymour, to come to the aquarium so that she can hit him up for a loan. Someone, presumably Hemmingway, calls Gerald and tells him that his wife is at the facility. The jealous Parker rushes to the building to confront Gwen. Meanwhile, a deaf mute pickpocket, Chicago Lew, is working his way through the facility. Suddenly, the body of Parker drops into the penguin tank, where it is discovered by schoolteacher Hildegarde Withers. It is then up to Withers to solve the crime, which she finally does, but not before Inspector Piper of the New York police arrests the wrong parties and brings them to trial.

Oliver is dynamite as Hildegarde Withers. This is the role for which she was born. With her fussy manners, tilted head, modulating voice, deprecating sniff and expressive eyes, she delivers her lines with an acerbic wit, making them all the funnier. Gleason, as Inspector Oscar Piper, matches her line for line. The rail-thin Piper is alternately fussy and competent and alternately tolerant of and exasperated by Withers. Piper often has a cigar in his mouth or hand which, like a cat's tail, often helps to convey the mood he is in. He is an excellent foil for the witty Miss Withers.

The repartee between Withers and Piper is some of the best ever written for the screen.

When asked her profession by Inspector Piper, Miss Withers responds, "I'm a schoolteacher. I might have done wonders with you if I had caught you young enough." Or, when Withers tells Piper that she knew that Parker was murdered and that's why she had the police called, Piper responds, "I'm surprised you thought the police necessary." While those lines may not seem all that amusing in print, just watch how funny they are when delivered by two consummate performers.

The aquarium setting is unique for this type of film, providing metal walkways and dark corners where misdeeds can occur. The shots of penguins and fish interspersed among the plot sequences adds to the interest of the production.

The mystery itself is also quite good. Parker's cause of death changes from what seems to be an obvious drowning to the fact that he was killed with a sharp object (probably Withers' hatpin) thrust into his ear. The change in the method of murder causes everyone, including the viewer, to reassess the case over the course of the movie. There are several interesting clues, such as the hatband later found in the penguin pool, the stains on Gwen Parker's stockings, and Chicago Lew writing that he knows who the murderer is. Hemmingway actually seems like the obvious murderer, but suspicion moves from character to character so often that perhaps someone less obvious is the killer.

The weakness in the film is its denouement, which occurs at the murder trial of Gwen Parker. Her attorney, Barry Costello, conducts one of the most ridiculous cross-examinations of a witness ever, accusing Miss Withers of knowing Parker many years before and being jealous because he left her, implying that Hildegarde was the killer. No attorney would ever be permitted to make such a ridiculous cross-examination in court, without any factual basis for his accusations. Obviously, the screenwriters had never observed a real trial.

Then, at the very end of his cross-examination, Costello reveals that he knew Parker was stabbed in the right ear when all of the publicity in the case indicated that he was stabbed in the left ear. Thus, based on that mistake, Withers fingers Costello as the murderer. However, although not shown in the film, one of the prior witnesses at the trial almost surely was the coroner and he would have testified that the victim was stabbed in the right ear. In any event, any defense attorney would have had access to the coroner's report so Costello had a number of opportunities to learn in which ear the stabbing took place. Once again, did the screenwriters conduct any research into criminal proceedings before writing the script?

Nevertheless, the outing of Costello does have some basis in the facts of the case. His explanation for being at the aquarium at the time of the murder and his quick decision to represent Gwen seem suspicious. Despite his detailed deduction as to how Chicago Lew could have been killed in jail by Philip Seymour, Costello is really the only one who could have done the deed. Thus, there are clues to the identity of the murderer — not just the one identified in the script.

One of the best parts of *Penguin Pool Murder* is its second surprise ending, after the murderer is identified. It is not the marriage proposal from Oscar Piper to Hildegarde Withers; that is a true movie cliché. No, the surprise is in avoiding the other true movie cliché. When Philip Seymour and Gwen Parker meet outside the jail, after their acquittal in court, it is clear that with Gerald out of the way, young love will finally bloom. But no, Seymour slaps Gwen and walks away; he has finally discerned Gwen's two-faced and disloyal character. What a great ending for the film! It effectively complements the engaging story that preceded it.

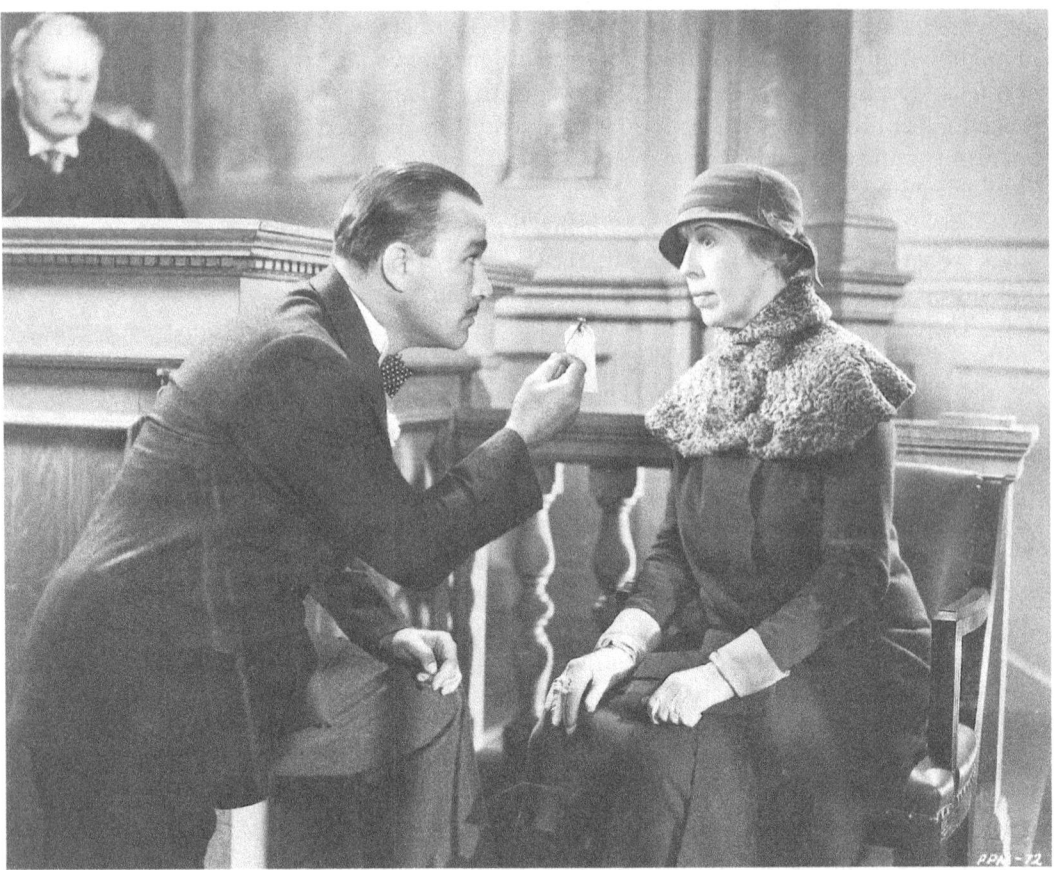

In the incredible climax to *Penguin Pool Murder* (1932), Barry Costello (Robert Armstrong) cross-examines Miss Withers (Edna May Oliver) about the murder weapon, her hat pin, and in the process reveals himself as the murderer. The judge is played by Wilfrid North.

*Note on the Source Material*: *Penguin Pool Murder* was based on Stuart Palmer's first Hildegarde Withers book, *The Penguin Pool Murder*, published in 1931. The plot of the book is nearly identical to the plot of the movie, although attorney Barry Costello has a different motive for killing Gerald Lester (Parker) in the book than in the film. According to the novel, Costello was a client of Lester's who felt he was defrauded during the stock market crash. Thus, the murder was a revenge killing. It was Costello who called Parker to tell him about his wife at the aquarium. By contrast, in the movie, Costello is the secret lover of Gwen Parker (his motive for the killing) and, although it is not entirely clear who called Parker in the movie, it was probably Hemmingway.

The courtroom ending of the movie, which is described above, actually comes from the book, so perhaps the criticism is better directed toward Palmer than the screenwriters. At least in the book, however, the judge does question the relevance of the Withers cross-examination by Costello. Also, since Withers is the first witness to testify in the book, the coroner had not yet been called to the stand to provide the cause of death, at which time he would have surely disclosed that the stabbing occurred in the right ear. In the movie, Withers is called by defense counsel to testify, so the prosecution must have put on its entire case by the time of Withers' testimony.

In print, the whodunit aspects of the story seem weak. There are only two suspects for the crime (other than Seymour and Mrs. Lester, who are obviously not guilty, since they were arrested) and between Hemmingway and Costello, Costello stands out as the killer, particularly after his antics at the prison where the pickpocket is found dead. While large portions of the dialogue from the book were carried into the screenplay, much of the wordplay between Withers and Piper is new to the film. It is much cleverer than the talk in the book.

The true reason why the movie is better than the novel is the perfect casting of Oliver and Gleason in the lead roles. They are perfect in the parts, filling out Palmer's creations as mere words could never do. Along with William Powell and Myrna Loy in *The Thin Man* (1934), Oliver and Gleason are the best-cast acting duo in all of the mystery movie series. It is a shame that, unlike Myrna Loy in the Thin Man series, Oliver left the Hildegarde Withers series before its conclusion.

## *Murder on the Blackboard* (1934)

Police work has certainly changed since 1934. In *Murder on the Blackboard*, when Mr. MacFarland, the principal of the school in which a murder has taken place, refuses to talk to the police, Inspector Oscar Piper asks him, "Do you talk or do I let the boys go to work on you?" Today, that type of police activity seldom takes place with Miranda warnings and similar rights woven into the fabric of American justice. One has to wonder, however, as to how commonplace that conduct was back in the 1930s except, of course, in the movies.

Then there is Hildegarde Withers' idea to trap the murderer by stating in front of all the suspects that policeman Donahue, who was attacked by the killer and who was then recovering in the hospital, would be able to identify the killer once he saw him or her again. The idea is that the murderer will fall for the trap and try to kill Donahue in his hospital bed. The ruse works and the killer is captured. Again, even a cursory review of true crime stories from modern-day newspapers discloses few if any instances where the police trap a killer by tricking him into revealing his own identity. Once again, one has to wonder how commonplace these police traps were back in the 1930s except, of course, in the movies.

It is also unlikely that the police would rely on a schoolteacher to do their investigating and crime-solving. It is also hardly likely that if the police agreed to set up a trap for the killer, they would allow Miss Withers to participate in the ruse, putting herself at risk. However, all of these examples are mystery movie conventions of the era and provide films like *Murder on the Blackboard* with a charm and innocence that contemporary mystery movies do not have.

It is a wonder that there is any learning going on at Miss Withers' schoolhouse. The principal, Mr. MacFarland, is a lecher, making unwanted advances to two of the teachers; the janitor, Otto Schweitzer, is a drunk and a blackmailer; another teacher, Addison Stevens, has proposed to teacher Jane Davis while being secretly married to music teacher Louise Halloran; and Jane Davis may have stolen a winning lottery ticket from Louise Halloran, who is her roommate as well as her colleague. When Halloran's body is discovered by Withers at the school, those are the four obvious suspects. A killing on Withers' home turf is an affront to the schoolteacher-detective's sensibilities and so, showing her usual disdain for the acumen of the police, she conducts her own investigation deducing the identity of the killer long before the police are able to do so.

*Murder on the Blackboard* is aided by its limited sets, as much of the action occurs in the schoolhouse, with its gloomy hallways, strange fire escape and dark cellar with secret passages. There is a particularly unusual element to the murder because even though Louise Halloran was bludgeoned to death, she was already dying from pernicious anemia. An empty can of benzene in Addison Stevens' classroom may be the best clue found by Withers since a regular diet of small doses of benzene could cause pernicious anemia. But, if Louise was already being poisoned, why murder her with a blunt instrument?

In the end, though, the mystery in *Murder on the Blackboard* does not work, primarily because of an egregious cheat. When Oscar Piper suspects Addison Stevens, Withers clears him by stating that she had checked his alibi at the library and it was a good one. Later, after exposing Stevens as the killer, Withers states that Stevens had signed for a valuable book that could not be removed from the library. He then hid the book, left the library, did his deeds, came back to the library and returned the book. It therefore appeared as if Stevens had been at the library the whole time.

The problem is that once Withers, who is supposed to be the competent detective, clears Stevens of the crime, the viewer has to clear him also. If instead the filmmakers had shown Withers investigating the alibi at the library, the viewer may have been able to determine the flaw in Stevens' alibi, thus keeping Stevens as a possible suspect. That is why this is such a serious flaw in the murder mystery. (Of course, if the police had checked the alibi on their own, instead of leaving it to a talented amateur, the murderer may have been discovered earlier.) Another significant flaw in the story is the contention that Halloran disclosed the name of her murderer in the music notes she wrote on her blackboard. Since no person on Earth could have ever understood that clue other than Withers, what was the point?

Nevertheless, whatever defects there may be in the mystery of *Murder on the Blackboard*, any Hildegarde Withers movie with Edna May Oliver in the lead is a joy to watch. While Withers may not be everyone's choice for their elementary schoolteacher, she is surely everyone's choice for one of their favorite movie detectives. Even some unfunny wordplay is funny when delivered by Oliver, with her fussy manner accentuated by her humorous facial expressions and cutting voice. James Gleason as the cigar-smoking Inspector Piper is also entertaining as usual. So, if a mystery fan can forget the defects in the mystery and enjoy the acting and the dialogue, *Murder on the Blackboard* is a film to watch.

*Note on the Source Material*: The film was based on Stuart Palmer's 1932 Hildegarde Withers novel *Murder on the Blackboard*. The book has a few more potential suspects than the film and the explanation for the schoolteacher's murder is more detailed and cohesive in the novel than in the film. That difference, unfortunately, simply highlights more of the defects in the plot, making the book less satisfactory than the film. It hardly helps the believability of the novel that at one point, the police employ a Viennese criminologist, Professor Pfaffle, as the acting inspector of the Homicide Squad and at other times it appears that Miss Withers is running the investigation of the murder of Anise Halloran (a slightly different name than in the movie).

A significant difference between the two works is that in the novel it is Oscar Piper who is slugged over the head in the cellar of the school, putting him out of action for most of the story. In the movie, it is policeman Donahue who suffers that fate. The filmmakers were shrewd enough to realize that the strength of the films was in the chemistry between Withers and Piper and their clever dialogue. The removal of Piper would have been a serious detriment to the film.

In the novel, the readers go along with Withers as she investigates Stevenson's alibi at the library. Thus, they can determine on their own that there may be a flaw in Stevenson's story. However, the book displays some of the other problems of the film: the inexplicable clue of the music notes on Halloran's blackboard, the hiding of the fact that Stevenson and Halloran were secretly married (although there is a good explanation in the book as to why they kept the wedding a secret) and how Stevenson could be dating Jancy Davis when he was married to her roommate.

## Murder on a Honeymoon (1935)

*Murder on a Honeymoon* is the most entertaining of the Hildegarde Withers movies. The setting of the film is the bright and wide open spaces of an island off the coast of California. The tone of the film is therefore much lighter than the previous features in the series, aided considerably by the genuine humor inherent in the Withers character and her relationships with Oscar Piper and others. *Murder on a Honeymoon* is a good mystery which is greatly enhanced by its light-hearted tenor.

On a seaplane flying to the Santa Catalina Islands, Miss Withers witnesses the death of fellow passenger, Roswell Forrest, just after he smoked a cigarette, took a slug of whiskey from another passenger's flask and inhaled some of Withers' smelling salts. The local police believe that the death was natural, a result of heart failure, but Withers believes it was murder. She telegrams Oscar Piper back in New York for information about the victim, and Piper is surprised to learn that Forrest was to be the state's witness against a gang of mobsters, who therefore put out a contract on his life. Concerned about Withers' safety, Piper flies to Catalina to protect his friend and to also solve the murder. Of course, it is Withers who actually solves the crime, after concluding that the cigarette Forrest smoked on the plane was laced with poison.

The film was based on Stuart Palmer's novel *The Puzzle of the Pepper Tree*; the filmmakers must have decided that Palmer's title was not strong enough to engender audience interest in the movie. The best alternate title for the picture might have been *Murder on a Seaplane*, surely a very descriptive title for the movie to follow. Instead, by going with *Murder on a Honeymoon*, a serious mistake was made. The honeymooners seem to be very minor characters in the film, but with the title of the feature focusing on the two, they become very important suspects to the viewer. In fact, the title of the movie is probably the best clue to the identity of the murderers provided anywhere in the film. Even the unexpected death of the husband, surprising though it may be, does not dissuade the viewer from focusing on the wife as the most likely murderer, based solely on the title of the movie.

*Murder on a Honeymoon* does not work as a whodunit, even though it meets the classic mold for works in the genre, with a killing among a limited number of suspects, each of whom has the potential to be the killer. However, no clues to the identity of the murderer are provided to the viewer, so the film comes up short in that category. *Murder on a Honeymoon* actually succeeds as a police (or schoolteacher) procedural, with Hildegarde and Oscar following a series of leads and in the process hitting dead ends from time to time, until they finally are able to identify the real killer. The trail goes from the body on the plane to the snatching of the body before an autopsy can be performed to the later discovery that the body is not that of the person it was supposed to be. The red herrings of the

Murder brings the detecting duo of Hildegarde Withers (Edna May Oliver) and Inspector Oscar Piper (James Gleason), center, to Santa Catalina Island in *Murder on a Honeymoon* (1935). One of the suspects is Joseph B. Tate (Leo G. Carroll, right), a Hollywood director, whose prop man (Irving Bacon, left) is holding a pelican that will be needed in the next scene of the movie being filmed.

airplane pilots, the ship captain and the motion picture director are clever diversions from the task of locating the true killer.

Edna May Oliver is simply delightful in the film, dishing out some wonderfully humorous insults to others, while taking a shot or two herself with haughty aplomb. For example, when the local doctor disparages Miss Withers' suspicions, calling her a reader of detective stories, she responds, "I worked with a detective on two other cases—Inspector Piper of the New York Police. He's no great shakes himself, but he's a giant compared to some I've seen since." And, if that line does not seem all that funny to read, it is hilarious to watch as Oliver delivers it in her disparaging tone. As to taking a hit herself, when Withers is accidentally squirted by a man spraying for bugs, she asks, "You have much trouble with pests?" He responds, "Yes, I do, lady. But you go right ahead. That's what we're here for." Oliver's expression when realizing she has been insulted is priceless. *Murder on a Honeymoon* is one of the most amusing of all the mystery movies.

James Gleason is the perfect foil to Oliver, as always, with the two seeming to be an older version of Nick and Nora Charles and other crime-solving couples of 1930s cinema. Even though the romance is gone, there is true affection between the two.

This was the last film in the series in which Edna May Oliver played Hildegarde Withers. In later films she was replaced by two fine actresses, Helen Broderick and then Zasu

Pitts, but, in fact, they could never truly replace Oliver. Her performances in these three films are truly unforgettable. She will remain in everyone's eyes for all time the true Hildegarde Withers, the schoolteacher turned detective from New York City.

*Note on the Source Material*: In 1958, the Four Preps, in the song "26 Miles," immortalized Santa Catalina as the Island of Romance. Twenty-five years earlier, Stuart Palmer, in his novel *The Puzzle of the Pepper Tree*, wrote about Santa Catalina as an island of murder. As for romance, the lyrics of the 1950s song clearly do not fit, since the killers turn out to be a young couple who were honeymooning on the island. (*The Puzzle of the Pepper Tree* would not have been a good title for the film, and it does not really work for the book either. The title refers to the location of the body of the victim after it was stolen from the doctor's office, which is a fairly minor part of the story.)

*Murder on a Honeymoon* is substantially based on Palmer's novel, although the seaplane passengers are slightly different in the book than in the movie. In fact, Miss Withers is not on board the plane when the murder occurs; she is already vacationing on the island and learns about Forrest's death after the plane lands. In the book, the poison is administered through chewing gum; in the film, a poisoned cigarette is used. As was often the case when a book is adapted for a film, the novel has more details than the movie, such as why the pepper tree was so easy to move (it had landed there after a recent storm and had not grown in) and whether the young couple was really on a honeymoon (the police checked and they had a marriage license).

Also, Oscar Piper does not make it to the island until the very end of the novel. For *Murder on a Honeymoon*, the filmmakers knew that one of the strengths of the movie series was the Withers-Piper relationship and so, in the film, Piper travels quite quickly from New York to California so that he can begin jousting with Withers onscreen as soon as possible. When Palmer's 1932 novel *Murder on the Blackboard* was made into the 1934 movie of the same name, a similar adjustment was made to the scope of Piper's involvement in the story.

## *Murder on a Bridle Path* (1936)

Seventy-five years after the release of *Murder on a Bridle Path*, the type of amateur detective story that the film embodies has gone out of favor in print mysteries. In the modern era, so to speak, most detective novels are either a variation on a police procedural (although often with some classic whodunit aspects) or are about a detective who is a professional, such as a private eye or an attorney. Gone are the days of talented amateurs such as Philo Vance, Lord Peter Wimsey, Miss Marple and Jessica Fletcher, who somehow become involved in murder investigations and then somehow solve the crimes before the police do.

There are several reasons for this change in style. One is the absurdity or lack of basis in reality of a non-professional ever solving a murder and surely not on a recurring basis. Another is the difficulty of devising a scenario in which the amateur first becomes involved in the crime investigation and thereafter somehow tags along on the official inquiry.

In the 1930s, however, and particularly with a film like *Murder on a Bridle Path*, the writers had no problem solving those difficulties. They simply ignored the problem. Thus, just after the body of Violet Feverel is discovered in Central Park, apparently thrown by her horse, Withers walks into the scene, having coincidentally found the runaway horse. In fact, she has discovered some blood on the horse's body, already causing her detective nostrils to flare. Since Feverel went riding at the break of dawn and Withers is dressed in a business suit (on a day she was probably supposed to be teaching in school), the whole scenario makes little sense.

Withers then accompanies Inspector Piper on his investigations, as though that is the most natural way in which to handle things. Withers even questions some of the witnesses on her own, identifying herself as being associated with the police. When Piper goes on dangerous parts of his investigation, such as entering the dark mansion of the Gregg family, Withers accompanies him, despite the significant risk to the schoolteacher. As a result, at the end of the film, Withers almost becomes the third victim of the murderer. And, as absurd as it all is, the audience accepts these incongruities because they are conventions of the era and, indeed, provide the mystery movies of the 1930s with some of their appeal.

Although Feverel's death appears to be an accident, the blood on the horse comes from a BB imbedded in the animal, indicating that the horse may have been shot from a distance to cause it to throw Feverel. She may then have been struck in the head by a blunt instrument, to mimic the effect of a blow from the shoe of the horse. There are a particularly large number of suspects, including the victim's ex-husband who was just released from jail on a fraudulent court order, the manager of Feverel's stable who may have been in love with Feverel, her former boyfriend who is now in love with her sister, and the butler at the Gregg mansion. Oscar Piper keeps accusing different suspects of the killing, with no facts to support his claims, but in the end, it is Withers who solves the crimes, more by luck than rational deduction.

*Murder on a Bridle Path* is a fun film. The strength of the series is still in the relationship of Withers and Piper, with Helen Broderick playing Withers for the only time in the series. She is fine in the part and if she had originated the role, no one would ever have had grounds to complain about her performance. However, as good as Broderick is, she pales in comparison to Edna May Oliver. When Broderick delivers a funny line, she is funny; when she delivers an unfunny line, she is not. Oliver, however, with her voice and expressions, could turn an unfunny line into a funny one just by her delivery.

A difficulty with *Murder on a Bridle Path* is that Withers really does little detective work. She just stumbles onto clues. If she looks on the ground where the murder occurred, she discovers a pipe which may be a clue. When Hildegarde illegally searches old Mr. Gregg's pocket, she finds a note concerning alimony payments, incriminating young Don Gregg. When she illegally searches the butler's room, she discovers the weapon that killed Feverel. There is not much true detective work going on in this film and at the end, the motive for the murders comes out of the blue.

Despite these negatives, *Murder on a Bridle Path* is always absorbing, with interesting suspects and motivations, a unique setting for Feverel's murder (the bridle path), another interesting setting of the dark Gregg mansion and the surprise death of another character, in a story that could have only been told in the 1930s. Unfortunately, it does have the stock character of High Pockets, the young black stable boy played by Willie Best in stereotypical fashion. However, High Pockets may be smarter than he seems, selling his lucky rabbit's foot to Withers for a tidy sum and then, after she leaves, pulling another rabbit's foot out of his shoe. Indeed, High Pockets may be the brightest character in the film, with his astute observations of what happened around the time of the murder of Feverel. The film also has an amusing moment at the end when Withers, who has pocketed a pipe from the crime scene without telling Piper, is embarrassed to find that the pipe was dropped by the medical examiner at the scene of Feverel's murder, so that it was not really a clue at all.

*Murder on a Bridle Path* is not a realistic portrayal of a crime investigation, but then, who cares? The film is another in what seems to be the always entertaining Hildegarde Withers series, set in the 1930s when apparently a schoolteacher really could become a successful detective.

*Note on the Source Material:* The film was based on Stuart Palmer's 1935 novel *The Puzzle of the Red Stallion*. The red stallion is Siwash, the horse Violet Feverel was riding on the Central Park bridle path when she was murdered. The book follows the film closely, with the same victims, the same killer and the same red herring, namely, the pipe that Withers finds at the murder scene. For some reason, *Murder on a Bridle Path* did not include two very cinematic scenes from the novel: the out-of-control ride by Violet's sister on Siwash which almost leads to her death and the afternoon spent at Beulah Park during an important day of horse racing.

On the other hand, there were changes made to the story to make it more cinematic. Abe Thomas, the butler at the Gregg mansion, has a wife in the novel. In the movie, he has the strange-looking son who adds to the "old dark house" nature of the Gregg abode. Also, the climax of the film, with Withers almost killed, is original to the movie.

As was often the case in the Hildegarde Withers series, *Murder on a Bridle Path* is better than the book on which it is based. The book has more talk than action and seems particularly dated 75 years after its publication. The film, on the other hand, even though it is almost as old as the book, seldom becomes boring and never seems dated. It goes to show, once again, that Hildegarde Withers and Oscar Piper were naturals as screen detectives.

## *The Plot Thickens* (1936)

*The Plot Thickens* is a difficult film to evaluate. On the one hand, it contains what is probably the best mystery in the entire Hildegarde Withers movie series. On the other hand, there is the disappointing performance by ZaSu Pitts as Hildegarde Withers.

The film involves the murder of wealthy John Carter, who is shot while sitting in his car just after pretty Alice Stevens has left him alone. Previously, Alice had a fight with her boyfriend Robert Wilkins, and when she called Carter to pick her up, Carter had a fistfight with Wilkins because of his jealousy about Alice. In addition to Wilkins being an obvious suspect in the Carter murder case, the butler of the house, Kendall, is a significant suspect. He is jealous of the relationship between Joe, the chauffeur, and Marie, the housemaid, and he sets out after the car driven by Carter, believing that Joe and Marie are in it. Thus, Kendall may have shot Carter believing he was Joe. Then there is the mysterious Frenchman who was threatening Carter at the beginning of the film.

Thus, there are a number of good suspects, always a plus for a murder mystery. Withers' one contribution to the crime investigation is her focus on a famous emerald she finds at Carter's house; it had been stolen years before from the Louvre in Paris. (Despite its value, Withers is allowed to keep it in her purse for the remainder of the film.) That leads to a trip to the Cosmopolitan Museum, the murder of a museum guard, the theft of the valuable Cellini Cup and the final capture of the gang, which involves a midget, a pretty young sculptress and Joe the chauffeur. In the end, the killing of Carter involved the theft of jewels and valuable artwork, not the personal motives highlighted at the beginning of the feature.

*The Plot Thickens* has a strong storyline, not only because of the number of good suspects but also because the whole focus of the investigation changes when the tale moves to the Cosmopolitan Museum. There the film morphs into a theft investigation more than a murder investigation, with the change of setting giving the film new life, not to mention a whole new set of potential villains. Then there is the fact that Carter's body was moved twice, once when his car was driven from the scene of the murder to the garage of his mansion and once again when someone moved the body from the garage to a room inside the house. This adds an overlay of complication to the murder investigation, somewhat unusual for a short mystery film.

The problem with *The Plot Thickens* is the performance by ZaSu Pitts as Hildegarde Withers. She has an irritating voice which is not offset by special mannerisms or eccentricities. She is completely unable to sell any of the purported zingers she throws at Oscar Piper. Piper responds to her barbs as though they were as witty as the ones from the prior films, which they are not, making it appear that Gleason is overacting. Edna May Oliver left large shoes to fill for any actress subsequently performing the Withers role but Helen Broderick was almost able to fill them. ZaSu Pitts does not even come close. It may be that the lines she is given are not as great as those given to the prior actresses in the series but even if they are, Pitts does not have the versatility to deliver them with the proper acerbic wit, as Oliver and Broderick were able to do.

Indeed, Withers has no business even being in this film. In the prior movies, Withers became involved in the murder cases either directly or by fortuitous circumstances, somewhat justifying her continued involvement in the crime investigation. In *The Plot Thickens*, Withers learns that Piper is investigating a murder unrelated to her and yet she still decides to become involved, for no justifiable reason. What is even stranger, the entire police department sees nothing unusual in her activities. (Even stranger than that, schoolteacher Withers has a full-time maid on duty at her apartment.)

Then, despite Withers' involvement in the inquiry, it is, in fact, Inspector Piper who actually makes most of the advances in the investigation, including locating the fake Cellini cup, unmasking the midget, discovering the real Cellini cup hidden in a sculpture and developing his own trap for tricking the killer into revealing himself. Based on their mutual experiences in the prior films, Inspector Piper may have Hildegarde Withers to thank for his improved investigatory techniques but by the time of *The Plot Thickens*, it is apparent that Piper no longer needs Withers' assistance. Since Pitts is more irritating than amusing in the role of the schoolteacher-detective, the whole reason for a Withers-Piper movie was slowly evaporating.

Although the performance of ZaSu Pitts and the manner of handling the Withers character in this film is particularly disappointing, in the end, the excellent mystery elements of the film trump those deficiencies. After all, *The Plot Thickens* aspires to be nothing more than a good murder mystery and in that regard the film is well worth a view.

*Note on the Source Material:* The Plot Thickens was based on Stuart Palmer's short story "The Riddle of the Dangling Pearl," first published in the November 1933 issue of *Mystery* and featured in *Hildegarde Withers: Uncollected Riddles* (Crippen & Landru Publishers, 2002). Palmer purportedly wrote over 50 Hildegarde Withers short stories, many of which have never been published in book form.

The "Dangling Pearl" refers to the pearl on the Cellini cup which swings back and forth in time with the vibration of the building. That phenomenon is used by Withers to determine that the Cellini cup found in the museum checkroom is a fake, because its pearl remains stationary at all times. The same clue was used in the movie, although there the pearl swung only when a clock chimed.

The second half of *The Plot Thickens* concerning the events in the museum comes from the short story, to which the movie is surprisingly faithful. Thus there is the killing of the guard who was likely to be able to detect the difference between the real and fake Cellini cup, a sculptress who hides the real cup inside her sculpture and a midget operating in the museum, hiding among some schoolchildren. The first part of *The Plot Thickens*, concerning the murder of John Carter, is completely original to the film. Thus, the filmmakers cleverly expanded a good short story into a full-length feature by adding a murder mystery to the plot. Luckily, they did not expand the story by adding comic relief, as other mystery films have done.

As good as the mysteries are in the film version of the story, the short story remains more true to the Withers-Piper characters than the film. In the story, it is Withers who finds the hidden Cellini cup in the sculpture and unmasks the midget, not Inspector Piper. If one is going to write a story about an amateur detective assisting the police, it would seem to be a requisite that the amateur solves the crime before the police. The filmmakers seem to have forgotten that principle of mystery fiction when devising the storyline of *The Plot Thickens*.

## *Forty Naughty Girls* (1937)

With this last film in the series, it is depressing to see what has happened to the Hildegarde Withers movies. The clever repartee and love-hate relationship between Hildegarde Withers and Oscar Piper, previously the highlights of these films, are now completely gone. Instead, the two characters have been reduced to slapstick comics. For example, on the way into a Broadway theater, Piper cannot find his tickets. Withers accidentally knocks his hat to the floor and, surprise, he finds the tickets in the inside band. Later, when Piper is interviewing a witness, every time the witness responds, a seamstress starts her sewing machine, drowning out the answer. The seamstress is almost deaf, providing some comic misunderstandings between Piper and her. Withers loses her purse in the tall ticket well on the way into the theater; Piper gets his hand stuck inside when he tries to reach for it. In the theater, Withers accidentally hits the person sitting next to her in the face, gets her dress caught in a door and then on a suit of armor which she unknowingly drags behind her, and then a stage elevator deposits her right into the middle of a dance number being performed on stage. How sad it all is.

Part of the problem is that ZaSu Pitts is totally miscast as Hildegarde Withers, at least as originally portrayed by Edna May Oliver. As a result, the part has now been completely rewritten for comedy purposes only. Her foil, Oscar Piper, becomes primarily a comedy element also. It was always irritating that in film after film Piper accused people of murder without any evidence, simply jumping to wild conclusions, but in *Forty Naughty Girls*, his serial finger-pointings at the wrong people are particularly exasperating. Gleason's fuming expression when he is shown to be wrong has clearly overstayed its welcome.

On a night when Piper brings Withers to see a hit Broadway musical titled *Forty Naughty Girls*, there is much backstage intrigue, swirling around Windy Bennett, the show's publicist. He is in love with one of the stars of the show, Rita Marlowe, who is engaged to be married to the play's producer, Ricky Rickman. Windy has also been making unwanted advances to another pretty young performer, June Preston, which causes her boyfriend Bert to punch out Windy. Also, Windy is blackmailing the show's author, Tommy Washburn, because Tommy plagiarized the play's script from a man who is now dead. Not surprisingly, Windy's body is discovered during the show, shot to death by a .32 caliber pistol, perhaps the one missing from the prop master's collection of stage guns. After another murder and some more slapstick, Withers fingers the surprise killer.

There are a few appealing aspects of the feature. While it does not take place in real time, most of the action occurs in the back of the theater while the musical is being performed in the front. Musical numbers are always heard in the background and from time to time scenes on the stage are shown. It is a unique backdrop for a murder mystery. Director Edward Cline sometimes allows his camera to prowl the backstage areas, particularly at the beginning of the show with the rush of performers entering and exiting the stage, giving the film a strong sense of movement. While there may not be forty of them, there are lots of pretty showgirls on display throughout.

Nevertheless, *Forty Naughty Girls* is dreadful. There is almost no true detective work done by Piper, at least until the end of the film when nitrate is discovered on the inside of a glove of Ricky Rickman, confirming that he is the killer. Withers does even less detective work than Piper. Her main contribution to the investigation is to smell each member of the cast as they come by, to see if they have the same perfume or cologne that she smelled on Windy's body. As to her discovery of the killer, Withers happens to go to Rickman's room "on a hunch," where she discovers an envelope from a private detective sticking out of the door. That envelope discloses that Rickman was suspicious of the Windy-Marlowe relationship, putting the kibosh on his statement that he had no idea the two were seeing each other, and confirming his motive for the killing of Windy. Of course, if that is detective work, anyone could have solved these murders if they happened to read the report which was shoved under Rickman's door. How the report got there in the middle of a Broadway show is unexplained. The question as to why Rickman killed Windy before confirming his suspicions about him by reading the detective report is never addressed.

Thus, *Forty Naughty Girls* provides a bit of a mystery but not much in the way of competent detectives or clues to aid the viewer in identifying the murderer. The film is mainly filled with lame attempts at humor, most of which fail miserably. It is stunning how fast the quality of the Hildegarde Withers series has dropped since its 1932 debut with *Penguin Pool Murder*. With the loss of Edna May Oliver in the lead role and the difficulty of writing the part for an actress such as ZaSu Pitts, the writers simply gave up, deciding to forego clever writing and subtle humor in favor of slapstick comedy and schtick. It was an unwise choice.

*Note on the Source Material*: The credits to *Forty Naughty Girls* state, "Story by Stuart Palmer." Presumably the film was based on Palmer's short story "The Riddle of the Forty Naughty Girls," first published in the July 1934 issue of *Mystery* and featured in *Hildegarde Withers: Uncollected Riddles* (Crippen & Landru Publishers, 2002). While the presumption seems obvious, there is, in fact, little in common between the short story and the film.

The short story does not involve a Broadway play. The setting is the Diana Burlesque, where the show being performed is *Forty Naughty Paris Girlies*. When the voluptuous Janey Vere de Vere is on stage and just about ready to complete her stripping, a tremendous bang is heard and a man in the right front box is discovered dead, with a bullet hole in the center of his forehead. It turns out that the man is either the current or ex-husband of Janey, but since she has a clear alibi, Piper and Withers must look elsewhere. However, with some clever detective work by Withers, Janey's alibi is finally broken.

There is more cleverness in Palmer's short story than in the entire feature film which was supposedly based upon it. However, the setting of a burlesque house would hardly have seemed appropriate for a Miss Withers film, although it would have been a great change of pace for the series. The only aspect of the story incorporated into the film is the finding of nitrate on the inside of the glove of the killer. It is a shame that the clever method of murder employed in the short story was not also used in the film.

## Afterwards

After leaving the Hildegarde Withers series, Edna May Oliver performed in character roles for several of the major Hollywood studios. Her specialty was historical classics, such as *A Tale of Two Cities* (1935) and *Romeo and Juliet* (1936) for MGM and *Drums Along the Mohawk* (1939) for 20th Century–Fox. She received an Academy Award nomination in the Best Supporting Actress category for the latter film. She even returned to RKO for the Astaire-Rogers picture *The Story of Vernon and Irene Castle* (1939). Oliver had such a familiar face that she was caricatured in cartoons such as *Porky's Road Race* (1937). She died in 1942 at the age of 59.

James Gleason was never idle after the Hildegarde Withers series ended. The apex of his career was probably in the early 1940s, with *Meet John Doe* (1941), directed by Frank Capra, and *Here Comes Mr. Jordan* (1941), for which he was nominated for an Oscar for Best Supporting Actor. He appeared in numerous mystery movies, often playing a policeman, such as *The Ex-Mrs. Bradford* (1936), two Falcon movies and *Arsenic and Old Lace* (1944). In the 1950s, Gleason made frequent appearances on television. He passed away in 1959.

Stuart Palmer continued writing Hildegarde Withers novels and short stories after the film series ended. In later books, Withers retired to Los Angeles but she still became involved in murder investigations. So did Oscar Piper, even though he still worked in New York City.

While there were no other films about the schoolteacher-detective, one more movie was based on a Hildegarde Withers short story. Palmer was a good friend of fellow mystery writer, Craig Rice, and they worked together on the screenplay for *The Falcon's Brother* (1942), the film in which the original Falcon, played by George Sanders, was killed and his brother, played by Tom Conway, replaced him in the series. Rice is most famous for her novels about John J. Malone, an attorney who becomes involved in murder investigations.

Starting in the late 1940s, Rice and Palmer collaborated on six short stories for *Ellery Queen's Mystery Magazine* which teamed Withers and Malone in the investigation of a crime. The stories were later collected in *People vs. Withers and Malone* (1963). One of those stories, "Once Upon a Train," was the basis for *Mrs. O'Malley and Mr. Malone* (1950). While John J. Malone was one of the detectives in the film, the Withers character was replaced by Mrs. O'Malley, a hillbilly character from Montana. Thus, the film is not, in actuality, a Hildegarde Withers film.

One of Palmer's significant contributions to the mystery field was as the writer for movies in several Hollywood mystery movie series. In addition to the Falcon series (for which Palmer contributed two scripts), Palmer wrote for the Lone Wolf series (one film) and Bulldog Drummond series (three films), along with writing for non-series mystery movies. Palmer also published mysteries that did not involve Hildegarde Withers. Palmer served as president of the Mystery Writers of America in 1954 and 1955. He passed away in 1968.

In 1971, a television movie about Hildegarde Withers, *A Very Missing Person*, starred Eve Arden as Withers and James Gregory as Oscar Piper. It was a pilot for a proposed television series which was never produced. There were no radio series about the character.

# 6

# Thatcher Colt
## *The Police Commissioner*

The movies of the Hollywood mystery series seldom featured a police detective as their lead character. Usually the police regulars in series were foils for an amateur detective, as Oscar Piper was to Hildegarde Withers, Steve McBride was to Torchy Blane, and Inspector Farraday was to Boston Blackie. There were, of course, exceptions to this rule, such as Charlie Chan of the Honolulu police force and Dick Tracy from an unnamed metropolitan police force. There was also Thatcher Colt, who, as police commissioner of New York City, had the highest official position of all of the movie detectives. Based on a character created by Anthony Abbot, Colt was the subject of two mystery films in the early 1930s and one feature film in the early 1940s.

## Background

### Novels

Anthony Abbot, *né* Charles Fulton Oursler, was born in 1893 in Baltimore, Maryland, a member of an old but not very rich Baltimore family. He dropped out of school before the end of eighth grade and went to work in a variety of jobs, from a water boy for a construction gang to a clerk in a law office. He eventually acquired an interest in writing and after putting some time in on newspapers became, in 1920, the supervising editor at Mac-Fadden Publications, whose long line included *Physical Culture*, *True Story* and *True Detective*. During the course of his long editing career, Oursler also worked for *Liberty* magazine and became a senior editor at *Reader's Digest*.

From the early 1930s to the mid–1940s, Oursler, using the pseudonym Anthony Abbot, wrote a series of detective stories about Thatcher Colt, the police commissioner of New York City. The title of most of the novels began with the word "About," meaning that between the title and the pseudonym, his mystery novels would appear at the beginning of any alphabetical listing of books. (Oursler later denied that this was his intention but his objective seems obvious.)

The Thatcher Colt novels were modeled somewhat on the popular Philo Vance novels of the day. For example, the narrator (and author) of the book, Anthony Abbot, is the secretary to the lead detective and, although he is present during the investigations, has little to do. Also, Colt is a citizen of the upper classes, well-dressed and very comfortable investigating crime among the elite. Colt lives in Manhattan in a mansion which has an extensive library and an elaborate gym. Luckily, though, Colt does not have the ego of the arrogant Mr. Vance.

Colt debuted in the 1930 novel *About the Murder of Geraldine Foster*, a story concerning the ax murder of a doctor's secretary. Later novels took Colt to the East River, Madison Square Garden and Buzzard's Bay to investigate suspicious deaths. Two of the novels in the series were based on true crime cases of the 19th century, i.e., the Lizzie Borden matter (involving the ax murder of Lizzie's father and stepmother) and the Hall-Mills case (about the death of a priest and a choir woman who were having an affair).

## Film Series

Columbia started a film series about Thatcher Colt in 1932 with the release of *The Night Club Lady*. The movie involves the murder of the owner of a nightclub at midnight on New Year's Eve while surrounded by the police. That film was followed by *The Circus Queen Murder* (1933), which tells the story of infidelity, jealousy and murder against the backdrop of a touring circus.

In both films, Adolphe Menjou played Colt. Menjou, who was born in Pittsburgh, Pennsylvania, in 1890, started appearing in silent films around 1915. He first came to prominence in *A Woman of Paris* (1923), a film melodrama which Charlie Chaplin directed. Menjou played a wealthy French playboy who had an affair with the female lead. Menjou continued to work regularly in silent films but when sound came to the cinema, his career temporarily stalled. He returned to the screen in 1930 and then in 1931 appeared in *The Front Page* as tough newspaper editor Walter Burns, for which he received an Academy Award nomination for Best Actor. The following year he starred in *The Night Club Lady*.

The other continuing performer was Miss Kelly, Colt's secretary, played by Ruthelma Stevens. The actress, who was born in 1903, began her film career with *The Night Club Lady*. After her two supporting roles in the Thatcher Colt movies, she appeared sporadically in films into the 1950s. The part of Miss Kelly was small in the first feature but became more significant in *The Circus Queen Murder* when she traveled with Colt on his vacation, only to become involved with intrigue at the circus.

Although *The Night Club Lady* was originally intended to be the start of at least a three-film mystery series, only one sequel was ever released. Columbia did not specialize in long-running mystery series in the 1930s. It was not until the 1940s that Columbia emphasized mystery movie series, such as the Lone Wolf and Boston Blackie series. However, Colt made it to the screen one more time, in PRC's *The Panther's Claw* (1942). In this case, Colt investigates the murder of an opera singer.

*The Panther's Claw* starred Sidney Blackmer as Colt. Blackmer, who was born in North Carolina in 1895, began his film career in 1914 with a bit part in the famous serial *Perils of Pauline*. Although he appeared in additional uncredited parts in silent films, his early successes were on Broadway, acting in many productions during the 1920s. During the sound era, he became a familiar character actor, with roles in many mystery series such as the Mr. Moto, Charlie Chan and Ellery Queen series. Blackmer is probably best-known today as the answer to a trivia question: Which actor played Teddy Roosevelt the most times in the movies?

## The Films

### *The Night Club Lady* (1932)

*The Night Club Lady* is a quintessential 1930s mystery movie, set in the supposed upper echelons of society, where men were tuxedos, ladies wear evening gowns, they all live in multi-room apartments with maids and other servants, and they all visit lavish nightclubs on New Year's Eve. Underneath the surface, though, there is blackmail, murder, drunkenness and deceit, calling for the investigative talents of Thatcher Colt, a police commissioner who is himself a member of the type of society in which these events occur.

*The Night Club Lady* commences with a montage of scenes of New York City on New Year's Eve, before focusing on the apartment of Lola Carewe, the owner of Lola's, a nightclub. Lola is understandably on edge that night since she has recently been receiving written death threats. Nevertheless, she decides to go to her club that evening, accompanied by her friend Mr. Rowland. At the nightclub, Lola receives another death warning, threatening Lola's murder at midnight. Thatcher Colt intervenes, first by saving Lola from a gunshot fired from behind a curtain and then by having numerous policemen surround her at her apartment in order to prevent the threatened killing. But as the clock is striking the hour of midnight, Lola has a seizure and drops to the floor, dead.

This first half of the film is stunning, enhanced by the effective camerawork. Scenes are shot from a variety of angles including high angles or close two-shots, the camera is often in movement (particularly at the nightclub scene) and there is even use of a zoom lens upon occasion. The nightclub set is particularly lavish, filled with numerous extras, tellingly portraying the decadent consumption of the rich during the Great Depression. Even though the film uses the cliché of a predicted death which the police cannot prevent, the murder scene is effectively filmed. There is a mixture of high shots, extreme close-ups of the potential victim and pans around the policemen, as one smokes a cigarette, another plays with some chips, another swings his key chain and another looks at his watch. There is no dialogue or mood music; there are just the sounds in the room as the tension slowly increases. The scene ends with its surprise—the scream of Lola and her drop to the floor.

If the second half of the film does not match the quality of the beginning, that is understandable. After the death of Lola, *The Night Club Lady* is a whodunit, with many dialogue scenes as the police interview the suspects. The film also becomes stagebound, as most of the rest takes place in Lola's apartment. Even the direction becomes less interesting, with fewer opportunities for camera innovation.

The interest in the second half of the film is mainly in the police procedural nature of the investigation, as Colt scours the world for data about the various suspects. Then, recognizing that Dr. Lengle acted suspiciously when he was called in to view Lola's body, Colt uncovers the unusual method of murder, at which point the story focuses on the potential culpability of the various suspects. The ending of *The Night Club Lady* is somewhat suspenseful, although it does employ another mystery cliché, trapping a killer into exposing herself.

Adolphe Menjou is perfectly cast as Thatcher Colt, playing him as sophisticated and debonair but also as an extremely sharp detective. Mayo Methot (better known as Humphrey Bogart's first wife) is attractive yet convincingly harsh and shrill as Lola Carewe. The one very irritating part of the film is the constant interruptions by Colt's friend Tony, usually drunk, who has no reason to be along on the investigation.

The explanation of the crimes will not stand much scrutiny. The method of murder and the fact that it was timed perfectly to occur at midnight on New Year's Eve is hard to swallow. Given the backstory of Lola's relationship with Basil Boucher, there was no reason for her to have a picture of him in her room, other than to provide an important clue to Colt. There are two very misleading matters related to the murderer, Mrs. Carewe (Boucher). She is referred to by Lola as her mother even though she is only her stage mother (whatever that means for someone no longer in films). In addition, when Mrs. Carewe is told that Dr. Lengle has been called, she expresses some objection to the choice, even though, as part of her murder scheme, Lengle had to be called in. The actual clues that give the killers away to Colt, i.e., Dr. Lengle changing arms on which to give an injection in Lola's body and the kiss mark on Boucher's picture, are never disclosed to the viewer. In other words, the viewer is given all of the information to indicate that Mrs. Carewe is not the killer and none of the information that she is.

Those criticisms are hardly unimportant in a mystery story, but the enjoyment of *The Night Club Lady* comes mainly from the suspense of the first half of the story and Colt's investigative methods in the second half. The murder weapon of a scorpion is innovative, and when it is learned near the end of the film that there is another scorpion still alive and in the possession of the killer, the tension increases.

Murder among the elite was a common subject of mystery movies of the 1930s, with *The Night Club Lady* being one of the best examples thereof. It is a quite an enjoyable experience as long as the mystery is not analyzed too closely.

*Note on the Source Material*: *The Night Club Lady* was based on Anthony Abbot's 1931 novel *About the Murder of the Night Club Lady*. In the book, Lola Carewe is known as the Night Club Lady, not because she owns a nightclub, but rather, because on many nights she reserves front row seats at half a dozen nightclubs, whether she uses them or not.

The film is a faithful adaptation of the book, with the same murders, the same unusual method of murder and in the end, the same killer. The differences between the two, which are not all that many, are illustrative of the difference between mystery films and mystery novels.

One change is small but significant. In the book, the death of Lola is prophesied for sometime before 3:00 AM on New Year's Day. The filmmakers moved the time to 12:00 midnight on New Year's Eve, surely a more cinematic moment, also allowing for twelve chimes of the clock to sound as the murder of Lola may or may not occur. Also, Lola's film death occurs in front of the audience, as she is surrounded by the police. In the book, her death occurs "off stage," after she enters a room and closes the door.

The book is more of a police procedural, with the murder of Lola taking place nearer to the beginning of the novel than in the film. This permits the novel to focus on the detailed investigation by Colt, including making contacts in Europe, interviewing all of the characters, checking on alibis, having autopsies conducted, locating the source of the deadly scorpions and trailing all of the suspects. In the film, while the police procedural nature of the story is not eliminated, there is much more emphasis on the threat to Lola and the police's attempts to protect her.

At the end of the novel, Colt gathers all of the suspects in Lola's apartment to try to determine the killer. In the film, that scene also occurs but there the audience knows that there is one more spider still around and that Colt, in re-enacting Lola's murder, could be putting himself at risk. And, indeed, that does happen, as Colt appears to have been bitten by the scorpion although in the end, it is disclosed that it was just a scheme by Colt to trap the real killer. Nevertheless, the change gives the movie more excitement than Colt merely explaining the crimes, as he does in the book.

*About the Murder of the Night Club Lady* is an excellent example of an early police procedural novel. In adapting the book to the screen, the makers of *The Night Club Lady* made all of the right decisions, in either modifying the story or emphasizing certain matters, to make the film into an effective cinematic experience. Both versions of the story are recommended.

## *The Circus Queen Murder* (1933)

The similarities between *The Night Club Lady* and this sequel are obvious. In the first film, the murder takes place at midnight on New Year's Eve. In the latter film, the crimes take place on Friday the 13th. In both films, Thatcher Colt is unable to prevent the death of a female victim, even with ample advance warning of the crime. In both cases, Colt puts his life at risk near the end of the film to trap the killer. In both films, Colt is the best-dressed detective in the entire history of films, wearing a tuxedo in much of *The Night Club Lady* and in the sequel, wearing three-piece suits with a flower in the lapel. There is one crucial difference, though. *The Night Club Lady* is a classic whodunit, with multiple suspects for the murders. *The Circus Queen Murder* is a mild mystery, with the killing taking place near the end of the film, with no doubt as to who the killer is.

Police Commissioner Colt is in need of a vacation and, by use of a knife thrown at a map of New York State, decides to take a trip to the town of Gilead. He also decides to bring his secretary, Miss Kelly, along for the trip, for reasons that are never made entirely clear. The Greater John T. Rainey Traveling Circus is performing in Gilead, and Colt becomes involved in some intrigue at the circus which involves a number of suspicious characters under the big top. One is Josie La Tour, the beautiful aerialist who is also an owner; she is having an affair with Sebastian, another high-flying performer. La Tour is married to Flandrin, another trapeze performer, who is none too happy about the affair between La Tour and Sebastian. Flandrin is then apparently murdered, but Colt deduces that he has faked his own death in order to enable him to murder La Tour during her circus performance on Friday the 13th. Despite Colt's entreaties, La Tour refuses to cancel her performance, resulting in the death of the circus queen during the afternoon show. Colt is at least able to save Sebastian from harm but he cannot then prevent the spectacular suicide of Flandrin.

The key scenes in the film occur near the end, with Flandrin hiding atop the circus tent near the aerial performers. Sebastian is first in the air, performing on a swing with a rope that has been frayed and eventually breaks. Luckily, he comes to no harm. Next up is the beautiful La Tour, who is killed high in the air by a poisonous dart blown at her by Flandrin. These scenes are both spectacular, with impressive stunts (shot from below) which emphasize the height of the acts and surprise endings to each scene. Even the later suicide of Flandrin is spectacular, resulting in the second grisly fall to the circus floor that day. These scenes are a long time coming in the story but they are well worth the wait.

Prior to that, there is not much happening in the film, although it still has its interest, mainly due to the circus setting. There is the circus trying to move to its next location in a rainstorm, Flandrin spooking the horse ridden by La Tour during a circus parade, the question of the correct number of cannibal performers, and a voodoo doll with a pin

**Greta Nissen plays aerialist Josie La Tour, the title character in *The Circus Queen Murder* (1933).**

through the heart thrown threw the window of La Tour's wagon. The story is further held together by the performance of Adolphe Menjou as Thatcher Colt. Menjou was born to play the dapper policeman, who investigates the crimes or potential crimes with a calm yet incisive demeanor. Even when Flandrin pulls a gun on him, Colt is quiet and unruffled, attempting to figure out a way to save the lives of both Miss Kelly and Sebastian.

Josie La Tour is played by Greta Nissen and at one point, Colt describes her as exceedingly attractive. That is surely an understatement, as Nissan's beauty shines in whatever scenes she appears, particularly when wearing her skimpy circus garb. If not for her Norwegian accent, Nissen might have been a major star in Hollywood in the 1930s.

*The Circus Queen Murder* has little plot but much atmosphere. It has a sparse mystery but excellent acting. It has an inconsistent narrative but a unique setting at a traveling circus. In the end, the positives outweigh the negatives, making this an enjoyable though hardly a classic mystery film.

*Note on the Source Material*: *The Circus Queen Murder* was very loosely based on Anthony Abbot's 1932 novel *About the Murder of the Circus Queen*. In the book, Josie La Tour is murdered while performing on the high wire at Madison Square Garden. (This was the third Madison Square Garden, which was located at 50th Street and Eighth Avenue in New York City. The facility was closed in 1967 and replaced by the current Garden, which was built above Penn Station on Seventh Avenue between 31st and 33rd Streets.)

There are numerous suspects, including her husband Flandrin, high wire performer Sebastian, and a part-owner of the circus, Marburg Lovell, who has a romantic interest in La Tour. Among the circus performers is a gang of Ubangis who have some knowledge of the crime. All of those elements were carried over into the film, although Lovell's interest in La Tour was downplayed in the film, Sebastian's interest in La Tour was emphasized in the film, and the Ubangis were turned into cannibals for the movie.

The difference between the two works is patent, with La Tour murdered at the beginning of the novel, making *About the Murder of the Circus Queen* a true whodunit. There are multiple suspects and multiple clues which have to be investigated. Later on, the Ubangi witch doctor is murdered, adding to the puzzlement. None of these aspects of the novel were carried over to the film. Indeed, after the murder of La Tour at the beginning of the book, little else from the rest of the book is incorporated into the film, even to the extent that the identity of the murderer and the method of murder are different in the novel than in the film.

## *The Panther's Claw* (1942)

After an absence of about ten years, another Thatcher Colt mystery finally made it to the cinema, in the form of *The Panther's Claw* (1942). Unfortunately, most viewers will quickly recognize that *The Panther's Claw* signifies an important drop in stature from the Thatcher Colt features from Columbia. First, *The Panther's Claw* is from PRC, perhaps the worst of the Poverty Row studies. Second, the film is directed by William Beaudine, who is best remembered today for helming many of the Bowery Boys films. Third, the budget of the film, if there is one, is paltry. There are no action scenes or even outdoor scenes in the entire movie. For example, the opening in a cemetery is shot in front of an embarrassingly unconvincing rear projection shot of several rows of tombstones. Except for the credits and a few moments at the beginning of the film, there is no background music. In other words, *The Panther's Claw* is a Poverty Row film at its worst.

The plot is not much better than the film's production values. The first crime being investigated is the blackmailing of a number of people, with the extortion notes signed with a black paw print, hence the title, *The Panther's Claw*. Later it is discovered that the prints actually came from an ordinary house cat, calling into question the title of the film. This blackmailing aspect of the plot disappears about halfway through the movie, once the police identify a Mr. Digberry as the blackmailer. His totally unconvincing explanation for blackmailing himself and others is that he needed an alibi to give to his wife for why he had withdrawn $1000 from the bank and lent it to someone whose name he refuses to reveal.

Lobby card for *The Panther's Claw* (1942).

Surely even the bumbling Mr. Digberry could have come up with a better explanation to give his wife for taking their money out of the bank, perhaps even one that his wife would have believed.

The film then segues into the second and more serious crime being investigated — the shooting death of opera singer Nina Politza. Once again, all of the evidence points to Digberry, but Colt is not so sure. After a little more investigation, Colt fingers the real criminal, who had concocted an elaborate scheme to frame Digberry for the killing. Given the cleverness of the frame-up, it is a little hard to believe that the murderer forgot to wipe his fingerprints from the murder weapon, but then none of the rest of the story makes much sense either.

Although Colt does not reveal all of his clues to the audience, the key clue for the viewer comes from the later killing of wigmaker Samuel Wilkins. Only two people knew that the police were bringing Wilkins in to identify the real murderer of the opera singer. One was Digberry, and he could not be guilty because the police suspect him of the crime. Thus, the other person who knew about Wilkins' proposed identification had to be the killer. Of course, why the police revealed to Digberry and the real murderer that Wilkins was being brought in to make his identification is hard to fathom. The police are just as responsible for the death of Wilkins as the murderer is.

*The Panther's Claw* has absolutely no pace at all. Scenes are dragged out by interminable dialogue, such as moments when Digberry does not quite understand what is being said to him. Little scenes are added for padding, such as Digberry making breakfast for himself, or a moment where a telephone operator puts a call through to Digberry, instead of the phone just ringing on its own. As is common for this type of mystery, an African-American elevator operator is added to the story, not for plot purposes, but for comic relief. *The Panther's Claw* had no pace in any event, so why slow the film down even more?

Sidney Blackmer is quite good as Thatcher Colt, almost as well-dressed as Adolphe Menjou and every bit as convincing as the astute police commissioner. Byron Foulger, a reliable supporting player in 1940s mystery movies, actually has the most screen time in the film, playing Mr. Digberry. This may be Foulger's largest role in any film and while he is appealing for a while, he wears out his welcome about halfway through. Of course, Foulger is doing the best he can with the lines he is given and the inexplicable actions his character has to take. The other performances are satisfactory, except for Joaquin Edwards who overacts outrageously as Enrico Lombardi, undercutting what little believability that character has.

*The Panther's Claw* is a poor mystery, a poor comedy and is also deadly dull. Even by PRC's low standards, the film is awful.

*Note on the Source Material*: The credits to *The Panther's Claw* indicate that the film was based on an original story by Anthony Abbot. Since the story was not identified by name and Abbot did not write any stories titled "The Panther's Claw," it has always been assumed that the movie was based on a story which Abbot wrote specifically for this feature. In fact, *The Panther's Claw* was based on "About the Perfect Crime of Mr. Digberry," one of only two short stories Abbot wrote about Thatcher Colt. The story was included in *To the Queen's Taste*, the 1946 collection of mystery stories edited by Ellery Queen.

Indeed, the movie is substantially based on the story, with key exceptions being that, in the story, Digberry's blackmail notes are signed by the Driller (there is no cat in sight), the red herring of the movies, Enrico Lombardi, is missing, and a very alive Mr. Wilkins comes to police headquarters at the end of the story to identify the actual murderer. The short story is really a police procedural as Colt follows clue after clue on the trail to the killer. The film plays more like a whodunit.

The most significant difference between the two works is that there was not enough plot in the short story to fill the seventy-minute running time of *The Panther's Claw*. The filmmakers therefore had to fill the movie with padding and comic relief, leading to the downfall of the movie. By contrast and partially because of its brevity, "About the Perfect Crime of Mr. Digberry" is an interesting story to read.

## Afterwards

After his two appearances as Thatcher Colt, Adolphe Menjou's career in Hollywood soared. In the 1930s, he had important roles in major films such as *Little Miss Marker* (1934) with Shirley Temple and *A Star Is Born* (1937) with Janet Gaynor and Fredric March. His career slowed somewhat in the 1940s, but for mystery fans, his next significant role was as the title character in *Mr. District Attorney* (1947). His other major crime role was as a police detective in *The Sniper* (1952). Menjou passed away in 1963.

Sidney Blackmer continued working regularly in films and on the stage after his starring role in *The Panther's Claw*. He won the 1950 Tony Award for Best Actor for *Come Back, Little Sheba*. His best-known film role for modern audiences is probably in *Rosemary's Baby* (1968), where he played the leader of the satanic worshippers. Blackmer died in 1973.

In total, Oursler wrote eight novels about Thatcher Colt, with the last being *The Shudders* (1943). He converted to Roman Catholicism in 1943 and thereafter concentrated on books about religion, writing under his given name, Fulton Oursler (dropping his first name). His most famous work is *The Greatest Story Ever Told*, published in 1949, a retelling of the life of Jesus Christ. Oursler passed away in 1952.

There were no further movies about Thatcher Colt after *The Panther's Claw*. Nor were there any television shows featuring the character. However, a radio program titled *Thatcher Colt* or *Thatcher Colt Mysteries* aired on NBC from 1936 to 1938. It originally starred Hanley Stafford as the New York City police commissioner.

# 7

# Inspector Trent
## *The Police Detective*

As noted in the previous chapter about Thatcher Colt, Hollywood mystery movie series usually did not feature a police detective as its lead character. Hollywood was usually much more interested in amateur detectives such as schoolteachers, reporters, teenagers and nurses, or private detectives like Michael Shayne, Nick Carter and Philip Marlowe. In the early 1930s, however, the situation was different. Hollywood did seem to have an interest in police detectives. In addition to the Charlie Chan series from Fox, Columbia Pictures produced the Thatcher Colt movies about the police commissioner of New York City and then Columbia developed a four-picture series about Inspector Trent, a detective also on the New York City police force, at least for a time.

## Background

The Inspector Trent series commenced with *Before Midnight* (1933). Three more films followed in 1934. In his four screen adventures, Trent investigates a murder which may be the result of a family curse, the murder of a boxer in an empty apartment, a murder at a Hollywood studio and a murder by gangsters related to the theft of a valuable jewel. Needless to say, Trent solves all of the cases in which he becomes involved.

Unlike Thatcher Colt, the character of Inspector Trent was original to the cinema. He supposedly works for the New York City Police Department, although in his first case, *Before Midnight*, Trent investigates a murder about 60 miles away from the big city. In the only other film in the series that is available for viewing, *The Crime of Helen Stanley* (1934), Trent suddenly works for the Los Angeles Police Department.

Inspector Trent was played by Ralph Bellamy in all four films. Born in 1904 in Chicago, Illinois, Bellamy started acting in regional theater right out of high school, at one time owning his own stock company, and finally worked his way to Broadway in 1929. Bellamy turned to films in 1931 and in his early screen appearances sometimes played second leads in major productions but usually played supporting roles in all types of films. By 1933, as of the start of the Inspector Trent series and just two years into his screen career, Bellamy had already appeared in about 20 films. The Inspector Trent series was an early opportunity for Bellamy to try to make a name for himself, by starring in a series of B-films.

There were no other regulars in the Inspector Trent series. However, Shirley Grey had roles in the last three films in the series, playing different parts.

## The Films

### *Before Midnight* (1933)

*Before Midnight* begins with Captain Frank Flynn of the New York Police Department relating the story of the Arnold case, one of Inspector Trent's most famous successes, to a policeman named Bill, challenging Bill to solve the crime from the clues that Flynn will give him. Flynn states that the story begins, as they say in books, on a great night for a murder. Flynn could have said that the murder takes place, as they say in books, on a dark and stormy night, because in *Before Midnight*, the murder of Edward Arnold takes place on one of the darkest and stormiest nights in murder mystery history, with the rain beating down in torrents, the booming of some of the loudest thunder claps ever, and a window being blown open just at the time of the murder.

The opening of *Before Midnight* is the strongest portion of the film. The dark house setting works well with the set-up to the Arnold murder, as Arnold has called Inspector Trent all the way from New York City to his Forest Lake estate because he believes that he is about to be murdered. Arnold's great-grandfather was murdered and on the night before that occurred, a pool of blood was found beneath the great-grandfather's portrait. Arnold is now concerned because the night before, he discovered another pool of blood under the portrait. Arnold then shows Trent the large clock in the foyer, stating that the clock always stops just a minute before the murder of an Arnold, implying that all of the previous Arnolds were murdered in the house. Suddenly the clock stops, a window swings open, and Arnold drops to the floor dead, cause unknown. The coroner later determines that he was poisoned. Luckily, while the famous Inspector Trent failed in his assignment to prevent Arnold's murder, he is already on the scene to investigate and, after one more murder, is able to identify the surprise killer stalking the Arnold mansion.

*Before Midnight* is an exceedingly complicated mystery which does not hold together all that well. If, as Trent says, it is impossible to have two hypodermic marks in the same place on a person's body, how did the point of the fountain pen happen to end up in the same hole as the one previously created by the hypodermic needle? Why did Fry put his own blood under the portrait? Why did the clock stop just before Arnold died?

Trent's investigative techniques leave a lot to be desired. He arrests a banker in town, on no evidence whatsoever, arguing that if the banker is guilty they have him locked up, and if he is not, it may cause the real killer to make a mistake. That is not much of a reason to arrest a prominent citizen without evidence and one imagines that a suit for false arrest is in the offing. At one point, Trent gathers all of the suspects in one room but, instead of questioning them, he advises them of the death of houseboy Kono, and then tells them they can leave. Trent never even asks them about their alibis for the time of Kono's death. Later, Trent has a policeman steal evidence from a suspect's purse. Apparently, policemen did not need search warrants in the early 1930s.

For all of that, *Before Midnight* is quite enjoyable. The effectiveness of the tale is enhanced by the expressionistic sets, such as the large Arnold foyer with its stone pillars and arches and wide steps leading to the upper floor, and the outside of the attorney's office with its bare hallway and shadow-enhancing glass in the office door. Director Lambert Hillyer varies his shot selection, such as the scene in which Arnold and Trent are talking with a roaring fire behind them, a camera which moves within scenes instead of always making cuts, and the use of contrasting light and dark to create shadows.

*Before Midnight* is in the style of a classic whodunit with a murder committed in a large mansion with a limited number of suspects living in or visiting the house. However, the film has an added feature of a howdunit, because it is not quite clear how the poison was introduced into Arnold's body. Also, two of the characters are not who they are supposed to be, adding to the intrigue.

The quality of *Before Midnight* drops substantially once Arnold is murdered, with the film never matching its strong opening. However, the sets, direction and complicated plot (with only negligible comedy relief) belie its B–nature status. With an excellent performance by a very young Bellamy as Inspector Trent, and the film's Philo Vance–type ending, with Trent allowing the murderer to commit suicide rather than face trial, *Before Midnight* is a good opening film for a new mystery series.

## *One Is Guilty* (1934)

[*This is one of only a few films discussed in this book which the author did not view.*]

In this second film in the series, Inspector Trent is back in New York City, investigating the murder of a boxer in an empty apartment at the Rexford Arms. Among the clues he discovers are a woman's scarf, two lipstick-stained cigarette butts and a watch with a missing minute hand. After another murder and some diligent detective work, Trent solves the case.

## *The Crime of Helen Stanley* (1934)

For some reason left unexplained, the Inspector Trent of *The Crime of Helen Stanley* works for the Los Angeles Police Department instead of the New York Police Department. That turns out to be fortunate since a murder has occurred at a Hollywood studio, Tru-Art Pictures, and who is better able to solve such a crime than Inspector Trent? The victim, Helen Stanley, was killed while performing a dance in front of the cameras in a nightclub scene for a film. At first blush, the killer seems obvious. Wallach, another actor in the film, was supposed to shoot the character being played by Stanley. Wallach is given a prop gun with two blank bullets in it. Wallach substitutes one real bullet for a blank bullet and at the appropriate time in the scene, fires a shot at Stanley. She drops to the floor, dead. Wallach, who is Stanley's husband although long-separated, is chased around the studio and, just before committing suicide by jumping off a high catwalk, confesses his crime.

Despite the fact that Wallach is clearly the murderer, any experienced mystery movie fan knows that it cannot be so, or there would be no movie left. Therefore, no viewer is surprised to learn that Wallach's gun did not fire the fatal bullet. Wallach had mistakenly fired the blank cartridge instead of the real bullet. Therefore someone else is the murderer. However, since Stanley was whirling around the dance floor when the shot came, Inspector Trent does not even know from which direction Stanley was shot.

*The Crime of Helen Stanley* was not the first or the last murder mystery to be set at a Hollywood studio. Others include *The Death Kiss* (1933) and *The Falcon in Hollywood* (1944). In addition to the obvious cost savings of using the real studio in which the real film is being shot as the setting for the shooting of the fictitious film, there is an intrinsic interest in filmmaking that all film fans have, which adds to the fun of watching these movies. In *The Crime of Helen Stanley* the viewer learns about the lighting used on the set and the wardrobe used by the extras, and observes the director looking at the scene through

Inspector Trent (Ralph Bellamy) discovers Betty Lane (Shirley Grey), bound and unconscious after someone stole her sister Helen's diary in *The Crime of Helen Stanley* (1934).

the camera lens to see how the shot will look on screen. This early scene in the film is also used to introduce the audience to the suspects for the upcoming murder.

Another familiar scene in a mystery movie is where a photograph of the crime may provide a significant clue to the identity of the killer. *The Crime of Helen Stanley* goes that one better, since the murder of Helen Stanley occurred while a movie camera was rolling. The cameraman, Lee Davis, finally gets the idea to have Inspector Trent view the rushes to see if they will disclose the direction from which the shot came. They do and Inspector Trent lays a trap for the killer in a re-enactment of the crime.

As is often the case in a B-movie mystery, the motive for the killing comes out of the blue, making the identity of the killer less than convincing. It also does not help that not one shadow of suspicion was ever cast on the character, until the very end. To accept the entire premise of Helen Stanley's murder, the audience must suspend its disbelief and swallow the incredible coincidence that two people shot at Helen Stanley at the exact same time, while she was performing in front of the cameras, and that one of them, Wallach, negligently left a blank cartridge in the gun that he was using.

Nevertheless, *The Crime of Helen Stanley* is a worthwhile diversion for the mystery movie fan. It holds the audience's interest throughout, with the scenes which directly concern the motion picture industry the clear standouts. The film meets the limited goal that all second features had, of trying to entertain the members of the audience who came to the theater primarily for the other movie on the bill.

## *Girl in Danger* (1934)

[*This is one of only a few films discussed in this book which the author did not view.*]

The last film in the Trent series is a little different than the prior films, although Trent is still not above searching a suspect's apartment without a warrant. Here, the main crime being investigated is a jewel robbery and the murder of one gangster by another. During the course of the proceedings, Trent is shot by one of the gangsters and his murder is announced in the next day's newspapers. Not surprisingly, Trent is alive and well at the end of the film, capturing the killer and his gang and rescuing the girl.

## AFTERWARDS

After completion of the Inspector Trent series, Bellamy generally played character parts in films and on television. He received an Oscar nomination for Best Supporting Actor for *The Awful Truth* (1937) where he competed with Cary Grant for the affections of Irene Dunne. Probably his most famous performance was as Franklin Delano Roosevelt in *Sunrise at Campobello*, first on Broadway where he won a Tony Award in 1958 and then in the 1960 film. In 1987, Bellamy won an honorary Oscar for his unique artistry and distinguished service to the acting profession.

For mystery movie fans, Bellamy played Ellery Queen in the first four films in the seven-picture series produced at Columbia in the 1940s, beginning with *Ellery Queen, Master Detective* (1940). Ellery Queen, as played by Bellamy, was sometimes more of a clown than a serious detective. The films may have been better if the part was written and performed in the more serious manner of Inspector Trent. From 1949 to 1954, Bellamy played private detective Mike Barnett in the television mystery series *Man Against Crime*. Bellamy died in 1991.

After the completion of the four-movie series at Columbia in 1934, there were no more films about Inspector Trent. Since the character was a screen original, it is not surprising that there were never any radio or television series about the character.

# 8

# Nick and Nora Charles
## *The Thin Man Series*

Dashiell Hammett wrote only five novels, and they provided the source material for two of the most famous detective movies of all time. Hammett's 1930 novel *The Maltese Falcon*, originally serialized in *Black Mask* magazine starting in 1929, spawned the famous 1941 movie starring Humphrey Bogart, Mary Astor, Sydney Greenstreet and Peter Lorre. Hammett's 1934 novel *The Thin Man* was turned into a film that same year starring William Powell and Myrna Loy. In many ways, *The Thin Man* was the more influential of the two films. It resulted in five sequels to the original film, stretched out over a 13-year period, and also created a subgenre of the detective movie: the male and female detecting duo.

## Background

### Dashiell Hammett

Hammett is still one of the most famous names in all of American mystery fiction. Born Samuel Dashiell Hammett in Maryland on May 27, 1894, the future writer dropped out of school in his early teens. After toiling at various jobs such as a freight clerk, cannery worker and nail-machine operator, he went to work for the Pinkerton National Detective Agency in Baltimore, Maryland, in 1915. Thereafter, he worked for the agency around the country, most notably in San Francisco. Hammett was able to use this background in detective work when he began writing mystery fiction. His days with the Pinkerton Agency probably inspired one of his most famous creations, the Continental Op, a San Francisco detective whose actual name was never disclosed to the reader.

Hammett joined the Army during World War I and worked in the Motor Ambulance Corps, where he contracted tuberculosis. After the end of the war, he returned to the Pinkerton Agency, married and had two children, quit his job, separated from his wife and started writing crime fiction. Starting in the 1920s, he was published regularly in the leading pulp magazines, including *Black Mask*, where his first four novels were serialized before being released in book format. His fifth novel, *The Thin Man*, was published in 1934. The novel related the story of a murder investigation by the famous detective Nick Charles, who was accompanied by his loving wife, Nora, and their dog, Asta. The novel had more humor than any of the other works of Hammett's.

## The Film Series

MGM bought the rights to *The Thin Man* and released a movie version in 1934. The film starred William Powell and Myrna Loy and it was so successful that five more films were released in the series, all starring Powell and Loy.

Powell was born in 1892 in Pittsburgh, Pennsylvania. As a teenager, he moved with his family to Kansas City, Missouri, and after graduating from high school, he moved on his own to New York City to attend drama school. He then had some success on Broadway before moving into pictures. His first film role was in *Sherlock Holmes* (1922), wherein John Barrymore played the great detective and Powell had a featured part as a reluctant agent of Professor Moriarty. Powell can be hard to recognize in the film as he was very young and did not yet sport his famous mustache. Thereafter, Powell was constantly at work in silent films, before being chosen by Paramount to be the first actor to play the most famous detective of the 1920s, Philo Vance, in a silent film titled *The Canary Murder Case* (1929). Partway through production, it was decided to make the film into a talkie and therefore Powell is credited as playing the first detective in a sound film.

Powell made a total of three Vance films at Paramount before moving to Warner Brothers for his last Vance film, *The Kennel Murder Case* (1933). While making the Vance movies, Powell was working steadily in other films. Right after *The Kennel Murder Case* (1934), he appeared in *Manhattan Melodrama* (1934) with Clark Gable. It was directed by W.S. Van Dyke and also starred Myrna Loy. Based on the chemistry he discerned between Powell and Loy, Van Dyke lobbied MGM to star the two as Nick and Nora Charles in a movie Van Dyke wanted to direct. Van Dyke got his wish and *The Thin Man* was produced.

Myrna Loy, *née* Myrna Williams, was born in Montana in 1905. She alternately lived in both California and Montana in her younger years, eventually settling in California. It was there at the age of 18 that she began dancing professionally. She first appeared in silent films in 1926 and because of her exotic looks often played villainous Asian roles. She also played that type of part in the early sound era, with her best-remembered early roles being Fu Manchu's daughter in *The Mask of Fu Manchu* (1932) and a murderous Eurasian halfbreed in *Thirteen Women* (1932). In that same year, her film roles started to broaden. She had a supporting comedy role in director Rouben Mamoulian's famous musical *Love Me Tonight* (1932), starring Maurice Chevalier, and in 1933 she performed in *Topaze*, a comedy with John Barrymore. As related above, after her supporting role in *Manhattan Melodrama*, Loy was cast in *The Thin Man*.

Other than Nick and Nora, the only other character to appear in all six films was Asta, their dog. As well known to crossword puzzle enthusiasts as mystery movie lovers, Asta was a wire-haired terrier who was played by several different dogs over the course of the long film series.

## The Films

### *The Thin Man* (1934)

*The Thin Man* may well be the best-loved detective movie of the 1930s. Noted mainly for its elements of wit and sophistication, *The Thin Man* is also a clever mystery, with multiple bodies, numerous suspects and a crafty plot twist near the end which involves the thin man of the title.

The story commences with absent-minded Clyde Wynant, a very thin man, meeting his daughter, Dorothy, and her fiancé, Tommy. Wynant is about to go out of town on a mysterious business trip but promises to be back in time for the holidays and Dorothy's wedding. Before he leaves town, Wynant discovers that some valuable bonds are missing from his safe so he goes to the apartment of his mistress, Julia Wolf, and accuses her. She admits her involvement but implies that she had a partner.

Time passes and even though her wedding is approaching, Dorothy has not heard from her father in over three months. Dorothy's mother, who has divorced Wynant and remarried, is still after Wynant for money. She goes to Julia Wolf's apartment to try to learn something about Wynant's disappearance. There she discovers Julia's murdered body and, in her dead hand, Wynant's watch chain. The police believe Wynant committed that murder and another one later in the film, but Nick Charles is not so sure. He decides to become involved in the investigation and at the end of the film unmasks the real killer at a dinner party held at his home.

*The Thin Man* is best-remembered today for the urbanity and modernity of the relationship between Nick and Nora Charles. They are a man and a woman who are truly in love and, perhaps more importantly, truly enjoy each other's company. They banter, accept each other's foibles, kiss and make up, and, if Asta's instincts are correct at the end of the film, have a mature sexual and loving relationship.

The dialogue between the two is sparkling, particularly the asides thrown away by Nora about Nick's somewhat unusual friends, many of whom seem to have a stretch of prison in their background. ("Oh, Nicky, I love you because you know such lovely people.") Finding that Nick has already had six martinis to her one, Nora asks the bartender to line up five more martinis for her. Nick also gets off his share of good lines. For example, when Nora says that if Nick is killed, she will not remain a widow for long, Nick concurs, saying, "Not with all your money."

The banter is important but the film would never have worked without the perfect casting of Powell and Loy. By 1934, Powell was already well-known to movie audiences for playing Philo Vance, but Nick Charles is no Philo Vance and Powell plays the roles completely differently. Nick is often tipsy but never out of control. He purports to be uninterested in the case while always bringing a high level of acuity to the analysis of the facts. At the same time, Charles is a little bit of a hardboiled detective, taking guns from assailants who are poised to use them. No matter which version of Nick is then on the screen, Powell is always convincing and engaging.

Loy is charming, witty and funny as Nora and she is about as attractive a detective's assistant as ever appeared on the screen. Always dressed in eye-catching outfits, whether just walking the dog or giving a dinner party, Loy is the epitome of the 1930s Hollywood version of a sophisticated lady. When she wrinkles her nose at Nick, well, it is easy to see why Nick loves Nora.

The rest of the male cast is outstanding, with bits by familiar supporting players such as Porter Hall as MacCauley, Harold Huber as Nunheim and Edward Brophy as Morelli, all of whom are realistic suspects for the killings. The one offbeat bit of casting is Nat Pendleton as Lieutenant Guild. Pendleton is better known today for comedy roles or very small parts in movies, but he is effective as the quite large and not so dumb policeman. Pendleton's counter-intuitive casting in *The Thin Man* is a decided plus. However, some of the female performances are disappointing. For example, Minna Gombell as Mimi Jorgenson and Natalie Moorhead as Julia Wolf often overact for little reason. It is always a joy, though, to see Maureen O'Sullivan in any movie, with her striking good looks and tantalizing voice. She has a significant role as the thin man's daughter and it is difficult to take one's eyes from O'Sullivan when she is on the screen.

What is often overlooked about *The Thin Man* is that there is quite a good murder mystery being told. Before Nick and Nora are even introduced, the background story of Clyde Wynant is told in detail, including his intended disappearance for reasons unknown, his former wife who is still interested in his money, his current girlfriend who is probably unfaithful to him, and the stealing of the bonds by his girlfriend and a person unknown. Amid all the banter and repartee, the focus of the film is never far from the mystery. Even in the Christmas Eve party scene in Nick's apartment, with its many strange characters, flowing alcohol and Nora being amazed at the quality of Nick's associates, various suspects arrive at the apartment with information that moves the plot forward.

While other films only have a limited number of suspects, *The Thin Man* has so many that when Nick brings them to his home for a dinner party, extra chairs are needed. While it appears that Wynant may have committed the two murders that the police are investigating, there is quite a surprise concerning the third murder that is discovered. The one flaw in the mystery, though, is that there are no good clues to the murderer and the audience has no rational basis for determining who the real killer is. Indeed, if Nick is to be taken at his word, he did not even know who the murderer was when he brought all the suspects together at the denouement.

*The Thin Man* is a movie of both style and substance, a mixture that is hard to find in any mystery movie of any decade.

*Note on the Source Material*: The film was based on the 1934 Dashiell Hammett novel *The Thin Man*. Since the book opens months after the disappearance of Charles Wynant, this is a rare novel in which the title character does not appear in the book. For mystery and trivia fans, another example is *Rebecca* by Daphne Du Maurier.

The movie follows the basic outline of the book, with the murder of Julia Wolf sparking a police investigation into the actions of Charles Wynant, an eccentric inventor who had disappeared months before Wolf's killing. Nick Charles, in New York for the Christmas holiday season, is dragged into the investigation by the thin man's daughter, Dorothy. Nick knows many of the characters involved from his dealings with them in the past when he was a private detective.

This is that rare situation where the film version of a famous novel is better than the book. Because the film plot is laid out in detail before Nick and Nora are introduced in the movie, it is easier for the viewer to follow the plot in the film than in the book. By contrast, much of the story in the book is related verbally by the characters to Nick, in retrospect. That allows the film's plot to be slightly more complicated than that of the novel, another rare event. With distinctive actors in the movie roles, large and small, the characters never run together as they do in the book. Also, while the killer and motive are the same in each medium, the screenwriters essentially jettisoned the second half of the book's story, substituting a more cinematic way to tell it (such as gathering all of the suspects together at the end of the feature so that Nick can finger the killer).

Hammett's genius was to create two unforgettable characters, Nick and Nora Charles, who are loving, sexual, witty and classy, and then throw them into a complex murder story. Husband-and-wife detectives were unknown in crime fiction until Hammett developed the idea, and Hammett imbued Nick and Nora with a degree of sophistication that would be hard for subsequent crime writers to match. Indeed, some of the book's memorable dialogue ("I love you, Nicky, because you smell nice and know such fascinating people") and the overemphasis on drinking in the novel are incorporated into the film.

However, the best dialogue in the movie is original to the screenplay, and with the perfect casting of Powell and Loy in the leads, the film comes alive as the book never quite does. Their chemistry is what sparks the movie, ratifying the screenwriters' decision to place more emphasis on the relationship between Nick and Nora in the movie than Hammett did in his book.

*Note on the Titles*: *The Thin Man* was popular enough to spawn a sequel. Even though the thin man of that title was not Nick Charles, the studio desired to capitalize on the name, calling its next film *After the Thin Man*. The title could be justified because this was Nick's first case after the thin man affair. However, with the third film in the series, *Another Thin Man*, the reference has to be to Nick and Nora's baby son who makes his first appearance in that film. There are no particularly thin characters in the movie. Therefore, the "Thin Man" has to refer to Nick Charles. Similarly, the fifth film in the series, *The Thin Man Goes Home*, involves Nick's return to his home town. The title can only be justified by Nick now being known as "The Thin Man."

Interestingly, unlike the Falcon, the Saint and the Lone Wolf, who are referred to in their films by both their real names and their sobriquets, Nick is never referred to as "The Thin Man" in any of the films. However, given the titles of the last five films in the series, it is no wonder that movie audiences are surprised when viewing the first film to discover that the thin man of the title is not Nick Charles.

## *After the Thin Man* (1936)

At the beginning of *The Thin Man*, the screenwriters concentrated on setting up the mystery story before introducing Nick and Nora Charles and their unusual lifestyle. In *After the Thin Man*, the opposite approach is taken. The writers spend the first 15 minutes or so of the movie emphasizing the relationship between Nick and Nora, Nick's friends and Nora's family before any of the mystery elements are introduced.

These early, non-mystery moments are some of the most amusing scenes in any crime film. They include a surprise New Year's Eve party thrown for Nick and Nora by people at the Charles house, using the Charles' food and spirits even though many of the guests do not even know Nick and Nora. There is also the introduction of Nick's acquaintances, including a purse snatcher, a truck driver, a newsboy and a boxer. At Nora's aunt's house, there is an elderly butler who finds it hard to carry Nick's heavy coat and there is even a variation on the old "Walk this way" joke.

The dialogue in these opening scenes is particularly crisp, with the highlight occurring after Nora has met a number of Nick's unusual friends. An elderly, well-dressed couple then waves to Nora, and when Nick asks who they are, Nora replies that Nick doesn't know them; "They're respectable."

*After the Thin Man* is a mystery, though, and a crime story is slowly introduced among the comedy moments. It features the sophisticates of the upper class, who dress formally for dinner, have cooks and butlers and attend lavish nightclubs on New Year's Eve. All is not well in that society, however, as Nora's cousin Selma is in an unhappy marriage with Robert Landis. Robert has disappeared and Selma's aunt wants Nick to find him. Nick and

The lovely Nora Charles (Myrna Loy) and her husband Nick Charles (William Powell) at a nightclub on New Year's Eve in *After the Thin Man* (1936). On the right is Dancer (Joseph Calleia), one of the owners of the nightclub.

Nora go to a Chinese nightclub which Robert often frequents, where they discover Robert, who is apparently in an affair with nightclub singer Polly. David Graham, Selma's former fiancé, who is still in love with Selma, has agreed to pay Robert $25,000 to leave town and (not coincidentally) clear Graham's path to Selma.

Dancer, the owner of the club, tells Polly to take Robert home, hoping to obtain a large check from Robert related to a forgery. In the meantime, Robert meets Graham and pays him $25,000 in bonds to leave town. All of the potential suspects then seem to converge on the scene. Polly has left the club with Robert. Dancer and the other owner of the club, Lum Kee, have gone on separate car rides for no explainable reason. Polly's brother Phil Byrnes (who turns out to be Polly's husband) is following Robert. Robert goes back to Selma's house for some clothes, infuriating Selma enough that she follows him outside with a gun.

Robert is then shot in the back while he is walking down the street. When Graham pulls up in his car, Selma is standing over the body with a gun. Believing Selma is innocent, Graham disposes of her gun in the river. However, because Selma is now unable to prove that her gun was not the murder weapon, she is arrested for Robert's killing. After two more murders, those of Phil Byrnes and of a gardener, Pedro, who was then a janitor in Polly's apartment building, Nick gathers all the suspects and after some byplay with the bunch, identifies the true killer.

Even after the opening scenes of *After the Thin Man*, the relationship and banter between Nick and Nora are the highlights of the film. Powell seems so natural as Nick that he hardly seems to be acting. Loy is stunningly beautiful as Nora. Nevertheless, sometimes the film does seem padded with comedy, as when Asta grabs a rock with an important note on it and will not give it to Nick, or when Nora cajoles Nick into cooking eggs for her in the middle of the night. These are minor points, however, as most of the comedy works quite well, especially as performed by one of the most likable movie couples of all time.

The mystery, however, has its flaws. Although there are ostensibly a number of suspects, Lum Kee and Dancer are quickly ruled out when ballistics evidence shows that their guns were not involved in the killing of Robert. Polly is eliminated because the killer was eavesdropping on her apartment. Polly's "brother" is himself killed so he cannot be the murderer of Robert. Selma cannot be the murderer since the police arrested her for the crime. Nora's Aunt Katherine and Dr. Kammer are not serious suspects. That leaves only Graham, and, indeed, he is the person Nick fingers for the crimes.

Nick catches Graham in a mistake, describing Pedro, the former family gardener whom he had last seen six years before, as having a long white moustache. However, an old family picture of Nora shows that six years before, the gardener had a short black moustache. Therefore, the only way Graham could have known about the longer white moustache is if he saw it on the day he killed the gardener. But why wasn't this photo shown to the audience when Nora first brought it to Nick, so that the viewer could have caught the same mistake in Graham's story? For some reason, screenwriters of mystery films were usually afraid to play fair with the viewers.

Also, Nick seems to be a one-trick private detective. His only investigative technique seems to be to gather all the suspects in a room, accuse each of them of the crime and then hope that the true killer will make a mistake. Even though Nick is two for two in the series with this approach, the technique would not seem to have a high likelihood of success over time.

On the other hand, *After the Thin Man* is such an enjoyable film that it is not helpful to over-analyze the mystery plot. Nick and Nora Charles clearly enjoy each other's company and so will any movie audience.

## *Another Thin Man* (1939)

Nick and Nora Charles return in *Another Thin Man*, a murder mystery and gangster movie set in Manhattan and Long Island. Nick and Nora now have a one-year-old son, Nick, Jr., but little else has changed in their lives. Nick and Nora still drink, banter and take their dog Asta with them wherever they go.

As *Another Thin Man* opens, an old family friend, Colonel McFay, summons Nick and Nora to his Long Island estate for help with a serious problem. It seems that Phil Church, a former employee of the colonel and a man who blames the colonel for his imprisonment for the last ten years, has threatened the colonel's life. Church has moved into the house down the road from the colonel and has been terrorizing the colonel ever since. Indeed, the night Nick and Nora arrive, a "dead" body is seen on the road near the colonel's home, the colonel's swimming pool bathhouse is set on fire and the colonel's dog is killed. The colonel fears for his life and as it turns out, with good reason. Later that night, the colo-

Phil Church (Sheldon Leonard), far right, tells Nora (Myrna Loy) and Nick Charles (William Powell) that he has twice dreamed about Nick dying and that unless the two get out of town immediately, it could happen in real life, in *Another Thin Man* (1939).

nel's murdered body is discovered. He was hit over the head with a blunt instrument and his throat was cut.

The obvious villain is Phil Church or one of his associates, i.e., Dum Dum, his assistant, or Smitty, his girlfriend. There is also a strange bespectacled man named Diamondback following Church. His motives are unclear but suspicious. Another set of suspects are Lois, the colonel's daughter; Dudley Horn, her fiancé; Freddie, another young gentleman in the house who has a crush on Lois; and Mrs. Bellam, the housekeeper who may be the real mother of Lois. In addition, the nurse for the Charles family immediately disappears once the murder of Colonel McFay is discovered. At the end of the movie, Nick manages to stay sober long enough to identify the surprise killer.

The highlight of the prior Thin Man movies was the relationship between Nick and Nora and, in that regard, *Another Thin Man* does not disappoint. Loy is particularly delightful in those lighter moments, such as when two policemen are trying to convince her to turn on Nick, by telling her about all the women Nick had before he was married. Loy is amusing as she listens to the stories in bemused silence, finally asking if the stories are really true. When the policemen answer in the affirmative, Nora says, "I always thought he was bragging."

Loy is as beautiful as ever in many chic outfits from her seemingly endless wardrobe.

She may be the best listener in films since Ginger Rogers listened to Fred Astaire sing to her in all of their films together. Without even saying a word, Loy can be funnier listening to the statements made by Powell than Powell is in saying them.

*Another Thin Man* has the most complex plot of any of the films in the Thin Man series, and that is both a positive and a negative. Any avid fan of mystery movies enjoys a complicated crime with multiple murders and many plausible suspects. *Another Thin Man* surely has those. Also, unlike the prior two films, Nick does not try to trick the murderer into a confession but instead, does some real investigating to discover the killer. That adds to the cogency of the crime plot.

However, there are simply too many suspects around (and for that matter, too many policemen around) to keep the whole story straight. Much of the plot is fueled by incredible coincidences, such as the murder of the colonel occurring on the night that Nick and Nora arrive at his home, giving the murderer a needed alibi. In the end, the mystery seems more convoluted than complicated, and Nick's explanations for the murders seem pat and unconvincing. With a 105–minute running time, the film drags occasionally. *Another Thin Man* would have been a substantially better film had it been shorter and more focused.

Those negatives are not insignificant when evaluating a mystery movie, but the Thin Man movies, including *Another Thin Man*, were always high-class productions, with excellent acting, clever writing and competent directing. Although *Another Thin Man* is the weakest film in the series to date, it is still better than many mystery films of its era. And when the story bogs down a little, there is still Myrna Loy to watch.

*Note on the Source Material*: *Another Thin Man* was based upon Dashiell Hammett's lengthy short story. "The Farewell Murder," first published in the February 1930 issue of *Black Mask* magazine. The investigator is the unnamed Continental Op and the "Farewell" in the title refers to the town in which the murder occurs.

The beginning of *Another Thin Man* is very similar to the beginning of the story as, in the story, the Continental Op is called out to the home of wealthy Mr. Kavalov, who is being threatened by his former business associate, Captain Sherry. On the ride, the Op sees a "dead" body in the road and that night a field is burned and a dog is killed. Later, Kavalov is killed and the Op is off to find the killer.

There are far fewer suspects in the story than the film. The Continental Op is a serious detective, so there is no clever banter among the parties as there is in the film. The killer, who partnered with Sherry in the crime, is a slightly different person than in the film, making the solution to the murder much more convincing in the story than in the movie. "The Farewell Murder" contains less humor but is a more convincing murder mystery than *Another Thin Man*. It is well worth a read.

## *Shadow of the Thin Man* (1941)

The Thin Man movies were always noted for their comedy elements, particularly in their depiction of the relationship between Nick and Nora. This time, however, the filmmakers went too far. *Shadow of the Thin Man* is more of a comedy than a mystery and after a while, the comedy elements and the mystery, what little there is, become quite tedious.

Nick and Nora happen to be at the race track when news comes of the murder of a jockey in the locker room shower stall, apparently related to the jockey's association with gamblers. Despite the entreaties of the police and the press, Nick refuses to become involved.

Later, Nick and Nora happen to be at the wrestling arena where Whitey Barrow, a newspaper reporter who is also somehow involved with the gamblers, is shot and killed. Because suspicion falls on a friend of Nick's, Nick finally agrees to investigate. After gathering all of the suspects at police headquarters, he identifies the least likely one as the killer of Barrow.

That plot drips out between numerous comedy set pieces, such as Nick having to drink milk in front of his son, Nick getting dizzy on a carousel with his son, Nora becoming enthusiastic at the wrestling match, a waiter at a restaurant convincing everyone in the Charles party to have sea bass for dinner, and Asta causing a riot at that restaurant. Some of it is amusing but there is simply too much of it. At times, the murder mystery seems to disappear.

On the positive side, there are some interesting performers and performances in the film. Stella Adler plays suspect Claire Porter. The soon-to-be famous acting teacher is, as expected, good in the part of the tramp-turned-society lady, and, in addition, she is also quite attractive. Lou Lubin plays "Rainbow" Benny, racetrack lout, murder suspect and murder victim. The nattily dressed but always frightened Benny is an interesting character who seems to come straight from the writings of Damon Runyon. Lubin is one of many actors in the Thin Man movies with very unusual faces. Barry Nelson, as reporter Paul Clarke, makes his film debut in *Shadow of the Thin Man*; for Donna Reed, playing Paul's girlfriend Molly, this was just her second film. Of the two, Reed stands out more, with her wholesome beauty shining through in a basically forgettable part.

The one grating performance comes from Dickie Hall as Nick, Jr. While he is not as bad as Donnie Dunagan in *Son of Frankenstein* (1939), this is still one of the worst performances ever by a child actor. He is so unconvincing as the Charles' offspring that he makes the audience uncomfortable whenever he is on screen. It is not surprising that Hall had only a few more credited appearances in his very short screen career. Perhaps he should have taken lessons from the dog playing Asta, who is at least a natural in that part.

Since Nick is still not much of a detective, he is back to gathering the suspects in a room and encouraging them to talk, in the hopes that one of them will make a slip, convicting himself. How ridiculous is that! What is the likelihood of that investigative technique ever working? Well, based on the Thin Man movies, its chances of success are 100 percent. In *Shadow of the Thin Man*, however, this method of crime investigation is particularly unconvincing. One character makes a slip about seeing the steps in the apartment building from Benny's room (which is impossible), leading Nick to the conclusion that Benny has recently changed rooms, convicting the least likely suspect of the crimes because of an offhand remark he recently made to Nick about having visited Benny in his room. It is all pretty silly and very wearying.

Crime films are different than mystery novels. At the end of a mystery book, the detective can simply explain his solution and his reasoning and the reader will not be bored by the presentation, because the reader is just reading. By contrast, in a film, where a talking head can become very boring very fast, the gathering of the suspects is a cinematic device to allow the detective to explain things in a more interesting setting. Even though the detective is still a talking head, his accusations against each of the suspects, the interplay between the detective and the suspects plus some cuts between all gathered in the room give the film a sense of movement and excitement, eliminating the boredom.

When the cinematic Charlie Chan or Hercule Poirot gather suspects at the end of a film, they either know who the killer is or are setting a trap for the killer. They are not just hoping someone will expose himself by making a misstatement. By contrast, when Nick Charles gathers the suspects at a time when he has no idea who the killer is, he changes from a competent detective into the luckiest person alive, undercutting the mystery and the believability of the movie.

Myrna Loy is still a joy to watch, dressing in many beautiful outfits throughout the film. However, those hats she wears are very distracting at times, except when people make funny comments about them. Surprisingly, Nick probably wears more different outfits in the film than Nora. For example, Nick wears four different suits or sport coats on just the first day of the case. Nick and Nora are the best-dressed detectives in movie history.

*Shadow of the Thin Man* is a very disappointing film, with an uninteresting mystery saddled with a ridiculous solution. Frankly, the film is tedious at times, something the prior films in the series never were. As to the perplexing title, by the end of the movie, its meaning finally becomes clear. In this fourth film in the series, Nick Charles has become just a shadow of the detective that he used to be.

## *The Thin Man Goes Home* (1944)

After an absence of three years from the cinema, Nick and Nora Charles returned in *The Thin Man Comes Home*, the fifth film in the series and the second comedy in a row. Beginning with the last film, *Shadow of the Thin Man*, the emphasis of the series shifted from mystery to comedy, and if that is what the viewer is interested in, this film is a delight. There are extended comedy scenes, such as Nick, Nora and Asta trying to make their way through crowded train corridors, Nora relating some of Nick's questionable detective exploits to Nick's parents, Nick allowing Nora to trail an innocent character all over town and Nora becoming involved in a spectacular jitterbug at the local bazaar. Asta also gets to do his usual comedy schtick, this time, for example, with a goat on the train and later, with a painting of a dog. Although there is clearly too much of it, some of the comedy in the film is quite funny.

There is also the relationship between Nick and Nora, sophisticated and loving as always, even if the banter does not come up to the prior films' quality. There is even some pop psychology thrown in, with Nick (or at least Nora) trying to impress Nick's dad with Nick's detective skills, as the elder Charles was always disappointed that Nick did not follow in his footsteps and become a doctor. What's not to love about this film?

The problem, of course, is that *The Thin Man Comes Home* is still a murder mystery and in that regard, the film is seriously lacking. The first event that relates in any way to a crime is the murder of Peter Barton and that does not occur until about one-third of the way through the film. Nick is then on the trail of the murderer, and in the process he learns many of the dark secrets of his hometown of Sycamore Springs. At the end of the film, Nick gathers all of the suspects at his father's home and, in Nick's usual style, identifies the surprise killer.

There are several interesting aspects of the feature. The switch of setting from the urban jungles of New York and San Francisco to the small-town atmosphere of Sycamore Springs is a change of pace for the series, although, in the end, life hardly seems less sordid in this town than in the teeming metropolises. The killing of Barton is a nice moment. He is surprisingly killed just as Nick opens the front door to him. No sound of a gunshot is heard; Barton just drops to the ground. When Nick gathers the suspects at the end of the film, Nick knows in advance who the killer is, a much better approach than in the prior

Nick Charles (William Powell) is upset with Nora Charles (Myrna Loy) for a newspaper interview she gave to Nick's hometown newspaper, implying that Nick has returned on a case, in *The Thin Man Goes Home* (1944).

films, where Nick did not know and gathered the suspects in the faint hope that the killer would make a slip.

The best aspect of the mystery is that there is one solid clue to the killer, Dr. Bruce Clayworth. The first time Clayworth goes to Crazy Mary's shack with Nick, Clayworth calls out to her before entering, to ensure that he will not get slugged by the crazy lady. The second time Clayworth goes with Nick, he never calls out, a clear indication that he already knows Mary is dead, making him the killer of both Mary and Barton. It is a fair clue and one that a knowing viewer will recognize, making *The Thin Man Comes Home* a rare mystery film that gives the audience a solid clue to the killer's identity. Also, since Clayworth is the town's coroner, he has a chance to substitute bullets after examining Barton's body, which is a nice twist for the mystery.

There are other reasons, of course, why the viewer will know that Clayworth is the killer. He is the least likely suspect in town, as he assists Nick somewhat in his investigations. Since Clayworth mentions several times how much more successful Nick was than he when they were in high school, from fishing to females, that is a pretty good indication that Clayworth may be the villain. That type of backstory is often used to set up a confrontation at the end of a mystery movie and that is exactly what occurs in *The Thin Man Comes Home*. After Nick identifies Clayworth as the killer, Clayworth grabs a rifle and attempts to kill Nick, partially to assuage his jealousy of Nick from high school.

While the core murder mystery holds together well, the stories of all the other residents of Sycamore Springs and their direct or indirect involvement in stealing secret plans for a foreign government is unconvincing. Also, it is not clear how Nick discovered that information. He narrates an interesting tale to all who are present at the film's end, but is he accurate? If this aspect of the story has been developed in greater detail during the feature, *The Thin Man Comes Home* could have been an excellent mystery.

Perhaps more than any other mystery movie, *The Thin Man Comes Home* is a matter of taste. If one is just interested in another chapter in the lives of the Charles family, comedy and all, the film is quite enjoyable. If one is interested in viewing a solid mystery, the sheer enormity of the comedy elements becomes grating at times, and as for the mystery, it had more potential than what was actually produced. For the pure mystery aficionado, *The Thin Man Comes Home* is disappointing.

## *Song of the Thin Man* (1947)

The Thin Man series lost its way with the prior two films, which placed too much emphasis on the comedy and not enough on the mystery elements. The Thin Man stories are supposed to be, after all, mysteries with comedy elements and not the other way around. However, for its last film, *Song of the Thin Man*, the series got back on track with a good crime story punctuated by the trademark Thin Man humor.

Nick and Nora are on board a gambling ship for a charity event. The entertainment is provided by jazz band leader Tommy Drake, its lead clarinettist, Buddy Hollis, and sexy blues singer, Fran Page. Drake is a true ladies' man, having previously stolen Fran from Tommy. Now Fran accuses Drake of having additional affairs. Drake announces he is leaving the band to go on a tour set up by Mitchell Talbin, a band booker. However, when the owner of the gambling vessel, Phil Brandt, refuses to pay Drake what he owes him and Talbin refuses to advance him $12,000, Drake is justifiably worried. Gambler Al Amboy is on board ship and he is interested in enforcing a gambling debt against Drake.

Drake sneaks into Brandt's office to search for his money where he is shot by an unseen assailant. When the police finger Brandt for the crime, he and his new wife, Janet Thayer, come to Nick for help. Janet's father, who disliked Brandt, is also a suspect. After a wide-ranging investigation, Nick brings the suspects back aboard the gambling ship and, with a ruse involving the very disturbed Buddy Hollis, exposes the true killer.

That brief summary of the plot discloses what a good mystery *Song of the Thin Man* is. There are numerous suspects, and because the killer may have thought he was shooting Brandt instead of Drake, the field is more wide open than first thought. The film spends a significant amount of time setting up the crime and the suspects, something the last two Thin Man films failed to do. Also, unlike many other mystery features, there is a solid early clue in the story, when Mrs. Talbin provides a weak excuse for why her valuable necklace is missing. Could she have used it to pay Drake's gambling debt, which was satisfied in some way on the night of the murder? Since Drake was a ladies' man, that gives a clear motive to Mitchell Talbin if Drake was involved with Mrs. Talbin.

That scenario drifts into the background as Nick's sleuthing goes forward, with Nick actually conducting a substantial investigation of the Drake murder, even proceeding on a clue to Poughkeepsie, New York. Throughout the film, suspicion believably floats from one character to another. However, *Song of the Thin Man* is not a talkfest. There is the surprise knifing of Fran Page, a shot taken at Brandt in the Charles apartment and the apparent kidnapping of Nick, Jr., by the then-apparent killer. There is also the requisite Charles humor, involving Nick, Jr., Asta, Nick's former associates and the use of jazz idioms that are hard to understand. To the extent there is padding in the feature, it is in the music — but the music never seems like padding since the jazz is enjoyable.

Among the other positives of *Song of the Thin Man* are the striking actresses who perform in the film. Gloria Grahame, a fixture of film noir (*In a Lonely Place* [1950] and *The Big Heat* [1953]), is sultry as Fran Page, particularly in the tight gold lame dress she wears when singing. Marie Windsor, another dangerous female of film noir (*The Narrow Margin* [1952] and *The Killing* [1956]), appears late in the film as Helen Amboy, the gangster's wife, in her own eye-catching outfit. Pretty Patricia Morison, who battled Sherlock Holmes in *Dressed to Kill* (1946), has a significant part as Phyllis Talbin, who cannot seem to keep track of her valuable necklace.

And even if Myrna Loy was finally starting to show her age in *Song of the Thin Man*, thirteen years after *The Thin Man* (1934), she still has that certain something that makes her stand out from the rest of the female cast. Part of it is simply her chemistry with William Powell, which only improved over the years. When Loy is on the screen, it is still hard to take one's eyes off of her, no matter what else is going on.

In the end, the missing necklace of Mrs. Talbin reappears, sealing the deal on the identity of the killer of Drake. It is always satisfying when the viewer can logically solve a murder puzzle based on an actual clue, rather than by asking yourself which person is the least likely suspect.

By 1947, the Thin Man series, a creature of 1930s Hollywood, may have seemed passé to some filmgoers, but *Song of the Thin Man* showed that there was still some life left in the old franchise. Even though styles may change, a good mystery, witty writing and first-rate acting never go out of date. Although this film did, in fact, turn out to be the swan song of the Thin Man movie series, Nick and Nora were astute enough to leave the cinema with the audience wanting just a little bit more.

## Afterwards

After the novel *The Thin Man* was published in 1934, Hammett did very little other writing. He lived with playwright Lillian Hellman for many years and devoted himself to political causes. He died in 1961.

There were no more Thin Man movies after *Song of the Thin Man* (1947). However, Nick and Nora Charles did make it to the radio and television. *The Adventures of the Thin*

*Man* ran on various radio networks from 1941 to 1950, with a few breaks in between. The series was based on the Thin Man movies, thus being a blend of mystery, urban sophistication, comedy and romance. Les Damon originated the role of Nick Charles on the radio, with Les Tremayne and Joseph Curtin also playing the role. Claudia Morgan played Nora Charles throughout the entire run of the series.

Nick and Nora came to television in 1957 for a show that ran on NBC for two seasons. In *The Thin Man*, Peter Lawford played Nick and Phyllis Kirk played Nora. The series was clearly inspired by the movies, with Nick a retired detective married to a society lady, and pulled into crime investigations by his former associates. Asta was also around. In 1975, ABC aired "Nick and Nora" as part of a late night mystery series. It starred Craig Stevens and Jo Ann Pflug.

During the course of the Thin Man series, which was spread out over 13 years, Powell appeared in numerous other films, such as the well-known screwball comedies *My Man Godfrey* with Carole Lombard and *Libeled Lady* with Jean Harlow, both from 1936, and the enduring family film *Life with Father* (1947). His last film role was as the Navy ship's doctor in *Mister Roberts* (1955). He died in 1984.

Loy also appeared in many other films during the Thin Man series, usually appearing with top male stars such as Clark Gable, Spencer Tracy and Robert Montgomery. She made a total of 13 films with Powell, such as *The Great Ziegfeld* (1936), in which she played one of Ziegfeld's wives, actress Billie Burke. She took a break from acting in the 1940s to focus on the war effort, resuming a regular screen career with *The Best Years of Our Lives* (1946), about returning war veterans. In that film, she played Fredric March's wife. Loy continued her career of playing film wives in movies such as *Mr. Blandings Builds His Dream House* (1948) with Cary Grant and *Cheaper by the Dozen* (1950) with Clifton Webb. She passed away in 1993.

# 9

# Perry Mason
## *The Defense Attorney*

Many people recognize the fictional crime-solving attorney Perry Mason, either from the numerous novels written about the character by Erle Stanley Gardner or from the long-running television show which first appeared on CBS in 1957. For most fans, the face of Perry Mason will always be Raymond Burr, who played Mason on television for nine seasons in the hour-long shows and then later reprised the role in a series of two-hour made-for-television movies.

Less well-known are the six Perry Mason films released by Warner Brothers in the mid–1930s. Perhaps the reason for their lack of impact today is that three different actors played the famous attorney in the series and the supporting cast often changed from film to film. Or, perhaps the reason is that the film series was so overshadowed by the very successful television series that followed it. Whatever the reason, the Perry Mason movie series should not be overlooked by the mystery fan, because as a group, the films are an interesting, if not wholly successful interpretation of some of the cases of the most famous attorney-detective in all of crime literature.

## Background

### Erle Stanley Gardner

Erle Stanley Gardner was himself an attorney, yet he never attended law school. Gardner was born on July 17, 1889, in Malden, Massachusetts. Since his father was a mining engineer, Gardner traveled often as a child, including long stays in Oregon and California. After graduating from high school in California, Gardner kicked around for a while until he took a job as a typist at a California law firm. There, although he never went to law school, he "read law" for three years, passing the California bar in 1911. In those years and in some states still today, a person can take the bar exam after studying for several years under a judge or a practicing attorney, without ever going to law school.

After becoming a lawyer, Gardner specialized in defending poor Mexican and Chinese clients in criminal cases, gaining him much fame but little money. Later, even after becoming a successful author and retiring from the active practice of criminal law, Gardner maintained his interest in the law, including becoming a strong advocate for prison reform. In 1948, he founded the Court of Last Resort, a private organization dedicated to securing the release of men who were believed to have been unjustly convicted of a crime. The organization was successful in many of its cases.

In the early 1920s, while still maintaining an active law practice during the day, Gardner began writing stories at night, turning out 4000 words of fiction on an almost daily basis. He sold his first story to the pulps in 1923 and thereafter, from 1923 to 1932, sold hundreds of stories to a number of different pulp magazines, often using a pseudonym because of the number of his works which were published. Most of his stories were mysteries, although from time to time he wrote some Westerns. By 1932, the last year Gardner wrote for the pulps, he was making a considerable living from his writing activities.

## The Novels

In 1933, Gardner's first novel about Perry Mason, *The Case of the Velvet Claws*, was published by William Morrow and Company, the firm that published all of the subsequent original hardcover editions of Mason books. In this first novel, Gardner had not yet developed the Mason mystery stories to their full degree. Mason does not even appear in court in the novel. In fact, Mason seems more like the average hardboiled detective of the day, doing his own investigating and bullying people into telling him what he wants to know.

Over the course of the next 80 novels, Gardner developed the Perry Mason formula that is well-known today. A client (often a pretty young lady) comes to him with a problem. Mason immediately throws all of his time, attention and resources into helping the client, with the story moving at a frenetic pace. Eventually there is a murder, with Mason's client accused of the crime. Despite the strong evidence against his client, Mason is able to finger the real culprit. Many of the novels ended in a fiery courtroom setting, with Mason's cross-examination of key witnesses eliciting important evidence as to the identity of the real killer. Often, an interesting legal issue, such as a difficult point of evidence, was debated in the novel.

Mason was assisted by his loyal and efficient secretary, Della Street, and his tough, sharp investigator, Paul Drake of the Drake Detective Agency. Mason's usual opponent in court was the district attorney, Hamilton Burger, who never prosecuted a successful case against Mason's clients, except, perhaps, in *The Case of the Terrified Typist* (1956). In about half of the cases, Mason's adversary on the police force was Lieutenant Tragg, the shrewd but gentlemanly homicide detective. In the earlier novels, Mason was often up against Sergeant Holcombe, with whom Mason had a testy relationship, at best.

## The Film Series

Warner Brothers immediately recognized the potential of a film series about Perry Mason, with the first film released only a year after the first novel, *The Case of the Velvet Claws*, was published. *The Case of the Howling Dog* (1934) was a faithful adaptation of the Gardner book of that title, with a very serious Mason, assisted by Della, representing a young woman accused of murdering her husband. The film concludes with the traditional courtroom surprise. The next three films were also based on Gardner novels about his famous detective, but here, the presentation is completely different. The stories are told in a light manner, with, for example, Mason dead drunk in one scene in *The Case of the Lucky Legs* (1935) and Mason marrying Della at the beginning of *The Case of the Velvet Claws* (1936).

In these first four movies in the series, Mason was played by Warren William, a very familiar actor to mystery movie fans. William was born in 1894 in Aitkin, Minnesota. He appeared in a number of plays on Broadway from 1924 to 1931, while at the same time appearing in small roles in some silent films. With the advent of sound, William, with his rich speaking voice, became an important player in Hollywood, appearing in significant films such as the soap opera *Three on a Match* (1932), the Busby Berkeley musical *Gold Diggers of 1933* (1933), the Frank Capra feature *Lady for a Day* (1933) and the original *Imitation of Life* (1934).

In the mid–1930s, William began playing famous detectives of the cinema. He portrayed Philo Vance in *The Dragon Murder Case* (1934) (a role he would repeat in *The Gracie Allen Murder Case* [1939]), Sam Spade in the second screen version of Dashiell Hammett's *The Maltese Falcon*, titled *Satan Met a Lady* (1936), and Perry Mason in the first four films in that series. William is best known today for playing the Lone Wolf in a long series of mystery movies commencing with *The Lone Wolf Spy Hunt* (1939). William died in 1948.

For the fifth film in the series, *The Case of the Black Cat* (1936), Ricardo Cortez was brought in to play the famous defense attorney. Cortez was born in New York City in 1900; his real name was Jacob Krantz. In 1922, he moved to Hollywood where he changed his name to Ricardo Cortez with the intent of him making him the next Rudolph Valentino. That idea never panned out and Cortez never became a major star in Hollywood, although he did appear in a variety of movies, from romances to melodramas. In the mystery field, he was the first person to play Sam Spade on the screen, in the 1931 version of *The Maltese Falcon*. He also appeared in two Charlie Chan films and a Mr. Moto picture. Cortez died in 1977.

For the last film in the series, *The Case of the Stuttering Bishop* (1937), Donald Woods played the attorney-detective. This was an unusual choice since Woods usually played character parts in films. Indeed, he had played a suspect in *The Case of the Curious Bride* (1935), just two years before. Woods was born in 1906 in Manitoba, Canada, and raised in California. Following his Hollywood debut in 1934, he appeared in over 75 films, numerous plays and then, starting in the 1950s, many television series. While Woods appeared in many mystery movies over his long career, *The Case of the Stuttering Bishop* contains his only performance as the lead detective. Woods passed away in 1998.

In the six-film series, Della Street was played by five different actresses, with Claire Dodd playing the role twice, in *The Case of the Curious Bride* (1935) and *The Case of the Velvet Claws* (1936). Allen Jenkins played Spudsy Drake, a comic version of the Paul Drake of the Gardner novels, in *The Case of the Curious Bride* and *The Case of the Lucky Legs* (1935). Jenkins had previously played Sergeant Holcombe in the first film in the series. Eddie Acuff took over the role of Spudsy Drake for *The Case of the Velvet Claws*. District Attorney Hamilton Burger first appeared in *The Case of the Black Cat* (1936) and reappeared in the last film in the series, *The Case of the Stuttering Bishop* (1937). Paul Drake, as contrasted with Spudsy Drake, also appeared in the last two films in the series, although in *The Case of the Black Cat* he was still not the strong, serious private investigator of the novels.

## The Films

### *The Case of the Howling Dog* (1934)

*The Case of the Howling Dog* is a true classic, equal to the best films in any of the Hollywood mystery movie series. It has one of the most complex plots of any of them, with

In this publicity shot from *The Case of the Howling Dog* (1934), a perplexed Perry Mason (Warren William) has arrived at the Foley house just after the shooting of the howling dog and Clinton Foley (Russell Hicks). Presumably, Mason will not be perplexed for long.

many potential suspects and clues aplenty. Even after a jury acquits Mason's client of murder, the film has one truly shocking surprise left. *The Case of the Howling Dog* is a movie that must be viewed by all true mystery fans.

As successful as Perry Mason's career has become, for $10,000 in cash he is willing to settle what appears to be a mundane dispute between two neighbors. Wealthy Arthur Cartwright comes to the famous defense lawyer with a problem. The dog of his next door neighbor, Clinton Foley, has been constantly howling over the last several days, putting Cartwright's nerves on edge. He wants Foley arrested if he will not stop his dog from wailing. Cartwright also wants to make a will, leaving his estate to Evelyn, the woman who is now living with Foley as Foley's wife. Cartwright makes it quite clear that Evelyn is not truly Foley's wife.

The next day, several unusual events occur. Cartwright's holographic will arrives in Mason's mail, but instead of leaving his estate to the woman who is living with Foley, he leaves it to Foley's real wife. While Mason is investigating matters at the Foley house, Mr. Foley shows Mason a note from Evelyn, which states that Evelyn has run off with Cartwright. Mason's operatives learn that Evelyn is actually married to Cartwright and that a few years before, Foley took Evelyn away from Cartwright while at the same time leaving his own wife, Bessie Foley. Now there is a quite attractive housekeeper named Lucy Benton living at Foley's house. Does the amorous Clinton Foley have a new love interest in his life?

That night, Bessie Foley arrives unannounced at her husband's house to confront him. She lets herself in with a key. When Clinton sees her, he lets the dog loose to attack her. A shot is heard and the dog collapses. Clinton then starts after Bessie with a knife, another shot is heard and Clinton drops to the floor dead. It seems clear that Bessie has committed the murder of her husband but then she does spot a door gently closing in the room, so perhaps someone else fired the fatal shot. Bessie is arrested and, given the facts, a guilty verdict seems likely. Luckily for Bessie, Arthur Cartwright had already retained Perry Mason to defend Bessie if the need ever arose. As expected, Perry is up to the task and obtains an acquittal for his client.

The movie is a classic-style whodunit, with multiple clues and multiple suspects. Director Alan Crosland keeps the story moving with cinematic effects such as dolly shots when the characters converse, allowing them to walk as they talk, giving the film a sense of movement. In a film with no background music, the killings of Clinton and the dog occur while a radio is playing the title song from *Dames* (1934), giving the murder sequence an eerie yet satirical effect. The climax takes place during a murder trial, as was common in Perry Mason stories. A trial setting is an excellent cinematic device to convey a substantial amount of information to the audience, while keeping the story interesting amid the questions, answers, objections and court rulings. The tension in the final cross-examination of Lucy Benton is aided by the sound of shovels and pick-axes working in the new Foley garage addition, in an attempt to locate the bodies that may literally be buried there.

Other important contributions to the success of the film are the performances, in both the main and supporting roles. Warren William is quite good as Perry Mason, self-assured, confident and a tough cross-examiner in court, although he does irritatingly wag his finger too much at the other characters. Three very attractive young actresses co-star: Dorothy Tree as Lucy Benton, Helen Trenholme as Della Street and Mary Astor as Bessie Foley. All are all quite good in their roles. Unfortunately, for those mystery fans who have seen the 1941 *The Maltese Falcon* (and who has not), it is hard to believe anything that a character played by Mary Astor says in a mystery film, and once again, she seems to be doing a lot of prevaricating here. Harry Tyler, as a taxi driver who becomes an important witness, and Helen Lowell, as Cartwright's deaf housekeeper, are also very good in small, but significant parts.

With all of these positives, it is still the mystery that makes the movie. There are many perplexing clues for the viewer, such as the howling dog and why his howling started and then stopped, the new garage that Foley is constructing but apparently does not need, Arthur Cartwright's decision to change the bequest in his will the night after meeting with Mason, the dog biting Lucy Benton, and the many documents on which the handwriting does not match. The solution is complex, with a total of three murders, two perpetrators and a few other people who may not have the purest of motives.

The film is a mystery lover's dream, with one of the most puzzling stories ever filmed. Few will be able to predict the movie's last surprise. After all the Perry Mason books and television shows that many have read or seen, is Mason's client actually guilty in the first film version of the character? Perhaps so, but since Mason obtained an acquittal from a jury, Mason's record in court remains spotless, and, in addition, based on the Constitutional principle of double jeopardy, Bessie Foley will never be tried again. What a wonderful mystery film! The ending has a surprise that few will forget.

*Note on the Source Material*: The film was based on *The Case of the Howling Dog* by Erle Stanley Gardner, published in book form in 1934, the year of the film's release. The film follows the book more closely than perhaps any other mystery movie followed the source on which it was based. Every important scene in the movie comes from the novel, and just about every important scene from the novel is depicted in the film. Even substantial portions of the film dialogue come from the book, such as when Mason's client complains that he does not believe her, Mason replies that he does not believe anything that he cannot make a jury believe. At the end of the movie, after the surprise ending, Della calls Mason a cross between a saint and a devil.

For those expecting to see Lt. Tragg in the movie, Sgt. Holcombe was Mason's usual police adversary in the books at this time. For those expecting to see District Attorney Hamilton Burger trying the murder case, in the book the case is tried by Assistant District Attorney Claude Drumm. Both of those characters appear in the film. However, Paul Drake was an important character in the book and it is not clear why his part was replaced by two private detectives in the film. The characterization of Della Street as an efficient and faithful secretary carries over from the book. That characterization would change in later films in the series.

There are a few interesting changes from the novel, necessitated by the dramatic demands of the cinema. The shooting of Clinton Foley, apparently by Bessie Foley, is depicted in the film, and while it appears that she has done the shooting, no gun is shown and there is that door mysteriously closing after the shooting. In the book, the reader only learns about the circumstances of Foley's death when Bessie tells her story to Mason. That change is probably for two reasons: the creation of a very dramatic scene for the cinema, and also because it confirms that Bessie shot in self-defense, meeting any Code requirements of the day.

The final courtroom scene in the movie, involving the cross-examination of Lucy Benton, is moved, at the request of Mason, to the Foley house, for no good legal reason. The judge readily grants the request, for no good legal reason, but what do you expect from a judge who does not wear his judicial robes in court? The non-legal reason, of course, is that it is much more dramatic to have the cross-examination at the Foley residence, with the sound of workers using shovels and pick-axes in the background, heightening the tension, leading to the discovery of the bodies under the garage. The change in venue does not happen in the novel.

Despite a few changes, the filmmakers were clever enough to recognize that the novel *The Case of the Howling Dog*, despite its complexities, would make an excellent mystery movie, and they chose to dramatize the book substantially as written. It resulted in one of the best film whodunits of the 1930s.

*Note on the* Perry Mason *Television Episode*: "The Case of the Howling Dog" first aired on April 11, 1959. The episode has little in common with the book, other than a howling dog and a similar murder victim. While it made sense to modernize the plot of a 1930s novel for a 1950s television audience, the writers went further, jettisoning the whole story of the novel and, by that act, jettisoning one of Erle Stanley Gardner's best whodunits.

The television episode is not bad, although the whole mystery does not hold together very well. Perhaps the TV viewer should be more interested in finding an answer to this question: Did the courts in California in the 1950s really take two-hour breaks for lunch?

## *The Case of the Curious Bride* (1935)

As good as *The Case of the Howling Dog* was, that is how bad *The Case of the Curious Bride* is. The first Perry Mason film was serious stuff, with Mason aggressively investigating the crime and defending his client, in the tradition of the novels of Erle Stanley Gardner. The second film is primarily silly stuff, with Mason often a figure of comedy, in the soon-to-be tradition of many of the movies in the Hollywood mystery series of the 1940s. Indeed, since Mason is played once again by Warren William, comparisons between this movie and William's Lone Wolf films come easily to mind. In *The Case of the Curious Bride*, William plays Mason as he would later play the Lone Wolf, with a touch of satire in his attitude and a lack of seriousness. William's approach to the role seriously undercuts the effectiveness of the film, although, of course, part of the problem is the way the role is written.

The screenwriters chose to turn Mason from a brilliant trial attorney into a gourmet cook who has an entourage who travels with him, including a newspaper reporter and even the county coroner. Perry is still a famous defense attorney, but he never makes even one appearance in court. For some reason, Paul Drake, the tough private investigator of the books, is turned into a comic figure, now known as Spudsy Drake. What were the filmmakers thinking? Had they forgotten the successful formula of *The Case of the Howling Dog*?

After another triumph in court, Perry Mason is cooking a gourmet dinner for his gang of groupies when an old friend, Rhoda Montaine, arrives. She tells Mason a tale of a friend of hers whose first husband, supposedly dead for four years, has now turned up alive. Mason, of course, suspects that Rhoda is talking about herself, but she flees the scene before Mason can get more details. Nevertheless, Mason decides to have the body of George Moxley exhumed. Imagine everyone's surprise when the coffin of Moxley is opened and there is only a wooden Indian inside. Later, Mason realizes that since Rhoda remarried, Moxley must be blackmailing Rhoda over the situation.

When Mason arrives at Moxley's apartment, Moxley is dead. The police eventually trace Moxley to Rhoda, and after Mason prevents Rhoda from fleeing the city by airplane, the police arrest her for the murder. Rhoda has a strong motive for killing Moxley and she was at Moxley's apartment around the time of the murder, so the case against her is strong. Despite the compelling evidence against Rhoda, Mason believes in her innocence. After some roundabout investigation of the crime, Mason gathers all of the suspects at his apartment and identifies the true killer.

There is so much wrong with this movie that it is hard to know where to begin. As noted above, turning Mason into a figure of comedy was a serious mistake. There is even a scene where Mason and Spudsy smell tear gas on a handkerchief and start crying while they are talking. It is hard to know who they resemble most, Laurel and Hardy or Abbott and Costello. Comedy scenes such as these slow the movie down to a grinding halt. Contrast this film with the Perry Mason television shows, with no humor (until the brief scene after the last commercial) and no wasted moments, as a complex story is cogently told in less than 60 minutes. Unfortunately, just the opposite occurs in *The Case of the Curious Bride*. Even though director Michael Curtiz uses constant dissolves between scenes in an attempt to increase the speed of the film, the pace still is incredibly slow.

Erle Stanley Gardner was an attorney and an accomplished one at that. Even though he permitted Mason to stretch the ethical principles of attorneys perhaps beyond the breaking point, Gardner was always accurate on the law. In *The Case of the Curious Bride*, however, the filmmakers appear to be unconcerned with legal niceties. Thus, Mason interviews his client in her cell with a newspaper reporter present. That eliminates the attorney-client privilege with regard to those discussions, a mistake no competent attorney would make. The police let Rhoda talk to her husband and then record the conversation over a secret intercom, thereby violating the spousal privilege of confidential communications. Of course,

*The Case of the Curious Bride* (1935) is publicized in this cigarette card, which shows Claire Dodd as Della Street and Warren William as Perry Mason.

a number of movies, mysteries or not, make mistakes in the presentation of the law, but these scenes go way overboard. Surely these scenes are symptomatic of some of the reasons why Gardner was so upset with Hollywood's treatment of his character and wanted significant input into the production when the famous attorney was brought to television.

For a murder mystery, there is a striking lack of suspects for the killer of George Moxley. After Rhoda, the only other potential killer is her husband and, perhaps, Oscar Pender, a character who arrives late in the film. No one else seems to have much of a motive or much of an opportunity. Without good suspects other than Rhoda, *The Case of the Curious Bride* is not much of a mystery. Also, without a dazzling courtroom scene at the end, *The Case of the Curious Bride* is not much of a Perry Mason story.

Most of the interest in the film comes from tangential items. *The Case of the Curious Bride* marks the first film appearance by Errol Flynn, who is strikingly handsome playing George Moxley in a brief flashback. Donald Woods, who plays Rhoda's husband, went on to play Mason in the last film in the series, *The Case of the Stuttering Bishop* (1937). Winnie Shaw, as Doris Pender, gets to sing a little bit on stage, as she also did in *Smart Blonde* (1936), from the Torchy Blane series. Frankly, Shaw's singing, rather than the mystery, is the highlight of the film.

*Note on the Source Material*: *The Case of the Curious Bride* was based on the 1934 Gardner novel of the same name. Surprisingly, given the film's lack of quality, the core plot of the movie comes from the novel. Thus, Rhoda Montaine comes to Mason's office with a story about a friend who needs help and Rhoda asks questions about what happens when a husband disappears but no body is found. It eventually turns out that Rhoda is being blackmailed by her first husband, Gregory Moxley, who Rhoda thought was dead when she married Carl Montaine. Moxley is killed in his apartment around the time Rhoda comes to visit him, and at the time of the murder, Oscar Pender is present, trying to obtain compensation from Moxley for the wrong done by Moxley to his sister. The father of Rhoda's husband tries to bribe Mason into taking a dive in the defense of Rhoda. The killer is the same, although in the film, the killing appears to be an accident while in the novel, it may have been self-defense.

The similarities between the plots of the novel and the film provide the movie with its strongest elements. It is the changes from the book, however, that doom the film. In the novel, just as in the film, Mason hides Rhoda in a phone booth at an airport, to prevent her from being arrested by two policemen and being accused of flight. Unfortunately, the film turns this incident into a moment of comedy rather than one of suspense, by emphasizing Spudsy's antics at the airport rather than the strategy of Mason to avoid having his client accused of flight. In the book, a character comes to Mason's office with tear gas in a handkerchief, to assist her in pretending to cry before Mason. In the movie, the screenwriters purloined the idea of the tear gas in a handkerchief, but used it instead to create the "Abbott and Costello moment" described above.

More importantly, Gardner takes the time, in his novel, to develop facts and circumstances so that there are at least five legitimate suspects for the crime. In addition to Rhoda, Carl and Oscar, the novel spends some time to provide murder motives to Dr. Claude Milsap, a friend of Rhoda's, and C. Phillip Montaine, Carl's father. The novel is a true whodunit with multiple realistic suspects; the movie is a mystery-comedy.

The Perry Mason of this time frame was not above stretching lawyers' ethics to win a court case. In the novel, he substitutes buzzers for doorbells in the apartment building in which Moxley was killed, confusing the district attorney at the time of trial. Instead of using this clever plot device for the film, the screenwriters substituted a character Mason hires to impersonate a former wife of Moxley's, in order to confuse the police. That scheme does not work; the police figure out the ruse quite quickly. That stunt is also played for laughs in the film, also undercutting the effectiveness of the plot point.

Perhaps most importantly, the filmmakers overlooked two courtroom scenes from the novel. The first involves a civil trial concerning the annulment of Carl and Rhoda's marriage. The second involves the climax in the courtroom during Rhoda's murder trial, always the highlight of a Gardner novel and the television show. By forgoing these events, the screenwriters overlooked some very interesting legal issues raised in the novel and also some exciting courtroom pyrotechnics by Mason. While the novel, *The Case of the Curious Bride*, is nothing special, it is still much more interesting to read than the movie is to view.

*Note on the* Perry Mason *Television Episode*: "The Case of the Curious Bride" (October 18, 1958) is a fairly faithful adaptation of the book although it is a little less complicated than the book. The rigmarole of substituting doorbells and buzzers at the building in which the murder occurred is incorporated into the television episode, thus giving the TV episode

Perry Mason (Warren William) meets with two of the swindled Lucky Legs contestants in *The Case of the Lucky Legs* (1935). Margy Clune (Patricia Ellis), who is Mason's client, is sitting and Thelma Bell (Peggy Shannon) is standing.

more of the feel of the Gardner novel than the movie. Luckily, the idea of tear gas in a handkerchief causing someone to cry was eliminated, as were all of the comedy elements.

## *The Case of the Lucky Legs* (1935)

It is incredible how far the quality of the Perry Mason series dropped, from its fabulous debut in *The Case of the Howling Dog* (1934) through just this third film in the series. *The Case of the Lucky Legs* is so bad that it makes the previous film, *The Case of the Curious Bride* (1935), a very disappointing movie, seem like a masterpiece.

One of the problems is that *The Case of the Lucky Legs* is a Perry Mason film in name only. When Mr. Bradbury first comes to Mason's office to employ him, Mason is passed out on the floor behind his desk from an all-night binge. Della Street finds nothing unusual or wrong about this. Mason (and for that matter, Della) takes nothing seriously in the film, even after a murder has occurred. Everything is treated in a flippant manner. And, for two movies in a row, Mason does not make an appearance in court. The strength of the Perry Mason books and the television shows were often the trial sequences. By foregoing those in several of the movies, Mason becomes just another run-of-the-mill detective, indistinguishable from the numerous film sleuths of the Hollywood mystery series.

*The Case of the Lucky Legs* commences with the most interesting scene in the film, at the Lucky Legs contest in Cloverdale, sponsored by the Leg-easy Hosiery Company. A number of local women appear behind a curtain and show off their legs, with the winner receiving a thousand dollar prize from the sponsoring company. Pretty Margy Clune is the unanimous winner, to the chagrin of her boyfriend Dr. Bob Doray, who does not want her demeaning herself in public. Mr. Bradbury, the owner of the department store where Margy works and a co-sponsor of the contest, is also in love with Margy. Margy attempts to collect her winnings from the show's promoter, Frank Patton, but he leaves town with all the money, although not before being accosted by a swindled winner from a prior contest. Margy then leaves Cloverdale to locate Patton and claim her prize.

Bradbury follows Margy to San Francisco and hires Mason to locate her. Instead, Mason finds the murdered body of Frank Patton in Patton's room at the Empire Apartments. He also recognizes Margy's legs when she is walking down the steps of the apartment building, fleeing the crime scene. The police suspect Margy of the murder but at the end of the film, Mason discloses that Bradbury was the murderer, resulting in an incredible conflict of interest for Mason, who was originally hired by Bradbury. Of course, for an attorney who lifts important evidence from a crime scene and takes it away in his pocket (an incident that does not come from the book), a little conflict of interest (which is properly explained away in the book) is probably of slight concern.

The problems with *The Case of the Lucky Legs* are caused, in significant part, by *The Thin Man* (1934), an excellent mystery involving the sophisticated Nick and Nora Charles and their witty banter and upper class attitude toward the imbibing of liquor. Warner Brothers apparently decided to emulate the style of that film and in the process gutted the original Gardner plot of its hardboiled crime elements and emphasis on the law. Those attributes were the essence of the early Perry Mason novels. Instead, the film emphasizes drinking, the "clever" and "witty" repartee of Mason and Della Street (which is not all that clever and witty) and the constant glib attitude toward the goings-on. Murder would seem to be a serious subject which should have been treated in a more solemn manner.

The ridiculousness of the story is highlighted at the end, when Mason discloses the killer's identity to the police and to a number of the suspects. This type of scene is often the highlight of a mystery movie. Here, however, Mason explains the crimes during his medical exam, which proceeds from location to location and medical test to medical test, constantly interrupting Mason's explanation. The filmmakers probably thought this was incredibly clever. In actuality, it was incredibly stupid.

Since there are very few suspects, the identity of the killer is obvious from the beginning, although readers of the Perry Mason novels may have suspected the woman across the hall from the murder room who appears for a moment and notifies the police of the crimes. That surprise conclusion, as unconvincing as it may have been, would, at the least, have shown some real cleverness on the part of the screenwriters. But, that was not to be and therefore, as a film bereft of cleverness, humor and mystery, *The Case of the Lucky Legs* is the low point of the Perry Mason films.

*Note on the Source Material*: *The Case of the Lucky Legs* was based on Gardner's 1934 novel. The core plot of the movie comes from the novel, as Marjorie Clune wins a Lucky Legs contest in her home town of Cloverdale, is defrauded by Frank Patton out of the prize money, follows him to California and is herself followed by J.R. Bradbury and Dr. Doray (here, a dentist) who are both in love with her. Bradbury hires Mason to locate Marjorie but, instead, Mason discovers the body of Frank Patton in his apartment with a knife in the back.

The novel is one of the weakest of the early Perry Mason books. The plot does not hold together very well and exhibits some of the faults of the movie. There are very few legitimate suspects and Mason never appears in court. The entire second half of the book, which did not make it into the movie, involves Mason chasing lead after lead, all in one night, worrying little about legal ethics.

Nevertheless, Mason takes the murder of Patton very seriously throughout the novel, and the attorney is never the subject of ridicule, as he is in the movie. As with most Mason novels, the story moves at a frenetic pace, and raises at least one interesting legal issue, which, in this case, is how to prove intent in order to prosecute Patton for fraud in conducting the Lucky Legs contests in the way he did. These last two elements are missing from the film, underscoring the view that the film, *The Case of the Lucky Legs*, is a Perry Mason movie in name only.

*Note on the* Perry Mason *Television Episode*: "The Case of the Lucky Legs" (December 19, 1959) is substantially better than the novel. The most important change between book and film is that the television program ends in court with much of the information about the crime and the suspects being revealed in courtroom interrogations. Also, some additional suspects were added to the plot for the TV episode, making the proceedings quite intriguing. Much like the book, the TV episode follows Mason's own investigation on the night of the murder, although it is not handled at the frenetic pace of the novel.

## *The Case of the Velvet Claws* (1936)

*The Case of the Velvet Claws* is another in what was rapidly becoming a long line of awful Perry Mason movies. It is always tempting to measure these six Perry Mason films against the Perry Mason of the Gardner novels or the Perry Mason of the long-running television program. That is not fair to these movie versions, which should rightfully be evaluated on their own, as mystery films from the 1930s without preconceived notions of the character from other media. However, even if such an unbiased evaluation were possible, *The Case of the Velvet Claws* is still dreadful.

The story commences with the marriage of Perry Mason to his secretary, Della Street. (This never occurred in the novels and there was no romance between the two in the television series, but that is a matter to be ignored in this discussion.) The marriage ceremony is performed by a night court judge so for the first movie in quite some time, Mason actually appears in court, although not as counsel for the defense. The time spent on Mason's failure to spend his wedding night with Della detracts from the murder mystery and takes valuable time away from developing a whodunit that makes some sense.

Mason is planning a strange honeymoon because in addition to Della, apparently his investigator, Spudsy Drake, is also along for the journey. While Spudsy does do some investigative work in the film, he is also there for comic relief, with his weightlifting, strange costumes and silly efforts to prevent the police from entering Mason's apartment. Spudsy is not amusing and is simply another distraction from the murder mystery.

The murder at issue is that of George C. Belter, the owner of the gossip magazine *Spicy Bits*. Belter's wife Eva has hired Mason, at gunpoint, to work to prevent *Spicy Bits* from publishing a story about her assignation with Peter Milnor, a local politician. George Belter throws Mason out of his house and tells Eve that he is still going to publish the story. Eve then brings out her gun and shoots Belter at point blank range. This presents a serious problem for Mason, since Eve is his client and Mason has never lost a murder case before. Yet Eve has clearly murdered Belter.

Mason's suspicions are aroused by two spent cartridge shells on the floor when, supposedly, there was only the one shot fired. On that evidence alone, Mason guesses that Eve's shot went out the window and later, another person came into the room and fired a fatal shot at Belter. When it appears that the housekeeper is blackmailing Carl Griffin, Belter's nephew, into marrying her, Mason concludes that Griffin is the killer.

That explanation of the clues and the identity of the murderer just given above make more sense than the manner in which the crime is explained by Mason in the film. So much time is spent on irrelevant matters in *The Case of the Velvet Claws* that it is hard to follow what Mason is actually investigating. The killer, Griffin, and the housekeeper and her daughter barely appear in the film until the end so their unmasking as the villains of the piece is of little interest to the viewer. According to Mason, Griffin shot Belter simply because Belter told Griffin that he had changed his will in his favor that morning and Griffin saw the opportunity to kill Belter after Eva's shot missed. There is no foundation laid as to any animosity between Griffin and Belter or, perhaps, that Griffin needed money, so the motive for the murder comes out of the blue and is totally unconvincing.

Warren William's performance is excellent, if he were playing the Lone Wolf, but he is not. William conveys a total lack of seriousness in the part of Perry Mason, as if a murder investigation and his status as a potential suspect are of no concern to him. (It is probably inappropriate here to mention Raymond Burr's performances as Mason — tough, confident, serious and astute — the proper way to play the role.) It is hard to have much confidence in William ever solving Belter's murder and clearing his client's name, once again undercutting the mystery element of *The Case of the Velvet Claws*.

As noted above, the main clue to the second shooter is the second spent cartridge shell. Mason puts the shell in his pocket and takes it out of the murder room, preventing the police from learning about it. Mason therefore breaks the chain of custody of the evidence, which will make it impossible to prosecute Griffin for his crime. Mason has Eva sign a statement that she shot at Belter, which Mason gives to the police even though he is Eva's attorney. While he later clears Eva of actual murder, he has helped her confess in writing to attempted murder, also a serious crime. As a result of Mason's actions, Eva should be off to prison for many years, if the district attorney were any good. Of course, these last two legal points are not addressed in the film, as the screenwriters clearly had very little knowledge of legal proceedings.

*The Case of the Velvet Claws* is wrong on the law, wrong on the characterization of the principals, wrong on the acting style, and wrong on its overemphasis on trivial matters to the detriment of the crime that is being investigated. The solution to the mystery amounts to guesswork and is unconvincing. It is hardly helped by the fact that the explanation is given while all of the characters, including Mason, are sneezing. The movie, *The Case of the Velvet Claws*, fails on its own, without any comparisons to the Mason novels or the television shows.

*Note on the Source Material*: *The Case of the Velvet Claws* was based on the 1933 Gardner novel of the same name. It was the first Perry Mason story ever published. Although Mason is already a successful lawyer at the beginning of his literary career, he does not appear in court in this first novel. Gardner would correct that oversight in his next few books and then throughout most of the remaining novels about the criminal defense attorney.

The movie takes the core plot of the book with, in the book, Eva Belter hiring Mason to prevent *Spicy Bits* from publishing a story about her and a politician, Mason learning that her husband George Belter is actually the owner of *Spicy Bits*, Mason confronting Belter about his ownership interest in the blackmailing magazine and the subsequent shooting death of Belter. Eva is quite the prevaricator, a characteristic also brought out in the movie.

The difference between the two works, though, is stark. The novel, *The Case of the Velvet Claws*, is all business, with no honeymoon with Della, no comic relief from Paul Drake and without Mason catching a cold, elements from the film that take away from the seriousness. With no time wasted on extraneous matters, Gardner had the time to set up a much more realistic murder mystery than in the movie, with multiple legitimate suspects for the murderer of Belter. There are also some real clues to the culpability of Griffin for the murder, unlike the movie, such as a previously unlocked door that is now locked and a wet umbrella that mysteriously appears in an umbrella stand in the Belter home on the night of the murder.

Mason never pockets that second shell in the book, as he inexplicably does in the movie. However, the Mason of the books does assist Eva in confessing to attempted murder, although there is a better explanation given in the book for Mason's actions. The novel, *The Case of the Velvet Claws*, is no masterpiece, but it is far better than the movie.

*Note on the* Perry Mason *Television Episode*: "The Case of the Velvet Claws" first aired on March 21, 1963. Just as in the book and the movie, this is a rare Mason tale wherein Mason does not appear in court.

*Note on the Titles*: A number of people question the meaning of the film's title and the use of the phrase "velvet claws." There is no explanation given in the film, but in the novel, Della Street describes Eva Belter as being "all velvet and claws," meaning feigning sweetness on the outside but being quite mean on the inside. That expression must have disappeared from the vernacular since 1933.

All of the Perry Mason films used the title from the books on which they were based except for *The Case of the Black Cat* (1936), which was based on the novel titled *The Case of the Caretaker's Cat* (1935). Presumably, the studio felt that the new title was more mysterious and interesting than the Gardner title, even though there is no black cat in the film.

The Gardner novels were known for their alliterative titles, such as *The Case of the Dangerous Dowager, ...Perjured Parrot, ...Haunted Husband, ...Drowning Duck* and the like. The only film to employ an alliterative title was *The Case of the Lucky Legs* (1935).

## *The Case of the Black Cat* (1936)

With *The Case of the Black Cat*, Warner Brothers got its production of Perry Mason movies back on the right track. Gone is Warren William and his insincere approach to the character and in his place is Ricardo Cortez, tough as they come, but still with a little humor in the characterization. Gone is the inebriated criminal defense attorney with his entourage of hangers-on; in their place is a determined attorney who is a loner except for his secretary and investigator. Gone is the romance (and the marriage) between Mason and Della

Street, and in its place is the appropriate professional relationship for a law office which deals in serious legal matters. Gone is Spudsy Drake, the ridiculous caricature of private investigator Paul Drake, and in his place is a more realistic, if slightly nerdy, version of the same character. And, perhaps most importantly, for the first time since *The Case of the Howling Dog*, Mason defends a client in court.

Mason is aroused from his bed late one night and called to the home of Peter Laxter, a wealthy client. Laxter wants Mason to rewrite his will and include several unusual provisions. Laxter wants to disinherit his granddaughter Wilma, whom he loves, because he is afraid that all of her suitors are only interested in the money she will inherit from him. Instead, Peter decides to leave all of the money to his two grandsons, Frank Oafley and Sam Laxter, of whom he is less fond. The new will also provides that the caretaker, Ashton, must always have a job at the Laxter house so long as Ashton needs one. Shortly after the new will is signed, Peter Laxter is burned to death in a fire at his house.

Mason gets back into the case when Ashton consults with the attorney. Although the heirs have followed Peter's will and kept him on as caretaker, Sam Laxter has threatened to kill the caretaker's cat. The cat and Sam have never gotten along very well, even before Peter died. Mason writes a letter to Sam on behalf of Ashton, raising the ire of both Sam and Frank and their shyster lawyer, Shuster (Clarence Wilson in the best performance in the film). However, what seems like a fairly trivial matter about a cat eventually leads to a search for hidden money and jewels, two deaths, the arrest of Mason's client for murder and a courtroom surprise with Mason, not unexpectedly, clearing his client of all wrongdoing.

While *The Case of the Black Cat* is an improvement over the most recent films in the series, it is still a disappointment. Even though the filmmakers were able to correct many of the problems of the last several Mason films, they were unable to recreate the feverish pace of the Erle Stanley Gardner novels. By contrast, the plot of *The Case of the Black Cat* moves quite slowly, never truly grabbing the viewer's interest. Part of the reason is that the death of Peter Laxter comes many minutes into the story and then a considerable amount of time goes by before the later killings occur. Before and during all of that, there is a lot of time spent on boyfriends, wills, cats and waffles, but not on any mysteries.

The climax occurs at the preliminary hearing of Douglas Keene, with Hamilton Burger for the prosecution and Mason for the defense. What mystery fan does not relish that setup? This is the opportunity for Mason to dazzle the audience with his courtroom technique, pulling facts from reluctant witnesses, parrying the objections of the district attorney and finding the evidence to clear his client and identify the true killer.

In fact, though, the filmmakers miss this obvious opportunity. There are very few witnesses called and no courtroom byplay of objections, court rulings and strong cross-examination of witnesses. Indeed, on the last day of the trial, Mason calls a surprise witness to the stand but instead of asking him any questions, simply tells the court, in a long series of flashbacks, what really happened and who the killers are. In terms of storytelling technique, there was actually no reason to have Mason appear in court in this film. While Mason's solution to the murders may be true, there are no facts given to support his story, and unlike the television show, no one confesses to the crimes. Nevertheless, the judge drops the charges against Mason's clients without any objection from the district attorney.

There are other less-than-convincing moments in *The Case of the Black Cat*. Mason never gives an explanation as to how he discovered what truly happened, assuming his explanation is correct. Suspects leave fingerprints all over crime scenes yet no one thinks to lift any of the prints and compare them to the prints of the suspects. The black cat of the title is white and gray. And, perhaps most surprising of all, an attorney, called in the middle of the night by his client to re-draft the client's will, actually leaves his warm bed and goes to the client's house to provide the required legal services. Shouldn't a mystery have some credibility?

*Note on the Source Material*: *The Case of the Black Cat* is a faithful adaptation of Gardner's 1935 novel *The Case of the Caretaker's Cat*. The killings and the killers are the same, as are the several suspects and the appearance of Shuster, the less than ethical attorney for Sam Laxter and Frank Oafley.

There are three significant changes in the presentation. The book starts out with Ashton coming to Mason's office and explaining the difficulties that he is having about his cat. Mason did not previously know any of the characters. Mason therefore obtains all of his facts about the death of Peter Laxter and related matters when they are told to him by other characters. In the movie, and consistent with the way this type of movie is usually filmed, the story opens with the situation at the Laxter home and what happened to Laxter, before Ashton makes his appearance at Mason's office.

The second third of the novel involves Mason chasing clues, tricking a minister into giving him some facts, having a run-in with Sergeant Holcomb, trying to locate the mysterious Watson Clammert, and trying to get Douglas Keene to the police station to give himself up before the police attempt to arrest him as a fugitive. This is the part of the novel that has the frenetic pace which is typical of the Mason stories. Nevertheless, given the time constraints of the movie, this section of the novel, while interesting, had to be jettisoned.

The novel ends with the preliminary hearing of Douglas Keene, with the trademark examination, cross-examinations, trial objections and rulings on the same. In the course thereof, important facts are obtained. Eventually, however, the assistant district attorney, in an unusual move, calls Mason as a witness, giving Mason the chance to give a monologue of his analysis of the events that occurred and who the killers were. Thus, part of the problem with *The Case of the Black Cat* comes from the end of *The Case of the Caretaker's Cat*, with Mason giving a speech about the murders instead of eliciting the information through the examination of the witnesses.

*Note on the* Perry Marson *Television Episode*: As was often the case with the television shows, "The Case of the Caretaker's Cat" (March 7, 1959) is not so much based on the Gardner novel as inspired by it. Thus, the episode involves the death of a wealthy man in a house fire, a previous change in his will and a caretaker who has a cat. However, there are different suspects and different characters and, in fact, the accused and the real murderer are different from the ones in the novel. Also, the only reason the caretaker has a cat on the television episode is so that the novel's title could be re-used. The cat is much more important in the book than in the television episode.

For mystery movie fans, it is refreshing to see Benson Fong playing the caretaker whom Mason represents on the murder charge. Fong played Charlie Chan's son Tommy in some of the 1940s Chan movies from Monogram. George E. Stone, who played the Runt in the Boston Blackie series, had a recurring role as the court clerk in many of the *Perry Mason* episodes. Stone had difficulties performing in the 1950s due to his failing eyesight, and in most of the *Perry Masons* he has no lines and is very difficult to even spot in the courtroom.

In "The Case of the Caretaker's Cat," however, he has several lines, including swearing in a witness.

## *The Case of the Stuttering Bishop* (1937)

If it was unfair to compare some of the prior entries in this series to the Gardner novels or to the Raymond Burr television series, *The Case of the Stuttering Bishop* demands such a comparison. The film is faithful to its source material and has the look of the famous television program, making it, by far, the best film in the series since *The Case of the Howling Dog*.

A man identifying himself as Bishop Mallory consults Mason about the crime of manslaughter and its statute of limitations. Eventually, Mason learns that 20 years earlier, a woman named Ida Gilbert accidentally killed a man in an auto accident. Her wealthy father-in-law, Ronald Brownley, a man with political connections who had objected to Ida's marriage to his son, had Ida charged with manslaughter. Ida fled to Australia with her husband, who abandoned her before their daughter Janice was born. Because she did not have funds to care for the baby, Ida allowed Bishop Mallory to find a home for Janice with a couple in America. Now, Ida wants the elder Brownley to recognize Janice as his granddaughter. Brownley, however, believes that another woman is his granddaughter and he intends to change his will to provide for that woman. Before that can happen, however, Brownley is shot several times by a woman in a raincoat. The police arrest Ida Gilbert, who, luckily for her, is then represented by Mason. After some courtroom fireworks, the identity of the actual killer of Brownley is exposed.

Donald Woods makes an excellent Perry Mason, displaying some of the hardboiled attitude of the Mason of the contemporary Gardner novels. Woods is handsome, serious and committed. Sporting a mustache to give him a little bit of an older look, he is much more convincing than either Warren William or Ricardo Cortez ever could be playing someone who could actually be a criminal defense attorney in court. Joseph Crehan plays Paul Drake and, for once, the part is written as it was in the books, with Drake a serious and competent investigator and an important ally for Mason. If Crehan seems just a little too old or a little too small for the part, that is only because of obvious comparisons with William Hopper, who played the role for so many years in the television series. Ann Dvorak is also fine as Della Street, although she has little to do. Nevertheless, while Perry and Della have more than the normal employer-employee relationship, gone is the romance and gone is the unconvincing verbal byplay between the two, a vast improvement over some of the previous films.

The whodunit itself is the most complex in the series and one of the most complex mysteries ever filmed. *The Case of the Stuttering Bishop* weaves a story of past events affecting contemporaneous actions and involves multiple characters, some of whom are not who they appear to be and others who appear to be phonies but then surprisingly turn out to be exactly who they are supposed to be. This complexity, though, is both a positive and a negative. It is obviously beneficial to have a challenging mystery for the viewer to both follow and solve. However, upon occasion, the story jumps from event to event or from character to character, without taking the time to explain the connection between the two, making the movie hard to follow. It would have taken only a little more effort by the filmmakers to have made *The Case of the Stuttering Bishop* as effective a complex mystery tale as Warners' *The Kennel Murder Case* (1933).

Although *The Case of the Stuttering Bishop* is much more serious than the previous four films in the series, it paradoxically has more legitimate laughs. Some comic relief is provided by Tom Kennedy playing hotel detective Jim Magooney. Kennedy is doing a mild imitation of his role as Gahagan in the Torchy Blane series (also from Warner Brothers), but he is more amusing here, proving that "less is more" when dealing with Kennedy. In an unrelated highlight moment, Mason pretends he is drunk outside a hotel door, so that he can evade the police. Suddenly, the door opens and a woman appears, shouting, "I thought I told you the next time you came home drunk you could sleep in the park, you termite."

Unlike many of the films in the series, Mason appears in court at a preliminary hearing, just as he did in most of the books and the television programs. As the prosecution presents its case, the facts of the crime are told effectively by the witnesses, with short snippets of testimony providing important information to the viewer. When Mason goes on the offensive, though, there is some excellent cross-examination, particularly of an eyewitness to the crime who said that shooter was a woman wearing a white raincoat. When Mason is done, it is clear that the shooter could have possibly been wearing a light yellow raincoat, expanding the potential killers by two.

The climax in a courtroom setting is everything a Perry Mason fan could want. The scene is the highlight of the movie and the best courtroom scene in the entire series. The only disconcerting matter is that the last name of District Attorney Hamilton Burger is not pronounced with the hard "g" as in the food but rather, with a soft "g," as in the word "merger." Where that pronunciation comes from no one knows.

The killer appears to be a least-likely suspect which, for Perry Mason fans, should come as no surprise. But then, Mason is himself surprised when the killer turns out to be one of the most likely suspects, a plot twist which makes the whole tale make sense in retrospect. The double surprise at the denouement is a fitting end to *The Case of the Stuttering Bishop* and to the film series itself, although now that the filmmakers finally seemed focused on bringing an authentic Perry Mason story to the cinema, it is a shame that the series ended with this film.

*Note on the Source Material*: *The Case of the Stuttering Bishop* was based upon Gardner's 1936 novel of the same name. The movie is faithful to the book, even to the extent that Jim Magooney, the hotel detective in the film, comes from the novel (where he has a much smaller role and different name). However, the end of the film is different than the end of the book. While most of the courtroom examination and cross-examination in the film comes from the novel, the part of the film where Mason pressures Janice Alma Brownley on the witness stand, forcing her mother to confess to the murder, is original, as is the surprise courtroom identification of Sacks as the actual killer. In the novel, the same events occur but not in the courtroom. Once again, that change in staging of the denouement brings the film, *The Case of the Stuttering Bishop*, much closer to the television series than any of the other films in the movie series.

Also, Mason is not surprised in the book, as he appears to be in the movie, that Sacks is the killer. In both works, Stockton has provided an alibi for the fake Janice for the time of the murder of Brownley, thus protecting his investment in the fake Janice. In the book, however, Stockton had prepared that alibi before the fake Janice arrived at his apartment, leading Mason to believe that the alibi was originally prepared for Sacks, to permit him to kill Brownley. That subtle clue from the novel is missing from the film.

As noted above, when viewing *The Case of the Stuttering Bishop*, the viewer sometimes gets the feeling that the film jumps from scene to scene, without some necessary explanatory transitions. This feeling is confirmed by reading the novel. For example, in the picture, as Bishop Mallory ends his interview with Mason at the beginning of the film, the bishop states, "I must disappear and have no further contact with you 'til you bring me into court as a witness. And you will have to be very clever to find me, Mr. Mason."

At that point in the movie, the statement is totally perplexing. In the book, the bishop states, and Mason agrees, that if it comes out that the bishop brought the real Janice to Mason, the bishop's later identification of Janice in court will have less credibility. That is why the bishop decided that he must immediately cut all ties with Mason. The explanation makes sense in the book. There is no explanation given in the movie.

At one point early in the film, when the investigation seems to come to a halt, Mason tells Della, "My guess is that I'll receive a call from a woman giving her name as Ida Gilbert or Mrs. Oscar Brownley." In the next scene, that is exactly what happens but for the viewer, those names come out of the blue. In the book, Mason uses similar language, but only after Paul Drake had investigated the bishop's story about a trumped-up manslaughter charge, thereby learning about the accident in which Mrs. Oscar Brownley was involved. The line therefore makes sense in the book. In the movie, however, it is another perplexing moment.

As good as the film is, another five minutes of explanatory dialogue or scenes would have made the movie much better, not to mention, easier to follow. In adapting a novel into a film, it is not just enough to pull scenes and dialogue from the book. They must be pulled together in a cogent manner.


*Note on the* Perry Mason *Television Episode*: "The Case of the Stuttering Bishop" (March 14, 1959) was only loosely based on the novel. In the show, much like the book, a stuttering bishop tries to prove that a young lady is the real heir to a millionaire's fortune. He is up against a fake heir and a rough private detective. The millionaire is murdered before he can change his will. However, the mothers of the real and fake heirs are not characters and Mason's client is the real heir, not her mother. Also, the killer on television is different than the one in the book. So, once again, the 1936 film is closer to the original novel than the television program.

In terms of realistic portrayals of lawyers, this episode hits it on the nose. At one point, Mason tells a witness that he only has one more question to ask. Then Mason asks three. A similar moment is repeated in courtrooms in the United States every trial day of the year.


*Note on the Actors*: Donald Woods, who plays Mason in this film only, previously appeared as a suspect in *The Case of the Curious Bride* (1935). It was not unusual for an actor to appear in a series in a minor role and then later graduate to the starring role in a series. Hungarian-born Paul Lukas was a suspect in the Philo Vance film *The Benson Murder Case* (1930). He then went on to play the sophisticated detective in one film, *The Casino Murder Case* (1935). Jane Wyman played a minor character in *Smart Blonde* (1937), from the Torchy Blane series. She then went on to play the perky reporter in *Torchy Blane ... Playing with Dynamite* (1939). Gerald Mohr played the Lone Wolf in three films in the series, starting with *The Notorious Lone Wolf* (1946). Mohr had previously played the murder victim in a Lone Wolf film titled *One Dangerous Night* (1943).

## Afterwards

Erle Stanley Gardner wrote Perry Mason novels until his death in 1970. He was so prolific that as late as 1973, some of the works were still being published for the first time. Even today, the Mason novels are seldom out of print, with over 200 million copies sold in the United States alone. In addition to the characters he created for his pulp magazine stories, Gardner also wrote mystery novels about other series characters, such as District Attorney Doug Selby, in nine novels commencing with *The D.A. Calls It Murder* (1937), and private eyes Bertha Cool and Donald Lam, under his pen name A.A. Fair, in over 25 novels beginning with *The Bigger They Come* (1939).

While there were no more film versions of the famous attorney, there was a successful radio show which was on the air for 12 years, from 1943 to 1955. The show, which was part soap opera and part mystery story, was usually broadcast in serial form in 15-minute episodes, from Monday to Friday afternoon. A number of actors portrayed Mason over the years, with John Larkin playing the role the longest. Gardner objected when CBS wanted to move the serial to television so CBS used the same writers, same general approach and many of the same actors, to create *The Edge of Night*, a daytime soap opera which specialized in mystery yarns instead of the usual soap opera storylines about romance and infidelity. *The Edge of Night* was on the air for over 30 years.

Of course, the most famous version of the Perry Mason character was the long-running one-hour series, which debuted on CBS in 1957. Gardner, who was unhappy with the way Mason was portrayed in the 1930s films, set up the production company, Paisano Productions (named after his ranch), to produce the shows. That gave him some control over the final product. Raymond Burr was Perry Mason, Barbara Hale was Della Street, William Hopper was Paul Drake, Ray Collins was Lieutenant Tragg and William Talman was District Attorney Hamilton Burger. In the early years, many of the scripts were based on Gardner novels. The show went off the air in 1966.

CBS then tried to bring back the character for a new series in 1973, starring different actors, but the show was not a success. It went off the air after one season. Burr and Hale returned as Perry and Della in a very successful sequence of two hour made-for-television movies which aired on NBC starting in 1985.

# 10

# Sophie Lang
## *The Lady Thief*

As noted in the introduction to this book, the female detective was a prime fixture in mystery movie series of the 1930s, from Hildegarde Withers to Nancy Drew to Torchy Blane. As noted in Chapter 4 of this book, the character of the gentleman thief, such as the Lone Wolf, Raffles and Arsène Lupin, was also a regular fixture of Hollywood mystery features of the 1930s. With the release of *The Notorious Sophie Lang* in 1934, Paramount commenced a new movie series which combined both of those aspects of 1930s mystery movie fare. Sophie Lang is the lead character and, at least in the first film, she is a thief extraordinaire. Sophie is thus the first and only female equivalent of the gentleman thief in a Hollywood mystery movie series.

## Background

### The Stories

Frederick Irving Anderson was born in 1877 in Aurora, Illinois. After a ten-year career as a newspaper reporter, he turned to writing fiction, contributing short stories to *The Saturday Evening Post* and other popular magazines of the day. Some of his mystery stories were collected in three volumes, many of which featured Deputy Parr of the New York City Police Department as the lead detective. Parr was sometimes assisted by Oliver Armiston, a crime writer whose plots were so ingenious that the underworld sometimes decided to use them as a guide for their own criminal capers.

The first collection of stories, *The Adventures of the Infallible Godahl* (1914), featured Armiston and master criminal Godahl, who was always one step ahead of the very fallible police. In Anderson's third collection, *The Book of Murder* (1930), most of the stories feature Parr and Armiston up against a variety of criminals. In these stories, Parr had his greatest successes in thwarting the villains, since he had the aid of the brilliant Armiston to assist him. The middle book was *The Notorious Sophie Lang*, published in England in 1925. The collection was never published in America and so it is now very rare and expensive, if it can be found at all. In stories collected from *The Saturday Evening Post*, Parr matched wits with, and always lost to, a beautiful and very intelligent jewel thief to whom the police had given the name "Sophie Lang."

## The Film Series

With the exception of the three films in the Sophie Lang series, none of Anderson's other works were adapted for the sound cinema. The first film in the Paramount series, *The Notorious Sophie Lang*, gives a credit to the stories by Frederick Irving Anderson but it is believed that the plot of the film is original to the cinema. In that 1934 film, Sophie, with the assistance of a woman known as Aunt Nellie, carries out brazen jewel robberies in New York City, while courting a gentleman thief from England. In *The Return of Sophie Lang* (1936), Sophie has reformed and is working as a companion to an older woman whose valuable jewel is stolen, requiring Sophie to recover it to clear her own name. In *Sophie Lang Goes West* (1937), Sophie is still reformed but nevertheless becomes involved in another jewel robbery and another romance.

Gertrude Michael played Sophie Lang in all three films in the series. Michael was born in Talladega, Alabama, in 1910. After graduation from high school, she attended college, appeared on the radio and, in 1929, began appearing in regional theater in Cincinnati. She moved to Broadway in 1931 and then to films, with a bit part in *Wayward* (1932), a romantic melodrama. Michael was soon signed to a long-term contract by Paramount. From 1932 to 1934, she appeared in almost 20 films in supporting roles, including a part in *Murder on the Blackboard* (1934) from the Hildegarde Withers series.

Her first starring role was as the title character in *The Notorious Sophie Lang*. This was a significant part for Michael and had the potential to make her a Hollywood star.

## THE FILMS

### *The Notorious Sophie Lang* (1934)

*The Notorious Sophie Lang* is a perfect crime caper, light-hearted in nature, similar to the gentleman thief movies of the era but with a tone more in line with that of more recent crime adventures such as the 1960 and 2001 versions of *Ocean's Eleven*.

Famous jewel thief Sophie Lang has returned to New York City after a five-year absence to commence her own one-woman crime wave. As the movie opens, Sophie is already making her escape from the Diamond Importers offices with a cache of diamonds in her possession. She then manages to get past the police perimeter in a stolen ambulance. Later, Sophie steals a valuable string of pearls from Telfen Jewelers, even though the police expect her to do so, having substituted a fake string of pearls into the mix and having a hidden camera ready to take pictures of her. Sophie also has time to romance a famous British jewel thief, Max Bernard. At the end of the film, despite the best efforts of Inspector Stone of the New York police, Sophie and Max appear to have escaped.

Inspector Stone has the same function as Deputy Parr in Frederick Irving Anderson's stories, trying to catch Sophie but always being at least two steps behind. Standard police techniques, such as establishing a perimeter around a crime scene, do not work. Innovative police techniques, such as creating a robbery setup at Telfon Jewelers to trap Sophie or trailing Max to locate the lady thief, do not work. In fact, the most effective trick used in the film is employed by Sophie, as she bugs Inspector Stone's home office to obtain important information. Sophie is so confident and brazen that she even steals some pearls right from the suit coat of Inspector Stone while he is wearing it.

Inspector Stone (Arthur Byron) finally meets Sophie Lang (Gertrude Michael) in person in *The Notorious Sophie Lang* (1934). However, Stone does not realize that the woman is Sophie Lang or that she is about to steal some valuable pearls from him.

In addition to the clever criminal vignettes sprinkled throughout the film, *The Notorious Sophie Lang* sports some excellent performances in the lead roles. Gertrude Michael is vivacious and witty as Sophie Lang, and she is attractive in the extreme, particularly late in the film when she has to run through the hotel in her short slip. Paul Cavanaugh is handsome and suave as the gentleman thief, Max Bernard; Arthur Byron is believably frustrated as Inspector Stone, although he does take his defeats with equanimity. The supporting performances are also winning, with the always delightful Alison Skipworth delightful once again as Aunt Nellie, Sophie's trusted assistant, and Ferdinand Gottschalk amusing as Augustus Telfon, who reluctantly agrees to assist the police, only to be robbed by the always clever Sophie. The comic relief is provided by Leon Errol as Stubbs, the policeman who follows Brand throughout the film. Errol does provide a few mild laughs while generally remaining unobtrusive.

Some of the early parts of the film are slow-moving but the pace accelerates at the end when Stone arrests Brand for a robbery he did not commit but unwittingly lets Sophie escape even though she is the one who committed the theft. There are other twists and turns, lies and back-stabbings and then some close calls for Sophie and Max before they apparently escape on a boat to England. The movie never turns serious; it is always all a lot of fun.

An in-vogue term for describing a certain group of Hollywood films from the early 1930s is pre–Code. The pre–Code era is the approximately five-year period beginning with 1929, when sound films first dominated the market, until mid–1934 when a strict production code was self-imposed by Hollywood. Pre-Code films were not above making villains into heroes and they were less strict about good triumphing over evil, as contrasted with post–Code films. On its face, *The Notorious Sophie Lang* is a pre–Code film, in the sense that criminals Sophie and Max are the heroes. But, at the end, in what almost seems like an epilogue, Code considerations seem to have taken the upper hand, as the police recover all of the valuables stolen by Sophie in New York, and Inspector Stone wires Scotland Yard to pick up Sophie and Max when their boat docks in London. Thus, good has triumphed over evil, a requirement of post–Code films.

For most fans of *The Notorious Sophie Lang*, it is probably better just to forget the ending and assume Sophie successfully absconds with the goods and the man she loves. That would probably have been the ending if the film were released just a few months earlier. With either ending, *The Notorious Sophie Lang* is highly recommended.

## *The Return of Sophie Lang* (1936)

After a two-year absence from the silver screen, Sophie Lang returns in another tale of crime and robbery. But, has Sophie really returned? The light-hearted, fun-loving Sophie of *The Notorious Sophie Lang* has been replaced by the always serious and usually morose Sophie of the sequel. Even though Gertrude Michael has returned for the title role, the blond-haired Sophie of the first feature is now a brunette who seems to have aged considerably since her first screen appearance. The new Sophie has reformed and seems quite happy to be the companion to a wealthy older lady who does not know Sophie's true identity. The love affair from the first feature with the gentleman thief Max Bernard is forgotten. There is a character in *The Return of Sophie Lang* who once again uses the pseudonym of Nigel Crane and really is jewel thief Max Bernard, but he is much older than the Max Bernard of the first film. There is no relationship between Sophie and Max, amorous or otherwise. It is as if *The Return of Sophie Lang* is not truly a sequel to *The Notorious Sophie Lang* but is a film *sui generis*.

The contrast between the openings of *The Notorious Sophie Lang* and its sequel are patent. In the first film, as the story begins, Sophie is already in the process of committing a clever robbery. In *The Return of Sophie Lang*, she is at a cemetery in England, viewing her own tombstone on a cloudy day, as the world believes that Sophie is dead. It will take some time before the film is able to drop the somber mood of this opening. While Sophie is at the cemetery, a young American reporter, Jimmy Lawson, delivers flowers to Sophie's grave, and this is clearly not the first time he has done so. Lawson never knew Sophie; her exploits made life exciting for Lawson from a distance. Of course, that is an absolutely ridiculous reason for Lawson being at the graveyard. It is simply an excuse for Lawson to meet Sophie, so that they will know each other when they later coincidentally meet once again on a ship sailing to America.

For five years, Sophie has been a companion to the elderly Mrs. Sedley, who has brought on board the ship the very valuable Kruger diamond. Also on board is a man known as Nigel Crane, who is really the famous jewel thief Max Bernard. Sophie and Max know each other either by reputation or from an encounter in the past, and Sophie worries that Bernard will try to get his hands on the Kruger diamond. Sophie believes the valuable is locked away in the boat's safe, but when she is off on a romantic interlude with Jimmy, Bernard lifts the jewel from Mrs. Sedley. The chase is then on and despite Bernard's constant efforts to pin the theft on Sophie, she finally recovers the jewel and convinces the police to arrest him for the crime.

The performances in *The Return of Sophie Lang* are all excellent, down to the smallest parts, with Sir Guy Standing giving the best performance in the film playing Bernard, a little older than most thieves of his type but surely just as suave and sophisticated as the rest of them. Through most of the film, Bernard is the focus of the tale, following a devious plan of theft, whether incriminating Sophie, getting the diamond off the ship by hiding it in Jimmy's coat or recovering it at gunpoint from Jimmy and Sophie in New York City. Standing carries the film with his debonair and charming performance.

The most significant problem is that much of *The Return of Sophie Lang* is quite boring; there is simply not much happening. Adding to the ennui is the somber atmosphere which carries over from the opening scene in the cemetery through almost the entire boat ride to America. Fortunately, the film does pick up quite a bit at the end, with Sophie posing as Mrs. Sedley in an attempt to recover the diamond for her loyal employer. At that point the tone of the film finally becomes more light-hearted and there are several storyline twists and turns, including Sophie's clever call to the police right under the noses of the villains.

All works out in the end. The diamond is recovered, Sophie is cleared of all wrongdoing, and Jimmy and Sophie are in love. It is a typical happy ending for a Hollywood film. But what true mystery fan does not wish that Sophie had a little more larceny in her heart and a little more mischief in her demeanor? That may not have been possible for this post–Code film, but it would have made *The Return of Sophie Lang* a much better movie.

## *Sophie Lang Goes West* (1937)

[*This is one of the few films discussed in this book which the author did not view.*]

Sophie is still reformed in this final film but she has apparently ditched Jimmy Lawson, her boyfriend from *The Return of Sophie Lang*. Since Sophie always seems to be a suspect whenever there is a theft of a jewel, she heads West to avoid the police, an idea that could have come in handy for the Lone Wolf and Boston Blackie in their 1940s film series. In her journey west to Hollywood, Sophie, as usual, runs into another jewel thief, this time supposedly also reformed, and a very valuable diamond, this time owned by the Sultan of Padaya. After some back and forth with the jewel, all ends well, with Sophie falling in love once again.

## AFTERWARDS

After the publication of the three collections of his short stories, the last one being in 1930, Frederick Irving Anderson continued to write short mystery stories on a sporadic basis. A few of these were published from time to time in mystery magazines but none were collected in book form. Anderson died in 1947.

There were no radio or television shows featuring the Sophie Lang character. Nor were there any other films about the lady thief after the three released in the 1930s. Despite the success of *The Notorious Sophie Lang*, Gertrude Michael never reached her potential in Hollywood. A nervous breakdown, accidents and alcohol-related illnesses put the brakes on her career. After 1937, her film work was infrequent. Most of her work in the 1940s was in Poverty Row features. Few of her later film appearances were in significant films. In the 1950s, Michael made numerous appearances on television programs. She passed away in 1964.

# 11

# Sarah Keate
## *The Nurse Detective*

The "Had I But Known" discipline of writing was once an important subgenre of detective and mystery fiction. Usually associated with Mary Roberts Rinehart and the publication of *The Circular Staircase* in 1908, this type of mystery has a beautiful heroine writing the story in the first person, usually becoming involved in a precarious situation which requires her rescue by the handsome hero at the end of the book. At some point during the narrative, the heroine writes something like, "Had I known then what I know now, these terrible things would never have happened." This type of story has been ridiculed over the years and is no longer written in the style of the early 1900s. However, suspense novels involving female protagonists are still a staple of contemporary mystery fiction.

Mignon G. Eberhart is usually included in the "Had I But Known" school of writers, probably because of language such as the following from the beginning of *Murder by an Aristocrat* (1932):

> But knowing what I now know, I could never again force myself to cross that green and tranquil lawn, pass the step where Emmeline stood and screamed, and enter the wide and gracious door.
> A door which led to horror.

However, in the Sarah Keate books, although the style is "Had I But Known," at least the substance is pure whodunit, with Keate assisting the police in solving murder cases. And, once the character moved to the cinema, with no on-screen narration, even the "Had I But Known" style of storytelling completely disappeared.

## BACKGROUND

### The Novels

Born in 1899 in Lincoln, Nebraska, Mignon Good Eberhart spent three years at Nebraska Wesleyan University, a small liberal arts college in her hometown, but never obtained a degree. In 1923, she married Alinson C. Eberhart, a civil engineer, with whom she traveled extensively. After working for a while as a freelance journalist, she decided to become a fulltime writer of mystery novels. Her first novel, *The Patient in Room 18*, published in 1929, introduced the character of Nurse Sarah Keate.

Redheaded Sarah Keate is a middle-aged, unmarried nurse who sometimes works in hospitals and sometimes in patients' homes. Wherever she is employed, murders seem to occur. Although Nurse Keate seldom solves the crimes, she is a shrewd observer of the suspects and the evidence. Writing in the first person, Keate recreates the atmosphere and settings of the killings and provides all of the clues for the reader to determine the killer on his own. The person who usually solves the homicides is Lance O'Leary, a young, no-nonsense homicide detective who first meets Keate when he is investigating several murders at a hospital in which she works, as related in the first book in the series. O'Leary is smart enough to use Keate's powers of observation to assist him in his detective work, even though he is often required to rescue Keate from dangerous situations.

From 1929 to 1932, Eberhart wrote five Sarah Keate books. All five were adapted into movies by Warner Brothers. In the mid–1930s, Eberhart wrote numerous short stories about her nurse-detective. One of those short stories was adapted into a film at 20th Century–Fox.

## The Film Series

The first Nurse Keate film was *While the Patient Slept*, a 1935 production which starred Aline MacMahon as Nurse Keate and Guy Kibbee as Lance O'Leary. The film involves a murder in an old dark house where Keate is attending to a patient who had a stroke.

MacMahon was born in 1899 in McKeesport, Pennsylvania. She achieved her first successes on Broadway before moving into films at Warner Brothers in 1931. Although she did have some dramatic film roles in the 1930s, she is better known during that time period for playing sassy working women, such as Trixie in *Gold Diggers of 1933* (1933). Nurse Sally Keate is another such role. After her one appearance as the nurse-detective, MacMahon had no other significant roles in mystery films. She retired from film work in the mid–1960s, returning to the stage. MacMahon died in 1991.

Guy Kibbee was born in 1882 in El Paso, Texas. He started his performing career as a teenager on Mississippi riverboats, eventually moving to the Broadway stage. In 1931, much like MacMahon, Kibbee started his film career at Warner Brothers, usually playing character parts, coincidentally appearing with MacMahon in *Gold Diggers of 1933* (1933). *While the Patient Slept* is a rare starring role for Kibbee, although he did play the title characters in *Babbitt* (1934) and in RKO's Scattergood Baines B–movie series in the 1940s. Kibbee retired from film work in 1949. He passed away in 1956.

The second film in the series was *The Murder of Dr. Harrigan* (1936), about the killing of the title character on a hospital elevator. For some reason, the name of the lead character was changed from Sarah Keate to Sally Keating (the name change continued for the next film in the series) and a younger actress was brought in to play the role, thus undercutting the spinsterish characterization of the nurse-detective from the Eberhart novels. Kay Linaker, who was born in Pine Bluff, Arkansas, in 1913, was 23 years old when she starred in *The Murder of Dr. Harrigan*, one of her first film roles. Linaker's prior acting experience was on Broadway. For mystery fans, Linaker is best known today for appearing in several Charlie Chan movies. After her film career ended, she began writing for television, going on to co-write the screenplay for *The Blob*, a 1958 science fiction classic. Linaker passed away in 2008.

The third film in the series was *Murder by an Aristocrat* (1936). For the first time in the movies, Nurse Keating actually solves the crime (the murder of a blackmailer in a large mansion filled with his relatives). Once again, the lead role went to a new actress for the series, Marguerite Churchill. Churchill, who was born in 1909 or 1910 in Kansas City, Missouri, began appearing in films at the beginning of the sound era. Her career was just about over by the end of the 1930s. Her best-remembered role today is probably as the love interest in *Dracula's Daughter* (1936). Churchill died in 2000.

With the next film, *The Great Hospital Mystery* (1937), the Sarah Keate films moved to 20th Century–Fox. The mystery involves the substitution of a body in a hospital and the killing of one of the hospital's employees. The nurse-detective's name was changed to Miss Keats and a new actress, Jane Darwell, tackled the role.

Darwell was born in 1879 in Palmyra, Missouri. Her acting career began in theater productions in Chicago and then, as early as 1913, she appeared in some silent films. However, her true film career began in the early 1930s, when Darwell was already in her 50s. She usually played character parts, often as the mother or grandmother of a character, such as her appearances in five films with Shirley Temple. Her most famous role, by far, was as Ma Joad in *The Grapes of Wrath* (1940), for which she won an Academy Award. Upon occasion she was cast against type, such as playing one of the lynch mob members in *The Ox-Bow Incident* (1943). Her last film appearance was in *Mary Poppins* (1964), a silent part where she tossed breadcrumbs to pigeons while Julie Andrews sang "Feed the Birds." Darwell died in 1967.

The fifth film in the series, *The Patient in Room 18* (1938), was based upon Eberhart's first Nurse Keate novel. The movie, produced at Warner Brothers, involves several murders at a hospital and the theft of a valuable packet of radium. Nurse Keate was played by Ann Sheridan, the fifth actress in five movies to play the role. Lance O'Leary, now a private detective, was played by Patric Knowles.

Ann Sheridan was born in 1915 in Denton, Texas. After winning a beauty contest in 1933, she came to Hollywood in 1934, eventually signing with Warner Brothers in 1936. After some small roles at Warners, she received early starring roles in the last two Sarah Keate films, *The Patient in Room 18* and *Mystery House* (1938). Some of her next roles are her most famous today: the female lead in three Dead End Kids crime movies, the most renowned being *Angels with Dirty Faces* (1938). Nicknamed the "oomph girl" by Warner Brothers, Sheridan continued working steadily in the 1940s, in such films as *King's Row* (1942) with Ronald Reagan and *I Was a Male War Bride* (1949) with Cary Grant. She passed away on January 21, 1967.

English-born Patric Knowles (1911–95) moved to Hollywood in 1935 after signing a contract with Warner Brothers. In the 1930s and 1940s, he had good supporting roles in major films such as *The Adventures of Robin Hood* (1938) and *How Green Was My Valley* (1941). While he did appear in a few mysteries, he is probably best known today for his appearances in horror films, namely a small role in *The Wolf Man* (1941) and the key role of Dr. Mannering in *Frankenstein Meets the Wolf Man* (1943).

Sheridan reprised her role as Sarah Keate in *Mystery House* (1938), a story about several murders at an isolated hunting lodge. Dick Purcell played Lance O'Leary, the third and last actor to play the part. Purcell was born in 1908 in Greenwich, Connecticut. He had steady work at Warner Brothers throughout the late 1930s, although seldom in significant parts. Purcell played the lead character in *Captain America*, a 15-chapter serial from Republic released in 1944. He died that same year at age 35, the victim of a heart attack.

## THE FILMS

### *While the Patient Slept* (1935)

A cliché can be defined as an element of an artistic work which is so overused that it loses its special effect. By that strict definition, the opening of *While the Patient Slept* is not a cliché. The film commences at the Federie mansion on a particularly dark and stormy night, with a large dog in the yard, barking at all who enter the grounds. As loud thunderclaps are heard, a butler walks around the house in a menacing fashion. The audience is then introduced to wealthy Richard Federie, who has gathered all of his heirs to make an unknown announcement to them. Later that night, there is a shotgun killing in the old dark house and the mystery begins.

While there is little that is unfamiliar about the opening of *While the Patient Slept*, it is still not a cliché because it is a very effective piece of filmmaking. The sounds of the thunder and the barking of the dog are used effectively. The constant downpour creates an overwhelming ambience of eeriness and dread. The large tower room set with its curved staircase, high ceilings, open space, curtained areas and multiple doors creates the perfect setting for the murder of a surprise character.

Before Richard Federie can make his announcement to his heirs, he receives a telegram which leads to a serious stroke. Nurse Keate is called in to minister to Richard, who is allowed to sleep in a bed specially placed in the tower room. While both Richard and Nurse Keate are sleeping, Adolph Federie, the son of Richard, is shot on the curved steps leading to the room. As a part of the intrigue, everyone seems to be after a knick-knack of an elephant, which contains a mysterious writing. Adolph had it in his hands when he was shot. Nurse Keate recovers the object, but it later goes missing again. At the end of the film, policeman Lance O'Leary, with the assistance of Nurse Keate, creates a trap, ensnaring the real murderer and revealing the secret of the elephant curio.

Much of the success of the film must be attributed to the acting duo of Aline MacMahon as Nurse Keate and Guy Kibbee as Lance O'Leary. MacMahon is a revelation—prim and proper as Nurse Keate but always ready to use her comedy background to land a zinger or two on O'Leary. Kibbee, who is a surprising choice to play an experienced policeman, is easygoing and unruffled, making him a perfect fit for the part. The easy repartee between the two actors, usually seen in character parts, is the highlight of the feature. Indeed, all of the performances are good, with the exception of Allen Jenkins as policeman Jackson. Jenkins gives his usual over-the-top performance, which is exceedingly discordant with the understated performances of MacMahon and Kibbee. Jenkins needed to turn it down several notches for this mystery movie.

The opening is the high spot of the film, with the rest of the movie becoming mundane, with the witnesses interviewed and re-interviewed, and the police jumping to the wrong conclusions. The surprise killer is one of the suspects, so that is a positive, but his motive comes out of the blue and there are no clues provided to the viewer so that the viewer can reach the proper deduction. If *While the Patient Slept* is viewed within the lens of a police procedural rather than a whodunit, the film works substantially better.

This Nurse Keate film has been compared to the Hildegarde Withers movies from the same era from RKO. Both have an older female detective sparring with a crusty policeman, with the female tossing deprecating one-liners at the detective and with a hint of romance in the air. There is an important distinction, though. Unlike Hildegarde Withers, Nurse Keate actually does little detecting in *While the Patient Slept* and it is O'Leary who actually solves the crimes with some clever deductions.

Toward the end of the film, it is cliché time again, but this time, the definition fits. There are hidden guns, locked attics, softly closing doors, hands behind a curtain that grab Nurse Keate, menacing shadows on the wall, and a surprise twin brother. Sometimes *While the Patient Slept* seems more like the silent horror film *The Cat and the Canary* (1927) or the 1936 serial *The Amazing Exploits of the Clutching Hand*, than a murder mystery. Unfortunately, those are not particularly good comparisons for a mystery movie. But on the whole, *While the Patient Slept* is an entertaining view.

*Note on the Source Material*: The film was based on Eberhart's 1930 novel, *While the Patient Slept*. The film is faithful to the book, with the same two murders committed by the same killer. Most of the suspects are the same although the relationships among them are slightly different in the book than in the film. Other features of the movie which are recognizable in the book are the twin brother, the jade elephant with the unexpected writing inside, the mysterious butler and cook, and the barking dog.

The plot of the book is more complicated and the characters better fleshed out than in the movie, which is hardly surprising given the short running time of the film. What is particularly interesting are the changes made in the plot of the book in its metamorphosis into film. The dark and stormy night motif is a film concoction, as is the irritating character of policeman Jackson, played by Allen Jenkins. The budding romance between O'Leary and Miss Keate is also a Hollywood creation.

In many ways, Hollywood took a solid, albeit old-fashioned mystery and added some typical elements of the cinema which Hollywood apparently felt were necessary for every mystery film of the era. Perhaps the filmmakers were right. Although the movie *While the Patient Slept* could have done without the Allen Jenkins character, the dark and stormy night atmosphere and the "romantic" repartee between O'Leary and Keate are decided plusses.

Even though the two works are somewhat contemporaneous, the book seems old-fashioned, with its individual chapter titles and Sarah Keate, as narrator, writing lines foreshadowing the later story. For example, just after her arrival at the Federie mansion, she writes, "There was that about the place that I definitely and positively did not like, and it was clear to me, even then, that it would not be a pleasant case. And it was not." The film, even though made over 75 years ago, seems more modern than the novel of the same period. Both, however, are interesting diversions.

## *The Murder of Dr. Harrigan* (1936)

In choosing to watch this second film in the Nurse Sarah Keate mystery series, now the Nurse Sally Keating mystery series, the viewer is probably expecting to see a film in which the star of the series, amateur though she may be, solves a murder mystery before the police do. Surprisingly, Sally Keating does not perform any detective work in the film nor does she solve any mystery. In fact, the main purpose for Keating being in the film appears to be to provide another suspect for the crime. To add to the strange structure of *The Murder of Dr. Harrigan*, the whodunit is not solved by anybody; it is solved by accident. Surely *The Murder of Dr. Harrigan* is a strange film to release in a mystery movie series.

Most of the action takes place in the Melady Memorial Hospital during the night shift of Nurse Sally Keating. Peter Melady, the founder of the hospital, who suffers from a serious heart condition, occupies a room on Miss Keating's floor. Melady has demanded that a surgeon at the hospital, Dr. Harrigan, perform heart surgery on Melady the next morning, which is peculiar because Melady and Harrigan despise each other. Melady also insists that Harrigan use a new anesthesia named slaipan which was developed for patients who cannot use ether. Melady controls the formula to slaipan and therefore calls the newspaper to announce the debut use of the drug the next day.

Melady's operation is destined not to occur. Harrigan suddenly decides to perform the operation that night and wheels Melady to the operating room on his own. Shortly thereafter, no one can find either Harrigan or Melady. After a search by Nurse Keating, Harrigan's stabbed body is accidentally discovered on the hospital elevator, which had been out of service for quite some time. Later, Melady's body is found in the morgue with the tag of a recently deceased charity patient on his toe. One of the potential motives for the crime turns out to be an ownership dispute over slaipan. When Miss Keating ends up with the formula, she is attacked by a person seeking the formula. The police shoot the assailant, thereby discovering the murderer.

A hospital setting is an excellent place for a murder mystery, with lots of doctors, nurses and patients readily available as suspects, and poisons and sharp objects easily obtainable for murder weapons. *Green for Danger* (1944) by Christianna Brand and the 1947 movie based thereon are two of the best-remembered examples of a murder mystery set in a hospital. Another excellent example is Ellery Queen's novel *The Dutch Shoe Mystery* (1931), although the movie based on that book, *Ellery Queen and the Murder Ring* (1941), is very disappointing. In *The Murder of Dr. Harrigan*, the filmmakers exploit the hospital setting to its fullest advantage, confining almost the entire story to the Melady Hospital. The claustrophobic effect created adds an atmosphere of dread to the happenings, increasing the tension in the first half of the film as the killing promised by the title of the film is about to occur.

The early parts of the movie are quite enjoyable. As the professional staff goes about its daily activities with the hospital patients, the viewer is introduced to the numerous potential suspects for the expected murder of Dr. Harrigan. However, there are so many suspects that the film does not have the time to distinguish the characters and provide individual information about their potential motives for a murder, along with whatever means and opportunity they might have. Indeed, the suspects are all one-dimensional and not interesting enough for the viewer to care if any one of them committed the crime. The filmmakers should have eliminated the two comedy patients, the dipsomaniac and the one suffering with nerves, and spent more time developing the other characters. If they had done so, the murder mystery would have hung together much better.

When the killer is finally unmasked, the audience's reaction may well be — who *is* that person? Since the explanation for what happened that night is provided, not by Lieutenant Lamb and not by Nurse Keating, but rather by George Lambert, a hospital intern who seems to be guessing, the whole matter is unconvincing. Again, why was Dr. Harrigan murdered? Why was Melady's body dispatched to the morgue? Once the movie is over, it is hard to remember the answers to those questions.

Joseph Crehan, a character actor who appeared in over 300 films, with many roles as a policeman, is quite good as Lieutenant Lamb, competent and intense. Crehan is also more stylishly dressed than he usually is in his film roles as a policeman. The rest of the cast is adequate enough, except for Kay Linaker as Sally Keating. Linaker is pretty but bland, with not enough personality to carry this film. She never connects with the audience on any sympathetic or emotional level, also undercutting the audience's interest in the whodunit. The direction by Frank McDonald is competent at best, adversely affected by some wobbly camerawork when the camera moves in to focus on an object.

As noted above, the key problem with the film is its underlying structure with Sally Keating, the purported heroine, doing nothing to solve the murder of Dr. Harrigan. Indeed, no one solves the homicide because if the murderer had not attacked Keating to obtain the formula, he would have gone undiscovered. It is hard for an audience to solve a movie murder when the characters themselves are unable to do so.

At the end of the film, Nurse Keating, always unmarried in the books, accepts a marriage proposal from George Lambert, intern and competent guesser of solutions to murder mysteries. A marriage for Nurse Keating would end her film detective career, almost for sure. Thus, what is the chance that Nurse Keating will not be married at the beginning of the next film in the series? And, if she is not, what is the point of doing a series of movie mysteries about the same nurse-detective?

*Note on the Source Material*: *The Murder of Dr. Harrigan* was based on Eberhart's 1931 novel *From This Dark Stairway*. For anyone who sees the movie before he reads the book, the whodunit in the novel will seem fresh, because the killer in the movie is not even a character in the

This publicity photo from *The Murder of Dr. Harrigan* (1936) shows George Lambert (Ricardo Cortez), and Nurse Sally Keating (Kay Linaker).

book, even though the underlying murder mysteries are virtually the same. Thus, in the novel, Dr. Harrigan's stabbed body is found on an elevator, Peter Melady goes missing just after his heart operation was supposed to begin, there is a dispute over the ownership of a revolutionary anesthetic and Nurse Keate is attacked by the murderer at the end.

The differences between the two works are significant. It is true that Nurse Keate does not solve the murder in the book; that is done by Lance O'Leary who makes a late appearance in the novel. Nevertheless, unlike the film, Sarah does make significant investigations on her own, including deducing where Peter Melady's body has gone, determining how the chewing gum got on Harrigan's body, locating the missing snuff bottle and catching an inconsistency in the story of the hospital orderly. Keate's detective work is crucial for O'Leary's investigation, and because Keate once again narrates the book, she is its key character. In the film, Keating sometimes seems to be more of a suspect than a lead character.

There is an important clue in the novel by which the reader can identify the killer. Since the stretcher which carried Peter Melady into the operating room was found in the operating room, how was his body removed from the hospital? The answer to that question leads conclusively to one individual as the killer. In the film, while the stretcher also remains in the operating room, since the murderer is different, nothing can be made of that clue. Indeed, the decision to change the killer in the movie results in no clues at all to the identity of the murderer in the film version.

*From This Dark Stairway* is an excellent whodunit with multiple clues, fleshed-out suspects and a believable solution. In transferring it to the screen for *The Murder of Dr. Harrigan*, and adding the figures of comic relief and a love interest for Keating, the filmmakers eliminated all of the nuances and strengths of the book, except one. Eberhart was always excellent at establishing the settings for her novels, in this case, creating an atmosphere of foreboding and anxiety in a busy hospital. As set forth above, the filmmakers were also able to do so, at least during the first half of the film.

## *Murder by an Aristocrat* (1936)

The key scenes of *Murder by an Aristocrat* occur one pleasant afternoon when Nurse Sally Keating, who is working at the Thatcher mansion attending to gunshot victim Bayard Thatcher, is given a break from her official duties. She proceeds outside the house to the garden where she sits on a chair, reading a book. There she observes the 3:20 PM mail plane flying low overhead, the butler mowing the lawn, the dog running out of the house barking and shaking, Mrs. Thatcher complaining that the dog broke a vase, Mrs. Thatcher driving away, and later, Dave Thatcher sneaking out of the house, Hilary Thatcher arriving at the house by auto (and after entering the house rushing away), Janice Thatcher returning to the house, and then the maid, Florrie, discovering Bayard's body, dead from a bullet wound. Nurse Keating essentially stands in for the viewer in these scenes, witnessing important clues for the murder investigation that is about to occur.

Inserted in between Keating's observations are some scenes that occur away from the Thatcher estate. These events include Dave Thatcher and District Attorney John Tweed fishing at a lake, with Dave disappearing for a few moments, and Mrs. Thatcher, calling home to Bayard Thatcher from a pharmacy phone, making sure that the clerk knows that the call was being placed at 4:00 PM. Mrs. Thatcher tells the clerk that her call with Bayard was suddenly cut off. Then there is another perplexing matter: no one heard a gunshot. Even Miss Keating, who was outside the manor the entire afternoon, heard nothing.

*Murder by an Aristocrat* is a classic-style whodunit, characteristic of its time. Everyone in the Thatcher family, each of whom is the potential aristocrat of the title, has a good motive for the murder of Bayard Thatcher. But the murderer of Bayard Thatcher is obvious. The mail plane and the dog running out of the house at 3:20 PM set the time of the murder. Mrs. Thatcher was the only one in the house at the time and her excuse that the dog knocked over a vase is silly. Her blatant attempt to fix her alibi at 4:00 PM is unconvincing. No true mystery fan will be surprised when Nurse Keating fingers Mrs. Thatcher.

On the other hand, the solution to the mystery is also the charm of the film. What mystery fan does not want to solve a murder at least once in a while, not on the basis of identifying the least likely suspect but rather, following some actual (and not obscure) clues to the killer? In that regard, *Murder by an Aristocrat* is quite satisfying. Also, for the first time in the movie series, Nurse Keating is the one who solves Bayard's murder, also a satisfying result.

The production itself is run-of-the-mill with uninspired direction and standard camerawork. Most of the performances are fine, with the actors being contract players at Warner Brothers, familiar to most mystery fans because they have appeared or will appear in other Warner Brothers mystery movies of the era. Marguerite Churchill, in her first and only performance as Sarah Keating, is pretty but bland, no different than Kay Linaker in the prior film.

The one performance that stands out is that of William Davidson as murder victim Bayard Thatcher. Davidson appeared in over 250 films in his career, usually playing small character parts. In *Murder by an Aristocrat*, he gets a chance to shine, particularly in the opening scene as Bayard sarcastically blackmails his relatives. Bayard comes across bombastic and dangerous. Davidson is always convincing as the egotistical Bayard and no one is surprised when Bayard becomes the murder victim.

Indeed, the opening scene is another highlight of *Murder by an Aristocrat*, as Bayard belittles his family's upper class attitudes and fake virtues, deriding them as "the motley remains of the glorious Thatchers." Later in the film, there is more implied social commentary as both an attempted murder and the actual murder raise more concerns among the family about bad publicity than about the victim. These mild moments of social criticism provide just a little spice to the murder mystery.

*Murder by an Aristocrat* sometimes resorts to mystery movie clichés. There is the dark and stormy night for the first set of events and then a hooded figure sneaking through the house on the night before the murder. Dave Thatcher conveniently ends his life near the end of the picture, either deliberately or through a drug overdose, allowing his wife to end up with District Attorney Tweed, her true love.

The movie avoids any comic relief, allowing all involved to focus on the whodunit, which has its intrinsic interest. Faults and all, *Murder by an Aristocrat* is worth a view for any mystery fan who likes a classic whodunit.

*Note on the Source Material*: The film was based on Eberhart's 1932 novel of the same name. Much like the movie, it was a rare Keate novel from the era in which Lance O'Leary did not appear and for that reason, Nurse Keate solves the murder.

The setting is the Thatcher mansion where the killing of Bayard Thatcher occurs, obviously committed by one of the aristocratic Thatchers, even though Adela Thatcher insists that the crime was committed by a burglar. Nurse Keate is on site to tend to Bayard after his recent gunshot wound, obviously caused by Adela's son Dave Thatcher, even though the family insists that it was an accident that occurred when Bayard was cleaning his gun.

The broad outline of the killing, the motives and alibis of the suspects and the identity of the murderer are the same in both works. The book, however, may be the most tedious work ever produced by Eberhart. The Thatcher family simply talks the case to death, going over and over the facts, with Sarah Keate present during the discussions for no reason other than the fact that she is the prime detective in a series about a nurse-detective. The film version pared the mystery down to its simplest elements and by showing more incidents about Bayard Thatcher before his death, instead of just talking about them, turned a mundane novel into an appealing movie.

## *The Great Hospital Mystery* (1937)

With *The Great Hospital Mystery*, the Nurse Keate series moved to 20th Century–Fox, and another new actress was tapped to play the lead role. However, instead of employing a pretty young actress for the part, the approach taken in the last two movies in the series, the filmmakers turned to Jane Darwell, a matronly-looking performer who was then 58 years old. With that recasting, Nurse Keate (renamed Keats for this film) now seems more like Hildegarde Withers than Torchy Blane, thereby bringing the character closer to Eberhart's original depiction of Nurse Keate. The change for this particular film is inspired and Darwell is one of the best features of *The Great Hospital Mystery*.

Another important positive for the film is its quick pace. The entire story takes place in less than twelve hours and includes a bank robbery, a car chase, a murder, an attempted murder and additional skullduggery in a hospital setting. While there is some comedy relief, the film never seems padded, with the storyline easily filling out the film's short length of 60 minutes.

It begins with a robbery at the Triborough Savings Bank and the killing of a guard. As the crooks leave, they force their way into a car driven by Allen Tracy, who had just dropped his sister off at the bank. Tracy is compelled by the robbers to drive them away but, with the police in hot pursuit, Tracy deliberately crashes the car to effectuate his escape. Tracy cannot, however, go to the police because he is on probation, so he goes to the Samaritan Hospital, where his best friend Tom Kirby is employed. Tracy is worried about his own well-being because he believes that the gang is following him with the intention of eliminating a potential witness. To help his friend, Kirby concocts a scheme to convince the gang that Tracy is dead by placing an already dead body in Tracy's hospital room. Matters go horribly wrong, however, when a gunshot wound is discovered in the body in Tracy's hospital room. That brings the police into the matter and, after a very real murder occurs, Nurse Keats assists the police in solving the case.

*The Great Hospital Mystery* is just what the title indicates — a mystery, not a whodunit. There are a limited number of suspects, the most logical one being Dr. Triggert, the head of the hospital. Most of the suspicion in the film is focused on Dr. Triggert and he is a good candidate, as he is a very dislikable character and also because he is played by perennial film villain Sig Rumann.

However, it is clear from the moment Mortimer Beatty enters the story that he is going to attempt to kill Allen Tracy. The robbers have tailed Tracy to the rear ambulance entrance of the hospital and when he hides inside, the crooks specifically state that they will watch for Tracy from the front of the hospital. Beatty is sitting in the waiting room in the front of the hospital when Tracy appears. Beatty is clearly faking his stomach pains, just to get into the hospital. He deliberately tricks the hospital staff into giving him a seventh-floor room because he overhears that Tracy has a room on that floor. *The Great Hospital Mystery* hardly hides the fact that Beatty is the killer, and thus, there is very little whodunit in the picture.

Nevertheless, *The Great Hospital Mystery* is an absorbing mystery, with elements which include Tom Kirby devising a scheme to fake Tracy's death by the substitution of a body that died by natural causes, the surprise discovery of a bullet hole in the corpse which supposedly died of heart failure, dark figures stalking the hospital halls and fire escapes, the sudden disappearance of Tracy, the surprise death of Kirby and that curious incident when it seems that Dr. Triggert has scheduled an unnecessary operation on Beatty to, it seems, get rid of him. In the latter instance, the motive of Triggert appears to be that Beatty has witnessed Triggert doing something improper in the hospital that evening. (Of course, with the confirmation that Beatty is the killer, the actions of Dr. Triggert in attempting to operate on Beatty, over his objections, make no sense.)

Joan Davis, playing inept probationary nurse Flossie Duffy, is the main comic relief. Davis is refreshing because it is rare in a movie mystery that the comic relief is female. Davis was always a likable performer and she is quite funny in this film, although her pres-

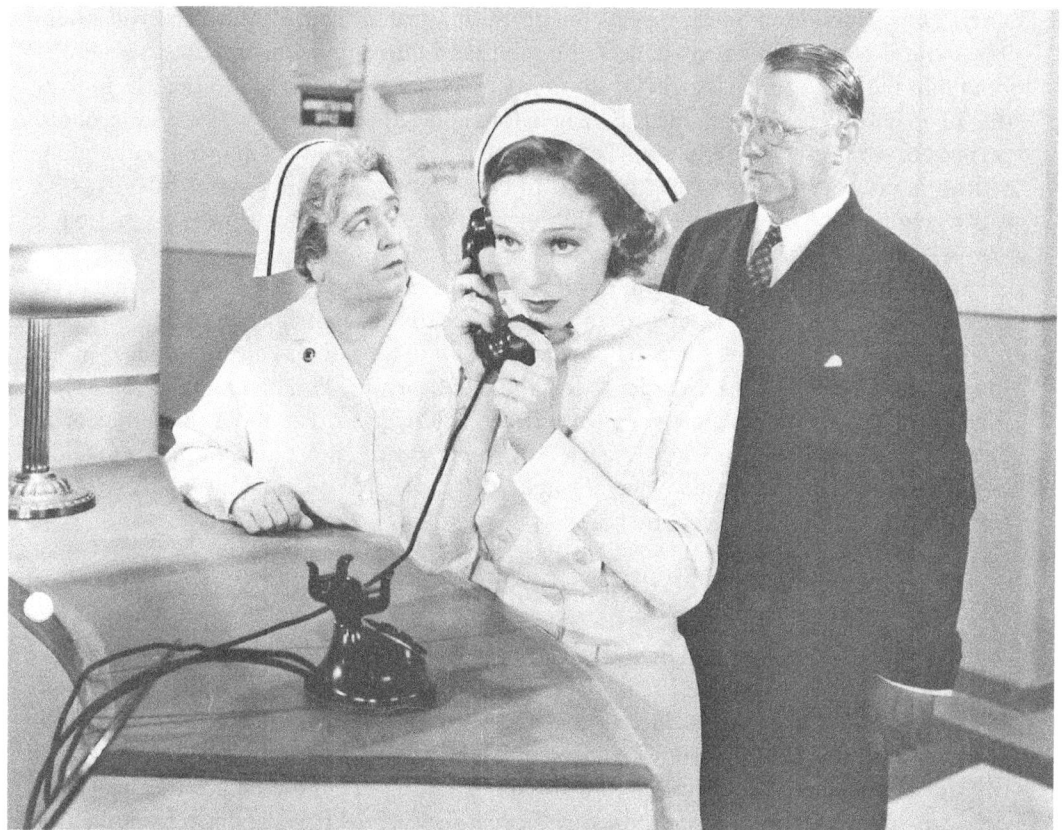

The only "age appropriate" nurse, Sarah Keate (Keats in this film), played by Jane Darwell (left), and Dr. Triggert, the hospital superintendent (Sig Rumann), stand by as Nurse Ann Smith (Sally Blane) makes a phone call in *The Great Hospital Mystery* (1937), based on a story titled "Dead Yesterday."

ence does start to wear thin toward the end. The most amusing performer in *The Great Hospital Mystery*, however, is William Demarest, playing the cold-blooded killer Mortimer Beatty. For most of the film, Demarest plays the part for laughs, generally making fun of the quality of the hospital and the lack of competence of its staff. For example, when Dr. McKerry examines Beatty and tells him, "Of course, your stomach seems a little swollen, but that does not worry me," Beatty replies, "Well, if your stomach was swollen, it wouldn't worry me either."

Frankly, Beatty is such an amusing character that the viewer is tempted to change his mind about the identity of the killer, no matter how explicit Beatty's involvement in the nefarious activities has previously been made. It therefore actually comes as a slight surprise that Beatty actually is the murderer. Perhaps then, in the end, *The Great Hospital Mystery* is a sneakily clever whodunit, not just an absorbing mystery.

*Note on the Source Material*: *The Great Hospital Mystery* was based on Eberhart's short story "Dead Yesterday," first published in *Pictorial Review* in September 1936. It is collected in *Dead Yesterday and Other Stories* (Crippen & Landru Publishers, 2007).

Surprisingly, since "Dead Yesterday" is a short story and *The Great Hospital Mystery* is a full-length movie (albeit fairly short), the film is substantially based on the Eberhart story. Thus, Nurse Ann Smith reports the death of a patient named Allen Tracy in Room 9 by natural causes, but when Nurse Keate returns to the room with Ann, there is a bullet wound in the body. Smith is arrested for murder but when it is discovered that the body is that of a charity patient who died the day before and not that of Allen Tracy, everyone is perplexed. Ann refuses to explain what happened. Later the body of mortuary attendant Switzer is discovered. The killer turns out to be a woman in Room 8 named Beatty, who was trying to kill Tracy so that he would not testify against her husband and other bank robbers in a trial that was then ongoing.

In moving the story from print to film, all of the mystery elements were carried over, even the broken valve on Tracy's room door and Beatty's statement that he saw a person leaving Tracy's room on all fours. The significance of these clues is better explained in the short story than in the film. In order to lengthen the story, the film includes the comedy of Joan Davis and the dispute between Kirby and Dr. Triggert. Also, more time is spent in developing the characters of Dr. Triggert, Mortimer Beatty and Ann Smith. These additions to the storyline bring incremental value to "Dead Yesterday," making *The Great Hospital Mystery* into the good feature that it is.

## *The Patient in Room 18* (1938)

There are two standout moments in *The Patient in Room 18*. The first involves the double murder of hospital patient Frank Warren and his doctor, Arthur Lethany, in the Room 18 of the title. First the killer locks private detective Lance O'Leary and hospital nurse Sarah Keate in O'Leary's hospital room, ensuring that they will not interfere with his plans. Then he pulls the hospital's electrical circuit breaker, cloaking the entire edifice in semi-darkness, resulting, for cinematic purposes, in the lightning of the thunderstorm creating sudden bursts of light and shadows while the evil deeds are being done. Then, Dr. Lethany enters Room 18, apparently to steal the $100,000 worth of radium which is strapped to Warren's chest. The killer enters from behind and knocks Lethany out with a blow to the head. Then he injects morphine into the arm of Warren, killing him. After dragging Lethany's body to the room closet, the shrouded killer makes his escape. All this time Higgins, the hospital janitor, has been watching the goings-on through the outside window.

The other moment is when Lethany's body is discovered in Room 18. Because O'Leary's butler, Bentley, has smelled a sweet, sickly odor inside, O'Leary opens the locked closet door of the room. As Nurse Keate screams, the standing body of Lethany falls, crashing into the room. Although the audience knows that Lethany's body is inside the closet, the sudden fall into the hospital room is a sudden, shocking moment.

Unfortunately, those two scenes are just about all that is entertaining about the film. The rest is standard mystery fare as Lance O'Leary, a patient at the hospital, along with his love interest, Sarah Keate, attempt to solve those two murders along with the later killing of Higgins. At the end of the film, O'Leary sets a trap and catches the killer.

Although all of the characters seem to have motive and opportunity, it is actually illusory. As to opportunity, the killer has to be a member of the hospital staff who knows where the hospital fuse box is and also how to find the morphine and inject it into Warren's arm. In other words, many of the potential suspects are immediately eliminated, especially since the killer is obviously a man, which the movie audience learns as it watches the first two killings onscreen. As to motive, while there is substantial intrigue whirling around the hospital, much of which involves shifting romantic interests, little of it relates to the killing of

Warren. In fact, it is obvious right from the time of the killings that the motive for Warren's murder is either the purloining of the valuable radium or a necessary act by the killer when Warren recognizes him stealing the radium. As a result, most of the backstory of the suspects is irrelevant to the murder investigation.

The comedy in *The Patient in Room 18* is also quite irrelevant to the story, particularly the interminable early scenes involving O'Leary's mental problems and his spats with Nurse Keate. The real problem with the film, though, is that it makes little sense.

The best example of this is with the "killing" of Lethany. After Lethany is slugged over the head, his body is locked in the Room 18 closet for at least for twelve hours. He appears to be dead when the door is opened. The reason the door is opened is because Bentley has smelled something in the closet, presumably a dead body. The police conducted an autopsy on the other two bodies so there is no reason for the viewer to assume that the police negligently skipped one in Lethany's case. The newspaper headlines confirm a second murder victim at the hospital when Lethany's body is discovered. Yet, in fact, Lethany is alive, resuscitated by private eye O'Leary after his fall from the closet, even though there are numerous doctors on site who should have been able to confirm that Lethany was still alive and then do a better job of bringing him back to consciousness. O'Leary then hides Lethany in the hospital basement, for reasons unexplained and difficult to discern. By the way, since Lethany is alive, what is the odor that Bentley smells coming from the closet door? The whole matter is ridiculous.

Two of the actresses, Ann Sheridan as Nurse Sarah Keate and Rosella Towne as another hospital nurse, are quite attractive. Some of the supporting performances, such as Cliff Clark as Inspector Foley, the policeman who verbally spars with O'Leary, Eric Stanley as Bentley, O'Leary's valet who has a prior prison record, and Frank Orth as Higgins, the usually drunk hospital janitor who witnesses Warren's murder, are excellent. However, the acting plus a few interesting moments in the story are not enough to carry *The Patient in Room 18*. It is a very disappointing film.

*Note on the Source Material*: The film was based on Eberhart's first novel about Sarah Keate, also titled *The Patient in Room 18*. Published in 1929, it details the first meeting between Keate and policeman Lance O'Leary. The film is a fairly close adaptation of the novel, although some of the characters are a little different and so are their motives. However, the killer is the same and so is the trap set for him (the chance to steal the packet of radium).

In the novel, Dr. Lethany is actually murdered in Room 18. There is no nonsense about him just being knocked out and O'Leary secretly reviving him and hiding him in the cellar. Why the filmmakers made that change to the novel is unknown, but it clearly undercuts the effectiveness of the movie. Also, the ineffective comedy moments are cinema-created. Thus, most of the changes from novel into film were negatives, except for the sequence showing the killing of Warren and the apparent killing of Lethany. In the book, their bodies are discovered after the fact, and that is the first time anyone knows of their deaths. The film version went for the more cinematic approach and showed the killings as they occurred.

*Note on the Changing Lead Performers*: With Ann Sheridan's ascension to the role of Sally Keate for *The Patient in Room 18*, a different actress played the lead role in each of the first five films in the Nurse Keate series. Given that the films were released in the short time period of three years, this lack of continuity in the lead performers is perplexing. It is quite likely that one of the reasons that the Nurse Keate mystery series is almost forgotten today is the inability of the audience to identify the character with any one actress.

Surprisingly, there are several other 1930s examples of constant turnover of lead performers in a mystery movie series. In six Hildegarde Withers movies, six Perry Mason movies and nine Torchy Blane movies, three different actors or actresses played the lead detective. Similarly, the Bulldog Drummond and Philo Vance series also had numerous actors in the lead role over the years, although in those two cases the films were produced over a long period of time at many different studios.

A continuity of actors in the lead role surely contributed to both the effectiveness and appreciation of a Hollywood mystery movie series. There were 44 Charlie Chan films released between 1931 and 1949 and yet only three actors played the role of the Chinese detective in all of those years. How well-remembered would that series have been if ten different actors had played the Chinese detective? Basil Rathbone and Nigel Bruce starred in 14 Sherlock Holmes movies from 1939 to 1946, making that series one of the best-remembered of all time. In addition, there were 14 Boston Blackie movies released in the 1940s with Chester Morris playing the title character in all of them and ten Crime Doctor movies during the same decade with Warner Baxter always playing the lead. Likewise, Warren William appeared in nine straight Lone Wolf films commencing in the late 1930s and continuing into the 1940s. When the part of the Lone Wolf was then turned over to less well-known performers, the series suffered.

Even the Thin Man series, with six films over a 13-year period, always starred William Powell and Myrna Loy as they aged gracefully over the years. How effective would that series have been if in the 1940s younger actors had been brought in to play the lead roles? Indeed, the continuity of the Thin Man series is a decided plus for those films. At the end of the second film, *After the Thin Man*, Nora Charles is pregnant and by the next film, *Another Thin Man*, Nick, Jr., has already been born. Nick, Jr., then grows up in the remaining films in the series.

In the other mystery series without a continuity of actors, there was often no continuity in the storylines either. Thus, in *The Case of the Velvet Claws* (1936), Perry Mason and Della Street are married. In the next film, *The Case of the Black Cat* (1936), the marriage is forgotten. In *Torchy Blane Runs for Mayor* (1939) Torchy is successful in her political campaign but in the next film, *Torchy Blane ... Playing with Dynamite* (1939), her new job as mayor is forgotten. And, of course, Nurse Keating accepted a marriage proposal at the end of *The Murder of Dr. Harrigan* (1936), which was then completely forgotten at the beginning of the next film, *Murder by an Aristocrat* (1936). In fact, in the latter film, she is engaged to someone else.

That leads to the question: How much better would the Sarah Keate series have been with one actress playing the nurse-detective in all six films? Obviously, any answer to that question would be speculative, but at least the studio was finally smart enough to bring Ann Sheridan back to the series for the last film, bringing a measure of continuity to the series at long last. However, a new actor was brought in to play Lance O'Leary in the last film, so in fact there was only a small measure of continuity between the last two features.

## *Mystery House* (1938)

Nurse Sarah Keate is apparently still having trouble holding a job at a hospital, and so she is now back to private duty nursing, this time for wheelchair-bound Lucy Kingery, who is at the hunting lodge of the Kingery family. After dinner, at a meeting of the shareholders of the Kingery family business, Herbert Kingery says to the owners that the business is in trouble, caused in part by the substantial fraud and embezzlement by one of the stockholders. While Kingery will not reveal the name of the embezzler, he advises the group that he intends to call in the police.

Once Kingery makes that speech to a group of people which includes the embezzler, mystery movie fans know that he is not long for this world. Kingery goes back to his bedroom and bolts the door, and then a shot is heard. All of the entrances to the bedroom are locked and so a shareholder, Lai Killian, breaks in through a back entrance and discovers Kingery's body. At the inquest, the death is ruled a suicide, because Kingery was alone in the locked room and a gun was found in his hand. (As an aside, the gun was not there when Kingery's body was discovered.) Kingery's daughter Anne does not believe the verdict and, with the help of Miss Keate, brings private detective Lance O'Leary on board to independently investigate. O'Leary comes to the hunting lodge on a snowy weekend when all of the suspects have returned at the request of Anne. There, after two more killings, O'Leary solves the murder.

If the viewer is willing to suspend his disbelief over the explanation of the murders, this last film in the Sarah Keate mystery series is one of the best. *Mystery House* runs less than one hour and it moves quickly. There is little wasted time — none on comedy relief and just a little on the romance between Keate and O'Leary. A locked room murder, such as the killing of Herbert Kingery, always has its special interest and since the murder of Gerald Frawley (the third victim in *Mystery House*) is very close to being a locked room murder, the film has special appeal. While the hunting lodge setting has some characteristics of an old dark house, it does not quite fit that description. Rather, on the weekend when O'Leary arrives, the lodge becomes snowbound, making it impossible to bring the sheriff in to investigate the last two murders or for any of the suspects to leave while a serial killer seems to be on the premises. *Mystery House* sometimes seems more like an Agatha Christie whodunit than an old dark house mystery. All of these attributes are decided positives for the film.

The problem with *Mystery House* lies with the solution to the murders. The least satisfying explanation of a locked room murder is the use of a mechanical device to accomplish the killings. It is not that a mechanical device is an uncommon method of murder in a locked room; it is actually used quite often in mystery novels and films. A good example occurs in *The Kennel Murder Case* (1933), based on S.S. Van Dine's Philo Vance book of the same title, and a less satisfactory one is shown in *The Mandarin Mystery* (1936), based on *The Chinese Orange Mystery* by Ellery Queen. It is just that the use of a mechanical device is one of the least convincing explanations for such a crime. Here two of the murders were caused by an old-fashioned gun mounted on a wall, whose trigger is tied by a cord to the door bolt, going off when the bolt is shut. In *Mystery House*, that device is used in two different rooms for two different killings. How did the killer ever rig those devices up in a house not his own and how did he know in advance that he would ever need them in a particular situation? If a gun was found in Kingery's hand after his death, which could not have been the murder weapon, why didn't ballistics figure that out, defeating the theory of Kingery's suicide? In fact, why didn't ballistics also figure out that Kingery was shot from at least a short distance away, also eliminating the theory of suicide?

Other aspects of the tale are unconvincing, such as the chauffeur lurking around the house, knocking O'Leary unconscious and apparently being in the murder room when the

Detective Lance O'Leary (Dick Purcell, in the suit), stands among all of the suspects, one of whom is the murderer and one of whom will be the next victim, at Hunting's End Lodge in *Mystery House* (1938). From left to right, the suspects are Gerald Frawley (Ben Welden), Gwen Kingery (Anne Nagel), Julian Barre (Anthony Averill), Joe Page (Anderson Lawlor) and Terice Von Elm (Sheila Bromley).

last killing occurs. His innocent explanation for all that he has done before is hardly credible, so the chauffeur can only be seen as a red herring, blatantly and unconvincingly employed by the screenwriters to deflect suspicion away from the prime group of suspects.

However, it may not be helpful to over-criticize the plot of *Mystery House*, tempting as it may be to do so, since the film is still fun to watch. Young and dark-haired Lai Killian is played by William Hopper, who played in over 100 films in his career, although with few memorable parts. For mystery fans, he will always be remembered for playing gray-haired Paul Drake on TV's *Perry Mason* in the 1950s and 1960s. Mystery fans may also wonder why, in a mystery series about Nurse Sarah Keate, she is not the one who solves the murders in *Mystery House*, although that anomaly also occurred in prior films in the series. Thus, there are a number of reasons, relevant or irrelevant to the quality of the film, as to why a mystery fan would want to watch *Mystery House*, so long as he does not pay too much attention to the explanation of the murders.

*Note on the Source Material: Mystery House* was based on Eberhart's 1930 novel *The Mystery of Hunting's End*. In the written work, Matil Kingery asks Lance O'Leary to come to the family hunting lodge to attempt to solve the murder of her father Huber, which occurred five years before. All of the suspects have been invited back to the lodge and Sarah Keate is also there as nurse to wheelchair-bound Lucy Kingery, the sister of Huber. As a result of a huge and unexpected snowstorm, all of the occupants are stuck in the lodge as several killings and attempting killings take place. After being stumped for several days, Lance O'Leary finally solves the case.

Eberhart's novel, even more than the film version, truly seems like a forerunner to Agatha Christie's *And Then There Were None*, as a group of individuals are trapped in an isolated place with a murderer in their midst. One wonders if the Eberhart novel provided some of the inspiration for Christie's classic novel, which was published in 1939, almost ten years after *The Mystery of Hunting's End*.

The plot of the film is substantially based on the novel, as the location, two of the murders and the method of murder by mechanical means are the same. One of the murders in the novel is different from one of the murders in the film and, unlike the film, none of the murders in the book are locked room murders, so in that regard, the film is more appealing. However, the unconvincing red herring of the chauffeur is original to the movie, so in that regard, the novel makes more sense. Other matters that were not carried over from the book to the film are an attack on O'Leary, the poisoning of the dog and the disappearance of the body of one of the murder victims.

The main difference between *The Mystery of Hunting's End* and *Mystery House* is that the novel is overlong and often seems like a talkfest. With its short length and little filler material, the film version moves quickly and is seldom boring.

## Afterwards

After *Mystery House* (1938), there were no further films about either Nurse Keate or Nurse Keating. Nor have there been any radio or television programs about the nurse-detective.

Eberhart wrote almost sixty mystery novels and numerous short stories during her long career. However, after the first five novels about Nurse Sara Keate, she only returned to that character two more times for a full-length story, *Wolf in Man's Clothing* (1942) and *Man Missing* (1954). Lance O'Leary was not a character in either of those last two novels.

Many of Eberhart's mysteries were romance mysteries, with a young woman often found in a dangerous situation caused by conflicting amorous interests. These stories were not part of any mystery series. However, she did write short stories about continuing characters such as Susan Dare, a young mystery story writer, and James Wickshire, an elderly New York banker, and novels about Jacob Wait, a police detective. In 1971, Eberhart won the Grand Master Award from the Mystery Writers of America. She died in 1996.

# 12

# Torchy Blane
## *The Investigative Reporter*

The 1930s were the heyday for mystery movie series starring female detectives, from Hildegarde Withers, a schoolteacher, to Sarah Keate, a nurse, to Nancy Drew, the famous teenage detective. Less well-known today, perhaps because she was not based on a character from literature, is Torchy Blane, the pretty, perky and pugnacious newspaper reporter, who hit the mystery movie scene in 1937 with Warners' *Smart Blonde*, the first film in a nine-movie series. While Torchy may not be as famous as those other female detectives from crime literature, there were, somewhat surprisingly, more films in the Torchy Blane series than in any of the other series featuring a female detective.

The youthful Torchy was paradoxically closest to the spinster Hildegarde Withers than to any of her other contemporaries. For example, Torchy and Hildegarde each solved crimes while jousting with her favorite policeman, whether Steve McBride or Oscar Piper, with each entertaining marriage proposals from her adversary at some point during the course of the proceedings. Neither female detective, however, actually made it to the altar. Similarly, the Hildegarde Withers series was sparked by the performance of Edna May Oliver, who originated the role on-screen, and the Torchy Blane series still merits a look today for the performance of Glenda Farrell, who originated the role of Torchy in that series and played her in seven of the nine films. Much like Oliver in the Hildegarde Withers movies, even when the Torchy Blane films were disappointing, Farrell was still a joy to watch.

### Background

#### The Stories

The characters of newspaper reporter Torchy Blane and her policeman love interest, Steve McBride, are original to the cinema. One would be hard-pressed to locate any mystery stories featuring a female detective named Torchy Blane.

The movies, though, give credit to Frederick Nebel, a well-known author of pulp mystery stories in the 1920s and 1930s. Nebel, who was born in 1903 in New York City, began his writing career in the 1920s, with his first story published in 1926 in the famous pulp magazine *Black Mask*. During the course of his mystery-writing career, Nebel created several series characters, such as Donny "Tough Dick" Donahue of the Interstate Detective Agency and Cardigan, an Irish detective, for the Cosmos Detective Agency. However, two of his most popular characters were the duo of MacBride and Kennedy.

MacBride was Captain Steve MacBride of the Richmond City Police Department. Kennedy, always known as "Kennedy of the Free Press," was a hard-drinking male reporter who often came up against MacBride while they were investigating crimes in Richmond City. The first MacBride and Kennedy story appeared in the September 1928 *Black Mask*. Nebel continued writing stories about the pair until 1936, with over 35 yarns being produced. The Torchy Blane movies are supposedly based on Nebel's stories about MacBride and Kennedy.

In later years, Nebel discontinued writing crime stories altogether, shifting to romance stories for the women's magazine market. In the 1950s, his health began to decline and by the early 1960s, his writing career was over. He died in 1967. Nebel's mystery novel *Sleepers East* (1933) became the basis of the Michael Shayne film *Sleepers West* (1941).

## The Film Series

When the MacBride and Kennedy stories were brought to the screen by Warner Brothers, MacBride remained a policeman but Kennedy was turned into the pretty blond female newspaper reporter Torchy Blane. Thus, a new movie character was born, having no relationship to the Kennedy of the Nebel stories. In all, there were nine films in the Torchy Blane series, commencing with *Smart Blonde* (1937). In each film, Torchy solves the crime before Steve McBride (note the change in spelling) is able to do, but usually not until McBride rescues Torchy from the clutches of the latest villain.

Torchy Blane was played by Glenda Farrell in the first four films in the series. Farrell was born on June 30, 1904, in Enid, Oklahoma. After working initially on the stage, she became a contract player at Warner Brothers in the 1930s, with small roles in famous films such as *Little Caesar* (1930) and *I Am a Fugitive from a Chain Gang* (1932), and even playing an important supporting role in the musical *Gold Diggers of 1935* (1935). In the famous horror film *Mystery of the Wax Museum* (1933), Farrell played an aggressive newspaper reporter, a character just like Torchy Blane but with a different name.

Steve McBride was played by Barton MacLane, just one of the many police roles MacLane performed during his long film career. MacLane was born on December 25, 1902, in Columbia, South Carolina. Much like Farrell, he worked on the stage before becoming a contract player at Warner Brothers in the 1930s. In addition to policemen, MacLane often played heavies, such as gangsters or Western villains. Nevertheless, it is the police roles for which MacLane is best remembered by mystery fans, from *The Case of the Curious Bride* (1935) to *The Maltese Falcon* (1941).

In those first four films, Torchy and McBride investigate several murders, competing with each other to see who will be first to solve the crimes. In the meantime, the two are engaged to be married although they never seem to make it to the altar.

In the fifth film, *Torchy Blane in Panama* (1938), two new actors were brought in to play the leads. Lola Lane played Torchy and Paul Kelly played McBride. Lane was one of the famous Lane sisters, who along with Rosemary and Priscilla Lane and Gale Page, appeared in several famous films about the love lives of four sisters, starting with *Four Daughters* (1938). Kelly began working in films in the early silent era, with regular screen work during the first two decades of the sound era. Despite the change in cast, the plot of *Torchy Blane in Panama* was similar to those of the prior films in the series.

Farrell and MacLane then returned to the series for three more films. However, in the last film, *Torchy Blane ... Playing With Dynamite* (1939), Farrell and MacLane were gone once again, replaced by Jane Wyman and Allen Jenkins. Wyman is most famous for her career after this film, winning the Oscar for Best Actress for *Johnny Belinda* (1948). Jenkins is one of the most recognizable actors in crime films in the 1930s and early 1940s, from playing Spudsy Drake in the Perry Mason series' *The Case of the Curious Bride* (1935) and *The Case of the Lucky Legs* (1936), to playing Hunk, Baby Face Martin's sidekick, in *Dead End* (1937), to playing Goldie Locke in some of the early Falcon films.

The last four Torchy films, no matter who played the leads, were similar to the other films in terms of style and their light-hearted tone. The impending marriage of Torchy and McBride, however, was downplayed somewhat in the latter films.

There were a number of other regulars. One was Gahagan, the policeman-chauffeur for Steve McBride. Gahagan was the comic relief in the Torchy Blane series, even though the films were not all that serious in the first place. Gahagan was played by Tom Kennedy, the only actor to appear in all nine films. Kennedy, who was born in New York City in 1885, began appearing in films in the early silent era, easily making the transition to sound films, always at work playing character parts such as dumb policemen and other working class roles. Despite his real-life background in boxing, he ended the Torchy Blane series in a wrestling ring in *Torchy Blane ... Playing With Dynamite* (1939).

Other regulars or semi-regulars were George Guhl, as the desk sergeant who was even dumber than Gahagan, and Joe Cunningham as Maxie, Torchy's editor at whatever paper she happened to be working at. Frank Shannon played Captain McTavish, McBride's boss, a more natural role for the Irish–born actor than the role for which he is most famous today—the Russian–born Dr. Zarkov in the Flash Gordon serials.

## The Films

### *Smart Blonde* (1937)

*Smart Blonde* is set in Hollywood's idea of 1930s New York City, with its fast-working reporters always looking for a scoop, police detectives willing to arrest people on little evidence, nightclubs with large orchestras and excellent singing acts, skyscraper hotels with huge and luxurious suites, and people always immaculately dressed. This background is hardly evocative of the real New York City of the time, but after all, this is a movie and not real life, and people who came into movie theatres in the middle 1930s were very willing to suspend their disbelief. While there may have been a lingering Depression outside the theater, once the ticket taker tore a patron's ticket, realism was left in the outside world. There are no poor people on *Smart Blonde*'s silver screen.

Businessman Fitz Mularkay has decided to sell all of his business interests (including his successful nightclub) so that he can marry socialite Marcia Friel, who disapproves of many of Fitz's activities. Torchy Blane, crack reporter for *The Morning Herald*, gets the first interview with Tiny Torgensen, the man who is going to buy Mularkay's businesses. After the interview, as Torchy looks on, Torgensen is shot dead in a cab. The murder investigation falls to Police Sergeant Steve McBride, who is also Torchy's boyfriend. Luckily for Steve (although he does not necessarily recognize his luck at the time), Torchy has decided to help him.

There are a number of suspects, including rival businessmen who may have wanted to buy Fitz's business, singer Dolly Ireland who was in love with Fitz until he threw her over in favor of Marcia, and Fitz's right hand man Chuck Cannon, who is upset about the pending sale. When Chuck is found dead, Fitz is suspected. Eventually, the murderer is discovered by Torchy and not surprisingly, the killer is not one of the most likely suspects.

There is a lot to like in the first film in the Torchy Blane series. Glenda Farrell is one of the most engaging performers in all of the 1930s mystery movies. Perky and vivacious, she draws the viewers into the story with her enthusiasm and cleverness. Plot deficiencies can easily be overlooked when Farrell is on the screen. Oddly enough, Barton MacLane has more screen time than Farrell as he plays perhaps the fastest talking policeman in the history of the cinema. One smart touch here is that McBride shows substantial initiative of his own and is himself an excellent policeman. The filmmakers made the right choice in making McBride a competent foil to the clever Torchy, rather than a figure of comic relief.

The police humor in the story is left to McBride's policeman-chauffeur Gahagan, played by Tom Kennedy. Other than his interest in using the police siren whenever possible, the role is without any humor. Luckily, Gahagan's screen time is kept to a minimum.

A significant problem with *Smart Blonde* relates to the storyline, as the plot runs round and round with little logic in its progress. Torchy finds a torn piece of paper under one body, which the police somehow missed. She then conceals that evidence from McBride so that she can use it for herself. Later she conceals an important photographic clue from McBride. Does it make any sense for Torchy to do that to the man with whom she is in love? McBride seems to careen from suspect to suspect in his efforts to solve the case. In fact, Torchy's habit of hiding evidence from him foils his attempts to quickly solve two murders, delaying the resolution of the story.

The overriding problem with the film, however, is the lack of clues for the viewer. While the viewer can follow McBride's investigation, seeing his clues as he discovers them, such as ballistics evidence and eyewitness testimony, Torchy hides her information from the audience, solving the crimes off-screen to the chagrin of the viewer. For much of the screen time, the story seems to make little progress and then the end of the film seems particularly rushed, as Torchy almost seems to jump to her conclusion of the identity of the murderer, with not many facts to back her up. It is a disappointing ending, particularly since most of her evidence is a surprise to the audience.

Wini Shaw, who famously sang "Lullaby of Broadway" in *Gold Diggers of 1935*, also gets to sing in this film and that is a decided plus. Jane Wyman has a small role as a hat check girl, which would be insignificant except for the fact that she would go on to play Torchy Blane in a later film. With engaging performers and an appealing 1930s milieu, *Smart Blonde* is an interesting film to watch. It is just unfortunate that it did not have a more cogent mystery story to tell.

*Note on the Source Material*: *Smart Blonde* was based on "No Hard Feelings" by Frederic Nebel, a short story published in the February 1936 issue of *Black Mask* magazine. It was one of the last of Nebel's stories about Kennedy and MacBride.

*Note on Torchy's Newspapers*: In *Smart Blonde*, Torchy works for *The Morning Herald*, as can be seen in the first shot in the film showing the newspaper and Torchy's article about Tiny Torgensen, and later, by the business card Torchy hands to Torgensen. Torchy continues to work for *The Morning Herald* in her next film, *Fly Away Baby*. In *The Adventurous Blonde*, Torchy works for the *Evening Herald*, as seen by the newspaper in which her stories appear and the name on a glass door at the newspaper office.

In *Blondes at Work*, Torchy has moved to *The Daily Star*, as evidenced by the rag in which her stories appear. She remained at that paper in *Torchy Blane in Panama*, but by the time of *Torchy Gets Her Man*, she is working for the *Evening Globe-Bulletin*, as shown by the newspaper which is visible during the movie's credits. (During the course of that film, however, Gahagan introduces Torchy as a reporter for *The Morning Herald*.)

In *Torchy Blane in Chinatown*, Torchy now works for *The New York Star*, as shown by the paper in which her stories appear. In *Torchy Blane Runs for Mayor*, her stories appear in *The Daily Star*, as can be seen in a montage of newspaper headlines. Despite being fired from *The Daily Star* during the course of that film, Torchy is back at *The Daily Star* for the last film in the series, *Torchy Blane ... Playing With Dynamite*.

It is not known why the filmmakers could not keep Torchy's newspapers straight. Interestingly, in the Frederick Nebel stories, newspaper reporter Kennedy always worked for the *Free Press*.

## *Fly Away Baby* (1937)

Although *Fly Away Baby* is not much of a mystery, it is still entertaining. It utilizes the standard formula of many of the Torchy Blane movies. There is a murder, Torchy finds more clues than the police, Torchy believes one suspect is the killer, and Torchy is determined to find enough evidence to bring that suspect to justice. In this film, though, there is an interesting variation as Torchy follows that suspect around the world on an airplane adventure until the crime can be solved.

*Fly Away Baby* opens just after the murder of jeweler Milton Devereux and the disappearance of a collection of diamonds. Steve McBride is on the case in his official capacity as a police detective, and for some reason Torchy is on the case in her unofficial capacity as a newspaper reporter. There are only a few potential suspects. One is Mr. Sills, Devereux's employee, who discovered the murder, and another is Guy Allister, Devereux's partner in the business. Actually, Sills and Allister are not really suspects since there are no motives that can be attributed to either of them and there are no clues that suggest their culpability. However, with few other significant cast members in the film, the viewer must keep a sharp eye on those two.

Torchy instead focuses on Sonny Croy, the arrogant son of a wealthy newspaper publisher. Croy had recently quarreled with Devereux over a loan and Devereux had threatened to tell Sonny's father that Sonny was living beyond his means. Torchy and McBride accidentally discover suspicious notes that Croy had made on a restaurant menu on the day of the murder, and Torchy later discovers the murder weapon, suggesting that the murderer came from outside the jewelry business building. Even with all this incredible luck, Torchy cannot prove her case against Troy because of his airtight alibi. Torchy, however, is nothing but persistent and she doggedly pushes ahead, and in the process of trying to nail Croy, exposes the real murderer.

If Sherlock Holmes was the world's greatest detective, Torchy Blane is surely the world's luckiest detective. She finds clues in all the wrong places and her ridiculous guesses about crimes always seem to come true. On the other hand, her successes are not entirely attributable to luck; sometimes she has some clever ideas. Torchy is smart enough to trace the serial number of the murder weapon, a German gun, with the German authorities, easily exposing the identity of the killer. On the other hand, it is hard to believe that no one on the police force thought of doing the same thing.

But it is probably not the mystery and it is surely not the detective work that brings viewers back to the Torchy Blane series time and time again. (It is not the comic relief of the unfunny Gahagan, either.) Rather, it is the relationship between Torchy and McBride and their banter back and forth. It is Torchy's ways of beating the other reporters to a scoop. It is Glenda Farrell's vibrant personality.

In *Fly Away Baby*, it is also the biting dialogue from the chief suspect, Sonny Croy, as he ridicules McBride for his lack of success in solving the Devereux murder. It is also the introduction of the audience to the flying vehicles of the day, whether the propeller plane that takes the wayfarers across America, the amphibian China Clipper (with its entrance through the roof) that takes the passengers across the Pacific or the Zepellin that takes the cast on the final leg of its journey. The film has a historical interest today that it did not have in 1937. At times, the movie is more of a travelogue than a crime story.

At the end of the film there are a few plot twists, with two surprising murders and a not very convincing main culprit. As was usual in the series, the explanation for the misdeeds cannot withstand much scrutiny. So, if a mystery fan is willing to overlook the flimsy mystery plot, the lack of clues and the feeble explanation for the crimes, *Fly Away Baby* can be quite entertaining.

## *The Adventurous Blonde* (1937)

This is pretty silly stuff. As the film opens, *Evening Herald* reporter Torchy is about to arrive in New York City by train to marry policeman Steve McBride, her adversary and love interest from the prior films. Four reporters from the rival paper *The Evening Globe* get a bright idea. As a gag on Torchy on her wedding day, they decide to stage a fake murder, have Torchy write a story about the murder which will be published in the *Evening Herald*, and then *The Evening Globe* can publish a story debunking Torchy's scoop. Everyone will then have a hearty laugh over the entire escapade.

The problem with this stunt is that the whole idea makes absolutely no sense. Does anyone truly believe that any newspaper would ever do such a thing? The whole escapade would bring shame on both the *Evening Herald* and *The Evening Globe*. Isn't there any real crime going on in New York City that these reporters can cover?

The silliness does not end there. When Torchy accompanies McBride on the murder investigation, McBride actually asks Torchy to interview some of the witnesses for him. Later, Torchy grabs McBride's badge and, just by showing it to other policemen, they are willing to provide her with all kinds of governmental services, including a police chauffeur. Both sets of newspaper reporters are permitted to interview suspects in their jail cells, and when *The Evening Globe* obtains a confession from a suspect, the police actually congratulate the reporters for helping them out. Much of *The Adventurous Blonde* is a comedy, but it should still make some sense. The film presents a totally unrealistic picture of both the newspaper industry and the police.

As for the mystery, the reporters choose an actor named Harvey Hammond as their fake victim. Hammond is willing to join in the fun for $500 and the publicity his upcoming new show will receive. With the help of his butler, a stocking is tied around Hammond's neck and he is left lying on his apartment floor with his head under the couch, waiting for McBride and Torchy to arrive. An assistant coroner, who is in on the prank, is also ready to declare Hammond dead, which he does.

Torchy reports the story to her newspaper, which publishes an extra about Hammond's death. The competitor then publishes an extra saying that the *Evening Herald* got it wrong. Imagine everyone's surprise when the real coroner arrives and declares that Hammond really is dead. The reason the viewer will have to use his imagination for this is because there must be few, if any, viewers who will not guess that Hammond will actually be murdered in the middle of the prank.

There are a number of suspects, all relating to Hammond's serial infidelity. There is Jenny Hammond, his wife, Theresa Gray, a lover whom he has just dismissed, Grace Brown, a young actress in whom he has recently taken an interest, and Hugo Brand, Grace's boyfriend. Again Torchy conducts more of an investigation of the crime than the police. It turns out that Theresa Gray is the wife of Mortimer Gray, the publisher of *The Evening Globe*, who authorized the stunt of the fake death of Harvey Hammond.

It is somewhat fitting that the solution to Hammond's murder (Mortimer Gray is the killer) relates to the newspaper stunt, giving some credibility to the beginning of the film. In the end, though, there is too much silliness in the framework of the story and too many coincidences in the investigation of the mystery to make the whole thing work. Although this is a disappointing film, Glenda Farrell is still a joy to watch and she is able to carry the film past many, but not all, of its deficiencies.

## *Blondes at Work* (1938)

Once again Torchy Blane demonstrates that she is the luckiest newspaper reporter in all of New York City. In *Smart Blonde*, she just happened to be present when Tiny Torgensen was shot and killed, the incident that started the mystery in that film. At the beginning of *The Adventurous Blonde*, she accidentally read a telegram sent to a woman who would become a murder suspect. In *Blondes at Work*, Torchy's luck continues. As the film opens, while Torchy is receiving a parking ticket, she sees department store heir Marvin Spencer being assisted down the street and into a taxi cab by millionaire Maitland Greer. Spencer is holding his side and appears to be sick. When Spencer's knifed body is later discovered, Torchy once again has the inside track on a murder investigation.

Torchy will need that inside information as she goes into a contest with her fiancé Steve McBride to determine who will be first to solve the murder, with neither one supposed to provide any assistance to the other. At that point, the film becomes a battle of the procedurals, with McBride's investigation moving forward based on a lipstick-stained handkerchief found in Spencer's hotel room. That leads to a woman of dark hair, possibly Italian or Spanish, which eventually leads to Louisa Reville, a girlfriend of Spencer's. After discovering the murder weapon, McBride arrests Maitland Greer for the crime.

Torchy employs a different tack, tracing the cab driver to Spencer's hotel and later locating the missing Louisa Reville. Having seen Greer accompany Spencer down the street, it is clear to Torchy that Greer is innocent, even though a jury convicts him of murder. Of course, Torchy is finally vindicated when the real killer confesses, although it was probably a case of self-defense.

*Blondes at Work* is really a screwball comedy with mystery interruptions. Most of the film involves the friendly competition between McBride and Torchy, with Torchy getting inside dope from the diary of Gahagan, unbeknownst to the lumbering cop. Come to think about it, is Gahagan really a policeman? His duties for the police department seem somewhat obscure in these films and his job description may well be "comic relief." If that is so, he should have been fired many films ago.

Lieutenant Steve McBride (Barton MacLane), left, and Sergeant Parker (Thomas E. Jackson), right, bring their best clue, a handkerchief with perfume on it, to Mr. Jay (actor unidentified), a fashion director, to see if he can identify the perfume, in *Blondes at Work* (1938). The two models between McBride and Jay are played, from left to right, by Carole Landis and Suzanne Kaaren.

While the parallel investigations by Torchy and McBride are interesting, once Greer is indicted for Spencer's murder, the mystery falls away. There are really no suspects other than Greer and Reville, and if Greer is not guilty (and he cannot be, because Torchy says he is not), then the only possibility left is Louisa Reville. She eventually confesses to the killing off-screen, further diminishing any surprise that her involvement in the murder might have brought. Indeed, the last third of the film is all comedy, with Torchy listening in on jury deliberations so that she can scoop the competition, resulting in a well-justified jailing of Torchy for contempt of court

Once again, Glenda Farrell and Barton MacLane are excellent as Torchy and McBride, carrying along both the crime and the comedy elements in an engaging manner. *Blondes at Work* is not for a mystery fan who is looking for a solid crime story; it is for the mystery fan who is looking for an amusing film, with some mystery elements.

In either case, the viewer will probably agree with Captain McTavish's opinion of McBride's police work, which he gives at the beginning of the film, when McBride defends Torchy's involvement in his police investigations. McTavish tells McBride, "You're supposed to track your own cases, without help from reporters or anybody else. If you can't do that, we'll put somebody in charge of the squad who will." Unfortunately, but not unexpectedly, in *Blondes at Work* McBride is once again unable to solve a murder without the assistance of the vivacious Torchy Blane. Perhaps someone else should be put in charge of the murder squad.

*Note on the Remake*: *Blondes at Work* appears to be a remake of *Front Page Woman* (1935), which would not be surprising. Warner Brothers had a habit of quickly remaking films under different titles, as discussed in Chapter 1, in relation to *Calling Philo Vance* (1940).

## *Torchy Blane in Panama* (1938)

This is far and away the worst Torchy Blane mystery to date. Indeed, the only mystery in the film is where the screenwriters hid the plot.

During a large New York City parade of the Loyal Order of Leopards (essentially ugly men dressed in short leopard outfits walking down the street), a bank is robbed and a teller is shot and killed. The one clue is that the currency that was stolen consisted of new bills, and a bank official is able to provide the police with their serial numbers. Even though Torchy arrives at the crime scene well after the police, she discovers an important additional clue: a lodge button wedged into the dead teller's cage. Now, in the course of a robbery at gunpoint, how could that button possibly have ended up where it did? But Torchy needs a clue so the writers provided her with one, even though it makes absolutely no sense.

Torchy tries to tell Steve about the button, but he brushes off her attempts to speak to him. Instead of Torchy insisting that Steve listen to her, she writes a story about the button for her newspaper, embarrassing her fiancé in front of the police captain. This is a particularly irritating plot point, repeated later in the film, with Torchy taking unjustified actions just because Steve will not listen to her. How hard is it for these two lovers to communicate?

Since the button came from a lodge member in California (who is now dead), Torchy assumes the killer is within the California delegation of the Leopards. For plot purposes, the owner had to be dead or the police would have identified him as the thief and killer immediately, ending the movie quite abruptly. How the button got into the hands of the true robber is never explained.

Torchy then comes up with the craziest idea possible. She surmises that since the currency is hot and the boat that is taking the California Leopards back home will travel through the Panama Canal, the robber must be intending to exchange the marked bills for other bills in that Central American country. Frankly, it seems as if Torchy concocted this ridiculous theory only because she wanted an all-expense-paid trip to Central America and she believes that her newspaper will provide her with one. For some reason, Steve, Gahagan and another newspaper reporter buy Torchy's theory and join her on the boat. Torchy has to parachute her way onto the vessel in the middle of the ocean.

On board ship, Torchy starts drinking with all of the California Leopards to see if any of them is the killer. This approach seems like a long shot for solving the crime (and a particularly tedious way to spend an evening) but the last Leopard she talks to seems to be particularly handsome, and since Torchy spends some extra time with him, he is clearly the criminal. Also, Gahagan notes that this man, Stan Crafton, does not know the secret Leopard handshake, so maybe he is an impostor. Of course, that cannot be the case because if he is an impostor, how did he ever obtain the three-year-old Leopard button that was found by Torchy at the bank?

Crafton sneaks off the boat in Panama in order to sell the hot money to a Panamanian at a reduced price, giving Crafton a profit from the bank robbery. Surprise! Torchy's crazy theory was correct after all. Torchy runs to Steve to tell him that Crafton is escaping but Steve brushes her off once again. Instead of insisting that Steve listen, Torchy decides to sneak off the boat. It is completely ridiculous that she does not make Steve listen to her story and prevent Crafton from escaping, but there was still more screen time to fill, so the movie could not yet end. Torchy is captured by Crafton in Panama, but Steve rescues her in the nick of time, undercutting the concept of a movie about a successful and independent female character.

The above is a detailed description of the plot of the film, just to show how ridiculous it is. Even the title makes little sense since Torchy spends almost no time in Panama. There was still not enough story to fill the hour running time of the movie so the filmmakers did just the wrong thing: gave more screen time to Gahagan than in any other film in the series to date. Put quite bluntly, Gahagan is not the least bit funny.

Lola Lane and Paul Kelly make their only appearances as Torchy Blane and Steve McBride, respectively, and while it is initially disconcerting to see them in the parts, they are both actually quite good. Glenda Farrell was often the only reason to watch the Torchy Blane features, but Lane is perky, pretty and passionate as Torchy, more than filling Farrell's shoes. However, the film itself is awful, but what would one expect from a mystery film that contains no mystery?

## *Torchy Gets Her Man* (1938)

This is the sixth movie in this crime series about Gahagan, police-chauffeur. It probably would have made more sense to create a string of mystery movies about an inquisitive female reporter who always seemed to become involved in mysteries which she solved before the police did. But Warner Brothers decided to go the opposite way, emphasizing the comedy antics of Gahagan at the expense of Torchy Blane, finally making Gahagan the principal character in this film.

Gilbert, a Secret Service agent, asks Steve McBride's help in setting up a sting to capture Bailey, a counterfeiter of $100 bills. Gilbert tells McBride that Bailey is likely to pass the phony bills at the racetrack, so McBride gets Gilbert a job at the track's $100 window. There, Gilbert, who is really Bailey, passes fake C–notes to unsuspecting patrons right under the nose of McBride. Torchy, anxious to discover what McBride is working on, trails Gilbert one night and accidentally learns that he is Bailey. After the requisite capture of Torchy by the villains and the requisite rescue of Torchy by McBride, the counterfeiters are captured and Torchy gets her story.

This film has three structural flaws. One of the older rules of mystery writing is that a mystery novel has to be about a murder. No less serious crime will suffice. And, although there are a number of notable exceptions to that rule, such as *The Moonstone* (1868) by Wilkie Collins (theft of a valuable jewel) and *Gaudy Night* (1935) by Dorothy Sayers (poison pen letters), most mystery novels, even to this day, follow the rule. Similarly, most full-length mystery movies also involve a murder, with the rare exception of films directed toward juvenile audiences, such as the Nancy Drew or Tailspin Tommy features.

In *Torchy Gets Her Man*, the crime is counterfeiting; there are no murders. As a result, there is not enough story to fill the hour running time so the emphasis is on Gahagan, who probably gets the most screen time of any character. Thus, the viewer gets to see Gahagan tricked into carrying the wrong messages back and forth to the Treasury Department, his unusual betting system at the track, and his hiring of a dog who only understands German to help follow the crooks. With Farrell, one of the most engaging performers in all of the mystery series, playing Torchy, why de-emphasize her part and focus on Gahagan?

The second structural flaw is that Torchy is not actually investigating any crime. She is simply trying to determine what McBride is investigating. Thus, when Torchy stumbles onto Gilbert and his gang of thieves, she does not even realize that Gilbert is a crook. She has to be told so by Gilbert.

The third structural problem is that Steve McBride is finally made into a bumbling policeman. How could McBride ever be fooled by such an obvious scam? At one point, Gilbert accurately describes McBride as having more brawn than brain, and another gang member states that he believes McBride has trouble putting two and two together. In prior films, while Torchy may have beaten McBride to the solution of the crime, McBride was still a hard-working cop developing clues on his own. The tension between Torchy and McBride in the prior films as they both smartly investigated crimes gave those films both some romance and some interest.

With *Torchy Gets Her Man*, the romance seems to have gone out of this relationship, as they barely converse with each other and they no longer talk about getting married. Unfortunately, with the poor scripts and unfunny comic relief, the viewers' interest also has gone out of the Torchy Blane series.

## *Torchy Blane in Chinatown* (1939)

Again, why is Gahagan a character in the Torchy Blane mystery series? He adds nothing to the storyline and as comic relief, his contribution is minimal. Yet, for two movies in a row, Gahagan has more screen time than Torchy. What were the filmmakers thinking?

At least in the case of *Torchy Blane in Chinatown*, the film is about murder, and three murders at that. Adventurers Allan Fitzhugh, Dr. Mansfield and Captain Condon smuggled jade burial tablets out of China and into the United States on behalf of Senator Baldwin. A gang of Chinese thugs demands a ransom for the jade and, to prove the sincerity of its threats, announces that it will execute Fitzhugh at midnight. Fitzhugh appeals to the New York City police, and Steve McBride promises protection for Fitzhugh at the Adventurers Club. McBride's security plans work and the midnight deadline passes with McHugh still alive. However, after McHugh leaves the club, his car is ambushed and McHugh is killed by gunfire, resulting in his head being shot off. A church bell then chimes and it turns out that the killing indeed took place at midnight. All of the policemen's watches were running fast.

There are subsequent death threats made against the two surviving adventurers via notes written in Chinese and then the killing or disappearance of the two other adventurers, until the fiancé of the Senator's daughter agrees to pay $250,000 to stop the threats. He proceeds by boat to the last buoy in New York Harbor where he is to turn the money over to the villains. However, when the three masked Chinese villains arrive, McBride tricks them by arriving in a submarine, captures the three members of the gang and reveals their true identities. Torchy then announces that she knew who the blackmailers were all the time.

The mystery itself is not all that bad, with numerous suspects for the villain or villains and some interest generated by trying to guess how the killers will accomplish their pre-announced killings with the proposed victims surrounded by the police. The execution, however, is a different matter. Even with a running time of less than 60 minutes, there was still not enough plot to fill the entire hour, so the filmmakers had to resort to something to stretch the story to its requisite length.

It might have been a good idea to focus on the (now forgotten) upcoming marriage of Torchy and McBride and have a little more cute banter between the two. Or, it might have been nice to focus on Torchy's independent investigation of the crimes, something that used to be done in the earlier films in the series but now also seems to have been forgotten by the filmmakers. Indeed, when Torchy announces at the end that she had already figured out who the killers were, the audience surely greets that statement with some skepticism, since Torchy has done absolutely nothing during the story except follow McBride around.

Instead of some clever writing, the screenwriters chose to focus on the unfunny Gahagan with his tiresome poetry, his looking through a keyhole at some Chinese actresses, his desire to take a sip of some drinks that may be poisoned and his solo rowboat ride in the dark of New York Harbor when he is supposed to be off-duty. At one point, McBride tells Gahagan to take the night off, saying, "You'll only be in the way." If only the screenwriters had taken their own advice about Gahagan for all of the Torchy Blane films.

Once again, McBride is made an object of ridicule, allowing several killings to take place right under his nose. He never makes the most basic investigation, such as checking the background of the three adventurers or checking on the poison in the cigarette that supposedly killed Mansfield. At one point while protecting Captain Condon, McBride hears an explosion in the Baldwin home and everyone rushes there to see what happened. When they return to the spot where they left Condon, he has disappeared. Who would ever fall for such a trick?

With all of the deficiencies, the only reason to view *Torchy Blane in Chinatown* is for the little things. Glenda Farrell is particularly attractive in her evening gown at the Baldwins' engagement party for their daughter and Victor Sen Yung makes a very brief appearance as a Chinese actor, shortly before obtaining his signature role as Jimmy Chan in the Charlie Chan series. Other than that, there is little reason for a mystery fan to watch the film.

*Note on the Source Material*: The script was based on a story by William Jenkins, under his *nom de plume* Murray Leinster, titled "The Purple Hieroglyph," first published in *Snappy Stories* in its March 1, 1920, edition. It was previously filmed as *Murder Will Out* (1930) and as a silent film, *The Purple Cipher* (1920). Born in 1896, Jenkins began writing stories for magazines in 1916 and, over the next several decades, contributed numerous stories for pulp magazines such as *Argosy* and *Snappy Stories*. He also began writing science fiction stories during this time period, and today he is best remembered for his output in that genre, including winning a 1956 Hugo award for best novelette. Jenkins died in 1975.

## *Torchy Runs for Mayor* (1939)

For crime aficionados, there may be nothing better than a film about a crusading newspaper reporter or brave attorney busting up the rackets in a big city teeming with gangsters and corrupt public officials. A good example is *Racket Busters* (1938), directed by Lloyd Bacon, where a lawyer and a truck driver break up the trucking racket in a large city. In

*Deadline U.S.A.* (1952), directed by Richard Brooks, newspaper editor Ed Hutcheson uses the last few issues of his newspaper to crusade against a gangster terrorizing his city. There is also *The Phenix City Story* (1955), directed by Phil Karlson, with attorney Pat Patterson leading the fight to rid "Sin City, U.S.A." of its criminal elements. And then there is *Torchy Runs for Mayor* (1939), the last film to star Glenda Farrell as the female investigative journalist.

*Torchy Runs for Mayor* is in the tradition of prior and future films about racketeers in the big city and the struggle of one individual to go head to head with the mob, but since this is a Torchy Blane film, the tale is light-hearted, rather than rough. Nevertheless, the strength of the core plot and some excellent performances, particularly in the villain roles, make this the best of the Torchy Blane films in quite some time.

Torchy is on a mission. She intends to expose Mayor Saunders as a pawn of the mob, led by Doc Dolan, the ostensibly upright citizen who is in reality a crime boss. Torchy has been running a string of newspaper stories about the two, getting her information from a secret wire she has placed in the mayor's office. By that device, Torchy has learned that Dolan has a little red book in his safe at home, in which he records his illegal transactions. If Torchy can find that book, she can expose Doc Dolan.

With a safecracking friend of hers, Torchy is able to steal the book, but then no regular newspaper in town will print her story. Torchy convinces Hogarth Ward to publish it in his small independent paper and also run for mayor, leading to the death of Ward when the gangsters believe that he has the book. When no one else will do so, Torchy is tricked into becoming the mayoral candidate against Saunders and surprisingly she wins the election, but not before she is kidnapped by Dolan, leading to her rescue by Steve McBride.

*Torchy Runs for Mayor* is sparked by some excellent performances, particularly John Miljan as Doc Dolan and Joe Downing as Spuds, Dolan's vicious henchman. They are truly menacing characters, whether punching Ward, an older newspaper editor, and knocking him cold or mercilessly executing him with a lethal injection of poison. When Miljan and Downing are on screen, the two bring *Torchy Runs for Mayor* back from its light-hearted tone to the serious crime drama it often tries to be. It was particularly clever of the screenwriters to make the crime boss into a physician, providing him with that unusual method of murder (at least at that time) of a lethal injection. Glenda Farrell and Barton MacLane are good as usual as Torchy and Steve. Frank Shannon, back once again as Captain McTavish, has one of his largest roles in the series and he is quite believable. Even Tom Kennedy as Gahagan is not so bad, actually being useful at the end of the film when a fight breaks out at the Dolan farmhouse.

There is not much mystery to the story, as it takes some time for the killing of Ward to occur. Since the murder is shown on-screen, there is no question as to who the murderer is. That is not a problem, though, as a film such as *Torchy Runs for Mayor* is not so much a whodunit but rather a how-will-the-crooks-be-caught film. The semi-climax is quite exciting, with a brawl through the Dolan farm, highlighted by fistfights, gunshots and even a man thrown through an upper window of the house. In the perhaps not unexpected climax, Doc Dolan is killed in a trap set for McBride by Dolan's own henchmen. It is an ironic and fitting end to the film.

*Torchy Runs for Mayor* does succumb to using the movie clichés of the genre, such as a little book that could be the downfall of the mob, if only it can be located, and an innocent character confessing to the murder of Ward for no credible reason. These are nitpicks at best, as overall the film is quite entertaining.

Torchy's career took a number of turns in this movie, as she was fired from her newspaper job and then successfully ran for mayor. Is there any chance she will still be the mayor at the beginning of the next film? Perhaps not, but what is sure, unfortunately, is that Glenda Farrell and Barton MacLane would leave the series after *Torchy Runs for Mayor*, to the detriment of the product.

## *Torchy Blane ... Playing with Dynamite* (1939)

There is a lot to be learned from this last film in the Torchy Blane series. Apparently, a judge can put a defendant in jail for nine months, just on the statements of a policeman, without any trial at all. A prisoner can break out of jail by merely paying off a guard, who will then simply give the keys and a gun to the prisoner and let her walk out of jail. And, perhaps most important of all, Torchy Blane's real first name is Ellen.

In this film, Torchy is on the trail of Denver Eddie, a notorious bank robber who always seems to be one step ahead of the police. Torchy is brought to a judge's chamber for speeding, where she coincidentally sees a woman, later identified as Jackie McGuire, being sentenced for shoplifting. When her publisher later informs Torchy that Jackie is Denver Eddie's moll, Torchy decides to go undercover by being arrested and then attempting to learn some information from Jackie while making friends with her in prison. The ridiculous plan somehow works and Torchy, Steve McBride and Gahagan capture Denver Eddie at a wrestling arena when wrestler Gahagan is thrown out of the ring onto him.

There were some bad films in the Torchy Blane series but this is the worst by far. There is nothing right about it. Torchy gets deliberately thrown in jail when she pulls the fire alarms on city alarm boxes 11 times, even though there are no fires. Apparently, this was supposed to be funny, but as firemen from all over the city are drawn to false alarms, at a cost and risk to the taxpayers, there is nothing funny about Torchy's acts which seem particularly inconsiderate of her fellow citizens.

The scenes in prison should have been suspenseful, but after about four minutes of film, Torchy is already walking out the door with Jackie, in the easiest prison escape in the entire history of prison films. At the end, the capture of Denver Eddie should have been exciting, but the filmmakers played it for laughs with Gahagan actually making the capture while he is wrestling in the main event. This is not funny; it is stupid.

Eddie Marr plays Denver Eddie and it is the movie's one striking performance. Jane Wyman was probably the best actress ever to play Torchy, eventually earning four Oscar nominations for Best Actress and winning for *Johnny Belinda* (1948). However, Wyman is awful in this film. She seems to be overacting to try to match Glenda Farrell's natural performance in the prior films in the series. Wyman equates comedy with mugging and incredibly wide eyes. The two, however, seldom contribute to the humor of a film and they certainly do not do so in this case. Allen Jenkins plays Steve McBride and although he is okay in the part, he cannot convey the genuineness of Steve McBride as Barton MacLane was able to do. Would MacLane have ever been caught in that ridiculous scenario at the wrestling arena in which Jenkins finds himself?

To make the plot, such as it is, work, the San Francisco police must not know that McBride and Gahagan are policemen. That is the only way that the storyline could get Gahagan into the squared circle at the finish. The explanation for not asking for help from the San Francisco police, as any other out-of-state cops would have done, is silly. McBride and Gahagan allegedly did not tell the San Francisco police that they were hot on the trail

After Torchy Blane (Jane Wyman, right) is deliberately arrested so that she can go undercover in jail in *Torchy Blane ... Playing with Dynamite* (1939), a prison guard (Jessie Perry) helps her escape.

of a dangerous killer in their city because they did not want to lose the reward for the capture of Denver Eddie. That is totally ridiculous and, unfortunately, is only one more manifestation of the sloppy plotting throughout the film. Another unfortunate characteristic of the production is its languid pace, effectively stifling any interest the film might have had.

If *Torchy Blane ... Playing with Dynamite* is the best that Warner Brothers could produce for the investigative reporter at this late date, it was time for the series to end. Luckily, someone at Warners apparently recognized this, because *Torchy Blane ... Playing with Dynamite* is the last film in the series.

## Afterwards

Glenda Farrell's career peaked in the 1930s and although she continued to work somewhat regularly in Hollywood in the 1940s, the films in which she appeared were usually of little significance. In the 1950s and 1960s, she made numerous guest appearances in television. Farrell passed away in 1971.

Barton MacLane continued working regularly in films in the 1940s and 1950s, usually in supporting roles. He then did substantial guest appearance work in television, becoming most familiar to television audiences from his recurring role as General Peterson in *I Dream of Jeannie* (1965–1969). MacLane died in 1969.

Although ostensibly based on stories written by Frederick Nebel, the Torchy Blane character was truly a movie original. Once the series ended in 1939, there were no more movies produced about the character and she was never the subject of a radio or television series.

# 13

# Alan O'Connor and Bobbie Reynolds
## *The Federal Agents*

Two new styles of Hollywood crime films developed in the mid-1930s, one involving a federal agent as the hero and the other involving male and female pairings as the lead detectives. An example of the first is *G-Men* (1935) with James Cagney, which is often cited as the seminal film with a government agent as the protagonist. It was followed by many films about the FBI and other federal agents. In the mystery series area, there were the Persons in Hiding films about the FBI and the Brass Bancroft films about a Secret Service agent. Examples of the second type of new crime movie are *The Thin Man* (1934) and its many progeny. In the mystery series area, in addition to the Thin Man movies, there were the three Joel and Garda Sloan films.

The Alan O'Connor-Bobbie Reynolds films were a clever attempt to combine these two subgenres of the mystery movie. O'Conner and Reynolds are federal agents who attempt to work together while exchanging witticisms, with the possibility of romance beneath the surface. The series started slowly but despite some shortcomings in the writing, acting and production, the movies do have their interest, even today. After four films were quickly made in 1936 and 1937, the series abruptly disappeared.

## BACKGROUND

Alan O'Connor is an investigator with a federal office, presumably the Federal Bureau of Investigation, although that is not made entirely clear, and the vast scientific and technical resources of the Bureau never seem to be at his disposal. Bobbie Reynolds is another agent in the same office although in the first film, *Yellow Cargo* (1936), she is working undercover, which is a surprise both to the viewer and Alan O'Connor.

The series was released by Grand National, an independent studio which was only in existence for a few years in the 1930s. The company did produce several mysteries, the most notable of which were two Shadow films starring Rod La Rocque. The O'Connor-Reynolds series consists of only four films, one from 1936, and then three produced and released very quickly in 1937. In these films, the two agents investigate a variety of criminal activity: smuggling of illegal aliens, kidnapping of a Navy officer, smuggling of gold and bank robbery.

Alan O'Conner was played by Conrad Nagel. Nagel, who was born in Iowa in 1897, became a major star in Hollywood during the silent era, usually playing the romantic lead. He easily made the transition to sound, being steadily at work in the early 1930s. He was such a well-known Hollywood figure that he was a founder of the Academy of Motion Picture Arts and Sciences and twice hosted the Academy Awards ceremony in the early 1930s. However, his career soon faltered, leading him to turn to the very low-budget O'Conner-Reynolds series at an independent studio.

Eleanor Hunt, who played the wide-eyed Bobbie Reynolds in all four films, was born in New York City in 1910. Her first major screen role was in *Whoopee* (1930), opposite Eddie Cantor. Unfortunately, that was probably the apex of her career, as thereafter she played in generally minor films and film shorts. If Hunt is remembered at all today, it is for the Alan O'Connor-Bobbie Reynolds series.

## THE FILMS

### *Yellow Cargo* (1936)

Smuggling of illegal aliens is the offense being investigated in *Yellow Cargo* and because that is an unusual crime for this type of film (although see *Secret Service of the Air* [1939] in the Brass Bancroft series), it provides the feature with a different feel than many B–movies of the era. Indeed, some of the film's main plusses are the unique ways in which the villains smuggle illegals into the country, such as disguising them as dead bodies in a hearse or as Asian extras in a movie the villains pretend to be shooting. Nevertheless, not much of consequence happens in the film until its entertaining conclusion, and therefore *Yellow Cargo* is a very disappointing start to the new mystery series.

Federal narcotics agent Alan O'Connor (spelled "Allan" in this film) is pulled into the Immigration and Naturalization Services on a special assignment to investigate the smuggling of illegal Asians by land and water on the West Coast. That night, two members of the criminal gang are bringing illegals into the country in a hearse, and the border guard who is supposed to be preventing such activity makes only a cursory inspection of the vehicle before allowing it to cross the border. However, when a motorcycle policeman stops the meat wagon for speeding, he looks in the back and discovers that the "corpses" are really illegal aliens. The officer receives a crack on the head for his efforts and the villains speed away, but not before one drops a piece of paper.

O'Connor is immediately on the job but perhaps he was not the best choice for the assignment because it takes him over two weeks to interview the injured officer and to be advised about the paper. In fact, instead of being a competent investigator, O'Connor may simply be one of the luckiest federal agents of all time. He had some acting experience so he uses the guise of an actor looking for work to investigate the smuggling. That is a particularly fortuitous idea since the villains are using a film studio as their front for smuggling the aliens, so a better ruse could not have been devised by O'Connor. Of course, if the smugglers were still using the mortuary gag, O'Connor would never have solved the case. Oh well, it is better to be lucky than good.

Newswoman Bobbie Reynolds, who is either a gossip reporter or interviewer of foreign celebrities or investigative reporter, but not very good at any of those vocations, is also suspicious of the studio. O'Connor, with Bobbie's help, finally exposes the gang and captures the villains.

Despite its short length, *Yellow Cargo* is particularly slow-moving. It is filled with the inexplicable actions of Bobbie Reynolds hanging out at the bogus film studio with her particularly unfunny cameraman, supposedly trying to get a story and learning very little. Eleanor Hunt plays Bobbie as if she were a ditz and not much else. The revelation at the end of the film that Bobbie is a federal agent is hard to believe, particularly because of her incompetent antics in the film, such as having a photo taken of the villains in the dark with the use of a large flash attachment, immediately disclosing her interloping to the villains and resulting in her capture. If Bobbie is a federal agent, then who is her incompetent cameraman? Indeed, if Bobbie is a federal agent, how can the government possibly function?

Nagel, however, is a joy to watch in the film. Handsome and always nattily dressed, he gives a breezy performance as Alan O'Connor, always rising above the quality of the material that he is given. None of the other actors in the film come close to Nagel's acting skills.

*Yellow Cargo* is a low-budget film and that shows in its limited use of music and overuse of tight shots to camouflage the threadbare nature of its sets. At the end of the film, however, there is an exciting car chase with very limited use of rear projection shots. The driving is actually taking place on country roads and the villains' clever use of a truck to throw O'Connor off their trail is ingenious. Many low-budget mystery films try to avoid substantial outdoor scenes in order to reduce costs. *Yellow Cargo* goes in the opposite direction, bringing the film to a satisfactory conclusion—almost. Unfortunately, the film ends with a whimper, with O'Connor taking a machine gun off of the villain as if it was a piece of candy, in one moment eliminating all excitement and credibility to the story.

Thus, despite a few positive attributes, *Yellow Cargo* is a second-rate movie which is boring in the extreme. However, with Nagel in the lead, there is at least some hope for the next three films in the series.

## *Navy Spy* (1937)

Lacking both an interesting premise and an exciting conclusion, attributes that *Yellow Cargo* almost had, *Navy Spy* has nothing going for it.

Navy Lieutenant Don Carrington is brought on board a Navy ship to protect him from villains who are after the formula for the vapor fuel that he invented. Since the paper on which the formula was written was destroyed in a fire, it is expected that an attempt will be made to kidnap Carrington and then try to make him talk. But how will the villains do that if Carrington is safely ensconced on a naval vessel? Simple. His girlfriend Ann writes him a note that she is in trouble, Carrington sneaks off the boat and then he is immediately captured by the heavies.

Federal agent Alan O'Connor is put on the job and another agent, Bobbie Reynolds, forces her way into the case as his assistant. Although they move at a leisurely pace, they somehow manage to follow the clues, find Carrington's location and, with the assistance of the Navy, capture the gang.

The most significant problem with *Navy Spy* is the lack of urgency displayed by O'Connor and Reynolds. They take forever to get to the ship where Carrington was last seen and then they take forever to get back ashore to begin the investigation proper. Everything moves at a slow pace, including the climax on board the ship where Carrington is hidden. Since the federal agents do not treat the pursuit as urgent and seem to have little interest in what they are doing, the viewer also has little reason for maintaining any particular interest in the goings-on.

O'Connor's investigation is all about coincidences. In Ann's dressing room he discov-

Disguised federal agent Alan O'Conner (Conrad Nagel), center with the mustache, has been captured by thugs who are after a secret formula for a vapor fuel in *Navy Spy* (1937). Among the villains is the leader of the gang, Barradine (Howard Lang), sitting in the car, and his right hand man Bertie (Don Barclay), second from the left. The other henchmen are unidentified.

ers a prescription bottle which was supposed to be for Carrington, something that logically should never have been in Ann's possession in the first place. That leads to a doctor's office. While O'Connor is burglarizing it, the villains come in and mention a meeting at a waterfront bar. O'Connor and Reynolds travel there, where they happen to overhear talk about the ship where Carrington is being held. The two then manage to get on board that ship before the villains return.

O'Connor and Reynolds must be the most fortunate federal agents in the world. The villains keep leading them to the next stage of their inquiry, by dropping hints right into their laps. Of course, in order to keep their jobs, O'Connor and Reynolds need to be very lucky, because their investigatory technique leaves a lot to be desired. Perhaps if they had just moved a little faster, they may have been able to find some clues on their own.

Much of the film is taken up with the banter between O'Connor and Reynolds (Reynolds is supposed to be on vacation and O'Connor was supposed to handle the assignment on his own). Once again, if this case were only worth the time of one federal agent, then it is hardly worth the time of the viewers either. Conrad Nagel and Eleanor Hunt have absolutely no chemistry together, although it would be hard to have any considering the dialogue they are required to speak. The acting is only fair at best, with, and unlike in the first film, Nagel surprisingly disappointing as Alan O'Connor.

It is difficult to come up with any reason to watch *Navy Spy*. Even the title makes no sense in the context of the storyline. There is no Navy spy in the story.

## *Gold Racket* (1937)

After two misfires, the Alan O'Connor–Bobbie Reynolds series finally produced a winner. There is nothing special about *Gold Racket*. The plot is not innovative, the production is not special, the performances are not exceptional and there are no surprises at the end. Yet *Gold Racket* is just what one would expect from a good second feature programmer — a competent mystery with a diverting story nicely compacted into its short running time of just slightly over 60 minutes.

This time the government is focusing on the smuggling of gold into the United States from Mexico. Since gold can be mined in Mexico cheaply and then sold in the States for $35 an ounce, its illegal importation can lead to a tidy profit, especially for McKenzie, a man who has substantial mining interests in Mexico. Because of the pressure from the government after the death of a federal officer at the hands of the smugglers, McKenzie devises a new method of transporting the gold into this country. He employs pilot Steve Williams to fly the gold into the United States, hoping to smuggle all of his gold assets out of Mexico before the feds close in.

O'Connor cleverly ties a gold bar taken from the villains to the Los Moradas region of Mexico. Once there, he spots Steve Williams at the Cafe LaTarantella, a bar run by Scotty Summers. Since Williams is a ladies' man, O'Connor calls in Bobbie Reynolds to assist him. She poses as a café nightclub singer and in that guise wins the attention of Williams. Bobbie learns some important information from him, leading to the eventual arrest of the gang.

*Gold Racket* works better than the prior films in the series for several reasons. O'Connor does some real detective work, tracing the gold in the bar to a particular region of Mexico. With the help of Bobbie, he purloins a nugget of gold from Steve's pocket, confirming the location of the mine from which the gold has come. It may all seem somewhat obvious but it makes the film believable.

Another positive is that Bobbie finally has a significant role. She is called in by Alan to assist him, rather than trying to force herself into a case in which she is not wanted, the unbelievable storyline of *Navy Ship* (1937). Given a chance to shine at last, Eleanor Hunt is very good as Bobbie, whether performing in the café, flirting with Steve Williams or standing up to the gang when she is captured at the end of the film. It helps that Hunt is quite attractive in the role.

There are several good suspense sequences. Early in the film, two of the gang attempt to kidnap O'Connor when he returns to an assayer's shop to retrieve a gold bar. It looks like the villains have the drop on him, but O'Connor is prepared, with federal agents in place to trap the crooks. It is a clever scene. Later in the film, Bobbie is supposed to keep Williams at the café while O'Connor searches his room. Bobbie is unable to hold Williams and when she phones O'Connor in Williams' room, O'Connor, after being somewhat indecisive, does not answer the phone. He is then trapped in Williams' apartment by three members of the gang.

The finale is good, though not spectacular. Alan and Bobbie have separately chased the smugglers to Winston, California, from where the last shipment of gold will finally be dispersed. Unbeknownst to O'Connor and Reynolds, the two have been fingered by a gang member, leading to Bobbie's capture. Here, however, unlike other mystery movies, O'Connor smartly calls in other federal agents to assist him, instead of doing everything alone, also adding to the cohesiveness of the film. As a result, Bobbie is rescued and the gang is captured with little trouble, except for some mild gunplay.

*Gold Racket* is nothing special but it was never intended to be. It never challenges the viewer but it never attempts to do so. *Gold Racket* is never more than a competent programmer, but it is still entertaining today. It more than adequately fits the bottom of the double bill.

## Bank Alarm (1937)

*Bank Alarm* is the second film in a row in the O'Connor-Reynolds series which is an unexpected pleasure for the B–mystery movie fan. It has some fascinating mystery elements, surprising for this type of film.

Federal agents Alan O'Connor and Bobbie Reynolds are called in to assist the local police as they investigate a string of brazen bank robberies. Recently, the villains have become so bold as to kill a jailed gang member. The robbers next steal the $40,000 Works Progress Administration payroll in Lone City, Nevada. The payroll is being held overnight at the local post office, which shares a building with the local hoosegow. Jerry Turner and another gang member get themselves arrested as vagrants and are incarcerated overnight. While the sheriff is sleeping right in front of their cell, they easily pick the jail's lock, steal the payroll from the post office next door and then return to their cell. The next day, the sheriff drives them to the edge of town and gives them each a dollar, not realizing that they have secreted the payroll under their jackets. The two escape unsuspected. This entire robbery sequence is a hoot.

The bills are all marked but that is not a challenge for Joe Karlotti, the leader of the gang. He brings a satchel full of the bills to the chief teller of the Second National Bank, Leon Curtis, who is part of the gang. Curtis is an excellent engraver and his job is to change the serial numbers on the bills, so that they will pass muster. His only mistake is one of bad luck. A serial number he uses for one of the bills happens to be identical to another bill at the bank, and when Overman, the head bookkeeper, notices the discrepancy, he takes the bills to Inspector Macy of the local police force. That leads to the murders of Overman and Macy. In the meantime, Curtis has also helped the gang rob his own bank, by having the burglar alarm decommissioned.

As a result of these very inventive criminal sequences, the first half of the film is always entertaining. If the second half does not quite measure up, that is not surprising. This is, after all, a B-movie. And, in fact, what almost ruins the second half is the insertion, for dubious reasons, of a B-movie convention, namely, comic relief; Bulb, the comic photographer played by Vince Barnett, reprises his unfunny role from the first film in the series, *Yellow Cargo* (1936). Barnett may be less funny in this film than he was in his previous outing. He is a 1930s Birmingham Brown, assisting the police for no apparent reason and trying to be funny, usually with little success.

*Bank Alarm*, just like the prior film *Gold Racket* (1937), is a clever police procedural. O'Connor and Reynolds follow the clues, making a fairly competent investigation as they work their way up to the leader of the gang. However, the two also decide to utilize Bulb in their investigations, instead of using an expert from the feds, severely undercutting the credibility of O'Connor and Reynolds.

Bulb is even used to guard Alan's sister Kay when she is threatened by the gang. It is

Federal agents Bobbie Reynolds (Eleanor Hunt) and Alan O'Connor (Conrad Nagel) inspect a counterfeit bill in *Bank Alarm* (1937).

hardly surprising to anyone that Bulb does not prevent Kay's kidnapping. The use of Kay, however, does bring a personal element to the film, mellowing O'Connor's Joe Friday "strictly business" approach to crimefighting. The use of Kay also brings some variety to the storyline, making *Bank Alarm* stand out among the other films in the series.

Conrad Nagel is excellent, as usual, as Alan O'Connor. There are two good performances among the villains. Wheeler Oakman plays Joe Karlotti. Oakman was always good in a villain's role, even becoming a little bit of a lecher at the end of the movie. Frank Milan plays Jerry Turner, the crook who romances Kay O'Connor. Milan had played Steve Williams in *Gold Racket*, another crook-as-romancer role. As good as he is in these films, he had few other roles in Hollywood.

The O'Connor-Reynolds series started slowly but it reached its prime in these last two films. It is a shame the series had to end so abruptly.

## Afterwards

Eleanor Hunt made only one more film after the Alan O'Connor-Bobbie Reynolds series ended. Her film career was over by 1941. She died in 1981.

Conrad Nagel's film career became spotty after the end of the O'Connor-Reynolds series but Nagel was nevertheless seldom out of work in the entertainment industry. He became the host and director of a radio program for many years, while also appearances on Broadway. From 1949 to 1952, he was the host of *Celebrity Time*, a television quiz program. He also guest starred regularly on television. Nagel passed away in 1970.

Alan O'Connor and Bobbie Reynolds were Hollywood concoctions, with no ties to literature, radio or comic strips. Once the four-film series was completed in 1937, the characters were never heard of again.

# 14

# Mr. Moto
## *The Japanese Detective*

The Mr. Moto series is often compared to the Charlie Chan series of the same era. Much like the Chan films, the Moto films were produced at 20th Century–Fox, with Sol M. Wurtzel as the executive producer, Norman Foster often the director and Philip MacDonald often the screenwriter. Among the many familiar actors employed in both series were Harold Huber, Lionel Atwill, Leon Ames, Lynn Bari and even Keye Luke. And, of course, the lead character is a crimefighter with an Oriental background.

Yet, for all of those similarities, the films in the two series were usually completely different. Even when a Chan film was about international intrigue, a somewhat rare occurrence, the films were primarily murder mysteries. The Moto films, on the other hand, were never murder mysteries (except for *Mr. Moto's Gamble*, which was written for the Chan series). Rather, the Moto films were primarily about international intrigue, set on a worldwide stage. Also, Moto was dissimilar in nature to the somewhat staid Charlie Chan. Moto was an expert in judo and gunplay and was never reluctant to mix it up with the villains, often dispatching them to their deaths without regret. Thus, although the Moto and Chan series were produced at the same time by the same studio with some surface resemblances, the differences between the series are much more significant than their similarities.

## BACKGROUND

### John P. Marquand

John Phillips Marquand was born on November 10, 1893, in Wilmington, Delaware. He lived in Rye, New York, until the age of fourteen. He then moved to New England, which he considered his true home, attending high school in Massachusetts, graduating from Harvard University in 1915 and then working as assistant magazine editor of the *Boston Evening Transcript* from 1915 to 1917. After serving in World War I as an artillery captain in France, Marquand had brief careers in journalism and advertising. At that point, he turned to writing novels and short stories, his first novel being *The Unspeakable Gentleman*, published in 1922. Thereafter, Marquand was a frequent contributor of short stories to several popular magazines of the day, most notably *The Saturday Evening Post*. Many of his novels were also serialized in shortened form in these magazines.

In the non-mystery field, Marquand generally wrote mildly satirical novels about life among the rich and socially prominent of New England. His most famous work, *The Late*

*George Apley* (1937), which falls into that vein of stories, won the Pulitzer Prize. But his other non–Moto works, while popular at their time, such as *H.M. Pulham, Esquire* (1941) and *B.F.'s Daughter* (1946) (both made into motion pictures), are seldom read today.

In 1935, Marquand moved to Peiping, China, at the suggestion of his editors at *The Saturday Evening Post*, who wanted one of their most important writers to acquire a first-hand knowledge of the Far East. The results of this expedition were *Ming Yellow*, a 1935 novel set in China and, of course, the Mr. Moto stories.

Mr. I.A. Moto is a secret service agent for Japan, roaming the pre–World War II globe, handling difficult situations on behalf of his country wherever they arise. Among his other attributes, Moto is skilled at judo and is an expert shot. Although Moto is always very polite to those with whom he speaks, he is willing to kill an adversary whenever necessary and without remorse. In the Marquand novels, Mr. Moto is never the main character. Rather, he is a key figure lurking in the background, until the surprise climax of the story. The main characters are usually Westerners who accidentally come into contact with Moto during one of his secret missions.

The first Moto novel, *Mr. Moto Takes a Hand*, also titled *No Hero*, was published in 1935. It was originally serialized in *The Saturday Evening Post*, as were the next three Moto novels. The last Moto novel from this era, *Last Laugh, Mr. Moto* (1942), also titled *Mercator Island*, was serialized in *Collier's*. Given the world situation by that time, novels with a Japanese agent as a hero were unlikely to have much of a following and the 1942 Moto novel was Marquand's last Moto work for many years.

## The Film Series

Mr. Moto became the subject of an eight-film mystery series made at 20th Century–Fox between 1937 and 1939. Only two of the films were purportedly based on a Marquand novel and the relationships between those films and the books that supposedly inspired them were tenuous, at best. The fifth film in the series, *Mr. Moto in Danger Island* (1939), was based on *Murder in Trinidad*, a novel by John W. Vandercook.

The Mr. Moto of the film series, renamed Kentaro Moto, is not always a Japanese secret agent. In fact, his profession seems to change from film to film, including being the owner of a company that sells Chinese artifacts, a confidential investigator for the International Association of Importers, a college professor of criminology and then an agent of the International Police. What does carry over from the novels is Mr. Moto's polite manner, which belies his expertise in judo and an apparent willingness to send his adversaries to their death.

In *Think Fast, Mr. Moto* (1937) and *Thank You, Mr. Moto* (1938), the Japanese detective is investigating smuggling, although in the latter film, he also works to protect a Chinese treasure. *Mr. Moto's Gamble* (1938) is the odd film in the series, with Moto investigating the death of a boxer in the ring. Then it is back to international intrigue for *Mr. Moto Takes a Chance* (1938), about a revolution in Southeast Asia, *Mysterious Mr. Moto* (1938), about an international group of assassins, and *Mr. Moto's Last Warning* (1939), about an attempted attack on the French fleet near the Suez Canal. *Mr. Moto in Danger Island* (1939) returns to the crime of smuggling, although in this case it is diamonds, and in *Mr. Moto Takes a Vacation* (1939) Moto is after an international jewel thief.

Peter Lorre played Mr. Moto in all eight films. Lorre was born in Hungary in 1904. After performing on the stage in Vienna and other European cities and also after appearing in a few small film roles, Lorre came to international fame in the Fritz Lang–directed German film *M* (1931), in which he played a child murderer who could not control his homicidal tendencies. In 1933, the Jewish Lorre fled Nazi Germany, first going to England where he played the villain in Alfred Hitchcock's *The Man Who Knew Too Much* (1934) and *Secret Agent* (1935). Lorre then moved to Hollywood where he continued appearing in crime films, although *Mad Love* (1935) was more of a horror film and *Crime and Punishment* (1935), in which Lorre played Raskolnikov, a murderer, was more of a psychological film. Thereafter, Lorre received his continuing role as the lead in the Mr. Moto series.

Lorre employed little makeup for the part of the Japanese detective, merely flattening his hair and wearing thick round glasses. Nevertheless, he convincingly portrayed the shrewd and secretive agent. Much like the novels, there were no other regulars in the series.

## THE FILMS

### *Think Fast, Mr. Moto* (1937)

*Think Fast, Mr. Moto* is a muddled mess. Its plot is sloppily developed and the production displays a serious lack of attention to detail. In reading the plot summary below, the reader should keep in mind one of the revelations at the end of the film. At all times during the feature, Mr. Moto was not acting as a policeman or a government agent; he was merely the owner of a business which was harmed by the smuggling of the Morloff gang. Given that knowledge, does any of the story make sense in retrospect?

In San Francisco, the Chinese New Year is being celebrated on the streets of Chinatown. A Chinese rug merchant (a disguised Mr. Moto) is being harassed by the police for selling goods without a license. Moto moves on but then spots a man with a Union Jack tattooed on his right wrist leaving a curio shop. Moto goes in, and while attempting to sell some diamonds to the curio shop owner, spots a dead body in a wicker basket below the counter. Actually, Moto deliberately drops an item from his hand, allowing him to look under the counter, thereby making the surprise discovery. Why Moto did that is left unexplained, especially since it appears that he entered the curio shop on an impulse. Moto is forced to flee the shop but not before demonstrating his judo skills on the shop owner and a policeman.

The theme of dead bodies in wicker baskets will be mentioned again in *Think Fast, Mr. Moto*, once in a newspaper story and once near the end when Mr. Moto explains that the villains disposed of problem individuals by killing them, depositing the bodies in wicker baskets and then throwing the baskets into the sea. Presumably, the villains used a similar method to dispose of their associate who decided to leave a wicker basket with a body in it on the floor of a curio shop with a hand sticking out for anyone to see.

Actually, this is not a bad start to *Think Fast, Mr. Moto*, as it adequately conveys the beginnings of some mystery story amid the backdrop of the Chinese festival. In any other film, there would then be some expository material, explaining who Moto is and what he is investigating. For some reason, that is skipped in *Think Fast, Mr. Moto*, making much of the rest of the movie hard to follow. If an audience is not invested in the knowledge of what crime has been or is being committed and the need for an investigation, that audience can have little interest in subsequent goings-on.

Moto reserves a stateroom on the *Marco Polo*, a Hitchings ocean liner on its way to

Shanghai. He coincidentally receives a room just opposite that of Bob Hitchings, the son of the owner of the liner. That coincidence was necessary because Hitchings will be an important character in the film. Moto is immediately suspicious of the ship's steward, Carson, who also has a flag tattoo on his right wrist. That sparks the question: Why do the villains have such a tattoo on their wrists? The most it can do is bring attention to them, which should be the last thing a quality group of smugglers should want. The real reason, of course, is that the tattoo, as silly as it is, moves the plot forward, as Moto can immediately identify some of the villains by that device. Note, however, that this plot point will soon disappear from the film.

After some comedy scenes and a display of card tricks by Moto, the *Marco Polo* docks in Honolulu where pretty Gloria Danton comes on board, immediately attracting Hitchings' attention. At first she plays hard to get but eventually the two appear to fall in love. At the end of the film, it is explained that Gloria is really Tanya, a white Russian who was forced by the gang leader Marloff to spy on Hitchings to discover his plans. Actually, though, Gloria makes no effort to do any investigation of Hitchings and it hardly makes sense for someone not a member of the criminal gang to be employed in such capacity, so it is clear that Gloria's only reason for being in the story is to provide a love interest for the film (along with the filler material that such a side story can bring).

In the best scene in the film, Moto discovers Carson searching his stateroom and a fight ensues. The battle goes out to the ship's deck, where Moto intentionally throws the steward over the railing and into the ocean to his death. The scene displays a sudden burst of violence in the previously staid film, and the maliciousness on the part of the lead detective is unprecedented for mystery movies of this era.

The *Marco Polo* docks in Shanghai and Hitchings is met on the dock by Joseph Wilkie, the Hitchings' long-time manager in Shanghai. The audience has been suspicious of this character for quite some time, even though this is his first appearance in the film. Wilkie is played by Murray Kinnell and his appearance alone confirms those suspicions. Often smoking a pipe, he seems just a little too well-dressed and sophisticated to be anything other than a villain. First impressions are important in life and in the movies, and the audience, in this case, will not be disappointed. (At least Wilkie does not have a flag tattoo on his right wrist, but then, why doesn't he, if other members of the gang do?)

At the hotel where Hitchings is staying, one of the telephone operators is an agent of Moto's who allows him to listen in on telephone conversations of the guests. Of course, since Moto is not a policeman or a government agent himself, it is unclear how he could have a hotel operator working for him so far away from his home base. No explanation is given. Moto then goes to a bazaar in the city, for no reason other than for subsequent plot purposes, i.e., to disclose his identity to one of the villains, who will later be able to unmask Moto when Moto is posing as a villain near the end of the film.

Moto rides in a rickshaw and he is followed by one of the villains in another rickshaw. ("Driver, follow that rickshaw.") The rickshaws are placed in front of a projection screen of travel through Shanghai which was probably taken from another film, since the footage was obviously shot from the back of a motor vehicle. As a result, the rickshaws appear to be moving at about 30 miles per hour. Moto proceeds to the police station, which has the following lettering above the door: "Chinese Police Station." One has to wonder if the police stations of the era in New York City are identified as "American Police Station."

The action moves to the International Club where the lead villain, Marloff, addresses Wilkie by name in front of Moto, sealing the deal on Wilkie's guilt. It is an inexplicable mistake on Marloff's part, ensuring that everyone will know that Wilkie is the villain. Later, Wilkie "accidentally" knocks a gun from Moto's hands and then, when all is just about lost for him, "accidentally" shoots Marloff while pulling a gun from Marloff's coat pocket, which is an almost impossible accident. Why not simply run a streamer across the bottom of the screen identifying Wilkie as the secret villain? How often is the most likely suspect actually the surprise villain?

Moto has sent his assistant, Lela, to call the police, but she is shot at close range with a gun with a silencer before she can get her whole message out. Once again, it is a stunning scene of violence for this type of film. Not surprisingly, however, since Lela is on the side of right, at the end of the film, the police announce that she will recover. Perhaps Lela was also wearing a bulletproof vest, just as Moto was inexplicably wearing one at the end of the film when he was shot in the chest. Presumably, Moto was wearing the vest throughout the entire film, because how does he know when he will be shot and where? But then, what is the explanation for the bloodstain on his white tuxedo if he was protected from the bullet by the vest?

*Think Fast, Mr. Moto* is a complete disappointment, with an inconsistent plot that makes little sense. Scenes follow scenes for no logical reason. By delaying an explanation of Mr. Moto's role in the story, and, indeed, what crime he is investigating, much of the story is hard to follow. There are a few good performances but they are not worth mentioning because they are defeated by the clumsy storyline. What a disappointing start to a mystery series from a studio that was then producing some excellent Charlie Chan movies.

*Note on the Source Material*: Some sources cite Marquand's story "That Girl and Mr. Moto" published in *The Saturday Evening Post* from September 12 to October 17, 1936, in six installments, as the basis for *Think Fast, Mr. Moto*. A check of the actual issues of the *Saturday Evening Post* discloses that the name of the story is *Think Fast, Mr. Moto*, which was published in book form in 1937. However, there are almost no similarities between the book and the film.

In the book, Wilson Hitchings, the nephew of the owner of Hitchings Brothers, a financial institution, travels from Shanghai to Honolulu to convince a distant relative, Eve Hitchings, to stop operating a gambling casino on the islands using the name Hitchings Plantation. The manager of the Hitchings interests in Hawaii is named Mr. Wilkie and as it turns out, he is not entirely honest. Mr. Moto appears in the story from time to time as a Japanese agent who is attempting to prevent the laundering of money through the Hitchings Plantation for use by revolutionaries in Manchuria.

Obviously, the film *Think Fast, Mr. Moto* has little relationship to the plot of the novel of the same name. Indeed, with its setting in Hawaii, its emphasis on the young hero from a different part of the world who is investigating a crime and in the process falling in love, and the limited (in terms of pages) but important involvement of an Oriental detective or secret agent, the novel has more in common with the first Charlie Chan novel, *The House Without a Key*, than the alleged movie version of the novel, *Think Fast, Mr. Moto*.

## *Thank You, Mr. Moto* (1938)

The body count is high in this second film in the Mr. Moto series. The Japanese detective kills two people early in the film, the villains kill a dealer in Chinese antiquities and an elderly Chinese woman, her son commits suicide with a knife to the belly and at the end, several of the villains bite the dust. Mr. Moto himself is not afraid to mix it up with his enemies, employing fisticuffs and a little judo from time to time. Clearly, these Moto films are not your typical 1930s Hollywood detective films; they are more in the style of the mystery films of the 1940s and beyond.

In the Gobi Desert, a mysterious assailant attempts to kill an Asian man while he is sleeping in his tent. The Asian reverses the situation, kills his attacker and buries him in the desert. It takes a little while for the viewer to realize that the Asian gentleman is actually Mr. Moto in one of his clever disguises. When the caravan arrives at Peiping, the police, at the insistence of a cultured gentleman by the name of Mr. Schneider, search Moto. When they find an ancient scroll hidden in his bamboo walking stick, the chase beings.

Mr. Moto escapes, but the hunt is still on for a series of seven ancient Chinese scrolls, valuable in and of themselves for their artwork and antiquity, but more so because when placed in the proper order, they provide the location of the hidden tomb of Genghis Kahn and the vast treasure supposedly located therein. The chase involves a Chinese family experiencing hard economic times but who refuse to divulge the location of the scrolls, a semi-dishonest dealer in stolen Chinese artwork and an international gang of thieves attempting to gain access to the legendary treasure. As the story progresses, death follows death but eventually Moto wraps matters up and ends the villainy, with the Genghis Kahn treasure never located.

*Thank You, Mr. Moto* certainly has its interest. As mentioned above, there is some jarring violence in the film, surely the two surprising ones at the hand of Mr. Moto but particularly the villains' shocking killing of an elderly royal, Madame Chung. These incidents make the film stand out from the standard fare of the mystery movie series of the era. A treasure hunt with a map divided into several pieces is always diverting. The Chinese traditions and the nobility of Prince Chung and his mother and their clash with the crass avarice of the villains provide an interesting cultural overlay to the crime story. Sidney Blackmer, playing the main heavy, Koerger, adds a level of class and sophistication to the part, although his class and sophistication does not prevent him from punching Madame Chung in the face while wearing a sharp ring. Peter Lorre is good, as always, as Mr. Moto.

But for all of the positives, *Thank You, Mr. Moto* suffers from the same problems as the first Moto film. Simply stated, the movie makes no sense. In this case, Moto is supposedly acting as a confidential investigator for the International Association of Importers. But, what exactly is he investigating for that association? Arguably, he does put an end to a smuggling ring but in the process, he deliberately destroys all of the ancient scrolls of the Chung family. Moto seems more interested in protecting Chinese culture and history than fulfilling some task as a private detective. Moto should have gone without pay for this assignment.

There are many other questions raised by the inconsistent plot. How did Mr. Moto discover the scroll that he first had on him in the desert? Why was Moto invited to that dinner party by Colonel Tchernov at the beginning of the film (other than for the obvious reason — the main plot of the story had to start somewhere)? Is there any viewer, even one who has never seen a film like this before, who does not know that there are blanks in the gun when Moto is shot at close range?

For B–movies, the Moto films are first-class productions with good direction, often by director Norman Foster, who helmed this film and five others in the series. Foster also directed a few films in the Charlie Chan series. There is also the fine acting expected from a 20th Century–Fox film, even a mystery programmer. However, it is clear after viewing

Mr. Moto (Peter Lorre) prevents Eleanor Joyce (Joyce Regan) from calling the police, finally revealing to her that he is a confidential investigator for the International Association of Importers, in *Thank You, Mr. Moto* (1937).

the first two movies in the series that the Moto films are lacking in the script department, making them difficult to understand and enjoy. Over the long haul, style without substance is not a winning combination, especially in a mystery series.

*Note on the Source Material*: The credits to *Thank You, Mr. Moto* state that the film is based upon a story by John P. Marquand. Presumably the reference is to the 1936 Marquand novel *Thank You, Mr. Moto*. The setting of the book is China, there is some interest in eight scroll paintings, there is an unscrupulous dealer in Chinese antiquities and there are some other characters (if not their names) in common with the film.

However, in the book, Moto, who is only a minor character, is an agent of the Japanese government who is trying to prevent a faction of that government from attempting a military takeover of China. There is no treasure of Genghis Kahn at issue. The book is written in the first person by an American, Tom Nelson, and there is much emphasis on his relationship with another American, Eleanor Joyce. While those two characters are carried over into the film, they are far less significant there. Indeed, there is very little of the novel in the film, meaning that none of the eight Moto films were truly based on a work by Marquand.

## *Mr. Moto's Gamble* (1938)

Because *Mr. Moto's Gamble* is a captivating mystery rather than a confusing tale of espionage, this is one of the best of the Moto films. By now, most mystery fans know the reason for the anomaly in the type of story material used for this Mr. Moto film as contrasted with the other seven films in the series. The script for *Mr. Moto's Gamble* was originally written for a Charlie Chan film, expected to be titled *Charlie Chan at the Ringside*. Production on that film started but during the first days of shooting, Warner Oland fought with the studio and left the set. The studio, in order to salvage some of its investment in the film already shot, had the script re-written for Mr. Moto and incorporated some of the footage already taken of Keye Luke as No. 1 son Lee Chan. Thus, *Mr. Moto's Gamble* has a strange combination of Lee Chan assisting a different Oriental detective than his father, although with similar results. To create a link between the two mystery series, Lee even says to Moto, at one point, that Charlie sends his best to Moto.

In this film, Moto is now a criminology teacher and Lee Chan is one of his students. Along with Lieutenant Riggs, they attend a boxing match between Bill Steele and Frankie Stanton, with the winner to fight the heavyweight champion of the world, Biff Moran, eight weeks later. Gambler Nick Crowder wagers $10,000 with bookie Clipper McCoy that Stanton will not come out for the fifth round. McCoy has already taken similar bets from gamblers in six other cities, so he is concerned that Stanton will throw the fight. Not unexpectedly, Stanton falls in the third round and is counted out, but not because he took a dive. Stanton is pronounced dead in the ring by a physician.

Because poison is found on Steele's gloves (it probably made its way into Stanton's bloodstream through the cut over his eye) Steele is arrested for murder. His boxing license is also suspended. Moto is not so sure of Stanton's guilt and so he works to get Steele's license reinstated, so that the title match with Moran can occur. At the arena, while Steele is winning the championship, Moto traps the real killer.

This excellent mystery weaves a complex tale of gambling and boxing with the backdrop of the boxing ring, the locker rooms under the arena and the training camp of Biff Moran. Moto first attempts to determine who made the out-of-city bets against Stanton, because they clearly indicate insider information. However, this is a case that is not easily solved as Moto cannot find his way through the labyrinth of dead ends to locate the mystery gambler. Also making matters difficult for Moto are the several good suspects, such as gambler Nick Crowder, who made money on his bet against Stanton, bookie Clipper McCoy, who is clearly not a person of high repute, and Philip Benton, whose company owns the boxing arena and seems to be a solid citizen. Benton may be the unlikeliest of the suspects, however, since, after all, he bet on Stanton so he lost money when Stanton died in the ring.

Some of the joys of watching *Mr. Moto's Gamble* are the number of familiar character actors in the film: Ward Bond, who would have more significant roles in 1940s mysteries such as 1942's *The Falcon Takes Over* in which he played Moose Malloy, George E. Stone, who would go on to play the Runt in the Boston Blackie series, Cliff Clark, enactor of a number of policemen in mystery movies including Inspector Donovan in the Falcon series, Lynn Bari, who was a pretty addition to many Hollywood mystery movies, Lon Chaney, Jr., just a few years before he would become a horror film icon, and John Hamilton, well known as Perry White from the *Adventures of Superman* television series. Harold Huber plays Lieutenant Riggs, as he previously played a policeman around that time in the Charlie Chan series. Huber is not bad in the role, although his characteristic overacting starts

From left to right, Lee Chan (Keye Luke), Inspector Riggs (Harold Huber) and Mr. Moto (Peter Lorre) attend a boxing match which will end in murder in *Mr. Moto's Gamble* (1938).

to creep into his performance in the second half of the feature. In addition, less well-known actors Douglas Fowley (playing boxing manager Nick Crowder) and Bernard Nedell (playing gambler Clipper McCoy) are nothing short of excellent in their roles. Even when the 20th Century–Fox mystery series were weak in plot the acting was always excellent.

Surprisingly, the use of Lee Chan in the film is the element that does not work. Lee was much more interesting and funny when he was interacting with his father, rather than with his criminology professor Mr. Moto. Also, the filmmakers made the same mistake that Monogram later made with Tommy Chan and Birmingham Brown in the low-budget Charlie Chan films. Most of Lee's scenes in *Mr. Moto's Gamble* are not with Mr. Moto but rather are with Maxie Rosenbloom, playing Knockout, making the two of them into a kind of comedy team. Abbott and Costello they are not. The two have no timing together and they are not the least bit amusing.

That is not to say that the film does not have some funny lines. When Lee ends up in jail and Moto conspires to keep him there, Lee says, in response to Knockout's question as to why Moto would leave them in jail, "I don't know, Wellington. Pop used to leave me in jail once in a while, too." At the boxing arena, when Moran is clobbering Steele and a patron tells Steele's girlfriend that Moran has not laid a hand on Steele, a wag in the crowd behind him says, "Better watch that referee, then. Somebody's giving him an awful beating." While the latter line is an old joke, jokes only become old when they are funny.

The old man with the walking stick is a disguised Mr. Moto (Peter Lorre) in *Mr. Moto Takes a Chance* (1938). He is tricking Bokor, the high priest (George Regas), on the left, from harming two American cameramen, Chick Davis (Chick Chandler, left center) and Marty Weston (Robert Kent). Two of Bokor's tribesmen (actors unidentified) look on.

The movie has a much more intricate plot than is usual in these types of films, so the viewers' interest never abates. Suspicion realistically shifts from character to character, with many viable suspects. The film is essentially book-ended by two boxing matches, with the inherent interest they have. In addition, the latter match has the added suspense of a gun hooked up to a timer aimed at Moto, with several interesting shots from behind the gun, with Moto essentially in the cross hairs. Even after the killer is exposed, there is one more surprise death.

The final unveiling of the killer (who could never have shot poison onto Stanton via a water gun while Stanton was boxing in the ring) and Mr. Moto's explanation for how he solved the case cannot withstand much scrutiny. So be it. *Mr. Moto's Gamble* is an entertaining mystery throughout. It would have been one of the good Warner Oland Charlie Chan films if it had been completed for that series. It is therefore one of the best of the Mr. Motos.

## *Mr. Moto Takes a Chance* (1938)

Although *Mr. Moto Takes a Chance* was the second Mr. Moto film produced by 20th Century–Fox, it was the fourth film released in the series. Apparently, the studio felt that the movie was weaker than *Thank You, Mr. Moto* and it wanted to follow the first film in the series, *Think Fast, Mr. Moto*, with a stronger entry. If that was the studio's reasoning, it was spot on, because *Mr. Moto Takes a Chance* may be the weakest film in the entire series.

The movie has two basic flaws. The first flaw (a common problem with many of these Moto films) is that the audience knows that Moto is investigating something in Southeast Asia, but it does not know exactly what he is doing there. The audience never learns until very late in the feature what the movie is about and when it does learn, the subject is disappointing. The MacGuffin is a revolution in an out-of-the-way place known as Tong Moi, located so far from the United States and so insignificant that it could have no true effect on American interests. Thus, throughout the film, the audience is not invested in Mr. Moto's activities.

Second, it is as dull as a movie can be. As a consequence of its weak storyline, not much happens in the picture until the very end. Surprisingly, though, the film has little obvious padding. There is of course the expected comedy relief, this time by newsreel cameramen Marty Weston and Chick Davis, but they never seem obtrusive or annoying. (They are also not very funny but that is another matter.) In addition, the filmmakers incorporate excessive stock footage of jungle life into the picture, sometimes making the film seem more like a Tarzan movie than a Moto feature. Nevertheless, the archive footage comes in small spurts, so it is not all that bothersome. Instead, the tedious nature of the film comes from an intrinsically lackluster plot, hardly ameliorated by some boring diversions into uninteresting subplots.

Famous flyer Victoria Mason, on an around-the-world trip, deliberately crashes her plane near the kingdom of Tong Moi in Southeast Asia, by pretending that the plane is on fire. Mr. Moto is coincidentally leading an archaeological dig in the same part of the world, although presumably that is a cover for something else that he is doing there. It takes some time for the audience to be told that Moto, on behalf of an unnamed government, is investigating a potential revolution in Tong Moi. Moto eventually discovers a hidden cache of explosives in a secret room below the temple of Tong Moi. With the help of Mason, who is also a spy on the side of right, Moto prevents the revolution by the local priest Bokor and his men. However, Rajah Ali then arrives and attempts to take over the revolution started by Bokor. With the help of the explosives, Moto is able to stop Ali's plans and save Mason and others from a deadly fate.

That is the entire plot of *Mr. Moto Takes a Chance*. If that is all there were to the film, it would probably fill only about fifteen minutes of screen time. To complete the allotted running time of the feature, there are the side stories of Ali's favorite wife apparently dying from simply having her picture taken for the newsreel, the attempted execution of the newsreel cameramen, Moto saving them by appearing as an old wise man in the temple, the romance between one of the cameramen and Victoria, and the rajah's dinner with local entertainment. Little of these frolics and detours move the story forward and all of them are quite boring.

Then there are the totally inexplicable parts of the storyline. Victoria Mason eventually turns out to be a spy, apparently working for the United States government. How many spies would go on an airplane trip around the world, with the great publicity that the story will have, blowing any cover that she might need on her next mission? Boker is a devious revolutionary, very willing to knife his munitions dealer in the back, yet he is afraid of Moto when he is disguised as a mystic-powered local elder. Every time one of Boker's men tries to kill Moto or the other foreigners, whether by poison darts or thrown knives, even at close range, they always miss. Despite the disguise as an archaeologist, Moto apparently always knew exactly where the munitions were hidden, because he finally goes right to them without hesitation.

Of course, almost any film has some interest and so does *Mr. Moto Takes a Chance*, with Moto being once again a particularly violent 1930s hero, killing at least three people at close range. Also, there is a clever plot device of the rajah killing all of the carrier pigeons that Moto uses to communicate with the outside world, unknowingly leaving Moto on his own to deal with the evildoers. The finale, with Moto's group fighting Bokor's group which is fighting the rajah's gang, with the munitions dealers also involved, may be unique in this type of film, although the lack of music in these scenes (as well as in the rest of the film) dampens the effect. None of these is enough to solve the problems with *Mr. Moto Takes a Chance*, a deadly dull film with an unconvincing plot.

## *Mysterious Mr. Moto* (1938)

*Mysterious Mr. Moto* is a solid entry in the not always solid Mr. Moto series. The film has a particularly evil group of villains, a plot which is sparked by several action sequences, and some fascinating interludes at a London tavern.

Paul Brissac, a Frenchman soon to be identified as a member of the League of Assassins, and a disguised Mr. Moto escape from Devil's Island. They are chased through the woods by prison guards and their dogs, finally fleeing in a hidden canoe. The two make their way to London where Moto signs on as the houseboy for Brissac, so that he can accomplish his secret mission of identifying the leader of the League of Assassins and the identity of its next intended victim. Moto soon learns that the target is Prague steel magnate Anton Darvak, a pacifist who has refused to sell the formula for a new type of steel to armament manufacturers. Moto saves Darvak from a certain death from a falling chandelier at the Coventry Galleries, instead tricking the leader of the League of Assassins into being killed in his own trap.

The storyline does not make a lot of sense but those difficulties are papered over by the action sequences. In addition to the exciting opening, there is the killing of a man by a lorry backing over him, a rousing and well-staged fight at a tavern, Moto taking on three men in a street fight and multiple opponents in another fight, a car chase, and Moto jumping from a high building ledge onto a padded wagon below. Even after the incident of the falling chandelier which should have been the conclusion of the film, a shootout and another fight at the art gallery still remain. There is probably more action in *Mysterious Mr. Moto* than in all of the Charlie Chan films of the same era put together.

One of the recurring motifs of *Mysterious Mr. Moto* is the musical clue that the villains use when they are about to start trouble, played in succession by an organ grinder, an accordion player, a violinist and a small orchestra. In addition to its uniqueness, the musical theme adds to the tension of the story, alerting the audience that significant trouble is upcoming. It is a clever suspense device.

For a B–movie, the scenes at the Blue Peter tavern, where the members of the League often gather, are striking. For plot purposes, it would have been sufficient to have employed only a few extras at the tavern. Instead, the pub is crammed with extras and filled with interesting vignettes, such as a man being tossed out of the bar just as Moto reaches the entrance, Moto being over-charged for his drinks, a woman selling flowers and using the proceeds to buy a drink, a man speaking and singing a song to the accompaniment of an accordion, a heavyset man making advances to a short ugly woman who slaps him, and an upper-class couple slumming in the pub to drink in some of the local color. While important plot developments do take place at the Blue Peter, the strength of the pub scenes comes from the variety of incidents that occur there and the nuanced and detailed evocation of the atmosphere of a typical British pub. These are surprising sequences for a low-budget film.

As to the identity of the head of the League of Assassins, few mystery fans will fail to guess that Darvak's friend David Scott-Frensham, played by Erik Rhodes in his usual style as an eccentric lightweight (see his performances in the Fred Astaire-Ginger Rogers films), is that mysterious person. This character has no reason to be in the film unless he is the secret leader of the villains. At least the movie gives a clue to his secret identity. He advises Moto that in order to protect Darvak, he has brought in two men from Scotland Yard. The viewer, however, can easily determine that David's two operatives are not officers of the law.

The conclusion of the film is particularly brutal, as Moto tricks David into his own trap, having him killed by the chandelier cut by Brissac in an attempt to kill Darvak. Nevertheless, it is not a surprising development to the seasoned Moto film fan, as Moto has often permanently dispatched his enemies in prior films without a hint of regret. Indeed, it is that mean streak in Moto that makes these films stand out, even when the storylines are not that persuasive. In *Mysterious Mr. Moto*, it is also the action sequences and the tavern scenes that make this one of the best of the Moto films.

## *Mr. Moto's Last Warning* (1939)

Without a doubt, the Mr. Moto films are B–movies but within that context, *Mr. Moto's Last Warning* has an outstanding cast. First and foremost, of course, is Peter Lorre as Mr. Moto. Giving his usual understated but then surprisingly violent performance, Lorre is always at the center of this feature, even though he has limited screen time. Lorre was a major character actor and sometimes star of many excellent films, both before and after he starred in the Moto series.

The head villain is Fabian, played by Ricardo Cortez. Cortez had been a leading man in Hollywood in the early 1930s, having previously played Sam Spade and Perry Mason. He makes an easy transition into playing the main heavy in this film, always in control of his henchmen yet displaying an aura of sophistication. When it comes to creating an appearance of sophistication, the master of that is George Sanders, here playing another villain, Eric Norvel, hiding behind his own air of refinement to obtain information from others. That same year, Sanders would become well-known playing the lead in the Saint mystery series.

Then there is John Carradine, obvious fake beard and all, playing an undercover British agent, and Robert Coote in an early screen role playing a "silly ass Englishman," much like Algy from the Bulldog Drummond movies. The one performance in the film that is a little too much is that of E.E. Clive playing the English general who assists Mr. Moto. Clive plays the part as an extremely broad caricature of an upper-class Englishman, amusing but not realistic.

Thus, a lot of the fun of *Mr. Moto's Last Warning* is in the actors and their performances but the plot is not bad either. Moto is in Egypt to prevent a spy ring from disrupting the peaceful relations between England and France by blowing up the French fleet as it steams through Port Said in the Suez Canal. Moto believes that the gang is led by Fabian, the ventriloquist at the local theater. Other members of the gang are Eric Norvel, who is trying to trick the admiral's wife into disclosing information about the movements of the fleet, and Danforth, a British secret agent who has wormed his way into Fabian's gang. After two murders by the villains and the attempted murder of Moto on two occasions, Moto finally saves the fleet and has the gang either captured or killed

The plot is thin and Moto only conducts a very limited investigation into the imminent sabotage of the French fleet. Much of the film concentrates on the villains, with an interesting setup as Norvel worms his way into the affections of the admiral's wife for devious reasons, Fabian being a ventriloquist with an aggressive wooden dummy allowing him to legitimately remain in Egypt while hatching his plot, Fabian finding that his gang member Danforth is really a British secret agent and having him killed, and then the villains putting explosives into Moto's room in an assassination attempt. Moto is actually off-screen for much of the film, yet the scenes without him are some of the strongest scenes in the film, having a spy vs. spy quality that is not often found in this type of feature.

Even after viewing five of these films, the violence in the Moto series is always surprising, given the time period in which they were produced. An agent masquerading as Moto is killed by Norvel, Danforth is cruelly left at the bottom of the sea by Fabian in a diving bell with no oxygen, and Norvel is similarly left at the bottom of the ocean by Moto when he cracks the shell of Norvel's diving helmet, ensuring a second death by suffocation. There are also a couple of good fights, with Moto once again displaying his judo skills.

So, while the plot of the movie may be thin, that deficiency is more than made up for by the performances and the action sequences. The Moto series seemed to improve as it went on and *Mr. Moto's Last Warning* is an example of that improvement.

As an aside, on two occasions, when the program for the theater in which Fabian performs is shown to the viewer, *Charlie Chan at Monte Carlo* with Warner Oland is listed as the film being played that night. This was a clever plug since fans of the Mr. Moto films were probably also fans of the Charlie Chan films.

## *Mr. Moto in Danger Island* (1939)

*Mr. Moto in Danger Island* (sometimes called simply *Danger Island*) is not a bad film. It is just that it is filled with the clichés of the genre, and with nothing innovative or intriguing in the storyline, there is scant reason for mystery movie fans to insert their copy into the DVD player for repeat performances.

This time out Mr. Moto, along with his ad hoc companion, wrestler Twister McGurk, is investigating diamond smuggling on the dangerous island of Puerto Rico. Moto is replacing the prior investigator, Graham, who was murdered on the island. Moto suspects that a mole among the governor's friends is the head of the smugglers, a view that is confirmed when the governor is murdered. Moto determines that the smugglers are using a hidden swamp on the island as their base of operations. After a police raid on the swamp, Moto tricks the head of the smugglers into revealing his identity.

Moto's investigative techniques here are unconventional, at best. As the boat upon which he is traveling approaches Puerto Rico, Moto pretends that he is experiencing an attack of appendicitis and that he will need an emergency operation once he reaches shore. This is all a ruse to trap the mole in the governor's inner circle by causing a kidnap attempt on Moto, which seems to be a very inefficient way of outing the villain. In fact, the information is dispensed so late to the potential suspects that none could have arranged the kidnapping of Moto, so the trick could never have been successful, which it is not. Indeed, the

Commissioner Gordon (Richard Lane), on the right, holds a letter accusing Mr. Moto (Peter Lorre, center), of being an imposter as Lieutenant George Bentley (Robert Lowery), in the rear, looks on, in *Mr. Moto in Danger Island* (1939). It is easy to determine that the comic relief in this film is incompetent professional wrestler Twister McGurk (Warren Hymer), on the left.

prime result of this stunt is that Moto and Twister are almost killed. The whole ploy is just a bad idea. One hopes that this type of trap is not included in the manual for whatever profession Moto is engaged in for this film.

Later, Moto has a letter written to Commissioner Gordon, exposing Moto as a fraud. The theory here is that Moto will be arrested, can escape, meet up with the real villains who will now think he is one of them and then garner some information about the smuggling operations. This escapade assumes that Moto will be able to escape from the police, escape the bullets of the police who are chasing him all over the island and then gain the confidence of the villains. What it really leads to is Moto and McGurk almost being killed again. That manual of Moto's really needs to be revised as soon as possible!

As to the clichés, one is Warren Hymer as incompetent wrestler Twister McGurk. Mr. Moto does not have any sons so McGurk is inserted into the storyline as the comic relief, under the misconception that every series mystery film requires a character solely for the purpose of providing laughs, however small they may be. In *Mr. Moto in Danger Island*, however, Mr. Moto's enthusiasm in having McGurk along on his adventure, for no apparent reason, undercuts Moto's seriousness and his aura of authority.

Another cliché occurs at the point in the film where the governor lets all of the suspects know that he will soon have an important meeting upstairs at the mansion with Major Castle, presumably to obtain information about the smugglers. As expected, once that occurs, the governor's life expectancy drops to just a few minutes; he is eliminated by a knife to the back.

Then there are the statements by Moto and the doctor at the island hospital that Captain Dahlen, a henchman of the smugglers who was shot while trying to escape, will be available to talk to Moto at eight that night, presumably to divulge important information about the smugglers. It is an obvious trap for the lead criminal who, on cue, throws a knife into Dahlen's body, resulting in the villain's immediate capture. No mystery fan will be the least surprised to find that Dahlen was already dead at the time Moto and the doctor made their announcements.

*Mr. Moto in Danger Island* sports an excellent cast of supporting actors. Two of the best of the mystery villains, Leon Ames and Douglass Dumbrille, are on board, as is Richard Lane, soon to be a regular in the Boston Blackie series, and Jean Hersholt, best known for the Academy Award named after him. Another positive is that there are also two good clues to the head smuggler-murderer, one when he takes charge of the smuggled diamonds that have been found by Major Castle's daughter and another when he shoots Dahlen during the escape from the swamp, clearly an attempt to eliminate anyone who can turn on him. It is always nice to have a few legitimate clues to the identity of a villain during a film.

However, the Moto films are supposed to be about international intrigue in exotic locations, so why is there not even a little stock footage of the real Puerto Rico and why is there not even one Hispanic person in the film? And what is it with the English-language newspapers spelling "Puerto Rico" as "Porto Rico"? This lack of attention to detail, with all of the other problems, makes *Mr. Moto in Danger Island* a disappointment.

*Note on the Source Material*: John W. Vandercook was a London-born American writer whose works included four mystery novels set in exotic locations that Vandercook explored in his younger days, such as Fiji and New Guinea. The hero of the novels was Bertram Lynch, an investigator for the League of Nations who was accompanied by Robert Deane, whom he met on board ship in the first book in the series, 1933's *Murder in Trinidad*. Deane also narrates the stories in the first person.

*Murder in Trinidad* was the basis for three movies. The first, produced at Fox in 1934, had the same title. The middle film was *Mr. Moto in Danger Island* (1939), from 20th Century–Fox. The third was *The Caribbean Mystery* (1945), also produced at 20th Century–Fox. The three films seem to have more in common with each other than with the book, each ending with the lead villain being tricked into revealing himself when he tries to kill a person who was already dead.

The novel concerns opium smuggling in Trinidad. There are some surface similarities between the novel and the Mr. Moto film, including smugglers using a swamp as their hideout, Lynch's predecessor on the island being murdered, Lynch and Deane setting themselves up as criminals so that they can intermingle with the smugglers in their swamp hideout, and Major Cassel and his daughter also being trapped in the swamp. Cassel was accused of murdering the governor on the island, by stabbing him in the back, similar to the incident in the film.

However, despite these many similarities, the two works are substantially different. The island swamp hideout of the villains in the book is a significant setting for the story, including the almost impossible approach thereto. Many characters and incidents were not carried over from the book to the movie, Major Cassel's alleged crime took place many years before the novel begins, the identity of the leader of the smugglers is different and the ending of the movie, with the trap set at the hospital, is original to the movie. Oh, and Twister McGurk is not a character in the novel. While *Mr. Moto in Danger Island* is the only film in the Moto series that was truly based on a novel, much of the film script is original.

## *Mr. Moto Takes a Vacation* (1939)

This last film in the Mr. Moto series is one of the best. It has a unique plot, good production values, good comic relief and excellent direction, all of which belie its B–movie status.

Archaeologist Howard Stevens discovers the crown of the queen of Sheba in a dig in Egypt. Not only does the crown have historical significance, valuable jewels adorn it. Moto, who has an interest in capturing the long-thought-dead jewel thief Metaxa, follows the crown on its journey by boat from Egypt to Honolulu and then on to San Francisco, where the artifact is to be put on display at the Fremont Museum. Despite the many security precautions at the museum, Metaxa almost absconds with it, but he is thwarted at the last moment by the mental acuity and physical fighting skills of Mr. Moto.

That short summary of the plot makes the storyline seem mundane and in many ways it is. What makes it interesting is that there are three different villains after the crown and when one villain is disposed of, the next one comes to the fore. By far the most aggressive of the villains is small-time hood Joe Rubia, who seems to work for jeweler David Perez. Perez has decreed that Moto must be eliminated and therefore much of the film concerns Rubia's attempts to accomplish that feat. However, when Rubia later believes that Perez is double-crossing him, he kills Perez. At the direction of Mr. Moto, Rubia and his partner are then captured as they try to break into the museum. The crown is now completely safe.

But no, fake insurance investigator Paul Borodoff is already in the museum and is about to steal the antique. He is prevented from doing so by Moto, and Mextaxa is finally captured. But no, Borodoff is not Mextaxa and so there is one more surprise villain for Moto to uncover. Thus, by employing three separate villains on the same quest and operating at the same time, *Mr. Moto Takes a Vacation* does display some ingenuity in its storyline.

Unfortunately, the viewer is well aware, long before Mr. Moto is, that Hendrik Manderson, the philanthropist who has financed the expedition to Egypt and is always at the museum, is actually Mextaxa. Manderson is just too unlikely a suspect and his character is portrayed just a little too eccentrically for him to be anyone other than the main villain. Nevertheless, because of the casting, there is a neat trick played on the viewer, since the curator of the museum, Professor Hildebrand, is also a suspect. Hildebrand is played by veteran B–movie villain Lionel Atwill, and so the viewer may have some lingering doubts as to the true identity of Mextaxa, despite all the indications pointing to Manderson.

Moto's comic sidekick, Archie Featherstone, may not be to everyone's taste but he surely garners some laughs. He is introduced walking on the deck of a ship, accidentally hitting people with his paddle, knocking the ship's steward down and causing a real ruckus. When he sees Mr. Moto, he calls him by his real name in the loudest of voices, undercutting Moto's attempts to travel incognito. It is all quite amusing. Featherstone starts to wear on the viewer as the film goes on, but at least he is part of the plot and not some irrelevant comic relief thrown into the film to burn up some screen time.

In terms of production values and direction, *Mr. Moto Takes a Vacation* emphasizes setting and mood. There are early film noir techniques, such as the conversations between the crooks in a shadowy room lit only by a single lamp, or chases down dark streets with the participants' huge shadows on buildings. There is the stylized killing of Manderson's servant Mr. Wong, who enters a Chinese restaurant and takes a seat at a table surrounded by curtains and beads while a furtive figure takes a seat in the immediately adjacent area, allowing a knife thrust into Wong through the curtains and the beads. Then there are those outdoors scenes which are shot in the dark in a driving rain, adding just a little more apprehension to the mood of the film.

While the rain is an important element of the plot (Mextaxa is caught, in part, by the wet footprints he leaves on the museum floor), there is no plot necessity to employ a hard rain which extended over many of the movie's scenes. The sole purpose of the driving rain is to provide some added atmosphere. This type of attention to detail in the production of the film is what makes *Mr. Moto Takes a Vacation* stand out from many of the other B–mystery films of the era. It is a fitting conclusion to the Mr. Moto series.

## Afterwards

After the end of the Moto book series in 1942, John P. Marquand continued writing novels about society and the upper classes, similar in concept to *The Late George Apley*. After a long hiatus, he wrote one more Moto novel, *Right You Are, Mr. Moto*, also called *Stopover: Tokyo*, which was published in 1957 after being serialized in *The Saturday Evening Post*.

In that work, an older Mr. Moto helps two American agents prevent a Communist takeover of Japan. Marquand died of a heart attack on July 16, 1960, in Newburyport, Massachusetts.

*Right You Are, Mr. Moto* was made into a movie, *Stopover Tokyo* (1957), but Moto was not a character in the film. In the James Bond era of the 1960s, Moto returned to the screen one more time in *The Return of Mr. Moto* (1965), in which Moto was an Interpol agent on the trail of international criminals. Moto was played by Henry Silva.

Mr. Moto came to the radio in May 1951 in a 23–episode NBC series which ran until October 1951. In terms of oldtime radio, this was very late in the cycle to be introducing a new crime series, as the genre was being taken over by television by that time. The series, titled *Mr. I.A. Moto*, starred James Monk as the inscrutable, crafty and courageous international agent extraordinaire. There were never any television shows about the character.

After the conclusion of the Moto series, Peter Lorre constantly worked in films, many of which were mysteries. He had significant supporting roles, such as Joel Cairo in *The Maltese Falcon* (1941) and Ugarte in *Casablanca* (1942). In the 1960s, Lorre turned to horror films, appearing in a trio of features with Vincent Price. Lorre passed away on March 23, 1964.

# 15

# Bill Crane
## *The Private Detective*

Starting in 1928 and continuing for over 60 years, Doubleday, the famous publishing house, released many of its mystery novels under the "Crime Club" imprint. Each book had the Crime Club symbol on its cover — the drawing of a man with a gun made out of the five letters which spelled the word "Crime." A number of well-known mystery novels had their first United States publications under the Crime Club imprint, including many written by Edgar Wallace and books from the Saint, Bulldog Drummond and Fu Manchu series.

An imprint was one method for a publisher to give a special status to some of its mystery novels. The use of an imprint was a common practice of mystery publishers of the era. Other well-known mystery imprints were the Red Badge Mysteries (Dodd Mead), Cock Robin Mysteries (Macmillan), Inner Sanctum (Simon and Schuster), and Rinehart Suspense Novels (Holt).

In 1937, Universal entered into an arrangement with Doubleday to select up to four Crime Club books per year for production as mystery movies. The films were produced by Irving Starr under the auspices of Crime Club Productions, Inc., and were released through Universal. In all, there were eight movies produced, but within that group there was only one mystery series: the three Bill Crane movies based on novels by Jonathan Latimer and starring Preston Foster.

## BACKGROUND

### The Books

Jonathan Latimer was born in Chicago in 1906. After graduating from Knox College in Illinois in 1929, he worked on two newspapers in his hometown before turning to the writing of fiction. Latimer's main claim to fame in print mysteries is his Bill Crane series, which is comprised of only five novels. Although usually referred to as the Bill Crane series, probably because of the movie mysteries about the character, the detective is referred to as William Crane throughout the novels. The first Crane book was *Murder in the Madhouse*, published in 1935, and the last was *Red Gardenias*, published in 1939. Although Crane's adventures usually take place in Latimer's home town of Chicago, Crane is actually employed by Colonel Black's detective agency, which is based in New York. Crane is aided in his investigations by colleagues Tom O'Malley and Doc Williams. Drinking is a fixture in the

Crane novels, leading critic William L. DeAndrea to see Crane as a bridge between Dashiell Hammett's Nick and Nora Charles and Craig Rice's John J. Malone.

Despite the film series based on his mystery novels, Latimer is best known today for his screenplays and teleplays for other mysteries. In 1939, just after the Bill Crane movie series ended, Latimer wrote the screenplay for *The Lone Wolf Spy Hunt*. He also wrote the scripts for several well-known mystery films such as *The Glass Key* (1942), based upon Dashiell Hammett's famous novel, *The Big Clock* (1948), based upon a well-known novel by Kenneth Fearing, and *Night Has a Thousand Eyes* (1948), based on Cornell Woolrich's suspense novel. In the 1950s, Latimer turned to television, writing for several mystery shows. He is most familiar to TV mystery fans for his work on *Perry Mason*, contributing numerous scripts to the long-running series.

## The Film Series

As noted above, Universal released three films about Bill Crane as part of its late 1930s Crime Club movie series. The first was *The Westland Case* (1937), in which Crane has only six days in which to find the necessary evidence to exonerate an innocent man who is headed to a date with the electric chair. The second was *The Lady in the Morgue* (1938), which involves a search for a woman's body which has disappeared from the morgue. In the final feature in the short series, *The Last Warning* (1938), Crane is called in to investigate blackmail but ends up solving a kidnapping and a murder.

Crane was played by Preston Foster in all three films. Foster was born in 1900 in New Jersey. He performed as a singer in opera and later as an actor on the Broadway stage, before he turned to films in 1929. Among his early work, Foster had supporting parts in significant films such as *The Last Mile* (1932), *I Am a Fugitive from a Chain Gang* (1932) and *The Informer* (1935). With the Bill Crane series, Foster received three of his few starring roles in Hollywood.

The other recurring role in the series was Doc Williams, Crane's assistant. The part was played by Frank Jenks in all three features. Jenks was born in 1902 in Des Moines, Iowa. During the 1920s, he was a song and dance man in vaudeville. In 1933, he moved to Hollywood, where he performed in numerous films, usually as a supporting player, such as a sarcastic reporter or policeman. The part of Doc Williams in the Bill Crane series was just such a role.

## THE FILMS

### *The Westland Case* (1937)

*The Westland Case* has a familiar set-up for a mystery movie. A man is days away from being executed for a murder he did not commit, and only one man can save him. Will there be enough time? This scenario can be found in *Charlie Chan in London* (1934) and many other films. The storyline is used so often because it is effective. The set-up brings a sense of urgency to a mystery movie.

In this case the incarcerated individual is Bob Westland, accused of murdering his estranged wife by shooting her with a rare type of gun. Westland is on Death Row with just six days left. He now hopes that he can be cleared because he has just received an anonymous note, claiming that the writer can provide an alibi for Westland for the night of the murder. Westland hires an attorney, Charlie Frazee, to help clear his name and Frazee, in turn, hires Bill Crane, a lazy but effective private detective. Crane determines that the writer of the anonymous note is Manny Grant, a small-time hood, but before Crane can talk to him, Grant is killed, gangster-style. Crane then learns that the bookkeeper of Westland's brokerage firm, Amos Sprague, has important information about the murder, but now Sprague is deliberately run down by a car. Undeterred, Crane continues to ferret out the clues, finally clearing Westland in the proverbial nick of time.

At the beginning of the film, the characterization of Bill Crane is off-putting. He is shown to be lazy and a lush. This is particularly disconcerting given that an apparently innocent man is scheduled to die in the electric chair in just a few days. One of Crane's ploys is to ask each of the friends of Bob Westland, one of whom is surely the real killer, to help in the investigation. That is an unlikely way to engender much faith in Crane's investigative competence, acuity or effort.

Even though Crane keeps pulling the pages off of a calendar on the wall of the warden's office to emphasize the fact that time is quickly running out, the film has little tension. The reason for the incongruity is the laid-back style of Crane and his tendencies to drink and sleep on the job. Another reason is that the viewer never really meets Bob Westland on a personal basis and thus there is no emotional attachment.

After a while, though, *The Westland Case* hooks the viewer. Assuming Westland is innocent, and that is a reasonable assumption on the part of the viewer, then *The Westland Case* has a clever locked room murder. There are only two keys to the death room, Westland's and his wife's, and his wife's key was found inside the locked murder room with the body. Then there is the fact that the murder bullet was fired by a rare war-time gun known as a Webley, and Westland owns such a gun, which is now missing. The only Webley that can be found is owned by Woodbury, a partner of Westland's, and Woodbury's gun is not the murder weapon. By the end of the movie, Crane has found another Webley at the bottom of the Chicago River and the bullets fired by a third one, the murder weapon, at a shooting range in Peoria. The intrigue of multiple guns, one of which is the murder weapon, is reminiscent of several of the Perry Mason novels by Erle Stanley Gardner.

Other puzzling aspects of *The Westland Case* are the fraudulent bonds in Westland's brokerage accounts, an incongruity in the time of the murder caused by the change in clocks to daylight savings time, a fake phone call to Westland on the night of the murder and tampered with telephone lines at a suspect's apartment. *The Westland Case* is an extremely complex murder mystery, which is a positive, but unfortunately there is simply not enough time in the short film to effectively work in all of the clues and events. Also, there is no way the viewer can figure out, on his own, the complicated chain of events of the night of the murder and the morning after. The film is therefore best viewed as a private detective procedural rather than a whodunit, and on that basis it works quite well.

The performances are excellent. Two deserve special mention. Clarence Wilson plays the attorney, Frazee, as an intense, frustrated, and yet romantic person. While Wilson overacts a little, he is always fun to watch. He also played an attorney in *The Case of the Black Cat* (1936) from the Perry Mason series, as well as in several other movies. Then there is Barbara Pepper playing Agatha Hogan, the new tenant of the apartment in which the killing occurred. The attractive blond plays the part as a petite version of Mae West. Pepper is attractive and funny and she is the focus of attention whenever she is on the screen.

*The Westland Case* grows on the viewer as it progresses. In the end, it is an intelligent mystery, something often hard to find in a B–mystery movie.

*Note on the Source Material*: Given its short length, *The Westland Case* is a surprisingly close adaptation of Jonathan Latimer's 1935 novel *Headed for a Hearse*. Even the character of Agatha Hogan, who would appear to be a typical screen concoction, comes from the novel (although her first name there is Myrna). So does Hogan's infatuation with Frazee, Westland's attorney (Finkelstein in the book). The film even uses some of the dialogue from the novel.

The differences between book and film highlight the differences between the two media. Latimer takes some time to introduce Bob Westland in his prison setting, and thus the reader does have more of an emotional attachment to the character than the movie viewer. Bill Crane drinks with great regularity in the novel, just as he does in the movie, but he is seldom lazy in the book and his indolent and sarcastic personality in the film is a screen concoction. On a superficial basis, that may make the film more interesting than the novel, but the novel is more realistic and focused. Also, while the film seems rushed, particularly at the end, as so many incidents plus Crane's character development must be squeezed into the film's short running time, the book is evenly paced, making it a good read. Both versions of the story are very entertaining mysteries, so if a viewer enjoys the film version, it is worth the effort to try to locate a copy of the book, which has been long out of print.

## *The Lady in the Morgue* (1938)

*The Lady in the Morgue* is the most complicated mystery in the Bill Crane series and, for that matter, one of the most complicated film mysteries of the 1930s. It is very difficult for the viewer to keep all of the characters separate or to keep up with the rush of events. Nevertheless, it's a fun movie to watch.

A surprising number of people are interested in the naked body of a lady now lying on a slab at the city morgue. It was found hanging from a hotel bathroom door, apparently a suicide. The woman had registered at the hotel as Alice Ross, but no one believes that is her real name. Wealthy Mrs. Courtland, who lives outside the city, believes the body may be that of her missing daughter Kathryn. She hires the Black detective agency, in the person of Bill Crane, to investigate. Gangsters Steve Collins and Frankie French believe that the dead lady is Arlene, Collins' wife, and for separate reasons, each wants to claim the body to bury it. Also involved is Chauncy Courtland, Kathryn's brother, who arrives at the morgue to try to determine the identity of the body. Before anyone can get a good look at the cadaver, the morgue attendant is killed and the body is stolen.

In addition to the multitude of suspects, there are a number of distinct mysteries being investigated. The first is the question of the identity of the corpse. The next is whether her death was murder or suicide. Finally, if it was murder, who committed the murder and was it the same person who killed the morgue attendant and then later, an employee at a mortuary? That is a lot of mystery to include in a 70–minute film.

Director Otis Garrett employs a number of techniques to move the story along. First, the antics of Bill Crane and Doc Williams from the first film in the series, *The Westland Case*, are substantially toned down. There is much less about drinking and sleeping in this film, giving more screen time to the actual tale. Garrett also moves between scenes with jump cuts, wipes, the next scene starting to appear in the middle of the shot from the prior scene and the like, giving the film a sense of speed and movement, even when there is a lot of talk. While these techniques are old-fashioned from today's perspective, they work quite well for *The Lady in the Morgue*.

Detective Bill Crane (Preston Foster) dances at a nightclub with one of the hostesses (actress unidentified) while looking for clues to the location of a missing body in *The Lady in the Morgue* (1938). The trumpet player, Sam Taylor (Roland Drew), will become important to the solution to the crimes.

There are also more adult-style scenes in *The Lady in the Morgue* than would be expected from this type of film. One is a party scene at a luxurious penthouse which involves a number of attractive but predatory females, out to get any wealthy man they can find. This scene has the feel of a pre–Code film. At the party Crane meets a woman who calls herself Kay Renshaw, a saucy blonde with a sharp wit and a titillating nature. Played by Barbara Pepper, she reminds one of Mae West, which is not that surprising since Pepper played a similar role in *The Westland Case*. Pepper appeared in over 100 films in a career that stretched over 30 years, but she never became a star. That is surprising because although there are a number of attractive women in *The Lady in the Morgue*, Pepper always stands out from the pack, even though she has a relatively small part.

As noted above, there are so many mysteries floating around in the film and so many disagreeable suspects that the film becomes overly confusing at times, particularly at the end. Nevertheless, the seasoned mystery fan will know that Chauncy Courtland, the only apparently good character in the film and the one who seems to be assisting Crane at times, will be one of the killers. There are good clues to his culpability, as explained by Crane at the end of the story. However, Courtland's murder of the morgue attendant was an accident; the other two murders were done deliberately by another character, providing an added climactic surprise.

As a result, the conclusion to *The Lady in the Morgue* is quite satisfactory for the true mystery fan. And, even though many of the earlier sections of the film are hard to follow, it is still fun to watch. *The Lady in the Morgue* is another good entry in the Bill Crane mystery series.

*Note on the Source Material*: *The Lady in the Morgue* was based upon Latimer's 1936 novel of the same name. Thus, the book involves the theft of a body known only as Alice Ross from the Chicago morgue, the murder of the morgue attendant and Crane's search for identity of Alice and for her killer. The complexity of the film is caused by the length of the novel, almost 300 pages, and the difficulties inherent in transferring a novel of that length into a film that lasts about one hour.

In Latimer's novels, Crane was often assisted by two other members of the Black detective agency, Tom O'Malley and Doc Williams. In *The Lady in the Morgue*, both help Crane. Consistent with the rest of the film series, only Doc Williams appears in the movie version.

There is a lot of fooling around with dead bodies in the novel, which was not included in the film's script. The film's strange penthouse party scene is inspired by a section of the book, but the film version is actually more ribald. That makes it even more surprising that the scene was included in a film which was released after the Production Code was in force.

## *The Last Warning* (1938)

Bill Crane and Doc Williams are back for their last screen adventure, this time called in by young John Essex to investigate a threatening note he received which was signed by "The Eye." The note refers to some unspecified debt of Essex's. Essex claims that he does not owe money to anyone. In fact, though, Essex owes a gambling debt to casino owner Steve Felson, so perhaps Felson is making the threat. More notes are found, some appearing as if by magic in locked rooms. John's sister Linda is then kidnapped and Felson is murdered. Lazy private investigator Bill Crane somehow finally catches on to the secrets behind the skullduggery at the Essex manor. He exposes the kidnappers and identifies Felson's murderer.

The first two films in the Bill Crane series were quite entertaining. By contrast, *The Last Warning* is simply awful. It does not have one redeeming feature. The problem with the film is one of attitude. From the beginning of the movie, Crane and Williams take nothing seriously, insulting everyone they see and seemingly being more interested in meeting young ladies than protecting the well-being of John Essex. Their demeanor toward the people who hired them raises the question as to how they ever obtain any clients. Private detectives in the real world would never behave as they do. Perhaps that is why it takes Crane and Williams so long to solve a fairly simple case. They are too busy making jokes to do a thorough investigation.

Although the mystery is uncomplicated, it still makes no sense. John Sussex has called Crane and Williams in for protection from the person writing the threatening notes and who also supposedly took a shot at Sussex, even though Sussex is the villain of the piece, writing the blackmail notes himself and signing them "The Eye." Since Sussex had no way of knowing in advance how incompetent Crane and Williams were, why call in private detectives when you are the one committing the crime? Of course, despite the illogic of Sussex calling in Crane and Williams, there are very few mystery fans who will not know that Sussex is, in fact, a blackmailer, kidnapper and killer all rolled into one. He is the only suspect who benefits from the whole criminal enterprise, there are no witnesses to the shot allegedly fired at him in conjunction with the first threatening note, most of the threatening notes are found by him, and he is the one person who clearly needs the ransom money. The only reason a viewer might hesitate to finger Sussex as the criminal is that the actor who plays him, Ray Parker, is so bad in the role that it might seem like piling on.

All of the acting in the film is unremarkable or worse, surprising because the inimitable E.E. Clive, who played Tenny in the Paramount Bulldog Drummond films, is in the cast. As smooth a performer as Clive was, in big parts and small, sometimes he took the part of an upper-class British gentleman to the extreme, making the character a caricature rather than a real person. That is what happens in *The Last Warning* as Clive overacts the part of Major Barclay to such an extent that he becomes a major irritant, not a humorous element of the film.

Then there are the mystery movie clichés. The first is a suspicious-looking butler, a classic red herring. Not surprisingly, even though the butler turns out to be a blackmailer, he is not the one Crane is seeking. Then there is the moment when one of the suspects, Carla Rodriguez, tells Crane she has something important to tell him. Is there any viewer who does not expect that Carla will be killed before she reveals her secret to Crane? Not surprisingly, later that evening, Carla is permanently dispatched with a knife to the back.

At the end of the film, as is customary, Crane fingers the villain and gives an explanation of the crimes committed during the movie. His account turns out to be unconvincing in every way. That is not surprising, however, since Crane has done little detective work, seemingly sleepwalking his way through most of the movie. Of course, Crane may have been sleepwalking because the film is so dull. Surely, much of the audience is sleeping right along with him.

*The Last Warning* is a complete waste of time. It is not surprising that there were no subsequent Bill Crane films. If a mystery fan wants to see a good Bill Crane movie, the first two films in the series are the only choices.

*Note on the Source Material*: *The Last Warning* was based on Latimer's 1938 novel *The Dead Don't Care*. Many of the problems with the film arise from the novel. Crane and his associate are particularly indolent in the novel, primarily preoccupied with drinking, dames and swimming. One character, Imago Paraguay, tells Crane that she has something important to tell him later that night and, of course, she ends up dead, although by poisoning, not by a stabbing as in the film. Penn Essex hires the private detectives, even though he is the villain, an anomaly which is never explained in the novel.

In other ways, *The Dead Don't Care* is better than the film version, with Camelia, the sister of Penn Essex, not involved in her own kidnapping, and the kidnapping actually being carried out by some thugs who put Camelia at real risk, leading to an exciting and suspenseful climax. The key scene in *The Dead Don't Care* is the sequence when Essex delivers the ransom money to the drop site as the police and Crane watch, only to discover later that the money has disappeared. While this scene also appears in *The Last Warning*, with the same surprising conclusion, it is lost among all of the irrelevant moments in the film. In essence, the filmmakers took a fairly good crime novel and, by emphasizing its comedy attitude to the detriment of its clever crime moments, turned out a very disappointing film.

## Afterwards

Although Jonathan Latimer concentrated on screenwriting after the conclusion of the Bill Crane movie series, he did publish a few more crime novels. He died in 1983.

Some of the Crime Club mysteries were dramatized on CBS's *The Eno Crime Club*, a mystery series that ran from February 9, 1931, until December 21, 1932. The Crime Club next received its own show, which ran on the Mutual Broadcasting System from December 2, 1946, to October 16, 1947. These shows were supposed to be adaptations of Crime Club novels but, in fact, about half of the scripts were original to the radio show. Apparently none of the Bill Crane novels were adapted for either radio show. There were no television shows about the private detective.

After the Bill Crane series ended, Preston Foster continued to work steadily in films. Among his crime roles were the title part in *Roger Touhy, Gangster* (1944) and the mastermind behind an armored car robbery in *Kansas City Confidential* (1952). In the 1950s, he turned to work in television and also returned to his musical roots, composing several popular songs. He passed away in 1970.

Similarly, Frank Jenks was quite busy during his long Hollywood career. In 1947, he appeared in two Philo Vance movies playing Ernie Clark, a part that is indistinguishable from the Doc Williams character in the Bill Crane series. Jenks then made a successful transition to television, working steadily in the medium from 1950 until his death in 1962.

# 16

# Joel and Garda Sloane
## *The Husband and Wife Team*

With the success of *The Thin Man* (1934) starring William Powell and Myrna Loy, other screen mysteries were created which attempted to display an adult and sophisticated relationship between the main detective and his love interest. For example, there was *Star of Midnight* (1935) starring Powell and Ginger Rogers, *The Case of the Lucky Legs* (1935) with Warren William and Genevieve Tobin (the third Perry Mason movie), and *The Ex-Mrs. Bradford* (1936) starring Powell and Jean Arthur. The most successful knockoff of *The Thin Man*, however, was *Fast Company* (1938), featuring amateur detective Joel Sloane and his wife Garda. The film was so popular that it quickly spawned two sequels, *Fast and Loose* and *Fast and Furious*, both from 1939.

## BACKGROUND

### The Novel

Born in New York City in 1907, Harry Kurnitz grew up in Philadelphia, attending the University of Pennsylvania. In 1930, he became a book and music reviewer for the *Philadelphia Record*. While there, he began writing fiction in his spare time.

Under the pseudonym Marco Page, Kurnitz wrote several mystery novels, the first of which was *Fast Company* (1937), about rare book seller Joel Glass and his wife, Garda. Glass' bookselling business was not very successful so he worked on the side for an insurance company, locating rare books which had been stolen. When successful, Glass received a finder's fee from the insurance company. In *Fast Company*, Glass' sideline led him to becoming involved in the investigation of the murder of Abe Selig, also a rare bookseller, but one who was not above selling stolen and/or forged books.

*Fast Company* was the only book Kurnitz wrote about Joel and Garda Glass. However, when *Fast Company* was bought by MGM, Kurnitz came on board as a screenwriter, receiving a credit under the name Marco Page. Kurnitz remained as a screenwriter for the two sequels to *Fast Company*, although he received credit in those movies under his real name. After the short film series ended, Kurnitz stayed in Hollywood and, during his long writing career there, contributed to the screenplays for over 40 films, including two of the Thin Man movies and *Witness for the Prosecution* (1957). He also wrote a number of popular Broadway plays, such as the musical *The Girl Who Came to Supper*, for which he was nominated for a Tony award in 1964, along with Noël Coward, who wrote the music and the lyrics.

## The Film Series

When *Fast Company* was brought to the screen in 1938, the name of the husband-and-wife team was changed to Joel and Garda Sloane. Sloane is still, however, a rare bookseller who investigates crimes because of his knowledge of rare books. In *Fast Company*, the main crime that Sloane investigates is the murder of dishonest bookseller Otto Brockler, another name change from the novel.

*Fast Company* starred Melvyn Douglas (1901–81) as Joel Sloane. Born in Macon, Georgia, he began appearing on the stage in 1919, generally performing with stock companies, until he made his Broadway debut in 1928. Douglas' debut in films was in the 1931 feature *Tonight or Never*. Douglas appeared in many prestigious films over the years, including *Ninotchka* (1939) and *I Never Sang for My Father* (1970). He won Oscars for roles in *Hud* (1963) and *Being There* (1979). For mystery fans, he played the famous cracksman in *The Lone Wolf Returns* (1935) and then played another famous cracksman in the title role in *Arsène Lupin Returns* (1938). Douglas also starred in *Steve Randall*, a 13–episode television series about a lawyer turned private eye which first aired in 1952.

Florence Rice, who played Garda Sloane, is virtually unknown today. The daughter of the famous sportswriter Grantland Rice, she was born in 1907 in Cleveland, Ohio. She came to Hollywood in the early 1930s and for a decade or so worked constantly. For mystery fans, she played a role similar to Garda Sloane in *Mr. District Attorney* (1941). Rice passed away in 1974.

The second movie in the series was *Fast and Loose* (1939). It involves a forged Shakespearean manuscript and three murders. Two new performers were brought in to play the lead roles.

Robert Montgomery, who played Joel Sloane, was born in New York in 1904, first appeared on Broadway in 1924 and then, when he received a contract from MGM, moved to Hollywood in 1929. In the early 1930s, he became one of MGM's most popular leading men, usually performing in breezy, sophisticated comedies, often co-starring with the studio's top female stars such as Norma Shearer, Joan Crawford, and Greta Garbo. He received Academy Award nominations for his roles as a psychotic killer in *Night Must Fall* (1937) and as a boxer who died before his time in *Here Comes Mr. Jordan* (1941). In the mystery field, he is best known for directing and starring in *Lady in the Lake* (1947), the adaptation of Raymond Chandler's novel, shot entirely from the point of view of the detective, Philip Marlowe, and *Ride the Pink Horse* (1947), the adaptation of Dorothy B. Hughes' novel about a war veteran who tangles with a gangster in a small New Mexico town. Montgomery died in 1981.

Rosalind Russell (1907–1976) played Garda Sloane. Russell, who was born in Connecticut, began appearing on the stage in the early 1920s. She began her screen career in 1934, usually playing comedy roles, although she did receive dramatic parts from time to time. Her career took off with her portrayal of reporter Hildy Johnson in *His Girl Friday* (1940). Over the course of her career, Russell received four Academy Award nominations for Best Actress, including one for *Auntie Mame* (1958), a role she originated on Broadway. *Fast and Loose* is one of five films in which she performed with Robert Montgomery. Garda Sloane was Russell's only significant role in the mystery field, although she did appear in the Philo Vance mystery *The Casino Murder Case* (1935).

The last film in the Joel and Garda Sloane series was *Fast and Furious* (1939), perhaps an apropos title since the three films in the series were released in just two years. The story

After the murder of book dealer Otto Brockler, Joel Sloane (Melvyn Douglas) questions one of the suspects, Brockler's secretary Julia Thorne (Claire Dodd), in *Fast Company* (1938).

involves a murder in a beach town and is unrelated to the rare book business. Once again, MGM brought in two new performers for the lead roles.

Franchot Tone, who played Joel Sloane, was born in 1905 in Niagara Falls, New York, and began appearing in films in 1932. Throughout the 1930s, he generally had supporting roles in major films and lead roles in minor films. He is best remembered for his performance as one of the sailors on Captain Bligh's ship in *Mutiny on the Bounty* (1935), for which he received an Oscar nomination for Best Actor. Tone did not appear in many significant mystery movies, one exception being *Phantom Lady* (1944), directed by Robert Siodmak, in which Tone played a villainous role. During the 1940s, Tone had few significant film parts and in the 1950s and 1960s, his work was generally limited to the stage and television, except for important character parts such as playing the president of the United States in *Advise and Consent* (1962). Tone died in 1968.

Ann Sothern (1909–2001) was the third Garda Sloane of the short film series. She was born in North Dakota and, after appearing in musicals on Broadway and bit parts in films, she obtained regular work in Hollywood in the 1930s. She generally appeared in comedies and musicals; in the Maisie movie series, a set of ten movies released by MGM starting in 1939, she played a showgirl who travels the world having adventures and romances. Sothern was later in two successful television programs, *Private Secretary* (1953–57) and *The Ann Sothern Show* (1958–61). For her last film performance, in *The Whales of August* (1987), she received an Academy Award nomination for Best Supporting Actress. Other than *Fast and Furious*, Sothern made no significant appearances in mystery movies.

## The Films

### *Fast Company* (1938)

While *Fast Company* was based on a mystery novel written by Marco Page, the influence of *The Thin Man* (1934) cannot be overlooked. Just as in *The Thin Man*, the principals are a very loving couple who exchange witty dialogue with each other and third parties throughout the day. They become involved in murder and other crime investigations. They alternately exasperate the police and then help the police solve the mystery. However, there is one clear difference between the two movies. There is little emphasis on drinking in *Fast Company*, a mainstay of *The Thin Man*.

As *Fast Company* opens, Ned Morgan has just been released from jail after serving a two-year term for stealing valuable rare books from dealer Otto Brockler. Ned is in love with Brockler's daughter Leah, and Leah is now hoping to find a job for the newly released convict. Garda Sloane asks her husband Joel, another bookseller, to help Ned in his quest for a new job. Before Joel can do so, Ned attempts to reconcile with Brockler on his own, leading to a nasty exchange between the two. Thereafter, when Joel intercedes with Brockler on behalf of Ned, he is turned down cold. In each case, Brockler threatens to send Ned back to jail, ending with, "I can do it, too."

To the chagrin of no one, later that night, Brockler is discovered with his skull smashed in. While Ned is the obvious suspect, there are plenty of other people who could have committed the crime. Two of Brockler's partners in the stolen and forged book business are Eli Bannerman, a sophisticated crook, and Sydney Wheeler, a neurotic book forger. Brockler's secretary, Julia Thorne, is also a prime suspect. Julia probably has some involvement in Brockler's illegal schemes because, as Garda notices, she wears very expensive jewelry and clothing for a mere secretary. After many plot machinations, including the sudden murder of Wheeler by Bannerman and the capture of the Sloanes by the villains, Joel unmasks the killer of Brockler and also has Bannerman arrested for his book-dealing crimes.

*Fast Company* may have more fascinating male villains than any other movie, and each is played by a wonderful character actor. George Zucco plays Otto Brockler, the first person murdered in the film. Zucco usually played characters whom the audience wanted to hate, and Brockler is just such a part. Brockler, who deals in stolen books, has apparently framed an innocent man into a two-year prison term and now threatens to do it again, even over the protests of his daughter who is in love with that man. How evil can one person be? Zucco is always convincingly wicked in the role and few people are upset when his character is murdered.

Louis Calhern plays Elias Bannerman, a man who tries to gyp his assistant Wheeler out of his fair share of their criminal spoils and then later decides to kill him anyway. Bannerman also hires a hit man to shoot Joel Sloane in the back. Calhern often played sophisticated villains in films and Bannerman is just the type of part that he always performed in a compelling manner. Sometimes, the slime seems to ooze out of his unctuous pores.

Dwight Frye was a horror film icon with a strong résumé in film mysteries also, such as playing Wilmer in the original *The Maltese Falcon* (1931). Frye was adept at playing strange, hyperactive characters and he nails the part of book forger Sidney Wheeler. The very large Nat Pendleton, who sometimes played a policeman in mystery films, here plays hit man Paul Terison with his usual blend of bullying and comedy. It is a joy to watch four great character actors come together for one film and create a collective atmosphere of evil and villainy.

There is one more villain in the piece and that is Brockler's secretary, Julia Thorne, played by the lovely Claire Dodd. The role is partly written as a blond femme fatale, soon to be seen in the film noir films of the 1940s. But in 1938, that concept had not yet been fully developed, at least not in the movies. While Julia is far from honest and is not above using her feminine wiles for criminal gain, Dodd, while attractive, exudes no sensuality in the role. Joel Sloane seems to be half-heartedly romancing Julia and Julia seems to be half-heartedly romancing Joel, while at the same time reluctantly romancing Bannerman. With a part that is so ambiguously and inconsistently written, it is not surprising that Dodd's performance is weak.

In a light-hearted whodunit, it is always important that the mystery itself be interesting and cohesive, so that there is a solid base on which to place the comedy elements. *Fast Company* does not disappoint. There are multiple suspects, a surprise murder of Wheeler, the attempted murder of Joel and an exciting conclusion as both Joel and Garda are about to be executed by Bannerman before they make a last-minute escape.

Even with all of these other attributes, the heart of the film is still the relationship between Joel and Garda Sloane. The dialogue is every bit as clever as that in the Thin Man movies, with witty repartee from both Joel and Garda. Melvyn Douglas is very good as Joel, coming close to the performances of William Powell in some of the Thin Man movies. Florence Rice is very appealing as Garda, even if she is not quite as attractive or tantalizing as Myrna Loy is in the early Thin Man movies. It is surprising that she seldom received other good roles in major films after her fine performance in this feature.

*Fast Company* is one of the lesser-known films of the mystery movie series of the 1930s, but it is excellent in every regard. It works as both a solid mystery and a light comedy. What a joy to discover an unexpected gem such as this film!

*Note on the Source Material*: The film *Fast Company* was based on the 1938 novel of the same name by Marco Page. Since Page was credited as one of the writers on the film, it is not surprising that the film follows the novel quite closely. Thus, as the plot of the book develops, Ned Morgan is released from prison after being framed for a book theft by Abe Selig (Otto Brockler in the film), Ned is in love with Abe's daughter Leah, Selig is murdered by being hit over the head by a small marble statue from his desk, Selig was involved in fencing stolen books with Elias Bannerman and Sydney Wheeler, Wheeler is killed by Bannerman in an isolated setting, and eventually, Glass exposes the killer of Selig (the same killer who is unmasked in the film).

The difference between the two works is one of emphasis. A few subsidiary characters are not carried over into the film. The plight of Ned Morgan and the enigmatic character, Julia Thorne, receive more prominence in the film, as does Garda Sloane and her relationship with her husband. Some of the clever dialogue from the book finds its way into the movie but additional clever repartee between Joel and Garda is added for the movie. While the capture of Glass near the end of the book is similar to what happens to Sloane in the movie, the film scene is written in a tighter manner than in the novel. The incident makes more sense in the film, as well as being more suspenseful.

The novel *Fast Company* is fair, at best. The subtle changes made in modifying it for the screen and the quality of the acting in the film are some of the reasons why the film is superior to the book.

## *Fast and Loose* (1939)

*Fast and Loose* is an example of a film that tries too hard with the comedy elements and not enough with the mystery elements, making the film not very funny and not very mysterious. It is an unworthy sequel to *Fast Company*, the first movie about Joel and Garda Sloane.

Joel Sloane's rare book business is having financial troubles so he is excited when Christopher Oates, a wealthy but befuddled oldtimer, commissions him to help him purchase an original Shakespearean manuscript from wealthy Nicholas Torrent. In order to obtain an invitation to the Torrent house, Joel agrees to investigate some suspicious matters at the Torrent house on behalf of Torrent's insurance carrier, Security Union Mutual. The agent, David Hilliard, has a first edition of *Paradise Lost* which was either stolen from, or lost at, the Torrent house without an insurance claim being made, raising suspicions with the insurance company. Joel proceeds to the Torrent mansion where he gets mixed up with three murders, a forged manuscript, a gambler known as Lucky Nolan and a shady lady named Bobby Neville. Joel is beaten up, shot at and has his car run off the road. At the end of the film, he solves the crimes, sort of, and presumably lives happily ever after with his loving wife Garda.

In terms of trying too hard for the comedy elements, the film opens with a note left for the milkman which reads, "Milkman: Please leave one quart of aspirin tablets." The telephone has a note on it which reads, "Dear Telephone: One peep out of you and we will cancel all agreements." Would anyone, under any circumstances, write such notes and place them in their house? Would anyone, under any circumstances, think those notes were funny? The notes are symptomatic of the forced humor in the film, such as old Mr. Oates being unable to remember anything or the Sloanes sharing a steak on their eyes when they both somehow get matching black eyes after a car crash. This is not the sophisticated humor of *The Thin Man*; it is pure silliness.

As for not trying hard enough with the mystery elements, there are three murders committed and the last two make little sense. The second victim is Wilkes, the manuscript forger, whose body is discovered well after his murder inside a suit of armor in the hallway of the Torrent mansion. Since the killing took place with many people in the house, how did the killer, by himself, stuff the body inside the armor, particularly without making any noise? The third murder is of Stockton, the owner of the stolen manuscript. His body is found in a locked library, which should have created an interesting locked room mystery, except that there is never any explanation as to how the locked room murder was actually committed. As silly as *Fast and Loose* is, it is still a mystery and there should therefore be some logic to the crimes being depicted.

In addition, from time to time Joel Sloane, the somewhat silly rare book dealer, suddenly becomes a hardboiled detective, knocking guns out of people's grasps or beating up some gangsters. Those acts are totally out of sync with his personality as portrayed in the remainder of the film. Although Joel is ostensibly the hero-detective of the film, he never really solves any of the crimes. People either seem to come to him with important information or they simply give themselves away. *Fast and Loose* is really not much of a detective film.

Robert Montgomery stars as Joel Sloane and his performance is weak. Melvyn Douglas portrayed the same role with a dash of aplomb. Montgomery acts as if he were in a daze throughout most of the film. Since Joel twice goes to gangster Lucky Nolan's casino, apparently with the sole purpose of getting beat up, perhaps Sloane is, in fact, in a daze throughout the film. If so, then Montgomery gives the perfect performance for that interpretation of the character.

Joel Sloane (Robert Montgomery) and Bobby Neville (Joan Marsh) have been arrested for the murder of Nicholas Torrent in *Fast and Loose* (1939).

The one bright spot is Rosalind Russell as Garda Sloane. Russell never looked more beautiful in films, and even though the dialogue given to her is not much better than that of Montgomery's, she at least delivers her lines in a convincing manner. While this was hardly a major role for her, and her character does seem to disappear in the middle third of the film, Russell is always enthusiastic in her performance, unlike Montgomery who seems to be bored. The Sloane family funds are running law, but that does not prevent Garda from wearing numerous expensive but attractive outfits and nightgowns, showing off the beauty of Rosalind Russell.

In addition to its other problems, *Fast and Loose* has no pace, with the story meandering among numerous characters and irrelevant scenes. The film has absolutely no suspense, with the film concluding not with a bang but with a whimper. There is little to recommend for the mystery movie fan in *Fast and Loose*. Indeed, there is little to recommend for the non-mystery movie fan either.

## *Fast and Furious* (1939)

Sometimes the third time is a charm; sometime it is a disaster. The latter, unfortunately, is an apt description for *Fast and Furious*, the third and final feature in the Joel and Garda Sloane trilogy. Amplifying the mistakes made in the prior feature *Fast and Loose*,

Gangster Lucky Nolan has sent a henchman (Max Wagner) to kidnap Garda Sloane (Rosalind Russell) but Joel Sloane (Robert Montgomery), center, intervenes, in *Fast and Loose* (1939).

there is so much emphasis on the comedy aspects that the first murder does not occur until over 30 minutes into the film. Before that, the audience, which presumably is looking forward to a good crime movie, is "treated" to an average screwball comedy.

Joel is talked into investing $5000 into a beauty pageant by his long-time friend, Mike Stevens. Mike is managing the pageant which is being held in the beach resort town of Seaside City. The pageant is owned by Eric Bartell and there are rumors that once the pageant ends, Bartell intends to abscond with all of the profits, leaving Stevens (and therefore Sloane), holding the bag. When Stevens learns about this, he accosts Bartell in his hotel room and demands the return of all of his money. Bartell agrees but while he is opening the safe in another room to obtain the cash, Stevens hears a shot. When Stevens enters the room with Sloane and the police, Bartell's body is discovered and all the money is missing. Stevens is immediately arrested for murder.

Joel decides that he needs to clear Stevens' name. It never occurs to him that since he works with valuable books (there are no books involved in this case), it makes absolutely no sense for him to become involved. After watching the investigation Sloane makes, the viewer will come to the same conclusion, since Sloane does practically nothing to locate the real killer other than to harass all of the suspects. Indeed, it is Garda who finds the most significant clue when she illegally searches the room of one of the suspects, beauty contestant (and Bartell's girlfriend) Jerry Lawrence. There, Garda discovers a passport and a receipt, the latter eventually leading to the stolen money which had been checked for storage at the local boat dock.

It is obvious from the time of the murder that one of two people committed the crime: Jerry, or Lily Cole, who worked with Bartell and was upset with his relationship with Jerry. Both were in or near the hotel room when Bartell was killed and both of them knew about the money in the safe. Therefore, no viewer will be surprised to learn that someone else committed the murder, for the flimsiest of motives, with Joel discovering the perpetrator's identity based on the flimsiest of clues. Neither the discovery of the murderer nor the reason for his discovery is all that convincing. To be blunt, *Fast and Furious* is not a very good mystery.

The foregoing discussion of *Fast and Furious* is somewhat misleading since, based on the plot summary, the reader might believe that *Fast and Furious* is primarily a murder mystery. It is not. In fact, very little of the film is about the mystery. Most of the time is taken up with the "witty" exchanges between Joel and Garda (Garda is apparently jealous that Joel is going to be a judge of the beauty pageant and be around lots of beautiful women). There is more wasted footage with Garda trying to trick Joel into going on a vacation, a hotel bellboy who is flabbergasted about what is going on, and a long screwball comedy moment with real lions in the Sloanes' hotel room. It is all pretty wearying stuff. There is one good moment, though, which brings memories of serial cliffhangers. Joel and Garda are locked in a theater storage room as the stage floor starts to descend on them because someone above apparently pulled the stage elevator switch. While the scene is harrowing and the escape clever, it does not, in retrospect, make much sense, since the person who is later identified as the killer had no reason to kill the Sloanes at that time (or at any time).

Franchot Tone is good in the role of Joel Sloane, giving essentially a comedy performance. Ann Sothern is better — perky, prickly and quite attractive as Garda. The character of Garda, though, has become one more of comedy relief than detective, illustrating what little respect the filmmakers had for the mystery material in the movie.

The Joel and Garda Sloane series started strong with *Fast Company* but tanked very quickly. Harry Kurnitz, the creator of the characters and a screenwriter on all three films, had clearly run out of ideas for his bookseller-detective. Mercifully, the series ended with this feature.

## Afterwards

Although the first film in the series, *Fast Company* (1938), was based on a book by Harry Kurnitz, under his pseudonym Marco Page, and Kurnitz was a screenwriter on the remaining two films in the series, Kurnitz never wrote another novel about Joel and Garda Sloane. He did, however, write other mysteries under the name Marco Page which involved crime within the world of art. *The Shadowy Third* (1946) was set in a symphony hall and *Reclining Figure* (1952) dealt with art objects and their forgery. Kurnitz passed away in 1968.

Despite their debut in a Kurnitz novel, Joel and Garda Sloane were essentially screen concoctions. Accordingly, after the short film series ended in 1939, there were no other films, radio shows or television shows about the mystery-loving couple.

# 17

# Nancy Drew
## *The Teenage Detective*

It is difficult for an adult to evaluate a movie made for youngsters, especially one that is a mystery. For a crime film, it is just too easy to point out the lapses of logic in the plot, lack of a complex story, incredible coincidences and the necessary omission of any serious violence. All of these probably mattered little to youthful audiences in 1938 and 1939 when the four Nancy Drew films were released. They probably found the films to be quite satisfactory.

More difficult to predict is whether a modern young audience, reared on color films, more adult themes, high production values, great special effects and violent images, would find the Nancy Drew films at all interesting. Perhaps they would, because Nancy Drew stories, along with the Hardy Boys and others, are still being sold today. Since there is apparently a current market for those books, there must be something in those stories that appeals to kids today. Or, perhaps that is simply the nostalgic fancies of a mystery-loving adult who read and was thrilled by all of those books when he was a youngster himself.

## Background

### The Novels

All of the Nancy Drew novels identify the author as Carolyn Keene and for many years, fans believed that Carolyn Keene was a real person. In fact, Carolyn Keene is a pseudonym, with the books being written by a number of authors over many years.

Edward Stratemeyer was born on October 4, 1862, in Elizabeth, New Jersey. At an early age, he started selling stories to children's story papers, graduating quickly into writing dime novels and then children's books. Stratemeyer created many of the famous early children's series, such as the Rover Boys and the Bobbsey Twins, before deciding to open his own company to produce books geared toward youngsters. In 1905, he started the Stratemeyer Syndicate, where he employed a system wherein he wrote the outlines for the books, but the books themselves were then written by ghostwriters who worked under the pen name assigned to the series. The ghostwriters also gave up any rights they had to the books.

The Stratemeyer Syndicate was very successful; its series included the Hardy Boys, Tom Swift and Bomba the Jungle Boy. In 1929, Stratemeyer thought of a series about a young female detective and outlined the plots of the first five novels to Grosset & Dunlap, the publisher of the Stratemeyer Syndicate novels. The publishing house liked the idea and Stratemeyer assigned the writing of the novels to Mildred Augustine Wirt, a 24-year-old writer born in Iowa but then living in Ohio.

The first Nancy Drew novel was *The Secret of the Old Clock* (1930) and that novel, as outlined by Stratemeyer and written by Wirt, established most of the conventions of the series. Pretty 16-year-old Nancy lives in the town of River Heights with her father, attorney Carson Drew, and their grandmotherly servant Hannah Gruen. Nancy's mother passed away when Nancy was only three. While dressing beautifully, driving her roadster and having luncheon with many people, Nancy solves an amazing number of mysteries that come to the small town. In *The Secret of Shadow Ranch* (1931), Nancy's cousins George Fayne (a dark-haired tomboy) and Bess Marvin (a giggly blond) were added to the cast of characters. In *The Clue in the Diary* (1932), Ned Nickerson, a male friend and sometimes assistant for Nancy, was added.

Twelve days after *The Secret of the Old Clock* was published, Stratemeyer passed away. The company was then taken over by his daughters, Harriet and Edna. Throughout the 1930s, Wirt wrote most of the Nancy Drew novels based on outlines written by one of the daughters. After Wirt parted with the Syndicate in 1953, Harriet wrote many of the books on her own.

## The Film Series

Warner Brothers brought Nancy Drew to the screen in a four-movie series, commencing with *Nancy Drew— Detective* (1938). There Nancy solves the mystery of the kidnapping of a wealthy older woman who was about to make a significant donation to Nancy's school. In addition to Nancy, her father Carson Drew and friend Ted Nickerson (a name change from the books) appeared. George, Bess and Hannah Gruen were nowhere to be seen although the Drew family did have a housekeeper who appeared in all four films.

Nancy was played by child star Bonita Granville, who was born in Chicago in 1923. Granville made her film debut at the age of nine in *Westward Passage* (1932), playing the lead character in the film when that character was a child. In 1936 in *These Three*, Granville played Mary Tilford, a young brat who lies about her schoolteachers, a role for which Granville received an Academy Award nomination for Best Supporting Actress. For the next several years, Granville worked steadily in films until receiving the role of Nancy Drew at the age of 15.

Ted Nickerson is a much more important character in the films than in the books. He was played by Frankie Thomas, although the credits in the first two Nancy Drew films list him as Frank Thomas, Jr. Thomas was born in 1921 in New York City to parents who were both actors on the Broadway stage. It was therefore natural for Thomas to also go into acting and at the age of 11, he began appearing in Broadway productions. When one of his Broadway plays, *Wednesday's Child*, was picked up by Hollywood, Thomas moved to Tinseltown to reprise his role for the movies. His father and mother also played parts in the film. He then appeared in other films before playing the lead character in *Tim Tyler's Luck* (1937), a 12–chapter serial in which Tim searches for his father in the African jungle. His next major film role was as Ted Nickerson in the Nancy Drew films.

With two appealing child stars in the lead roles, the thankless part of Nancy's father, Carson Drew, was given to familiar character actor John Litel. Litel, who was born in 1892 in Wisconsin, appeared in over 150 films in his movie career, usually in character parts playing lawyers, judges, and criminals. His first film role was in 1930 and by the time of *Nancy Drew— Detective* (1938), he had already appeared in over 20 films.

## THE FILMS

### Nancy Drew — Detective (1938)

Nancy Drew's first screen mystery involves the disappearance of wealthy and elderly Mary Eldridge on the same day on which she was going to donate $300,000 for the building of a swimming pool at her alma mater, the Brinwood School for Girls. Nancy, a student there, is immediately suspicious. Later that day, Nancy spots a Dr. Spires being dragged into a mysterious car whose license number is partially covered by mud. Later that night, Dr. Spires tells Nancy and her father, Carson Drew, that he was kidnapped earlier that day, blindfolded, and taken to a country estate to attend to an elderly woman who had been injured. Nancy immediately assumes that the injured woman is Miss Eldridge and off she goes to locate her.

The rest of the movie relates to Nancy's attempts to locate the place where Miss Eldridge is being held captive. She is assisted by Ted Nickerson, her neighbor (and potential boyfriend), and thwarted from time to time by the bungling of local policeman Captain Tweedy. The investigation involves carrier pigeons, a surveillance ride in an airplane, and a clandestine entry into the nursing home where Miss Eldridge may be held captive. In the end, Nancy locates Miss Eldridge and with the help of the police captures the gang of criminals who were holding her.

*Nancy Drew — Detective* displays all of the problems with children's mysteries—coincidences drive the plot, the criminals are reluctant to resort to violence even when it is the best thing for them to do, and the whole thing is, frankly, just a little hard to believe. While those would all be serious problems in an adult mystery, they are not significant problems here. Young people watching *Nancy Drew — Detective* back then probably had the willingness to suspend disbelief.

The film is also carried past its structural problems by the performance of Bonita Granville in the title role. She is much like a young Glenda Farrell from the Torchy Blane series, sticking her nose in where it does not belong but, in the end, usually being right. Granville is as cute as they come and her winning personality, always perky and enthusiastic, makes the film quite watchable, even today. While Granville's Nancy Drew is not quite the sophisticated Nancy Drew of the book series, she is still the best thing about the movie.

Frankie Thomas is also excellent in the film, exasperated when Nancy drags him into another difficult situation but always ready to assist in the investigation. He is also quite good at physical comedy and he garners more laughs in this film than many adult comic relief figures do in other movie mysteries. His character, Ted Nickerson, is quite a Renaissance boy, operating a short wave set, knowing where carrier pigeons are registered, building a wooden crate, and creating a radio transmitter from an old x-ray machine. Sometimes *Nancy Drew — Detective* seems like more like a Tom Swift adventure than a Nancy Drew mystery.

Unlike the later films in the series, the mystery in *Nancy Drew — Detective* is always at the forefront, notwithstanding the substantial moments of comedy relief, making it the best of the series. The movie is not for adults, unless they desire a nostalgic trip back to their younger days. For youngsters, however, *Nancy Drew — Detective* appears to be worth a view, even though it is in black and white with no special effects and no violence.

*Note on the Source Material*: The credits indicate that *Nancy Drew — Detective* is an original story but it is actually a fairly close adaptation of *The Password to Larkspur Lane*, the 1933 book by Carolyn Keene. The book does not start as the film does, with the disappearance of Mary Eldridge. As the book opens, Nancy spots a pigeon falling to the ground after being injured by an airplane. When Nancy rescues the wounded animal, she finds that it is a carrier pigeon and that there is a perplexing message in its small metal tube.

Other movie scenes are very recognizable from the book, such as the kidnapping of Dr. Spires, his telling Nancy and Carson Drew of being brought blindfolded to treat an injured woman at a large house, Nancy and a friend trying to locate the house by following the carrier pigeon, threats made to Carson and Nancy, and Nancy and a friend sneaking into the sanitarium by pretending to be a patient and her nurse. In the movie, Ned dresses up as the nurse; in the book, a female friend of Nancy's is involved and it all makes more sense.

The main difference between the two works is that while Ned has substantial screen time in the film and is really a co-detective with Nancy, he is only a minor character in the book, which always stays focused on Nancy and her investigation. In the novel, when Nancy is captured by the villains at the sanitarium, she makes her own escape and even destroys the villains' airplane without any assistance. The Nancy Drew of *The Password to Larkspur Lane* is a little more sophisticated and substantially more self-reliant than the title character of *Nancy Drew — Detective*.

As an aside, *The Password to Larkspur Lane* is a rare early Nancy Drew book which was not ghostwritten by Mildred Wirt. It was actually written by a male author, Walter Karig, who also wrote two other books in the series.

## *Nancy Drew ... Reporter* (1939)

There is no other way to describe it: this film is painful to watch. And the shame is that *Nancy Drew ... Reporter* commences with an interesting mystery told in an interesting manner.

High school student Nancy Drew is participating in a contest at the local newspaper, the *River Heights Tribune*, to determine which student can submit the best story over a three-day period. Nancy is uninterested in the actual assignment she receives so she works her way into covering the coroner's hearing into the murder of wealthy Kate Lambert. (That is a surprise in and of itself as it was unusual for either print or film juvenile mysteries to involve a homicide, although each of the next two films in the series also involves a murder.)

The background of the homicide is then told by the witnesses at the inquest. As each testifies, the viewer learns a little bit more of the backstory of the crime. This is a style of storytelling which would become famous on the *Perry Mason* television series of the 1950s and 1960s. Most of the witnesses first appear in the middle of their testimony, one even shown answering a question that is not heard on-screen. This film technique provides important information to the viewer quickly, without becoming boring. The result of the hearing is then learned by the viewer when a guard asks a spectator leaving the building what the verdict was, another clever way of providing important information to the viewer.

Eula Denning, the ward of the decedent, is held over for trial on the flimsiest of evidence, even though everyone, including attorney Carson Drew, believes that the evidence is overwhelming. However, during her testimony, Eula explains that if Mrs. Lambert was poisoned by a product used in photography, then the prints of the murderer will still be on the tin of the substance since due to a chemical reaction those prints cannot be wiped away. Thus, Nancy is off to find the tin and also to discover what a mysterious man with a cauliflower ear (later identified as Soxie Anthems) has to do with the case.

That is not a bad start to *Nancy Drew ... Reporter*. And then all of the silliness begins. First, Nancy has to trick Ted Nickerson into helping her. That brings into the picture the juvenile antics (and face-making) of Ted's very young sister Mary and her little friend Killer Parkins. The two provide comic relief of the worst quality, yet they keep reappearing throughout the film. Nancy decides to visit Eula Denning in jail and wants Ted to take Eula's picture, a practice frowned upon by the authority. That permits more antics by Nancy and Ted as they attempt to take Eula's picture without the guards realizing it. Then Nancy, using a childlike routine, tricks her father into representing Eula. Thereafter, Nancy tricks Ted into impersonating a boxer, for a reason that is impossible to explain, resulting in Ted being knocked cold in the boxing ring by Soxie Anthems. Note that Soxie sees Ted with Nancy in the gym but never catches on to Nancy's motives, even though Soxie has had contact with Nancy several times before in the movie.

Just when the viewer believes that matters could not get worse, they do. Nancy and Ted tail Soxie and his girlfriend to a Chinese restaurant where, since the two detectives, along with juveniles Mary and Killer, do not have enough money to pay for the dinner, literally have to sing for their supper. The Chinese restaurant has a band, even during the daytime, and since Mary is quite a singer (and has incredible backup from the other three), the owner tears up the check. Then Nancy and Ted talk Sergeant Entwhistle into going undercover as an old lady in order to trap the killer. Can anyone explain why Nancy wants Entwhistle to go undercover and why a policeman would ever do so in such a ridiculous garb? Nancy wins the newspaper contest by having an untrue story placed on the front page of the *Tribune*. Nancy surely has a lot to learn about newspaper ethics.

In addition to the silliness, the story has a defective underlying premise. If Miles Lambert poisoned his aunt Kate in order to obtain an inheritance, what involvement did Soxie and his girlfriend have in the crime? The answer is none, other than to give Nancy a lead to chase and chase and chase. The childish and silly Nancy always has to turn to Ted Nickerson for help, instead of relying on her own wits. Thus, this Nancy Drew of the Warner Brothers film series is the farthest thing from the sophisticated and clever Nancy Drew of the Carolyn Keene novels.

## *Nancy Drew ... Trouble Shooter* (1939)

Having described *Nancy Drew ... Reporter* as "painful to watch," there is not much left to describe *Nancy Drew ... Trouble Shooter*, yet it is actually worse than the previous film. Somehow, *Nancy Drew ... Trouble Shooter* has less mystery and more tedious comedy than *Nancy Drew ... Reporter*.

Carson Drew receives a letter from his friend Matt Brandon, who is being held in the local jail near Sylvan Lake for the murder of Henry Clark. Henry disappeared over a month earlier and neither he nor his body have been seen since. Matt and Henry had been feuding for years and on the night of Henry's disappearance, Matt had threatened Henry. However, without a body and with no real evidence against Henry, it is hard to see why Henry is being held by the sheriff at all.

In response to Matt's letter, Carson Drew does what any attorney would do in that situation. He closes his law practice in River Heights and moves his daughter and house-

**Having just escaped from a locked hotel room with the help of the hotel engineer (Charles Marsh), left, Nancy Drew (Bonita Granville) and Ted Nickerson (Frankie Thomas) spot boxer Soxic Anthems going into a hotel room to meet the killer of Kate Lambert, in *Nancy Drew ... Reporter* (1939).**

keeper to the country so that he can defend Matt. Nancy then inadvertently causes the discovery of the body. Next, while Carson seems to be doing little on behalf of his client, Nancy discovers several clues, including the seeds for the rare plant that was growing where the body was buried and the gun that could be the murder weapon. In the end, Nancy fingers the killer and saves Matt from a trial (and presumably an acquittal since there was no significant evidence against him, in any event).

The mystery in *Nancy Drew ... Troubleshooter* does not work at all. The real killer, Clinton Griffith, is obvious from the minute he enters the film. Since, by movie convention, Matt cannot be guilty, Griffith is the only other potential murderer. Griffith makes himself even more obvious by pushing the sheriff into arresting Matt.

Although Nancy does piece together a few important clues in her search for the real murderer, she obtains the most important evidence by luck. Houseboy Apollo actually witnessed the murders but, for some reason, thought he was seeing ghosts. Nancy combines Apollo's story with her knowledge of the facts of the murder, resulting in her inspection of Griffith's barn where she finds the murder weapon. Other than that, there is not much mystery to the film. In fact, the mystery elements of *Nancy Drew ... Troubleshooter* are so simplistic that they probably consume only about 15 minutes of the running time.

The rest of *Nancy Drew ... Troubleshooter* is about comedy and schtick. There are

Nancy's poor driving habits, Carson's (and then Ned's) infatuation with a pretty neighbor, Nancy's jealousy of her father's new relationship, Nancy's attempt to cook dinner, and Ted doing pratfalls with the boat he is building. Then there is the character of Matt's black servant Apollo, played by Willie Best. Believing he has seen a ghost when he spots Ned with flour all over his face, Apollo actually runs through a fence in fast motion, a particularly demeaning way to treat Apollo just for comedy relief. Surprisingly, that is not the most demeaning treatment of the Apollo character in the film. The real embarrassment for the viewer comes from Nancy and Ted's demeaning treatment of Apollo. The character seems to be about the same age as Nancy and Ted, yet they nonchalantly treat him as an inferior houseboy, just as the adults do.

Although there is some suspense created at the end of the film when the two teenage investigators are locked in a barn by the killer and later trapped in an out-of-control airplane, these scenes are still played more for laughs than suspense, undercutting their effectiveness. With the exception of Bonita Granville's always engaging performance as the title character, *Nancy Drew ... Troubleshooter* does not work on any level. Frankly, after a good first film in the series, the quality of these Nancy Drew features has deteriorated to a spectacular degree.

## *Nancy Drew and the Hidden Staircase* (1939)

In this film, Nancy fakes a suicide note to convince the police that a murder was a suicide, hides important evidence (a bullet shell) from the police, sends her father a fake telegram to attempt to get him out of town, and drugs two elderly women so that she and Ted can do some investigation in an old mansion without interruption. Nancy no longer seems to be a role model for the youth of America. Perhaps a better title for this film would have been *Nancy Drew ... Juvenile Delinquent*.

The film is based upon a somewhat crazy premise. The elderly Turnbull sisters live in a large mansion pursuant to the terms of their father's will. The document provides that the sisters must live in the mansion every day for 20 years or the property will be forfeited to the city. In order to ensure that the Turnbulls will not lose their property, attorney Carson Drew has collected affidavits from numerous parties testifying to the sisters' continuous occupancy of the house for the last two decades. Now, with just two weeks remaining in their 20-year "prison term," the sisters have decided to donate the property for a children's hospital.

At that point some strange incidents occur. A man appears at the Drew home to attempt to find those affidavits. He is chased away by Ted Nickerson, who is working that summer as an ice man. Then Phillips, the Turnbulls' chauffeur, is murdered and Nancy is surprised to discover that he was the man who came to the house and terrorized her over the affidavits. Thereafter there are some thefts of small objects from the Turnbull home, frightening the sisters. Luckily, an enthusiastic Nancy is on the case and along with a reluctant Ted solves the mystery.

Nancy actually does some nice investigative work with a spent bullet shell, proving to herself and Ted that Phillips' death was murder and not suicide. Of course, that investigation was better left to the police than Nancy. On the other hand, since the police force of River Heights is represented by the incompetent Officer Tweedy, and since Tweedy did not discover the cartridge shell in his own investigation, maybe Nancy was the appropriate person to do the analysis.

As was the case with all of the Nancy Drew movies, there is not much of a mystery in *Nancy Drew and the Hidden Staircase*, and what mystery there is does not hold together

Nancy (Bonita Granville) and housekeeper Effie Schneider (Renie Riano) learn that, because of one of Nancy's schemes, Ned Nickerson has lost his job at the ice company in *Nancy Drew and the Hidden Staircase* (1939). The iceman is played by Jack Mower.

very well. One way for the viewer to solve this type of movie mystery is to identify a character who is in the movie for no apparent reason. That person will always be the villain. In this case, on two occasions when Nancy visits the Turnbull sisters, their neighbor, Mr. Talbert, is also present for reasons hard to discern. He must therefore be the villain and, as it turns out, he is. Even though Talbert is the least likely of suspects, there is absolutely no surprise in his unmasking as the criminal.

There are inconsistencies in the plot, such as why the Turnbulls' chauffeur was involved in the crimes at all, but perhaps they do not matter. *Nancy Drew and the Hidden Staircase* was intended for a youth audience and not for adults. For youngsters, a story which involves a large mansion with a secret passageway in the basement, an exciting conclusion with Nancy and Ted trapped in the passageway as it is filling with water, and a little bit of mild humor may be all that they desire in a film. For adults, while the storyline is clearly lacking, it is still interesting to go back to a time when young ladies wore hats, drove roadsters with a rumble seat in the back, and had ice delivered to their houses on a daily basis by the ice man. Thus, while *Nancy Drew and the Hidden Staircase* is hard to recommend, it does have its interest.

*Note on the Source Material*: The novel *The Hidden Staircase*, published in 1930, was the second in the Nancy Drew series. It was part of the original three-book set of Nancy Drew mysteries written by Mildred Wirt and based on outlines by Edward Stratemeyer. The three original books were devised as a "breeder" set, providing children with the opportunity to become familiar with the character of Nancy while also getting them to want to purchase more books in the series.

Despite the similarities in title between that novel and the film, the two works have little in common. While the book does concern an old mansion occupied by two sisters, some thefts that occur there, and a secret passage to the adjoining house, the plots are substantially different. Ned Nickerson is not a character in the book. The villain is a lawyer who is harassing Carson Drew and even takes him prisoner at one point in the story. Also, there is no chauffeur murdered in the book. *Nancy Drew and the Hidden Staircase* is essentially an original work.

## AFTERWARDS

Given Nancy's popularity at the time, the four-picture Warner Brothers series was a disappointment in financial (and also artistic) terms. However, its lack of success did not affect the popularity of the books, which continued to sell exceedingly well for many years. There were a total of 34 published between 1930 and 1956. Starting in 1959, the original books were re-written for the purpose of modernizing them. In the process, the original 34 books were shortened. Thereafter, additional books covered Nancy's detective career at varying ages of her life. In all, over 300 titles about the young River Heights detective have been published and there is always the possibility of more.

Bonita Granville had numerous supporting roles in Hollywood films in the 1940s, including appearing in two Andy Hardy movies. As she got older, though, her number of film roles steadily decreased. In 1947, she married Jack Wrather, a producer who later bought the rights to the TV series *The Lone Ranger* and *Lassie*. Granville was a producer on *Lassie*, narrated a few episodes and even introduced a few of the multi-part episodes or previews of episodes on-screen. Her last significant film role was in *The Lone Ranger* (1956), one of the first feature films to be based upon a television series. It was produced by Wrather Productions. Granville died in 1988.

Frankie Thomas continued appearing in films until he joined the military in 1942. His last film was *The Major and the Minor* (1942). When Thomas returned from the war, he received steady work in radio and then daytime television. He attained lasting fame for starring in the television series *Tom Corbett, Space Cadet*, which was on the air for five years starting in 1950. Following the end of that program, Thomas gave up performing. He passed away in 2006.

After the end of the Nancy Drew series, John Litel continued appearing in films, still usually in small roles. He appeared in many movie mysteries including entries in the Brass Bancroft, Ellery Queen and Crime Doctor series. He also had a regular role as the father of Henry Aldrich in the 1940s movie series about the radio character. In the 1950s, he appeared regularly on television. Litel died in 1972.

Nancy Drew never made it to the radio and it took her many years before she had a regular television program. In 1977, ABC created an hour-long show, *The Nancy Drew Mysteries*, which alternated on Sunday nights with the hour-long, *The Hardy Boys Mysteries*. The updated Nancy was played by Pamela Sue Martin and Carson Drew was played by familiar television performer William Schallert. The series alternated with the Hardy Boys for a year and a half, and then the two shows were combined into one hour-long program. Nancy got the short end of the stick in the combined shows and Martin left the series, being replaced by Janet Louise Johnson. Nancy's involvement on the show ended shortly thereafter.

In 2002, a television pilot for *Nancy Drew* was not picked up as a regular series. In 2007, the teenage detective finally made it back to the big screen in the aptly titled *Nancy Drew* with Emma Roberts as the young detective and Tate Donovan as Carson Drew.

# 18

# Mr. Wong
## *The Other Chinese Detective*

What do Swedish–born Warner Oland, American–born Sidney Toler, Hungarian–born Peter Lorre and English–born Boris Karloff have in common? The answer is somewhat surprising. They each played Asian detectives in mystery movie series of 1930s Hollywood. For some unfathomable reason, the Hollywood studios were reluctant to use actors of Asian descent in the lead roles in their 1930s series about Asian detectives.

There was, however, one exception. While Karloff played Mr. Wong in the first five movies in the Wong series, Keye Luke succeeded to the lead in the last Wong film. Although Luke was raised in Seattle, Washington, he was born in Canton, China, in 1904. After becoming famous playing Charlie Chan's No. 1 son Lee Chan, Luke became, in *Phantom of Chinatown* (1941), the first performer of Asian descent to play the lead Asian detective in a Hollywood mystery movie series.

## BACKGROUND

### The Stories

*The Saturday Evening Post* had its serializations of the Charlie Chan novels by Earl Derr Biggers and later the Mr. Moto books by John P. Marquand. The competitive franchise of *Collier's The National Weekly* was the Mr. Wong stories by Hugh Wiley. From 1934 to 1938, *Collier's* magazine published a total of 12 Wong stories, each story contained in a single issue of the 5¢ weekly. The stories were eventually collected in *Murder by the Dozen*, published by Popular Library in 1951.

In the stories, Wong, who resides in Chinatown in San Francisco, is described as an important agent in the United States Department of Justice. His specialty seems to be investigating opium smuggling from the Far East. Although he is known as James Lee Wong to his family, he is simply known as James Lee to the public at large. Despite his government job, most of his cases are of a private nature, such as a shooting death during a film production by a gun that was supposed to contain only blanks, a missing diamond from an engagement ring, stolen gold bricks, and a fraudulent medium who is fleecing a wealthy widow. Some of Lee's cases do involve his government position, such as investigations concerning the murder of a federal agent and narcotics smuggling.

There are few physical descriptions of James Lee provided by Wiley. In one story, he is described as a Chinese man, about six feet tall and weighing about 165 pounds. It is also mentioned that he is a Yale graduate. The drawings of James Lee in *Collier's* seem to make him relatively young, surely younger than Boris Karloff played him in the movies. The stories do not emphasize James Lee's Chinese heritage and, unlike Charlie Chan, James Lee does not spout aphorisms. However, when James Lee is with another character of Chinese descent, they often trade Chinese expressions or sayings.

Hugh Wiley was born in 1884 in Zanesville, Ohio. He left school while still a teenager yet became a successful engineer and contractor. After serving in the army during World War I, Wiley began writing professionally, with his first stories appearing in *The Saturday Evening Post* as early as 1919. Some of his stories involved intrigue and mystery in an Oriental setting or with Oriental characters, and others were stories of black America told in an exaggerated (and, by today's standards, insensitive) manner.

## The Film Series

In 1938, Monogram Pictures brought the James Lee Wong stories to the cinema, perhaps trying to siphon off some of the interest that the Charlie Chan and Mr. Moto series were then generating. The movie Mr. Wong was not, however, the James Lee of the Wiley stories, but rather was an older, professorial private detective who regularly became involved in assisting the San Francisco police in their murder investigations. The one characteristic of Wong which carried over from the Wiley stories was Wong's expertise in chemistry and similar sciences. Much like the Wiley stories, the movies did not emphasize the Chinese heritage of Wong.

Monogram, a Poverty Row film studio, scored a coup when it signed the English–born Boris Karloff (1887–1969) for the title role. Born William Henry Pratt, Karloff emigrated from England to Canada in 1909 and began working intermittently on the stage, finally winding up in Los Angeles on a road company tour in 1917. Like many of the Hollywood stars of the 1930s, Karloff started his movie career in silent films, with some of his first roles as early as 1919. He had fairly steady work during the 1920s but never became a featured player or a star. With the advent of sound films, Karloff continued to work, including performing in a small role in the first sound Charlie Chan film, *Behind That Curtain* (1929). Karloff then had an important role in director Howard Hawks' *The Criminal Code* (1931), where he repeated his stage role as a prisoner who became a killer. Later that same year, Karloff was chosen for the role of the Monster in *Frankenstein* (1931) and his career as a star of horror films began.

Throughout the 1930s, Karloff appeared primarily in horror films, although from time to time he branched out into non-horror movies such as *The Lost Patrol* (1934), *The House of Rothschild* (1934) and, for mystery fans, *Charlie Chan at the Opera* (1936). By 1938, the first Hollywood horror film cycle had ended and Karloff was willing to lower his standards somewhat, agreeing to appear in a B–movie series at one of the lowest budget movie companies in Hollywood. When horror films came back in vogue, Monogram decided to have Karloff complete his six-film contract with the studio by appearing in a horror film. For the final Wong movie, Keye Luke was brought in to play the starring role. Luke was already known to mystery fans through his appearances as Lee Chan in that long-running Fox mystery series. Luke's career is discussed in more detail in Chapter 3 of this book.

Grant Withers appeared in all six Wong films playing Captain Street, the earnest but slightly incompetent policeman who always had to turn to Mr. Wong for assistance in his murder investigations. For some reason, Street's first name is Sam in *Mr. Wong in China-*

*town* and Bill in later films. Withers was born in 1905 in Pueblo, Colorado. He began appearing in films near the end of the silent era and, although his career started in a promising manner, by the mid–1930s he was already receiving only supporting roles in films. Most of the films in which he appeared in the 1930s are long forgotten. The Mr. Wong series constituted his only significant appearances in mystery movies.

Starting with *Mr. Wong in Chinatown* (1939), the third film in the series, Marjorie Reynolds made several appearances as newspaper reporter Bobbie Logan, who exasperated Captain Street by sticking her nose into his murder investigations. At the same time, Reynolds was appearing in Monogram's Tailspin Tommy series as Berry Lou Barnes. Reynolds' career is discussed in Chapter 21 of this book on the Tailspin Tommy series.

## The Films

### *Mr. Wong, Detective* (1938)

In *Mr. Wong, Detective*, Boris Karloff gives an excellent performance as the lead detective but a poor performance as Mr. James Lee Wong. While that may seem contradictory, it is not. Karloff is unconvincing as a Chinese investigator. It is simply not enough to give him a strange hairstyle, larger eyebrows, a moustache, thick eyeglasses and a little makeup around the eyes and expect him to appear to be Chinese. He makes no attempt at a Chinese accent, employing that familiar Karloff voice with the slight lisp.

On the other hand, if Wong is viewed as an older, professorial type of American detective, with a quiet but incisive manner, Karloff is excellent. His performance is less like his mad scientist roles of the 1940s and more like his Ardeth Bey in *The Mummy* (1932). Karloff was always good when he toned down his performance and it works quite well in this film. Thus, Karloff is convincing throughout *Mr. Wong, Detective*, except near the beginning when he wears Oriental garb and emphasizes the Chinese ancestry of his character.

The core plot of *Mr. Wong, Detective* has its interest. Businessman Simon Dayton comes to Wong with a problem. For the last two months, ever since his company decided to ship a load of chemicals abroad, there have been suspicious problems such as factory deliveries held up, railroad shipments damaged, cancellation of reservations of ships previously chartered and office files rifled. Now Dayton feels that he is being followed. Wong agrees to help and schedules an appointment for the next day at Dayton's office. Before Wong can meet with Dayton that day, Dayton's dead body is discovered in his office. An obvious suspect is Carl Roemer, who has been accusing Dayton of stealing a secret formula from him. Roemer came to Dayton's office on the day of the murder brandishing a gun. However, it is difficult to charge Roemer with murder because Dayton was not shot; he died by poison gas.

Other obvious suspects are Dayton's two business partners, who succeed to his interest in their company upon Dayton's death. However, their later deaths, in the same manner as Dayton's, eliminate them from the mix. There are also some spies who are after the shipload of chemicals, although it is never entirely clear what they are doing in the story. At the end, Wong announces the surprise murderer and the even more surprising method of murder.

The core mystery plot regarding Dayton, his partners and Carl Roemer is interesting, but there is not enough of it to fill a full-length feature. Most movie mysteries of the era

Mr. Wong (Boris Karloff), far right, has turned the tables on some foreign agents in *Mr. Wong, Detective* (1938). The villains are, from left to right, Olga, aka Countess Dubois (Evelyn Brent), Anton Mohl, aka the Baron (Lucien Prival), and Lescardi (Frank Bruno).

would have filled the extra time with unfunny comic relief, usually about an incompetent policeman. *Mr. Wong, Detective* avoids that cliché. Captain Street is not one of those incompetent officers who makes wild assumptions about the crime, accusing different people on scant evidence, a common attempt at comedy in a Hollywood mystery. That does not mean, however, that Street is competent because he clearly is not. He does very little investigation of the murders and no investigation of the crime scenes. Luckily, Wong is an expert detective with some scientific knowledge. Wong first discovers and then determines the significance of glass fragments found at each of the murder scenes. The fragments are the most significant clues in the film.

Instead of comic relief, the extra time in *Mr. Wong, Detective* is filled with the mysterious spies or foreign agents or unscrupulous business persons known as the Baron and Olga. It is never quite clear who they are or what they are doing in the film. Their part of the story is quite confusing and quite boring. Unfortunately, these detours from the main story detract substantially from the clever mystery story being told.

With the quick arrest of Roemer by the police, it is clear that he did not commit the killing of Dayton. The police never arrest the right person in this type of mystery movie. And for that reason, *Mr. Wong, Detective* is one of the cleverest of the 1930s mystery movies for, in fact, it turns out that Roemer is the killer. Roemer used the loud sirens of police cars to explode the glass vials of poison gas which he hid in each of the victim's rooms. Thus, in an ingenious twist, the police were actually complicit in the murders. Once that explanation is given by Mr. Wong, the murders and their relationship to Roemer's actions throughout the film make complete sense. All of Roemer's activities in the film were designed to bring the police to an upcoming crime scene with their sirens blaring, thus killing his intended victim. Also, Roemer is the only one who had the motive (revenge) to kill all three partners in the business. Thus, in retrospect, the mystery holds together very well. That is a rarity in mystery movies and even in mystery novels.

Unfortunately, *Mr. Wong, Detective* is very slow-moving, with minimal action and almost no scenes shot outdoors. As a half-hour television program, it would have been dynamite. As a feature film, it drags on too long. Nevertheless, if one can get past the style, the substance of the mystery is of the highest quality.

## *The Mystery of Mr. Wong* (1939)

The time-honored method of identifying the murderer in this type of mystery movie is to choose the least likely suspect. That does not work in *The Mystery of Mr. Wong* because most of the suspects are equally suspicious. Another potential technique for solving this mystery of Mr. Wong is for the viewer to rely on the clever clues sprinkled throughout the story which should lead inexorably to the real killer. Unfortunately, that also does not work here because Wong solves the murders based on clues he hides from the viewer. The audience is therefore left with the one remaining alternative method for identifying the murderer, and that is to choose the character who has no reason to be in the story, other than as the murderer.

Wong is invited to a party at the San Francisco mansion of wealthy Brandon Edwards, and since this is a mystery film, there is much intrigue at the Edwards abode. Edwards is a collector of rare Chinese artifacts such as the precious Eye of the Daughter of the Moon jewel, which he has just had stolen, smuggled out of China and delivered to him. Two members of Edwards' household, Chinese maid Drina and Russian singer Strogonoff, have a scheme to obtain the jewel. Valerie, Edwards' wife, is in love with Edwards' secretary Peter Harrison. Perhaps as a result of that, Edwards has decided to write Valerie out of his will, although the will has not yet been signed as of the beginning of the party.

The best scene comes early, with the killing of Edwards. As part of the entertainment at the party, the guests are playing a complex game of charades. Brandon, Valerie and Harrison perform in a short murder mystery, with the guests required to guess the title of the drama. Harrison performs the part of the jealous husband of Valerie who discovers Brandon, playing Valerie's secret lover, in a clinch with Valerie. Harrison shoots Brandon, who drops to the floor. The game continues and Wong guesses the title of the mystery, but once the episode is over, Brandon is still lying on the floor, dead from a gunshot wound. To add to the surprise, Brandon was not shot by Harrison with the stage gun; he was shot from the balcony in the back of the room.

Thus, *The Mystery of Mr. Wong* has a good set-up for its murder mystery, but little after that has much value. The film quickly becomes a talkfest and an uninteresting one at that. Even Karloff is disappointing. He makes no effort to portraying a Chinese detective; he performs the role of Mr. Wong as if the character has no Asian heritage in his background.

As to identifying the killer, there is a second criminologist at the Edwards mansion at the time of the murder, Ed Janney, a friend of Wong's and also of Street's, the investigating policeman. Janney has absolutely no reason for being in the film, unless he is the killer and so, of course, he is. At the end, Wong discloses all of the reasons why he knew Janney was the killer, none of which had previously been provided to the audience. What a disappointing resolution. The audience's only choice was to make a guess as to the identity of the murderer, based on a movie cliché rather than on real clues.

Janney's disclosure as the murderer cannot withstand much scrutiny. He wrote a threatening letter to Edwards on paper that was so unusual that the paper could be traced back to the university at which Janney taught. Now, some unsophisticated mug might make that mistake but Janney was supposed to be a noted criminologist. It is highly unlikely that he would make such an obvious error. Also, since Janney did not know what skit was being performed in the charade and that a gun with blanks would be fired, how did he know to go to the balcony and shoot Edwards at the exact moment that the stage gun was shot? How did he know that Drina had stolen the incriminating letter, requiring Janney to poison her with doctored cigarettes he just happened to have on him?

It may be unfair to over-analyze a B–murder mystery, but when one makes as little sense as *The Mystery of Mr. Wong*, it leaves itself open to such criticism, particularly since the solution to the mystery in the prior film, *Mr. Wong, Detective*, holds up very well. *The Mystery of Mr. Wong* is a very disappointing follow-up.

## *Mr. Wong in Chinatown* (1939)

*Mr. Wong in Chinatown* begins in a compelling manner, as an unknown, frightened Chinese woman dressed in black appears at Mr. Wong's door late one night, asking for help. Willie leaves the woman in the front room while he goes to a back room to get Wong. As the woman sits at a desk, a window opens, a hand and a blow gun appear, the sound of the firing of a dart is heard, the woman feels her neck and then she drops to the floor — but not before writing something on a notepad. When Wong gets there, the woman is dead. It is a mysterious and striking opening to a murder mystery, portending good things to come.

It turns out that the woman was Princess Lin Hwa from China and that she was in America to purchase airplanes for her brother's military back in China. Hwa brought a substantial sum of money with her to America, some of which is missing. Perhaps she was killed because of her political ties back in China or perhaps it was the money that brought about her execution. Wong becomes involved because the killing occurred in his home. There are two more killings and an abduction of Wong before he identifies the individual behind the killings.

After the strong opening, *Mr. Wong in Chinatown* becomes quite boring, quite fast. The police and Mr. Wong make a very slow investigation of the case, with the story becoming very confusing almost from the beginning of the inquiry. There is no pace or excitement to the tale and the film slows to a crawl when newspaper reporter Bobby Logan and her uninteresting banter with Inspector Street come to the forefront. The film creates such an atmosphere of ennui that even the last-minute rescue of Wong from a taxi which explodes, a fistfight between the villains and the butler of banker Davidson, and the climactic abduction of Wong do not inject any excitement into the story. Even Karloff is so un-animated in the title role that he puts a damper on the few action moments in the feature.

The story itself is inexplicable. It appears that the police have divided the work on the murder investigation, with the cops doing a small part of the legwork and Wong doing the bulk of it. As unrealistic as that is, at least it saves taxpayers some money. Street constantly tries to prevent Logan from becoming involved in the investigation and yet, at the end of

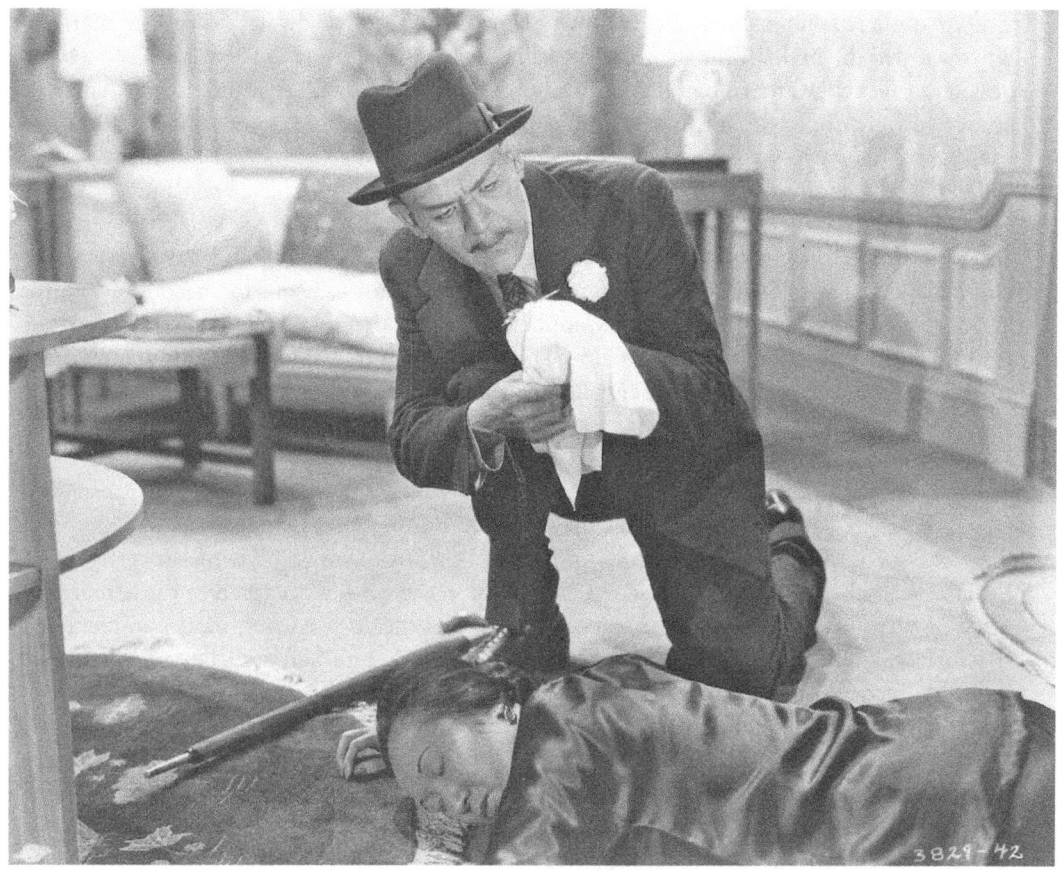

Mr. Wong (Boris Karloff) has discovered the second murder by poison dart in *Mr. Wong in Chinatown* (1939). The first victim was Princess Lin Hwa from China and the woman on the floor (Bessie Loo) was the companion of the princess.

the feature, he changes his mind and allows her to accompany him on all of his activities, even the particularly dangerous ones.

The mystery itself is written in a lazy manner. Why do the villains demand that Wong come to the Davidson house and then why do they abduct him? There is no logic to the plot point and was no doubt done just to try to provide some excitement to the end of the film. Because it is necessary for Street to rescue Wong on the freighter, it just so happens that Captain James loses his hotel key at the Davidson home, giving Street that one lucky clue to point him toward James' ship. Since there is no evidence against Davidson, Wong happens to be at his house when Davidson takes a call about a headstone at a pet cemetery, allowing Wong to guess that Davidson killed a dwarf and buried him there.

Wong actually says to Davidson, "One does not bury the body of a vicious dog in a pet cemetery under an expensive headstone." Wong therefore concludes that Davidson must have murdered the dwarf and buried him among the dead animals. Actually, though, most people do not bury any dog under any headstone, much less an expensive one. More importantly, most murderers do not bury their victims at all, much less under any headstone. The body of the dwarf must have been a surprise to the people who were working at the pet cemetery on the day of the funeral.

Also, there is no explanation as to why Davidson killed the dwarf, or for that matter, why he killed the maid of the princess. In fact, what was the dwarf doing in the film? Does anyone really believe that a banker could have committed these three murders, particularly since two were done with a Chinese blowgun? Whether believable or not, at least 20 minutes before his "surprise" unveiling as the killer, every viewer knows that Davidson is the killer, because he simply has too much screen time for what should have been a minor part.

Apparently Princess Lin Hwa did not believe that Davidson was the killer-type either. The clue she left Wong as she was dying reads, "Captain J," which could have meant the ship's Captain James or maybe the reference was to Captain Jackson, the head of a phony airplane manufacturer. Since neither were her killer, the princess led Wong on the wrong trail from the very beginning of the film. Thus, *Mr. Wong in Chinatown* is an unconvincing mystery told in an ineffectual and sloppy manner.

## *The Fatal Hour* (1940)

Who writes this stuff? And after they write it, do they ever read it?

At issue in *The Fatal Hour* is the murder of Detective Dan Grady while investigating a smuggling scheme in San Francisco's Chinatown. His body is discovered in the San Francisco Bay, shot in the back and weighted down so that the corpse would not soon come to the surface. Captain Bill Street, his friend from childhood and an associate of his in the San Francisco police department, is naturally upset. When the chief assigns the case to Street, he adds, not unexpectedly, "You will have command of every resource of the department." Just a few minutes later in the film, Mr. Wong comes to police headquarters to offer his assistance. Street tells him that he cannot officially call Wong in on the case because "I'm more or less doing it on my own." What suddenly happened to all of the resources of the department that were available to Street?

By just this fourth film in the story, Karloff has completely given up on portraying any of the supposed Chinese attributes of the character. He plays Wong solely as an elderly but savvy criminologist, although the most important course that Wong took in Criminology was probably "Coincidences 101." Discovering a rare Chinese figurine in Grady's desk, Wong goes to Beldon's Jewelers to have it appraised. While there, young Frank Beldon happens to go through the store. When Wong and Street later proceed to the Club Neptune, a hangout where Grady was last seen, Wong coincidentally also spots young Beldon there, tying Beldon's Jewelers to the smugglers. Without that coincidence, Wong would never have made the connection. Before going into Club Neptune, Wong decides to go around to the back of the building, for no particular reason, but while there, he happens to see the smugglers arrive by boat and make an attempt to deliver items to the club. Wong discovers in one minute what it probably took Grady weeks of surveillance to ascertain. In other words, if you pass the course in Coincidences, none of the other courses in Criminology are required since they would be superfluous.

The first half of *The Fatal Hour* is particularly weak, with everyone overacting about the loss of Dan Grady, and significant screen time being given to the always superfluous character, newspaper reporter Bobby Logan, played by Marjorie Reynolds. In the second half, things picks up considerably, with three murders committed in a short period of time. At this point, there is a shift in the storyline, away from Grady and toward the fact that Beldon's is under a court-ordered receivership, with the receiver being John Forbes, played by well-known character actor Charles Trowbridge. It will not take long for the viewer to

In *The Fatal Hour* (1940), Mr. Wong (Boris Karloff), center, inspects some of the jade found in murder victim Mr. Beldon's office. Police Captain Bill Street (Grant Withers), left, and policeman Clancy (James C. Morton), right, look on.

guess that Forbes is the head of the smuggling ring and the murderer. Forbes has no real reason to be in the film and his veneer of culture and sophistication, as convincingly portrayed by Trowbridge, makes him immediately suspicious.

There are some good mystery elements in the film about the timing of the killing of Tanya Sarova and Forbes' method of disguising the time of death to give himself an alibi. That is not to say that the scenario makes any sense, since it required Street and Wong to be at Forbes' apartment at the exact time a gun was shot during a radio broadcast. Nevertheless, the method of killing does show some ingenuity on the part of the screenwriters, redeeming them somewhat from their sloppiness in the first half of the feature.

The last murder to occur in *The Fatal Hour* is that of Griswold, the writer and performer of the radio play that was used for the alibi of Forbes in the killing of Tanya. Griswold has come to police headquarters, presumably to tell the police about the radio program, which, if the police learned about it, would compromise Forbes' alibi. Surprisingly, Griswold is stabbed to death in the reception area of the police station. Even though Wong concludes that Forbes committed that murder in addition to Grady's, note that it is almost physically impossible for Forbes to have committed Griswold's murder. Forbes was in Street's office with Street and Wong most of the time, so the killer must have been someone else, not that anyone else had a motive for Griswold's killing.

Wong never addresses that anomaly in his film-ending recitation of the solution to the crimes. Perhaps this is just another example of the careless writing, taking away from the interesting circumstances surrounding the murder of Tanya Sarova. Or, perhaps, it is a manifestation of something else Wong learned in criminology school, i.e., never let inconvenient facts get in the way of crime theories.

## *Doomed to Die* (1940)

In terms of quality, Monogram's *Doomed to Die* has some similarity to the studio's 1940s Charlie Chan movies. It has an excellent set-up to the story, but the execution falters and the explanation for the crimes has little credibility.

As the film commences, a fire at sea on a large ship, the *Wentworth Castle*, leads to significant loss of life. The story then moves to San Francisco where shipping magnate Simon Wentworth, the owner of the *Castle*, has just completed his will, leaving his entire estate to his daughter. Attorney Victor Martin is concerned that Wentworth may be considering suicide but Wentworth defuses his concern. After Martin leaves, Paul Fleming, who wants to consolidate his shipping line with that of Wentworth's, comes to the Wentworth office, but Wentworth throws him out. Finally, Paul's son Dick arrives to ask Wentworth for permission to marry Wentworth's daughter. Wentworth demurs and shows Dick the door to the outer office. Immediately thereafter, a shot is heard and Wentworth is found dead.

This opening is the highlight of the film, with its introduction of numerous characters who could have some motive for killing Wentworth. In addition, the fire on the *Castle* opens up a completely different set of motives for the murder, implying that there will be other potential suspects introduced along the way. This is surely a case for the great criminologist Mr. Wong, who agrees to assist the police in the investigation in a semi-official capacity.

So what does Mr. Wong do with his authority? He finds the missing murder weapon and hides it from the police. At the end of the film, he even states that he traced the weapon to the true killer, surely something that would have been easier for the police to do if they had been provided with the weapon. Later, Wong deliberately destroys the print of a reconstructed agreement so that Street cannot have it. Wong then tells the lab to make a new print for him but not to let Street see it. Wong should have been arrested as an accessory after the fact; instead, he is hailed as the man who solved the murder of Wentworth.

Mr. Wong may, however, have been justified in these questionable activities because the actions of the police are so unorthodox. When Street goes out to the dangerous waterfront to arrest Kai Ling, he brings newspaper reporter Bobby Logan along with him, potentially putting her in serious danger. Later, he asks Bobby to interview some of the witnesses, so that he can secretly listen in on his office intercom. If there were a crime of being an incompetent after the fact, Street should have been arrested for that.

In terms of clichés, there are people shooting their guns in the dark, for no logical reason. Near the end, Paul Fleming falsely confesses to the killing of Wentworth in order to protect his son. In terms of comic relief, there is the particularly unfunny dialogue between Street and Bobby, who in this film is more irritating than ever. The one amusing character is Ludlow, chauffeur to the Wentworth family. When he is being questioned by Wong and the police, he is always sarcastic and belittling, deftly deferring suspicion from himself. Kenneth Harlan gives a fine performance in that role.

In the wrap-up, Wong accuses the chauffeur of committing the murder because Ludlow witnessed an agreement related to some smuggling. That is hardly sufficient evidence to convict Ludlow. But then the attorney, Victor Martin, for no reason, admits that he saw the chauffeur's signature on the agreement, and he says this right in front of the chauffeur. Ludlow then accuses Martin of double-crossing him, thereby revealing Martin as the killer of Wentworth.

Of course, if the lawyer had simply kept quiet, he would have had no problem and the chauffeur would not have accused Martin of anything. Thus, the ending has no believability. Even then, there is no explanation given as to why Wentworth was killed by Martin and in the context of the story, the viewer is hard-pressed to provide an explanation on his own. Frankly, it is all pretty depressing stuff.

After a viewer invests 70 minutes or so in the feature, the whole thing still makes no sense. Thus, a good set-up for a mystery has been done in, partly by a poor production, but mainly by very sloppy writing. *Doomed to Die* is another disappointment in the Mr. Wong series.

## *Phantom of Chinatown* (1940)

Watching these films in chronological order, *Phantom of Chinatown* can be a jarring experience and not just because of the spiffy hat that Captain Street wears. Boris Karloff is gone as Mr. Wong and in his place is Keye Luke, formerly of the Charlie Chan series and an actor of Chinese descent. As fine an actor as Karloff was, he never really fit the role of a Chinese detective and, in actuality, he stopped trying to bring any Asian authenticity to the role after the first movie in the series. With Luke, of course, there can be no issue as to whether his performance is "Chinese enough." The better question is whether, at the age of 36, Luke has the gravitas to play the wise detective from the East. Adding a mustache to give him an aura of maturity may not be enough.

The story is initially told in flashback by Dr. John Benton, who is lecturing his university colleagues concerning his recent archaeological expedition to the Mongolian desert. He is aided in his recitation by newsreel-style footage shot by Charles Fraser, the expedition's cameraman. Benton's story includes his discovery of the tomb of a Ming emperor, whose coffin contains a scroll that may reveal the secret of the Temple of Eternal Fire. (This is of great financial importance to China as it could reveal an enormous untapped reserve of oil.) On the trip, Mason, the co-pilot of the support plane for the group, disappeared during a windstorm and is presumed dead.

During the lecture, Dr. Benton takes a drink from the pitcher of water in the room, starts to choke, and falls to the floor, dead. It is later determined that he has been poisoned by an unusual Oriental vegetable poison. That brings Captain Street of the San Francisco homicide squad into the picture and later, young university student James Lee Wong. With Wong's assistance, Street captures the villain and recovers photos of the ancient Chinese scroll, which are returned to Win Len, a representative of the Chinese government. Street also promotes a romance between Jimmy Wong and Win Len.

When Street is first introduced to Mr. Wong in *Phantom of Chinatown*, the two do not know each other, even though they have just appeared together in five films. This is quite puzzling. However, if *Phantom of Chinatown* is viewed as a prequel to the previous five films, it all makes sense. Luke does play the role younger than Karloff; Wong is even called "Jimmy" by some of the characters. Viewed in that way, Luke does have the gravitas to play the part as a younger version of the soon-to-be great criminologist. Luke's casting and performance are nice changes for the series. Indeed, with several other Chinese performers in the film, such as the attractive Lotus Long as Win Len, the workers at the Chinatown telephone exchange and Wong's cook Foo, *Phantom of Chinatown* has more authenticity as a film about Asian characters than any of the features in the Charlie Chan and Mr. Moto series.

Another nice change is the elimination of the character of Bobby Logan, the officious newspaper reporter who was the comic relief in three films in the series. *Phantom of Chinatown* eschews a comic relief figure, instead finding some humor in the clash between American and Chinese cultures. Director Phil Rosen, who has never been known for his directorial acumen, surprisingly brings a little bit of style to the shot selection and the staging of scenes, adding to the effectiveness of the feature.

Even with those positives, it is hard to have strong feelings, good or bad, about *Phantom of Chinatown*. The plot does have some interest, particularly the early flashback scenes regarding the discovery of the tomb and the scroll. There is a somewhat suspenseful scene at the end when Wong makes himself the object of a trap, resulting in Wong's life being in danger. However, most of the story is mild and bland. The ending is particularly confusing, with Fraser and Mason (who managed to escape the desert unharmed) fighting with each other in a falling-out among thieves, with each having killed a different victim in the film. But how did either of them obtain the unusual Chinese poison?

Though *Phantom of Chinatown* is quite ordinary, it is still better than most of Karloff's Wong films. With Keye Luke, a mystery fan favorite in the lead for the first time in his career, *Phantom of Chinatown* has just enough appeal that the true mystery movie lover should find some interest in it.

## Afterwards

With the advent of the second horror film cycle in 1939, Karloff was busy during the 1940s, with much of his movie work in the horror genre. He also had a significant stage success during that decade in *Arsenic and Old Lace*, a mystery spoof. In the 1960s, Karloff's career was revitalized once again with appearances in a number of significant horror films such as *The Raven* (1963). Later, he played an aging horror film star in *Targets* (1968), directed by Peter Bogdanovich.

Karloff appeared in two television series with mystery elements. One was the 26–episode *Colonel March of Scotland Yard*, where he played a one-eyed investigator for Scotland Yard's Department of Queer Complaints. The stories were based on works by John Dickson Carr, writing under the name Carter Dickson. The series was filmed in London in 1952 but not syndicated in America until several years later. Also, Karloff was the host of *Thriller*, an anthology series of horror stories which ran for two seasons starting in 1960. In addition to introducing the stories, Karloff appeared in five of the show's 67 episodes. Karloff passed away in 1969.

With the end of the Mr. Wong series, Grant Withers continued to appear regularly in films throughout the 1940s into the mid–1950s and thereafter, he made numerous guest appearances in television. Withers committed suicide at the age of 54 in 1959.

Hugh Wiley wrote short stories into the 1940s, although none were about the Asian detective. Wiley's writings after that time focused on subjects of interest to him, such as early Chinese jade and bronze as well as engineering, a field to which he also returned. He died of influenza in 1968. There were no radio or television series about the Oriental detective.

# 19

# Barney Callahan
## *The Roving Reporter*

While it was rare for a newspaper reporter to go sleuthing in early detective fiction, it was very much different in the cinema. On the silver screen, in addition to several single crime films featuring a newspaper reporter as the prime detective, it was not unusual for reporters to become the lead detectives in mystery movie series. In the 1930s, there was the Torchy Blane series, discussed in Chapter 12 of this book. In the 1940s, it was the Big Town series from Pine-Thomas Productions, about a big city newspaper whose managing editor and reporters often became involved in crime investigations in order to obtain a good story.

The Torchy Blane series had some inspiration in the writings of Frederick Nebel, a well-known author of pulp mystery stories in the 1920s and 1930s. The Big Town film series was adapted from the *Big Town* radio series which debuted on CBS on October 19, 1937. Less well known today (and probably then) are the Roving Reporters films from 20th Century–Fox, which were released in the late 1930s. Perhaps the reason for its lack of fame is that the series was an original and not based on works from any other medium. Or, perhaps the reason is that the series was particularly low-budget, without any name performers.

## BACKGROUND

In 1938, 20th Century–Fox commenced their new mystery series, the Roving Reporters, even though there is only one reporter involved in all of the films and the tag line "Roving Reporters" is never used within a film. It is used, however, above the title of the features. The reporter is Barney Callahan of the *Evening Chronicle* or the *Daily Chronicle*, depending on the film. He is assisted in his three film adventures by Snapper Doolan, his photographer. Together the two somehow become involved in and then solve one murder mystery per film, even though, on the surface at least, they seem fairly incompetent.

In *Time Out for Murder* (1938), Callahan, with the assistance of a female bill collector, clears a bank clerk of the murder of a wealthy bank client. In *While New York Sleeps* (1938), Callahan probes the death of an insurance company investigator, which may be murder or suicide. In the final film in the series, *Inside Story* (1939), the plot concerns Barney's interest in a clip joint hostess and the murder in which she has become involved.

Callahan was played by Michael Whalen in all three films. Whalen was born in 1902 in Wilkes-Barre, Pennsylvania. Before entering films in 1935, he was a manager of a Woolworth's department store and performed in vaudeville. His early screen appearances were for 20th Century–Fox where he had significant roles in two Shirley Temple films, before starring in the Roving Reporters series.

Chick Chandler played Snapper Doolan throughout the three-film series. Chandler was born in 1905 in Kingston, New York. He made his film debut in a 1925 silent film, but his career did not take off until the early 1930s. He eventually received a contract at 20th Century–Fox. Prior to his role in the Roving Reporters series, he appeared in minor supporting roles in *Murder on a Honeymoon* (1935) from the Hildegarde Withers series and *Mr. Moto Takes a Chance* (1938).

The Roving Reporter films seemed to have a repertory group of supporting players. Cliff Clark was in all three films playing Inspector Collins, the policeman frustrated by Callahan's interference, a type of role very familiar to Clark. Jean Rogers, most famous for playing Dale Arden in *Flash Gordon* (1936), also appeared in all three films as the female lead, although always playing a different character. June Gale and Jane Darwell also appeared in multiple films in the series.

## THE FILM SERIES

### *Time Out for Murder* (1938)

Is that really Cliff Clark playing a policeman again? In how many movies did he appear as a police detective and in how many movies did his character fail to solve the murder? All the same, Clark, much like Thomas Jackson, Barton MacLane, Sam Levene and James Gleason, is always good to see in any crime film. Clark can always be counted on for a good performance, even if the film itself was otherwise lacking and even if Clark's character cannot correctly crack the case.

While *Time Out for Murder* has its faults, there is a good little mystery lurking in there somewhere. Johnny Martin, who works for a bank managed by his uncle Phillip Gregory, goes to the apartment of a wealthy bank client, Peggy Norton, to deliver a bank statement. While there, Johnny opens a locked drawer for Peggy, breaking his pen knife in the process and leaving his fingerprints for the police to later discover. Peggy gives Johnny a case of valuables from the drawer, asking him to take them to the bank for safekeeping while she goes away on a trip. Peggy is then shot and killed. The police search for Johnny, who has not yet returned to the bank and, unfortunately for him, is still holding Peggy's jewels when he is found. Johnny is arrested for murder. The case seems airtight but newspaper reporter Barney Callahan believes the killer may be one of his good friends, racketeer Dutch Moran. At the end of the film, there is an abduction, an armored car robbery, a shootout and the revelation of the killer of Peggy Norton, which comes as a true surprise.

It is probably not worthwhile dwelling for long on the negatives of *Time Out for Murder*; they are very obvious. There is Barney Callahan's trombone playing, Snappy Doolan's idiocy and repetitive practical joke of handing a hot flashbulb to unsuspecting people and the insertion into the story of female bill collector Margie Ross, who unconvincingly becomes involved in investigating the Norton killing. The performances are never more than adequate with the exception of Douglas Fowley who convincingly plays Dutch Moran, reminding the viewer a little of Jimmy Cagney in similar parts. The direction of H. Bruce Humberstone is unremarkable.

One of the strengths of the film is the motif of the telephone time service, where peo-

Reporter Barney Callahan (Michael Whalen), center, discovers a phonograph needle which may be an important clue in a murder case in *Time Out for Murder* (1938). Looking on are photographer Snapper Doolan (Chick Chandler) and bill collector Margie Ross (Gloria Stuart).

ple call the operator and obtain the correct time. Initially, these vignettes seem to be used as devices for bringing Johnny's girlfriend Helen Thomas into the story and as a comedy prop for Snapper Doolan. If that were all the telephone time service were intended to be, that still may have been sufficient because those scenes at the telephone service also bring lovely Jean Rogers into the film, playing Helen Thomas. However, there is a more important plot purpose for those scenes. The telephone time service is cleverly used to disguise the actual time of death of Peggy and provide one character with an alibi.

The film has numerous clues that may relate to the murder, such as the call to the operator at Peggy's apartment building to establish what is probably the wrong time of the killing, the chewing gum in Peggy's apartment, the fact that Moran has been paying many of Peggy's bills and the fact that Phillip Gregory disputes Johnny's statement that it was Gregory who sent Johnny to Peggy's apartment. After a while, it seems clear that Moran is not the killer and therefore the only logical substitute is Gregory. His disagreement with Johnny over the facts of the case is inexplicable unless Gregory is the killer.

As it turns out, and in a true surprise, Gregory is not the murderer. While the identity of the killer comes out of the blue, it is still an unanticipated plot twist, keeping *Time Out for Murder* interesting right to the end. And, unlike many other whodunits, the ending has its independent excitement, with two of Moran's men freelancing on an armored car robbery, Margie Ross somehow riding along on the robbery and the ensuing car chase and shootout. It is all somewhat confusing and it may not make much sense but it is better than bringing all of the suspects into one room and accusing each of them of the crime, a common ending to movie mysteries. At least in a bit of realism, the not-too-bright Callahan does not really solve Peggy's murder. The solution is dropped into his lap.

Given its clever plot, *Time Out for Murder* should have been much better than it turned out to be. In particular, the unfunny comedy padding should have been eliminated. Nevertheless, the film is worth a look, as a good example of the type of second feature mystery programmer produced by a major studio in the 1930s.

## *While New York Sleeps* (1938)

This film has a great title that suggests a tale of crime on the mean streets of the Big Apple, in that shadowy and clandestine time between dusk and dawn when only those with nefarious motives prowl the byways of the concrete jungle. In fact, the title has nothing to do with the plot, proving once again that you cannot judge a movie by its title.

In New York City, there has been a series of bond messenger murders, with the valuable bonds they were carrying now missing. Barney Callahan has little interest in the crimes until his friend, insurance detective Steve Martin, who was apparently investigating the bond robberies, is shot and killed. In Martin's apartment Barney finds a hand buzzer which the police have overlooked. (It is truly surprising that the police in these types of films so often overlook a piece of physical evidence which the lead detective spots immediately.) As a result of that clue, Barney becomes suspicious of nightclub owner Joe Marco, a well-known practical joker. It is not clear why a well-known practical joker would bring a trick device along on a killing, but not much else about the film makes any sense either.

At this point in the feature, the mystery comes to a screeching halt. The viewer is treated to some of Marco's practical jokes, there are a couple of musical numbers presented at the club, Barney's romance with his girlfriend Judy King goes on the fritz when Judy's boyfriend from Johnstown, Pennsylvania, shows up, and there are more fun and games with Inspector Collins. These scenes seem interminable, without any real humor (unless one enjoys, along with Marco, practical jokes such as exploding cigars and collapsing chairs). The moment where Barney tries to end Judy's romance with her boyfriend by use of a forged letter is particularly mean-spirited, without an ounce of humor. The only high point of these scenes is Jean Rogers playing Judy King. Rogers has never looked lovelier since playing Dale Arden in *Flash Gordon* (1936). It is a shame that she never became a bigger star in Hollywood.

Late in the film, the mystery gets back on track, with a few legitimate suspects finally appearing at the nightclub and with the "surprise" killing of Marco which surprises no one. Once again, Callahan does not solve the case. He merely happens to be near Nora Parker's apartment when the bonds are being recovered by Red, who leads him back to the killer and the bond thieves, who immediately admit their guilt. Callahan is not much of a newspaper reporter, as he fakes evidence in a police investigation and calls in the news of Marco's death to his paper before the killing may have actually occurred. Yet Barney is a better reporter than a detective since, once again, the solution to the crimes is simply handed to him. He does no real detective work.

There are some aspects of this film to appreciate. The cast may be a little better than *Time Out for Murder*, since it includes Harold Huber (whose overacting as Joe Marco actually works well for this film), William Demarest, Sidney Blackmer, Marc Lawrence and Joan Woodbury. Also, Chick Chandler as Snapper Doolan actually has a few funny moments. Other than those minor matters, it is hard to find anything positive to say about *While New York Sleeps*.

*Time Out for Murder* provided promise that the remainder of the Roving Reporters series would be pleasurable viewing. With *While New York Sleeps*, however, that hope comes to a swift end. It is not surprising that the series ended after just one more film.

## Inside Story (1939)

[*This is one of the few films discussed in this book which the author did not view.*]

*Inside Story* was the first film directed by movie star Richard Cortez, who had a background in mystery movies, having previously played Sam Spade and Perry Mason for the cinema. The movie was based on a short story by Ben Ames which had previously been filmed by Fox as *Man Trouble* in 1930. The case involves a clip joint hostess (Jean Rogers) who becomes involved with a murder at her club, her efforts to discover the real killer and her attempts to escape from an onerous boss. A review of a synopsis of the film's plot indicates that it is typical for the series, leading one to conclude that the best thing about the film could be, once again, pretty Jean Rogers.

### AFTERWARDS

Since the Roving Reporters series was a Hollywood original, and not a very successful one at that, there were no further films, radio series or television series about Barney Callahan or Snapper Doolan or, for that matter, any other reporters who liked to rove.

After the series ended, Michael Whalen continued working sporadically in Hollywood, while at the same time often returning to his stage roots. Of interest to mystery fans, Whalen played the role of Philip Lombard, the potential hero or villain of Agatha Christie's *Ten Little Indians*, in the initial Broadway production, which opened in New York City in 1944. Later Whalen did significant guest work in television. He died in 1974.

Chick Chandler continued working regularly in Hollywood after the end of the Roving Reporters series, usually playing a figure of comic relief. He had no other significant roles in mystery movies. Later, he appeared regularly on television. He died in 1988.

# 20

# Brass Bancroft
## *The Secret Service Agent*

Warner Brothers was a major player in the Hollywood detective series of the 1930s. During that decade, the studio released six Perry Mason films, nine Torchy Blane films, four Nancy Drew films and even three Philo Vances. By the early 1940s, however, Warners had completely exited the mystery series field, although during the decade, it did release several outstanding non-series detective movies such as *The Maltese Falcon* (1941) and *The Big Sleep* (1946).

Warners' last crime series, which commenced in 1939 and ended the following year, featured Secret Service agent Brass Bancroft. An original concoction by the studio, the series was of low quality and would be forgotten today if not for the presence of Ronald Reagan in the lead role. The Brass Bancroft series was a disappointing conclusion to Warner Brothers' productions of mystery movie series.

## BACKGROUND

Brass Bancroft's introduction into the Secret Service and his first adventure is related in *Secret Service of the Air* (1939), wherein Bancroft, a pilot in private industry, is brought into the Secret Service to help the federal government combat the smuggling of illegal aliens into the United States by air. Thereafter, Bancroft remained with the Secret Service and in his next two films, *Code of the Secret Service* and *Smashing the Money Ring*, both from 1939, he fought two different gangs of counterfeiters. Bancroft then ended his screen career with *Murder in the Air* (1940), in which he fought spies attempting to steal secret government plans.

The United States Secret Service division of the Treasury Department was created on July 5, 1865, for the purpose of preventing the circulation of counterfeit currency within the United States. In 1867, its responsibilities were expanded to include the task of "detecting persons perpetrating fraud against the government." That broad mandate was then interpreted to include the prevention of smuggling into the United States, and thus, *Secret Service of the Air* accurately reflects one of the crimes that is within the jurisdiction of the Secret Service. In the early 1900s, the Service began providing protection for the president of the United States and today, the most well-known function of the Secret Service is protection of members of the executive branch. Nevertheless, none of the Brass Bancroft films concern those duties of the Service.

William H. Moran was the director of the Secret Service from 1917 to 1936. The credits to the first two movies in the Brass Bancroft series state that they were based on materials compiled by W.H. Moran, possibly from his unpublished memoirs which were purchased by Warner Brothers. It is believed, however, that all four films had original scripts with no relationship to any materials provided by Moran.

Ronald Reagan starred as the young pilot and Secret Service agent Brass Bancroft. Reagan was born on February 6, 1911, in Tampico, Illinois. He began his career in entertainment as a sports broadcaster for a Des Moines radio station, with one of his duties recreating baseball games of the Chicago Cubs from telegraph reports. He then moved to Hollywood and in 1937 appeared in his first film, *Love Is on the Air*, playing a radio reporter, a role with which he had obvious familiarity. Reagan had an early screen success in *Brother Rat* (1938), playing one of the three young cadets involved in some romantic misadventures, which led to his casting in the Brass Bancroft films.

Eddie Foy, Jr., appeared in all four films playing comic relief character Gabby Walters, a friend of Bancroft's. Foy, who was born in 1905 in New Rochelle, New York, was the son of famous song and dance man Eddie Foy. After the death of his wife, Foy, Sr. incorporated all of the children into his vaudeville act, using the name "The Seven Little Foys." Foy, Jr. began appearing in films at the beginning of the sound era, usually in music-related roles. The Brass Bancroft series was the only mystery film series in which he appeared.

## THE FILMS

### *Secret Service of the Air* (1939)

The beginning of *Secret Service of the Air* is promising. The story could have been ripped out of today's headlines, as it involves the federal government trying to thwart illegal smuggling of aliens into this country from Mexico. In the early moments of the movie, there is a sudden and surprise burst of violence, as an airplane pilot disposes of his cargo of aliens in an unusual manner, while the plane is still in the air. But when the main storyline of *Secret Service of the Air* begins, it is all clichés and comic relief, very disappointing after the strong opening.

In addition to smuggling illegal aliens into America, the criminals have recently brutally murdered a government agent. Tom Saxby of the Secret Service is determined to eliminate the smugglers so he recruits Brass Bancroft, a commercial transport pilot, to infiltrate the gang. Saxby concocts a deception wherein Bancroft is arrested and convicted of a trumped-up charge and then sent to jail, where he can obtain information about the smugglers from Ace Hamrick, the gang's incarcerated pilot. The subterfuge works and Bancroft learns enough in prison to become a flyer for the gang in Mexico. There, as a result of another ruse concocted by Saxby, Bancroft breaks up the gang and captures the leader.

Even though *Secret Service of the Air* is a second feature only, it is still a very disappointing film. One problem with the film is that it moves too quickly in setting up the deception created by Saxby. Once Bancroft is recruited by Saxby, he is arrested, tried and convicted on the phony charges, arrives at jail, escapes with Ace Hamrick almost before they meet, and then they are both quickly re-captured by the police. There is no time spent showing Bancroft acclimating to prison life or gaining Ace's confidence. Then, when Bancroft moves to Mexico, he becomes a pilot for the smugglers almost immediately. There is no time spent laying the groundwork for Bancroft proving his bona fides to the smugglers.

As a result of the failure to take the time to lay a foundation for the movie's twists and turns, nothing seems real or convincing about the film, which is particularly disappointing as Warner Brothers knew how to handle this type of story. For better examples of the implementation of this plot device, see *Bullets or Ballots* (1936), with Edward G. Robinson going undercover, or *White Heat* (1949), with Edmond O'Brien infiltrating a gang.

Other parts of the plot make little sense. For example, Bancroft and Hamrick escape from prison while on a work crew outside the jail, by simply driving away in an accomplice's car parked nearby. If it were always so easy to escape from jail! Then there is the problem of tricking Cameron, the leader of the smugglers, into flying across the border into the United States with the illegal aliens on board the plane. Luckily for Saxby, the gang begins to suspect Bancroft and they decide to wire Saxby's hotel room to listen in when he talks to Bancroft. Saxby knows about the eavesdropping and tells a tale of Bancroft flying back to the States to locate counterfeit plates. That is all Cameron needs to get on the plane and then to be captured with the evidence.

However, Saxby's complex plot required the gang to suspect Bancroft, learn about Bancroft's meeting with Saxby, and then to wire the room so they could listen to the conversation between the two federal agents. In other words, for Saxby's plan to work, it required the smugglers to do something that no one on the government side of the case would ever expect them to do. This is just one example of faulty plotting in the film. Others include Bancroft's lame explanation to the smugglers as to how he got out of Alcatraz so quickly or why the gang would believe Bancroft over Hamrick when Hamrick accuses Bancroft of being a government agent. The list could go on and on.

While some of the movie seem rushed, other parts move too slowly. Bancroft's romantic problems at the beginning of the film are quite boring. Throughout the film, Eddie Foy, Jr., is particularly irritating as the unfunny comic relief, once even looking at a brush in his hand, pretending it is a mirror and commenting that he needs a shave. What? Isn't comedy supposed to make some sense? When Foy is on the screen, the plot comes to a stop.

If not for Ronald Reagan's continuing role in this series, these movies would have been forgotten long ago. At least in *Secret Service of the Air,* there is a chance to marvel at how young he once was. That is one of the few reasons to watch this film.

## *Code of the Secret Service* (1939)

According to the Turner Classic Movies website, Ronald Reagan thought so little of *Code of the Secret Service* that he encouraged Warner Brothers not to release it. Even with the small investment the studio had made in the feature, they were not willing to give it up, and so the film was released to, not unexpectedly, less than stellar reviews. Over the years, the reputation of *Code of the Secret Service* has not improved, and therefore few modern viewers expect to receive very much from the film. That is a fortunate attitude because *Code of the Secret Service* delivers very little.

In his new case for the Secret Service, Bancroft is on the trail of counterfeiters who have stolen Treasury engraving plates, allowing them to produce counterfeit bills of the highest quality. Bancroft meets Treasury agent Dan Crockett in Mexico, where it is believed the counterfeiters are headquartered. Crockett is shot and killed by the villains, who frame Bancroft for the murder. Bancroft escapes and discovers the hideout of the gang in a monastery. While Bancroft is trying to convince some Mexican troops to storm the monastery, he and Elaine, an innocent bystander, are captured by the gang. Bancroft and

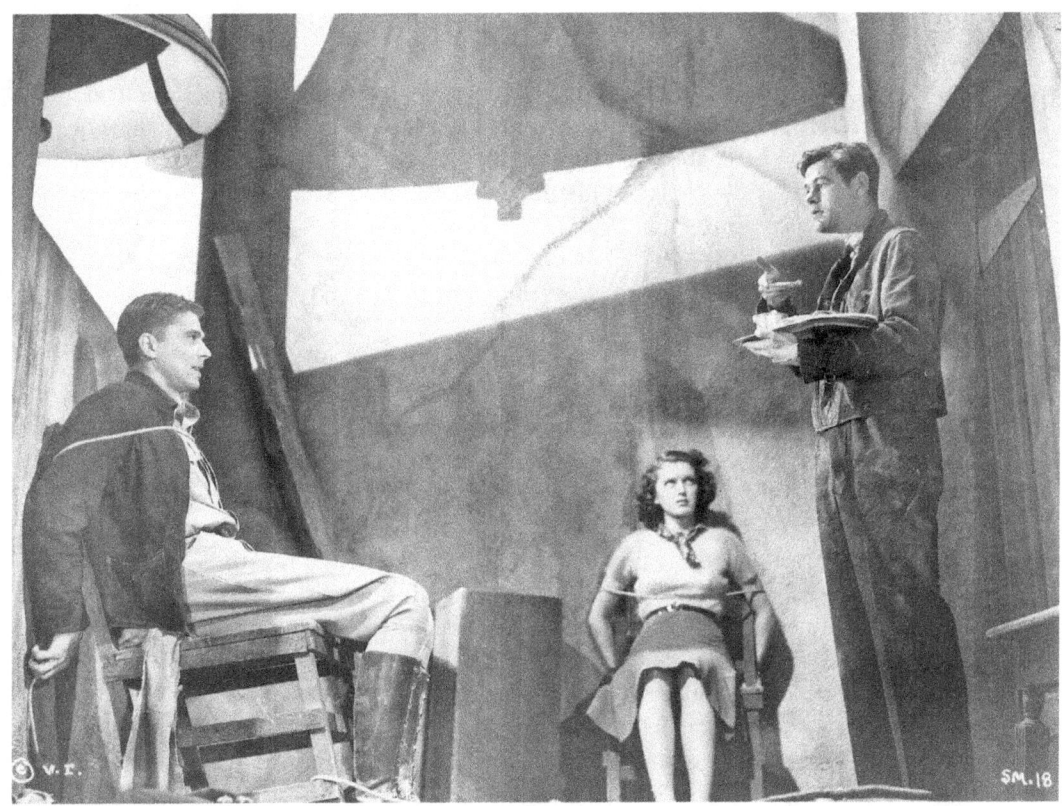

Brass Bancroft (Ronald Reagan), left, has been captured by counterfeiters along with Elaine (Rosella Towne). Bancroft has already escaped his bonds and is about to attack the henchman (actor unidentified) carrying the food in *Code of the Secret Service* (1938).

Elaine eventually escape and recover the stolen plates, but none of the gang members are captured. They are all killed, several in their own explosion at the monastery.

In some ways, *Code of the Secret Service* seems like a movie serial, as Bancroft escapes from peril after peril just in the nick of time. The film ends in a car chase around steep and narrow mountain roads. Even though it is the villain's car which finally goes over the cliff, this sequence is still a serial cliffhanger cliché. The movie is also a poor man's *The 39 Steps* (1935), with Bancroft escaping from a train, being saved from a bullet by a book he was carrying, being handcuffed to the reluctant heroine and the two having to escape the villains together. Unfortunately, Brass Bancroft is no Richard Hannay and director Noel M. Smith is no Alfred Hitchcock. The viewer therefore should either watch a real serial or rent a copy of Hitchcock's masterpiece, rather than taking the time to watch *Code of the Secret Service*.

As with the first film in the series, *Secret Service of the Air*, Reagan makes an engaging hero. Even though these films were no more than second features, they provided a rare chance for Reagan to be the lead in a film produced at a major studio. Probably then, but surely after all these years, Reagan is the best thing in *Code of the Secret Service*. Eddie Foy, Jr., the comic relief, is as irritating and unfunny as he was in the prior film. Rosella Towne is also back from the prior film but in a different and more substantial role. Towne is quite attractive and is a plus for the movie. (Unfortunately, though, she is no Madeleine Carroll.) Joseph King replaces John Litel as Tom Saxby, Bancroft's boss, but the role is so negligible that the difference is hardly noticeable.

It is rare to see a film like this set in Mexico, particularly one that sometimes takes on aspects of a Western, and the novelty of the setting is a plus. In the end, though, there is nothing new going on here, and what is going on here is shot in a lackadaisical and unenthusiastic manner. This film is really just for fans of Ronald Reagan, and for those fans, there are better Reagan films.

## *Smashing the Money Ring* (1939)

During the course of *Smashing the Money Ring*, there are two sets of montages of life behind prison bars. It must have been easy for the B–unit at Warner Brothers to obtain that footage, since Warners had been making prison movies for quite some time. There were *I Am a Fugitive from a Chain Gang* (1932), with Paul Muni sentenced to a Southern prison for a crime he did not commit, *20,000 Years in Sing Sing* (1932) (actually made by First National which merged into Warner Brothers), with Spencer Tracy taking a murder rap for his girlfriend and heading to the penitentiary, *San Quentin* (1937), with Humphrey Bogart sentenced to a jail where the warden is in love with Bogart's sister, and *Each Dawn I Die* (1939) with James Cagney playing a newspaper reporter who is framed for a crime and sentenced to the Big House. And that is just a partial list, with many Warner Brothers gangster films having at least a few scenes behind prison walls.

While part of the Brass Bancroft mystery series, this film is more prison yarn than mystery, in the tradition of the famous Warner Brothers prison films of prior years. For a viewer hoping to see a mystery movie, *Smashing the Money Ring* is the wrong choice. For a viewer hoping to see a good prison picture, there are far better alternatives available.

As the film opens, it seems that there is a counterfeiting ring operating from right inside the Big House. The movie follows the chain of the fake money as it makes it way outside prison walls to a distribution ring on board a gambling ship named the *Kismet* where the counterfeiters pass the bills to unwary customers. The ship's owner, Steve Parker, an ex-convict himself, tries to stop the racket but is threatened by one of the crooks, Dice Matthews. Parker decides to tip off the police about Dice and in order to protect himself, Parker slugs a cop, expecting to spend 30 days in jail. Instead, Parker is given a one-year sentence, to be served at the same institution where Dice is sent.

This opening is the strongest part of the film, as it weaves its tale of counterfeit bills being printed inside a penitentiary to those same bills being spread outside the penitentiary, amid the backstory of animosity between Parker and Dice. It takes some time for the Secret Service to become involved, and that involvement is minimal until the story proceeds inside prison walls. There the focus is on Brass Bancroft, as he goes undercover as an inmate to try to locate the counterfeiting plates.

After that point, the story is all clichés: a tough warden, a tougher captain of the guards, a likable prisoner running the prison library, a fight among the convicts almost ending in a knifing, and then the requisite escape from jail. Bancroft actually does little to figure out who the crime boss is, solving the case by somehow surviving a shooting at close range, thus being able to subsequently relate the name of the crime boss to the surprised prison warden. Bancroft is still so unprepared to solve the case that as he is telling the warden about his discovery, the crime boss gets the drop on him once again, almost resulting in another close range shooting of Bancroft!

The plot cannot withstand much scrutiny. Were they really counterfeiting money in jail? If they had such good plates there, why not move them out of the jail, making the illegal operation work in a much smoother manner? What was hidden by Parker inside the prison algebra book? That is never explained. If Dice did not kill Parker (and apparently he did not), then why was anyone else interested in murdering Parker?

*Smashing the Money Ring* does have its good points, as there is an intrinsic interest in scenes at a prison, the escape is exiting, and the identity of the leader of the gang of counterfeiters is surprising. However, there is really nothing new here.

*Note on the Remake*: *Smashing the Money Ring* was a partial remake of Warners' 1936 prison movie *Jailbreak*. Thus, in addition to being a prison movie, *Smashing the Money Ring* continued another Warner Brothers tradition: remaking older films but changing the title so that when the unsuspecting moviegoer purchased a ticket for the second film, he would not realize that he had recently seen a similar movie. This same issue is addressed at the beginning of the discussion of *Calling Philo Vance* (1940) in Chapter 1 of this book.

## *Murder in the Air* (1940)

Secret Service agent Brass Bancroft goes undercover to expose a gang of saboteurs by posing as Steve Swenko, a spy who was killed in a train crash ironically caused by sabotage. Using a letter hidden in the heel of Swenko's shoe, Bancroft obtains an introduction to Joe Garvey, the head of an allegedly patriotic organization of naturalized American citizens, but which is, in reality, a front for the saboteurs. Now a part of the spy organization, Bancroft is given the assignment to board a dirigible, make contact with Rumford, the secretary to a representative of the League of Nations, and follow his plans to destroy the dirigible and help to steal the secret plans. However, after Bancroft boards the dirigible, Garvey finds out the truth about him and wires Rumford, who knocks Bancroft out while the dirigible is crashing in a storm. Presumed killed in the crash, Bancroft nevertheless recovers after a short stay in the hospital, just in time to help shoot Garvey and Rumford out of the sky.

On its face, the core plot is quite appealing, with an interesting story arc where Swenko's wife appears, obviously recognizes Bancroft as an impersonator, and deviously attempts to trap him on behalf of Garvey. There are other nice touches, such as when Bancroft first appears at a hotel asking for Garvey and is accosted by policemen who try to beat the truth out of him. When Bancroft does not flinch, the policemen, now revealed to be fakes, are willing to introduce Bancroft to Garvey.

That said, *Murder in the Air* is painfully unexciting. There is lots of stock footage to pad the story. The direction by Lewis Seiler is mundane at best. Seiler just appears to be going through the motions for this B–feature, employing only standard camera setups and angles. His direction does nothing to add to the pace or excitement. In the hands of a more enthusiastic director, *Murder in the Air* could have been a much better film.

An additional reason for the lack of excitement is that this story has been done many times before and many times since, and there is little new in this rendition of the old chestnut of a spy or policeman going undercover into the enemy camp. Eddie Foy, Jr., is painfully unfunny as Gabby Waters, and the emphasis on his antics early in the film dampens, to a large degree, any excitement there may have been in the story. At 55 minutes, this is the shortest film in the series and despite that fact, it is still boring in many spots. The

While posing as spy Steve Swenko in order to infiltrate a gang of saboteurs, Brass Bancroft (Ronald Reagan) meets Swenko's wife Hilda (Lya Lys), who is obviously not convinced of Bancroft's bona fides, in *Murder in the Air* (1940).

introduction of the science fiction device of the inertia projector is hardly a plus for the feature.

Despite being produced at a major studio, the Brass Bancroft features were anything but major films. Their only claim to fame today is as a training ground for Ronald Reagan who, after this film, was off to better things. Mercifully, the Brass Bancroft films came to an end with this feature.

## Afterwards

With the conclusion of the series, Reagan stayed at Warner Brothers, where he received his two best-remembered roles. One was in *Knute Rockne — All American* (1940), where he played George Gipp, aka "The Gipper," the ill-fated Notre Dame football player ("Win just one for the Gipper!"). The other was in *Kings Row* (1942), where Reagan played Drake McHugh, whose legs were unnecessarily amputated ("Where's the rest of me?"). Reagan thereafter had an unspectacular film career. In television, he was the host of *Death Valley Days* in the mid–1960s. Reagan was then elected governor of California in 1966 and president of the United States in 1980. He passed away on June 5, 2004.

Eddie Foy, Jr., continued appearing in films, playing his father on several occasions, as for example, in *Yankee Doodle Dandy* (1942), a film about George M. Cohan. The story of Eddie Foy and his musical offspring was brought to the screen in *The Seven Little Foys* (1955), starring Bob Hope as Eddie Foy, Sr. Eddie Foy, Jr., passed away in 1983.

Since Brass Bancroft was a studio concoction, there were no other films made about the character. Similarly, there were no radio or television shows about the Secret Service agent.

# 21

# Tailspin Tommy
## *The Young Aviator*

After Charles Lindbergh's successful solo flight across the Atlantic in 1927, interest in airplanes and aviators grew rapidly, and the creators of feature films, serials and comic strips were happy to oblige their audiences and readers with stories on the subject. *Wings* (1927), which won the Oscar for Best Picture, was one of the earliest full-length films about aviation. *The Airmail Mystery* (1932) and *The Phantom of the Air* (1933) were Universal serials of the early 1930s which emphasized flying and flyers. And then there were the comic strips based on aviation, such as *Scorchy Smith* (first appearance in 1930) and *Smilin' Jack* (first appearance in 1933).

The very first newspaper comic strip about airplanes and flyers, however, was *Tailspin Tommy*, which made its bow in 1928. It was so popular that in the mid–1930s, Tommy and his friends became the subject of two serials released by Universal. Then, in 1939, they became the stars of a motion picture series produced at Monogram Pictures. The four films in the Tailspin Tommy series combined aviation and aviators with crime and spy stories and were primarily directed toward a juvenile market.

## BACKGROUND

### Comic Strip

The comic strip *Tailspin Tommy* debuted as a daily strip on May 21, 1928, and added a Sunday feature on October 20, 1929. Hal Forrest was the original cartoonist for the strip, and the stories were written by Glen Chaffin. In 1933, Forrest bought out Chaffin's interest in the strip and that is why Forrest has the only credit in the Monogram film series.

Forrest was born in Philadelphia, Pennsylvania, in 1895. He attended the Art Institute of Chicago from 1911 to 1915 and during World War I, he enlisted and was assigned to the aviation section of the Signal Corp in Texas. While still in the reserves, Forrest started drawing an aviation cartoon which, after the excitement caused by Lindbergh's solo flight, developed into the *Tailspin Tommy* newspaper comic strip.

The strip told the story of young Tommy Tomkins, who lived with his widowed mother in Littlefield, Colorado, a small town about a hundred miles from Denver. Tommy, who had an interest in airplanes from an early age, talked "airplane" so much that he even acquired the nickname "Tailspin Tommy" before he ever rode in a plane. As an older Tommy worked on autos at the local garage, he took a correspondence school course in aviation in the hope of learning to fly a plane.

Tommy's life changed forever one day when he spotted a plane in trouble and ran to help out. The plane was flown by mail pilot Milt Howe, who made a successful emergency landing near Littlefield. Howe took Tommy under his wing, so to speak, and got him a job in Texas fixing airplanes at Three Points Airlines, which was owned by Paul Smith. There, Tommy met his girlfriend-to-be, Betty Lou Barnes, a waitress at the airport café.

Tommy eventually obtained his pilot's license, as did Betty Lou and Tommy's childhood friend Skeeter Milligan, who had followed Tommy from Colorado to Texas. The three then became involved in airplane adventures all over the world.

## Serials

The first serial based upon a comic strip, *Tailspin Tommy* (1934) also spawned the first sound serial sequel, *Tailspin Tommy in the Great Air Mystery* (1935). The two serials were closely related, with much of the action of the first serial set in the town of Littleville, where Tommy Tomkins, his friend Skeeter Milligan, and Tommy's girlfriend-to-be, flying ace Betty Lou Barnes, were introduced to each other. It was Betty Lou who gave Tommy the nickname "Tailspin Tommy." This was a change from the comic strip, where Tommy received that nickname at a young age because he was so interested in planes.

Although the main plot to *Tailspin Tommy* was original to the serial, a number of incidents came from the comic strip, such as Tommy earning his flyer's license, a payroll robbery, an attempt to hijack valuable shipments being transported by air and the filming of a World War I movie, *The Midnight Patrol*. (The plot idea of the filming of a movie at Three Points Airlines was carried over into *Stunt Pilot*, the second film in the Monogram series.) Tommy eventually earned his pilot's license and helped defeat the sabotage occurring at Three Points Airlines.

The sequel, *Great Air Mystery*, took less from the comic strip but maintained its spirit with an emphasis on aviation and the adventures of Tailspin, Skeeter and Betty Lou. It picked up where the first one left off, with the opening chapter set partly in Littleville before Tommy, Skeeter and Betty Lou became involved in evil doings in a Central American island known as Nazil. Airplane stunts and cliffhangers abounded in each serial. Although the three main characters came back in the second serial, only Noah Beery, Jr., reprised his role (Skeeter Milligan). Clark Williams replaced Maurice Murphy as Tommy and serial favorite Jean Rogers replaced Patricia Farr as Betty Lou.

## Film Series

In 1939, independent studio Monogram Pictures commenced a four-movie Tailspin Tommy series. All four films were released in 1939, a clear indication of the quick shooting schedules and low budgets of the movies. The films tell the story of Tommy Tomkins, a young aviator at Three Points Airlines, who, in addition to being a pilot, is an inventor. During the course of the series, Tommy invents an airplane bombing system and a device to track airplanes in flight. Tommy's girlfriend Betty Lou Barnes apparently also works for the airlines, as does Skeeter Milligan, another young pilot. Paul Smith is the owner of Three Points Airlines.

While each of the films is as much about aviation and personal relationships as they are about crime, the movies always have a significant crime-related component. In *Mystery Plane* (1939), Tommy fights off a gang of criminals who are trying to steal his innovative airplane bombing system. In *Stunt Pilot* (1939), Tommy investigates a murder that occurred in the sky. In *Sky Patrol* (1939), Tommy thwarts a gang of munitions smugglers. In *Danger Flight* (1939), he prevents a payroll robbery.

Tailspin Tommy was played by John Trent in all four movies. Trent, whose given name was LaVerne Brown, was born in Orange County, California, in 1906. He became a pilot while in college and did some barnstorming through Virginia before becoming a co-pilot for TWA, one of the largest airplane companies of the era. He then did a screen test and appeared in a few films before starring in the Tailspin Tommy series, which must be considered the highlight of his acting career.

Milburn Stone played Skeeter Milligan for the entire series. Stone, who was born in 1904 in Kansas, appeared in vaudeville and on the stage before moving to Hollywood in 1935. There, he never seemed to obtain any roles more significant that bit parts or character parts in B–movies or serials. Skeeter Milligan was Stone's only continuing role in a movie series.

Pretty Marjorie Reynolds played Betty Lou Barnes in all four films. Reynolds, who was born in Buhl, Idaho, in 1917, began her film career as a child actress in the silent era and then moved into sound films in the early 1930s, usually in uncredited roles. Reynolds finally received more significant roles later in the decade, such as appearing as the female lead in several B–Westerns, before receiving the role of Betty Lou. Around the same time, she also appeared in three of the Mr. Wong mystery movies, also from Monogram Pictures.

Jason Robards played the small role of Paul Smith in all four films. Born in 1892, he appeared first in silent films and then worked steadily in sound films, usually in small roles in B–movies. The role of Paul Smith was a typical film part for Robards.

## THE FILMS

### *Mystery Plane* (1939)

As Tommy Tomkins' first feature film adventure begins, Tommy is trying to interest the U.S. military in his airplane bombing system by providing them with a test of the device's accuracy as it drops missiles from a high altitude plane. Once it is clear that Tommy's device actually works, a group of villains attempts to steal the designs for the system so that they can sell them to a foreign power. Their method for accomplishing their evil plan is to kidnap Tommy and his friends Skeeter and Betty Lou and then threaten harm to Betty Lou if Tommy does not cooperate by drawing a copy of the plans for them.

After holding out for a while, Tommy apparently finally concedes. Unfortunately for the villains, Paul Smith, the owner of Three Points Airlines, suspects that Tommy and his friends have been kidnapped, locates the hiding place and arrives with the authorities to capture the criminals. In the meantime, Tommy, Skeeter and Betty Lou have already escaped and stolen a plane. In the ensuing chase in the air, the remaining criminals are killed.

*Mystery Plane* is not necessarily a crime movie; it seems more in the nature of an adventure film. It is clearly intended for a juvenile audience. Thus, it takes almost half the movie before a crime is even contemplated. Prior to that, the film focuses on an important event in young Tommy's life when he was about nine years old. He met the famous flyer Brandy Rand, who was conducting a flight exhibition at a county fair. Tommy helped to rescue Brandy when he landed in a lake after leaping from a plane using a parachute. This was one of the most significant events in young Tommy's life as he worshiped Brandy as a hero.

Unfortunately, while these scenes are mildly interesting, they are puerile in content and tone and consume far too much of the film's short running time. They might, however, have been interesting to a young audience.

Matters become more interesting as the film moves to contemporary times, with the grown-up Tommy now about 25 years of age. Here, though, the problem is a lack of suspense or tension, even after Tommy, Skeeter and Betty Lou have been captured. The female villain, Anita, who captures Betty Lou, seems like one of the nicest people around. The head villain seems particularly unintimidating. The most he does to try to get Tommy to cooperate is to cause Betty Lou to scream one time, off-screen. Surprisingly, a much older and wearier Brandy Rand is one of the gang and he is not very threatening either, since he appears to be drunk most of the time. Indeed, the criminals are so innocuous that Tommy, Skeeter and Betty Lou are able to overpower three of the villains by themselves, without much effort.

The lack of menacing villains is symptomatic of the lack of excitement throughout the film. Tommy and Skeeter are captured by the villains by simply waving them to a stop on a country road. Betty Lou is later captured off-screen. The authorities come to the villains' hideout in a slow-speed boat ride. Over and over again, potentially exciting moments are handled in an unexciting way.

There are two striking scenes. The first involves Tommy and Skeeter taking their plane to a high altitude to conduct the bombing test. The oxygen tanks on the plane fail, and Tommy and Skeeter lose consciousness. The plane then streaks toward the earth, with Tommy waking up just in time. It is one of the few exciting moments in the film.

The other moment occurs at the end. Brandy finally realizes his errant ways and, in order to prevent Tommy and the gang from being shot out of the sky, deliberately flies his plane into the ocean, killing all of the villains aboard. For a movie that appears to be intended for a younger audience, and probably for that reason has such tame villains, this is a particularly brutal plot resolution.

Obviously, *Mystery Plane* was intended to fill the bottom of a movie double bill and did not aspire to great heights. If that was its goal, the film achieved it. *Mystery Plane* may still have some interest because of its origins in a comic strip and younger viewers may appreciate it, but other than that, there is not much to recommend it.

*Note on the Source Material*: Each of the films had the writing credit "Original Story by Hal Forrest." While it may be that all of the films were based on a comic strip continuity, it would be difficult to identify every one of them. However, the opening of the film, wherein young Tommy Tomkins helps to rescue pilot Brandy Rand, may be inspired by the opening story of the comic strip where young Tommy Tomkins helps to rescue pilot Milt Howe.

## *Stunt Pilot* (1939)

The Tailspin Tommy series was more about aviation than crime, with lots of planes doing rolls and flips and crashing to the earth, usually without serious injury to the passengers on the planes. *Stunt Pilot* is no exception, with the first two-thirds of the film about a motion picture studio making a film at Three Points Airlines, with lots of stunts, two crashes (without injuries), allegedly defective planes and the usual trappings of aviation movies. When the mystery finally comes near the end of the feature, it is tepid at best, with an obvious perpetrator and the means of proving the crime apparent from the outset.

As the film opens, Tommy is engaged as a stunt pilot for the Hollywood film being shot at Three Points Airlines. However, after a near-fatal crash in an old plane, he quits because he believes that Sheehan, the director of the film, has de-emphasized safety in favor of obtaining authentic crash footage. The movie company calls in Earl Martin, an arrogant but experienced stunt pilot, to complete the film. Before his film work commences, Martin takes Betty Lou into the air in a defective plane, resulting in another crash, this time with Betty Lou at risk. That leads to a fistfight between Tommy and Martin.

The climax of the Hollywood film in production is a dogfight in the air, with Skeeter volunteering to play the role of the hero because he needs the money for an operation for his sister. Skeeter is supposed to shoot Martin's plane out of the air with a machine gun mounted on his plane. The machine gun is supposed to have blanks instead of real bullets. Tommy replaces Skeeter in the plane and, when the air scene is shot, real bullets are fired by Tommy's machine gun, resulting in Martin crashing to his death. Tommy is arrested on somewhat specious circumstantial evidence. Nevertheless, there is finally a real mystery. However, the film then wraps up quite quickly, with Tommy identifying the true killer and helping to capture him on a train.

*Stunt Pilot* was made for juveniles and not for ardent mystery fans, but even the young viewer will know who the killer is, far in advance of the time when the film characters figure it out. The means of discovery, by use of the photos from a machine gun camera, will surprise no one, not even the youngest viewer. Even the death of Martin comes as no surprise, once several of the characters discuss the real machine gun bullets that are at the movie site.

Once again, the tempo of the movie is slow, partly caused by its lackluster direction. The flying sequences are boring and seem quite familiar. Until the murder of Martin, the film has little interest and after the murder of Martin, the film unfortunately still does not have much interest.

There are a few positives. There is a brief education into the production of films, such as the use of the sound equipment, ground signals to the planes to provide direction to the pilots flying above, and another hidden plane in the air shooting some of the flying scenes. In that regard, *Stunt Pilot* is similar to *The Death Kiss* (1933) and *The Falcon in Hollywood* (1944), two murder mysteries set on a Hollywood studio lot in which the viewer learns a little about film production while attempting to solve a murder. The other plus is John Trent, playing Tailspin Tommy. The young and handsome actor is earnest and sincere in the role, giving the film much more credibility than the script provides. Nevertheless, this is a tough film for an adult to view and one suspects that it is a tough film for children to view, even when watching it on a cinema screen back in 1939.

*Note on the Source Material*: This film's script was based on one of the most popular storylines in the comic strip, involving the shooting of a World War I movie, *The Midnight Patrol*, at Three Points Airlines. During the filming, stunt pilot Bruce Wilkins is killed in a staged dogfight after someone substitutes real bullets for the blanks in the machine gun used by another stunt pilot. Tommy Tomkins is one of the suspects. The filming of a movie at Three Points Airlines was also told in the last few chapters of the 1934 serial *Tailspin Tommy*.

## Sky Patrol (1939)

In this third entry in the weak Tailspin Tommy series, Tommy and the gang match wits with a group of smugglers who are attempting to sneak a large cache of munitions out of the country and apparently into the hands of a foreign government. In the process, a young aviator learns a life lesson in courage and in overcoming phobias.

With little explanation, Tommy and Skeeter have given up their day jobs at Three Points Airlines and are now apparently in the military, training young pilots for the Sky Patrol, a force that seeks airborne spies, smugglers and anyone else who may be operating outside the law. Carter Meade, the son of the head of the Sky Patrol, Colonel Meade, has difficulty shooting a gun and would rather not be in the Sky Patrol. Tommy helps him pass his last flying test and off into the skies goes Carter Meade.

On one of his patrols, Carter discovers an unregistered amphibian plane flying out over the ocean. When Carter tries to ground the amphibian, the smugglers on board shoot Carter's plane out of the sky. Carter parachutes into the ocean and the smugglers kidnap him. Everyone, including Carter's father, believes that Carter is dead. Tommy persists in trying to locate the missing amphibian plane and the boat to which it was flying, believing that Carter may still be alive and imprisoned on the vessel. At the conclusion of the movie, Tommy crashes his own plane into the ocean in a ruse to board the smugglers' boat and, as a result of this unorthodox approach to crime investigations, rescues Carter and blows up the ship.

Skeeter Milligan barely appeared in the prior feature in the series; his part is much more prominent in *Sky Patrol*. That unfortunately is not a plus. While Milburn Stone is okay in the Skeeter part, the role is now mainly one of comedy relief only, with Skeeter continually unable to pronounce the word "amphibian," wanting to blast the munitions warehouse without any positive evidence of what is happening there, and never being able to give a speech which he had previously prepared. Little of this is funny. Noah Beery, Jr., who played the role of Skeeter in the two Universal serials, was far better in the role.

On the other hand, the third member of the young trio, Betty Lou Barnes, barely appears in this film. That is unfortunate, as Marjorie Reynolds is quite attractive and it is easy to see why she went on to better projects in Hollywood once the Tailspin Tommy series ended.

While *Sky Patrol* does focus more on a crime story than prior films in the series, the presentation is just as tepid. Even the ending of the movie, with some fisticuffs, shootings and a terrific explosion, seems quite boring, probably because of the uninspired direction, clichéd storyline and inexplicable actions of the heroes and villains. As to the uninspired direction, where are the quick cuts or unusual camera angles that could add suspense and excitement to the battle at sea? As to the clichéd storyline, is there any viewer, young or old, who does not know, almost from the beginning, that youthful Carter Meade will end up being a hero and have the courage to shoot his weapon when necessary? As to the inexplicable actions of the characters, did Tommy really intentionally scuttle his aircraft in the middle of the ocean, just so he could get on the smugglers' boat? Is there any reason why henchman Mitch would go back to the hold where Tommy and Skeeter are being kept prisoner, other than the necessity of the screenwriters devising a means for Tommy and Skeeter to escape from their captors? There is little to like in the plot of this film.

Typical of the Tailspin Tommy series, this film is directed more toward a juvenile audience than adult mystery fans. However, it is hard to believe that even the youngsters in the audience would find *Sky Patrol* anything but boring.

*A Note on the Previews*: At the end of the first film in the series, *Mystery Plane*, Paul Smith tells the gang that a movie company wants to make a war picture at Three Points Airlines. Tommy, Skeeter and Betty Lou then say to the audience, in unison, "That's the next one — *Tailspin Tommy in the Movies*." The next film, titled *Stunt Pilot*, did involve a film company shooting at Three Points Airlines. At the end of *Stunt Pilot*, the sheriff asked if Tommy and the gang were interested in training pilots for the border patrol. They agreed and announced that the next film would be *Sky Patrol*. This time they got the next title right.

At the end of *Sky Patrol*, Tommy suggested that Three Points Airlines encourage youths to hang around the airport, see what goes on and learn about flying. The group could be called "Scouts of the Air." *Sky Patrol* then ended with an announcement that the next film in the series would be called *Scouts of the Air*. As it turned out, the next film in the series was called *Danger Flight*. However, it was clearly the film contemplated at the end of the prior film, with the main storyline involving one scout who helps Tailspin Tommy on two significant occasions.

## *Danger Flight* (1939)

This last film in the series is the best, with Tommy Tomkins making a daring flight in a storm to deliver needed medical supplies to an accident site and then becoming mixed up in a payroll robbery. Being the best film in this series, however, is faint praise for *Danger Flight* as the entire Tailspin Tommy series was disappointing and, indeed, trivial in many ways.

Because a gang of thieves attempted to steal a large payroll which was being transported by automobile to an isolated location where a dam is being constructed, Tommy agrees to fly the payroll from Three Points Airlines to the site in order to prevent another robbery attempt. When there is an accident at the dam, Tommy must bring emergency medical supplies to the site by air. He takes off in a storm and, because he cannot land, drops the supplies by his only parachute. On the flight back, Tommy gets lost in the storm and, because he can no longer escape by parachute, crashes in the woods.

Tommy is found by a young scout of the air, Whitey Lewis, who is proclaimed a hero. Whitey's older brother Mike, who previously attempted to steal the payroll, tricks Whitey into becoming an accomplice in a new robbery attempt. Tailspin and Whitey are then captured by the gang, but they make a daring escape and, with the help of the police, finish off the villains.

The Tailspin Tommy movies were directed toward a young audience and perhaps for that reason, it is unfair for adults to criticize the same. Maybe a young audience would enjoy stories about a young boy assisting a famous flyer in trouble (*Mystery Plane*), helping to solve a murder (*Stunt Pilot*) and, in *Danger Flight*, rescuing Tommy and foiling the payroll robbers. Also, the series may have had special interest for children of its era, with its emphasis on airplanes, which were probably still somewhat of a fad in the late 1930s. That distinguishes the Tailspin Tommys from other youth-oriented series of the time, such as the films about the Dead End Kids and their progeny. It is unlikely that sophisticated children from today would have the same interest in airplanes that kids from the 1930s may have had.

For those youngsters, *Danger Flight* does have its moments. Tommy's rescue flight in the rain, his return without a parachute, his loss of contact with the ground and his inability to see the Three Points landing field are suspenseful. Those scenes are highlighted by

From left to right, Skeeter Milligan (Milburn Stone), Tailspin Tommy (John Trent) and Betty Lou Barnes (Marjorie Reynolds) discuss whether Tommy should fly a plane at night, in a storm, in *Danger Flight* (1939).

some sudden appearances of trees, some cutting back and forth with the air field, the sudden stopping of the propeller while Tommy's plane is in flight, and even a point-of-view shot before the crash. It may not be Alfred Hitchcock but it is still done pretty well.

The second half of the story is cleverly written, making it seem to everyone that Whitey is involved in the payroll robbery. There are also some pretty tough elements to the story. Mike Lewis callously involves his brother Whitey in the payroll robbery, knowing that it will look to everyone as if Whitey deliberately threw in with the robbers, permanently ruining his life. At the end, Mike is shot on-screen at close range and Whitey is pushed down some basement steps. These scenes of sudden violence are surprising for a film geared to young audiences and bring back memories of the deliberate high-speed plane crash into the ocean in *Mystery Plane*, the first film in the series.

The ending is also reminiscent of the 1950s television series, *Highway Patrol* with its use of roadblocks, radio communications between the police and the use of aircraft to track the villains. One difference is that the television series used helicopters instead of planes.

It is difficult to recommend *Danger Flight* to any mystery fan since, despite its virtues, the crime element takes a back seat to the story about airplanes and the rehabilitation of a potential juvenile delinquent. Nevertheless, if there is one film in the series to watch, *Danger Flight* is it.

## Afterwards

The end of the Tailspin Tommy movie series just about marked the end of John Trent's acting career. He went back to his flying roots, becoming a test pilot and then flight manager for Douglas Aircraft until his retirement in the 1960s. He passed away in 1966.

After the conclusion of the Tailspin Tommy series, Milburn Stone continued his indifferent career in films, either playing small character parts or occasionally starring in a B–movie or serial. His big break came in television, where Stone played Doc Adams on the CBS-TV Western *Gunsmoke* from 1955 to 1975. Stone eventually won an Emmy for the role. Stone passed away in 1980.

Marjorie Reynolds had the most successful film career of any of the regulars in the Tailspin Tommy series. Her best-remembered role was as Linda Mason, the object of attraction for both Bing Crosby and Fred Astaire in *Holiday Inn* (1942). On television, she played Peg Riley, the wife of William Bendix, in *The Life of Riley*, from 1953 to 1958. Reynolds died in 1997.

Jason Robards appeared in over 200 films in his film career, with most of his roles being small, forgettable parts. He is best known today for being the father of Jason Robards, Jr., a noted stage and film actor. Robards is therefore often referred to today as Jason Robards, Sr., even though he was never billed in that manner during his career. Robards died in 1963.

Tailspin Tommy became the subject of a short-lived 1941 radio program on a CBS regional network. The *Tailspin Tommy* comic strip barely survived the end of the film series in 1939. Although at one time the strip was in 250 newspapers, its popularity steadily declined in the late 1930s and it ceased publication in 1942.

# 22

# Persons in Hiding
## *The FBI Story*

The Federal Bureau of Investigation and the film industry have always had a symbiotic relationship. In exchange for the FBI generating material for the cinema, the film industry provided positive publicity and complimentary stories about the FBI for many years. In the 1930s alone, among other films about the FBI, there were *G-Men* (1935), *Mary Burns, Fugitive* (1935), *Public Enemy's Wife* (1936) and *Missing Evidence* (1939), all of which were gangster or crime films. The FBI ended the decade fighting Fifth Columnists in *Confessions of a Nazi Spy* (1939). All of these films provided glowing portrayals of the federal agency.

In 1939 Paramount inaugurated a new mystery series dedicated to chronicling the exploits and successes of the FBI. It is usually referred to as the *Persons in Hiding* series because the four films were supposedly based upon chapters in J. Edgar Hoover's book of the same name. These low-budget films are often overlooked today, overshadowed by the more famous Hollywood movies about the FBI which were released both before and after. Perhaps one reason that the films in the *Persons in Hiding* series are little-known today is that they were generally very disappointing.

## Background

### The FBI

The Federal Bureau of Investigation had its beginnings in 1908 when Attorney General Charles Bonaparte created a special force within the Department of Justice to combat interstate crime. The first agents were actually employees or investigators from other parts of the government, such as the Secret Service, who were brought over to the Justice Department. At that time, the agents did not carry firearms and were unable to make arrests on their own. (These shortcomings were corrected in the 1930s.) Originally named the Bureau of Investigation, it eventually became the Division of Investigation before being renamed the Federal Bureau of Investigation in 1935.

J. Edgar Hoover became the first director of the organization in 1924 and continued in that position until his death in 1972. He is credited with professionalizing the Bureau, including hiring more qualified agents and instituting the use of scientific methods, such as centralizing fingerprint files and utilizing the latest techniques of forensic laboratories. In the 1930s, the FBI concentrated on gangsters, in the 1940s Nazis, and in the 1950s Communists. The FBI publicity machine was so effective during the Hoover era that few questioned the professionalism and integrity of the Bureau.

After Hoover's death, however, some alarming facts were revealed. These included illegal wiretaps, maintaining secret files on a number of prominent individuals, personal vendettas by Hoover, and some substandard investigations into crimes. The pristine reputation of the Bureau was damaged.

While Hoover was in charge, he tried, with great success, to control the films made about the Bureau. Thus, most films about FBI investigations before Hoover's death contain positive portrayals of the FBI. That has not always been the case with films about the Bureau made after the passing of Hoover and the damaging revelations about the Bureau's past. More recent films have often been critical of the Bureau's activities.

## The Book

*Persons in Hiding* was first published in 1938. The author is identified as "J. Edgar Hoover, Director, Federal Bureau of Investigation, United States Department of Justice," although many suspect that the book was ghostwritten by person or persons unknown. After an obsequious foreword by Courtney Ryley Cooper, a well-known writer of his day (and the person many people believe actually wrote the book), *Persons in Hiding* tells the apparently true stories of a number of criminals who were chased by the FBI in the 1930s. It also contains much overwrought preaching by Hoover on the subject of criminals, the judicial system, the duty of average citizens to be vigilant against crime and the problems associated with parole. In addition, as Bob Hertzberg wrote in *The FBI and the Movies*, Hoover constantly irritates the reader as he "explains away the scourge of gangsterism with dime-store psychology that passes for the insight of a great criminologist."

Several *Persons in Hiding* chapters are devoted to well-known crooks such as Ma Barker, Alvin Karpis and Baby Face Nelson. Others concern criminals who may have been famous then but are forgotten today. Most chapters end with a conviction or a death or some other form of punishment, enforcing the theme of the book that crime does not pay. *Persons in Hiding* concludes with a chapter titled "Looking Forward," which gives Hoover's viewpoint on the causes of, and the solutions to, crime and corruption.

## The Film Series

As noted above, films about the G–men were popular in the late 1930s. Paramount attempted to capitalize on that popularity by producing a series based on a book by the most famous lawman of that time, or perhaps of all time. On its face, the book *Persons in Hiding* was a good source for a film series, with its chapters telling the stories of the crimes and punishments of several notorious individuals. In fact, though, there is more preaching than detail in the book and perhaps for that reason, the films are all original works, with only tangential ties to the Hoover book.

The first film in the series, *Persons in Hiding* (1939), tells the tale of Dot Branson (played by Patricia Morison) and Gunner Martin (played by J. Carrol Naish), a husband-and-wife team of bank robbers, who find their comeuppance when they turn to kidnapping, thus bringing the FBI onto their trail. *Undercover Doctor* (1939) also stars Naish, this time as a high society physician who, on the sly, patches up gangsters shot by the police. The third film, *Parole Fixer* (1939), is about fraudulent releases of convicts from prison and the crimes they commit once they are sprung. Robert Florey was the director. The concluding movie

Dot Branson (Patricia Morison) is enjoying the fruits of her crimes and her passion for expensive perfume, when things are still going well for her and her cohort in crime, Gunner Martin (J. Carrol Naish), in *Persons in Hiding* (1939).

*Queen of the Mob* (1940), is about a gang of criminals run by the villainous Ma Webster (Blanche Yurka).

Carrol Naish appeared in three of the films, playing a different character in each. Interestingly, with the exception of some of the smaller roles, the FBI agents were played by different actors in each film. The best-known performers in that group are Ralph Bellamy, Lloyd Nolan, Lyle Talbot and Jack Carson. Presumably, Hoover did not want any FBI agent, even a fictional one, to become more famous than Hoover, so there was no one heroic FBI agent who appeared in all of the films and who could tie all of the films together into a cohesive series.

## THE FILMS

### *Persons in Hiding* (1939)

*Persons in Hiding* tells the story of Dot Branson and Gunner Martin, husband and wife, who are bank robbers and kidnappers. Because of the similarity in criminal protagonists, *Persons in Hiding* seems like an early version of *Bonnie and Clyde* (1967), although, obviously, without the violence and, unfortunately, without the style. *Persons in Hiding* is a second-rate crime film, made more disappointing by the fact that it had the potential to be an excellent gangster movie.

Dot, a hair stylist at a small town beauty parlor, is tempted by the fur coat and expensive perfume of one of the parlor's wealthiest clients and haunted by the poverty in which she grew up. She is determined to go places in life and not necessarily in an honest manner. Her opportunity arises when a person in the beauty salon is robbed by a petty crook named Freddie "Gunner" Martin. Dot decides to go on the road with Martin, using her brains and his brawn to move the small-time crook (and Dot) up the ladder of criminal success. Martin is in love with Dot so as part of her scheme, Dot marries him.

At the beginning of their partnership in crime, Dot's plans work to perfection, as she and Gunner pull bigger and bigger jobs, even escaping from the local police on the one occasion that they are caught. However, an ill-advised kidnapping of wealthy Burt Nast brings the FBI into the picture. With their use of fingerprints, smart interrogation techniques, extensive manpower and the knowledge of Dot's fondness for expensive perfume, the G-men are able to bring Dot and Gunner to justice.

*Persons in Hiding* does have its appeal, both in the personality of Dot and the efforts of the FBI to capture her and her husband. There are two particularly interesting scenes, first when Dot visits her stepparents back on the farm where Dot grew up. The father is lazy; the mother is unsophisticated. The setting is a real window into the reasons why Dot eventually turned to a life of crime. The other interesting moment could only occur in a 1930s gangster movie, at a time in America when gangsters were sometimes more popular than the policemen who tracked them down. Dot calls a newspaper to give Gunner Martin credit for a crime he did not commit, in the belief that publicity was a must for any successful crook of that era. In a strange way, back in the 1930s, that may have been true.

However, *Persons in Hiding* is brought down by its uninspired direction and shabby production values. Even though the movie is from Paramount Pictures, a major studio, it has the look of an opus from Monogram Pictures, a Poverty Row company. While Patricia Morison is good as Dot Branson, J. Carrol Naish is severely miscast as Gunner Martin. With Naish's small size and quiet manner, Martin comes across more like a small-town tailor than a hardened gangster. Clyde Barrow he is not. Without a good performance in this key role, much of the film is unconvincing and lame.

Other weaknesses abound. While the FBI agents are the heroes, little time is spent acquainting the viewer with the several agents involved, thus preventing the viewer from identifying with any of them. While Dot and Martin commit lots of crimes, very few of them are actually shown on-screen, undercutting any suspense and interest that their crime wave may have generated. An early montage of stock footage of their crimes consists mainly of snippets of film of cars traveling at high speeds with highway signs floating on the screen. It is a rare for the standard montage of the villains' criminal exploits to be uninteresting, but *Persons in Hiding* somehow manages that feat. Indeed, given all of the crimes that occur in the film, the movie is surprisingly slow-moving.

*Persons in Hiding* is a film of missed opportunities. Even though it has a relatively strong plot, it is, ultimately, a poor man's *Bonnie and Clyde*, and a weak beginning to the *Persons in Hiding* mystery series.

*Note on the Source Material*: *Persons in Hiding* was very loosely based on Chapter VIII of Hoover's book, "The Woman Behind the Crime." The chapter is actually about George "Machine Gun" Kelly and his wife Kathryn Thorne Kelly. The few incidents carried over from the chapter to the movie are the cold and calculating nature of the woman behind the criminal, a kidnapping of a wealthy individual (Kathryn wants to kill their captive after receipt of the ransom money but is overruled by the other members of the gang), the kidnap victim's recollection of events while in captivity leading the FBI to Kathryn and her husband, and, near the end of the chapter, Kathryn's willingness to turn her husband over to the authorities in exchange for the release of her parents from incarceration. However, the film is essentially an original work.

## *Undercover Doctor* (1939)

*Undercover Doctor* is a vast improvement over *Persons in Hiding*, and it also provides a much better role for J. Carrol Naish. *Undercover Doctor* is nothing special and it surely has its flaws, but viewing the movie is not a bad way for an avid mystery fan to spend 65 minutes.

A small town physician Bartley Morgan unexpectedly becomes involved with a criminal mob run by gangster Eddie Krator. Forced to operate on one of Krator's gang members (shot during a robbery), Morgan likes the money so much that he decides to work for the mob on a regular basis. Morgan also uses his criminal wages to move to Manhattan and build up a practice of affluent patients. Things are going so well for Morgan in the big city that he is set to marry Cynthia Weld, daughter of a prominent and wealthy family, even though he is probably in love with Margaret Hopkins, his original nurse from back home. However, due to some efficient but also lucky police work, and an important call by Margaret to the FBI about the location of Krator's hideout, Morgan and the rest of the gang are captured by the Bureau.

One of the strange things about *Undercover Doctor*, given its lineage, is that it barely demonstrates any clever or innovative investigative techniques of the FBI. Sure, there is a little about fingerprint evidence and an incident of tracing a fishing reel back to the store that sold it to the criminal. However, most of the FBI's success is based on luck and coincidence. Thus, Agent Anders happens to have surgery performed by Morgan on a gunshot wound, giving him the accidental opportunity to compare his scar to that of one of the Krator gang. Anders then suspects, because of the similarity of the scars, that Morgan may be involved in criminal activities. When Anders goes to the doctor's office to investigate, he happens to see the phone number of the FBI written on a pad, leading to the conclusion that Margaret had tipped off the FBI the night before (and failed to dispose of the pad sheet that night, as most people probably would have).

In fact, the FBI does not look very impressive in *Undercover Doctor*. The first time the federal agents surround the Krator gang at one of its hideouts, three of the criminals manage to get away, even though there are numerous policemen encircling the place. After finally capturing Krator, the FBI lets the local sheriff hold him in a local jail cell; Krator escapes easily. Margaret is clearly an accessory after the fact to some of Morgan's crimes, but Agent Anders does not arrest her. Instead, he takes her out to dinner. It is somewhat surprising that J. Edgar Hoover ever let this film be made.

Then there are the amusing moments. After Krator is captured, there is a newspaper headline quoting Krator as saying that no jail can hold him. What a surprise that he escapes from captivity in the next scene. (What is really surprising is how easy the escape is.) Throughout the feature, Morgan is a surgeon, fixing bullet woods and broken limbs. At the end, however, he suddenly has the ability to do plastic surgery, as if that were not a completely different skill.

Yet for all of that, *Undercover Doctor* is somewhat engaging. Naish is well-cast as Dr. Morgan, gradually growing from a wimpy local drunken doctor to an arrogant physician for the mob. Lloyd Nolan is easygoing and likable as Agent Anders. It is interesting to see Broderick Crawford in an early film in his career, playing Krator as gruff and tough as they come, essentially becoming a criminal version of Broderick Crawford's famous television role as policeman Dan Matthews in *Highway Patrol* (1955–59).

There is further interest in *Undercover Doctor* in the relationship between Morgan and Margaret although, admittedly, their interaction is hardly handled in either a nuanced or original manner. The backstabbing of the criminal characters and their suspicious attitudes towards each other provide entertainment, as do the two shootouts in the film, machine guns and all. The finale, where the tough gangster Krator is caught by the FBI while he is sleeping under anesthesia, is irony at its best. *Undercover Doctor* is a B–mystery diversion only but within that context, it is worth a look.

*Note on the Source Material*: *Undercover Doctor* was loosely based on Chapter V of *Persons in Hiding*, "Doctor of Crime," which is surely a more relevant title for the subject matter than the title used for the film. The real-life physician was Joseph P. Moran, whose life of crime started when a woman died following an "illegal operation," resulting in a prison term for him. Similar to Dr. Morgan in *Undercover Doctor*, Moran had a drinking problem. Also, if a member of the wrong criminal gang came to his office for emergency surgery, Moran was not above advising the police, helping to establish his good intentions with the police. However, much like the first film in the series, *Undercover Doctor* is essentially an original story with only minimal ties to Hoover's book.

## *Parole Fixer* (1940)

In this third film in the series, the FBI is investigating attorney Tyler Craden who, through illegal and unethical means, arranges paroles for unrepentant criminals. Two examples are shown in the film. In the first instance, Craden pushes for the release of Big Boy Bradmore, by composing a sympathy-generating letter to the parole board, supposedly from Bradmore's elderly mother. That is enough for Bradmore to be released from jail. Shortly thereafter, Bradmore kills an FBI agent. The second instance is the parole of Steve Eddson. In this case, Craden tricks a number of wealthy female philanthropists into writing letters and gathering petitions for the release of Eddson, resulting in his parole over the vehement objections of one of the parole board members. Shortly thereafter, Eddson is involved in a kidnapping of the daughter of one of the philanthropists. All of Craden's ruses work because he is blackmailing the head of the parole board, Gustav Kalkus, over a failed business deal. Kalkus is a reluctant but eventually malleable crony of Craden's.

The beginning of *Parole Fixer* is pretty silly stuff. The film could have incorporated a sophisticated discussion of the pros and cons of parole, when best to use it, and who best to decide it. Instead, and as the title suggests, *Parole Fixer* is a caricature of the parole process, solely for the purpose of making the point that parole is bad. If the letters and the petitions are not silly enough, adding a corrupt parole board head brings the picture into a fantasy world, where all criminals are totally evil, local and state officials are corrupt, the general public is innocent and easily manipulated, and only the FBI gets it right. The first half of *Parole Fixer* is somewhat insulting to its audience and in that sense, at least, has some of the spirit and attitude of J. Edgar Hoover's book, *Persons in Hiding*.

The second half focuses on the kidnapping of Enid Casserly and her boyfriend Bruce Eaton. On its face, that is an encouraging development. A good kidnapping will always jump-start a crime movie, with suspense created by the natural tension between the often conflicting goals of rescuing the victims vs. capturing the criminals. Then there is the almost always tension-filled scene of the payment of the ransom money.

Unfortunately, there is none of that in *Parole Fixer*. Here, the victims are kidnapped offscreen, there is never an attempt to pay the ransom money, and the

Publicity photo for *Parole Fixer* (1940), showing FBI agent Scott Britton (William Henry) with Enid Casserly (Virginia Dale), the kidnap victim he rescues.

Bureau uses the ridiculous trick of injecting its own ransom note into the mix to cause infighting among the thieves. There is no suspense in any of these scenes, somewhat surprising since Robert Florey, an often excellent director, is at the helm of the movie. Perhaps the reason is that the budget of *Parole Fixer* was so low that even Florey could not inject any excitement. The running time is under one hour, but it seems much longer.

At least *Parole Fixer* does illustrate some clever FBI investigative techniques, including tracing fingerprints, comparing mud on shoes and car brake pedals, and tracing of phone calls. Of course, the FBI still has incredible luck, with the always careful Eddson somehow leaving a scrap of paper in his suit coat pocket with valuable phone numbers written upon it, which the agents quickly discover upon a search of Eddson's room. Without that lucky discovery, all the fingerprint and mud evidence would have been of little use to the Bureau.

There is an attempt to create some excitement at the end when Bradmore escapes from the FBI but then is gunned down by the federal authorities following a car chase. It is the most exciting moment in the film, but it is still pretty lame. Indeed, most of the interest in the film comes from its actors. It is interesting to see Anthony Quinn and Richard Denning early in their screen careers but sad to see Gertrude Michael, star of the Sophie Lang mystery series, in a throwaway role. All of these actors were too good to appear in a film such as *Parole Fixer*, which is never more than second-rate.

*Note on the Source Material*: At this point in the series, the screenwriters stopped basing the films on J. Edgar Hoover's book. *Parole Fixer* was not based, even slightly, on *Persons*

*in Hiding.* Chapter VII of the book, titled "First Aid to Crime," is about a "renegade attorney" but none of the incidents from that chapter appear in the film. Chapter X, titled "Bill Dainard Was Paroled," involves the issue of parole and a paroled convict becoming involved in a kidnapping, but there is really no similarity between that chapter of the book and *Parole Fixer* except, perhaps, for the theme of the two works. Hoover writes in Chapter X, "Parole was not conceived for men who cannot or will not benefit by it." If *Parole Fixer* has a message, that is surely it.

## *Queen of the Mob* (1940)

The fourth film in the series, *Queen of the Mob*, is also the last film in the series. These FBI films have little going for them and except for a few moments in *Persons in Hiding* and *Undercover Doctor*, they are completely forgettable.

Ma Webster has three sons (Eddie, Charlie and Tom), along with an outsider, George Frost, in her criminal gang. Her fourth son Bert has turned to the side of good and is now an attorney with a wife and young son.

As the film opens, Ma is posing as an elderly bank customer when her gang comes in to rob the bank. The crooks take Ma hostage and threaten to kill her, unless the bank officials refrain from calling the police immediately. The ruse works and the robbery is a success. That leads into a montage of additional thefts before this section of the film culminates in a kidnapping and the receipt of $300,000 in ransom money. However, the bills are marked. When a criminal entrepreneur, Pan, offers to buy the $300,000 in hot money for $100,000 of cold money, the gang shoots him and takes all of his money. However, the good bills had previously been marked by Pan and the numbers are now in the possession of the FBI, so the Webster gang now has $400,000 of practically useless bills.

The remainder of the film details the FBI's pursuit of the Webster gang, the death of two of Ma's sons, and the few interactions between Bert Webster and the gang. The film ends in a shootout, with the third son killed and Ma surrendering to the federal agents.

*Queen of the Mob* is a complete bore. Parts of the film are padded, such as a long and unfunny scene wherein Billy Gilbert plays a baker who is questioned by the FBI. The kidnapping and recovery of the ransom money take place off-screen. A Christmas Eve robbery of a local store, which results in the death of one son and the capture of another, also goes unseen. While the death of another son while boarding a plane in FBI custody and the final shootout are shown to the viewers, they are mainly just a hail of gunfire and some actors pretending to be hit. There is no style in the storytelling and no excitement in the viewing.

There is an attempt made to inject some pathos into the film, as Ma Webster seldom gets to see her good son Bert, and only sees her grandson once, on Christmas Eve. On that occasion, Ma cannot even tell the boy that she is his grandmother. But while the attempt may have been a good idea, these scenes engender little emotion in the viewer. Ma is hardly a tragic figure; she is a cold-blooded killer. Also, Blanche Yurka, who plays Ma, is an actress of limited range. But it is unlikely that a better actress could have done much with the lame script.

One may ask: Why was a non-family member, George Frost, included in the gang? Few viewers will be surprised to discover that the Frost character was inserted into the plot so that Ma could have someone to kill late in the movie. Once again, and presumably inadvertently, the FBI does not look very competent in the film. They miss an early opportunity to catch Ma at a society affair when they show up late to the party. They allow one of the Webster sons to be killed when they are trying to transport him to prison. Incidents which reflect badly on the FBI are not all that surprising for this film series. Frankly, the FBI has not looked very good throughout these four movies.

The 1930s were a heyday for films about the FBI, and J. Edgar Hoover was very involved in making sure that each of the films released showed the FBI in a positive light. For some reason, though, Hoover must have overlooked the *Persons in Hiding* series. In addition to its agents taking questionable actions in the films, the FBI does not appear to be very accomplished while appearing in such low-budget, poorly produced features.

*Note on the Source Material*: *Queen of the Mob* was loosely based on the criminal career of Ma Barker and her sons and therefore has some relationship to Chapter II of *Persons in Hiding*, titled "The Mother Lode of Crime." However, none of the incidents in the movie come from the book except, perhaps, the ending. In Hoover's version of the story, the FBI surrounded a house containing Ma Barker and a son. In the ensuing shootout, Ma Barker was killed, along with the son. As with many of the tales told by Hoover, there is some controversy today as to whether Hoover's account of the career and death of Ma Barker was totally accurate.

## Afterwards

While there were no more films based on the book *Persons in Hiding*, the FBI continued to be the subject matter of numerous films, even up to the present day. Some of the more notable films featuring the FBI were *They Came to Blow Up America* (1943), where the FBI was after Nazis, *Roger Touhy, Gangster* (1944), where the FBI was back fighting gangsters, *The House on 92nd Street* (1945), a procedural about spies and espionage, *I Was a Communist for the F.B.I.* (1951), in which the Bureau took on the Red Menace, *The FBI Story* (1959), a fictionalized history of some of the important investigations of the Bureau, and more recently, *Public Enemies* (2009), the story of the capture of John Dillinger.

While there were at least two radio series based on the exploits of the FBI, neither were based on Hoover's book, *Persons in Hiding*. In 1965, an hour-long television series, *The F.B.I.*, debuted on ABC. It starred Efrem Zimbalist, Jr., as Agent Lewis Erskine. His boss, Arthur Ward, was played by Philip Abbott. Other recurring agent roles were played by William Reynolds and Stephen Brooks. Each episode was made with the cooperation and approval of the FBI and was supposedly based on a case from the files of the Bureau.

*The F.B.I.* was produced by Quinn Martin, who is well-remembered today for producing a number of TV crime series including *The Fugitive* and *Cannon*. *The F.B.I.* was Martin's most successful show, being on the air for nine seasons, ending its run in 1974. The show is still recalled fondly today by mystery fans, both for the quality of the program and for the fact that since Ford Motor Company was its original sponsor, all of the agents and all of the criminals drove Fords.

# Appendix
## 1930s Mystery Series Listed

BRASS BANCROFT
   Secret Service of the Air (1939)
   Code of the Secret Service (1939)
   Smashing the Money Ring (1939)
   Murder in the Air (1940)

TORCHY BLANE
   Smart Blonde (1937)
   Fly Away Baby (1937)
   The Adventurous Blonde (1937)
   Blondes at Work (1938)
   Torchy Blane in Panama (1938)
   Torchy Gets Her Man (1938)
   Torchy Blane in Chinatown (1939)
   Torchy Runs for Mayor (1939)
   Torchy Blane...Playing with Dynamite (1939)

CHARLIE CHAN
   Behind That Curtain (1929)
   Charlie Chan Carries On and Eran Trece (1931)
   The Black Camel (1931)
   Charlie Chan's Chance (1932)
   Charlie Chan's Greatest Case (1933)
   Charlie Chan's Courage (1934)
   Charlie Chan in London (1934)
   Charlie Chan in Paris (1935)
   Charlie Chan in Egypt (1935)
   Charlie Chan in Shanghai (1935)
   Charlie Chan's Secret (1936)
   Charlie Chan at the Circus (1936)
   Charlie Chan at the Race Track (1936)
   Charlie Chan at the Opera (1936)
   Charlie Chan at the Olympics (1937)
   Charlie Chan on Broadway (1937)
   Charlie Chan at Monte Carlo (1938)
   Charlie Chan in Honolulu (1938)
   Charlie Chan in Reno (1939)
   Charlie Chan at Treasure Island (1939)
   Charlie Chan in City in Darkness (1939)
   Charlie Chan in Panama (1940)
   Charlie Chan's Murder Cruise (1940)
   Charlie Chan at the Wax Museum (1940)
   Murder Over New York (1940)
   Dead Men Tell (1941)
   Charlie Chan in Rio (1941)
   Castle in the Desert (1942)
   Charlie Chan in the Secret Service (1944)
   The Chinese Cat (1944)
   Black Magic aka Meeting at Midnight (1944)
   The Jade Mask (1945)
   The Scarlet Clue (1945)
   The Shanghai Cobra (1945)
   The Red Dragon (1945)
   Dark Alibi (1946)
   Shadows Over Chinatown (1946)
   Dangerous Money (1946)
   The Trap (1946)
   The Chinese Ring (1947)
   Docks of New Orleans (1948)
   The Shanghai Chest (1948)
   The Golden Eye (1948)
   The Feathered Serpent (1948)
   The Sky Dragon (1949)

NICK AND NORA CHARLES
   The Thin Man (1934)
   After the Thin Man (1936)
   Another Thin Man (1939)
   Shadow of the Thin Man (1941)
   The Thin Man Goes Home (1944)
   Song of the Thin Man (1947)

THATCHER COLT
   The Night Club Lady (1932)
   The Circus Queen Murder (1933)
   The Panther's Claw (1942)

BILL CRANE
   The Westland Case (1937)
   The Lady in the Morgue (1938)
   The Last Warning (1938)

BULLDOG DRUMMOND
   Bulldog Drummond (1929)
   Temple Tower (1930)
   Bulldog Drummond Strikes Back (1934)
   The Return of Bulldog Drummond (1934)
   Bulldog Jack aka Alias Bulldog Drummond (1935)
   Bulldog Drummond at Bay (1937)
   Bulldog Drummond Escapes (1937)
   Bulldog Drummond Comes Back (1937)

*Bulldog Drummond's Revenge* (1937)
*Bulldog Drummond's Peril* (1938)
*Bulldog Drummond in Africa* (1938)
*Arrest Bulldog Drummond!* (1938)
*Bulldog Drummond's Secret Police* (1939)
*Bulldog Drummond's Bride* (1939)
*Bulldog Drummond at Bay* (1947)
*Bulldog Drummond Strikes Back* (1947)
*The Challenge* (1948)
*13 Lead Soldiers* (1948)
*Calling Bulldog Drummond* (1951)

NANCY DREW
*Nancy Drew — Detective* (1938)
*Nancy Drew...Reporter* (1939)
*Nancy Drew...Trouble Shooter* (1939)
*Nancy Drew and the Hidden Staircase* (1939)

SARAH KEATE
*While the Patient Slept* (1935)
*The Murder of Dr. Harrigan* (1936)
*Murder by an Aristocrat* (1936)
*The Great Hospital Mystery* (1937)
*The Patient in Room 18* (1938)
*Mystery House* (1938)

SOPHIE LANG
*The Notorious Sophie Lang* (1934)
*The Return of Sophie Lang* (1936)
*Sophie Lang Goes West* (1937)

ARSÈNE LUPIN
*Arsène Lupin* (1932)
*Arsène Lupin Returns* (1938)
*Enter Arsène Lupin* (1944)

PERRY MASON
*The Case of the Howling Dog* (1934)
*The Case of the Curious Bride* (1935)
*The Case of the Lucky Legs* (1935)
*The Case of the Velvet Claws* (1936)
*The Case of the Black Cat* (1936)
*The Case of the Stuttering Bishop* (1937)

MR. MOTO
*Think Fast, Mr. Moto* (1937)
*Thank You, Mr. Moto* (1938)
*Mr. Moto's Gamble* (1938)
*Mr. Moto Takes a Chance* (1938)
*Mysterious Mr. Moto* (1938)
*Mr. Moto's Last Warning* (1939)
*Mr. Moto in Danger Island* (1939)
*Mr. Moto Takes a Vacation* (1939)

ALAN O'CONNOR AND BOBBIE REYNOLDS
*Yellow Cargo* (1936)
*Navy Spy* (1937)
*Gold Racket* (1937)
*Bank Alarm* (1937)

PERSONS IN HIDING
*Persons in Hiding* (1939)
*Undercover Doctor* (1939)
*Parole Fixer* (1940)
*Queen of the Mob* (1940)

THE ROVING REPORTERS
*Time Out for Murder* (1938)
*While New York Sleeps* (1938)
*Inside Story* (1939)

JOEL AND GARDA SLOANE
*Fast Company* (1938)
*Fast and Loose* (1939)
*Fat and Furious* (1939)

TAILSPIN TOMMY
*Mystery Plane* (1939)
*Stunt Pilot* (1939)
*Sky Patrol* (1939)
*Danger Flight* (1939)

INSPECTOR TRENT
*Before Midnight* (1933)
*One Is Guilty* (1934)
*The Crime of Helen Stanley* (1934)
*Girl in Danger* (1934)

PHILO VANCE
*The Canary Murder Case* (1929)
*The Greene Murder Case* (1929)
*The Bishop Murder Case* (1930)
*The Benson Murder Case* (1930)
*The Kennel Murder Case* (1933)
*The Dragon Murder Case* (1934)
*The Casino Murder Case* (1935)
*The Garden Murder Case* (1936)
*Night of Mystery* (1937)
*The Gracie Allen Murder Case* (1939)
*Calling Philo Vance* (1940)
*Philo Vance's Gamble* (1947)
*Philo Vance's Secret Mission* (1947)
*Philo Vance Returns* (1947)

HILDEGARDE WITHERS
*Penguin Pool Murder* (1932)
*Murder on the Blackboard* (1934)
*Murder on a Honeymoon* (1935)
*Murder on a Bridle Path* (1936)
*The Plot Thickens* (1936)
*Forty Naughty Girls* (1937)

MR. WONG
*Mr. Wong Detective* (1938)
*The Mystery of Mr. Wong* (1939)
*Mr. Wong in Chinatown* (1939)
*The Fatal Hour* (1940)
*Doomed to Die* (1940)
*Phantom of Chinatown* (1940)

# Bibliography

Aaker, Everett. *Encyclopedia of Early Television Crime Fighters: All Regular Cast Members in American Crime and Mystery Series, 1948–1959.* Jefferson, NC: McFarland, 2006.
Brooks, Tim, and Earle Marsh. *The Complete Directory to Prime Time Network TV Shows 1946-Present.* New York: Ballantine, 1981.
Conquest, John. *Trouble Is Their Business: Private Eyes in Fiction, Film, and Television, 1927–1988.* New York: Garland, 1990.
DeAndrea, William. *Encyclopedia Mysteriosa.* New York: Macmillan, 1994.
Dunning, John. *On the Air: The Encyclopedia of Old Time Radio.* New York: Oxford University Press, 1998.
Everson, William K. *The Detective in Film.* Secaucus, NJ: Citadel Press, 1972.
Gribbon, Mark. "The Malefactor's Register." *http://markgribben.com/?p=308.*
Halliwell, Leslie. *Halliwell's Filmgoer's Companion.* 8th ed. New York: Scribner's, 1985.
Hanke, Ken. *Charlie Chan at the Movies: History, Filmography and Criticism.* Jefferson, NC: McFarland, 1989.
Herzberg, Bob. *The FBI and the Movies.* Jefferson, NC: McFarland, 2007.
Huang, Yunte. *Charlie Chan: The Untold Story of the Honorable Detective and His Rendezvous with American History.* New York: W.W. Norton, 2010.
Jewell, Richard B. *The RKO Story.* New York: Arlington House, 1982.
Lackman, Ron. *The Encyclopedia of American Radio.* New York: Checkmark, 2000.
Lertie, Arthur, and Kevin Burton Smith. *James Lee Wong, a/k/a Mr. Wong. http://www.thrillingdetective.com/wong.html/.*
Loughery, John. *Alias S.S. Van Dine.* New York: Scribner's, 1992.
Mitchell, Charles P. *A Guide to Charlie Chan Films.* Westport, CT: Greenwood Press, 1999.
Paris, Barry. *Louise Brooks.* New York: Alfred A. Knopf, 1989.
Pitts, Michael R. *Famous Movie Detectives,* Metuchen, NJ: Scarecrow Press. 1979.
_____. *Famous Movie Detectives II.* Metuchen, NJ: Scarecrow Press. 1991.
Rehak, Melanie. *Nancy Drew and the Women Who Created Her.* Orlando: Harcourt, 2005.
Remington, Steve. "Hal Forrest and Tailspin Tommy." *http://www.collectair.com/tailspin.html.*
Rovi, Bruce Eder. *Hugh Wiley.* http://www.answers.com/topic/hugh-wiley/.
Steinbrenner, Chris, and Otto Penzler. *Encyclopedia of Mystery and Detection.* New York: McGraw-Hill, 1976.
Treadwell, Lawrence P., Jr. *The Bulldog Drummond Encyclopedia.* Jefferson, NC: McFarland, 2001.
Turner Classic Movies Movie Database. *http://www.tcm.com/index.jsp.*
Tuska, Jon. *The Detective in Hollywood.* Garden City, NY: Doubleday, 1978.

# Index

Numbers in ***bold italics*** indicate pages with photographs.

"A" Is for Alibi (novel) 32
Abbott, Anthony 185, 188, 191, 193
Abbott, Philip 369
Abbott and Costello 25, 71, 139–140, 221, 290
About the Murder of Geraldine Foster (novel) 186
About the Murder of the Circus Queen (novel) 191
About the Murder of the Night Club Lady (novel) 188–189
"About the Perfect Crime of Mr. Digberry" (story) 193
Academy Award (Oscar) 7, 42, 43, 47, 48, 169, 183, 186, 199, 243, 260, 270, 275, 297, 309, 310, 311, 318, 352
Ace of Jades (novel) 168
Across the Pacific (1942 film) 159
Acuff, Eddie 217
Adler, Stella 209
The Adventures of Charlie Chan (radio program) 159
The Adventures of Robin Hood (1938 film) 6, 243
The Adventures of Sherlock Holmes (1939 film) 45, 101
Adventures of Superman (television series) 289
The Adventures of the Infallible Godahl (story collection) 235
The Adventures of the Thin Man (radio program) 213–214
The Adventurous Blonde (1937 film) 263–264
Advise and Consent (1962 film) 46, 310
After the Thin Man (1936 film) 204–206, ***205***, 254
The Airmail Mystery (1932 serial) 352
Alexander, Joan 39
Alias Bulldog Drummond (Bulldog Jack) (1935 film) 42, 46, 55–56
Allen, Gracie 7, 29, ***30***, 131, 132, 139
Allister, Claud(e) 48, 49, 52, 57, 60, 70, 82
Amazing Chan and the Chan Clan (television series) 159

The Amazing Exploits of the Clutching Hand (1936 serial) 244
Ames, Ben 343
Ames, Leon 282, 297
And Then There Were None (novel) 132, 257
Anderson, Frederick Irving 235, 236, 239
Andrews, Julie 243
Angel, Heather 44, 59, ***67***, 70, 73
Angels with Dirty Faces (1938 film) 243
The Ann Sothern Show (television series) 310
Anna Karenina (1935 film) 6
Another Thin Man (1939 film) 204, 206–208, ***207***, 254
Apana, Chang 85–86
Arbo, Manuel 91–92
Arden, Eve 184
Argosy (magazine) 269
Armstrong, Robert ***172***
Arrest Bulldog Drummond! (1938 film) 69–70
"The Arrest of Arsène Lupin" (story) 160
Arsène Lupin (1917 film) 161
Arsène Lupin (1932 film) 2, 45, 161, 162–163, 165
Arsène Lupin (play) 163
Arsène Lupin, an Adventure Story (novel) 163
Arsène Lupin, Gentleman-Burglar (story collection) 160
Arsène Lupin Returns (1938 film) 161, 163–165, ***164***, 309
Arsenic and Old Lace (1944 film) 183
Arsenic and Old Lace (play) 338
Arthur, Jean 10, 13, 308
Astaire, Fred 48, 208, 360
Astor, Mary ***20***, 200, 219
Atwill, Lionel 123, 125, 282, 298
Auer, Mischa ***50***
Auntie Mame (1958 film) 309
Averill, Anthony ***256***
The Awful Truth (1937 film) 199

"B" Is for Burglar (novel) 32
Babbitt (1934 film) 242

Bacon, Irving ***176***
Bacon, Lloyd 269
Bank Alarm (1937 film) 279–***280***
Barclay, Don ***277***
Bari, Lynn 282, 289
Barnett, Vince 279
Barrymore, John 2, 44, 45, 61, 63, 65, 68, 161, 162, 163, 165, 201
Barrymore, Lionel 162
Batman (1943 serial) 68
Batman and Robin (1949 serial) 128
Baxter, Warner 2, 90, 254
Beatty, Robert 81
Beaudine, William 191
Beck, Jackson 39
Beck, Thomas ***103***
Before Midnight (1933 film) 195, 196–197
Begley, Ed 159
Behind That Curtain (1929 film) 47, 86, 89–91, 97, 158
Behind That Curtain (novel) 86, 91, 92, 97, 129, 159, 328
Behind the Mask (1946 film) 141
Being There (1979 film) 309
Belasco, Leon 38
Bell, James ***37***
Bellamy, Ralph 195, ***197***, 199, 363
Bendix, William 360
Bennet, Spencer Gordon 86
Bennett, Joan 48
The Benson Murder Case (1930 film) 6, 17–19, 29, 233
The Benson Murder Case (novel) 6, 19, 29
Berkely, Busby 217
Berry, Noah, Jr. 353, 357
Best, Willie 143–144, 148, 178, 323
The Best Years of Our Lives (1946 film) 214
B.F.'s Daughter (novel) 283
The Big Clock (1948 film) 301
The Big Heat (1953 film) 213
The Big Sleep (1946 film) 344
Big Town (radio program) 339
The Bigger They Come (novel) 234
Biggers, Earl Derr 85–86, 98, 99, 112, 124, 129, 131, 327
The Bishop Murder Case (1930 film) 6, 14–***17***, ***15***, 18

375

# Index

*The Bishop Murder Case* (novel) 16–17
*The Black Camel* (1931 film) 87, **94**–96, 131
*The Black Camel* (novel) 2, 96, 131, 159
*The Black Gang* (novel) 54
*Black Magic* (1944 film) 88, 137–138, 142
*Black Mask* (magazine) 200, 208, 258, 259, 261
Blackmer, Sidney 186, 193, 194, 342
Blackwell, Carlyle, Jr. 41
Blane, Sally **251**
*The Blob* (1958 film) 242
*Blondes at Work* (1938 film) 260, 264–266, **265**
Blore, Eric 25
Bogart, Humphrey 187, 200
Bogdanovich, Peter 338
Bonanova, Fortunio 143
*Bonanza* (television series) 159
Bond, Ward 289
*Bonnie and Clyde* (1967 film) 364
*The Book of Murder* (story collection) 235
*Boston Evening Transcript* (newpaper) 282
Boyd, William 18
Brand, Christianna 246
Brent, Evelyn **330**
Brian, Mary 102
*Bride of Frankenstein* (1935 film) 45
Bridge, Alan (Al) 139
*Broadway Melody* (1929 film) 169
Broderick, Helen 170, 176, 178, 180
Bromley, Sheila **256**
Brooks, Louise **9**, 10, 11
Brooks, Richard 270
Brooks, Stephen 369
Brophy, Edward 33, 202
*Brother Rat* (1938 film) 345
Bruce, Nigel 254
Bruce, Virginia 28, 165
Bruno, Frank **330**
Buchanan, Elsa 101
Buchanan, Jack 42
*Bulldog Drummond* (1922 film) 41–42
*Bulldog Drummond* (1929 film) 42, 46–49, 54, 67
*Bulldog Drummond* (novel) 40, 42, 49, 54, 58
*Bulldog Drummond* (play) 48
*Bulldog Drummond* (radio program) 83
*Bulldog Drummond Again* (play) 60
"Bulldog Drummond and the Oriental Mind" (story) 73–74
*Bulldog Drummond at Bay* (1937 film) 42, 56–58, 76
*Bulldog Drummond at Bay* (1947 film) 45, 58, 74–76, **75**
*Bulldog Drummond at Bay* (novel) 46, 57, 58, 75–76
*Bulldog Drummond Comes Back* (1937 film) 44, 45, 60–62, 66, 72
*Bulldog Drummond Escapes* (1937 film) 43, 44, 45, 58–60, **59**, 65, 72
*Bulldog Drummond Hits Out* (play) 41
*Bulldog Drummond in Africa* (1938 film) **67**–69, 79
*Bulldog Drummond Strikes Back* (1934 film) 42, 45, 49–52, **50**, **53**, 60, 64
*Bulldog Drummond Strikes Back* (1947 film) 45, 76–77
*Bulldog Drummond Strikes Back* (novel) 52, 77
*Bulldog Drummond's Bride* (1939 film) 45, 72–74
*Bulldog Drummond's Peril* (1938 film) 64–67, 72
*Bulldog Drummond's Revenge* (1937 film) 62–64, **63**, 67, 73
*Bulldog Drummond's Secret Police* (1939 film) 49, 70–72
*Bulldog Drummond's Third Round* (1925 film) 42
*Bulldog Jack* (*Alias Bulldog Drummond*) (1935 film) 42, 46, 55–56
*Bullets or Ballots* (1936 film) 346
Burke, Kathleen 51
Burns, George 30, 31, 32
Burr, Raymond 215, 227, 234
Butterworth, Charles 51, **53**
Byron, Arthur **237**

Cagney, James 274, 340
Calhern, Louis 311
Calleia, Joseph **205**
*Calling Bulldog Drummond* (1951 film) 41, 46, 58, 80–83
*Calling Bulldog Drummond* (novel) 82
*Calling Philo Vance* (1940 film) 7, 22, 32–34, 266
Campbell, Louise 44, **63**, 64
*The Canary Murder Case* (1929 film) 2, 6, 7, 8–11, **9**, 12, 201
*The Canary Murder Case* (novel) 6, 10–11
*Cannon* (television series) 369
Cantor, Eddie 275
Capra, Frank 45, 183
*Captain America* (1944 serial) 243
*Captain Blood* (1935 film) 6
*The Caribbean Mystery* (1945 film) 297
Carradine, David 159
Carradine, John 294
Carroll, Leo G. 176
Carroll, Madeleine 348
Carson, Jack 363
Carter, Ben 139–140, 146, 152
*Casablanca* (1942) 299
*The Case of the Black Cat* (1936 film) 217, 228–230, 254, 302
*The Case of the Caretaker's Cat* (novel) 228, 230
"The Case of the Caretaker's Cat" (television episode) 230–231
*The Case of the Curious Bride* (1935 film) 217–220, **218**, 220–223, **222**, 224, 233, 259, 260
*The Case of the Curious Bride* (novel) 32, 223
"The Case of the Curious Bride" (television episode) 223–224
*The Case of the Howling Dog* (1934 film) 23, 216, 217–220, 221, 224, 229, 231
*The Case of the Howling Dog* (novel) 32, 219–220
"The Case of the Howling Dog" (television episode) 220
*The Case of the Lucky Legs* (1935 film) 216, 217, **224**–226, 228, 260, 308
*The Case of the Lucky Legs* (novel) 225–226
"The Case of the Lucky Legs" (television episode) 226
*The Case of the Stuttering Bishop* (1937 film) 217, 222, 231–233
*The Case of the Stuttering Bishop* (novel) 232–233
"The Case of the Stuttering Bishop" (television episode) 233
*The Case of the Terrified Typist* (novel) 216
*The Case of the Velvet Claws* (1936 film) 216, 217, 226–228, 254
*The Case of the Velvet Claws* (novel) 216, 227–228
"The Case of the Velvet Claws" (television episode) 228
*The Casino Murder Case* (1935 film) 7, 25–27, **26**, 38, 233, 309
*The Casino Murder Case* (novel) 27
*Castle in the Desert* (1942 film) 88, 131–134, **133**, 158
*Castle on the Hudson* (1940 film) 32
*The Cat and the Canary* (1927 film) 86, 244
Cavanaugh, Paul 237
CBS 339
*Celebrity Time* (television series) 281
Chaffin, Glen 352
*Challenge* (novel) 41, 68–69, 79
*The Challenge* (1948 film) 46, 69, 78–79
Chan, Frances 88, 137
Chandler, Chick 340, **341**, 342, 343
Chandler, Raymond 5, 293, 309
Chaney, Lon, Jr. 289
Chaplain, Charlie 186
Charles Scribner's Sons 31
*Charlie Chan* (radio program) 159
*Charlie Chan and the Curse of the Dragon Queen* (1981 film) 159
*Charlie Chan at Monte Carlo* (1938 film) 114–115, 155, 158, 245
*Charlie Chan at the Circus* (1936 film) 107–108
*Charlie Chan at the Olympics* (1937 film) 112–113, 115
*Charlie Chan at the Opera* (1936 film) 110–112, **111**, 127, 328
*Charlie Chan at the Race Track* (1936 film) 108–110, 125

*Charlie Chan at the Wax Museum* (1940 film) 126–127
*Charlie Chan at Treasure Island* (1939 film) 118–120, ***119***
*Charlie Chan Carries On* (1931 film) 87, 91–94, 125, 126
*Charlie Chan Carries On* (novel) 87, 92–93, 110, 124, 125–126
*Charlie Chan in Egypt* (1935 film) 102–104, ***103***
*Charlie Chan in Honolulu* (1938 film) 88, 115–117
*Charlie Chan in London* (1934 film) 43, 45, 87, 99–101, ***100***, 143, 301
*Charlie Chan in Panama* (1940 film) 99, 122–***124***
*Charlie Chan in Paris* (1934 film) 94, 101–102, 125, 158
*Charlie Chan in Reno* (1939 film) 117–118
*Charlie Chan in Rio* (1941 film) 96, 130–131
*Charlie Chan in Shanghai* (1935 film) 41, 87, 104–106
*Charlie Chan in the Secret Service* (1944 film) 88, 134–135, 139, 142
*Charlie Chan on Broadway* (1937 film) 113–114
*Charlie Chan's Chance* (1932 film) 91, 97–98, 129
*Charlie Chan's Courage* (1934 film) 98–99, 154
*Charlie Chan's Greatest Case* (1933 film) 44, 97–98
*Charlie Chan's Murder Cruise* (1940 film) 94, 124–126
*Charlie Chan's Secret* (1936 film) 87, 106–107, 138
*Cheaper by the Dozen* (1950 film) 214
Chesterfield 12
Chevalier, Maurice 201
*The Chinese Cat* (1944 film) 88, 135–137
*The Chinese Orange Mystery* (novel) 32, 255
*The Chinese Parrot* (1928 film) 86, 99
*The Chinese Parrot* (novel) 86, 99, 154, 159
*The Chinese Ring* (1947 film) 150–151
Christie, Agatha 14, 16, 23, 77, 132, 168, 255
Churchill, Mauguerite 242, 248–249
Cianelli, Eduardo 73
*Cimarron* (1931 film) 169
*The Circular Staircase* (novel) 168, 241
*The Circus Queen Murder* (1933 film) 186, 18–191, ***190***
*City in Darkness* (1939 film) 121–122
Clark, Cliff 253, 289, 340
Cline, Edward (Eddie) 182
Clive, E.E. 45, ***50***, 59–60, 61, 63, 71, 73, 101, ***164***, 165, 294, 306
*The Clue in the Diary* (novel) 318

*Code of the Secret Service* (1939 film) 344, 346–348, ***347***
Cohan, George M. 85
*Collier's* (*The National Weekly*) (magazine) 283, 327, 328
Collins, Ray 234
Collins, Wilkie 267
Colman, Ronald 2, 42, ***43***, 44, 48, 49, ***50***, 51, 52, ***53***, 54, 56, 68, 80
*Colonel March of Scotland Yard* (television series) 338
Columbia 2, 45, 74, 165, 186, 195, 199
*Come Back, Little Sheba* (play) 194
Compton, Joyce 45
Conan Doyle, Arthur 6
*Condemned* (1929) ***148***
*Confessions of a Nazi Spy* (1939 film) 361
Connolly, Walter 159
Conroy, Frank ***103***
Conway, Tom 46, 78, 79, 80, 183
Cooper, Courtney Ryley 362
Coote, Robert 294
Cortez, Ricardo 128, 217, 228, 231, ***247***, 294
Costello, Lou 71
Coulouris, George 83
*The Counterfeit Traitor* (1962 film) 81, 115
Coward, Noël 308
Crawford, Broderick 170, 366
Crawford, Joan 309
Crehan, Joseph 231, 246
*Crime and Punishment* (1935 film) 284
*The Crime Doctor's Strangest Case* (1943 film) 44
*The Crime of Helen Stanley* (1934 film) 195, 197–199, ***198***
*The Criminal Code* (1931 film) 328
*Crooked House* (novel) 14
Crosland, Alan 219
Cunningham, Joe 260
Curtis, Alan 8, 34, 35, 36, ***37***, 39
Curtiz, Michael 20–21, 221

*D.A. Calls It Murder* (novel) 234
Dale, Virginia ***367***
Dalya, Jacqueline 131
*Dames* (1934 film) 219
Damon, Les 214
*Danger Flight* (1939 film) 354, 358–***359***
*Dangerous Money* (1946 film) 147–148
*Dark Alibi* (1946 film) 144–146, ***145***, 152
Darling, W. Scott 152
Darwell, Jane 243, 249–250, ***251***, 340
*David Copperfield* (1935 film) 6
Davidson, William 23, 249
Davis, Joan 250–251
*The Dead Don't Care* (novel) 306
*Dead End* (1937 film) 260
*Dead Men Tell* (1941 film) 129–130
"Dead Yesterday" (story) 251–252

*Dead Yesterday and Other Stories* (story collection) 251
*Deadlier Than The Male* (1967 film) 83
*Deadline U.S.A.* (1952 film) 270
*Deadly Shade of Gold A* (novel) 32
*The Death Kiss* (1933 film) 197, 356
*Death Valley Days* (television series) 350
de Brulier, Nigel 104
de Cordoba, Pedro 122
de Croisset, Francis 163
Demarest, William 112, 251, 342
Denning, Richard 367
Denny, Reginald 44–45, 60, 61, ***63***, 65, 70, 71, 73
Dietrich, Marlene 88
*Dinner at Eight* (1934 film) 161, 162
*Docks of New Orleans* (1948 film) 151–152
*Dr. Jekyll and Mr. Hyde* (1920 film) 161
*Dr. Socrates* (1935 film) 32
Dodd, Claire 217, ***222***, ***310***, 312
Dodd Mead 300
*Don Juan* (1927 film) 161
Donovan, Tate 325
*Doomed to Die* (1940 film) 336–337
*A Double Life* (1948 film) 42
Doubleday 300
Douglas, Melvyn 2, 161, ***164***, 165, 309, ***310***, 312, 314
Douglas, Warren 150
Downing, Joe 270
*Dracula* (1931 film) 93, 95
*Dracula's Daughter* (1936 film) 242
*The Dragon Murder Case* (1934 film) 7, 22–25
*The Dragon Murder Case* (novel) 24–25
Drake, Oliver 156
*Dressed to Kill* (1946 film) 213
Drew, Roland ***304***
*Drums Along the Mohawk* (1939 film) 183
Du Maurier, Sir Gerald 48
Dumbrille, Douglas ***133***, 134, 297
Dunagan, Donnie 209
Dunne, Irene 199
*The Dutch Shoe Mystery* (novel) 246
Dvorak, Ann 231

*Each Dawn I Die* (1939 film) 348
Eberhart, Mignon G. 241–242, 247, 251, 253, 256, 257
*The Edge of Night* (television series) 234
Edwards, Jauquin 193
*813* (1920 film) 161
*Ellery Queen and the Murder Ring* (1941 film) 246
*Ellery Queen and the Perfect Crime* (1941 film) 45
*Ellery Queen, Master Detective* (1940 film) 199
*Ellery Queen's Mystery Magazine* 183
Ellis, Patricia ***224***

## Index

Emery, Gilbert 90
Emery, John 39
Emmy 360
*The Eno Crime Club* (radio program) 307
*Enter Arsène Lupin* (1944 film) 161–162, 165–167, **166**
*Eren Trece* (1931 film) 91–94, 126
Errol, Leon 237
*The Ex-Mrs. Bradford* (1936 film) 183, 308

Fairbanks, Douglas, Jr. 32
Fairlie, Gerard 41, 45, 58, 60, 72, 78, 82, 84
*The Falcon in Hollywood* (1944 film) 197, 356
*The Falcon Takes Over* (1942 film) 289
*The Falcon's Brother* (1942 film) 46, 183
"The Farewell Murder" (story) 208
Farr, Patricia 353
Farrell, Glenda 259, 261, 264, 265, 267–268, 269, 270, 271, 319
*Fast and Furious* (1939 film) 308, 309, 311–313, 314–316
*Fast and Loose* (1939 film) 308, 309, 313–*314*, **315**
*Fast Company* (1938 film) 308, 309, **310**, 311, 316
*Fast Company* (novel) 308, 312–313
*The Fatal Hour* (1940 film) 121, 334–336, **335**
*The F.B.I.* (television series) 369
*The FBI Story* (1959 film) 369
Fearing, Kenneth 301
*The Feathered Serpent* (1948 film) 89, 115–156
"Feed the Birds" (song) 243
*The Female of the Species* (book) 61–62, 72
Ferrer, Jose 39
Fetchit, Stepin 104
Fields, W.C. 48
*The Final Count* (novel) 41, 54, 61, 70
First National 348
*Flash Gordon* (1936 serial) 340, 342
Florey, Robert 362, 367
*Fly Away Baby* (1937 film) 261, 262–263
Flynn, Errol 6, 222
Fodor, Ladislaus 122
Fong, Benson 88, 134, 136, 140, **141**, 146, 147, 158, 230
Forde, Eugene 114
Forman, Carol 152
Forrest, Hal 352, 355
*Forty Naughty Girls* (1937 film) 170, 181–183
Foster, Norman 120, 282, 287
Foster, Preston 300, 301, **304**, 307
Foulger, Bryon 193
*Four Daughters* (1938 film) 259
The Four Preps 177
Fowley, Douglas 290, 340
Fox Film Corporation 2, 42, 72, 86, 89, 137, 139, 145, 158, 195, 297

Foy, Eddie, Jr. 345, 346, 347, 349, 351
Francis, Alec B. **15**
Francis, Kay 32
*Frankenstein* (1931 film) 328
*Frankenstein Meets the Wolf Man* (1943 film) 243
Freeman, Helen 61
*From This Dark Stairway* (novel) 247–248
*The Front Page* (1931 film) 186
*Front Page Detective* (television series) 39
*Front Page Woman* (1935 film) 266
Frye, Dwight 95, 311
*The Fugitive* (television series) 369

*G-Men* (1935 film) 274, 361
Gable, Clark 201, 214
Gale, June 340
Garbo, Greta 309
*The Garden Murder Case* (1936 film) 7, 27–29, 38, 45
*The Garden Murder Case* (novel) 29
Gardner, Erle Stanley 215, 219, 220, 221, 227, 229, 234, 302
Garfield, John 32
Garrett, Otis 303
*Gaudy Night* (novel) 267
Gaynor, Janet 193
Geldert, Clarence **15**, *17*
Gilbert, Billy 368
Girardot, Etienne 21, 23, 28
*Girl in Danger* (1934 film) 199
*The Girl Who Came to Supper* (musical) 308
*The Glass Key* (1942 film) 301
Gleason, James 169, 170, 173, 174, **176**, 180, 183, 340
*Gold Diggers of 1933* (1933 film) 242
*Gold Diggers of 1935* (1935 film) 259, 261
*Gold Racket* (1937 film) 154, 278–279, 280
*The Golden Eye* (1948 film) 154–155
Gombell, Minna 202
*Gone with the Wind* (1939 film) 47
*The Good Earth* (1936 film) 88
Gordon, C. Henry 113
Gottschalk, Ferdinand 237
*The Gracie Allen Murder Case* (1939 film) 7, 25, 29–32, **30**
*The Gracie Allen Murder Case* (novel) 31, 32, 39
Grafton, Sue 32
Grahame, Gloria 213
*Grand Hotel* (1932 film) 161
Grand National 274
Grant, Cary 199, 214, 243
Granville, Bonita 318, 319, **322**, **324**, 325
*The Grapes of Wrath* (1940 film) 243
*The Great Detective Stories* (story collection) 39
*The Great Hospital Mystery* (1937 film) 249–252, **251**

*The Great Ziegfeld* (1936 film) 214
*The Greatest Story Ever Told* (book) 194
*Greed* (1924 film) 170
Green, Nigel 83
*Green for Danger* (1947 film) 246
*Green for Danger* (novel) 246
*The Greene Murder Case* (1930 film) 6, 7, 12–14, 18
*The Greene Murder Case* (novel) 6, 13–14, 29
Greenstreet, Sydney 200
Gregory, James 184
Grey, Shirley 195, **198**
*Greystoke* (1984 film) 42
Griffies, Ethel 134
Grindé, Nick 14–15
Grosset & Dunlap 317
Guhl, George 260
*Gunsmoke* (television series) 360

Hale, Barbara 234
Hall, Dickie 209
Hall, Porter 59, 65, 202
Hamer, Gerald 73
Hamilton, John 289
Hammett, Dashiell 35, 200, 203, 208, 213, 301
Hardwicke, Cedric 84
*The Hardy Boys Mysteries* (television series) 325
Harlan, Kenneth 336
Harlow, Jean 204
Harvey, Forrester 71
Hawks, Howard 328
Hayworth, Rita (Rita Cansino) **103**, 104
*Headed for a Hearse* (novel) 303
Healy, Ted 25
*The Heiress* (1948 film) 42
Hellman, Lillian 213
Henie, Sonja 39
Henry, William **367**
Hepburn, Katharine 44
*Here Comes Mr. Jordan* (1941 film) 183, 309
Hersholt, Jean 297
Hervey, Irene 106
Hicks, Russell **218**
*The Hidden Staircase* (novel) 324–325
*Highway Patrol* (television series) 359, 366
Hillyer, Lambert 196
*His Girl Friday* (1940 film) 309
Hitchcock, Alfred 44, 284
*H.M. Pulham, Esquire* (novel) 283
Hodgson, Leyland **166**
Hogan, James 64
Hohl, Arthur **53**
*Holiday Inn* (1942 film) 360
Holland, Edna **145**
Holt 300
Homans, Robert E. **141**
Hoover, J. Edgar 361–362, 365, 368
Hope, Bob 351
Hopper, William 231, 234, 256
*Hound of the Baskervilles* (1932 film) 44

*Hound of the Baskervilles* (1939 film) 38
*House of Rothschild* (1934 film) 328
*The House on 92nd Street* (1945 film) 369
*The House Without a Key* (1926 serial) 86, 98
*The House Without a Key* (novel) 86, 98, 286
*How Green Was My Valley* (1941 film) 46, 243
Howard, John 43–44, 56, 61, *63*, 64, 65, *67*, 68, 73
Howard, Shemp 128
Huber, Harold 114, 115, 121–122, 130–131, 143, 202, 282, 289, *290*, 342
*Hud* (1963 film) 309
Hughes, Dorothy B. 309
Hughes, Mary Beth 131
Hulbert, Claude 55
Hulbert, Jack 42, 55
Humberstone, H. Bruce 23, 111, 340
Hunt, Eleanor 275, 276, 277, 278, *280*
Hurst, Brandon 13
Hyde-White, Wilfred 39
Hymer, Warren *296*

*I Am a Fugitive from a Chain Gang* (1932 film) 259, 301
*I Dream of Jeannie* (television series) 273
*I Never Sang for My Father* (1970 film) 309
*I, the Jury* (novel) 35
*I Was a Communist for the F.B.I.* (1951 film) 369
*I Was a Male War Bride* (1949 film) 243
*Imitation of Life* (1934 film) 217
*In a Lonely Place* (1950 film) 213
*Indiana Jones and the Kingdom of the Crystal Skull* (2008 film) 80
*The Informer* (1935 film) 301
*Inside Story* (1939 film) 339, 343
*Interpol Calling* (television series) 162
*Invaders from Mars* (1953 film) 47
*The Invisible Man* (1933 film) 45
Irving, Margaret 111
*Island of Lost Souls* (1932 film) 51
*It's a Gift* (1934 film) 48
*It's a Mad, Mad, Mad, Mad World* (1963 film) 170
*It's a Wonderful Life* (1946 film) 162

Jackson, Thomas E. *265*, 340
*The Jade Mask* (1945 film) 88, 138–139
*Jailbreak* (1936 film) 349
*The Jazz Singer* (1927 film) 87
Jenkins, Allen 217, 244, 245, 260, 271
Jenkins, William 269
Jenks, Frank 34, 35, *37*, 301

*Je Sais Tout* (periodical) 160
*Johnny Belinda* (1948 film) 260, 270
Johnson, Janet Louise 326
Johnson, Richard 83
Jolson, Al 87
Jones, F. Richard 47
Jones, Haywood 152
Jory, Victor 56

Kaaren, Suzanne *265*
*Kansas City Confidential* (1952 film) 307
Karig, Walter 320
Karloff, Boris 110, *111*, 327, 328, 329, *330*, *333*, 334, *335*, 337, 338
Karlson, Phil 141–142, 144, 270
Kaus, Gina 122
Keene, Carolyn 317, 320
*Keeper of the Keys* (novel) 87
Kelly, Paul 259, 267
Kennedy, Joyce 54
Kennedy, Tom 232, 260, 261, 270
*The Kennel Murder Case* (1933 film) 7, 19–*22*, *20*, 32, 33, 36, 201, 231, 225
*The Kennel Murder Case* (novel) 21–22, 33–34, 255
Kent, Robert *293*
*Key Largo* (1948 film) 162
Kibbee, Guy 242, 244
*The Kidnap Murder Case* (novel) 31, 39
Kilburn, Terry 46
*The Killer That Stalked New York* (1950 film) 162
*The Killing* (1956 film) 213
King, Joseph 348
King, Luis (Louis) 104
*King Kong* (1933 film) 55
*The King Murder* (1932 film) 12
*The King of Kings* (1927 film) 45
*King of the Underworld* (1939 film) 32
*Kings Row* (1942 film) 243
Kinnell, Murray 95
Kirk, Phyllis 214
*Knock-Out* (novel) 52
Knowles, Patric 243
*Knute Rockne All American* (1940 film) 350
Korvin, Charles 161–162, *166*
*Kung Fu* (television series) 159
Kurnitz, Harry 308, 316
Kuwa, George 86

Lachman, Harry 129, 133
*Lady for a Day* (1933 film) 217
*Lady in the Lake* (1947 film) 309
*The Lady in the Morgue* (1938 film) 301, 303–305, *304*
*The Lady in the Morgue* (novel) 305
*The Lady Vanishes* (1938 film) 155
Landis, Carole *265*
Lane, Lola 259, 267
Lane, Richard *296*, 297
Lang, Fritz 48, 284
Lang, Howard *277*
Larkin, John 234

La Rocque, Rod 274
LaRue, Jack *22*
*Lassie* (television series) 325
*Last Laugh, Mr. Moto* (novel) 283
*The Last Mile* (1932 film) 301
*The Last Warning* (1938 film) 301, 305–306
*The Late George Apley* (novel) 282–283, 299
Latimer, Jonathan 300, 303, 305, 306, 307
Laurel, Stan 21, 71
Lawford, Peter 214
Lawlor, Anderson *256*
Lawrence, Marc 342
Layne, Tom, Jr. 88, 113
LeBlanc, Maurice 160, 162, 163, 167
LeBorg, Reginald 36, 160
Leighton, Margaret *81*
Leinster, Murray 269
Leni, Paul 86
Leonard, Sheldon *207*
*The Letter* (1940 film) 7
Levene, Sam 340
Lewton, Val 129
Leyton, Drue *100*, 101
*Libeled Lady* (1936 film) 214
*The Life of Jimmy Dolan* (1933 film) 32
*The Life of Riley* (television series) 360
*Life with Father* (1947 film) 214
*Lifeboat* (1944 film) 44
*The Lightning Raider* (1919 film) 87
Linaker, Kay 131, 242, 246, *247*, 249
Lindsay, Margaret 23
*The List of Adrian Messenger* (1963 film) 99
*The List of Adrian Messenger* (novel) 99
Litel, John 318, 325, 348
*Little Caesar* (1931 film) 259
*Little Miss Marker* (1934 film) 193
Livingston, Margaret 11
Lodge, John 42, 56
Lombard, Carole 214
*The Lone Ranger* (1956 film) 325
*The Lone Ranger* (television series) 325
*Lone Wolf and His Lady* (1949 film) 45, 101
*The Lone Wolf Returns* (1935 film) 161, 164, 309
*The Lone Wolf Spy Hunt* (1939 film) 38, 164, 217, 301
Long, Lotus 338
Loo, Bessie *333*
Lorre, Peter 95, 283–284, *288*, *290*, *293*, 294, *296*, 299, 327
*Lost Horizon* (1937 film) 42, 44
*The Lost Patrol* (1934 film) 328
*Lost Weekend* (1945 film) 43
Louise, Anita 74–*75*
*Love Is on the Air* (1937 film) 345
*Love Me Tonight* (1932 film) 201
*Love Story* (1970 film) 43
Lowe, Edmund 7, 27–28, 38–39
Lowell, Helen 219
Lowery, Robert 128, *296*

Loy, Myrna 2, 51, 173, 200, 201, 202, **205**, 206, **207**–209, 210, **211**, 213, 214, 254, 308, 312
Lubin, Lou 209
Lugosi, Bela 87, 93, **94**–95
Lukas, Paul 7, 18, **26**, 27, 28, 38, 233
Luke, Edwin 88
Luke, Keye 87, 88, 89, 94, 101, 102, 113, 114, 155, **157**, 158, 159, 282, 289, **290**, 327, 328, 337, 338
"Lullaby of Broadway" (song) 261
Lys, Lya **350**

*M* (1931 film) 284
MacBride, Donald 128
MacDonald, Philip 99, 102, 282
MacDonald, John 32
MacFadden, Hamilton 95
MacLane, Barton 259, 261, **265**, 270, 271, 272–273, 340
MacMahon, Aline 242, 244
MacMahor, Horace 44
Macmillan 300
*Mad Love* (1935 film) 284
*Madame X* (1929 film) 88
*The Major and the Minor* (1942 film) 43, 325
*The Maltese Falcon* (1931 film) 217, 311
*The Maltese Falcon* (1941 film) 200, 219, 259, 299
*The Maltese Falcon* (novel) 32, 35, 200, 217
Mamoulian, Rouben 201
*Man Against Crime* (television series) 199
*Man Missing* (novel) 257
*Man Trouble* (1930 film) 343
*The Man Who Knew Too Much* (1934 film) 284
*The Man Who Laughs* (1928 film) 86
*The Mandarin Mystery* (1936 film) 255
Mander, Miles 166
*Manhattan Melodrama* (1934 film) 201
*Mapp v. Ohio*, 367 US 643 (1961 court case) 121
March, Frederic 193, 214
Marion, George F. 14
Marquand, John Phillips 282–283, 286, 288, 299, 327
Marr, Eddie 270
Marsh, Charles **322**
Marsh, Joan **314**
Martin, Pamela Sue 325
Martin, Quinn 369
Martin, Ross 159
*Mary Burns, Fugitive* (1935 film) 361
*Mary Poppins* (1964 film) 243
*The Mask of Fu Manchu* (1932 film) 201
McDonald, Frank 76, 246
McNeile, Herman Cyril (Sapper) 40, 43, 45, 48, 58, 60, 61, 64, 66, 68–69, 70, 72, 73, 80
Meek, Donald 39
*Meet John Doe* (1941 film) 183

*Meeting at Midnight* (1944 film) 137–138
Menjou, Adolphe 186, 187, 190, 193
Menzies, William Cameron 47
*Mercator Island* (novel) 283
Merkel, Una 51
Methot, Mayo 187
MGM 2, 6, 7, 14, 161, 183, 201, 308, 309, 310
Michael, Gertrude 236, **237**, 239–240, 367
*Michael Shayne, Private Detective* (1941 film) 128
Milan, Frank 280
Miljan, John 270
Milland, Ray 43, **59**, 68, **100**, 101
Miller, Walter 86
*Ming Yellow* (novel) 283
*Missing Evidence* (1939 film) 361
*Mission: Impossible* (television series) 33
*Mr. Blandings Builds His Dream House* (1948 film) 214
*Mr. District Attorney* (1941 film) 309
*Mr. District Attorney* (1947 film) 193
*Mr. I.A. Moto* (television series) 299
*Mr. Moto in Danger Island* (1939 film) 283, 295–298, **296**
*Mr. Moto Takes a Chance* (1938 film) 88, 283, **291**–293, 340
*Mr. Moto Takes a Hand* (novel) 283
*Mr. Moto Takes a Vacation* (1939 film) 283, 298–299
*Mr. Moto's Gamble* (1938 film) 282–283 289–291, **290**
*Mr. Moto's Last Warning* (1939 film) 283, 294–295
*Mister Roberts* (1955 film) 214
*Mr. Wong, Detective* (1938 film) 151, 329–331, **330**
*Mr. Wong in Chinatown* (1939 film) 150–151, 328, 329, 332–334, **333**
Mitchell, Grant 28
Mohr, Gerald 233
Monk, James 299
Monogram Pictures 88, 89, 134, 144, 149, 154, 158, 290, 328, 352, 353, 364
Montgomery, Robert 214, 309, **314**, **315**
*The Moonstone* (novel) 267
Moorhead, Natalie 202
Moran, Lois 90
Moran, William H. 344
Moreland, Mantan 88, 134, 136, 138, 139–140, **141**, 143–144, 146, 147, 150, 154, 155, 159
Morgan, Claudia 214
Morison, Patricia 213, 362, **363**, 364
Morley, Karen 163
Morris, Chester 2, 254
Morton, James C. **335**
Mowbray, Alan 101
Mower, Jack **324**
*Mrs. Miniver* (1942 film) 46
*Mrs. O'Malley and Mr. Malone* (1950 film) 183
Muller, Marcia 168
*The Mummy* (1932 film) 104, 329

Mundin, Herbert 107
Muni, Paul 32
*Murder by an Aristocrat* (1936 film) 242, 248–249, 254
*Murder by an Aristocrat* (novel) 241, 249
*Murder by the Dozen* (story collection) 327
*Murder in the Air* (1940 film) 344, 349–**350**
*Murder in the Madhouse* (novel) 300
*Murder in Trinidad* (1934 film) 297
*Murder in Trinidad* (novel) 283, 297–298
*The Murder of Dr. Harrington* (1936 film) 242, 245–248, **247**, 254
*Murder on a Bridle Path* (1936 film) 170, 177–179
*Murder on a Honeymoon* (1935 film) 169, 175–177, **176**, 340
*Murder on the Blackboard* (1934 film) 173–175, 177, 236
*Murder on the Blackboard* (novel) 169, 174–175
*Murder Over New York* (1940 film) 127–129, 137
*Murder Will Out* (1930 film) 269
"Murders in the Rue Morgue" (story) 108
Murphy, Maurice 353
"The Musgrave Ritual" (story) 71
*Mutiny on the Bounty* (1935 film) 310
Mutual Network 83, 159
*My Man Godfrey* (1936 film) 214
*The Mysterious Dr. Fu Manchu* (1929 film) 87
*Mysterious Mr. Moto* (1938 film) 283, 293–294
*Mystery House* (1938 film) 243, 254–257, **256**
*The Mystery of Hunting's End* (novel) 256–257
*The Mystery of Mr. Wong* (1939 film) 331–332
*Mystery of the Wax Museum* (1933 film) 259
*Mystery Plane* (1939 film) 353, 354–355, 358
Mystery Writers of America 257

Nagel, Anne **256**
Nagel, Conrad 274–275, 276, **277**, **280**–281
Naish, J. Carrol 68, 159, **166**, 362, **363**, 364, 365, 366
*Nancy Drew* (2007 film) 325
*Nancy Drew and the Hidden Staircase* (1939 film) 323–325, **324**
*Nancy Drew — Detective* (1938 film) 318, 319–320
*The Nancy Drew Mysteries* (television series) 325
*Nancy Drew...Reporter* (1939 film) 320–321, 322
*Nancy Drew...Trouble Shooter* (1939 film) 321–322
*The Narrow Margin* (1952 film) 213
Nash, Mary 123

Nash, Ogden 5
*National Treasure* (2004 film) 80
*Navy Spy* (1937 film) 276–278, **277**
NBC Blue Network 159
Nebel, Frederick 258–259, 261, 262, 273, 339
Nedell, Bernard 290
Neill, Roy William 133
Nelson, Barry 209
*The New Adventures of Charlie Chan* (television series) 159
Newland, John 46
"Nick and Nora" (television series) 214
*The Night Club Lady* (1932 film) 186, 187–189
*Night Has a Thousand Eyes* (1948 film) 301
*Night Must Fall* (1937 film) 309
*Night of Mystery* (1937 film) 7, 14, 29
*Ninotchka* (1939 film) 309
Nissen, Greta **190**
"No Hard Feelings" (story) 261
*No Hero* (novel) 283
Nolan, Lloyd 363
North, Wilfrid **172**
*The Notorious Lone Wolf* (1946 film) 233
*The Notorious Sophie Lang* (1934 film) 235, 236–238, **237**
*The Notorious Sophie Lang* (story collection) 235
Nowell, Wedgewood 161

Oakman, Wheeler 280
*Ocean's Eleven* (1960 film) 236
*Ocean's Eleven* (2001 film) 236
Oland, Warner **50**, 51, 86–88, 91, **94**, 99, **100**, 101, **103**, **111**, 114, 116, 117, 158, 159, 291, 327
Oliver, Edna May 69, 170, **172**, 173, 174, **176**, 178, 180, 181, 182, 183, 295
O'Moore, Pat 46, 74, 75
"Once Upon a Train" (story) 183
*One Dangerous Night* (1943 film) 233
*One Is Guilty* (1934 film) 197
*One Step Beyond* (television series) 46
O'Neal, Ryan 43
Ortega, Santos 83, 159
Orth, Frank 253
Oscar (Academy Award) 7, 42, 43, 47, 48, 169, 183, 186, 199, 243, 260, 270, 275, 297, 309, 310, 311, 318, 352
O'Sullivan, Maureen 203
Oursler, Charles Fulton 185, 194
*The Ox-Bow Incident* (1943 film) 243

Pabst, G.W. 11
Page, Marco 308, 311, 312, 316
*The Painted Veil* (1934 film) 87
Pallette, Eugene 7, 10, 13, 18, **22**, 23, 25, 33

Palmer, Stuart 168, 174, 175, 177, 179, 180, 182, 183
*Pandora's Box* (1929 film) 11
*The Panther's Claw* (1942 film) 121, 186, 191–193, **192**
Paramount (Pictures) 2, 6, 7, 11, 17–18, 31, 43, 44, 45, 50, 56, 201, 235, 236, 361, 364
Paretsky, Sara 168
Park, E.L. 86, 90
Parker, Ray 306
*Parole Fixer* (1939 film) 362, 366–368, **367**
Parsons, Milton 129, 134
*The Password to Larkspur Lane* (novel) 319–320
Paterson, Pat **103**
Pathé 86
*The Patient in Room 18* (1938 film) 243, 252–253
*Patient in Room 18* (novel) 241, 253
Pendleton, Nat 28, **164**, 165, 202, 312
*The Penguin Pool Murder* (1932 film) 169, 170–173, **172**
*The Penguin Pool Murder* (novel) 168, 169, 175–173, 182
*People vs. Withers and Malone* (story collection) 183
Pepper, Barbara 302, 304
*Perils of Pauline* (1914 serial) 186
Perry, Jessie **272**
*Perry Mason* (radio program) 234
*Perry Mason* (television series) 117, 215, 234, 256, 301, 320
*Persons in Hiding* (book) 362, 364–365, 366, 367–368, 369
*Persons in Hiding* (1939 film) 362, **364**–366
Petrie, George 39
Pflug, Jo Ann 214
*Phantom Lady* (1944 film) 310
*Phantom of Chinatown* (1940 film) 327, 337–338
*The Phantom of the Air* (1933 serial) 352
*The Phantom of the Opera* (1925 film) 110
*The Phenix City Story* (1955 film) 270
*The Philadelphia Story* (1940 film) 44
*Philo Vance* (radio) 39
*Philo Vance Returns* (1947 film) 8, 37–38
*Philo Vance's Gamble* (1947 film) 8, 34–35
*Philo Vance's Secret Mission* (1947 film) 8, 35–**37**
*Pictorial Review* (magazine) 251
Pidgeon, Walter 46, 80, **81**, 82
*The Pilgrim's Progress* (1910 film) 87
Pilkington, Tom **166**
Pine-Thomas Productions 339
Pitts, ZaSu 170, 176–177, 179, 180, 181, 182
*The Plot Thickens* (1936 film) 170, 179–181
*A Pocket Full of Rye* (novel) 14

Poe, Edgar Allan 108
*Porky's Road Race* (1937 cartoon) 183
Powell, David 161
Powell, William 2, 6, 7, 10, 13, 15, 17–18, **20**, 21, **22**, 23, 27, 27, 33, 38, 44, 173, 200, 201, 202, **205**, 206, **207**, **211**, 213, 214, 254, 308, 312
PRC (Producers Releasing Corporation) 7, 34, 36, 38, 186, 191
Price, Vincent 299
Prival, Lucien **330**
*Private Secretary* (television series) 310
Producers Releasing Corporation (PRC) 7, 34, 36, 38, 186, 191
*Public Enemies* (2009 film) 369
*Public Enemy's Wife* (1936 film) 261
Pulitzer Prize 283
Purcell, Dick 243, **256**
*The Purple Cipher* (1920 film) 269
"The Purple Hieroglyph" (story) 269
*A Purple Place for Dying* (novel) 32
*The Puzzle of the Pepper Tree* (novel) 175, 177
*The Puzzle of the Red Stallion* (novel) 179

Quartermaine, Charles 14
Queen, Ellery 255
*Queen of the Mob* (1939 film) 363, 368–369
Quinn, Anthony 68, 367
Quon, Marianne 88, 134

*Racket Busters* (1938 film) 269
*Raffles* (1930 film) 42
*Raffles, the Amateur Cracksman* (1917 film) 161
Raines, Ella 166
Ralph, Jessie 28
Randell, Ron 45–46, 74, **75**
Rathbone, Basil 2, 6, **15**, **17**, 33, 38, 71, 254
*The Raven* (1963 film) 338
Ray, Allene 86
Reagan, Ronald 243, 344–346, **347**, 348, **350**
*Rebecca* (1940 film) 44, 132
*Rebecca* (novel) 132, 203
*Reclining Figure* (novel) 316
*The Red Dragon* (1945 film) 142–144
*Red Gardenias* (novel) 300
Reed, Donna 209
Regan, Joyce **288**
Regas, George **50**, **293**
Reliance Pictures 45
*The Return of Bulldog Drummond* (1934 film) 42, 52–55, 67
*The Return of Bulldog Drummond* (novel) 64
*The Return of Charlie Chan* (TV movie) 159
*The Return of Mr. Moto* (1965 film) 299

*The Return of Sophie Lang* (1936 film) 236, 238–239
*The Return of the Black Gang* (novel) 84
Reynolds, Marjorie 329, 334, 354, 357, ***359***, 360
Reynolds, William 369
Rhodes, Eric 294
Riano, Renie ***324***
Rice, Craig 183, 301
Rice, Florence 309, 312
Rice, Grantland 309
Richards, Grant 7, 29
Richardson, Ralph 42, 52, 55, 68
Richmond, Kane 128
"The Riddle of the Dangling Pearl" (story) 180–181
"The Riddle of the Forty Naughty Girls" (story) 182–183
*Ride the Pink Horse* (1947 film) 309
*The Riders of the Whistling Skull* (1937 film) 156
*Right You Are, Mr. Moto* (novel) 299
Rinehart, Mary Roberts 168, 241
RKO 2, 87, 169, 183, 242
Robards, Jason 354, 360
Roberts, Emma 325
Robinson, Frances 39
*Roger Touhy, Gangster* (1944 film) 307, 369
Rogers, Ginger 208, 308
Rogers, Howard Emmett 82
Rogers, Jean 340, 341, 342, 343, 353
*The Roman Hat Mystery* (novel) 32
*Romeo and Juliet* (1936 film) 183
*Rosemary's Baby* (1968 film) 194
Rosen, Phil 134–135, 139, 140, 141, 143, 144, 338
Rosenbloom, Maxie 290
Rosing, Bodil ***17***
Rumann, Sig 250, ***251***
Russell, Rosalind 2, 25, ***26***, 309, 314, ***315***
Ruth, Roy Del 51
Ryan, Sheila 36, ***37***

St. Clair, Malcom 11
Salkow, Sidney 75
*San Quentin* (1937 film) 348
Sanders, George 46, 183, 294
Sapper (Herman Cyril McNeile) 40, 43, 45, 48, 58, 60, 61, 64, 66, 68–69, 70, 72, 73, 80
*Satan Met a Lady* (1936 film) 217
*The Saturday Evening Post* (magazine) 235, 282, 283, 286, 249, 327, 328
Sayers, Dorothy 6, 267
*The Scarab Murder Case* (1936 film) 39, 40–41
*The Scarab Murder Case* (novel) 39
*The Scarlet Claw* (1944 film) 73
*The Scarlet Clue* (1945 film) 133, 139–***141***, 145, 146
Schallert, William 325
*Scorchy Smith* (comic strip) 352
Sears, Zelda 14
*Secret Agent* (1935 film) 284

*The Secret of Shadow Ranch* (novel) 318
*The Secret of the Old Clock* (novel) 318
*Secret Service of the Air* (1939 film) 275, 345–346, 347
*Secrets of the Lone Wolf* (1941 film) 80
Seiler, Lewis 349
Sellon, Charles 48
Sen Yung, Victor 88, 116, 117, 128, 129, 130, ***133***–134, 147, 148, 150, 154, 155, 158, 159, 269
*Seven Keys to Baldpate* (novel) 85
*The Seven Little Foys* (1955 film) 351
Seward, Billie ***119***
Seymour, Dan 34–35
*Shadow of the Thin Man* (1941 film) 208–210
*The Shadow Returns* (1945 film) 141
*Shadows Over Chinatown* (1946 film) 146–147
*The Shadowy Third* (novel) 316
*The Shanghai Chest* (1948 film) 152–154, ***153***
*The Shanghai Cobra* (1945 film) 141–142
*Shanghai Express* (1932 film) 88
Shannon, Frank 260, 270
Shannon, Peggy ***224***
Shaw, Winnie (Wini) 222–223, 261
Shearer, Norma 309
Sheridan, Ann 243, 253, 254
*Sherlock Holmes* (1922 film) 6, 44, 161, 201
*Sherlock Holmes and the Voice of Terror* (1942 film) 44
*Sherlock Holmes Faces Death* (1943 film) 71
Sherwood, Yorke ***50***
*The Shudders* (novel) 194
Silva, Henry 299
Simon and Schuster 300
"The Simple Art of Murder" (essay) 5
Siodmak, Robert 310
Skipworth, Alison 237
*The Sky Dragon* (1949 film) 89, 156–158, ***157***
*Sky Patrol* (1939 film) 354, 357–358
*Sleepers East* (novel) 259
*Sleepers West* (1941 film) 259
Sloane, Everett 83
*Smart Blonde* (1937 film) 222–223, 233, 258, 259, 260–261, 264
*Smashing the Money Ring* (1939 film) 344, 348–349
*Smilin' Jack* (comic strip) 352
Smith, C. Aubrey 45, 51
Smith, Noel M. 347
*Snappy Stories* (magazine) 269
*The Sniper* (1952 film) 193
Sojin 86
*Some Girls Do* (1968 film) 83
*Son of Frankenstein* (1939 film) 209
Sondergaard, Gale 166

*Song of the Thin Man* (1947 film) 212–213
*Sophie Lang Goes West* (1937 film) 236, 239
Sothern, Ann 310–311, 316
*The Spanish Cape Mystery* (novel) 32
Spillane, Mickey 35
Stafford, Hanley 194
Standing, Sir Guy 45, 239
Stanley, Eric 253
*A Star Is Born* (1937 film) 193
*Star of Midnight* (1935 film) 308
Stephenson, James 7, 33
*Steve Randall* (television series) 309
Stevens, Craig 214
Stevens, Ruthelma 186
Stone, George E. 23, 230, 289
Stone, Milburn 354, 357, ***359***, 360
*Stopover: Tokyo* (1957 film) 299
*Stopover: Tokyo* (novel) 299
*The Story of Vernon and Irene Castle* (1939 film) 183
*Strand* (magazine) 73
Stratemeyer, Edward 317, 325
Stratemeyer, Harriet 318
Stroheim, Erich Von 170
Stuart, Gloria ***341***
*Stunt Pilot* (1939 film) 353, 354, 355–356, 358
Sullivan, Francis L. 54
*Sunrise at Campobello* (1958 play) 199
*Sunrise at Campobello* (1960 film) 199
*Suspicion* (1941 film) 44
*Swing Time* (1936 film) 170

*Tailspin Tommy* (comic strip) 352–353, 356, 360
*Tailspin Tommy* (1934 serial) 353, 356
*Tailspin Tommy* (radio program) 360
*Tailspin Tommy in the Great Air Mystery* (1935 serial) 353
Talbot, Lyle 23, ***157***, 363
*A Tale of Two Cities* (1935 film) 42, 183
Talman, William 234
*Targets* (1968 film) 338
Tashman, Lilyan 48
Taylor, Kent ***30***
*The Teeth of the Tiger* (1919 film) 161
Temple, Shirley 193, 243, 340
*Temple Tower* (1930 film) 42, 49, 72
*Temple Tower* (novel) 49, 72
*Ten Little Indians* (play) 343
*Terror by Night* (1946 film) 101
*Thank You, Mr. Moto* (1938 film) 283, 286–***288***
*Thank You, Mr. Moto* (novel) 288
"That Girl and Mr. Moto" (story) 286
*Thatcher Colt* (radio program) 194
*These Three* (1936 film) 318
*They Came to Blow Up America* (1943 film) 369

# Index

*They Made Me a Criminal* (1939 film) 32
*The Thin Man* (1934 film) 2, 7, 38, 173, 201–204, 213, 225, 308, 311
*The Thin Man* (novel) 200, 203–204, 274
*The Thin Man* (television series) 214
*The Thin Man Goes Home* (1944 film) 128, 204, 210–212, ***211***
*Think Fast, Mr. Moto* (1937 film) 283, 284–286, 292
*Think Fast, Mr. Moto* (novel) 286
*The Third Round* (novel) 66, 70, 72
*13 Lead Soldiers* (1948 film) 46, 79–80
"Thirteen Lead Soldiers" (story) 80
*Thirteen Women* (1932 film) 201
*The 39 Steps* (1935 film) 347
Thomas, Frankie (Frank) 318, 319, ***322***, 325
Thomas, Jameson 104
Thorndike, Oliver ***75***
*Three on a Match* (1932 film) 217
*Thriller* (television series) 338
*Tim Tyler's Luck* (1937 serial) 318
*Time Out for Murder* (1938 film) 339, 340–342, ***341***
*Time to Kill* (1942 film) 44
Tobin, Genevieve 308
Todd, Ann 54
Toler, Sidney 88, 89, 116, 117, ***119***, 121, 1244–125, 128, ***133***, 134, 138, ***141***, 144, ***145***, 148–149, 150, 156, 157, 327
Tom, Layne, Jr. 88, 113
*Tom Corbett, Space Cadet* (television series) 325
Tomlinson, David 82
Tone, Franchot 310, 316
*Tonight or Never* (1931 film) 304
Tony Award 194, 199, 308
*Top Hat* (1935 film) 48, 170
*Topaze* (1933 film) 201
*Torchy Blane in Chinatown* (1939 film) 88, 262, 268–269
*Torchy Blane in Panama* (1938 film) 259, 262, 266–267
*Torchy Blane ... Playing with Dynamite* (1939 film) 233, 254, 259–260, 262, 271–***272***
*Torchy Gets Her Man* (1938 film) 262, 267–268
*Torchy Runs for Mayor* (1939 film) 254, 262, 269–271
*The Torn Curtain* (1966 film) 115
Towne, Rosella 253
Tracy, Spencer 32, 214
*The Trap* (1946 film) 148–150, 154
Tree, Dorothy 219
Trenholme, Della 219
Trent, John 354, ***359***, 360
Trowbridge, Charles 334, 335

Tuttle, Frank 11
*Twentieth Century* (1934 film) 161
20th Century-Fox 2, 88, 131, 134, 137, 139, 141, 145, 158, 183, 242, 243 249, 282, 283, 287, 290, 297, 339, 340
"26 Miles" (song) 176
*20,000 Years in Sing Sing* (1932 film) 32
Tyler, Harry 219

*Undercover Doctor* (1939 film) 362, 365–366
United Artists 42
Universal 161, 166, 300, 301, 352
*The Unspeakable Gentleman* (novel) 282
Usher, Gary ***111***
Ustinov, Peter 159

Valerie, Joan 128
Vance, Louis Joseph 161
Vandercook, John W. 283, 297
Van Dine, S.S. 6, 7, 10, 12, 14, 16, 21, 25, 29, 30, 31, 33, 39
Van Dyke, W.S. 201
Varconi, Victor 95
Verdugo, Elena ***157***
*A Very Missing Person* (TV movie) 184
Villiers, James 83
Vinson, Helen 22
Vitaphone 39

Wagner, Max ***315***
Walton, Douglas 101
Warner, H.B. 45, 68
Warner Brothers 2, 6, 7, 32, 81, 201, 215–216, 225, 228, 232, 242, 243, 248, 259, 267, 272, 318, 325
*Watch on the Rhine* (1943 film) 7
Watkins, Pierre ***153***
*Wayward* (1932 film) 236
Weaver, Marjorie 128
Webb, Clifton 214
*Wednesday's Child* (play) 318
*Weeks v. United States*, 232 US 383 (1914 court case) 121
Weldon, Ben ***256***
Weldon, Robert 129–130
Wentworth, Patricia 168
*Werewolf of London* (1935 film) 88
West, Mae 302
*The Westland Case* (1937 film) 301–303
Westman, Nydia ***63***
*Westward Passage* (1932 film) 318
Wever, Nick 83
Whalen, Michael 339–340, ***341***, 343
*The Whales of August* (1987 film) 310
*What Price Glory?* (1926 film) 7

*While New York Sleeps* (1938 film) 339, 342
*While the Patient Slept* (1935 film) 242, 243–245
*While the Patient Slept* (novel) 245
*White Heat* (1949 film) 346
Whiteman, Paul 11
*Whoopee* (1930 film) 275
Wiley, Hugh 327, 328, 338
William, Warren 2, 7, 23, 38, 163, 165, 216–217, ***218***, 219, 221, ***222***, ***224***, 227, 228, 231, 254, 308
William Morrow and Company 216
Williams, Clark 353
Williams, Earle 161
Wilson, Clarence 229, 302
Windsor, Marie 213
*Wings* (1927 film) 352
*The Winter Murder Case* (novel) 6, 39
Winters, Roland 89, 144, 150, 151, 152, 156, ***157***, 158, 159
Wirt, Mildred Augustine 318, 320, 325
Withers, Grant 328–329, ***335***, 338
Witherspoon, Cora 125
*Witness for the Prosecution* (1957 film) 308
*Wolf in Man's Clothing* (novel) 257
*The Wolf Man* (1941 film) 243
*The Woman in Green* (1945 film) 29
*A Woman in Paris* (1923 film) 186
*The Woman in the Window* (1944 film) 48
Woodbury, Joan 342
Woods, Donald 217, 222, 231, 233
Woolrich, Cornell 301
Wrather, Jack 325
Wray, Fay 55
Wright, Willard Huntington 5, 6, 7, 31, 32, 39
Wright, William 8, 37–38, 39
Wurtzel, Sol M. 282
Wyman, Jane 233, 260, 261, 270, ***272***

*A Yank on the Burma Road* (1942 film) 159
*Yankee Doodle Dandy* (1942 film) 351
Yarbrough, Jean 78
*Yellow Cargo* (1936 film) 274, 275–276, 279
*You Can't Take It with You* (1938 film) 162
Young, Loretta 51
Young, Robert 87, 96
Young, Roland ***15***
Yurka, Blanche 363, 368

Zimbalist, Efrem, Jr. 369
Zucco, George 70, 116–117, 165, 311

www.ingramcontent.com/pod-product-compliance
Lightning Source LLC
Chambersburg PA
CBHW081534300426
44116CB00015B/2624